# Attachment Theory and Res

*A Reader*

Edited by

Tommie Forslund
and
Robbie Duschinsky

**WILEY** Blackwell

This edition first published 2021
© 2021 John Wiley & Sons Ltd

The right of Tommie Forslund and Robbie Duschinsky to be identified as the authors of the editorial material in this work has been asserted in accordance with law.

*Registered Offices*
John Wiley & Sons, Inc., 111 River Street, Hoboken, NJ 07030, USA
John Wiley & Sons Ltd, The Atrium, Southern Gate, Chichester, West Sussex, PO19 8SQ, UK

*Editorial Office*
111 River Street, Hoboken, NJ 07030, USA

For details of our global editorial offices, customer services, and more information about Wiley products visit us at www.wiley.com.

Wiley also publishes its books in a variety of electronic formats and by print-on-demand. Some content that appears in standard print versions of this book may not be available in other formats.

*Library of Congress Cataloging-in-Publication Data*
Names: Forslund, Tommie, editor. | Duschinsky, Robbie, editor.
Title: Attachment theory and research : a reader / Tommie Forslund, PhD, researcher in Developmental Psychology at Stockholm University, Stockholm, Sweden; researcher at SUF Resource Center, Region Uppsala, Uppsala, Sweden, Robbie Duschinsky, Head of the Applied Social Science Group and Senior University Lecturer, University of Cambridge, Cambridge, UK. Fellow and Director of Studies, Sidney Sussex College, Cambridge, UK.
Description: First edition. | Hoboken : Wiley, 2021. | Includes bibliographical references and index.
Identifiers: LCCN 2020048348 (print) | LCCN 2020048349 (ebook) | ISBN 9781119657880 (paperback) | ISBN 9781119657897 (adobe pdf) | ISBN 9781119657903 (epub)
Subjects: LCSH: Attachment behavior. | Developmental psychology.
Classification: LCC BF575.A86 F67 2021 (print) | LCC BF575.A86 (ebook) | DDC 155.5/1241–dc23
LC record available at https://lccn.loc.gov/2020048348
LC ebook record available at https://lccn.loc.gov/2020048349

Cover Design: Wiley
Cover Image: Denis Pogostin/iStockphoto

Set in 11/13pt Dante by SPi Global, Pondicherry, India
Printed and bound by CPI Group (UK) Ltd, Croydon, CR0 4YY

C103932_260221

# Attachment Theory and Research

# Contents

# Introduction

## Tommie Forslund and Robbie Duschinsky

Attachment theory originates in the work of the British psychoanalyst and child psychiatrist John Bowlby and the Canadian clinical psychologist Mary Ainsworth. Bowlby sought a scientific explanation for the affectional bonds that children form with their caregivers, as manifested by attempts to seek and maintain proximity to and comfort by their caregivers, and by negative reactions following prolonged separations and losses. He eventually formulated the core tenets of attachment by drawing from multiple scientific disciplines, including ethology, psychoanalysis and cognitive psychology (Van der Horst, 2011). Bowlby's emphasis on the importance of early care may come across as self-evident today. However, it was anything but an orthodox position when he formulated attachment theory, at which time the importance of children's actual experiences with their caregivers were not sufficiently acknowledged (Bowlby, 1940, 1951, 1969/1982). Ainsworth, who collaborated closely with Bowlby, then extended his account by conducting extensive empirical observations of caregiver–child interaction, and by identifying individual differences in infants' expectations of the availability of their caregivers (Ainsworth et al., 1978; Van Rosmalen et al., 2015, 2016).

Already in their lifetime, their work influenced various aspects of policy to do with children. One important shift to which they contributed was recognition of the negative effects of hospitalization for children when, as was common policy, their caregivers were not permitted to visit or allowed to visit only very irregularly (Bowlby et al., 1952; Van der Horst & Van der Veer, 2009). Ideas from attachment theory have also been influential for parents, teachers, child protection services and policy-makers. Key concepts and ideas that entered into circulation included Bowlby's emphasis on the importance of early care for socioemotional development, his concern about major separations of infants from their caregivers, and his emphasis on the value of continuity in child–caregiver relationships. Ainsworth's ideas also gained recognition, particularly her identification of the importance of caregiver sensitivity for children's socioemotional development. She is also known for her account of the sensitive caregiver as a "secure base" from which the child can explore the environment, and as a "safe haven" to which the child can return for comfort and protection. For instance, the "First 1000 Days" policy agenda acknowledges the developmental importance of early care, and makes explicit reference to attachment theory (House of Commons Health and Social Care Committee, 2019). Further, preschool curricula often make reference to attachment theory and the importance of creating a secure base to facilitate children's exploration and, through this, their learning.

Since the passing of Bowlby and Ainsworth in the 1990s, ideas about attachment seem to have become more, rather than less, appealing and popular. One reason may be their alignment with current concerns about the importance of early experience for brain development (Gerhardt, 2014; Wastell & White, 2017). In a 2018 survey conducted by the British government of organizations working with children in need of help and protection, attachment theory was, by a large margin, cited as the most frequently used underpinning perspective (Department for Education, UK, 2018). In social work policy and practice, Smith and colleagues (2017) have argued that attachment theory "has become the 'master theory' to which other ways of conceiving of childcare and of relationships more generally become subordinated" (p. 1606). In family courts, attachment theory and research is referenced in relation to children's best interests and used to inform decision-making (Keddell, 2017).

Yet the account of attachment theory and research that is available in much clinical and child welfare practice, as well as in popular and policy contexts, can sometimes be distorted or hazy (Furnivall et al., 2012, Reijman et al. 2018; Morison et al., 2020). For instance, popular accounts of attachment theory often miss Bowlby's (1988) qualifications of his earlier emphasis on the importance of early care: in his later work he placed emphasis on the potential for both continuity and change in psychological development. The popular account of attachment theory likewise misses that Ainsworth was using a technical definition of "sensitivity.". She meant the ability of a caregiver to perceive and to interpret accurately the signals and communications implicit in a child's behavior, and given this understanding, to respond to them appropriately and promptly. This meaning is not implied by uses of the word "sensitive" in ordinary language, which is typically assumed to mean warm and caring. Popular accounts of attachment theory also tend to overestimate the amount of information that can be gained from observations of individual persons' attachment quality (e.g. Granqvist et al., 2017). It has recently been highlighted that popular accounts of attachment theory sometimes influence family court decision-making, resulting in a large number of attachment scholars writing a consensus statement with recommendations for how to use attachment theory and research in decision-making concerning child protection and child custody (Forslund et al., 2021).

Already in 1968, Ainsworth wrote to Bowlby with concern: "attachment has become a bandwagon" – a popular and oversimplified cause. She specifically worried that a breakdown of communication was occurring between active attachment researchers and their publics, causing both excessive enthusiasm for the paradigm in some quarters and unfair rejections in others. Furthermore, appeals to attachment by practitioners often neglected what she considered essential about the paradigm, for instance by focusing on laboratory-based classifications of infants' attachment quality rather than on their perception of the caregiver's availability based on their actual experiences of care (see also Ainsworth & Bowlby, 1991).

What factors contributed to this bandwagon? One was that Bowlby was a great popularizer. He used television, radio, magazines and books published by the popular press to get his key messages out to clinicians, policy-makers and the wider public. However, Bowlby knowingly simplified his messages in these forums, and he often kept his more subtle conclusions and qualifications for his scholarly work. Indeed, he was explicit that in his popular writings he exaggerated matters; it was a kind of marketing strategy for his more complex theoretical reflections (see, e.g. Bowlby, 1987). While this strategy created a version of attachment theory that could circulate much more easily, it was in some important regards a misleading or even distorted picture of his conclusions.

The cut-price popular account of attachment that Bowlby set in motion was evocative, provocative, quite general and had the appearance of scientific credibility. This contributed to its flexibility, its urgency and its exceptionally wide appeal to various people concerned with family relationships and child development (Duschinsky, 2020). For instance, Bowlby's warnings about the dangers of child–mother separations were too imprecise. Major separations are indeed potentially harmful for young children (for a discussion, see, e.g. Forslund et al.,2021). However, in failing to qualify what kinds of separations he was writing about, Bowlby conveyed the impression that even ordinary separations, including limited use of day-care, was a risk factor for long-term harm. By contrast Ainsworth gave no public interviews, and she never wrote a magazine or popular article. Her energies were firmly focused on establishing the scientific basis of attachment as a research paradigm. With exceptions such as Patricia Crittenden (e.g. Spieker & Crittenden, 2018), and Peter Fonagy (e.g. Fonagy & Higgitt, 2004), the next generation of attachment researchers followed Ainsworth's approach of focusing on research and ignoring public understandings and misunderstandings of attachment. As Susan Goldberg (2000) observed, after Bowlby "many attachment researchers (myself included) have been reluctant to take on this responsibility" (p. 248). This left popular misunderstandings influenced by Bowlby's crudest statements too frequently unchallenged.

Half a century later, important theoretical papers and empirical studies conducted by the successors of Bowlby and Ainsworth are often stuck behind paywalls and in books or encyclopaedias that are out of print or otherwise out of reach of potential readers. It is far too difficult for practitioners and publics to access attachment theory and research, and some of the books specifically targeted for practitioner audiences contain serious inaccuracies (e.g. Pearce, 2016). It is no wonder, then, that the image in wider circulation differs from the views held by attachment researchers (Duschinsky et al., 2020). Additionally, the diversity of stances within attachment research is too little visible from the outside, which can make attachment theory seem monolithic and unchanging.

In fact attachment theory and research has become both more complicated and much more diverse over time, when compared with the original formulations of Bowlby and Ainsworth. For instance, Ainsworth's model with three patterns of attachment has been expanded to include a fourth category of attachment termed "disorganized/ disoriented attachment" (Main & Solomon, 1986), as well as other characterizations in terms of dimensions (e.g. Fraley & Spieker 2003), additional categories (Landini et al., 2015), or scripts (Waters & Roisman, 2019). An "attachment disorder" category has also emerged within psychiatric nosology (Zeanah et al., 2016). Attachment measures have also been developed for children of various ages, for adolescents, and for adults, enabling research on attachment across the life span. Research on caregiver behavior thought important for children's attachment quality has also expanded to include various behaviors beyond sensitivity, including attention to the role of alarming caregiver behaviors (see Madigan et al. 2006). There has also been growing concern with the relationship between child attachment and child temperament (e.g. Belsky & Rovine, 1987). Attachment theory and research have also expanded from an initial focus on one "primary caregiver", to an interest in children's often multiple attachment relationships and their respective importance for child development (see Dagan & Sagi-Schwartz 2018). The initial emphasis on child–caregiver relationships has also expanded to include attachment relationships between romantic partners, and a variety of attachment-based interventions have been developed (see Mikulincer & Shaver 2018).

Over the decades the volume of empirical research has grown too large to be easily captured, in part due to the various developments and extensions of the theory, as well as the accumulation of empirical studies (Verhage et al., 2020). The *Handbook of Attachment,* edited by Jude Cassidy and Phil Shaver (2016), is a landmark attempt at integrating the current status of attachment theory and research, but the book stands at over a thousand pages, illustrating the challenge. Jeremy Holmes' and Arietta Slade's (2013) *Attachment Theory* also provides quite a comprehensive picture, but in the form of six edited volumes, it comes at a cost that renders it out of reach except for those with access to university libraries. Robbie Duschinsky's (2020) *Cornerstones of Attachment* (free to download from the Oxford University Press website) characterizes some of the key elements of attachment theory and research through a study of five nodal research groups, but is by no means a comprehensive survey.

For a variety of reasons then, over time the positions of classic and contemporary attachment researchers in their diversity and depth seem to have become lost in the public reception of the paradigm. Whilst there is much consensus, there are also relevant differences between researchers on several grounds, including but not limited to the following:

- What is attachment and how it should be conceptualized?
- How shall attachment be measured and are assessments valid across cultures?
- How does a child develop attachment relationships with various caregivers?
- What caregiver behaviors are important for child attachment?
- Are ideas about temperament compatible with attachment theory?
- To what extent do attachment experiences contribute to later development?
- What is the standing of the attachment disorder diagnosis?
- What are the implications of attachment theory and research for interventions?

Our intention with this book has been twofold. First, we wanted to provide a book that is sufficiently short and accessible, but which nonetheless gives an interesting introduction to the main tenets of attachment theory and its developments and diversity. Second, we wanted to increase the accessibility of some important but relatively inaccessible texts in attachment theory and research. We hope that this *Reader* offers some access to the richness and excitement of attachment theory and research, as well as to its diversity and current limitations. There is of course no way that a single volume can capture all that it should. Our selections have ultimately been oriented by three principles:

1. The first and most important principle has been to select important papers "off the beaten track." This includes papers never published in English, that are out of print or that are otherwise especially difficult to find. We have not included works already reprinted in other anthologies, or readily available for free online.
2. A second principle has been to select papers that offer something surprising that runs against common assumptions about attachment theory and research.
3. A third principle has been that in each chapter there should be something that will surprise or intrigue even a specialist.

*Attachment Theory & Research: A Reader* is intended as both a reference point and as an invitation to further exploration, with potential relevance for diverse readers including students, clinicians and other professionals, policy-makers and other interested individuals. Access to previously inaccessible and unpublished work should also make it relevant to researchers in developmental and social psychology. The book comprises fifteen papers and includes, for instance, an unpublished paper by John Bowlby, an unknown paper by Mary Ainsworth, and an important paper by Mary Main and Erik Hesse on disorganized attachment that has previously only been published in Italian. We have placed the papers in chronological order, largely coinciding with a progression from main tenets and classic attachment theory towards later research and selected applications and extensions.

In the first paper, John Bowlby (1960) discusses the concept of "separation anxiety" and lays out some of the theoretical proposals that would take center stage in his canonical trilogy *Attachment and Loss* (1969/1980). He takes as his starting point the anxiety that almost all children, from a certain age, show upon separation from their caregivers. He critiques contemporary views in which attachment and separation anxiety were seen as "secondary" to a child's concerns about being fed, or a consequence of distortions of "psychic energies." He then draws primarily on ethology to argue that attachment and separation anxiety are important "primary" phenomena that humans share with other animals, and which are mediated by "instinctual response systems" that have been retained in evolution due to their survival value. He also elaborates on the "protest-despair-detachment" sequence of behavior that he and his colleagues observed in response to being separated from caregivers and cared for by unfamiliar nurses on shift duty, and describes separation anxiety as a normative and inescapable corollary of attachment. He then critically discusses psychoanalytic theories of separation anxiety contesting the idea that children may be spoilt by excessive love and gratification. He argues that fear of separations and withdrawal of love can lead to problems with hostility and anxiety.

In the second paper, John Bowlby discusses the concepts of "anxiety," "stress," and "homeostasis," structured around the premise that we must consider basic biological principles in order to understand conditions that elicit anxiety and fear. He discusses both the nature of states held relatively stable by living organisms ("homeostasis"), and the nature of stable pathways along which development proceeds ("homeorhesis"), and argues that anxiety and fear are experienced when stable states are threatened by instability. Drawing from dynamic systems theory he elaborates on five types of homeostasis and homeorhesis, including three that are presumed to be older from an evolutionary perspective (physiological, morphological, ecological homeostasis) and two that he argues are more recent (representational, and person–environmental homeostasis). He then discusses the role of disturbance of representational and personal–environmental homeostasis in psychological growth as well as ill health. To this end, he discusses the concepts of "stress," "stressors" and "trauma," and emphasizes the importance of processes designed to restore homeostasis and homeorhesis. Finally, he elucidates similarities and differences between the concepts of "anxiety" and "fear," and the terms "security" and "safety," and discusses conscious and unconscious anxiety and fear. Given the longstanding interest in the link between caregiving, attachment quality, and child development, we believe that this paper is important to publish.

In the third paper, Mary Ainsworth (1984) presents the foundational ideas of attachment theory, summarizes research and discusses the future prospects of the paradigm. She discusses how the attachment system interacts with other behavioral systems, most notably the exploratory system. She then describes her own ground-breaking research regarding development of attachment and variations in attachment quality, focusing on the role of the caregiver's "sensitivity." To this end, she describes her development of the now classic strange situation procedure and differences between dyads classified as "secure," "avoidant" and "ambivalent/resistant." She also reviews research regarding attachment quality and subsequent development, elaborating on Bowlby's account on developmental pathways, and discusses loss of an attachment figure as a factor that may influence development. She considers the difference between healthy and unhealthy "mourning," and elaborates on Bowlby's notion of "incompatible models" of memory. This valuable presentation of Ainsworth's mature position on attachment theory and methodology, published in an obscure encyclopaedia, has remained unknown and, to the best of our knowledge, never cited.

In the fourth paper, Phillip Shaver, Cindy Hazan, and Donna Bradshaw (1988) discuss attachment in relation to romantic relationships. They note that research on romantic love has traditionally been descriptive and atheoretical, and argue for an attachment-based perspective informed by an evolutionary framework. They review a number of remarkable similarities between infant–caregiver attachment and adult romantic love, and apply Ainsworth's patterns of attachment to adult romantic relationships, describing two of their ground-breaking studies. Their discussion includes how self-designated attachment type was associated with participants' descriptions of their most important love relationship, descriptions of the self and descriptions of their attachment relationships during childhood. They then discuss limitations of their own research, emphasizing the preliminary measures of attachment constructs, and outline future research avenues. Crucially, they draw upon Bowlby's and Ainsworth's reasoning and suggest that romantic love relationships should entail an integration of three behavioral systems: attachment, sexuality and caregiving, and discuss the potential dynamics between these systems. Finally, they discuss grief in response to loss of a romantic attachment figure, using attachment theory to explain why loss can be so painful.

In the fifth paper, Alan Sroufe (1989), one of the leaders of the Minnesota longitudinal study of attachment and adaptation, discusses the importance of children's early attachment experiences and relationships for the development of the self, for social behavior and for relationship functioning. He approaches the topic from an "organizational perspective" and the concept of "dyadic regulation." Infants are seen as constantly embedded in formative relationships with their caregivers, and the self is seen as a "social creation," with the experiences that make up infant–caregiver relationships preceding, giving rise to and organizing children's development. He provides a detailed discussion of different stages in the development of the self and of regulation as going from regulation by the caregiver, via coordinated sequences of behavioral interaction, to increasingly independent self-regulation. He then draws on Bowlby and describes this organization as manifested in "internal working models" of self and others that are complementary in nature and generalized to subsequent relationships. Finally, drawing on findings from the Minnesota longitudinal study, he discuss secure attachment in relation to the concept of autonomy, potency of self and the feeling of the self as worthy of care.

In the sixth paper, Mary Main and Erik Hesse (1992) discuss theory and research regarding the origins of disorganized/disoriented attachment. They discuss the predicament a child faces when the attachment system and the fear system are simultaneously activated by caregiver behavior, with children both pushed away from frightening stimuli and pulled toward their caregivers. In so doing, they describe disorganized/disoriented attachment and the approach–avoidance conflict that is thought to arise when a caregiver is associated by a child with alarm. They then discuss links between unresolved traumatic experiences, as measured by lapses in monitoring of reasoning and discourse upon discussing traumatic loss and abuse in their interview instrument the "Adult Attachment Interview," and momentary "frightened" caregiving behavior, focusing on non-maltreating caregivers. Finally, they discuss adult unresolved/disorganized states of mind, and infant disorganized/disoriented attachment, in relation to a propensity for "dissociation" and "trance-like states." This paper is perhaps Main and Hesse's most detailed account of the psychological mechanisms inferred to underpin disorganized attachment and unresolved states of mind. However it has previously only been published in Italian.

In the seventh paper, Owens and colleagues (1995) present the results of an early empirical study regarding the concordance between adults' state-of-mind regarding attachment to caregivers and attachment quality to romantic partners. They discuss Freud's "prototype hypothesis," which Bowlby partly carried forward through his notion of "monotropy," and which suggests that early working models are to an extent generalized to subsequent relationships. Yet, they also note that Bowlby argued that internal working models are amenable to change following new experiences, and that we tend to have multiple attachment relationships, including more than one parent and romantic partners. They then pose important questions regarding how different working models, from different types of relationships, may be associated with and influence one another. They measure state-of mind regarding caregivers using the Adult Attachment Interview, and use a similar interview-based instrument – the Current Relationships Interview – to examine romantic attachment quality. They present and discuss their results, which challenge the prototype hypothesis, and provide a detailed discussion of important future research avenues.

In the eighth paper, Phillip Shaver (2006) discusses theory and research pertaining to the "dynamics of romantic love" and, in doing so, follows up on developments regarding their theory regarding the interplay between attachment, caregiving and sex. He critiques attempts to conceptualize romantic love primarily as affects, feelings and attitudes, and argues for the advantages of their conceptualization in terms of behavioral systems. He then addresses the challenge of how to best integrate the three systems, acknowledging that the theory may have failed to include the exploratory and affiliative systems. Also, he discusses the tendency to bestow loved ones with precious and irreplaceable qualities in relation to the caregiving system. He reviews both research examining associations between the three systems and research using priming. While many of their hypotheses have been corroborated, he argues that much is still uncertain regarding the origins of the interrelations between the systems and their dynamics, and elaborates on future research that may help resolve these issues.

In the ninth paper, Marinus van IJzendoorn and Marian Bakermans-Kranenburg (2012) discuss attachment theory in relation to temperament theory and emphasize a recent rapprochement, with caregiving acknowledged as influencing children's temperamental characteristics and temperament as influencing caregiving behavior. They refute an early hypothesis that variations in attachment behavior can be explained by temperamental characteristics and discuss alternative conceptualizations that focus on transactions. They give particular attention to Belsky's differential susceptibility model, which suggests that some children have a higher constitutional susceptibility to environmental influences than other children. In contrast to the more one-dimensional stress-diathesis model, this susceptibility is seen as "for better or worse," with genetically susceptible children faring worse than other children in suboptimal environments, but better than other children in enriched environments. They also apply the differential susceptibility model to caregiving, and discuss whether differential susceptibility may extend to caregiving practices.

In the tenth paper, Charles Zeanah and Mary Margaret Gleason (2015) review theory and research regarding "attachment disorders." They describe two distinct disorders: reactive attachment disorder (RAD), in which children display absence of attachment behavior, and disinhibited social engagement disorder (DSED), in which children display a lack of social reticence and show indiscriminate social behavior toward unfamiliar adults. While both disorders arise due to social neglect, they argue that their differentiation is motivated by differences in presentations, courses and correlates, and responsiveness to intervention. They also elaborate on differences between attachment disorders and patterns of attachment and discuss child vulnerability factors, since social neglect alone is not sufficient to explain the development of attachment disorders. They also discuss clinical correlates and co-morbidity, differentiating RAD from autism spectrum disorder and DSED from ADHD (Attention Deficit Hyperactivity Disorder), and discuss attachment disorders in relation to internalizing and externalizing problems. They also discuss the effects of deprivation on neurobiology, linking deprivation to structural and functional deviations in brain development. Finally, they discuss research on interventions, which have largely focused on adoption, and discuss different responsiveness between RAD and DSED.

In the eleventh paper, Matt Woolgar and Emma Baldock (2015) present the results of a study examining if there is a tendency to overdiagnose "attachment disorders" and "attachment problems" among adopted and looked-after children. Using one hundred consecutive referrals to a specialist unit in the UK, they examine whether attachment disorders and problems are identified in a higher extent in community-based referral letters than by specialists, and whether overdiagnosing of attachment disorders and attachment problems is at the expense of diagnosing more common problems such as ADHD and ODD (Oppositional Defiant Disorder). They elaborate on the potential allure of attachment disorders and attachment problems, and argue that the more common diagnoses should be considered as "first line diagnoses." One reason for this, they argue, is that whereas there is good access to evidence-based interventions for these more common problems, specific interventions for attachment disorders and problems are still at an early stage. Their findings not only suggest that there is a problem of over-diagnosing attachment disorders and problems, but also that these phenomena are ill understood. Based on their own findings and those of others, they then argue that the current diagnostic system for attachment problems is inadequate to meet the needs of clinicians, that there is confusion about an appropriate diagnostic framework and a lack of agreed upon standards for assessing attachment disorders.

In the twelfth paper, Ashley Groh and colleagues (2017) summarize and present the results of a recent series of meta-analyses on the association between child–mother attachment quality and (1) social competence, (2) internalizing problems, (3) externalizing problems and (4) temperament. They also examine whether effects endure or diminish over time, and if effects vary systematically depending on factors such as type of sample, child sex and socio-economic factors. They discuss results concerning differences between children classified as secure and insecure as well as regarding the four attachment categories, including some unexpected results regarding avoidant and resistant attachment. While the meta-analyses present robust support for the role of attachment quality in child development, they also elaborate on a number of empirical issues in need of inquiry. For instance, they note that the effects of attachment quality are small to moderate by Cohen's criteria. They also highlight that there is a scarcity of research on mediating mechanisms. They close by discussing potential problems with examining attachment in the strange situation in the form of four mutually exclusive categories.

In the thirteenth paper, Mary Dozier and Kristin Bernard (2017) describe their attachment-based intervention; the "Attachment and Biobehavioral Catch-up." They review theory and research on the importance of caregiver sensitivity for infants' development of biological and behavioral regulation, and emphasize the caregiver as a crucial co-regulator. They then describe their own ten-session home-visit programme the ABC, which was developed with a focus on caregivers at risk for inadequate and problematic care (e.g. abuse and neglect). They discuss how the ABC is designed to help caregivers (1) enhance nurturing behavior, (2) follow their children's leads and (3) reduce frightening behavior, and describe the importance of frequent and positive "in the moment" comments by the parent coach. They then review research showing positive effects of the ABC on caregiving sensitivity as well as on infants' attachment quality and self-regulatory ability, and describe an adaptation of the ABC for caregivers with toddlers. Finally, they discuss the need for further examination of the effectiveness of the ABC when implemented in the community.

In the fourteenth paper, Fabien Bacro and colleagues present theory and research on children's multiple attachment relationships and representations. They note that there is still a lack of consensus regarding the nature, structure and relative importance of each attachment relationship in children's development, and emphasize that parental roles have become more egalitarian in many countries. They then compare three theoretical models regarding how attachment relationships may become organized and influence child development: the hierarchical model based on Bowlby's notion of monotropy; the integrative model, in which different attachment relationships are thought to become integrated; and the independent model, in which different relationship models are seen as exerting independent effects on child development. In doing so, they review research examining whether children show preferences for certain caregivers, to what extent there is concordance in children's attachment quality with their mothers and fathers, and the respective influence of attachment to mothers and fathers for child development. Based on the increased number of children exposed to parental divorce they also review research regarding how different family contexts may influence children's attachment representations, and highlight the importance of the parental relationship post separation. Finally, they discuss research regarding placement trajectories and attachment quality in children placed in foster care, focusing on the risk for unstable placements and the need to repeatedly create new attachment relationships. They emphasize recent research by Bacro and colleagues who linked multiple placements to an increased risk for externalizing problems with disorganized attachment acting as a mediating mechanism. This chapter, which was written for the current anthology, includes research that has to date only been published in French.

In the fifteenth paper, Mary True presents theory and research on disorganized attachment and its origins, focusing on cultural differences in caregiving practices and the transferability of the strange situation procedure between cultures. She focuses particularly on her and her colleagues' research with Dogon mothers and infants in Mali, and presents new analyses motivated by advances in theory development. She describes Main and Hesse's theory of frightening/frightened caregiver behavior, and Lyons-Ruth's theory of dysfluent communication, and how her and her colleagues' initial findings were in line with both these "relational" theories of disorganization. However, she also notes that maternal sensitivity predicted attachment security in a "well baby exam" but not in the strange situation procedure, and that she and her colleagues did not observe any avoidant infants in the strange situation. She then contrasts the "proximal" caregiving practices of the Dogon with the "distal" caregiving practices in Western countries, and raises the question of whether the Dogon infants may have experienced overstress in the strange situation due to the rarity of experiencing such separations. She then presents and discusses her new analyses regarding the relational hypothesis and the overstress hypothesis, together with a meta-analysis examining whether the frequency of avoidant classifications is lower in Africa. The chapter was written for the current anthology.

## Suggested Further Reading

R. Duschinsky (2020). *Cornerstones of attachment research*. Oxford: Oxford University Press. Free to download here: https://global.oup.com/academic/product/cornerstones-of-attachment-research-9780198842064
   An in-depth appraisal of the respective contributions of five important research groups that have shaped theory and research on attachment: those led by Bowlby, Ainsworth, Main and Hesse, Sroufe and Egeland and Shaver and Mikulincer.

L. A. Sroufe, B. Egeland, E. A. Carlson, & W. A. Collins (2009). *The development of the person: The Minnesota study of risk and adaptation from birth to adulthood*. Guilford.
   A detailed account of the classic Minnesota longitudinal study, including its theoretically driven focus on important developmental at different time-points tasks and its key findings. A summary paper was also published by Sroufe as: L. A. Sroufe (2005). Attachment and development: A prospective, longitudinal study from birth to adulthood. *Attachment & Human Development*, 7(4), 349–367.

Jeremy Holmes and Arietta Slade (2018). *Attachment in therapeutic practice*. SAGE.
     One of the best books discussing the implications of attachment theory and research for psychotherapeutic practice.

Vivien Prior & Danya Glaser (2006). *Understanding attachment and attachment disorders: theory, evidence and practice*. Jessica Kingsley Press.
     The best existing textbook outlining attachment theory and research. However, the book is over ten years old, so there are important subsequent developments not covered here.

Howard Steele and Miriam Steele (Eds.). (2018) *Handbook of attachment-based interventions*. Guilford.
     A very helpful overview of the multiplicity of attachment-based interventions and evidence regarding their respective effectiveness.

Omri Gillath, Gery C. Karantzas, & R. Chris Fraley (2016). *Adult attachment: A concise introduction to theory and research*. Academic Press.
     A comprehensive overview of theory and findings from the social psychological tradition of attachment research, set out in an accessible Question & Answer format.

K. E. Grossmann, K. Grossmann, & E. Waters (Eds.). (2006). *Attachment from infancy to adulthood: The major longitudinal studies*. Guilford Press.
     A good overview of classic attachment research, with chapters presenting and discussing key findings from the first wave of major longitudinal studies to include attachment assessments.

Patricia Crittenden (2016). *Raising parents*, 2nd edn. Routledge.
     A lively starting point for engaging with the Dynamic Maturational Model of attachment and its clinical applications. An anthology of Crittenden's papers is also available: A. Landini, C. Baim, M. Hart, & S. Landa (Eds.). (2015). *Danger, development and adaptation: seminal papers on the Dynamic-Maturational Model of Attachment and Adaptation*. Brighton, UK: Waterside Press.

David Howe (2011). *Attachment across the lifecourse*. Palgrave Macmillan.
     An excellent overview of the findings of attachment research as relevant to different periods in the human life course. A strength is that the book is written clearly, and can easily be read by a non-specialist. It does not generally take much of a critical perspective on the research or theory.

Robert Karen (1994). *Becoming attached*. Oxford University Press.
     A readable and engaging introduction to the first generation of attachment researchers. Less scholarly, more journalistic.

Frank van der Horst (2011). *John Bowlby: From psychoanalysis to ethology: Unravelling the roots of attachment theory*. Blackwell .
     A meticulous intellectual biography of John Bowlby, covering his intellectual journey towards ethology as a main source of theoretical inspiration.

Jude Cassidy & Phillip Shaver (2018). *Handbook of attachment: Theory, research, and clinical applications*, 3rd edn. Guilford.
     A terrific, comprehensive account of attachment research that covers all the key topics in the "developmental" and "social psychology" traditions, with chapters written by leading experts.

Mario Mikulincer & Phillip R. Shaver (2016). *Attachment in adulthood*, 2nd edn. Guilford.
     A comprehensive integration of research in the social psychology tradition of attachment research.

# References

Ainsworth, M. (1968). Letter to John Bowlby, 27th April 1968. Wellcome Collections John Bowlby Archive, PP/Bow/K.4/12.

Ainsworth, M. D. S., Blehar, M. C., Waters, E., & Wall, S. N. ([1978] 2015).*Patterns of attachment: A psychological study of the strange situation*. Psychology Press.

Ainsworth, M. S., & Bowlby, J. (1991). An ethological approach to personality development. *American psychologist, 46*(4), 333–341.

Belsky, J., & Rovine, M. (1987). Temperament and attachment security in the strange situation: An empirical rapprochement. *Child Development, 58*, 787–795.

Bowlby, J. (1940). The influence of early environment in the development of neuroses and neurotic character. *International Journal of Psychoanalysis, 21*, 154–178.

Bowlby, J. (1951). Maternal care and mental health (Vol. 2). World Health Organization.

Bowlby, J. (1969/1982). *Attachment and loss: Attachment.* Pimlico.

Bowlby, J. (1987) Baby Love. *Hampstead and Highgate Express, April 3,* 1987.

Bowlby, J. (1988). Developmental psychiatry comes of age. *American Journal of Psychiatry, 145,* 1–10.

Bowlby, J., Robertson, J., & Rosenbluth, D. (1952). A two-year-old goes to hospital. *The Psychoanalytic Study of the Child, 7*(1), 82–94.

Cassidy, J. & Shaver, P. (Eds.). (2016). *Handbook of attachment: Theory, research, and clinical applications (3rd edn.).* Guilford Press.

Dagan, O., & Sagi-Schwartz, A. (2018). Early attachment network with mother and father: An unsettled issue. *Child Development Perspectives, 12*(2), 115–121.

Department for Education (2018). Children in need of help and protection: Call for evidence. https://www.gov.uk/government/consultations/children-in-need-of-help-and-protection-call-for-evidence

Duschinsky, R. (2020) *Cornerstones of attachment research.* Oxford University Press.

Duschinsky, R., Bakkum, L., Mannes, J., Skinner, G., Turner, M., Mann, A., Coughlan, B., Reijman, S., Foster, S., & Beckwith, H. (2020). Six attachment discourses: Convergence, *divergence and relay. Attachment and Human Development,* Forthcoming.

Gerhardt, S. (2014) *Why love matters: How affection shapes a baby's brain* (2nd edn.). Routledge.

Fonagy, P., & Higgitt, A. (2004). Early mental health intervention and prevention: The implications for government and the wider community. In B. Sklarew, S. W. Twemlow, & S. M. Wilkinson (Eds.), *Analysts in the trenches: Streets, schools, war zones (pp. 257–309).* Analytic Press.

Forslund, T., Granqvist, P., van IJzendoorn, M. H., Sagi-Schwartz, A., Glaser, D., Steele, M., Hammarlund, M., Schuengel, C., Bakermans-Kranenburg, M. J., Steele, H., Shaver, P. R., Lux, U., Simmonds, J., Jacobvitz, D., Groh, A. M., Bernard, K., Cyr, C., Hazen, N. L., Foster, S., . . . & Duschinsky, R. (2021). Attachment goes to court: Child protection and custody issues. *Attachment & Human Development,* 1–52.

Fraley, R., & Spieker, S. (2003). Are infant attachment patterns continuously or categorically distributed? A taxometric analysis of strange situation behavior. *Developmental Psychology, 39*(3), 387–404.

Furnivall, J., McKenna, M., McFarlane, S., & Grant, E. (2012). *Attachment matters for all: An attachment mapping exercise for children's services in Scotland.* Centre for Excellence for Looked after Children in Scotland (CELCIS). www.celcis.org/knowledge-bank/search-bank/attachment-matters-all

Goldberg, S. (2000). *Attachment and development.* London: Routledge.

Granqvist, P., Sroufe, L. A., Dozier, M., Hesse, E., Steele, M., van IJzendoorn, M., Solomon, J., Schuengel, C., Fearon, P., Bakermans-Kranenburg, M., Steele, H., Cassidy, J., Carlson, E., Madigan, S., Jacobvitz, D., Foster, S., Behrens, K., Rifkin-Graboi, A., Gribneau, N., ... & Duschinsky, R. (2017). Disorganized attachment in infancy: A review of the phenomenon and its implications for clinicians and policy-makers. *Attachment & Human Development, 19,* 534–558.

House of Commons Health and Social Care Committee (2019). *First 1000 days of life. Thirteenth report of session 2017–2019. HC 1496.* Health and Social Care Committee.

Keddell, E. (2017). Interpreting children's best interests: Needs, attachment and decision-making. *Journal of Social Work, 17*(3), 324–342.

Kohm, L. M. (2007). Tracing the foundations of the best interests of the child standard in American jurisprudence. *Journal of Law & Family Studies, 10,* 337–376.

Landini, A., Baim, C., Hart, M., & Landa, S. (Eds.). (2015). *Danger, dDevelopment and adaptation: Seminal papers on the Dynamic-Maturational Model of Attachment and Adaptation.* Waterside Press.

Madigan, S., Bakermans-Kranenburg, M. J., Van Ijzendoorn, M. H., Moran, G., Pederson, D. R., & Benoit, D. (2006). Unresolved states of mind, anomalous parental behavior, and disorganized attachment: A review and meta-analysis of a transmission gap. *Attachment & human development, 8*(2), 89–111.

Main, M., & Solomon, J. (1986). Discovery of an insecure-disorganized/disoriented attachment pattern. In T. B. Brazelton & M. W. Yogman (Eds.), *Affective development in infancy (pp. 95–124).* Ablex Publishing.

Mikulincer, M. & Shaver, P. R. (2016) *Attachment in adulthood,* 2nd edn. Guilford.

Morison, A., Taylor, E., & Gervais, M. (2020). How a sample of residential childcare staff conceptualize and use attachment theory in practice, *Child & Youth Services, 41*(1), 3–27.

Pearce, C. (2016). *A short introduction to attachment and attachment disorder.* Jessica Kingsley.

Reijman, S., Foster, S., & Duschinsky, R. (2018). The infant disorganised attachment classification: "Patterning within the disturbance of coherence." *Social Science & Medicine, 200,* 52–58.

Smith, M., Cameron, C., & Reimer, D. (2017). From attachment to recognition for children in care. *British Journal of Social Work, 47*(6), 1606–1623, p. 1606.

Spieker, S. J., & Crittenden, P. M. (2018). Can attachment inform decision-making in child protection and forensic settings? *Infant Mental Health Journal, 39*(6), 625–641.

Van der Horst, F. C. (2011). *John Bowlby: From psychoanalysis to ethology: Unravelling the roots of attachment theory.* Wiley.

Van der Horst, F. C., & Van der Veer, R. (2009). Why we disagree to disagree: a reply to commentaries by Robertson and McGilly, and Lindsay. *Attachment & Human Development, 11*(6), 569–572.

Van Rosmalen, L., Van Der Horst, F. C., & Van der Veer, R. (2016). From secure dependency to attachment: Mary Ainsworth's integration of Blatz's security theory into Bowlby's attachment theory. *History of Psychology, 19*(1), 22–39.

Van Rosmalen, L., Van der Veer, R., & Van der Horst, F. (2015). Ainsworth's strange situation procedure: The origin of an instrument. *Journal of the History of the Behavioral Sciences, 51*(3), 261–284.

Verhage, M. L., Schuengel, C., Duschinsky, R., van IJzendoorn, M. H., Fearon, R. P., Madigan, S., ... & Collaboration on Attachment Transmission Synthesis. (2020). The collaboration on Attachment Transmission Synthesis (CATS): A move to the level of individual-participant-data meta-analysis. *Current Directions in Psychological Science, 29*(2), 199–206.

Wastell, D., & White, S. (2017). *Blinded by science: The social implications of epigenetics and neuroscience.* Policy Press.

Waters, T. E., & Roisman, G. I. (2019). The secure base script concept: An overview. *Current opinion in psychology, 25,* 162–166.

Zeanah, C. H., Chesher, T., Boris, N. W., Walter, H. J., Bukstein, O. G., Bellonci, C., Benson, S., Bussing, R., Chrisman, A., Hamilton, J., Hayek, M., Keable, H., Rockhill, C., Siegel, M., & Stock, S. (2016). Practice parameter for the assessment and treatment of children and adolescents with reactive attachment disorder and disinhibited social engagement disorder. *Journal of the American Academy of Child & Adolescent Psychiatry, 55*(11), 990–1003.

# 1

# Separation Anxiety[1]

## John Bowlby

### Observations of Young Children

Since 1948 the Tavistock Child Development Research Unit has been concerned with recording the manifest responses which commonly occur when children between the ages of about 12 months and 4 years are removed from the mother figures[2] to whom they are attached and remain with strangers. Preliminary papers and a scientific film have been published (Robertson & Bowlby, 1952; Robertson, 1953a, 1953b; Bowlby, 1953, 1954) and a comprehensive report by James Robertson and the writer is in preparation. In it we shall draw not only on Robertson's own observations and those of other workers reported in the scientific literature, notably those of Burlingham and Freud (1942, 1944), and Heinicke (1956), but also on reports given us by mothers and nurses with first-hand experience of the problem. Since there is a high consensus in these reports we regard it as firmly established empirically that all children of this age, except those who have already suffered considerable deprivation of maternal care or are seriously ill, react to the experience with shock and anxiety. Our confidence in the validity of these observations is something we wish to emphasize since it is not uncommon for those whose theories lead to expectations of a different kind to cast doubt on them. In our view it is the theories which are mistaken, not the observations, and it is with the theoretical issues raised by these data that this paper is concerned.

It is evident, however, that the nature and dynamics of the responses to the rupture of a social bond cannot be understood until there is some understanding of the nature and dynamics of the bond itself. It was because of this that in a recently published paper (Bowlby, 1958) I discussed how best the nature of the young child's tie to his mother could be conceptualized. In it I advanced the view that instead of the tie being motivated by a secondary drive or one wholly based on orality, which are the most commonly held views today, it may be mediated by a number of instinctual response systems which are partially independent of one another and which wax and wane in activity at different periods of the infant's and young child's life. I suggested that much psycho-analytic theory, by concentrating attention too narrowly either on the meeting of 'physiological' needs (e.g. for food and warmth) or on orality, may have led to the picture as a whole being seen out of perspective; and that other responses, particularly clinging and following which seem to reach their zenith in the second and third years, require far more attention than they have yet been given.

The reasons leading me to advance these views are clinical: traditional theory has seemed to me to account neither for the intense attachment of child to mother-figure which is so conspicuous in the later months of the first year and throughout the second and third years of life, nor for the dramatic responses to separation from her

Source: John Bowlby, "Separation anxiety," pp. 89–113 from International Journal of Psychoanalysis 41:1 (1960).

which are the rule in these years. A formulation, based on a theoretical framework stemming from modern instinct theory, has seemed to me more promising. It is the line of thought begun in the previous paper that I shall pursue further in this one.

First let us consider the data.

Our observations[3] concern healthy children of 15 to 30 months admitted to a hospital, perhaps for investigation or elective surgery, or to some other residential institution and there cared for in traditional ways. By traditional ways we mean that the child is handled by a succession of strange nurses, mainly students, who will variously bathe, feed, and change him. The nurses will be on shift duty, and often within a few weeks most will have moved to other departments. No matter how kind each may be in her fragment of care, there will be no nurse whom he can come to know or with whom he can enter into a stable relationship. He may see his mother for a short time each day, but it may be less often. In this context a child of 15 to 30 months who has had a normal relationship to his mother and has not previously been parted from her will commonly show a predictable sequence of behaviour. This sequence can usefully be broken into three phases according to what attitude to his mother is dominant. We describe these phases as those of protest, despair, and detachment.[4] Though in presenting them it is convenient to differentiate them sharply, it is to be understood that in reality each merges into the next, so that the child may be for days or weeks in a state of transition from, or alternation between, one phase and another.

The initial phase, that of *Protest*, may last from a few hours to a week or more. During it the young child appears acutely distressed at having lost his mother and seeks to recapture her by the full exercise of his limited resources. He will often cry loudly, shake his cot, throw himself about, and look eagerly towards any sight or sound which might prove to be his missing mother. All his behaviour suggests strong expectation that she will return. Meantime he is apt to reject all alternative figures who offer to do things for him, though some children will cling desperately to a nurse.

During the phase of *Despair*, which succeeds protest, his preoccupation with his missing mother is still evident, though his behaviour suggests increasing hopelessness. The active physical movements diminish or come to an end, and he may cry monotonously or intermittently. He is withdrawn and inactive, makes no demands on the environment, and appears to be in a state of deep mourning. This is a quiet stage, and sometimes, clearly erroneously, is presumed to indicate a diminution of distress.

Because the child shows more interest in his surroundings, the phase of *Detachment* which sooner or later succeeds protest and despair is often welcomed as a sign of recovery. He no longer rejects the nurses, accepts their care and the food and toys they bring, and may even smile and be sociable. This seems satisfactory. When his mother visits, however, it can be seen that all is not well, for there is a striking absence of the behaviour characteristic of the strong attachment normal at this age. So far from greeting his mother he may seem hardly to know her; so far from clinging to her he may remain remote and apathetic; instead of tears there is a listless turning away. He seems to have lost all interest in her.

Should his stay in hospital or residential nursery be prolonged and should he, as is usual, have the experience of becoming transiently attached to a series of nurses each of whom leaves and so repeats for him the experience of the original loss of his mother, he will in time act as if neither mothering nor contact with humans had much significance for him. After a series of upsets at losing several mother-figures to whom in turn he has given some trust and affection, he will gradually commit himself less and less to succeeding figures and in time will stop altogether taking the risk of attaching himself to anyone. Instead he will become increasingly self-centred and, instead of directing his desires and feelings towards people, become preoccupied with material things such as sweets, toys, and food. A child living in an institution or hospital who has reached this state will no longer be upset when nurses change or leave. He will cease to show feelings when his parents come and go on visiting day; and it may cause them pain when they realize that, although he has an avid interest in the presents they bring, he has little interest in them as special people. He will appear cheerful and adapted to his unusual situation and apparently easy and unafraid of anyone. But this sociability is superficial: he appears no longer to care for anyone.

We have had some difficulty in finding the best term to denote this phase. In previous papers and in the early drafts of this one the term 'denial' was used. It gave rise to many difficulties, however, and is now abandoned in favour of the more purely descriptive term 'detachment'. An alternative is 'withdrawal', but this has two disadvantages for my purpose. In the first place there is a danger that it might convey the picture of an inactive child withdrawn from the world, a picture that is the opposite of what often obtains. In the second, in psycho-analytic writing it is commonly associated with libido theory and the idea of instinct as a quantity of energy which can be withdrawn, a model I am not using. Not only does the term 'detachment' have neither of these disadvantages, but it is a natural counterpart of 'attachment'. The nature of the defence process, or processes, that give rise to it is of course a matter for detailed study. In an earlier publication (Bowlby, 1954) I have discussed briefly its relation to repression and I hope at a later date to give this further attention.

Returning now to the empirical data, I wish to emphasize that the behaviour seen in the phases of Protest and Despair is not, as is sometimes alleged, confined to children whose relations to their mothers are already impaired. Though we have no large series of well-observed cases to quote, we are satisfied that there is clear evidence that it occurs in children whose previous relationships would be judged to have been anything between excellent and fairly unfavourable. It appears to be only in children whose relationships are already severely impaired, and who may therefore already be in a phase of Detachment, that such behaviour is absent.

In examining the theoretical problems raised by these observations it is convenient to consider them with reference to these three phases of behaviour. The phase of Protest raises the problem especially of separation anxiety; Despair that of grief and mourning; Detachment that of defence. Each of them is central to psychoanalytic theory and will therefore need detailed discussion – the first in this paper, the second and third in succeeding ones. The thesis to be advanced is that the three types of response – separation anxiety, grief and mourning, and defence – are phases of a single process and that when treated as such each illumines the other two.

Often in the literature they have been considered piecemeal. The reason for this appears to be the inverted order in which their psycho-pathological significance was discovered: for it was the last phase which was recognized first, and the first last. Thus the significance of defence, particularly repression, was realized fully by Freud in the earliest days of his psycho-analytic work and provides the basis of his classical theorizing: his first paper on the subject is dated 1894 (Freud 1894). His grasp of the roles of grief and separation anxiety on the other hand, although not wholly absent in his earlier work, was none the less fragmentary. Thus, although early alive to the place of mourning in hysteria and melancholia (Freud, [1897] 1954), twenty years were to elapse before, in *Mourning and Melancholia* (1917), he gave it systematic attention. Similarly in the case of separation anxiety: although in the *Three Essays on Sexuality* (1905) he gave it a paragraph (p. 224), and in the *Introductory Lectures* (1917) three pages (pp. 339–341), it is not until 1926 that in his important late work, *Inhibitions, Symptoms and Anxiety* (Freud, 1926), he gives it the central place in what was to be his final theory of anxiety. 'Missing someone who is loved and longed for' he affirms, 'is the key to an understanding of anxiety' (pp. 136–137), and it is on this datum that the whole argument of his book rests.

The reason for this inverse recognition of the three phases is clear: always in the history of medicine it is the end result of a pathological sequence which is first to be noted. Only gradually are the earlier phases identified, and it may be many years before the exact sequence of the whole process is understood. Indeed it was understanding the sequence which baffled Freud longest. Does defence precede anxiety, or anxiety defence? If the response to separation is pain and mourning, how can it also be anxiety? (Freud, 1926, pp. 108–109 and 130–131). It can now be seen that during the thirty years of his main psycho-analytic explorations Freud traversed the sequence backwards, from end result to initial stage. Not until his seventieth year did he clearly perceive the source and course of the processes to which he had devoted half a lifetime of study. The effects on psychoanalytical theorizing have inevitably been confusing.

By 1926 a substantial corpus of psycho-analytic theory was already being taught. As regards anxiety, castration anxiety and superego anxiety were cornerstones of thought and practice in Vienna and elsewhere, whilst Melanie Klein's hypothesis relating anxiety to aggression had recently been formulated and, linked to the concept of the death instinct, was soon to become a key concept in a significant new system. The full weight of Freud's ideas on separation anxiety and its relation to mourning came too late to influence the development of either of these two schools of thought.

Moreover, apart from the prophetic early reference by Hug-Hellmuth ([1913] 1919) and a brief word by Bernfeld ([1925] 1929), some years were to pass before the clinical papers drawing attention to the pathogenic significance of separation experiences were published. Some of the earliest, by Levy (1937), Bowlby (1940, 1944), and Bender and Yarnell (1941), presented empirical evidence suggesting an aetiological relationship between certain forms of psychopathic personality and severely disrupted mother–child relationships. At about the same time, Fairbairn ([1941] 1952, [1943] 1952) was basing his revised psycho-pathology on separation anxiety, having been preceded by some years by Suttie (1935) and to be followed a few years later by Odier ([1948] 1956); whilst Therese Benedek (1946) was describing responses to separation, reunion and bereavement which were to be observed in adults during the war. Meanwhile the firsthand observations of Dorothy Burlingham and Anna Freud (1942, 1944) of how young children respond to separation were being recorded, and Spitz (1946) was about to shock those who had eyes to see with his account of extremely deprived babies. Despite all this work by qualified analysts, however, and a number of important papers by Goldfarb (1943) and others, separation anxiety has never gained a central place in psycho-analytic theorizing. Indeed Kris (1956), writing as a participant in the Viennese scene, remarked recently how, when in 1926 Freud advanced his views regarding separation anxiety, 'there was no awareness amongst analysts … to what typical concrete situations this would apply. Nobody realized that the fear of losing the object and the object's love were formulae to be implemented by material which now seems to us self-evident beyond any discussion.' He acknowledged that only in the past decade had he himself recognized its significance, and could have added that even today there are schools of analytic thought which deny its importance. The continuing neglect of separation anxiety is well illustrated by a recent and authoritative survey of 'the concept of anxiety in relation to the development of psycho-analysis' (Zetzel, 1955) in which it is not once mentioned.

In the event, it is clear, some of the ideas Freud advanced in *Inhibitions, Symptoms and Anxiety* fell on stony ground. This was a pity, since in that book, written at the end of his professional life, he was struggling to free himself of the perspective of his travels – defence, mourning, separation anxiety – and instead to view the sequence from his new vantage point: the priority of separation anxiety. In his concluding pages he sketches out a new route: anxiety is a reaction to the danger of losing the object, the pain of mourning to the retreat from the lost object, defence a mode of dealing with anxiety and pain. This is the route we shall be following.

## Principal Theories

No concept is more central to psycho-analytical theory than the concept of anxiety. Yet it is one about which there is little consensus of opinion, which accounts in no small measure for the divisions between different schools of thought. Put briefly, all analysts are agreed that anxiety cannot be explained simply by reference to external threat: in some way processes usually thought of as internal and instinctive seem to play a crucial role. But how these inner forces are to be conceptualized and how they give rise to anxiety, that has always been the puzzle.

As a result of this state of affairs we find, when we come to consider how analysts conceive separation anxiety, some widely differing formulations; for each formulation is strongly influenced by the particular outlook regarding the nature and origin of anxiety which the analyst happens to have. Moreover, the place given to separation anxiety within the wider theory of anxiety varies greatly. For some, like Hermann and Fairbairn, separation anxiety is the most important primary anxiety; for others, like Freud in both his earlier and later work, it is only the shortest of steps removed from being so; for others again, like Melanie Klein and her associates, separation anxiety is deemed to be secondary to and of less consequence than other and more primitive anxieties. This being the present state of thought, inevitably the discussion has to touch on all aspects of the theory of anxiety. Yet it will be my plan to restrict the wider discussion as far as possible in order to concentrate on the task in hand, namely to understand separation anxiety and its relation to mourning.

A review of the literature shows that there have been six main approaches to the problem of separation anxiety; three of them are the counterparts, though not always the necessary counterparts, of theories regarding the nature of the child's attachment to his mother. In the order in which they have received attention by psychoanalysts, they are: –

i.     The first, advanced by Freud in *Three Essays* (1905), is a special case of the general theory of anxiety which he held until 1926. As a result of his study of anxiety neurosis (1894) Freud had advanced the view that morbid anxiety is due to the transformation into anxiety of sexual excitation of somatic origin which cannot be discharged. The anxiety observed when an infant is separated from the person he loves, Freud holds, is an example of this, since in these circumstances the child's libido remains unsatisfied and undergoes transformation. This theory may be called the theory of *Transformed Libido*. It resembles in many ways the sixth main approach, which is the one adopted here.

ii.    The anxiety shown on separation of young children from mother is a reproduction of the trauma of birth, so that birth anxiety is the prototype of all the separation anxiety subsequently experienced. Following Rank ([1924] 1929) we can term it the *Birth-Trauma* theory. It is the counterpart of the theory of return-to-womb craving to account for the child's tie.

iii.   In the absence of the mother the infant and young child is subject to the risk of a traumatic psychic experience, and he therefore develops a safety device which leads to anxiety behaviour being exhibited when she leaves him.

Such behaviour has a function: it may be expected to ensure that he is not parted from her for too long. I shall term this the *Signal* theory, employing a term introduced by Freud (1926) in *Inhibitions, Symptoms and Anxiety*. It is held in three variants according to how the traumatic situation to be avoided is conceived. They are: (*a*) that the traumatic situation is an economic disturbance which is caused when there develops an accumulation of excessive amounts of stimulation arising from unsatisfied bodily needs; (*b*) that it is the imminence of a total and permanent extinction of the capacity for sexual enjoyment, namely aphanisis (Jones, 1927). (When first advanced by Jones as an explanation of anxiety, the theory of aphanisis was not related to the anxiety of separation; two years later, however, he sought to adapt it so as to fit in with Freud's latest ideas). Finally (*c*), there is the variant proposed by Spitz (1950) that the traumatic situation to be avoided is one of narcissistic trauma. It should be noted that in the history of Freud's thought the Signal theory stems from, and is in certain respects the counter-part of, the theory which explains the child's tie to his mother in terms of secondary drive.

iv.  Separation anxiety results from the small child, owing to his ambivalence to his mother, believing when she disappears that he has eaten her up or otherwise destroyed her, and that in consequence he has lost her for good. Following Melanie Klein ([1935] 1952) we can call it the theory of *Depressive Anxiety*.

v.  Following the projection of his aggression, the young child perceives his mother as persecutory: as a result he interprets her departure as due to her being angry with him or wishing to punish him. for these reasons whenever she leaves him he believes she may either never return or do so only in a hostile mood, and he there-fore experiences anxiety. Again following Melanie Klein, this can be termed the theory of *Persecutory Anxiety*.

vi.  Initially the anxiety is a primary response not reducible to other terms and due simply to the rupture of the attachment to his mother. I propose to call it the theory of *Primary Anxiety*. It is the counterpart to theories which account for the child's tie to his mother in terms of component instinctual responses. It has been advanced by James (1890), Suttie (1935) and Hermann (1936), but has never been given much attention in analytic circles.

The hypothesis I shall be adopting is the sixth, since it stems directly from my hypothesis that the child is bound to his mother by a number of instinctual response systems, each of which is primary and which together have high survival value. Soon after birth, it is held, conditions of isolation tend to activate crying and a little later tend to activate both clinging and following also; until he is in close proximity to his familiar mother – figure these instinctual response systems do not cease motivating him. Pending this outcome, it is suggested, his subjective experience is that of primary anxiety; when he is close to her it is one of comfort.

Such anxiety is not to be conceived merely as a 'signal' to warn against something worse (though it might sub-sequently come to have this function). Instead, it is thought of as an elemental experience and one which, if it reaches a certain degree of intensity, is linked directly with the onset of defence mechanisms. It is because of this, and because I wish to distinguish it sharply from states of anxiety dependent on foresight, that I have termed it Primary Anxiety.[5]

Although I believe states of primary anxiety due to separation to be among the most frequent and pathogenic of such states, it is postulated that primary anxiety will arise in other circumstances also – perhaps whenever any instinctual response system is activated but not terminated. Primary anxiety due to separation seems likely, there-fore, to be but one example of a common condition. It has, however, several special features. Not least of these is its specially close linkage in infants and young children to the experiences of fright and fear. When frightened, infants and young children look to their mother for security and if they fail to find her are doubly upset: both com-fort and security are missing.

It is interesting, though by no means easy, to compare the theory of primary anxiety with Freud's two theories. The similarity to his original one of Transformed Libido is close. Although on occasion Freud spoke as though libido could only be transformed into anxiety after it had first been repressed, this does not appear to be basic to his formulation. Indeed, in his discussion of the conditions which lead anxiety to become pathological the process inculpated is repression (Freud, 1909, p. 26); in the absence of repression, we may therefore infer, there would still be anxiety, but it would be within normal limits. If this is a correct reading, then the main difference appears to be that, whereas in the theory advanced here primary anxiety is an immediate consequence of the persistent activation without termination of certain instinctual response systems, in Freud's theory anxiety is conceived as being the result of a 'transformation' which the libido undergoes.

The theory of primary anxiety appears to differ more from Freud's second theory, that of Signal Anxiety, than from his first. The principal difference here is that Freud postulates that a fairly complex process of motor learning must have occurred. The other difference, though it is not logically necessary for his position, is that he postulates also some awareness in the infant of causal relationships. The theory advanced here on the other hand makes no such assumptions and, instead, sees the anxiety as primitive and dependent only on simple orientational learning. Nevertheless, it must be remembered, Freud also postulated the existence of a primitive biologically based anxiety which is evoked by separation, and it is therefore useful to compare the two views. In Freud's theory this primitive anxiety is conceived as resulting from the instincts serving the infant's *bodily needs*, e.g. for food, becoming active and not being satisfied: in the theory here advanced it is conceived as resulting from the *instinctual response systems underlying attachment behaviour* (notably crying, following, and clinging) becoming activated and remaining so. Thus in both cases the primitive anxiety is conceived as resulting from instinctual systems which, whilst gratified by the mother's actions or presence, remain ungratified in her absence; or, in terms of the conceptual framework used here, from instinctual responses which, whilst terminated by the mother's actions or presence, remain unterminated in her absence. The essential difference therefore lies in the nature of the instinctual systems postulated as being involved.

At first sight the theory of primary anxiety may also seem to have something in common with the Birth Trauma theory. For instance, some might argue that, if anxiety is experienced at birth, it is no more than one example of primary anxiety arising from separation. However, this seems to me improbable since, like Freud (1926, pp. 130–131), I am not satisfied that true separation anxiety is present in the earliest months.[6] The birth trauma theory is not regarded as having explanatory value.

Whilst the theory of primary anxiety postulates that separation anxiety is itself an unlearnt and biologically based anxiety, it is far from blind to the existence and pathogenic importance of anxieties which are dependent on learning and anticipation. In the human it seems useful to distinguish at least two main forms of anticipatory behaviour – that based on primitive forms of learning, such as conditioning, and that based on memory organized by means of symbols. As soon as infants can be conditioned, which is very early, they can acquire a simple form of anticipatory behaviour and, in so far as the events to which they are conditioned are disagreeable, such for example as pain, hunger, or lack of human contact, they may be supposed to experience anxiety. This I shall term *Conditioned Anxiety*. Cognitively, it is still rather a primitive form of anxiety and in many ways more closely resembles primary anxiety than the form next to be described. Later, when the infant develops his capacity for using symbols and can thereby construct a world of objects existing in time and space and interacting causally, he is able to develop some measure of true foresight. Should the foreseen events be of a kind he has learned are disagreeable, he will once again experience anxiety. This I shall term *Expectant Anxiety*. Once this level of psychic organization is reached many kinds of danger, real and imaginary, may be foreseen and responded to. For example, whatever may occur at more primitive levels, at this level both persecutory and depressive anxieties play a crucial role; for anything which leads the child to believe he either has destroyed or alienated his mother, or may do so, cannot fail to exacerbate his expectant anxiety of temporary or permanent separation.

It is to be noted that originally the theories of persecutory and depressive anxiety were advanced by Melanie Klein independently of the problem of separation anxiety; and that, moreover, persecutory and depressive anxieties are conceived by her as existing, initially at least, in very primitive form either from birth or from the earliest weeks. Their manifestations at a higher level of psychic organization, she holds, are to be understood as stemming from these primitive roots. I remain sceptical of this view. It is therefore necessary to emphasize that such formulations are not indispensable to the concepts of persecutory and depressive anxiety: there is no need for their role at a higher level of psychic organization to be conceived as stemming from more primitive roots. That they play an immensely important role in the more developed psychic organizations, not least in exacerbating separation anxiety and raising it to pathological levels, there can be no doubt. In this paper, therefore, persecutory and depressive anxieties will be treated as of major consequence in the elaboration of separation anxiety at a higher level of psychic organization, whilst leaving as an open question their existence and role at a more primitive level.[7]

## Primary Anxiety, Fright, and Anxiety Dependent on Learning

It is my belief that the theory of instinctual responses deriving from ethology and advanced in my previous paper permits a new approach. The heart of this theory is that the organism is provided with a repertoire of behaviour patterns, which are bred into it like the features of its anatomy and physiology, and which have become characteristic of its species *because of their survival value to the species*. Such, it was suggested, are many of the responses characteristic of the family life of Man, namely those mediating relationships between the sexes and between parents and young. This provides an instinct theory having much in common with Freud's theory of part-instincts and his notion of the 'blind' strivings of the id.

Before applying this theory to separation anxiety as the particular problem under examination, however, it is necessary to review the whole problem of anxiety and fear reactions afresh. In doing so four conditions will be delineated each of which, it is believed, although in essence very different from the others, contributes in a special way to our problem. These are primary anxiety, fright, conditioned anxiety, and expectant anxiety.

In grasping the theory to be advanced it is vital to distinguish sharply between the concept of self-preservation and that of species survival: probably all biologists would regard the first, when conceived as an 'instinct of self-preservation', as one of the most influential of misleading theories, the second as one of the most pregnant concepts in the history of biology. The notion of an instinct of self-preservation posits a force or set of forces which is designed to ensure that *a particular individual* is preserved. The notion of species survival, which stems from evolution theory, points on the other hand to the fact that any biological character which is advantageous to *the species* tends to be perpetuated (through processes of natural selection and heredity), whilst any that are not so advantageous tend, over the course of generations, to be dropped out. It is true that often what is advantageous for the species is also advantageous for the individual; but there is no guarantee of identity of interest, and where they conflict it can be that it is the interests of the individual which go to the wall. That anatomical and physiological characteristics are subject to this rule has long been recognized. The conspicuous plumage of many birds, which is indispensable to their success in mating, may be most disadvantageous to their safety. The interests of individual survival are sacrificed; the interests of species propagation are paramount. That psychological characteristics are subject to the same law has, thanks largely to the superficial plausibility of the self-preservation theory, been slow to be appreciated. Yet it is clear that all psychological characteristics which have been developed because of their species survival value *must* be so subject, and these must include any characteristics to which the term instinctual is applied. For these reasons, in discussing the theory of anxiety and fright reactions, no references will be made to the concept of self-preservation. Instead we shall be thinking in terms of species-specific behaviour patterns, or instinctual response systems as I prefer to call them,[8] which are present because of their survival value to the species and which operate, at least initially, in the blind and automatic way regarded by Freud as characteristic of the id.

In the previous paper I described some of the characteristics of what I termed instinctual response systems which are to be culled from the recent work of ethologists: 'The basic model for instinctive behaviour is thus a unit comprising a species-specific behaviour pattern (or instinctual response) governed by two complex mechanisms, one controlling its activation and the other its termination. Although sometimes to be observed active in isolation, in real life it is usual for a number of these responses to be linked together so that adaptive behavioural sequences result.' I proceeded to consider 'how as humans we experience the activation in ourselves of an instinctual response system'. When the system is active and free to reach termination, it seems, we experience an urge to action accompanied, as Lorenz (1950) has suggested,[9] by an emotional state peculiar to each response. There is an emotional experience peculiar to smiling and laughing, another peculiar to weeping, yet another to sexual foreplay, another again to temper. When, however, the response is not free to reach termination, our experience may be very different; we experience tension, unease, anxiety. It is this line of thought I wish to pursue.

The hypothesis advanced is that, whenever an instinctual response system is activated and is unable for any reason to reach termination, a form of anxiety results. The blockage may be of many different kinds. In some cases the environment may fail to provide the terminating conditions, as for example when there is sexual arousal in the absence of an appropriate partner. In other cases two or more instinctual responses may be active but incompatible, for example, attack and escape. In other cases again, the blockage may be associated with fear or guilt, or some deeper inhibition. No doubt the particular form of blockage will influence outcome; here, however, I wish to emphasize only the common feature. No matter what the nature of the blockage, it is postulated, if an instinctual response system is activated and unable to reach termination, changes occur both in behaviour (namely in psychological and physiological functioning) and also in the subjective experience of the individual himself. When it rises above a moderate level it gives rise to the subjective experience of anxiety. To distinguish it from other forms of anxiety I am terming it primary anxiety.

Whether in fact every kind of instinctual response system which is active and unable to reach termination is accompanied by primary anxiety needs further exploration. So too do the behavioural accompaniments of anxiety. Both the physiological and the psychological components seem likely to be in large part unlearnt and thus in some respects to resemble instinctual responses. The psychological components are of course of great consequence for psychoanalysts; since, however, they are intimately related to defence mechanisms, it will be best to postpone a discussion of them until a later paper.

Let us now consider *fright*. Fright, it is suggested, is the subjective experience accompanying at least two related instinctual response systems – those leading on the one hand to escape behaviour, and on the other to alert immobility or 'freezing'. It is to be noted that as so defined it *does not presuppose any conscious awareness of danger*. Instead, it is conceived as being the accompaniment of certain instinctual response systems whenever they are activated. Like all instinctual response systems, those governing escape and 'freezing' are conceived as systems built into the organism and perpetuated by heredity because of their survival value. it is possible that there are more than two kinds of instinctual response systems associated with fright, but, since they do not form the subject of this paper, this possibility will not be explored.[10]

Unlike some response systems, such as those relating to sexual behaviour which are sometimes activated by purely internal changes, the systems governing escape and 'freezing' seem almost invariably to require some external condition for their activation. Amongst those to which they appear to be naturally sensitive are loud noises, sudden visual changes (e.g. fast-moving objects), extremes of temperature, physical pain, and mere strangeness.[11] At this elemental level of instinctual behaviour, the individual does not structure his universe into objects interacting causally to produce situations, some of which are expected to prove dangerous and others harmless. On the contrary, so long as he is operating on this level his responses are rapid and automatic. They may or may not be well adapted to the real situation. The individual flees or remains immobile not because he has any clear awareness of danger but because his flight or 'freezing' responses have been activated. It is because the response is automatic and blind that I regard the term 'fright' as better than 'fear' to denote its subjective accompaniment. (The word 'fear', it is suggested in the Appendix, may most conveniently be limited to denote the subjective state accompanying escape and 'freezing' whenever the cognitive component of these responses is at a higher level, namely whenever there is a clear conception of what object it is which has activated them.)

Thus far in our analysis primary anxiety and fright, though having in common the character of being automatic and blind, are conceived as very different states. Whereas primary anxiety is the subjective accompaniment of many, perhaps all, instinctual response systems when impeded, fright is the accompaniment of a couple or so of related response systems when activated. In the infancy of many species, however, special conditions operate which lead to a close connectedness between the two which I believe to be of vital importance for understanding separation anxiety. This becomes clear as soon as we examine the *situations which terminate escape responses*,[12] a matter usually given scant attention.

When the escape response of an animal is activated at only low intensity, mere removal from the activating conditions suffices to terminate it. This is no longer so when it is activated at high intensity. On such occasions in the natural environment animals escape not only *from* situations but *to* situations. A frightened rabbit bolts to its burrow, a fox to its earth, a band of baboons to their selected tree. Not until they have reached their preferred *haven of safety* do they rest. Burrow, earth, and tree are terminating situations, in each case be it noted often limited (on the principle of monotropy)[13] to a *particular* burrow, a *particular* earth and a *particular* tree (or group of trees). In humans the subjective accompaniment of reaching the haven of safety is a sense of security.

Young animals also escape *to* a situation. In their case, however, the situation is often not a place but *another animal* – usually the mother. This is true of individuals of many genera, from fish to primates. The human toddler escapes from a situation which has frightened him to his mother; other primate infants do the same (Harlow & Zimmerman, 1958; Yerkes, 1943). Probably for all, *the haven of safety which terminates escape responses and brings a sense of security is proximity to mother*.[14]

Thus we find that escape responses share with crying, clinging, and following the same terminating situation. The frightened baby, it might be said, is both 'pushed' toward his mother by his escape responses and 'pulled' toward her by his clinging and following responses. This is a striking conclusion. Primary anxiety, due to the non-termination of response systems mediating attachment behaviour, and fright, due to the activation of escape responses, are more intimately related than our initial sharp differentiation of them seemed to make likely. The question arises, even, whether the two groups of response system – namely those mediating escape and those mediating attachment behaviour – are really different. May we, instead, be dealing with the activating and terminating ends of a single group of systems? The possibility needs examination.

Reflection suggests that neither view may be adequate. In the first place, as we have seen, escape is closely linked with the very different response system of 'freezing'. Furthermore the terminating conditions of escape are often different from those of the response systems mediating attachment; thus the mere presence of the individual in a special location, or proximity to a mate, may each prove a haven of safety. Not only is 'freezing' very different from the behaviour patterns of crying, clinging, and following, but to be present in a location, if not to be in the proximity of a mate, is very different from the conditions which terminate attachment behaviour. Thus it seems useful for some purposes to distinguish two sets of instinctual response systems. Nevertheless, the discussion serves to show how intricately linked, through the existence of common activating and terminating conditions, these different systems tend to be and how misleading it would be were we to make a sharp division of them into two separate groups. Indeed, the adoption of a theory of instinctual behaviour such as that advocated here enables us to get away from any notion that each 'instinct' is entirely distinct from every other. Instead, it provides a flexible conceptual tool which promises to do justice to the complexities of the data.

So far we have been dealing only with those subjective experiences which accompany behaviour that is still at a primitive level. As conceived here, both primary anxiety and fright are the subjective components of instinctual response systems which are activated by certain conditions (part internal and part external, part unlearned and part learned by processes of conditioning) and which operate automatically. Not until the individual can structure his universe in terms of objects existing in time and space and causally related to one another can he develop the notion of a situation which is *potentially* dangerous. This leads us to differentiate a new class of behaviour with its own characteristic subjective accompaniment: these I shall term respectively *avoidance behaviour* and *expectant anxiety*.

As soon as the individual, whether human infant or a member of an infra-human species, has reached a stage of development in which some degree of foresight is possible, he is able to predict situations as dangerous and to take measures to avoid them. In this he is exercising a far more complex function that is required for instinctual responses and one which Freud habitually attributed to the ego.

At least three sorts of danger situation are distinguishable, though for reasons already given there is some overlap between them. They are:

a.  Situations in which the individual believe he is likely to be assailed by external stimuli which he finds (either 'naturally' or through learning or both) to be disagreeable and/or noxious and which, if realized, would activate his instinctual response systems of escape and freezing.
b.  Situations in which the individual believes he is likely to lose that external condition which terminates his escape responses, namely his haven of safety.
c.  Situations in which the individual believes certain of his instinctual responses will be activated without conditions for terminating them being likely to be present. Some such situations are already covered under (*a*) or (*b*); an example of one which is not is the prospect of sexual arousal in the absence of conditions for satisfaction.

The anticipation of any of these kinds of situation, and particularly the first two which appear to be the main ones, at once motivates him to take action intended to avoid their developing. Such 'action' may be of many kinds and will vary both in regard to the decisiveness with which a plan is made and in regard to whether or not it is actually executed. Irrespective of the mode of action resulting and irrespective, too, of which kind of danger situation is anticipated, the subjective states accompanying anticipation and avoidance appear to be the same: they are those of expectant anxiety.

The division of danger situations into two main classes, namely (*a*) and (*b*) above, is consistent with the empirical findings presented in a recent paper by Dixon, de Monchaux and Sandler (1957): a statistical analysis of patients' fears showed that they tend to cluster into 'fear of hurt' and 'fear of separation'.[15] As these authors point out, moreover, it is consistent with Freud's distinction between anxieties relating to castration and those associated with loss of object. It will be clear, however, that the two classes I have defined are more inclusive than Freud's: in the scheme presented here castration anxiety and separation anxiety each represent a particular albeit important example of a broader class. The third class defined above, (*c*), was the first to be discussed by Freud and is present in his theorizing from 1894 onwards.

It may perhaps be asked why the term 'anxiety' has been chosen to denote, in combination with a qualifying word, two such different emotional states as are referred to by 'primary anxiety' and 'expectant anxiety'. There are two reasons. First, as Freud pointed out (1926, p. 165), anxiety carries with it a note of uncertainty. This is true both of primary anxiety, where it is uncertain whether or not the individual will reach a terminating situation, and of expectant anxiety, where the subject is uncertain whether or not he can prevent the danger situation materializing. The second reason is that I believe both classes play a large part in the genesis of neurotic anxiety. A note on questions of terminology, with particular reference to Freud's usage, will be found in the Appendix.

This is a convenient moment to attempt a summary. We have now differentiated three classes of situation and three classes of behaviour, together with the corresponding subjective accompaniments to which they commonly give rise. The word 'commonly' is of importance, since situations can evoke behaviour (and its corresponding subjective experience) only when the organism is in an appropriate state. In the following tabulation the organism is assumed to be in such a state:

| Situations | Behaviour | Subjective accompaniment |
|---|---|---|
| 1. Which activate an instinctual response system without providing for its termination | Persistent activation of response | Primary anxiety |
| 2. Which activate instinctual response systems mediating escape or 'freezing' | Escape or 'freezing' | Fright |
| 3. Which, if no action is taken, it is anticipated will so develop that | | |
|    (a) instinctual response systems mediating escape or 'freezing' will be activated | | |
|    (b) the haven of safety will be lost | Avoidance | Expectant anxiety |
|    (c) an instinctual response system will be activated in conditions unlikely to provide for its termination | | |

In real life more than one situation may be present at once and behaviour of more than one kind and level result. Thus at the sound of an air-raid warning each member of a family may experience expectant anxiety in regard to the possibility of harm coming both to themselves and their loved objects and may take precautions accordingly; whilst the whistle of a bomb may excite both escape and clinging responses simultaneously. Although in them the function of foresight, dependent on an appreciation of causal relationships, may be well developed, the example serves to emphasize that the primitive non-foresightful instinctual responses none the less persist. During the course of development, it seems, we move from a condition in which we possess only the more primitive response systems to a condition in which we are equipped not only with these but also with the capacity for foresightful action. During maturity the extent to which primitive instinctual responses, action based on foresight, or both in combination are likely to mediate our behaviour on a particular occasion is a complex matter. It is one to which I hope to give further attention in a later paper on defences.

Before proceeding to a systematic discussion of separation anxiety, I wish to emphasize afresh that, although we have become caught up in sketching part of a revised theory of anxiety, this is not the purpose of the paper. Our problem is that of trying to understand separation anxiety. Adequately to formulate a comprehensive theory of anxiety would require a broader approach: in particular it would need to give close attention to anxiety arising from the threat of psychic disorganization.

## Ingredients of Separation Anxiety

From the foregoing it will be clear that, according to the hypothesis advanced, separation anxiety is initially a form of primary anxiety, with or without the addition of fright, and that, as the infant develops, anxiety based on learning comes to be added. The reasoning behind this hypothesis has already been presented. My confidence in it springs from my belief that it provides a better explanation of observations of infants and young children than do other hypotheses and is enhanced by the fact that it seems also to fit comparable observations of the young of other species. These will be reviewed.

In very many species of bird and mammal the young show signs of anxiety when removed from their parents. The 'lost piping' of young ducklings who have become attached to and have temporarily lost a mother figure is a familiar example. The behaviour of infant chimpanzees in such situations is well recorded. Since it resembles closely, though in slightly exaggerated form, what we see in humans and seems almost certainly to be homologous, it is instructive to examine it. I shall draw on three accounts. Two (Kellogg & Kellogg, 1933; Hayes, 1951) give detailed information about two infant chimpanzees who were 'adopted' and brought up in a human home; the third, that by Yerkes (1943), who had prolonged experience of young chimpanzees living in captivity with their own parents, presents generalizations based on many cases. All three agree on the intensity of protest exhibited and, by implication, the anxiety experienced when a baby chimpanzee loses its mother-figure.

Mrs. Hayes recounts how Vicki, a female whom she adopted at 3 days, would, when aged 4 months, cling to her foster-mother 'from the moment she left her crib until she was tucked in at night. … She sat on my lap while I ate or studied. She straddled my hip as I cooked. If she were on the floor, and I started to get away, she screamed and clung to my leg until I picked her up. … If some rare lack of vigilance on her part let a room's length separate us, she came charging across the abyss, screaming at the height of her considerable ability.'

The Kelloggs, who did not adopt their female chimp, Gua, until she was 7 months old and who kept her for 9 months, report identical behaviour. They describe 'an intense and tenacious impulse to remain within sight and call of some friend, guardian, or protector. Throughout the entire nine months … whether indoors or out, she almost never roamed very far from someone she knew. To shut her up in a room by herself, or to walk away faster than she could run, and to leave her behind, proved, as well as we could judge, to be the most awful punishment that could possibly be inflicted. She could not be alone apparently without suffering.'

It is of course possible to assume that such behaviour always contains an element of foresight – foresight that physiological needs will not be met. Its strength and immediacy, together with what we know about the primacy of clinging, make this, however, seem unlikely. Furthermore, as was stressed in the previous paper, such a theory is unnecessary.

Except for being less mobile, human infants during the second half of their first year seem to respond similarly to the lower primates. By this age they have become much more demanding of their mother's company. Often when she leaves the room they are upset and do their utmost to see that contact with her is resumed, either by crying or following her as best they can. Such protest behaviour, I am postulating, is accompanied initially only by primary anxiety.

Later, in both humans and chimpanzees, conditioned and expectant anxiety develop as a result of learning. Their development in chimpanzees is of course well attested. Comparing Gua with their son, who was 2½ months older than she, the Kelloggs report: 'Both subjects displayed what might be called anxious behaviour (i.e. fretting and crying), if obvious preparations were being made by the grown-ups to leave the house. This led (in Gua) to an early understanding of the mechanism of door closing and a keen and continual observation of the doors in her vicinity. If she happened to be on one side of a doorway, and her friends on the other, the slightest movement of the door toward closing, whether produced by human hands or by the wind, would bring Gua rushing through the narrowing aperture, crying as she came.' From this account, it seems clear, by a process of learning Gua was able to anticipate and so to avoid the danger of separation.

Similarly with human infants: it is signs that mother is going to leave them that come to evoke conditioned and expectant anxiety most commonly. At what period during the infant's first year the capacity for foresight develops is difficult to say. Experiment, however, should be easy. If Piaget's views are confirmed we should expect it to be present from about 9 months.

Not only do attachment behaviour and anxiety responses appear similar in humans and other species, but the same is true of fright responses in the absence of the mother. In such circumstances the young of many species freeze. Robertson noted this in young children soon after starting observations in 1948. Before a child had got to know him and whilst therefore he was still a frightening stranger, a young child in hospital would occasionally respond to his approach by suddenly becoming immobile, as if trying not to be there, though watching him intently the while. In the course of observations made in connexion with his film study, Robertson (1953a) was able to record this response on two occasions when a strange male colleague approached Laura (he himself by this time having become a familiar and reassuring figure). On each occasion Laura reacted by lying down with eyes closed and failed to respond as she usually did to Robertson's friendly words: indeed only a flicker of the eyelids showed she was not asleep. When told that the man had gone, however, she at once sat up.

Comparable behaviour in infant rhesus monkeys has recently been reported by Harlow and Zimmermann (1954). In the course of their experiments with model mothers they introduced eight baby monkeys for three-minute periods 'into the strange environment of a room measuring 6 feet by 6 feet by 6 feet and containing multiple stimuli known to elicit curiosity-manipulatory responses in baby monkeys. The subjects were placed in this situation twice a week for eight weeks, with no mother surrogate present during alternate sessions and the cloth mother present during the others. ... After one or two adaptation sessions, the infants always rushed to the mother surrogate when she was present and clutched her, a response so strong that it can be adequately depicted only by motion pictures. After a few additional sessions, the infants began to use the mother surrogate as a source of security, a base of operations. They would explore and manipulate a stimulus and then return to the mother before adventuring again into the strange new world. The behaviour of these infants was quite different when the mother was absent from the room. Frequently they would freeze in a crouched position.' Experimental work has also been done with goats and with similar results.[16]

If now we return to our account of chimpanzees it is especially to be noticed that, as in the case of Vicki, Gua became strongly attached to a *particular* figure. In her case it was the male foster-parent, who in fact did most for her: 'Her attachment became so strong that she had been in the human environment for fully a month before she would let go of the trouser leg of her protector for any length of time, even though he might sit quietly at a table for as long as an hour. Almost without respite she clung to him in one way or another. If through a temporary lapse in her vigil he should succeed in taking a step or two away from her, it would surely precipitate a frantic scramble after the retreating trousers, to which she would thereafter hang on determinedly.' Furthermore, it was only when her 'protector' was making preparations to leave the room that fretting and crying were exhibited.

These reports draw our attention afresh to the pronounced tendency for instinctual responses to become focused on a particular individual and not merely on a class of individuals. This was emphasized in the previous paper, where I proposed the term monotropy to describe it, and again earlier in this paper when we were discussing how the escape responses of animals tend also to become directed towards a particular object – in this case either a person or a place. Plainly, in the cases of both Vicki and Gua, the crying, clinging, following, and escape responses were fairly narrowly monotropic. Any mother-figure would not do: it always had to be someone who was known and trusted and, with decided preference, one particular person who was best known and most trusted. As every mother knows, human infants are no different: after a certain age mothering from any kind person will not do.

It seems almost certain in fact that every child who has not been institutionalized develops during his first year a clear preference for one person, namely the person who cares for him and whom I am calling 'mother', and this remains the case even though, in addition, he is likely to include a few others to whom he will turn as second best if mother is absent. It is because of this marked tendency to monotropy that we are capable of deep feelings; for to have a deep attachment to a person (or place or thing) is to have taken them as the terminating object of our instinctual responses. It is probably when these responses include those mediating attachment and escape that there exists what Erikson (1950) and others have described as 'basic trust'.

Unless this high degree of selectivity of the object terminating the response systems mediating attachment and escape behaviour is understood, reactions to separation from loved objects will remain a closed book. This is where, on occasion, formulations stemming from the theory of secondary drive break down. So long as the care-taker ministers efficiently to the child's physiological needs, it is sometimes reasoned, the child has nothing to grumble about: and so he ought not to grumble. This outlook would be ridiculous were it not so tragic – both for the child and for the well-intentioned caretaker.

As presented here, separation anxiety is the inescapable corollary of attachment behaviour – the other side of the coin. As soon as the instinctual response systems mediating such behaviour have matured and, by a process of learning of a simple kind, become oriented towards any object whatsoever, the child will become prone to experience primary anxiety at separation from it. Plainly this formulation implies that there is a period early in the infant's life during which he is not prone to separation anxiety as a specific form of anxiety. This needs discussion.

In my previous paper I discussed the perceptual and cognitive aspects of the child's tie to his mother and pointed to the evidence that prior to about 6 months the infant's differentiation, as measured by his responsiveness, between familiar mother-figure and stranger is present but only evident on careful observation. After about 6 months, however, differential responses are very striking. In particular I referred to the recent work of Schaffer, who observed the responses of twenty-five healthy infants aged under 12 months to admission to hospital for elective surgery. Of those over 28 weeks of age all but one fretted piteously, exhibiting all the struggling, restlessness, and crying with which we are familiar in rather older children. On the other hand, of those aged 28 weeks and under all but two are reported to have accepted the new environment without protest or fretting; only an unwonted silence indicated their awareness of change. Similarly, infants in the two age-groups exhibited very different responses both to visitors during the period of separation and also to their mothers on return home. Those over

28 weeks behaved negatively to strangers, but to their visiting mothers were demanding and clinging: those under 28 weeks, on the other hand, seemed hardly to differentiate between stranger and mother (though it was noticed that they became more vocal during their mother's visit).[17] On return home those over 28 weeks clung tenaciously to their mother and cried and were distressed if left alone by her: those under this age showed no such behaviour but instead appeared bewildered, scanning their surroundings with a blank expression (Schaffer 1958; Schaffer & Callender, 1959).

These observations, if confirmed, strongly suggest that separation anxiety on losing mother is not exhibited before about 28 weeks. As Schaffer points out, this is strikingly in keeping with a prediction made by Anthony (1956) on the basis of Piaget's findings.[18]

To conclude, as I am inclined to, that human infants younger than about 28 weeks do not experience differentiated separation anxiety on losing mother is not to suppose that they experience no anxiety whatever before this age. Though during these weeks the selection of a loved object may still be only embryonic, the instinctual responses comprising attachment behaviour are not. We know that crying and sucking (and in less degree clinging also) are fully active in this period and, in so far as a terminating situation is not quickly established for them, we may presume that primary anxiety is experienced. Moreover, sucking becomes monotropic fairly early, in as much as the infant quickly comes to prefer a particular object to suck – breast, bottle, or dummy. When he loses it he is upset. How significant for later personality development these primitive forms of separation anxiety are seems to me an unsolved problem. Though of great theoretical and practical interest, it is however one which is not of central concern to this paper and will therefore not be pursued further.

Let us now turn to the course of events which follows this early and controversial period. After the age of 6 months variations in the intensity of attachment behaviour, and *pari passu* in the intensity of separation anxiety, occur both in the short term and in the long. As regards *short-term changes*, every mother discovers that her child varies considerably from day to day and week to week. Some days he is intensely 'mummyish', on others much less so. It may help reconcile her to it to know that infant chimps are no different. Of Gua the Kelloggs write: 'During her fifteenth month, when she seemed to be in an "accelerating" phase of her cycle of affection for the chosen experimenter, she would scream and rush after him whenever he opened the door of the house. If left behind, she would run from one window to another pounding upon them and wailing', despite the presence of a familiar substitute. 'In the same stage of development she began to cry again to be carried by the individual of her preference and nothing would calm her till she had her way.' Although the Kelloggs seem unable to account for all the variations, some of them were obviously the result of particular conditions. Thus 'after a brief sickness, during which her dependency necessarily increased, Gua behaved again for some weeks almost as she had at the beginning, even though she was then many months older.'

The very close connectedness of the response systems mediating escape and those mediating attachment has already been emphasized. Inevitably anything which frightens the primate infant serves to intensify his attachment behaviour and, in the absence of his mother, to magnify his anxiety. Yerkes, generalizing about infant chimps brought up with their mothers in captivity, describes how 'even at 2 years of age, after it can feed itself and move about independently, the youngster will rush to its mother or to other adults in any emergency.'

Human mothers are familiar with such patterns of behaviour. Just as the child in his second or third year seems to be becoming more independent, he has a phase when he becomes more demanding again. Sickness, fright, or a period of separation often account for it. So too does the mother's own mood. As often as not when a young child becomes fretful and anxious it is because his mother has been upset, either with him or with someone or something else, and has consequently been brusque and irritable with him. She is less patient, her tone of voice changes, her expression is different: these are the things to which young children are keenly sensitive. Furthermore, it is not uncommon for mothers to use the fear of separation – or withdrawal of love which is substantially the same thing – as a sanction to enforce good behaviour. Sometimes this is done as a deliberate policy, more often almost unconsciously. No matter how expressed, however, it is a powerful sanction and, as Fairbairn and many others have emphasized, inevitably increases the child's proneness to separation anxiety. It is this aspect of the theme that Sullivan picked on almost exclusively, thereby making his views in the weight he gives to parental influence in the genesis of neurotic anxiety the counterpart of Klein's in the weight she attributes to constitutional factors. This debate is referred to again in the next section where we consider why one child rather than another becomes prone to excessive separation anxiety.

Nevertheless, even though experiential factors of one kind or another can frequently be seen to account for short-term variations in intensity of attachment behaviour, on some occasions it is very difficult to trace the reasons. Perhaps in human children it is the same as it was with Gua, whose 'attachment would wax and wane in a slow irregular rhythm' during the nine months she was with the Kelloggs. Systematic records are obviously required.

As regards the *long-term changes*, both in chimps and humans the instinctual response systems mediating attachment and escape behaviour slowly modify. Not only do they become less readily activated and, when activated, active at a lower level of intensity, but they come to be organized around an increasing range of objects. These two kinds of change appear to be taking place during the same period of the life span and consequently are not always easy to differentiate.

The processes underlying the long-term reduction in the frequency and intensity of their activation, with its concomitant reduction in separation anxiety, are unknown. As we have seen, their ready activation in early childhood is easily accounted for by their survival value. Since as the child grows older they become less necessary, it may well be that there is operative a maturational process designed to restrict their activity, as sexual activity is restricted at the menopause. Nevertheless experience and learning certainly play a considerable part also. As time goes on, the better grounds a child has to believe that his parents love him and will return to him, the less apprehensive will he be both before their departure and whilst they are away; the weaker the grounds, the more anxious on these occasions.

Although I believe such views to be theoretically plausible and, so far as there are relevant data, empirically well based, it must be recognized that they are not those which have been advanced by leading psycho-analysts, many of whom have thought that the growth of independence is impossible without the frustration of earlier needs. Freud held that it is possible to give a child too much affection and that it is this which prolongs the phase of dependence and promotes increased separation anxiety; a critique of this view is postponed to the next section. Melanie Klein shares the same outlook but invokes a different mechanism. In questioning how the child ever detaches himself from his mother, she suggests that 'the very nature of this overstrong attachment ... tends to drive him away from her because (frustrated greed and hatred being inevitable) it gives rise to the fear of losing this all-important person, and consequently to the fear of dependence upon her' (Klein & Riviere, 1937). Although a process of this kind is well known as one which underlies a *premature* development of independence,[19] I believe it to be the result of avoidable frustration and to lead to independence of a special and often pathological kind. I know of no reason to suppose it is responsible for its healthy growth.

As regards the second component of the long-term changes, the increasing range of objects toward whom attachment behaviour is directed, probably this is also a result both of maturational change and of learning. Thus the very capacity to include, even at a lower level of preference, a number of different people is something which may well become increased between, say, 18 months and 3 years by maturational processes. Even so, precisely who is included is obviously learned, and the number who become trusted by any particular child, whilst always limited, is evidently in large part the result of experience.

Once again it is instructive to hear of comparable changes in chimpanzees. Reading Yerkes's account, one gains the impression that, in chimps, initially the shift may be entirely one of object and that intensity of response remains unchanged. Generalizing again from his observations of chimps in captivity, he writes of the developing infant: 'Gradually a striking change in behaviour becomes evident. The initial specific clinging dependence upon the mother gives place rapidly to a generalized dependence on the extending social environment. ... Need for social stimulation, such as is provided by companions, becomes so strong during late infancy and early childhood that isolation causes varied symptoms of deprivation.' As the chimpanzee child grows older, however, the intensity of the attachment responses themselves seems to diminish: 'Maternal dependence normally is outgrown during infancy, and similarly, extreme social dependence tends to be outgrown during childhood and adolescence.'

Primary anxiety arising from separation either from mother-figure or companions is thus a function of age. The period when the individual is especially vulnerable is whilst the response systems mediating attachment and escape are not only easily activated at high intensity but are narrowly directed towards one, or at most a few, figures. Once there is a diminution in the readiness with which the response systems are activated, or the growing child, chimp or human, becomes able to accept temporary substitutes more readily, vulnerability decreases. So far as my own observations go, I have the impression that in humans these changes do not often take much effect until the child has reached about 2 years 9 months, though the age varies considerably from child to child.

## Origin of Separation Anxiety of Pathological Degree

Earlier in the paper I have made it clear that, on the hypothesis advanced, primary anxiety will occur whenever any (or at least one of a number of) instinctual response systems is activated and not terminated. The primary anxiety arising when a young child is separated from his mother is thus only a special case of a more general phenomenon. Nevertheless, clinical experience suggests that it is of peculiar pathogenic significance and, if this is so, the problem remains *why* it should be so. The following explanation appears plausible. In the first place, the phase during which the human infant's capacity for locomotion is limited is a long one. As a result, whether or not his attachment responses are terminated turns for some years on the initiative of others, especially his mother: he is entirely dependent on their goodwill. In the second, there is the close linkage between the instinctual response systems mediating attachment behaviour and those mediating escape, so that, whenever a young child is separated from his mother and such substitutes as he will accept, there is the risk of his experiencing not only primary anxiety but also fright, and both in conditions where there is no one available to provide comfort and security. This makes the situation doubly alarming to him and accounts for the intensity of distress we observe. Finally, because of their tremendous importance for survival, both these classes of response system appear to have special characteristics: first, they are permanently ready for activation and also readily activated; secondly, when active they are often so at great intensity; and, finally, they are not completely terminated except by the preferred mother-figure. In several of these respects they differ from other response systems, such for example as those mediating sucking behaviour. Thus the latter vary much in their readiness for activation, in many infants being inert after food has been taken and only becoming sensitive at intervals; they are often not exhibited at great intensity, and, as regards termination, are usually more easily provided for than are those mediating attachment and escape – a bottle, a thumb, or a comforter may suffice. By contrast the instinctual response systems mediating attachment and escape behaviour are permanently 'at the ready' for intense activation. Primary anxiety due to separation, sometimes suffused with fright, is thus immanently present from the time these response systems have become active and narrowly directed in the early months to the time when they diminish in intensity and/or the object becomes more easily replaceable (from around the third birthday). Probably at no other time in his life is the individual at risk of such intense primary anxiety and such 'unterminatable' fright.

In considering why separation anxiety can so easily reach pathological intensity two further aspects of these systems require emphasis. One is the readiness with which hostility is engendered when they are impeded. The exact conditions under which hostility is evoked require much more detailed study than they have yet been given, but it has long been common knowledge that separation from the mother, rejection by the mother, and a situation in which the mother is attending to some other individual – father, sibling, or visitor – are all apt to give rise to it.[20] It is my belief that it is situations such as these, rather than the frustration of oral desires, that engender the most frequent and intense hostility in infants and young children, hostility, moreover, which is inevitably directed towards the loved object itself. This is of the greatest relevance when we come to consider why in some children expectant anxiety in regard to separation exists at a level above the normal.

The second is that the period when they are most active is also the period when patterns of control and of regulating conflict are being laid down. Our data demonstrate that when primary anxiety arising from separation is allowed to persist, defences of a primitive nature (such as those giving rise to detachment described earlier) come into play. There is reason to suppose that the early and intense activation of such defensive processes may create patterns which in later life are of pathogenic significance. This is a theme I have touched on in an earlier paper in connexion with critical phases of development (Bowlby, 1957) and which I hope to pursue further.

Whether or not these reasons prove to be the right ones, there can be little doubt that separation anxiety is an exceedingly common component of neurotic anxiety. This was early recognized by Freud. 'One of the clearest indications that a child will later become neurotic', he observed, 'is to be seen in an insatiable demand for his parents' affection' (Freud, 1905, p. 223); this, of course, is another way of describing the child who exhibits, in excess, expectant anxiety in regard to separation and loss of love. Few would dispute this view today. There are, however, several hypotheses current in regard to why some children develop in this way and others do not; and it is in fact on this issue that the views advanced here differ most from those of Freud.

Hypotheses which have been advanced by psycho-analysts not only give very varying weight to constitutional and environmental factors but also inculpate different and in some respects contradictory factors in each class.

It is therefore useful to tabulate the five main hypotheses which have been advanced to account for why a particular individual suffers from an excess of separation anxiety. They are:

1.  *Constitutional Factors*
    a.  Some 'children have inherently a greater amount of libidinal need in their constitution than others,' and so are more sensitive than others to an absence of gratification (Freud, 1917).
    b.  Some children have inherently a stronger death instinct than others, which manifests itself in unusually strong persecutory and depressive anxiety (Klein, 1932).
2.  *Environmental Factors*
    a.  Variations in the birth process and severe traumata occurring during the first weeks of post-natal life may increase the (organic) anxiety response and heighten the anxiety potential, thereby causing a more severe reaction to later (psychological) dangers met with in life (Greenacre, [1941] 1952, [1945] 1952).
    b.  Some children are 'spoiled' by excess of early libidinal gratification: they therefore demand more of it and, when not gratified, miss it more (Freud, 1905, 1917, 1926).
    c.  Some children are made excessively sensitive to the possibility of separation or loss of love either through the experience of actual separation (Edleston, 1943; Bowlby, 1951), or through the use of separation or loss of love as a threat (Suttie, 1935; Fairbairn, [1941] 1952).

It should be noted that whereas hypotheses 1 (*a*), 2 (*b*) and 2 (*c*) are framed to account for the liability to an excess in particular of separation anxiety, 1 (*b*) and 2 (*a*) are intended to account for the liability to an excess of anxiety of any kind.

I do not believe there is any clear evidence in support of the first four of these hypotheses. Since with our present research techniques there is no way of determining differences in constitutional endowment, the first pair unavoidably remain untested (though of course not disproved). As regards the next pair, the evidence in regard to 2 (*a*) is far from clear; indeed in her paper Phyllis Greenacre is careful to explain that she regards it as no more than a plausible hypothesis. Evidence in regard to 2 (*b*) seems at the best equivocal: the subjection of a child to neurotic overprotection or to excessive libidinal demands from his mother sometimes appears like excess of affection but clearly cannot be equated with it. Evidence in regard to the fifth hypothesis, 2 (*c*), however, is abundant and affirmative. Therefore, without necessarily rejecting the first four, the fifth hypothesis, that an excess of separation anxiety may be due either to an experience of actual separation or to threats of separation, rejection, or loss of love, can be adopted with confidence. Probably a majority of analysts today utilize it in their work in some degree.

It is strange that in his writings Freud practically never invoked it. On the contrary, in addition to postulating hypothesis 1 (*a*), that some children have a constitutionally greater need of libidinal gratification than others, he committed himself early and consistently to hypothesis 2 (*b*), that an excess of separation anxiety is due to an excess of parental affection – in other words, the traditional theory of spoiling. Thus in the *Three Essays* (1905), after commending the mother who strokes, rocks, and kisses her child and thereby teaches him to love, he nevertheless warns against excess: 'An excess of parental affection does harm by causing precocious sexual maturity and also because, by spoiling the child, it makes him incapable in later life of temporarily doing without love or of being content with a smaller amount of it' (p. 223). The same theme runs through much of his theorizing about *Little Hans* (1909), though it is in his discussion of this small boy's separation anxiety that he comes nearest the view adopted here: he attributes part of it to the fact that Little Hans had been separated from his mother at the time of his baby sister's birth (pp. 114 and 132). However, both in the *Introductory Lectures* (1917, p. 340) and in *Inhibitions, Symptoms and Anxiety* (1926, p. 167) he makes no reference to such origins and instead explicitly adopts the theory of spoiling.

Since in my view there is no evidence to support this theory, the question arises why Freud should have favoured it. One reason seems to be that in his early work he was misled by the show of affection and overprotection which is so frequently present as an over-compensation for a parent's unconscious hostility to a child. This is suggested by the passage in *Three Essays* immediately following that already quoted: '... neuropathic parents, who are inclined as a rule to display excessive affection, are precisely those who are most likely by their caresses to arouse the child's disposition to neurotic illness' (1905, p. 223). In fact, when we come to investigate such cases psycho-analytically we find, I believe invariably, that the child's heightened anxiety over separation and loss of love is not a reaction to any real excess of affection from his parents, but to the unconscious hostility and rejection which lies behind it or to the threats of loss of love his parents have used to bind him to them.[21] Children who have received a great deal of genuine affection seem to be those who in later life show in highest degree a sense of security.

In addition to this, it seems probable that another reason for Freud's misperception of the origins of excessive separation anxiety was the delay in his recognition of the close bond of child to mother and the length of time over which it normally persists at high intensity; only if the child's strong attachment is perceived as normal is its severance or threat of severance recognized as dangerous. It is true that by the time he wrote *Inhibitions, Symptoms and Anxiety* he was of opinion that a main cause of man's proneness to neurosis lies in 'the long period of time during which the young of the human species is in a condition of helplessness and dependence ... (which) establishes the earliest situations of danger and creates the need to be loved' (1926, pp. 154–155). Yet, so far as I know, he never drew from this the natural conclusion that disruptions or threats of disruption of the primary bond are likely to prove a major hazard.

It will thus be seen that the views advanced in this paper differ from Freud's not so much on the nature of separation anxiety itself but on the conditions which determine its presence in excessive degree. On this issue indeed the two views are the opposite of one another. It is perhaps because of this and because Freud's hypothesis of spoiling has been built deep into psycho-analytic theory that there has been so much reluctance in many analysts to accept as valid the evidence which supports the hypothesis here advanced. It is time to return to this.

In my view the best opportunity for uncovering the conditions which lead an individual to become prone to an excessive degree of separation anxiety is either by direct observation of a child undergoing an anxiety-provoking experience or by a clinical examination in an analytically oriented child guidance clinic, in which treatment is given to both child and parent and a detailed history can be obtained both of main events in the child's life and of parental attitudes towards him. When we review the reasons why in some children expectant anxiety in regard to separation and loss of love exist in pathogenic degree, observations made in such settings suggest there are four main ones:

1. One determinant is undoubtedly the actual experience of a period of separation. In addition to our own observations (Bowlby, 1951, 1954; Robertson, 1953a), those of Edelston (1943), Prugh *et al.* (1953), Heinicke (1956) and Schaffer (1958) provide abundant evidence that the child who returns after not too long a period with strangers, whether in hospital or elsewhere, will soon attach himself with great tenacity to his mother and show intense anxiety at any threat of a repetition of the experience. Many cases of older children and adults who respond to separation with unusual anxiety are most readily understood in terms of the persistence of such a psychological state.

2. Another determinant is the excessive use by parents of threats of separation or withdrawal of love as sanctions.

3. Another is the child's experience of rejection by the mother, especially where her positive feelings are mixed with unconscious hostility.

4. Another is any actual event, such as a parent's or sibling's illness or death, for which the child has come to feel responsible and, therefore, guilty and unloved.

There are many papers by analysts which report cases falling under one or a combination of these last three heads (including an early one of my own: Bowlby, 1940) and others by clinical psychologists.[22] In a study predominantly concerned with the consequences of actual separation, however, it would be inappropriate to discuss this large and controversial area more fully. Nevertheless it should be noted that these four sources are not necessarily exhaustive: for example, any set of conditions which results in the child feeling guilty and therefore in danger of not being loved will be effective. At the same time, it is my view that only if each of the four sources listed above has been thoroughly explored and excluded is it wise to postulate other factors. Unfortunately such exploration is, I believe, only possible in the case of younger children and when their mothers are also willing to undertake treatment.

Merely to describe these sources of increased separation anxiety, however, is insufficient: we need also to understand the nature of their effects on the emotional development of the child. It is when we come to consider these effects that the interaction of expectant anxiety and hostility, to which attention has already been drawn, is seen to be so crucial. For each of these experiences – separation, threats of separation, actual rejection or expectation of rejection – enormously increases the child's hostility, whilst his hostility greatly increases his expectation of rejection and loss. Such vicious circles are a commonplace of psycho-analytic practice. Since it is in emphasizing their frequency and immense clinical importance that Melanie Klein has made her special contribution, this is a convenient point at which to reconsider her ideas.

The clinical observations made by Melanie Klein in the twenties, it will be recalled, were that some children who are attached to their mother in unusual degree are, paradoxically, also possessed of strong unconscious hostility directed towards that very mother. In their play they demonstrate much violence towards mother-figures and become concerned and anxious lest they may have destroyed or alienated them. Often after an outburst they run from the analytic room, not only for fear of consequences from the analyst, but also, it seems, to assure themselves that their mother is still alive and loving. These observations are now amply confirmed and demonstrate without doubt that the presence of unconscious hostile impulses directed towards a loved object greatly increases anxiety. This is readily intelligible. As Freud pointed out, we would not expect loss of love or castration 'if we did not entertain certain feelings and intentions within us. Thus such instinctual impulses are determinants of external dangers and so become dangerous in themselves' (1926, p. 145). The presence of hostile impulses directed to a parent, especially when unconscious, inevitably increases expectant anxiety. In so far as there is concern for the object's safety, it is depressive in character; in so far as there is fear of losing his or her love, it is persecutory. The role of such depressive and persecutory anxieties, springing from unconscious hostility, in persons suffering from an increased level of expectant anxiety in regard to being separated or unloved cannot be overemphasized; and this remains so whether or not we accept Melanie Klein's particular hypothesis in regard to their origin.

But just as unconscious hostility directed towards the loved object increases expectant anxiety, so does expectant anxiety, especially in regard to whether or not one is loved, increase hostility. It is of both great theoretical and great practical importance to determine, if we can, how these vicious circles begin. Does increased anxiety precede increased hostility, is it the other way round, or do they spring from a common source? Jones ([1929] 1948) recognizes the great difficulty of unravelling the sequence when looking backwards from data provided by the patient in analysis; and I believe this holds for young children as well as for older patients. Indeed it is at this point that I believe Melanie Klein's method has led her to one-sided conclusions.

Logically it is clearly possible for excess anxiety to precede excess hostility in some cases, for the sequence to be reversed in others, and for them to spring from a single source and so be coincidental in yet a third group. Such possibilities, however, are not allowed for by Melanie Klein's formulation. It is to be noted that she attaches no importance to instinctual tensions as such and does not subscribe to the view, advanced by Freud and again here, as well as by many other writers, that primary anxiety is the result of such tension. Instead, her basic tenet is that increased anxiety is always both preceded and caused by increased sadism: that it may sometimes be independent of, sometimes itself provoke, and often spring from the same source as the increased sadism is not conceded.

In my view both an excess of separation anxiety and an excess of hostility are very commonly provoked by the same experience. Further and more important is that, because the hostility is directed towards the loved object, it is often repressed and, being repressed, tends to generate further anxiety. Thus, on this hypothesis, the increased libidinal need for the object and the increased unconscious hostility directed toward it are both active in promoting neurotic anxiety. This is a view which, it will be seen, derives from the theories both of Freud and of Melanie Klein. It also links with Freud's early expressed belief (*Little Hans*, 1909) that in some way repression plays a crucial role in the genesis of pathological anxiety. Here, however, a distinction needs to be drawn between anxiety which is intense and anxiety which is pathological. Whilst it seems clear that repression is not a necessary condition for the genesis of *intense* anxiety – as is shown by the behaviour of young children in the weeks following return home after a time away from their mothers with strangers – it may well be a necessary condition for its development into *pathological* anxiety. Perhaps when there is no repression of love or hate intense anxiety provoked by separation or rejection subsides, and it is only when repression sets in that the anxiety becomes pathological. This hypothesis will need further examination.

Before ending this section a word must be said about the other pathological form of separation anxiety, namely its absence or presence at unusually low levels. It has already been emphasized that some measure of separation anxiety is the inevitable counterpart of a love relationship. The absence or attenuation of separation anxiety is thus a frequent accompaniment of absent or exiguous love relationships. The psychopathic character, the origin of which is so often a major disturbance in the early mother-child relationship (Bowlby, 1944; Greenacre, [1945] 1952), is commonly the one who shows little or no separation anxiety. Either he has never experienced a continuous loving relationship or, more frequently, the relationship he has had has been disrupted so severely that he has not only reached but remained in a phase of detachment. As a result he remains detached and so incapable of experiencing either separation anxiety or grief. Lesser degrees of this condition are, of course, more common than the extreme degrees, and sometimes give the impression of unusually vigorous independence. Analysis, however, shows that the springs of love are frozen and that their independence is hollow.

It is not unlikely that the possibility of promoting early and often apparently vigorous independence in some young children by a measure of frustration of their need for attachment has contributed to the notion that too much affection is bad for a child. There is no doubt that, in the short run, the child who is given more affection is sometimes more strongly attached and so, therefore, more prone to separation anxiety than are some of those who are treated more toughly (though by no means more so than all of them). However, since such 'dependence' in the well-loved child is outgrown and later provides the basis for a stable independence, it would be a mistake to suppose it pathological. On the contrary, as in the case of grief, the capacity to experience separation anxiety must be regarded as a sign of the healthy personality.

Though I believe that much of the variation between different individuals in respect of their proneness to pathological anxiety is to be understood as resulting from experiences such as we have been discussing, it seems probable that part of it is due to other factors. Thus it is most unlikely that all human infants are equipped by inheritance with instinctual response systems prone to develop responses of the same degree of intensity; whilst in others brain damage, caused before, during, or after birth, may make for undue sensitivity. Whatever the reason for it may be, those in whom the potential intensity is high will be greater risks for becoming entangled in the vicious circle of anxiety–hatred–more anxiety–more hatred–than will others. Only direct observations made whilst the child is developing in relation to his mother during the first two or three years of life can, I believe, throw light on this issue. It is to this task that research needs to be directed.

## Conclusion

Although in the course of this paper we have strayed into areas of difficult and abstract theory, my interest in the problem stems from clinical observation. At first I was struck by the calamitous after-effects which are sometimes to be found following a prolonged separation or series of separations occurring in early childhood. Next, in my work with James Robertson, we were both struck by the intensity and universality of separation anxiety when very young children are removed from their mothers, by the processes of grief, mourning, and defence which habitually follow if child and mother are not reunited, and by the acute exacerbation of separation anxiety after the child's return home. Finally, like most other clinicians, I have been impressed both by the frequency with which separation anxiety is exhibited at high levels in neurotic patients and by its ubiquity at more modest levels in the everyday life of all of us. It has been the attempt to understand and explain these observations which has led to this exploration of theory.

It will have been seen that the hypothesis advanced to account for separation anxiety is an immediate corollary of that advanced to account for the child's tie to his mother. In the earlier paper reasons were advanced why it was both legitimate and economical to conceive the child's tie as being the direct outcome of a number of instinctual response systems – crying, smiling, sucking, clinging, and following – which have become bred into the species as a result of their survival value. When they are activated and the mother-figure is available, attachment behaviour follows. Similarly, as we have discussed in this paper, when they are activated and the mother-figure is temporarily not available, protest behaviour and separation anxiety follow. This formulation not only has the merit of appearing to account for the facts but is also simple. Furthermore, it brings separation anxiety into immediate relation to grief and mourning, which in this scheme are seen respectively as the subjective experience and the psychological processes which occur when the responses mediating attachment behaviour are activated and the mother-figure is permanently unavailable, or at least believed to be so. A liability to experience separation anxiety and grief are thus the ineluctable risks of a love relationship, of caring for someone. This intrinsic connexion between separation anxiety and grief, and both with attachment to a loved object, to which Freud called attention in the final pages of *Inhibitions, Symptoms and Anxiety*, is also the theme of succeeding papers on grief and mourning in infancy.

## Appendix: A Note on Terminology

In a passage in *Beyond the Pleasure Principle* (1920, p. 12) Freud seeks to differentiate between the conditions denoted respectively by the German words 'Schreck', 'Furcht', and 'Angst', namely 'fright', 'fear', and 'anxiety': "'Anxiety" describes a particular state of expecting the danger or preparing for it, even though it may be an unknown one. "Fear" requires a definite object of which to be afraid. "Fright", however, is the name we give to the state a person gets into when he has run into danger without being prepared for it; it emphasizes the factor of surprise.' As we have seen, six years later in *Inhibitions, Symptoms and Anxiety*, he further differentiates the concept of anxiety, postulating two forms, one an 'automatic phenomenon' characteristic of id impulsiveness, the other a 'rescue-signal' characteristic of ego foresight.

The concepts and terminology advanced here have much in common with Freud's. Thus what I am terming respectively 'primary anxiety' and 'expectant anxiety' correspond closely to Freud's two forms of anxiety. The notion of primary anxiety, moreover, is very close to his original notion that anxiety is in some way connected with an 'excess of excitation' which cannot be discharged (see his paper on anxiety neurosis [Freud, 1894]).

In general the concept of 'fright' advanced here also resembles Freud's, though it identifies it more precisely than did Freud with primitive instinctual response systems. Both concepts agree, however, that in fright the cognitive component is at a simple level and that, in contrast to fear, there is no 'definite object of which to be afraid'.

Unfortunately in colloquial English the word 'fear' is used in many senses, often being synonymous with expectant anxiety and sometimes with fright. It is therefore doubtful how wise it is to make any attempt to give it a precise technical meaning. Were we to do so, I suggest it might be reserved for the subjective state accompanying the responses of escape and 'freezing' whenever the cognitive component of these responses is at a higher level, namely whenever there is a clear conception of what object has activated them. Such a usage would, I believe, be close to what Freud had in mind.

Most other workers conceive anxiety in ways similar to that advanced here. Thus Goldstein (1939) contrasts it with fear and postulates that anxiety is experienced when the organism is unable to cope with a situation and, as a result, is in danger of disorganization. This is a concept to which we shall be returning in a paper to follow in which the nature of depression will be discussed. Recently Gerard (1958), approaching the problem from the point of view of neurophysiology, has remarked: 'Anxiety is largely connected with frustrated drives ... with unfinished business ... with events to come.' Like Goldstein, he emphasizes uncertainty and the unsolved nature of the problem. Several writers, on the other hand, for example McDougall (1923) and Basowitz *et al.* (1955), whilst agreeing in general approach, seem to me in their description to be too preoccupied with behaviour dependent on foresight (and therefore with expectant anxiety) and to give too little attention to the more primitive processes underlying primary anxiety. McDougall in fact uses the term 'anxiety' as synonymous with 'expectant anxiety', and the term 'fear' to denote what I am terming 'fright'.

## Notes

1  An abbreviated version of this paper was read before the British Psycho-Analytical Society on 5 November, 1958.

2  Although in this paper I shall usually refer to mothers, it is to be understood that in every case I am concerned with the person who mothers the child and to whom he becomes attached, rather than to the natural mother.

3  This account is adapted from those given in Robertson and Bowlby (1952) and Robertson (1953a).

4  In the previous paper and the early drafts of this one the term 'denial' was used to denote the third phase. The problem of terminology is discussed more fully after the phase of detachment has been described.

5  As explained in my previous paper (Bowlby 1958), 'the terms primary and secondary refer to whether the response is built-in and inherited or acquired through the process of learning.'

6  See section 'Ingredients of Separation Anxiety' below.

7  For this abridged version a critical examination of psycho-analytical theories relating to separation anxiety has been omitted. It is being published as a separate paper: Bowlby, J. (1960). Separation anxiety: A critical review of the literature. *Journal of Child Psychology and Psychiatry*, 1 (4), 251–269.

8  In an earlier paper (Bowlby 1957) I have used the term 'instinctual response' to refer both to the behaviour and to the hypothetical internal structure which, when activated, is presumed to lead to the behaviour. To avoid this confusion I am now using the term 'instinctual response system' for the hypothetical internal structure, and limiting the term 'instinctual response' to the active behavioural response, including both the motor behaviour pattern and its physiological and psychological concomitants.

9  A similar view, though coupled with a materially different theory of instinct, was advanced by McDougall (1923).

10 The possibility that a single emotion, fright, may accompany more than one instinctual response system suggests that Lorenz's hypothesis that each response is accompanied by an emotional state peculiar to itself may need modification.

11 See the discussion by Thorpe (1950, p. 390). Several workers (e.g. Hinde 1954a) have shown that, paradoxically, strangeness evokes both escape and curiosity, and that there is a complex balance between the two competing response systems.

12 Such situations have been termed 'consummatory situations' by Bastock, Morris and Moynihan (1953) and by Hinde (1954b). In my view, however, partly because of the usefulness of the verb 'to terminate', a preferable term is 'terminating situation'.

13 'The tendency for instinctual responses to be directed towards a particular individual or group of individuals and not promiscuously towards many' (Bowlby (1958, p. 370).

14 The term 'haven of safety' has been introduced by Harlow and Zimmermann (1958). In describing their very interesting experiments with rhesus monkeys they write: 'One function of the real mother, human or sub-human, and presumably of a mother surrogate, is to provide a haven of safety for the infant in times of fear or danger.' See also Harlow (1958).

15 The secondary drive theory, which they invoke to account for the child's tie to his mother and for separation anxiety, is not necessary to an interpretation of their data.

16 In his experiments with goat kids Liddell (1950) has demonstrated the very different responses to fright-evoking stimuli of identical twins according to whether or not they were with their mother: the twin with his mother roamed about naturally and seemed relaxed, whereas the one without his mother froze almost immobile in a corner of the room.

17 Of Schaffer's twenty-five subjects, sixteen were aged over 28 weeks and nine 28 weeks and under. Of the two younger infants who deviated from the usual behaviour, one was already 28 weeks of age, and so on the margin of the older age group, and the other was thought to be missing his dummy.

18 Anthony writes: 'It would also follow that before the seventh month the infant cannot be separated from an object-mother firmly and substantially localized in space, as an organized reality. His separation feeling must therefore lack the quality of separations at a later stage.'

19 See, for instance, Winnicott's (1953) conception of the development of the false self and Balint's (1952) of conditions which give rise to neurosis and the need for a 'new beginning'.

20 Analytic literature is full of references to hatred arising in such situations. That separation from mother itself provokes it has been used by Freud (1920, p. 16) as a possible explanation of the cotton-reel incident: 'Throwing away the object so that it was "gone", 'he suggests, 'might satisfy an impulse of the child's … to revenge himself on his mother for going away from him'. Dorothy Burlingham and Anna Freud (1944), Spitz (1953), Robertson (1953a, 1953b) and Heinicke (1956) have all reported first-hand observations of intensely hostile behaviour following separation. It is Fairbairn's ([1951] 1952) view that the origin of the infant's aggression towards his libidinal object, and therefore of his ambivalence, lies in the trauma of separation from mother and the consequent libidinal deprivation and frustration.

21 There is another situation which may lead a child to become excessively clinging and which may also masquerade as "spoiling." It is when a mother, for unconscious reasons of her own, communicates to a child her desire that he should not leave her. This is a common finding in cases of so-called school phobia (Johnson et al. 1941).

22 In a comparison of twenty 6-year-old children reported as overdependent with twenty controls, Stendler (1954) found that six of the over-dependent children were 'over-protected' and eleven had suffered major disturbances in their lives between the ages of 9 months and 3 years.

# References

Abraham, K. ([1911] 1927) Notes on the psycho-analytical investigation and treatment of manic-depressive insanity and allied conditions. In: *Selected Papers on Psycho-Analysis*. London: Hogarth

Anthony, E. J. (1956) The significance of Jean Piaget for child psychiatry. *British Journal of Medical Psychology*, 29, 20–34

Anthony, S. (1940) *The Child's Discovery of Death*. London: Kegan Paul

Balint, M. (1952) New beginning and the paranoid and the depressive syndromes. In: *Primary Love and Psycho-Analytic Technique*. London: Hogarth

Basowitz, H. et al. (1955) *Anxiety and Stress: an Interdisciplinary Study of a Life Situation*. New York: McGraw Hill

Bastock, M., Morris, D., & Moynihan, M. (1953) Some comments on conflict and thwarting in animals. *Behaviour*, 6, 66–84

Bender, L., & Yarnell, H. (1941) An observation nursery: a study of 250 children on the psychiatric division of Bellevue Hospital. *American Journal of Psychiatry*, 97, 1158–72

Benedek, T. (1946) *Insight and Personality Adjustment: A Study of the Psychological Effects of War*. New York: Ronald Press

Bernfeld, S. ([1925] 1929) *The Psychology of the Infant*. London: Kegan Paul.

Bowlby, J. (1940) The influence of early environment in the development of neurosis and neurotic character. *International Journal of Psychoanalysis*, 21, 154–178

Bowlby, J. (1944) Forty-four juvenile thieves: their characters and home life. *International Journal of Psychoanalysis 25*, 19–52 and 107–127

Bowlby, J. (1951) *Maternal Care and Mental Health W.H.O. Monograph, No. 2*. London: HMSO

Bowlby, J. (1953) Some pathological processes set in train by early mother-child separation. *Journal of Mental Science, 99*, 265–272

Bowlby, J. (1954) Psychopathological processes set in train by early mother-child separation. In: *Proceedings of Seventh Conference on Infancy and Childhood March, 1953*. New York: Josiah Macy, Jr., Foundation

Bowlby, J. (1957) An ethological approach to research in child development. *British Journal of Medical Psychology, 30*, 230–240

Bowlby, J. (1958) The nature of the child's tie to his mother. *International Journal of Psychoanalysis, 39*, 350–373

Burlingham, D. & Freud, A. (1942) *Young Children in War Time*. London: Allen and Unwin

Burlingham, D. & Freud, A. (1944) *Infants without Families*. London: Allen and Unwin

Deutsch, H. (1937) Absence of grief. *Psychoanalytic Quarterly, 6*, 12–22

Dixon, J. J., De Monchaup, C., & Sandler, J. (1957) Patterns of anxiety: an analysis of social anxieties. *British Journal of Medical Psychology, 30*, 107–112

Edelston, H. (1943) Separation anxiety in young children: a study of hospital cases. *Genetic Psychology Monographs, 28*, 3–95

Erikson, E. H. (1950) *Childhood and Society*. New York: Norton

Fairbairn, W. R. D. ([1941] 1952) A revised psychopathology of the psychoses and psychoneuroses. In: *Psycho-Analytic Studies of the Personality*. London: Tavistock

Fairbairn, W. R. D. ([1943] 1952) The war neuroses: their nature and significance. In: *Psycho-Analytic Studies of the Personality*. London: Tavistock

Fairbairn, W. R. D. ([1951] 1952) A synopsis of the development of the author's views regarding the structure of the personality. In: *Psycho-Analytic Studies of the Personality*. London: Tavistock

Freud, A. (1952) The mutual influences in the development of ego and id. *Psychoanalytic. Study of the Child, 7*, 42–50

Freud, A. (1953) Some remarks on infant observation. *Psychoanalytic Study of the Child, 8*, 9–19

Freud, S. (1894). The neuro-psychoses of defence. *The Standard Edition of the Complete Psychological Works of Sigmund Freud, Volume III (pp. 41–61)*, London: Vintage

Freud, S. ([1897] 1954) 'Notes III' in *The Origins of Psycho-Analysis: Letters to Wilhelm Fliess, Drafts and Notes, 1887–1902*, New York: Kessinger Publishing

Freud, S. (1905). Three essays on the theory of sexuality. *The Standard Edition of the Complete Psychological Works of Sigmund Freud, Volume VII (pp. 123–246)*, London: Vintage

Freud, S. (1909). Analysis of a phobia in a five-year-old boy. *The Standard Edition of the Complete Psychological Works of Sigmund Freud, Volume X (pp. 1–150)*, London: Vintage

Freud, S. (1917). Mourning and melancholia. *The Standard Edition of the Complete Psychological Works of Sigmund Freud, Volume XIV (pp. 237–258)*, London: Vintage

Freud, S. (1917). Introductory lectures on psycho-analysis. *The Standard Edition of the Complete Psychological Works of Sigmund Freud, Volume XVI (pp. 241–463)*, London: Vintage

Freud, S. (1920). Beyond the pleasure principle. *The Standard Edition of the Complete Psychological Works of Sigmund Freud, Volume XVIII (pp. 1–64)*, London: Vintage

Freud, S. (1926). Inhibitions, symptoms and anxiety. *The Standard Edition of the Complete Psychological Works of Sigmund Freud, Volume XX (pp. 75–176)*, London: Vintage

Gerard, R. W. (1958). Anxiety and tension. *Bulletin of the New York Academy of Medicine, 34* (7), 429–444

Goldfarb, W. (1943) Infant rearing and problem behavior. *American Journal of Orthopsychiatry, 13*, 249–265

Goldstein, K. (1939) *The Organism*. New York: American Book Co.

Greenacre, P. ([1941] 1952) The predisposition to anxiety. In: *Trauma, Growth and Personality*. New York: Norton

Greenacre, P. ([1945] 1952) The biological economy of birth. In: *Trauma, Growth and Personality*. New York: Norton

Greenacre, P. ([1945] 1952) Conscience in the psychopath. In: *Trauma, Growth and Personality*. New York: Norton

Greenacre, P. (1952) *Trauma, Growth and Personality*. New York: Norton

Harlow, H. F. (1958) The nature of love. *American Psychologist, 13*, 673–685

Harlow, H. F. & Zimmermann, R. R. (1958) The development of affectional responses in infant monkeys. *Proceedings of the American Philosophical Society, 102*, 501–509

Hayes, C. (1951) *The Ape in our House*. New York: Harper

Heinicke, C. M. (1956) Some effects of separating two-year-old children from their parents: a comparative study. *Human Relations, 9*, 105–176

Heinicke, C. M. (1957) The effects of separating two-year-old children from their parents: a comparative study. *Paper read at the International Congress of Psychology*, Brussels.

Hermann, I. (1936). Sich-Anklammern—Auf-Suche-Gehen: Über ein in der Psychoanalyse bisher vernachlässigtes Triebgegensatzpaar und sein Verhältnis. *Internationale Zeitschrift für Psychoanalyse, 22* (3), 349–370

Hinde, R. A. (1954a) Factors governing the changes in strength of a partially inborn response. *Proceedings of the Royal Society, B 142*, 306–331

Hinde, R. A. (1954b) Changes in responsiveness to a constant stimulus. *British Journal of Animal Behaviour, 2*, 41–55

Hug-Hellmuth, H. Von ([1913] 1919) *A Study of the Mental Life of the Child*. Washington: Nervous and Mental Disease Pub. Co.

James, W. (1890) *A Textbook of Psychology*. New York: Holt

Johnson, A. M., Falstein, E. I., Szurek, S. A., & Svensden, M. (1941) School phobia. *American Journal of Orthopsychiatry, 11*, 702–711

Jones, E. ([1927] 1948) The early development of female sexuality. In: *Papers on Psycho-Analysis*. 5th edn., London: Baillire

Jones, E. ([1929] 1948) Fear, guilt and hate. In: *Papers on Psycho-Analysis*. 5th edn., London: Baillire

Kellogg, W. N., & Kellogg, L. A. (1933) *The Ape and the Child*. New York: Whittlesey

Klein, M. (1932) *The Psycho-Analysis of Children*. London: Hogarth

Klein, M. ([1935] 1952) A contribution to the psychogenesis of manic-depressive states. In: M. Klein, P. Heimann, S. Isaacs & J. Riviere (Eds.). *Developments in Psycho-Analysis*, London: Hogarth

Klein, M., & Riviere, J. (1937). *Love, Hate, and Reparation: Two Lectures*. London: Hogarth Press

Kris, E. (1956) The recovery of childhood memories in psychoanalysis. *Psychoanalytic Study of the Child, 11*, 54–88

Levy, D. (1937) Primary affect hunger. *American Journal of Psychiatry, 94*, 643–52

Liddell, H. (1950) Some specific factors that modify tolerance for environmental stress. In: H. C. Wolff, S. G. Wolff, Jr. & C. C. Hare, (Eds.). *Life Stress and Bodily Disease*. New York: Association for Research in Nervous and Mental Disease

Lorenz, K. Z. (1950) The comparative method in studying innate behaviour patterns. In: *Physiological Mechanisms in Animal Behaviour*. No. IV of Symposia of the Society for Experimental Biology. London: Cambridge University Press

McDougall, W. (1923) *An Outline of Psychology*. London: Methuen

Odier, C. ([1948] 1956) *Anxiety and Magic Thinking*. New York: International Universities Press

Prugh, D., Staub, E. M., Sands, H. H., Kirschbaum, R. M. & Lenihan, E. A. (1953) Study of emotional reactions of children and families to hospitalization and illness. *American Journal of Orthopsychiatry, 23*, 70–106

Rank, O. ([1924] 1929) *The Trauma of Birth*. London: Kegan Paul

Robertson, J. (1953a) Film: 'A Two-Year-Old Goes to Hospital'. London: Tavistock Child Development Research Unit

Robertson, J. (1953b) Some responses of young children to the loss of maternal care. *Nursing Times, April 1953*, 382–386

Robertson, J. (1958) Film: 'Going to Hospital with Mother'. London: Tavistock Child Development Research Unit

Robertson, J. & Bowlby, J. (1952) Responses of young children to separation from their mothers. *Courrier de la Centre Internationale de l'Enfance, 2*, 131–142

Schaffer, H. R. (1958) Objective Observations of Personality Development in Early Infancy *British Journal of Medical Psychology 31*, 174–183

Schaffer, H. R. & Callender, W. M. (1959) Psychological effects of hospitalization in infancy. *Pediatrics 24*, 528–539

Spitz, R.A. (1946) Anaclitic depression. *Psychoanalytic Study of the Child, 2*, 313–341

Spitz, R.A. (1950) Anxiety in infancy: a study of its manifestations in the first year of life. *International Journal of Psychoanalysis, 31*, 138–143

Stendler, C. B. (1954) Possible causes of overdependency in young children. *Child Development, 25*, 125–146

Suttie, I. D. (1935) *The Origins of Love and Hate*. London: Kegan Paul

Thorpe, W. H. (1950) The concepts of learning and their relation to those of instinct. In: *Physiological Mechanisms in Animal Behaviour*. Symposium IV of S.E.B. London: Cambridge University Press

Winnicott, D. W. (1953). Psychoses and child care. *British Journal of Medical Psychology, 26* (1), 68–74

Yerkes, R. M. (1943) *Chimpanzees: A Laboratory Colony*. New Haven: Yale University Press

Yerkes, R. M. & Yerkes, A. W. (1936) Nature and conditions of avoidance (fear) response in chimpanzees. *Journal of Comparative Psychology, 21*, 53–66

Zetzel, E. R. (1955) The concept of anxiety in relation to the development of psycho-analysis. *Journal of the American Psychoanalytic Association, 3*, 369–388

# 2

# Anxiety, Stress, and Homeostasis

## John Bowlby

*From the John Bowlby Archive, Wellcome Collections London, PP/Bow/H10*

*This paper was transcribed by Tommie Forslund and Robbie Duschinsky from John Bowlby's notes. Some of the text had already been written on a typewriter by Bowlby, but most was in the form of handwritten notes, with additions, deletions, rewordings, and various footnotes suggesting rounds of reworking the text.*

The thesis of this essay is that, in order to understand the conditions that elicit anxiety and fear, it is necessary first to consider basic biological principles. The principles concern (a) the nature of the states held relatively steady by a living organism (categories of homeostasis), and (b) the nature of the stable pathways along which development usually proceeds (categories of homeorhesis). Anxiety and fear are experienced, it is suggested, when some form of instability is appraised as being present or imminent and, especially, when instability is appraised as increasing and difficult to correct, or when risk of instability is appraised as increasing and difficult to reduce.

These appraisal processes, like any others, may or may not reach a phase of being felt. Because traditionally the words 'anxiety' and 'fear' refer to something felt, it is thought wisest to restrict their use to occasions when appraisal processes actually reach the phase of being felt. The term 'unconscious anxiety', though somewhat contradictory, is of course in common use. If used, it would apply to those same appraisal processes when they are in a phase of not being felt.

## Homeostasis

In order to survive in any environment, especially those undergoing changes, large or small, living organisms must maintain themselves in a comparatively steady state. Such steady state can be measured along numerous parameters, which can be grouped into a few major categories of homeostasis. Some refer to the organism's interior state, some to its relation with the outside world.

*Source:* John Bowlby, Anxiety, Stress and Homeostasis (unpublished manuscript), Bowlby Archive, Wellcome Collection, 1969. Reproduced with permission from Guy Dawson, The Bowlby Centre.

*Attachment Theory and Research: A Reader*, First Edition. Edited by Tommie Forslund and Robbie Duschinsky.
© 2021 John Wiley & Sons Ltd. Published 2021 by John Wiley & Sons Ltd.

The category of homeostasis first described by Claude Bernard, and for which Walter Cannon (1932)[1] coined the term, concerns a set of physiochemical measures interior to the organism. This category can be termed physiological homeostasis. Another set of measures also interior to the organism that are usually held even steadier, by healing processes, are those relating to body structure: this category can be termed morphological homeostasis. A third set of measures also held steady is well recognised by field biologists, namely the tendency for animals of any one species to remain within the limited range of environmental conditions to which the species is adapted – its ecological niche. Maintenance of an animal within its ecological niche is effected by a variety of behaviour patterns, the activation of which are sensitive to features of the environment. This category can be termed ecological homeostasis.

These three categories apply to all species of animal, and the first two apply also to plants. The biological control systems that maintain these categories of homeostasis are, for morphological homeostasis, physiological systems; for ecological homeostasis, behavioural systems; and for physiological homeostasis, both physiological and behavioural systems.

These three categories of homeostasis are intimately linked: by maintaining an animal within its ecological niche, the behavioural systems maintaining ecological homeostasis are acting in ways that greatly facilitate maintenance of morphological and physiological homeostasis.

I believe that at least two other categories of homeostasis can be recognised; they become increasingly evident in the higher animal phyla and play a great part in the lives of higher vertebrates and man. One of these categories refers to a special aspect of the organism's interior state, the other to a special aspect of its relation to the environment. We start with the latter.

Individuals of a species do not roam at random throughout the whole area of ecologically suitable terrain. On the contrary, they usually spend the whole of their lives within an extremely restricted segment of it. For example, a vole lives within a few square yards of thicket, a troop of baboons within a few square miles of prairie, human hunters and gatherers within a few hundred square miles of forest or plain. Even migrating birds, which may travel thousands of miles between nesting and wintering grounds, use only special parts of each; many nest each year at or very near the place they were born.

Nor do animals of higher species mix indiscriminately with others of their kind. Individual recognition is the rule. With certain individuals close bonds may be maintained for long stretches of the life-cycle. With a number of others there may be a less close but sustained relationship. Other animals may either be of little interest or else be carefully avoided.

Maintenance of an animal within that particular part of the ecological environment which it happens to frequent and in proximity to those particular individuals of its species with which it happens to associate I propose to term personal-environmental homeostasis.[2] Ethological evidence shows that preferences of personal companions and of environment usually develop early in life and are mediated by learning processes of an imprinting kind. In general, whatever is familiar is preferred to whatever is strange.

In order for an animal to maintain personal-environmental homeostasis, and in order, too, for it to find its way to particular parts of that environment and to treat appropriately different individuals in it, the animal must have available two working models, one of the *environment* and the other of the *self as agent*. There is good reason to believe that working models of both these types are built in the brain. In addition, there is evidence suggesting that, once built, these working models remain relatively stable, namely, relatively impermeable to dissonant information.

Maintenance of working models in a stable and relatively unchanging state I propose to term representational homeostasis. Representational stability appears to be maintained by cognitive processes that accept information compatible with an existing model and that reject, or scrutinise with great caution, information that is, or at least seems, incompatible.

The survival value of morphological, physiological and ecological homeostasis is, of course, not in doubt. The survival value of the latter two categories of homeostasis – personal environmental and representational – is by contrast, open to debate. Nevertheless, there is good reason to believe that at least the first of the two aids survival. By maintaining a familiar physical environment and familiar companions an animal is more likely to be able to

1 [Eds. Cannon, W. B. (1932). *The wisdom of the body*, NY: Norton.]

2 [Eds. Some of the ideas presented here would later appear, in abreviated form, in the two-page section 'Maintaining a stable relationship with the familiar environment: a form of homeostasis' in Chapter 9 of Bowlby, J. (1973) *Separation*, London: Pimlico.]

find food and drink, and more especially to achieve protection from natural hazards – from predators, from eating poisonous foodstuffs, from falling and drowning, from cold and rain.

The survival value of representational homeostasis may seem more problematic. Nevertheless a good case can be advanced. It seems not unlikely, for example, that perceptual constancy, the advantages of which are not disrupted, is itself an aspect of representational homeostasis. Indeed, another way of describing representational homeostasis would be 'conceptual homeostasis'.

When the uses to which a working model is put are considered, the advantages of 'conceptual constancy' become apparent. Once a working model has been built it becomes a tool with which information is processed, classified and filed, plans are framed, and their execution is monitored. Whenever a working model is undergoing revision of more than minor degree it is to that extent unserviceable. Perception and inference are less certain or even confused; planning is less prompt, execution less practiced. Furthermore, since shared plans can only be conceived and executed in collaboration with others provided that working models are also shared, an individual holding an idiosyncratic model of the world or of himself is likely to find himself facing the world alone.

Whilst it seems likely that the revision of working models tends always to be resisted, their cautious extension in familiar directions may be accepted fairly readily. Science is a social process whereby extensions of working models can come to be agreed; whilst in a scientific community even agreed revisions of working models are, in the long term, not impossible.

Two sciences have been concerned with the phenomena of personal-environmental homeostasis: they are *ethology*, notably the work on imprinting, and the *object-relations approach within psychoanalysis*, notably the views advanced by Fairbairn. In neither case, however, have workers been greatly concerned with the homeostatic properties of the phenomena studied. Insofar as psychoanalysts have invoked the concept of homeostasis, they have formulated it either in terms of maintaining a hypothetical psychic energy, or tension, within certain limits (e.g., Freud, Menninger) or else in terms of self-esteem (Engel; Sandler & Joffe). Within the scheme advanced here, maintenance of self-esteem is viewed as constituting a special case of representational homeostasis. Formulations regarding quantities of psychic energy or levels of tension are not found useful.[3]

Other disciplines interested in the phenomena are the school of cognitive psychologists studying cognitive dissonance (Festinger, 1957)[4] and certain traditions in the philosophy of science (e.g. Kuhn, 1963).[5] It is noteworthy, however, that in both cases there is a tendency to be more concerned with the disadvantages than the advantages of 'conceptual constancy'.

Within any of the five categories of homeostasis described states are never maintained more than relatively stable nor, except rarely, do set-points and limits persist unchanged during the life-cycle. In describing any kind of homeostasis it is necessary always to specify the period of time during which stability is maintained. What appears homeostatic over a longer period may appear unstable over a shorter one. For example, the annual migrations of geese from wintering ground to breeding ground and back again to wintering ground are stable over years but would appear unstable were the period of concern confined to a few months. Similarly, the behaviour of a commuter is stable over months but would appear unstable over hours and also over particular weeks. A form of homeostasis that applies over the longest periods of all is genetic homeostasis, namely maintenance of a population's gene-pool in a steady state over successive generations, which entails maintaining gene frequencies stable whilst preserving genetic variability.

The five categories of homeostasis listed all concern an individual organism. By contrast <u>genetic</u> homeostasis concern a population. There are other categories of homeostasis also that are found only at a supraindividual

---

3 [Eds. The following text was located at the very end of Bowlby's manuscript notes, with the prefix "8A". Since it fits with the theme discussed here, and the authors that are referenced, it may have been meant as an addition to, or as an alternative to, the current paragraph. Alternatively, at least one manuscript page is missing since the text would start mid-sentence. "Menninger (1954, 1963). Other and quite different versions have been formulated by Engel (1963, 1962) and by Sandler and Joffe (Joffe & Sandler, 1968; Sandler & Joffe, 1969). In the Engel version, the parameter held constant is the 'stability of the ego' or 'intactness of the psychic self', the maintenance of which persisting interaction with (what is here termed) the personal environment is believed to be essential. In the Sandler–Joffe version the parameter held constant or above a minimum level is conceived as a 'feeling of safety' or well-being. Within the sequence advanced here Engel's 'stability of the ego' is regarded as a product of the successful maintenance of personal environmental and representational homeostasis, whilst Sandler's 'feeling of safety' is regarded as an indication of the extent to which all of the various categories of homeostasis under consideration are being successfully maintained. Formulations regarding quantities of psychical energy or levels or tension are not found useful."]

4 [Eds. Festinger, L. (1957). *A theory of cognitive dissonance*, Stanford: Stanford University Press.]

5 [Eds. Kuhn, T. (1963) *Structure of scientific revolutions*, Chicago: University of Chicago Press.]

level. Examples are <u>familial</u> homeostasis as seen in the human family (Jackson, 1957),[6] <u>social-group</u> homeostasis as seen in many primate groups in the wild and also in human groups (Lawson, 1963),[7] and <u>demological</u> homeostasis as seen in studies of population densities of animal species (Wynne-Edwards, 1962).[8] Though each of these other categories of homeostasis is of great interest, both for behavioural science in general and for understanding human problems in particular, their examination lies outside the scope of this essay.

## Homeorhesis

Throughout the natural life-cycle of an individual of any species there are progressive changes in most of the homeostatic set-points, e.g. body measures change, pulse-rate drops, hormone levels change, habitat area increases, representational models become more differentiated and detailed. These developmental changes are indices of growth and maturation and usually follow a fairly predictable course. There is thus stability in the pathway of change. The tendency for organisms to maintain relatively steady developmental pathways, despite variation of environment and despite limited deviation along the route, is termed by Waddington (1957)[9] homeorhesis. The term he gives to each stable pathway is 'creode'.

For each measure and category of homeostasis there is (probably) a corresponding measure and category of homeorhesis. This is certainly so in the case of most morphological, physiological and ecological measures, all of which show a fairly high degree of homeorhesis in all species. In the case of the other two categories of measure (personal-environmental and representational) the position is less clear, because understudied. I suspect, however, that in these cases too there is a fairly high degree of homeorhesis.

When a species is endowed genetically with a high degree of developmental homeorhesis, the course of development of individuals is rendered relatively independent of even large fluctuations of environment. This can make for adults of a fairly high average degree of adaptedness to the usual environment even should their development have occurred in atypical environments. If this genetic strategy is carried too far, however, the species loses its adaptability. In the long run the species' environment might change so much that the single creode characteristic of its development might prove maladaptive, and, with no adaptability left, the species would become extinct.

An alternative genetic strategy is to provide a range of alternative creodes each suitable for one of a range of probable or potential environments and each tending to be the one followed when development happens to take place in that particular environment. An example is the capacity of a mammal's immunological system to develop persisting responses appropriate to particular features met with in the environment. Whilst an increased epigenetic adaptability of this kind has obvious advantages there are limits to the variety of environments to which any one repertoire of creodes is adapted. Furthermore, every increase in species adaptability, by increasing developmental instability, is probably bought at the cost of greater risk that some individuals will develop along maladaptive lines. Examples from the field of immunology are liability to anaphylactic responses or those arising from rhesus incompatibility.

In ordinary language an individual (or species) endowed with a high degree of homeorhesis is regarded as 'tough'. No matter what the environment (within limits) he seems to come through untouched. Conversely, an individual (or species) with low homeorhesis and high adaptability is regarded as 'sensitive'. How he develops depends on the particular environment in which he grows up. The result may be high adaptedness to that environment but it may also lead to deviant development and low adaptedness.

In some species, development in an atypical environment, i.e. one markedly different from the species environment of evolutionary adaptedness, can result in an organism becoming adapted to that atypical environment. Such adaptedness can be achieved in a number of ways. Some entail a shift in one or other homeostatic parameter, others a shift in one or another homeorhetic pathway. Waddington gives as an example the several possible ways

---

6 [Eds. Jackson, D. D. (1957) The question of family homeostasis. *Psychiatric Quarterly*, 31 (1), 79–90.]

7 [Eds. The reference is likely to Edwin Lawson, though exactly which text was meant by Bowlby is unclear. Lawson's only publication of 1963 was Lawson, E. D. (1963). Development of patriotism in children – a second look. *The Journal of Psychology*, 55 (2), 279–286.]

8 [Eds. Wynne-Edwards, V. C. (1962). *Animal dispersion in relation to social behavior*. Edinburgh: Oliver and Boyd.]

9 [Eds. Waddington, C. H. (1957) *The strategy of genes*. London: Allen & Unwin.]

in which development at high altitude may result in an organism becoming adapted to living at low pressures of atmospheric oxygen:

i.  by means of a shift in homeorhetic pathway, the area of lung alveoli is increased; this method permits both blood oxygen pressure and pulse rate to be maintained within usual homeostatic limits;
ii.  by means of a shift in one of these homeostatic measures, namely increasing heart-rate, the other homeostatic measure, blood oxygen pressure, and also homeorhesis of lung development are permitted to remain unchanged;
iii.  by means of a shift in the other measure of homeostasis, namely reduction in blood oxygen pressure, other measures can remain unchanged, though energy output is reduced.

Because adaptedness to any particular environment is never absolute and may be purchased at some cost to homeostatic steady states or homeorhetic stable pathways, it is often not possible to make unitary judgments about what is healthy and what not. A main long-term criterion, however, can always be applied, namely the degree to which any one solution contributes more or less successfully to species survival.

# Health and Ill-Health

Every form of ill-health, physiological and psychological, can (probably) be defined in terms of disturbances in one or another category of homeostasis or one or another category of homeorhesis, of a kind that temporarily or permanently impairs capacity for survival to some degree.

For example, physiological ill-health can be defined:

<u>either</u>

i.  as a disturbance in morphological or physiological homeostasis that temporarily or permanently impairs capacity for survival,

<u>or</u>

ii.  as a disturbance in morphological or physiological homeorhesis that temporarily or permanently impairs capacity for survival.

An example of (i) is measles. In the short run it can cause disturbances of various forms of physiological homeostasis. In the longer term the organism may become either better adapted (e.g. immune) or less well-adapted (e.g. brain damaged), or both. In either case there is a permanent shift of developmental pathway.

An example of (ii) is rickets which causes disturbances of morphological homeorhesis in an unfavourable direction.

Not infrequently the acute phase of illness represents a disturbance of homeostasis, and the persistent sequelae a disturbance of homeorhesis. Rickets is one example. Another is a badly mended fracture that leads to disturbances of growth in other parts of the body.

So long as a disturbance of any of these kinds lasts, it is likely to be experienced as painful or uncomfortable, and as handicap.

It seems probable that all forms of psychological ill-health can be defined in terms analogous to those applied to physiological ill-health but with reference to personal-environmental and representational homeostasis and homeorhesis.

For example the distress of separation or bereavement can be viewed as due to a disturbance of personal environmental homeostasis; delusions, hallucinations and thought disorder as constituting disturbances of representational homeostasis. Depression is usually associated especially with disturbance in representation of self.

The more chronic conditions can be viewed as disturbances of homeorhesis. Thus, phobias, addictions and sexual anomalies constitute disturbances in personal-environmental homeorhesis. The same is true of psychopathic personality. Thought disorder constitutes a disturbance in representational homeorhesis.

Other forms of psychological ill-health can be defined in a contrary way, namely, in terms of representational homeostasis that has been so rigid that necessary revision or working models of environment or of self are blocked. Examples are the various pathological variants of responses to loss.

It is not the purpose of this essay, however, to pursue matters of ill-health further.

## Disturbances of Homeostasis

### Stress and stressors

When a steady state is disturbed, processes are elicited that tend to restore it. Usually they are successful, but sometimes they are not.

Success turns on the degree of disturbance and on the capacity of the organism to respond. When disturbance is of limited degree, restoration may be an easy routine matter. When disturbance is of greater degree (or the organism is functioning below par) restoration be may difficult: on the one hand, it may take longer to achieve and, on the other, mobilisation of processes usually held in reserve may be necessary to achieve it.

Failure to restore homeostasis leaves the organism permanently changed in lesser or greater degree. Provided death does not ensue, there is a permanent shift of one or more measures of homeostasis and so of the course of development. Such shifts can be advantageous for survival, either in the short or in the long run. Others are disadvantageous. Because several different changes may occur following a single disturbance, some of the changes may be advantageous whilst others are disadvantageous; and it may then be difficult to determine where the balance lies.

In physiology the term 'stress' is used to refer to the state of an organism when some measure of homeostasis is disturbed in some degree and processes are elicited that have as their predictable outcome restoration of whatever steady state has been disturbed. A difficulty usually arises, however, because the degree of disturbance to which the term 'stress' is applied by different workers varies greatly.

At least four different usages can be discerned. Starting with the broadest, they are:

a. any disturbance of homeostasis, no matter how trivial or routine;
b. disturbances of such degree that homeostasis can be restored only by mobilising processes usually held in reserve;
c. disturbances of such degree that homeostasis is not fully restored and the course of development is changed;
d. as in (c) but restricted to disturbances following which the course of development is changed for the worse.

The term 'stressor' is used to refer to any condition, external or internal to the organism, that has a stressing effect. The definition of what is a stressor varies, therefore, in parallel to the definition of stress that is being adopted.

Logically, there is much to be said for the broadest definition of stress or stressor. By adopting it we are saved the difficult task of deciding between different degrees of homeostatic disturbances, and are also adopting a usage analogous to the one found useful by physicists. In the physics, stress in a material is measured in terms of force per square inch; which means, of course, that a feather exerts a stress, however trivial it may seem, in the material on which it rests just as does a ton of lead.[10]

However desirable the broadest usage may be, in clinical practice the term 'stress' tend to be restricted to disturbances of a degree beyond the routine and trivial; for example, as in usage (b), to those that that can be restored only by mobilising processes usually held in reserve. (This appears to be the way Selye [1950][11] uses the term: the processes making up his defense reaction are in fact restrictive processes of a kind not usually required). There are, however, several difficulties in any restrictive usage. First, there may be several different processes

---

10  In physics any condition causing a stress is commonly termed a 'load', though 'stressor' would be equally appropriate. A review of current usage in different fields of the term 'stress' is given by Richter [Eds. Richter, D. (1960). Some current usages of the word "stress" in different fields. In Tanner, J. M. (Ed.), *Stress and psychiatric disorder*, Oxford: Blackwell, pp. 31–33].

11  [Eds. Selye, H. (1950). Stress and The General Adaptation Syndrome. *The British Medical Journal*, 1383–1392.]

usually held in reserve: how many and which ones have to be mobilised before the disturbance can be classified as stressful? Secondly, some of these reserve processes may be mobilised in minimal degree even in routine responses to homeostatic disturbance. Thus, it is unlikely that any clear line of demarcation can be drawn between a routine disturbance and one of any degree beyond the routine.

Another term also applied to disturbances of homeostasis is 'trauma'. Although originally meaning simply 'wound' and still used in that sense, e.g. traumatic surgery, the term has acquired a more limited usage in the psychological sciences. When we speak of a 'mental trauma' we usually mean a disturbance of such degree that the course of development is, or at least is likely to be, changed for the worse.[12] This usage is identical with the most restricted usage of the term (namely [d] above). Conditions causing mental trauma can be termed 'traumatisation' (or possibly 'traumatisers').

It has been noted that a homeostatic disturbance can occasionally be of a degree that is not fully restored and so causes development to change; but that the change process can be in a direction of advantage to the organism. Such disturbances are habitually referred to as stressful, but not, of course, as traumatic. Indeed stress having this type of effect is sometimes referred to as 'strengthening experience'. In practice, however, it is often difficult to know what the balance of long-term effect of a major stressor will prove to be and so whether the stress produced is to be judged as traumatic or strengthening.

In what follows the terms 'stress' and 'stressors' are used fairly broadly. The varying degrees of disturbance and the varying outcomes are indicated by adjectives such as 'routine', 'major', 'intense', 'strengthening', and 'traumatic'.

[When] behavioural systems are under load, irrespective of which category of homeostasis being disturbed, it seems to be current practice to refer to the individual's condition as one of psychological (or emotional) stress. We consider the behavioural systems engaged in restoring steady states within each category of homeostasis in turn, starting with the simplest cases.

Any disturbance of personal-environmental homeostasis is responded to by attempts by behavioural means to restore the steady state disturbed. Loss of a loved figure is responded to by search; a damaged home by attempts to rebuild it. As long as attempts to restore to state continue, the individual's condition is habitually referenced to as one of psychological or emotional stress. Once success is achieved, stress ceases and relief is felt. Should the attempts fail and finally be abandoned on the other hand, stress also ceases. It is then replaced by despair and depression.

An analogous set of responses and sequences follow any disturbance of ecological homeostasis. Thus, reduction of oxygen pressure elicits attempts to escape into fresh air; a large rise or fall in temperature elicits attempts to find a more equable ambient temperature; an environment lacking water of food elicits attempts to find a more congenial habitat. Insofar as it is again behavioural systems that are under load the condition is likely to be references to as one of psychological and emotional stress.

The position regarding disturbances of <u>morphological</u> and <u>physiological</u> homeostasis is a little more complicated because, in the regulation of steady states of those sorts, two types of regulatory systems are called upon, physiological as well as behavioural. The term 'physiological stress', it should be noted, however, is habitually used to refer only to the load placed upon the relevant physiological systems. Insofar as a load may also be placed on relevant behavioural systems, the condition is referred to as one not of physiological but of psychological (or emotional) stress. An illustration is as follows: a person is suffering from incipient heat stroke in a desert. Physiological systems to reduce temperature are active and under heavy load. His condition would, further, be referred to as one of physiological stress. Yet simultaneously he might be struggling to escape the sun by climbing to a cave half-way up a cliff, but be finding the feat almost beyond him. His mental state might then be referenced to as one of psychological (or emotional) stress.

The position regarding disturbances of representational homeostasis is also a little complicated because, here again, two types of regulatory systems are called upon: psychological systems as well as behavioural ones. Current usage, it appears, is to refer to the condition as one of psychological (or emotional) stress when there is any disturbance of homeostasis, irrespective of which type of regulatory systems is relied upon. Let us consider the two types of systems successively.

---

12 The *Oxford English Dictionary* (1916) gives as the second meaning of 'trauma' (derived from psychoanalysis): "a disturbing experience which affects the mind or nerves of a person so as to induce hysteria of 'psychic conditions'; a mental shock".

Representational homeostasis, it is postulated, is maintained and restored in large part by the activation of perceptual-cognitive processes that filter and interpret sense data in ways that maintain current working models intact. Whenever the validity of a working model is called in question by the reception of incompatible yet mighty information, there is disturbance of representational homeostasis; and the perceptual-cognitive processes activated are consequently under load. An example is a person whose basic beliefs and assumptions about the world, whether framed in religious, political or scientific form, are called seriously in question by someone whom the person regards with respect. One the one hand, the person wishes to retain his original beliefs; on the other, he finds it difficult to ignore the contrary opinion. It is clearly in accordance with current usage to refer to condition as being one of psychological stress.

An alternative way of maintaining representational homeostasis is, by appropriate behaviour, to select the information likely to reach us so that it accords with our present working models. Whatever we suspect of being incompatible is almost automatically avoided, and a substantial effort may have to be made to give it attention. Much of this selection is achieved behaviourally by selecting what we read and listen to, though, as already indicated, much censoring is done also after our sense-organs have been exposed to the unwanted information. Should a person be forced against his wish to listen to incompatible views, as in a brain-washing session, the experience would clearly be regarded as stressful; and his condition would be described as one of psychological (or emotional) stress.

To sum up, the terms 'physiological stress' and 'psychological (or emotional) stress' are used today respectively to refer, not to a disturbance of any particular category of homeostasis, but to the type of regulatory system that is called upon to restore the disturbance. Whenever physiological systems are activated the organism is (or may be) described as undergoing physiological stress; whenever either behavioural or psychological systems are activated the organism is (or may be) described as undergoing psychological (or emotional) stress.

Thus far, the discussion has considered only actual disturbances of one or another category of homeostasis. In examining problems of psychological stress and anxiety, however, it is situations of *threatened* disturbance that are often of special importance.

## Threats of Disturbance of Homeostasis

A stressor has been defined as any change in the internal state or external environment that disturbs a steady state and thereby elicits regulatory processes that have as their predictable outcome restoration of whatever steady state has been disturbed. Living organisms, however, usually do not wait for a stressor to act. More often than not they are forewarned and take one or another type of action the consequences of which are either to avoid the stressor's striking or else to mitigate or cancel its effects.

It is evident that, in the development of an animal's capacity to take appropriate avoiding action, learning plays a major role. Every experiment in which an animal suffers punishment if it fails (e.g. when the buzzer goes it must press the right bar, or must turns down the right branch of a maze) is concerned with such learning. Nevertheless, there is good evidence that, in addition to all the cues portending trouble that are learned, there are other sorts of cues that lead animals to withdraw but that do not have to be learned. The strong tendency to avoid anything strange, which appears to be universal in birds and mammals, is one of the best investigated examples. The response of birds to the alarm call of their own species, and often to those of relative species, is another.

That many of the cues that elicit avoiding action should be responded to instinctively is hardly surprising. For if every individual had to learn for itself the hard way what was dangerous and what safe casualty rates would be enormous. To respond to everything strange with caution or escape may perhaps lead on many occasions to unnecessary timidity; but if on even only a few occasions it saves life it is intuitively worthwhile. Better to be safe than sorry.

The obverse of avoiding the strange is to remain close to the familiar. Remaining close to the familiar is, of course, the state of affairs maintained in personal-environmental homeostasis; and a principal position of this essay is that <u>maintenance of personal environmental homeostasis is a particularly efficient method of forestalling and avoiding disturbances to morphological and physiological homeostasis, and also to ecological homeostasis.</u> A corollary of that proposition is that the reason that, during evolution, higher vertebrates have become equipped with environmentally stable behavioural systems that have the effect of keeping an animal within its own familiar environment and close to its own familiar companions is that such systems, by maintaining that animal within a relatively safe arena, all make a major contribution to species survival.

The persistence of traditional customs in social groups, not only of man but also of some sub-human primates (e.g. food habits of chimpanzees) and of some birds (e.g. migrating habits of geese), can be looked at in the same light. Although obviously the details of such customs are learned, there seems to be a strong tendency in the young to adopt the customs of the group in which they are [illeg.] and a strong tendency in other members to enforce conformity.

The same seems to obtain for a working model of the world. Each social group has its own such model which is acquired by the young during the course of their education. Despite the existence of well-known exceptions in economically advanced countries, it seems likely that these conformist tendencies are an expansion of a genetic bias to develop in a conformist way in any environment that is not too far removed from the species environment of evolutionary adaptedness.[13]

Exploration and innovation are not overlooked. Even in animal societies and in tradition-rooted human societies such exploration and innovation occur. Where westernised societies are unusual is in the amount of exploration and innovation that they encourage and, especially, in the high valuation nowadays put upon it. But it needs to remembered that such shift in balance between tradition and innovation is not only historically very recent but is giving rise to much unforeseen and unwanted instability. Whilst in the short run the survival value of western innovation is undeniably high, its survival value in the long run remains unproven.

It is true that a familiar environment, familiar companions, and traditional customs and worldview may well not be the *best possible* for survival. Yet the very fact that a young creature has been born and reared in that environment and has been cared for by others who have adopted those customs, is testimony that the environment and the customs together are a combination capable of sustaining life. In wild creatures, therefore, and in almost all human communities also, it is no surprise that there is strong bias to preserve a conservative way of life.

The evolution of personal-environmental and representational homeostasis, it is therefore suggested, has provided higher vertebrates with an additional set of regulatory systems that contribute to survival. Evolved later than the systems that maintain morphological, physiological and ecological homeostasis, this additional set of systems acts as an *outer ring*. As a consequence of their evolution many hazards are avoided that would jeopardise safety by stressing the capability of the *inner ring* of regulatory systems evolved earlier. Seen in this light the evolution of personal-environmental and representational homeostasis appears as a way of doubling safety measures.

In concluding this section, special emphasis is given to the hypothesis that the outer ring systems that maintain personal-environmental and representational homeostasis are as 'bred in the bone' namely are as environmentally stable as are the inner ring systems that in an immediate way maintain morphological, physiological and ecological homeostasis. Thus, threats to outer ring steady states are responded to just as promptly and just as instinctively as are threats to inner-ring steady states. Moreover, just as an animal learns cues that forewarn it of threats to morphological, physiological and ecological homeostasis, so does it also learn cues that forewarn it of threats to personal-environmental and representational homeostasis. If this hypothesis is correct it would be expected that any disturbance, actual or potential to personal-environmental and representational homeostasis will engender no less stress and no less anxiety than do disturbances, actual or potential to those categories of homeostasis that, because more obviously contributing to survival, are better known and understood.[14]

## A Distinction Between Fear (or Alarm) and Anxiety[15]

It is stated in the introduction to this essay that it is useful to distinguish between fear and anxiety. On the one hand, it is posited that we try all times to withdraw or escape from a situation or object that we find alarming, and on the other, we try to go towards and to remain with some person or in some place that makes us feel secure.

---

13  In expressing that view, the existence of opposite tendencies follows.

14  The concept of personal environmental homeostasis is distinct from and much broader than that of territoriality. Whilst very many species of bird and mammal show marked preference for a particular home range and particular companions (see Jurell & Loizos, 1966), far fewer maintain and defend an exclusive territory. [Eds. Jewell, P. A., & Loizos, C. (1966). *Play, exploration and territoriality in mammals* (p. 18). London: Symposia of the Zoological Society]

15  [Eds. Some of this section is draw upon in Bowlby, J. (1973) Separation, London: Pimlico, Appendix III 'Problems of terminology'.]

The first type of behaviour is commonly accompanied by a sense of fright or alarm. What is experienced when the second type of behaviour is implicated, it is suggested, is best termed 'anxiety'.

Applied in the context of the theory of homeostasis now proposed this means that, whenever a person is focussing attention on the source of some homeostatic disturbance (or the threat of it) and on how to avoid it, what he feels is best termed 'fear' or 'alarm'; and that, whenever a person is focussing attention on restoring homeostasis and the difficulties of doing so, what he feels is best termed 'anxiety'. Whilst it is evident that both types of feeling can be present together, not infrequently one or the other predominates. The belief that in the two situations there is a real distinction in feeling is supported by the fact that the terms proposed have roots the meaning of which shade in two quite different directions. Thus, the English word 'fear' has cousins in old high German and old Norse with meanings that indicate 'ambush' and 'plague'; whilst alarm derives from sixteenth century Italian meaning 'to arms' and implies, therefore, 'surprise attack' (Onions, 1966).[16] By contrast, 'anxiety' has cousins in Greek and Latin in meanings that center on grief and 'sadness'; and is related to the German 'Angst' that, in addition to signifying dread, could in the seventeenth century also mean 'longing'. In addition 'anxiety' has as further cousins both 'anguish' and 'anger' (Lewis, 1967).[17] Insofar as separation from an attachment figure is accompanied by anxiety and often also by anger, and loss by anguish and despair, the usage is in keeping with its historical roots. It is also in keeping with Freud's belief that 'missing someone who is loved and longed for. . .' is '. . .the key to an understanding of anxiety.'[18]

## Inter-relations of Fear (or Alarm) and Anxiety

Although reasonably distinct in tone, those feelings termed respectively 'alarm' and 'anxiety' are nonetheless linked with one another in a very intimate way. A number of studies show clearly that the way children and animals behave toward mildly frightening objects varies greatly in differing social conditions.

It seems likely that comparable experiments would show similar results in adult humans (though I have not read of any). Walking through a wood at night with and without companions would be an appropriate type of test.

There is, of course, good reasons why in a group living species of animal should be more wary when isolated than when with its conspecifics. For in such species, when a predator threatens, the safety of every animal turns on the defensive efforts, either of all of them, or of the adult males together.

It is no accident that being together with 'kith and kin' buys relief from fear and anxiety, and engenders a feeling of security. Here again the etymology of words habitually in use, namely 'security' and 'safety', is revealing and stem from the Latin 'salvus' (Onions, 1966).[19]

The word 'safe' refers to absence of injury. As such it is appropriately used to describe <u>a situation in which injury is highly improbable</u>. The word 'security', on the other hand, has a very different origin. It incorporates the Latin <u>se</u> and <u>cura</u> and refers to a feeling of not being burdened by cares or grief. As such it is appropriately used to denote a <u>feeling of being unthreatened.</u>[20]

Now it is already evident that to feel fear or anxiety is only indirectly correlated with actual danger. In the same way, to feel secure is only indirectly correlated with actual safety. Thus members of a family may feel relatively secure when they are together, even if danger threatens; whilst conversely, each one alone might feel anxious even in the absence of any danger. Loneliness, like 'conscience doth make cowards of us all'.[21]

It is now possible, perhaps, to see some of the pitfalls that beset anyone in trying to formulate theories concerning fear (or alarm), anxiety, and feelings of security and of the situations that give rise to such feelings. First, there is a problem of distinguishing between avoiding a disturbance to homeostasis, on the one hand, and restoring homeostasis after it has been disturbed, on the other. Secondly, there is the fact that fear (or alarm) is

---

16 [Eds. Onions, C. T. (1966). *The Oxford dictionary of English etymology.* Oxford: ClarendonPress.]

17 [Eds. Lewis, A. ( 1967). Problems presented by the Ambiguous Word "Anxiety" as used inPsychopathology. *Israel Annals of Psychiatry & Related Disciplines* 5: 105–21.]

18 [Eds. Freud, S. ([1926] 2001) *Inhibitions, symptoms, and anxiety.* Standard Edition, 20:87–156.London: Hogarth Press, pp.136–7.]

19 [Eds. Onions, C. T. (1966). *The Oxford dictionary of English etymology.* Oxford: ClarendonPress.]

20 Sandler (1960) uses the term 'feeling of safety' as equivalent to any feeling of security, which is etymologically better suited. Sandler does not discuss how this 'feeling of safety' is related to actual safety. [Eds. Sandler, J. (1960). The background of safety. *International Journal of Psycho-Analysis,* 41, 352–356.]

21 [Eds. The quote is from the 'to be, or not to be' soliloquy by Hamlet, in Shakespeare's *Hamlet,* Act 3, Scene 1.]

frequently elicited, not by actual danger but by indicators only loosely correlated with actual danger. Thirdly, there is the fact that two of the most basic variables that determine whether fear or anxiety is experienced, and if so how intensely, namely strangeness versus familiarity and isolation versus companionship, tend to be highly idiosyncratic for each individual. So long as threats are public and common to all – an earthquake, a bellowing bull, a rifle pointed at someone – it is easy to classify them as 'real', evident, and verifiable. When, by contrast, there is threat or disturbance to someone's personal environment and to his stability within it – isolation, the possibility of home being demolished, uncertainty whether parents will remain together – the fear and anxiety generated are not to be regarded as 'unreal' or unverifiable or at the least exaggerated. What naturally engender fear or anxiety, does not always fall within what is conventionally regarded as 'reasonable'.

In the usage proposed, which is only tentative, the term 'ecology' refers to those characteristics of the environment to which all members of a species (or at least of one sex) respond more or less similarly, e.g. air or water, gradients of temperature and light. By contrast, the term 'personal environment' refers to those special characteristics of the ecologically preferred environment to which members of a species respond in distinctive ways, notably other individuals of the species and home-ranges, such as [illeg.]

(As a term, personal environment is cumbersome and will probably need to be replaced. We might consider 'wicology' for the science, which would give wicological homeostasis. This derives from a root giving a number of words in the northern European languages (Wic, Wik, Wijk) and of which 'bailiwick' is an derivative. They all refer to a [illeg.] or a district and are usually equivalent to a home-range. It is of some interest that both 'eco' as in ecology and 'wico' as suggested here are related to the Greek oikos (= house).

[*Bowlby's pagination suggests that three manuscript pages are missing, or were not written*]

It is when he feels secure that he can explore the merits of alternative working models and compare the extent to which these models fit with his experience and the models he has been using hitherto.

Whereas the revision of working models tends always to be resisted and therefore to be achieved only with difficulty, their conscious elaboration may be accepted fairly readily. Science is a social process whereby extensions of working models can come to be agreed; whilst in a scientific community an agreed change of working model can occur, it usually entails long and often heated debate.

Two sciences have been concerned with the phenomena of personal environmental homeostasis: they are ethology, notably the work on imprinting, and the objects-relations approach within psychoanalysis, notably the views advanced by Fairbairn. In neither case, however, have workers invoked homeostatic principles to interpret the phenomena studied.

## Fear and Anxiety, Conscious and Unconscious

In the account of fear and anxiety sketched several elements are distinguished. They can be arranged in two sequences according to whether disturbance of homeostasis is appraised as actual or only threatened. Because threats of disturbance are much commoner than actual disturbance, and also as a rule precede actual disturbance, the sequence resulting from threat is presented first.

I.   Disturbance appraised as threatened
   a.   Statistical likelihood of disturbance occurring in any of several categories of homeostasis, the likelihood in each case being detectable either from stimuli arising from the actual presence of a potential stressor or from stimuli arising from an indicator correlated with a probable presence of a potential stressor;
   b.   Appraisal of such stimuli as warning signals or signals of threat;
   c.   Preparatory responses that have the effect of preparing an individual to take any of a great variety of actions, including those preventive or corrective of disturbance;
   d.   Avoiding actions that commonly have the effect of preventing actual disturbance, but that may fail;
   e.   Continuous monitoring both of threat and of any changes occurring in its degree of imminence, and also of the effects of preventive actions;
   f.   Continuous estimating of the degree of success in preventing disturbance likely to be achieved by preventive actions, or by plans for preventive action;
   g.   In the light of such estimates, the revision, if necessary repeated, of plans for preventive action.

2.   <u>Disturbance appraised as actual</u>
   a.   Actual disturbance occurring in any of several categories of homeostasis, the disturbance in each case being caused by the action of a stressor and itself constituting a stress of some kind and degree;
   b.   Indicators of disturbance (stress), some of which act automatically in eliciting preparatory and/or corrective actions and some of which come into being as indicators only after 'raw' stimuli have been appraised as indicative of stress;
   c.   Preparatory responses that have the effect of preparing an individual to take any of great variety of actions, including corrective actions;
   d.   Corrective actions that usually have the effect of cancelling disturbance and restoring homeostasis, but that may fail;
   e.   Continuous monitoring both of disturbance and of any changes occurring in it and also of the effects of corrective actions;
   f.   Continuous estimating of the degree of success in restoring homeostasis likely to be achieved by corrective actions, or by plans for corrective actions;
   g.   In the light of such estimates, the revision, if necessary repeated, of plans for corrective actions.

It is probably wise to assume that any of the components in either sequence, when present, can either be conscious and felt or can remain unconscious and unfelt. What this statement implies is that every element in a sequence may be conscious and felt, or that no element in a sequence may be conscious and felt, or that any one or more elements may be conscious and felt and that others remain unconscious and unfelt.

To illustrate some of the clinical conditions that call for explanation it may be useful to give a few typical examples of people responding to disturbance, or threat of disturbance, without being fully aware of what is going on. A number of different patterns are well known to occur in patients before a holiday break. Patient A may be aware of anxiety but fail to relate it to the impending break and instead attribute it to something quite different. Patient B, by contrast, may show no overt anxiety, nor feel any, yet show by his actions that threat of disturbance has been appraised and appraised correctly: he may become remote, have little to say and may even miss the last session. Patient C may claim to be feeling no anxiety nor to have cause for any, yet be surprised to find himself tense and sweaty. Patient D may claim that he was never informed that a break was impending.

The assumption that any one or several elements in the sequences listed can be conscious and felt or unconscious and unfelt is in keeping with clinical experience. Taken in conjunction with knowledge that the appraisal processes involved vary from individual to individual, and also for any one individual on different occasions, and in addition may be of any degree of accuracy or inaccuracy, this assumption (and the schema of which it is based) might be expected to provide sufficient parameters to account for the great variety of psychological states, met with in and out of clinic, that are at present described in terms of anxiety, either conscious or unconscious, and of defences against anxiety. Whether or not that expectation is fulfilled requires extensive examination of the data.

# 3

# Attachment

## Mary D. Salter Ainsworth

"Attachment" is a term inextricably linked to the contribution of John Bowlby. His theory of attachment, although focused on the nature and development of affectional bonds, is a comprehensive psychological theory encompassing issues of motivation, emotion, and cognition as well. Although in his earliest statements it appeared to be concerned primarily with the normal course of development, his aim from the beginning was to account for individual differences in intimate relationships and the way they are handled, including some developmental outcomes that may be clearly identified as pathological. It is an open-ended theory that, from its earliest formulations, has stimulated research which in turn has influenced later theoretical formulations. Both theory and research have had an impact on child-care practices, especially in hospitals, residential institutions, and social agencies. It is the intent of this chapter to present the essentials of attachment theory and to consider the findings of some of the research to which it has given rise. This review has to be highly selective; the literature has become so voluminous that it is impossible in one chapter to refer to all the relevant research or to consider reformulations of attachment theory stemming from other theoretical paradigms.

## Deprivation and Separation

Bowlby's starting point was research stemming from the hypothesis that separation from the mother in early childhood could lead to pathological outcomes that were difficult to reverse (Bowlby, 1944). Subsequent reviews of the literature (Ainsworth, 1962; Ainsworth & Bowlby, 1953; Bowlby, 1952) led to a distinction between "maternal deprivation" as insufficiency of interaction of a child with the mother figure and "mother–child separation" as discontinuity of the bond of child to mother after it had become established. Although prolonged deprivation beginning before an infant had become attached to its mother was shown to have a very adverse effect on development (e.g., Goldfarb, 1943), in most of the research literature deprivation and separation were confounded, dealing with infants and young children removed from home and parents to whom they had already become attached and placed in an unfamiliar environment among unfamiliar caregivers, none of whom had sufficient interaction with the child to substitute as an adequate mother figure. Noting similar adverse effects, Bowlby directed research that shifted its main focus from outcome to process in an attempt to understand the sequence of responses a young child shows when separated under depriving circumstances and, also, to account for the sequence of

*Source:* Republished with permission of John Wiley & Sons, from Ainsworth, M. D. S. "Attachment," pp. 559–602 from *Personality and the Behavioral Disorders*, Vol. 1 (2nd ed.), eds. Norman S. Endler, Joseph McVicker Hunt, 1984; permission conveyed through Copyright Clearance Center, Inc.

readjustments in the child's behavior toward his or her family when eventually they are reunited. These responses are reviewed in the introductory sections of each of the three volumes of his *Attachment and Loss* series (Bowlby, 1969, 1973, 1980) and are so focal to his theory that they will be summarized here.

Three phases of response to major separation may be identified in children between the ages of one and four years: (1) *protest,* in which the child, both distressed and angry, tries by all means possible to regain the mother; (2) *despair,* in which the child becomes withdrawn and apathetic, with muted protest, and seems to have lost hope that the mother will return; and (3) *detachment,* in which the child's longings for the mother and anger at her abandonment of him or her seem to have disappeared. The intensity and duration of the responses are influenced by a number of variables – for example, age at separation, length of separation, presence or absence of individualized care by substitute caregivers, frequency of parental visits, and so on. Indeed, as Robertson and Robertson (1971) subsequently showed, sensitive attention to preparation for separation, familiarization with foster parents and foster home, and highly individualized substitute care can not only moderate the protest phase but also prevent the onset of despair and detachment – at least in a temporary and relatively brief separation.

Responses to the mother when reunited with her are related to the phase of response that the reunion interrupted. If the child had still been protesting separation, the child's feelings on reunion are likely to be ambivalent, with anger and distress intermingled with approach and clinging – and quite often also intermingled with short-lived indications of detachment. The conspicuous pattern of behavior after the initial reunion we would now consider expressive of "anxious attachment." After long separations in which detachment has become well consolidated, the child may continue to behave with indifference to the mother and her whereabouts although usually with occasional unprovoked aggression toward her. How long detachment persists before it gives way to behavior indicative of anxious attachment, and how long it is before the attachment again becomes normally secure, is influenced at least in part by how parents respond to the difficult behaviors implicit in both detachment and anxious attachment.

Bowlby was struck with the many points of resemblance between a young child's response to separation from the mother and the phases through which adults pass in responding to permanent loss of a loved person – to the extent that he believed much the same kind of processes must be implicated. The similarities seem more plausible when one considers that the young child's capacity to span long gaps of time and ability to understand the reasons for the separation are ill developed. To the child a long separation is the equivalent of permanent loss. Even in an adult's processes of recovery from loss Bowlby saw parallels with recovery from separation in early childhood, and in the pathological forms of mourning that have been identified in adults he saw resemblances to the pathological outcomes of early separation. A series of papers in the 1960s presented his comparisons between the mourning of children and that of adults, but he did not discuss these in the *Attachment and Loss* series until his third volume (Bowlby, 1980). Nevertheless, considerations such as these quickly took the scope of interest beyond the attachment of a young child to her or his mother and extended it to the nature of intimate relationships throughout the life span.

The questions raised by an examination of responses to separation and loss were many and weighty and yet not satisfactorily accounted for by then-current theories. Why should a child be so distressed away from home when all the child's basic drives are being met competently? Why should the child respond with anxiety and / or detachment rather than joy when finally reunited with the person she or he had so obviously been longing for? What could account for detachment, and for the fact that it so often and so intensely gives way to behavior seemingly quite opposite? What principles of development and what processes could account for the similarities between adult reaction to, say, the death of a spouse and a young child's response to being placed in a hospital for medical treatment?

The issues raised by these questions were the nature of the bond between an infant and its mother figure and how this bond develops, the role played by this bond in the subsequent course of development, and the ways in which this bond affects or is affected by other affectional bonds formed either early in development or later on; an explanation for continuity in development and also for obvious change within the context of continuity; an explanation for deviations from the normal course of development that may lead to clearly pathological outcomes, and the ways in which such outcomes might be prevented, reversed, or ameliorated. Issues such as these form the background of attachment theory.

Bowlby addressed himself first to the origin and nature of the infant's tie to its mother. He could not accept current theoretical accounts thereof, most of which accounted for the bond in terms of an infant's dependency on its mother as the chief gratifier of basic drives – or, indeed, as provider of primary reinforcers. Whereas learning theorists placed chief emphasis on hunger, most psychoanalytic theorists emphasized oral gratifications. Why then did one-year-olds protest the absence of the mother when other caregivers offered food and other basic gratifications? Convinced that current theories could provide no satisfactory answer to this question, Bowlby proceeded to formulate a new theoretical paradigm – in the sense that Kuhn (1962) used the term "paradigm."

Innovative though the new theory proved to be, it was nevertheless based on research and theory stemming from a number of scientific disciplines: contemporary biological science, especially evolutionary theory and ethological principles and research; laboratory and field studies of animal behavior, especially those dealing with primates; control-systems theory; cognitive psychology's information processing and relevant neurophysiological principles; and developmental research. In regard to the latter, Bowlby himself stimulated research into the development of mother–infant interaction and infant–mother attachment and wove the findings into his theoretical formulation. Clearly, Bowlby was also deeply indebted to psychoanalytic theory. He greatly admires Freud's contribution, although he believes Freud's metapsychology was shaped to biological principles that are now outmoded. Indeed, it is Bowlby's hope that his theory will bring Freudian theory up to date, substituting new biological foundations for those that are outmoded. Specifically, he rejected Freudian instinct theory, together with the theory of psychosexual development and the concepts of fixation and regression.

## Bowlby's Theory of Infant–Mother Attachment

### Behavioral system

The concept of the "behavioral system" is fundamental to attachment theory – a concept borrowed from ethology. Like the ethologists Bowlby concerned himself with species-characteristic behavioral systems – those that involve sequences of actions, occurring in nearly all members of the species (or members of one sex) despite environmental variations, often without opportunity for learning, and yielding survival advantage in the environment in which they evolved. Many behavioral systems are shared across species – for example, those involved in obtaining food, avoiding danger, exploring the environment, reproducing, caring for the young, and, Bowlby suggests, attachment of the young to parent(s) – although specific component behaviors in each system and the way they are organized together may vary from one species to another. Motivation is implicit in the behavioral system and need not be reduced to anything more fundamental.

Behavioral systems vary on a continuum from the extreme of environmental stability to the extreme of environmental lability. In regard to the systems with which he is most concerned – caregiving to the young by parents and attachment of the young to parents – Bowlby claims a genetic ground plan for the human species despite substantial lability with individual experience and cultural pressure. He gives little attention to even more labile behavioral systems, although one might well suppose that he thinks of them as resembling Piagetian schemata, differentiating out of more fundamental behavioral systems but becoming autonomous of their origins at least insofar as motivation is concerned. Motivation, for Bowlby, is implicit in the behavioral system, just as for Piaget it is implicit in the schema. Chess playing may become an autonomous behavioral system (or set of strategies) that is self-motivating once established – but Bowlby remains concerned with behavioral systems that are relevant to species survival, which chess playing presumably is not.

A behavioral system characteristic of any species has evolved because it increased the probability of survival of the species (or population) in the original environment in which the species emerged – that is, the "environment of evolutionary adaptedness" (Bowlby, 1969). Once activated, a behavioral system has one or more "predictable outcomes" – outcomes that are likely to ensue under ordinary circumstances but do not inevitably follow. Only one of these predictable outcomes, however, is likely to have yielded the survival advantage that accounted for the behavioral system's having evolved in the way it did, and this outcome is identified as the "biological function" of the system. Other predictable outcomes are coincidental as far as concerns the specified behavioral system, although they may be identified as functional for other behavioral systems.

The activity of behavioral systems is episodic; they start and stop. More accurately, they become more or less intensely activated. When one behavioral system is activated more intensely than any other, it determines what the individual will do at that particular time. The causes of a behavioral system's becoming more intensely activated are complex. According to Bowlby (1969) five classes of factor are implicated. Two of these are specific to the system at issue: a specific environmental stimulus and the way the behavioral system is organized in the central nervous system. The other three are unspecific: the hormonal state of the organism; the general state of the nervous system, particularly its state of arousal; and the total stimulation impinging on the organism. These unspecific factors may act to potentiate (or depotentiate) several systems but not any one system specifically. (Particularly in regard to the specific factors, one can suppose that experiential factors as well as genetic are involved.) The causes of deactivation of a behavioral system, and thus for the behavior's stopping, are assumed to be similarly complex.

If more than one behavioral system is activated simultaneously at comparable intensity, there may or may not be incompatibility or conflict. If the two systems are compatible – as in the case of an infant's simultaneously retreating from an alarming situation and seeking proximity to its mother – there is usually no conflict. If the two systems are incompatible, any one of a variety of patterns of behavior may be exhibited – a variety that displays common ground between ethologists and psychoanalysts – for example, intention movements, redirected behavior, and so on.

Behavioral systems are likely to include several component behaviors or behavioral sequences. In infancy and/or in simple organisms these tend to be fixed-action patterns that, once activated, are inclined to run their course regardless of environmental feedback. In adult or complex organisms a behavioral system may have many components, and how these become organized together is of considerable moment. They may be organized in a chain, with each component activating the next, as is most likely for fixed-action systems, or they may become organized into a plan hierarchy, as is most likely for "goal-corrected" behavioral sequences.

Bowlby placed much emphasis on goal-corrected behavior – behavior that, once activated, is constantly being corrected by environmental feedback. At this point control-systems theory became crucial for his position. He was concerned about demonstrating that a behavioral system can be "instinctive," in the sense of being species-characteristic and genetically programmed, and still operate purposively. He referred to control systems, such as servomechanisms, into which the designer has built a program, including a "set-goal." For example, the set goal of aircraft interception is built into an antiaircraft missile, as well as a program enabling it to alter direction in accordance with the evasive maneuvers the victim aircraft may undertake. An analog in animal behavior, Bowlby suggested, is the stoop of the falcon on its prey, except that in the case of the falcon the program and the set-goal are the products of evolution and are built into the genetic program characteristic of the species, regardless of the fact that such behavior is not manifest at the time of hatching and indeed requires some experience before it operates effectively.

## Feelings and defensive processes

Both affect and defensive processes are of substantial significance for attachment theory. In his account of them Bowlby drew on cognitive psychology's information-processing theory (Bowlby, 1969, 1980). Such a model presents no difficulty for the concept of unconscious processes; input is conceived as capable of influencing mood and behavior and of being stored in long-term memory without necessarily having been initially processed at the ultimate stage required for conscious appreciation.

Bowlby (1969) suggested that affects play an important role in appraising input, whether they are felt or unfelt (i.e., conscious or unconscious), and because they may influence behavior they may also communicate information to others. When the appraisal processes are felt, however, they play a valuable monitoring role, informing the individual about the progress and short-term consequences of his or her actions – a role essential for goal-corrected behavior. Furthermore, it is clear that Bowlby stressed the affective components of attachments, whether they are positive (e.g., feeling joyful, delighted, secure) or negative (e.g., feeling distressed, anxious, sad, angry, jealous).

Bowlby's (1980) application of information-processing principles to an understanding of defensive processes is a very significant contribution, allowing the inclusion in his theory of psychoanalytic insights about repression and other unconscious defensive processes without needing to accept the concept of psychic energy implicit in what he considered an outmoded instinct theory. As an illustration, let us consider his account of repression as defensive exclusion from perception and of reaction formation in a more flexible concept of diversionary activity – processes that may be available even to the young child, except perhaps in the first half of the first year. Although most input is routinely excluded from reaching the highest (conscious) level of information processing, some of it may be defensively excluded – the kind of information that when processed in the past has led to suffering (such as being rebuffed or rejected by an attachment figure). One effect of defensive exclusion is that the behavioral system at issue ultimately becomes deactivated; the environmental stimuli that ordinarily activate the system no longer do so – as in detachment when neither separation from nor reunion with the attachment figure activate attachment behavior. Whereas this input is indeed processed at some level, it is no longer matched with relevant information in long-term storage and hence does not activate the relevant behavioral system. Simultaneously, the individual may busy himself or herself with some form of activity that diverts him or her further from processing the information being defensively excluded. This diversionary activity is likely to relate to another behavioral system that is already activated intensely enough to direct behavior now that the other competing (attachment) system is deactivated. Thus in a one-year-old the diversionary activity may well be exploratory activity.

## Infant–mother attachment

Bowlby (1969) defined "attachment behavior" as a class of actions that have as their predictable outcome gaining or maintaining proximity to or contact with an attachment figure – or, in early infancy before an attachment has been formed, with a caregiver. The component behaviors of the attachment behavioral system are of two kinds: (1) signaling behavior, such as smiling or crying, that promotes proximity/contact by inducing the caregiver or attachment figure to approach and to remain close and (2) active behavior, such as rooting, sucking, reflex clasping, or, later, approach and clinging, through which an infant seeks or maintains proximity/contact through its own actions.

It is Bowlby's claim that the human infant, like infants of many other species, is genetically biased toward attachment behavior and, indeed, is biased to become attached to a mother figure, because this increased the probability of survival in the environment of evolutionary adaptedness. By inference from evidence he considered in his 1969 volume, he concluded that the "biological function" of attachment and attachment behavior is protection; he suggested that in the original environment in which the human species emerged, it was protection from predators that was especially crucial.

Present-day human infants living in varied environments throughout the world still behave as though it were a matter of life or death to achieve proximity to a caregiver or attachment figure whenever the attachment system is intensely activated, even though no obvious danger – and, certainly, no threat from a predator – exists. It is as though the preprogramming, once it becomes represented in the genetic ground plan of the species, continues to serve a survival function. Indeed, as Bowlby (1973) pointed out, there is good reason to believe that children are less at risk when a responsible caregiver is at hand and that even adults are more likely to survive dangerous situations when with companions than when alone. Thus for a baby to demand company even though not hungry, uncomfortable, or in pain or for a young child to be intensely distressed when separated from attachment figures is only to be expected as genetically biased behavior, and it in no way indicates that the child has been overindulged or "spoiled."

Attachment behavior may have predictable outcomes in addition to protection. As in all mammals, one such outcome is that the infant is fed. Bowlby (1969) considered this a coincidental outcome, not accounting for the infant's bond to its mother figure. In this he was influenced by Harlow's (e.g., 1958, 1961) finding that contact seeking in infant rhesus macaques is directed in preference to a surrogate figure comfortable to cling to rather than to one which regularly provides milk and that the former rather than the latter serves the infant as a haven when frightened and then later as a secure base for exploring an unfamiliar environment. He was also influenced by reports by Ainsworth (1967) and Schaffer and Emerson (1964) that human infants can and commonly do become attached to fathers and others who play no part in feeding them.

Another predictable outcome of attachment behavior is that the infant learns from the caregiver with whom proximity is maintained – another coincidental outcome since it is unlikely to have accounted for attachment behavior having been evolved. To be sure, learning about the environment is important for the continued survival of the young of any species, but it may be identified as the biological function of exploratory behavior. Indeed, attachment and exploratory behavior are linked in a functional way, for when an infant is within reasonable proximity to an attachment figure and the environment is full of interesting features, attachment behavior tends to be activated less intensely than exploratory behavior, and the infant is likely to explore. On the other hand, if the attachment figure is or threatens to become unavailable, attachment behavior is intensely aroused, and exploration is abandoned. The infant thus can use the attachment figure as a secure base from which to explore and to learn about his or her world and ways of coping with it (Ainsworth, e.g., 1967).

Proximity to an attachment figure also promotes learning how to communicate with others in ways that eventually overshadow but never entirely supplant the signaling behaviors of early infancy. Some (e.g., Richards, 1974) emphasize the learning of communication as the most important outcome of the mother–infant relationship. However, important as this outcome is for later relations with attachment figures and other conspecifics, it seems to be an *outcome* of attachment and attachment behavior rather than the outcome of proximity maintenance that accounts for attachment behavior having been evolved.

Attachment behavior and its manifestations can only be understood in relation to other behavioral systems. Some of these, when activated, work synchronistically with the attachment system; others work antithetically. Like exploratory behavior, what may be termed "affiliative" or "sociable behavior" – seeking proximity to or interaction with persons other than attachment figures – is antithetical in the sense that when one is more intensely activated than the other, it dominates behavior to the exclusion of the behavioral manifestations of the other system (Bretherton & Ainsworth, 1974). The food-seeking system, on the other hand, tends to work in synchrony with the attachment system. When a baby is hungry, attachment behavior, as well as food-seeking behavior, becomes more intensely activated; being picked up by the mother tends to lower the intensity of activation of attachment behavior and, indeed, also of food-seeking behavior if feeding ensues as it sometimes – but not always – does.

Another behavioral system that works in synchrony with the attachment system is fear behavior. Bowlby (1973) distinguished between two components of situations that activate fear behavior: (1) environmental stimuli, arousing *alarm*, and (2) the unavailability of an attachment figure, arousing *anxiety*. When both components are present, both fear and attachment systems tend to be activated at high intensity; the individual simultaneously seeks to avoid the alarming stimulus and to regain proximity to an attachment figure, and in this sense the two systems usually are in synchrony. On the other hand, the presence of an attachment figure (and thus the absence of anxiety) may keep the activation of the fear system at low intensity even when stimuli occur that would otherwise be alarming, and anxiety at the absence of an attachment figure may not become intense until something alarming occurs. Thus to predict the course of attachment behavior in any situation with any accuracy, the state of activation of other behavioral systems needs to be taken into account (cf. Bischof, 1975).

In regard to alarm, Bowlby (1973) identified certain "natural clues to danger," including not only loud noise and sudden approach but also aloneness and strangeness. Loud noise may presage natural disasters; sudden approach and strangeness may be associated with predation. Aloneness not only increases vulnerability to danger but also implies the absence of the security provided by a trusted companion. Even though such clues by no means always indicate danger, behaving fearfully in response to them is likely to have yielded enough edge of survival advantage for members of the human species to have become genetically biased to such response.

Bowlby acknowledged that fears may be learned through both individual painful experience and observation of the behavior of others and that the intensity of fearful reactions to even natural clues of danger may be considerably reduced by various desensitization influences. Nevertheless, a "compound fear situation" that combines several natural clues to danger may activate fear in an adult, especially if the adult encounters them when alone; any human companionship, especially the presence of a trusted figure, may mitigate such fear.

Bowlby (1969) suggested that the causes of activation of attachment behavior are both internal (e.g., pain, discomfort, illness, fatigue, hunger) and external, including alarming situations of all kinds, the departure or absence of an attachment figure, the return of such a figure after an absence, and rebuff, especially rebuff by an attachment figure. In general, if an attachment figure is present and believed to be responsive, other conditions, both internal and external, are less likely to activate attachment behavior at high intensity than they are if no attachment figure is nearby or if the attachment figure is expected to be unresponsive, either because of present behavior or expectations from past behavior. One outcome of intensive research into attachment behavior during the past decade has been to highlight the significance of context if one is to predict behavior (Ainsworth, e.g., 1982; Sroufe, Waters, & Matas, 1974).

## Development of attachment in the first year of life

Bowlby (1969) identified four phases in the development of attachment to mother, the first three of which are relevant to the first year – and these are in essential congruence with phases identified by Ainsworth (e.g., 1967, 1972). The fourth phase, a phase of goal-corrected partnership, will he discussed later in another section.

*Phase 1*

Bowlby emphasized two features of infant behavior beginning at birth: (1) the responsiveness of the infant to the various elements of stimulation most likely in the ordinary expectable environment to emanate from other people and (2) the behavioral components of the attachment system operative in early infancy. He assembled research evidence that the infant is especially tuned in to respond to stimuli emanating from other people, and more recent research evidence yields further support, some of it indicating also that the infant synchronizes behavior remarkably well with such stimulation. The behavioral components of the attachment system operative at birth or soon afterward – including sucking, rooting, crying, smiling, vocalizing, and reflex grasping and clasping – he conceived initially as fixed-action patterns that may become organized into a system on the basis of chaining. During this first phase, a baby, although predisposed to be socially responsive, responds with attachment behavior indiscriminately – to the stimuli offered by people rather than to any person as a unique individual.

*Phase 2*

The range of stimuli to which the baby is responsive tends gradually to narrow. The baby becomes increasingly discriminating, distinguishing its mother figure (i.e., its principal caregiver) from others and tending to direct its attachment behavior more specifically to the mother figure than to others. It is difficult to pinpoint the beginning of discriminating behavior for this depends on modality, with olfactory, tactual, kinesthetic, and vestibular clues being discriminated first, then auditory clues, and only later visual clues. At about six weeks, however, a baby can visually discriminate its mother from another when en face, although it is not until considerably later that a baby seems able to do so across a distance (e.g., Ainsworth, 1967). Both Schaffer (e.g., 1971) and Ainsworth (e.g., 1972) held that although discrimination of and consequent behavior differential to the attachment figure is a necessary condition for the emergence of attachment, it is not itself sufficient. Bowlby (1969) left the issue open, depending on the criteria used to specify the onset of attachment.

*Phase 3*

With the emergence of locomotion in the second half of the first year, proximity-seeking behavior becomes much more active and partly replaces the discriminating signaling behavior of Phase 2. The fixed-action characteristic of earlier attachment behavior gives way to goal-corrected (i.e., purposive) behavior, and organization of behavior into chains gives way to organization into a plan hierarchy. Within the context of an overall plan, specific behaviors are more or less interchangeable; there may be a variety of alternative behaviors through which an infant may approximate its proximity set-goal of the moment. From this point onward it becomes unproductive to consider the component behaviors discretely; it is their pattern of organization that is significant (Ainsworth, 1972). As Sroufe and Waters (1977a) have argued, attachment is essentially an organizational construct.

Although in earlier phases an infant has undoubtedly been building up primitive expectations about its mother's behavior as a result of experience in interaction with her, in Phase 3 the infant's "working model" of her – cognitive representation, or representational model – becomes more clear-cut and available to the infant even when the mother is not present perceptually. This model – together with similar models of other familiar persons, of self, and of the physical environment and together with the way the infant has centrally organized its attachment system and with the current environmental situation – will determine the infant's plan for the maintenance of proximity to attachment figure(s). It is doubtless no mere coincidence that locomotion, goal-corrected (intentional) behavior, and the beginnings of the use of representational models occur at about the same time and that more or less simultaneously separation distress emerges – a clear indication that a baby has become attached to its mother figure.

## Criteria of attachment

Schaffer's fundamental criterion of a baby's having become attached to a specific figure was that the figure is no longer interchangeable with others; he emphasized separation anxiety as the behavioral criterion thereof and pinpointed the mean age at which this criterion is met at about seven lunar months (Schaffer, e.g., 1971; Schaffer & Emerson, 1964). Yarrow (1967) reported that a majority of infants at six months of age showed marked distress when shifted from a foster mother to an adoptive home, and all the infants in his sample who were eight months of age or older at the time of the shift did so. Although separation distress is indeed likely to occur in major separations involving complete shifts of caregivers and rearing environments, its absence in many brief everyday separations does not necessarily indicate absence of attachment. Much depends on the infant's representational model of its mother, the state of activation of the attachment system relevant to other behavioral systems, and the nature of the specific situation in which the infant finds itself. It is the whole pattern of organization of a child's behavior as it is manifested across a variety of behavioral and environmental contexts that enables one to identify a child's attachment figures.

## The issue of monotropy

Throughout his discussion of the early phases of the development of attachment, Bowlby (1969) acknowledged that an infant may become attached to more than one figure, although he emphasized that attachment figures are necessarily few in number. Nevertheless, he does not consider all a child's attachment figures equal in significance; a baby tends to become especially attached to one figure – the principal caregiver or mother figure. This tendency Bowlby attributes to a principle of "monotropy," which implies the likelihood of a hierarchy of attachment figures – one principal attachment figure together with one or a few subsidiary figures.

Under nonstressful conditions it may be difficult to identify the principal attachment figure, for a child may seek proximity to, interaction with, or even contact with several persons, seeming to prefer first one and then another. But under stressful conditions that activate attachment behavior at high intensity, a child will by preference seek proximity to and contact with the principal figure rather than a secondary attachment figure if both are equally available to the child. Lamb's (1977) findings support this notion. Under the conditions of his home observation with both mother and father present, infants approached, smiled at, vocalized to, and even sought contact with the father more frequently than the mother, but when they cried and wanted comforting, they sought contact with the mother.

Lamb emphasized the role of the father as playmate and considered this role equally significant for development as that played by the mother. Bowlby (1969) distinguished the role of playmate from the fundamental caregiving role of the attachment figure – although mother as well as father and others may on occasion assume the playmate role. These considerations raise the issue of the place of attachment in the multifarious social relationships a person enters into during the course of a lifetime – an issue that will be touched on in the last section of this chapter. For our present purposes it is enough to emphasize that to attribute to two figures equal significance in influencing a child's development does not necessarily mean that they are equal in significance to the child as attachment figures.

## The Caregiving Behavioral System

Bowlby (1969) postulated a maternal behavioral system complementary to the infant attachment system and dovetailing with it. The predictable outcome of this system is maintenance of proximity of the infant and its biological function, protection. However, a mother is obviously capable of goal-corrected behavior, and hence the organization of the system is that of a plan hierarchy. Furthermore, the component behaviors differ from infant attachment behaviors; they may be identified as caregiving behaviors.

Obviously, infant signaling behaviors achieve their predictable outcome because caregivers are tuned in to respond to such signals – although some are more responsive than others. It would appear that a critical aspect of the environment to which infant behavior is preadapted is a mother figure available to receive infant signals and predisposed to respond to them.

Bowlby (1969) hypothesized that developmental anomalies would ensue should the environment in which a baby is reared differ too widely from the original environment. One such anomaly is failure to become attached – known to occur as a consequence of severe and prolonged "maternal deprivation" beginning in early infancy. So strong is the predisposition of an infant to become attached, however, that infants can and do become attached to mothers whose responses to infant behavior are quite distorted, even abusing. In such cases the developmental anomaly lies in the way in which the attachment becomes organized (e.g., Egeland & Sroufe, 1981).

During the past decade a number of studies have concerned themselves with father–infant interaction (e.g., Lamb, 1976; Parke, 1979). It is clear that fathers are capable of assuming a caregiving role even with very young infants, although what proportion indeed do so is not known and is undoubtedly greatly influenced by cultural constraints and individual circumstances. It is plausible to assume that human males as well as females have evolved a genetic predisposition toward caregiving behavior, although it may not be as readily activated as in females. Thus Rosenblatt (e.g., Rosenblatt, Siegel, & Mayer, 1979) has shown that even in rats – a species in which the male ordinarily displays no caregiving behavior – males may be induced to do so by prolonged exposure to newborn rat pups.

## The bonding of parent to infant

There seems little doubt that a mother is very likely to form an affectional bond with her infant, although it is perhaps better not to class this bond as an attachment because a mother is unlikely to rely on an infant for her feeling of security or to demand caregiving from a child and attempt to use the child as a secure base for her activities. Bowlby has not addressed himself to the question of how this bonding takes place.

By extrapolation from research with other species, for example, Rosenblatt's (1979) research with rats, maternal caregiving behavior is largely activated and maintained by the presence of infants, their characteristics, and their behavior, with hormonal state being implicated largely in the immediate postpartum period seemingly serving to "prime" maternal behavior. In this context Klaus and Kennell's (e.g., 1976) claim is plausible that bonding is greatly facilitated by the experience of close bodily contact with the baby immediately after its birth. Certainly such experience seems to be highly charged with positive emotion and may well make it easier for the mother to respond sensitively later to infant signals and needs, with consequent positive influence on infant development. This squares with research on a number of species of animals that indicates separation of infant from mother at birth may well have an adverse effect on maternal caregiving behavior subsequent to the separation – although the time constraints and the particular effects differ among species.

It would be a mistake, as Klaus and Kennell readily acknowledge, to assume that immediate postpartum experience is a necessary condition for mother–infant bonding in humans – mothers denied it for whatever reason nevertheless can and usually do form such bonds. Furthermore, the criteria for ascertaining whether such a bond has been established are as yet unclear. The criteria suggested by Klaus and Kennell tend to define a maternal bond in terms of sensitive responsiveness to infant signals – and yet research into mother–infant interaction suggests that a substantial minority of mothers are far from sensitively responsive. Clinical experience supports the notion that some mothers who are clearly insensitive nevertheless somehow feel strongly bonded. More research is needed.

It may he assumed that many fathers also form affectional bonds to their infants and that early and frequent or prolonged exposure to the presence of the infant facilitates such bonding – but relevant research into the conditions of father–infant bonding has yet to be undertaken. Meanwhile, one may speculate that the caregiving behavioral system has genetic underpinnings in both sexes and that these may be supported by individual experience and cultural influences or made more difficult by developmental anomalies resulting from the parent's own atypical rearing experiences, by other cultural influences, or by other circumstances.

## Patterns of Attachment of Infant to Parent

Whatever the difficulties of assessing the relative strength or significance of a child's attachments to different figures (or, indeed, of comparing two children in regard to the strength of their attachments to their mothers), there is strong evidence of striking qualitative differences in attachment in different dyads. There is also strong evidence that the qualitative nature of an infant's attachment to a specific figure is largely influenced by the history of the interaction the infant has had with that figure.

Interest in these qualitative differences was kindled by Ainsworth and Wittig (1969) who devised a laboratory situation – "the strange situation" – intended to highlight attachment behavior and its relationship to other behavioral systems through the introduction of cumulative stresses similar to those a baby commonly encounters in an unfamiliar environment. It emerged that this procedure was also powerful in highlighting individual differences in patterns of infant–mother attachment. The situation was devised in the context of a longitudinal study of infant–mother attachment of 26 white, middle-class infants in the Baltimore area. The babies with their mothers were introduced to the strange situation when they were 51 weeks old.

The dyad was introduced to a playroom in which there was a massive array of toys, expected to elicit exploratory behavior. A series of episodes followed: First, baby and mother were alone together; then they were joined by a stranger; then there was a separation episode in which the mother left the baby with stranger, followed by an episode of reunion with the mother; a second separation followed in which the baby was first left entirely alone and then rejoined the stranger; finally, the mother returned for a second reunion episode. (Details of the procedure, including scoring and classification of behavior, are given in Ainsworth, Blehar, Water, and Wall, 1978).

## Principal attachment patterns

Three main patterns of behavior were identified, discriminable most clearly in the infant's behavior toward its mother in the reunion episodes. At first these were labeled Patterns A, B, and C. Later, on the basis of a comparison with behavior at home, Pattern B infants were identified as securely attached and both Pattern A and Pattern C infants as anxiously attached to their mothers.[1]

### Pattern B: securely attached

This pattern was most frequent in all the white, American middle-class samples so far reported, accounting for about two-thirds of the infants. In the strange situation these infants tended to show heightened proximity-and-contact-seeking and contact-maintaining behavior in the reunion episodes, with little or no resistant or avoidant behavior. In the preseparation episodes they showed little attachment behavior, and when alone with the mother exploratory behavior was predominant. Most, but not all, were distressed in the separation episodes, particularly in the second separation.

### Pattern C: anxiously attached and resistant (or ambivalent)

This pattern was least frequent in middle-class samples, accounting for approximately 10%. In the preseparation episodes exploratory behavior occurred either without positive affect or little or not at all, and in the separation episodes intense distress was characteristic. Upon reunion with the mother Pattern C babies tended to want proximity/contact with the mother, but they were very difficult to soothe. Some were passive, relying on signals rather than on active proximity-seeking behavior; others were more active but angrily resistant to both mother and stranger, mingling this with contact-seeking behavior. Furthermore, Pattern C infants were likely to show fear of the stranger.

### Pattern A: anxiously attached and avoidant

This pattern occurred in about one-quarter of the infants in the middle-class samples. Most conspicuous among them was avoidance of the mother in the reunion episodes, either a steadfast ignoring of her or a mingling of avoidant and proximity-seeking behaviors. Pattern A babies tended to maintain at least the semblance of exploratory behavior throughout all episodes. They seemed more friendly with the stranger than with the mother.

In addition to classification in accordance with pattern, strange-situation behavior was also scored episode by episode. The scores included measures of exploratory behavior, crying, and six kinds of interactive behavior (of which proximity/contact seeking, contact maintaining, avoidance, and resistance were most useful) scored separately for mother and stranger. For a sample of 106 infants Ainsworth et al. (1978) reported a multiple discriminant-function analysis that discriminated the three patterns on the basis of these scores at a high level of statistical significance, thus strongly confirming the validity of the criteria used for the classification.

## Patterns of attachment and infant behavior at home

Ainsworth et al. (1978; Ainsworth, 1979) reported in some detail the relationships between the A, B, and C patterns and infant behavior at home during the first year of life. At home each dyad had been visited once every three weeks from 3 to 54 weeks of age, each visit lasting approximately four hours – resulting in approximately 72 hours of observational data for each. The findings may be summarized as follows. In comparison with Pattern

A and Pattern C babies, Pattern B babies cried less, especially in response to brief everyday separations; greeted the mother more positively when she returned after an absence; were angry less often; were more likely to respond positively both to being picked up and to being put down by the mother; had more varied modes of communication; and were more cooperative in response to maternal commands. Pattern A and Pattern C babies in the first quarter when face-to-face with their mothers were less responsive to maternal initiatives and more likely to terminate interaction. All these differences supported the identification of Pattern B babies as more securely attached to their mothers than A or C babies.

Despite the striking differences in their strange-situation behavior, A and C infants showed more similarities than differences in their behavior at home. However, Pattern A babies seemed to have more difficulties relevant to close bodily contact with their mothers; by the fourth quarter they almost never "sank in" when held, molding their bodies to the mother's, and their contact-seeking and contact-maintaining behaviors were more tentative and less active. The most striking difference was frequency of anger, however, with Pattern A babies significantly more angry than Pattern C babies.

## Patterns of attachment and maternal behavior at home

An examination of maternal behavior throughout the baby's first year supports the claim that patterns of attachment of infant to mother reflect the history of their interaction (Ainsworth, 1979; Ainsworth et al., 1978). Overall ratings showed mothers of the securely attached babies to be more sensitively responsive to infant signals and less rejecting, interfering, and ignoring than the mothers of anxiously attached babies. Particular importance is attached to sensitive responsiveness to infant signals and other behavioral cues, for this distinguished the mothers of securely attached babies from other mothers across all contexts of interaction – in prompt responsiveness to crying and in qualitative features of behavior relevant to close bodily contact throughout the first year and in regard to behavior relevant to both face-to-face and feeding interaction in the first quarter.

The mothers of the anxious-avoidant and anxious-resistant babies, although similarly insensitive to infant signals, differed strikingly in a number of ways. The mothers of the anxious-avoidant (Pattern A) babies tended to be more rejecting, especially in the context of close bodily contact – for which they had a deep aversion. They also were more rigid and compulsive and interacted more often with an impassive facial expression.

## Interpretation of congruence between infant and maternal behavior

The congruence between maternal behavior and a secure attachment pattern in the infant is easily understood. Experience of maternal responsiveness to signals leads the baby to build a representational model of its mother as accessible and responsive – which is the criterion of secure attachment to her. Perhaps it is, especially, her prompt response to crying and the infant's positive experiences in close bodily contact with her that lead the infant to have confidence in her even when attachment behavior is activated at high intensity – when the infant most wants to be close to her. The relationship between maternal behavior and the other two attachment patterns requires more discussion.

A baby whose mother has been inconsistently responsive to its signals builds up a representational model of her as someone who cannot be trusted to be accessible and responsive, and herein lies the baby's anxiety. Because of this relative lack of confidence in the mother, the baby tends to be more readily upset by brief separations and is more likely to be afraid of unfamiliar people and situations – indeed, more fearful overall. At the same time this infant is more frequently angry than the secure infant, because attachment behavior is more frequently frustrated by the mother's unresponsiveness. So whenever attachment behavior is intensely activated, the infant's desire to be close to its mother is suffused with anger. This much both Pattern A and Pattern C babies have in common. These dynamics are most overtly displayed in the anxious-ambivalent Pattern C babies, however, both at home and in the strange situation. But, whereas the mothers of Pattern C babies have afforded them some comforting experience when in close bodily contact, albeit inconsistently, this is believed not to be the case with the mothers of Pattern A babies.

It is suggested that the aversion to close contact characteristic of the mothers of the Pattern A babies is manifested in frequent enough rebuff of the baby when it seeks close bodily contact to cause the baby to be apprehensive of rebuff whenever its attachment behavior is intensely activated; the baby is not merely uncertain of its mother's responsiveness. It is believed that this expectation of rebuff and its associated anger is so painful to the baby that, over time, the baby has come to avoid close bodily contact with its mother. This avoidance is most conspicuous in moderately high stress situations when the Pattern A baby, like other babies, wants close contact – but it is also manifest in more subtle ways at home. This avoidance has much in common with the detachment that young children commonly show for shorter or longer periods following major separations (Ainsworth & Bell, 1970). Main (e.g., 1977) has been particularly concerned to clarify the processes underlying mother avoidance. For our purposes here, however, it is perhaps sufficient to point out the congruence between mother avoidance in the strange situation and the processes of perceptual defense elucidated by Bowlby (1980).

It is suggested that Pattern A babies under stress systematically exclude from perception (i.e., from highest-level processing) information that might intensely activate attachment behavior. Thus they tend not to be distressed when the mother leaves the room in the separation episodes of the strange situation and when she returns to the reunion episodes, resorting instead to diversionary activity, which in this situation commonly consists of what appears to be exploratory behavior. That the information had some effect at another level of processing, however, is suggested by heartbeat changes. Sroufe and Waters (1977b) found that Pattern A babies showed the same kind of acceleration of heart rate as did Pattern B and Pattern C babies at mother's departures and returns. They also reported that the "exploratory" behavior they showed in the separation and reunion episodes was not accompanied by the characteristic deceleration of heart rate at moments of special interest – and thus seems to be essentially diversionary activity rather than genuine exploration.

## Infant attachment to fathers

Freud (1938) asserted that an infant's relation with its mother is the prototype of all subsequent object relations. Thus one might expect that the pattern of an infant's attachment to its father would resemble the pattern of that infant's attachment to its mother. Two studies (Lamb, 1978; Main & Weston, 1981) have thrown doubt upon Freud's assertion by demonstrating that a baby who is secure in attachment to the mother is not necessarily secure in attachment to the father and vice versa. The implication is that it is the history of the interaction a baby has with each figure which determines the nature of the attachment formed with each. It is plausible that the more salient the father's role is throughout infancy and the less clear the mother's role is as principal caregiver, the more autonomous the baby's attachment to each might be. However, it is also a reasonable hypothesis that an infant's experience with the principal caregiver – mother figure – would influence the infant's expectations of other figures and, hence, responses in interaction with them.

Main and Weston (1981) compared the readiness of 12-month-old infants to establish a positive social relationship with an unfamiliar adult and to respond affectively to his changing moods to the patterns of their attachment to parents both separately and jointly. It was the joint (secure/nonsecure) patterns that were of most interest. Babies securely attached to both parents showed the greatest relatedness to the new adult, and those insecurely attached to both parents showed the least relatedness, whereas those that were securely attached to one parent but insecurely attached to the other fell in between. Since it made no difference which parent accompanied the baby to the session with the new figure, it would seem that it was somehow the way the infant had centrally organized its behavior which determined his or her reaction to the new person. On the other hand, the way the infant had centrally organized its behavior was obviously influenced by attachments to parents.

Since no one so far has made a systematic study of the nature of infant interactions with both parents (separately and together) throughout the first year and related that to the patterns of attachment to each at year's end, the issue remains open. Meanwhile, it would seem that both major hypotheses are promising and perhaps not mutually exclusive – that the history of interaction with a specific figure has much to do with the qualitative nature of the eventual attachment to him or her, whereas at the same time the expectations and representational models of previous and/or principal attachment figure(s) may at least at first affect interaction with and perhaps eventual attachment to another figure.

Nevertheless, it is clear that under conditions of moderate stress – as in a strange situation – babies can and do use father as well as mother as an attachment figure, as Kotelchuck (1976) first demonstrated. Indeed, babies can use another caregiver as an attachment figure, as Fox (1977) showed in the case of the metapelet in Israeli kibbutzim. However, such studies can give no clear indication of the relative significance of different attachment figures in influencing the child's development nor of which figure is indeed the principal attachment figure.

## The Development of Child–Mother Attachment Beyond Infancy

Bowlby (1969) suggested that Phase 3 of the development of attachment persists until near the child's third birth-day or longer – and then gives way to Phase 4, the phase of "goal-corrected partnership." In Phase 3 the child, although certainly capable of goal-corrected behavior and organization according to plans, is limited by what Piaget (1926) called "egocentrism." The child can adapt his or her behavior to expectations of how the mother will behave but is still incapable of seeing things from her perspective and, hence, of inferring the nature of her plans and motivation. Thus the child cannot act effectively to influence her to bring her plans into better harmony with his or her own. For Bowlby, the transition to Phase 4 comes with the child's achievement of at least some ability to perceive the world from another's point of view and so to comprehend better the mother's plans and motiva-tion. The acquisition of language facilitates better communication with the mother in order to reach joint and mutually agreeable plans in situations in which their initial separate plans may have diverged. It is when both part-ners can alter their plans in accordance with their understanding of the other partner's plans that Bowlby would describe their partnership as mutually goal-corrected. Although some dyads probably never attain this degree of mutuality, Bowlby conceived of the goal-corrected partnership as the final phase of development of attachment and as characteristic of mature relationships in which there is an attachment component.

Three studies addressing the issue of developmental changes in strange-situation behavior (Feldman & Ingham, 1975; Maccoby & Feldman, 1972; Marvin, 1977) are in essential agreement, despite somewhat different scoring procedures. However, only Marvin's study will be reported here, for his study included a wider age range and specifically addressed itself to Bowlby's hypothesis about the role of perspective taking in the development of attachment.

His was a cross-sectional study with three age groups – two-, three-, and four-year-olds – which he compared with Ainsworth and Bell's (1970) group of one-year-olds. In general, he found separation distress to decline with age, until by age four most children maintained exploratory play throughout the separation episodes without dis-tress. Beyond age two, children who protested separation seemed reassured when the stranger returned. The whole situation seemed to become less stressful as age increased; hence, attachment behavior was activated at progressively lower intensity. Although two-year-olds sought proximity to the mother as strongly as one-year-olds, the maintenance of physical contact seemed less important to them and to the children in the older age groups.

Marvin supplemented his study with tests of capacity to delay in the face of frustration and to take the conceptual perspective of another. He found that three-year-olds had much better frustration tolerance than two-year-olds but that they were little better in perspective taking, whereas most four-year-olds succeeded in the per-spective-taking test. In later studies Marvin and his associates (Marvin & Greenberg, 1982; Marvin, Mossier, & VanDevender, Endnote 1) have assembled evidence that strange-situation behavior in four-year-olds is indeed associated with the extent to which mother and child agree on a mutual plan concerning her temporary absence during which the child is left alone. All these findings tend to support Bowlby's hypotheses about the processes implicated in the transition between Phases 3 and 4 of the development of attachment.

## Stability and Change of Patterns of Infant–Mother Attachment

Stability of infant–mother attachment patterns has been examined by retesting the dyad in the strange situation after a lapse of time. Substantial stability has been found in white, middle-class samples tested at 12 months and retested at 18 months, ranging from 96% in the same A, B, and C classifications (Waters, 1978) to about 80% (Connell, 1976; Main & Weston, 1981). Such stability may be attributed either to resistance to change of the central organization of the infant's behavior to its parents or to a tendency for the interaction between them to continue to be much the same over time; indeed, both factors are probably implicated.

To be sure, there is evidence that attachment patterns change in response to environmental influences. Vaughn, Egeland, Sroufe, and Waters (1979) found only 62% stability upon retest in a large sample of infant–mother dyads of low socioeconomic status, with the shifts from secure to anxious attachment or vice versa associated with increasing or decreasing stress impinging on the mother and presumably affecting her interaction with the infant for worse or better. Under such circumstances one could expect changes also in the infant's representational model of its mother and in the organization of attachment to her, although it is suggested that the inner changes are likely to lag somewhat behind the changes in maternal behavior.

In the second and third volumes of his *Attachment and Loss* series, Bowlby (1973, 1980) cited evidence from clinical research of circumstances that can shift the pattern of secure attachment in the direction of more anxiety, and these circumstances are by no means limited to infancy or the preschool years. They include experiences of major separation from or permanent loss of an attachment figure as well as mere threats of separation or loss. Nevertheless, there is now substantial evidence that early attachment patterns tend to make some subsequent "pathways of growth" more likely than others. The next section will consider such evidence, at least as it pertains to the first five or six years.

## Attachment Patterns and Later Development

Research into continuity in development was handicapped for many years by the constraint of searching for correlations of the same or similar behavioral measures over two or more points separated in time. This approach is likely to be doomed to failure, especially if the time span covers a period of rapid development during which the major developmental issues faced by a child shift substantially and, hence, the contextual significance of a given behavior also shifts (Sroufe, 1979). However, a number of researchers concerned with the predictive value of infant attachment patterns escaped this impasse by addressing the issue of how early attachment to a parent influences *other* aspects of a child's subsequent behavior. In all but one of the studies cited below that are concerned with this issue, the infant–mother attachment pattern was assessed by the strange-situation procedure at some time between 12 and 18 months.

Securely attached infants become toddlers who at 21 months had higher scores on the Bayley Mental Scale – perhaps because they were more cooperative with the examiner and displayed more of a "game-like spirit." They were superior in the quality of their exploratory play in a free-play laboratory situation and more advanced in language acquisition (Main, 1983). They were also more cooperative both with their mothers and with an adult playmate – more obedient to their mothers' commands and interventions and with more evidence of "internalized controls" – whereas those previously identified as nonsecure displayed active disobedience more frequently (Londerville & Main, 1981).

In a tool-use problem-solving situation 24-month-old toddlers who had been identified as securely attached as infants were more enthusiastic, affectively positive, and persistent in problem solving; less frustrated by very difficult problems; and better able to seek and/or accept help from their mothers. Those who had been identified earlier as anxious-avoidant babies sought help only from the experimenter and were conspicuously noncompliant with the mother, indeed tending to display unprovoked aggression toward her. Those who had been identified earlier as anxious-ambivalent babies were overdependent and quickly frustrated by the problem, giving up and/or manifesting other "frustration behavior" (Matas, Arend, & Sroufe, 1978). Securely-attached toddlers also showed more "affective sharing" with their mothers (Waters, Wippman, & Sroufe, 1979).

In a preschool setting three-and-a-half-year-olds who had been identified as securely attached to their mothers on the basis of earlier strange-situation behavior were more socially competent with peers than those who had been identified as anxiously attached. They also scored higher on a measure of ego-strength/effectance (Waters et al., 1979). Lieberman (1977) also found a positive relationship between secure attachment and social competence with peers in three-year-olds, although her assessments of both sets of variables were made at the same age, and she found home visits more useful as a basis for assessing quality of attachment at this age than behavior in the strange situation.

In a preschool setting five-year-olds identified as securely attached when infants were more "ego-resilient" – better able to adapt resourcefully to changing personal and environmental circumstances – than those who had been identified as anxiously attached. They were also ranked by their teachers as more self-confident and more socially competent. In regard to ego-control, they were judged to be moderately controlled, whereas the anxious-avoidant children emerged as overcontrolled and the anxious-ambivalent children, as under-controlled (Arend, Gove, & Sroufe, 1979).

In summary, a substantial body of evidence has already emerged that different patterns of infant–mother attachment are associated with different degrees of success in coping with later age-appropriate issues throughout the preschool years, suggesting that they are associated with what Bowlby (1973) termed different "pathways" of growth. It seems very unlikely that this evidence could have been assembled if attachment patterns were wholly and immediately responsive to changes in maternal behavior. Indeed, in the preschool settings assessments were made of child behavior when the mother was absent; hence, any relationship with peer competence, self-confidence, ego-resilience, and ego-control had to stem somehow from the child's inner organization of behavior. It seems likely, as Bowlby suggested, that by the end of the first five years patterns of organization have become increasingly but not wholly resistant to change with changing circumstances, and that after about 15 years of age substantial change is difficult indeed.

## Anxious Attachment and Some Disorders Associated With It

There is little doubt that a major separation from attachment figures in early childhood can turn a hitherto secure attachment into an anxious one. However, Bowlby (1973) introduced clinical evidence suggesting that threats of abandonment or suicide (which some parents make when emotionally stressed), violent quarrels between parents, and other circumstances such as the death of a relative were also effective contributors to anxiety – lest attachment figures be lost through death, desertion, or family disintegration – and hence may lead to anxious attachment. Indeed, anxious attachment is a main theme of Bowlby's volume, *Separation*, as suggested by its subtitle, *Anxiety and Anger*. Let us consider anger before proceeding to other aspects of anxious attachment after the earliest years have passed.

### Anger

Bowlby (1973) suggested that anger is a ubiquitous accompaniment of anxiety and that it can be functional as well as dysfunctional in this context. When it is directed toward attachment figures, it would seem to be dysfunctional because of the risk of alienating them, but it *can* be functional and probably began thus. A child s angry protest at the actual or impending departure of an attachment figure and the child's active efforts to detain or regain him or her may well accomplish their purpose. The child's angry reproaches after the mother has returned from an absence may prevent a repetition of the experience or, at least, lead her to arrange less anxiety-provoking conditions for her next absence.

However, when anxiety is a persistent characteristic of a relationship with an attachment figure, anger is likely to be dysfunctional, tending to threaten the bond and to alienate the partner. Perhaps intermittent "hot displeasure" in an otherwise affectionate and secure relationship does not detract from its essential security, but persistent "deep-running resentment" or frequent aggressive outbursts are characteristic of anxious rather than secure attachment. To mingle intense anxiety and intense anger toward an attachment figure occasions severe conflict, for when one fears the loss of a loved one, expressing the anger may contribute to his or her desertion. Thus anxious attachment is riddled with ambivalence – as indeed was found to be the case even with one-year-olds.

Bowlby (1973) considered in some detail several disorders that clinicians have designated as phobic as stemming from anxious attachment; he suggests that these are at least as well accounted for by attachment theory as by the traditional psychoanalytic explanations. He referred to the distinction often made between a "phobic" condition – intensely fearing some situation and urgently avoiding it by withdrawing from it – and the "pseudo-phobic" condition – in which what is most feared is the loss of an attachment figure toward whom the person tends to retreat. It is the latter condition Bowlby considered most intimately related to anxious attachment – and, indeed, he implied that in many cases which have been identified as "phobic," it is the underlying anxious attachment that is the crucial factor. Let us consider his discussion of "school phobia" in some detail.

### School phobia

This disorder is one in which a child is very anxious when pressed to attend school and, indeed, refuses to go. Having examined the clinical literature, Bowlby (1973) distinguished four main patterns of family interaction characteristic of such disorders, which may occur separately but commonly occur in combination. Summaries of the first two patterns are as follows.

*Pattern A*

The mother herself is chronically anxious about attachment figures and keeps the child at home as a companion, perhaps being unaware of why she does so and rationalizing that the child is unfit to face the rigors of school life. As a consequence of having lost or having been deprived of loving care from attachment figures, the mother unconsciously inverts the roles of a caregiver–child relationship, expecting the child somehow to care for her. Often such a mother has a mother who similarly inverted roles, so she remains in a close, anxious, ambivalent relationship with her own mother who constantly demands attention. While submitting to her child's importunities, she tends to have excessive expectations of him or her and to resent any rebuff or slackening of the child's care for her that his or her behavior may imply; this leads her to alternate between overt loving and hostile behavior toward the child.

*Pattern B*

The child fears that something dreadful may happen to an attachment figure (usually the mother) while he or she is at school and remains home to prevent its happening. Bowlby suggested that such fears, rather than solely expressing unconscious hostile wishes toward the parent stemming from the child's own inner dynamics, are often attributable to real-life experiences – a consequence of threats of abandonment, suicide, withdrawal of love, and the like, or of concealment of true events surrounding a death or serious illness so that the child believes the parent might die or become ill if he or she is not there.

The other two patterns represent variations on the same theme of anxious ambivalent relationships with attachment figures. Furthermore, after reviewing the relevant literature, Bowlby (1973) concluded that the agoraphobic adult has much the same kind of real-life basis for fear of leaving home as do school-refusing children and that many of them had reported themselves to have been school refusers in childhood. Bowlby's chief plea to clinicians is to be alert to the possibility that there may be a real-life basis for a patient's fears and anxieties and to do their best to gain the relevant information to illuminate the picture of family interaction.

## Secure Attachment and the Growth of Self-Reliance

In infancy there are a number of indications that secure attachment is likely to facilitate the growth of self-reliance, foremost among which are the tendencies of securely attached infants to respond positively to being put down after having been held and to turn to exploratory behavior, using the mother as a secure base. Ainsworth, Bell, and Stayton (1971) also reported that a healthy balance between attachment and exploratory behavior was associated not only with maternal accessibility, acceptance, and sensitive responsiveness to signals but also with maternal respect for the infant as an autonomous person.

Bowlby (1973) assembled evidence that secure attachment facilitates self-reliance also in preschool children (e.g., Baumrind, 1967), older children and adolescents (e.g., Peck & Havighurst, 1960), and adults (e.g., Korchin & Ruff, 1964). He concluded, "an unthinking confidence in the unfailing accessibility and support of attachment figures is the bedrock on which stable and self-reliant personality is built" (p. 322). He noted also that timely and steady encouragement toward increasing autonomy and open communication are characteristic of family interaction associated with self-reliance.

It is a myth of present-day western society to equate attachment with an immature dependence, thus implying that it is the antithesis of independence or self-reliance. According to this line of thought, the sensitive responsiveness of an attachment figure to a child's signals, behavioral cues, and communications must eventually overindulge the child, smother him or her with protectiveness, and retard the growth of self-reliance. This is odd, because among a child's behavioral cues are those indicating that she or he enjoys the adventure of exploring new things, dislikes being interrupted when absorbed in autonomous activity, and is gratified upon achieving mastery of a new skill or problem on her or his own. An attachment figure cannot be truly sensitive in responsiveness to a child's cues and choose to ignore these.

## Pathways for the Growth of Personality

Bowlby (1973) considered two models that attempt to account for substantial continuity in personality development: (1) the classical Freudian model, emphasizing fixation and regression, in which from the beginning development is conceived as proceeding in a straight line, with individual differences attributable to constitutional differences – which determine the particular line development will take – and experiential factors – which make for fixations and regression to fixation points when difficulties are encountered – and (2) a model in which genetic endowment leaves a diversity of pathways initially open but experience narrows the possibilities until each individual tends to continue along or close to the particular pathway determined by experience.

Favoring the second model, Bowlby drew on the theory of epigenesis proposed by Waddington (1957), which was formulated in evolutionary terms. To the extent that the equipment characteristic of a species is insensitive to environmental influences, the risk of an individual's development proceeding along a maladaptive pathway is minimized; should there be gross changes in environmental conditions, however, the species itself is at risk. To the extent that a species' equipment is sensitive to environmental influences, there is a diversity of developmental pathways open to an individual, many of which may prove to be maladaptive in a stable environment; should there be gross changes in conditions, however, species survival is maximized, for at least a few individuals might be expected to adapt to and survive in the new environment. Waddington suggested that many species evolve processes that help to avoid the risks of both extremes by allowing sensitivity to environmental influences in the early stages of development but later buffering the developing individual against environmental impact and maintaining the individual on the developmental pathway he or she is already on. The self-regulatory property of these processes he termed "homeorhesis."

According to Bowlby, pressures that tend to keep development in the same pathway are thus both the stability of the environment and the homeorhetic processes in the individual. The family environment in which many persons are reared remains essentially the same over time. Furthermore, the way individuals organize their experiences within themselves – including the representational models they construct of their environment, themselves, and significant persons in their lives – have a homeorhetic tendency to maintain the direction of their development. Thus through both environmental and self-regulatory processes the interactions a child has with family members in her or his early years contribute to the persistence of development along whatever pathway it gets started on.

Nevertheless, there is clearly hope for clinical intervention to be effective in shunting development from a maladaptive pathway to one more promising. Such intervention, Bowlby suggested, is most likely to be effective if simultaneous attempts are made to change the patient's inner organization through inducing the patient to change his or her representational models *and* the family environment that tends to work against such change – a suggestion pointing toward family therapy alone or combined with some mode of individual therapy. Presumably, the younger the child, the more emphasis should be placed on intervention with the family and the more likely that this alone will alter the child's representational models and shift development to a more promising pathway – as indeed Fraiberg's (1980) reports of intervention with "at risk" infants would suggest.

## Responses to Loss

The breaking of an affectional bond is one of the events that may shift a person from the pathway of growth along which she or he has been proceeding to one less adaptive. Bowlby (1980) focused on loss through death for a variety of reasons: the theoretical importance attached by psychoanalysts to mourning a lost figure, the fact that research into loss has tended to focus on loss through death, and his own observations of the similarities between adult mourning and young children's responses to separation.

From a review of the literature on responses to the death of a spouse (e.g., Parkes, 1972) he identified four phases of mourning: (1) a phase of numbing, interrupted by outbursts of extreme distress and anger, lasting from a few hours to months; (2) a phase of yearning and searching for the lost figure, as though not completely believing that the loss was final, also characterized by distress and anger; (3) a phase of disorganization and despair, in which all hope of reunion is abandoned and old patterns of thinking, feeling, and action must be discarded; and (4) a final phase of some degree of reorganization, in which the representational model of the self is revised appropriate to the new situation. Throughout the first three phases at least, the bereaved person is likely to experience feelings of loneliness that cannot altogether be banished by comforting and attentive friends. Except for the absence of loneliness, Bowlby noted similar reactions in parents' responses to stillbirths, deaths in early infancy, and learning that their child is fatally ill – except that in the latter case, the second phase tends to be one of disbelief in the prognosis, with the last two phases usually deferred until the child has died.

In regard to loneliness, Weiss (1982) distinguished between loneliness associated with loss of an attachment figure (or, as in adolescence, yearning for one that has not yet been identified) and loneliness attributable to lack of friends and of a broader social network, perhaps occasioned through moving to a new environment. What alleviates one type of loneliness may not alleviate the other. Friends and a supportive social network may not banish the loneliness of one who is lacking an attachment figure. Secure attachment of child to parent or of, say, wife to husband cannot altogether compensate for the lack of familiar others.

## Defensive processes in mourning

It is commonly accepted that healthy mourning eventually paves the way to reorganization and openness to the formation of new affectional bonds, whereas unhealthy mourning is mourning that leads to pathological outcomes. Bowlby (1980) suggested, however, that much the same kinds of defensive processes are involved in both – all of which imply the exclusion of unwelcome information from higher-level processing. The distinction between healthy and pathological mourning rests upon how long these processes are maintained and the extent to which they disrupt mental functioning. Two processes, however – involving redirection of anger and the cognitive disconnection of emotional response from the causative situation – seem especially characteristic of pathological mourning.

## Disordered mourning

Bowlby (1980) identified two major variants of mourning that commonly lead to pathological outcomes – chronic mourning and prolonged absence of conscious grieving, of which the former is the more frequent. Chronic mourning fails to reach a phase of reorganization; it may result in a variety of disorders, especially depression, but also agoraphobia, hypochondria, and alcoholism. Prolonged absence of conscious grieving is an indefinite prolongation of the numbing phase and may betray itself as unhealthy through the emergence of seemingly unfounded ailments or by suddenly giving way to severe depression. Adults showing this pattern, Bowlby noted, present themselves as self-sufficient and independent, scorning tears or sentiment, and proud of carrying on as though nothing had happened. Perhaps some displayed no grief at loss because they had indeed formed no affectional bond with the lost person, but often enough there are signs that there had indeed been a bond but that the pain of the loss had been defensively excluded from conscious processing.

*Related cognitive processes*
Earlier, reference was made to Bowlby's (1980) account of defensive processes; now two further features of that account are needed. First, he drew on the distinction between episodic and semantic storage of information (Tulving, 1972). In the episodic type information is stored sequentially of events as they occur. In the semantic type the information is in generalized form, usually derived from what one has been told by others. Bowlby suggested that the representational models of self and attachment figures rest on both kinds of stored experience and that there may well be discrepancies between the two sources. Thus, for example, a child may have discrepant representational models, one based on memories of what the parent has pressed the child to believe (that she or he is loving, caring, and acting always in the child's best interests, whereas the child is ungrateful and unworthy of love) and another based on a series of memories of actual events – including episodes in which the parent was inaccessible, unresponsive, rejecting, and punitive, and in which the child's bids for love or care went unrecognized and the child's distress and/or anger seemed quite justified. When the former set of models is strongly held because of parental pressure, information incompatible with it is likely to be excluded from conscious processing.

A second relevant feature omitted from the earlier account of defensive processes is the concept of a number of complex control systems, loosely and hierarchically organized, with a "principal system" at the top of the hierarchy that initially scans all incoming information, quickly evaluating it in terms of knowledge stored in long-term memory, and decides whether it should be accepted for further conscious processing or discarded (Erdelyi, 1974). Bowlby suggested studies of information processing under hypnosis imply that there may be more than one principal system and that information excluded by the system which is usually dominant may nevertheless reach consciousness within another system segregated from the first. The phenomenon of dissociation is thus explained in terms of information which is cognitively disconnected from an event by one principal system and which is stored as linked to that event by another system. Cognitive biases based on such processes, and built up in the course of individual experience, are proposed as important influences on how a person responds to loss.

## Childhood Experiences and Cognitive Biases Relevant to Disordered Mourning

Anxious attachment to parent figures predisposes toward chronic mourning, leading the individual to consciously hope to retain or regain the attachment figure who has died (Bowlby, 1980). The chronic mourner is particularly likely to have in sematic storage a memory of himself or herself as worthless and of the lost attachment figure as ideal – and a discrepant set of models based on episodic memories that alternate with the first. The chronic mourner, however, clings to the model of the ideal loved one and the worthless self and thus tends to exclude information that might help him or her to revise models and reorganize his or her life.

Prolonged absence of conscious grieving seems associated with a long history of assertion of independence of affectional bonds – a deactivation of attachment behavior not complete enough to have prevented bond formation with the person now lost. Such a pattern is likely to be associated with parental rejection, often combined with pressure to refrain from crying or otherwise expressing intense feeling.

Individual variations of mourning disorders, their experiential backgrounds, and apparent defensive processes are further complicated by other significant variables that may either facilitate or work against the cognitive biases that may result in disorders of mourning; detail of Bowlby's discussion cannot be given here.

### Pathology associated with loss

A number of studies have suggested that childhood loss – especially loss of a parent – increases the probability of emotional disorders, including major illnesses, later on. Most specifically linked to childhood loss are suicide – as well as suicidal attempts and ideation (e.g., Adam, 1973) – and depression. Bowlby specifically highlighted the methodologically careful study by Brown and Harris (1978) which distinguished between childhood loss as a predisposing factor and later loss as a precipitating factor in the etiology of depression and which examined the role played by other real-life circumstances. The majority of "severe events" that seemed to have precipitated depression entailed actual or expected loss of someone with whom the depressed person had a close relationship. The fact that 20% of a control group had suffered similar severe events without becoming depressed suggested difference in vulnerability. Evidence was found that childhood loss may have contributed to vulnerability to depression – loss of a parent through either death or prolonged separation before the eleventh birthday, with the effect most striking if the lost parent was the mother. Those whose depression was diagnosed as psychotic were much more likely than the neurotic depressives to have experienced loss through death rather than through separation or desertion.

Drawing on Seligman's (e.g., 1975) concept of "learned helplessness" Bowlby (1980) suggested that in depressive disorders feelings of helplessness pertain to affectional bonds, beginning with bonds to parent figures. Such helpless feelings are likely to stem from failure to establish secure attachments to parents despite persistent effort, so later loss is interpreted as yet another failure: from experiences that lead children to form representative models of attachment figures as unavailable, rejecting, and/or punitive and of themselves as unlovable, incompetent and inadequate: or from actual experiences of childhood loss, with failure to replace the lost person with another responsive attachment figure. Thus childhood loss is viewed as only one of several kinds of impairment of individuals' confidence in their ability to maintain affectional bonds, so when they are later faced with loss of a significant figure, they are particularly likely to cognitively disconnect their misery from the loss itself and become totally preoccupied with feelings about themselves as miserable and without hope. Thus Bowlby suggests that depressive preoccupation is a form of defensive "diversionary activity" that bolsters the primary defense of cognitive disconnection.

## Conditions influencing responses to childhood loss

There are three occasions for loss of a parent or parents in childhood – through death, through parental divorce or separation which eventuates in the permanent loss of one parent, or through temporary separation from parents which while it lasts may be quite equivalent to permanent loss to the very young child.

### Loss through death

Bowlby (1980) drew on the few systematic studies available of loss through death (e.g., Furman, 1974), studies of psychiatric disorder that implicate childhood loss as a possibly causative factor, and supplemented these with a number of case studies. He concluded that when a young child's parent dies, the child is most likely to react healthily if there was a secure relationship with both parents before the loss and if the surviving parent (or trusted substitute) is available and comforting and gives the child confidence that the support will continue. Much hinges on what the child is actually told about the death and on whether the child is allowed to share in the family grieving rather than having it concealed from him or her, so as to work against a false hope of reunion, shorten mourning, and facilitate the reorganization of the child's life based on secure attachments to the surviving adults and/or to new figures.

Under unfavorable conditions children's responses to loss of a parent tend to be more disturbed and to have longer adverse effects. When the child has reason to feel somehow responsible for the death, when her or his attachment to the surviving parent is anxious, if the surviving parent withdraws into grief and becomes emotionally inaccessible to the child, when new caregivers are both unfamiliar and unresponsive – all these conditions make it difficult for the child to adapt without resorting to strong defensive maneuvers which themselves may have a long-term adverse effect on development. Concealment from the child that death has occurred or euphemistic explanations may lead the child to nourish false hopes of reunion. Attempts to falsify the account of circumstances surrounding death may be at variance with what the child knows, and the discrepancy may push the child toward cognitive disconnection of his or her feelings from the events that gave rise to them. Finally, all these conditions may well have differential effects on children of differing levels of development.

### Loss through parental divorce

Despite the fact that parental divorce or permanent separation has perhaps become the most frequent cause of a child's loss of a parent, at least in western society. Bowlby (1980) did not include it in his discussion. Much the same variations in conditions as those that influence responses to loss through death probably influence variations in response to loss through divorce, but there are at least two other considerations that are important for the latter.

How complete the break is with the noncustodial parent varies widely, and thus whether the loss is complete or partial, permanent or temporary. A child's hope of reunion with the lost parent is usually more realistic than in the case of loss through death; hence in cases in which the loss through divorce turns out indeed to be complete and permanent, mourning is more likely to be indeterminate and the reorganization of the child's life postponed. Furthermore, much would seem to hinge upon whether the lost parent was the child's principal attachment figure (usually the mother) or a subsidiary figure, and if the latter, upon whether the emotional significance of the relationship approached that of the relationship with the principal figure or was much less.[2] Indeed, the growing literature on the effects of divorce on family relationships is a potentially very rich source of information about the vicissitudes of attachments and other affectional bonds (e.g., Hetherington, Cox, & Cox, 1981; Wallerstein & Kelly, 1980; Weiss, 1975).

### Temporary separation

As implied earlier, for a very young child temporary separation while it lasts may be experienced as equivalent to permanent loss. The major adverse condition is being placed in a situation in which all caregivers are unfamiliar and none of them are consistently available or sufficiently responsive to the child to be satisfactory substitutes for the attachment figures who are no longer available. Rebuffs from adults too busy to give their attention may contribute to the child's feeling of having been totally abandoned. Separations under more favorable conditions may be less distressing and have far fewer adverse and long-term effects. Thus Robertson and Robertson (1971), who themselves acted as foster parents for a series of four children between the ages of one-and-a-half and two-and-a-half years and separated from their parents for periods from 10 days to 4 weeks, described ways in which the misery of separation can be mitigated and many of its adverse effects averted, even though they could not altogether prevent yearning for the absent mother. However, none of the children displayed behavior characteristic of the despair and detachment phases of response to separation, and none protested separation intensely. Furthermore, upon reunion with their parents and afterward the children, particularly the older two, reestablished their previous relationship with their parents fairly readily and with a minimum of the behaviors associated with anxious attachment or detachment.

*Early cognitive development and responses to separation and loss*
It is obvious from the usual readiness with which a very young infant adapts to removal from its natural mother and placement with an adoptive or foster mother that caregivers are more or less interchangeable for the infant and that the infant has not yet become attached to its natural mother. Neither temporary separation nor permanent loss need have any adverse effect in early infancy, unless the baby is unfortunate enough to be placed in an environment in which no substitute figure is available consistently enough for the baby to become attached to anyone.

It is now generally accepted that before a baby can become attached to anyone, its cognitive development must have proceeded to the point that the baby is able to conceive of the existence of that person even though she or he is not present to perception – that is, to have some representational model of that person, however crude or primitive. It is to Piaget (e.g., 1954) that we are indebted for the first description of the development of the concept of permanence of objects (and persons) throughout the first two years of life.

By six months of age most infants have acquired enough "object permanence" to have become attached to a mother figure. This is shown by Yarrow's (e.g., 1967) findings that most six-month-olds were severely distressed by transfer from a foster home to an adoptive home, whereas younger infants adapted readily to the change of caregiver. Indeed *all* the babies in Yarrow's sample who were transferred to an adoptive mother as late as eight months of age or older responded with severe distress. This fits reasonably well with Piaget's observation that babies at about eight months of age are far enough advanced in the development of the concept of the object to search for hidden objects and that the concept of an object's existing when not present to perception is acquired earlier than this in the case of the mother as object. Indeed, Bell (1970) demonstrated that infants securely attached to their mothers developed the concepts of both person permanence and object permanence more quickly than infants whose attachment was of anxious quality. Nevertheless, recent research (e.g., Bower, 1974; Gratch, 1977) suggests that the development of the concept of the permanence of objects (and presumably also of persons) begins earlier in infancy than Piaget had supposed.

Although some psychoanalytic theorists equate the concept of "libidinal object constancy" with the Piagetian concept of object permanence (e.g., Spitz, 1965), others define it differently (e.g., Mahler, Pine, & Bergman, 1975). These differences are of some moment for they are linked to the criterion for the onset of affectional bond formation (i.e., capacity for "true object relations"), which varies according to theorist from as early as 6 months of age for the majority of infants to as late as 24 months. Reviewing the various usages of libidinal object constancy, both Bowlby (1980) and Fraiberg (1969) concluded it to be an unsatisfactory concept.

Nevertheless, it seems generally agreed that the capacity for attributing continuing existence to the mother figure when she is not present to perception, for conceiving her as independent of self, for storing a representational model of her that can be retrieved from storage after a significant period of absence from perception – that is, a well-developed concept of person permanence – is required before an infant can mourn the loss of its mother. Bowlby (1980) concluded from a review of research giving careful descriptions of behavioral details that the responses of children as young as 16 months to loss corresponded so well with the responses of older children and adults that one could infer the processes of mourning to be essentially the same. He was cautious, however, about extending this conclusion to infants between 6 and 16 months, despite clear evidence from separation distress and cognitive studies that they are capable of the concept of person permanence to some degree. The issue as yet unresolved by research is whether the limitations to the capacity for mental representations result in a cognitive response to loss in the 6-to-16-month-olds that is different enough to make the term "mourning" inappropriate.

# Affectional Bonds Throughout the Life Span

An affectional bond may be inferred when one's partner in a relationship is not readily interchangeable with another, involuntary separation from whom would be likely to cause distress and whose loss would occasion substantial grief. An "attachment" is one kind of affectional bond which, in accordance with all the implications of Bowlby's theory, is characterized by an internalized control system aimed at the maintenance of a specified degree of proximity to the partner in the interests of gaining or maintaining feelings of security. Or, as Bretherton (1980) has suggested, attachment essentially implies a security-regulating system involving an internal organization of behavior with reference to the partner, based in large part on representational models of partner and self. It is assumed that not all kinds of affectional bonds are attachments, although some may involve an attachment component – that is, one's security is largely vested in the availability and responsiveness of the partner – and other components as well. Although the assumption is that relationships involving affectional bonds are long lived rather than transitory, this does not crucially distinguish them from other long-lived relationships in which it is the *role* of the partner that is important rather than the partner as unique individual, so some other individual might play the same role equally well.

Despite general agreement that affectional bonds are formed only to persons of special emotional significance in one's life, are few in number even over the course of a lifetime, and have a disproportionately strong influence on the course of one's life in comparison to the many others with whom one has relationships, research has tended to be concerned with more general issues of social behavior and social development – at least until fairly recently. It seems useful at this juncture to extrapolate from attachment theory – and from infant–parent attachment, which has heretofore been the main focus of research – to a consideration of other affectional bonds about which there has been very little systematic investigation.

## Attachment of child to parent figures

So far it has been established that attachments of a child to parent figures are first formed at some time in the second six months of life and that the qualitative nature of these attachments not only tends to be stable at least throughout the pre-school years but also tends to have pervasive influence on what pathway development takes. There is every reason to believe, however, that attachments to parent figures become less centrally important to a child during the school years, penetrating fewer aspects of the child's life than they did earlier. New relationships are formed, and eventually, during adolescence, the person seeks a heterosexual partner and, whether then or in early adulthood, is likely to find one with whom a new affectional bond can be established. Although for most this new bond may be expected to override child–parent attachments, it seems very unlikely to supplant them entirely. Systematic research is sadly lacking, however, in regard to the course of development of child–parent bonds beyond infancy, into early adulthood, and later.

As the child's activities come increasingly to have their focus outside the home, there is remarkably little information about changes in behavior that mediates continuing attachment to parents. It is usually assumed that the attachment to parents weakens, but there is little or no descriptive evidence either of the weakening or of the ways in which attachment continues to be manifested. Clinicians generally agree that the essential nature of the child's emotional attitudes to the parents does not change even after the child has reached mature adulthood and has made a major emotional investment in a marital bond. Certainly, there seems much reason for hypothesizing that young adults as well as adolescents tend to continue to rely on parents as attachment figures, to seek their care in emergencies, and – if the attachments are secure – to gain comfort and reassurance from confidence that parents can he counted on when needed. Yet many believe that parents and their adult offspring can enter into a new kind of mutually contributing relationship in which the son or daughter can, on occasion and/or in certain respects, be caregiver to a parent and yet, on other occasions and in other respects, still have the parent as attachment figure, while the parent, likewise, can alternate as caregiver and attachment figure to the child. Can this be so? Or does the earlier child–parent attachment override this possibility?

Is it possible for the roles of parent and adult son or daughter to be healthily reversed when the parent reaches old age – despite the fact that in earlier life such reversal of roles is rare and usually judged to be pathological? Certainly, in many cultures the aged parent would still be viewed by offspring as stronger and wiser and, hence, as a source of security. Does such veneration preclude playing a caregiving role to the aged parent? Research has not yet tackled issues such as this one. In any case it seems likely that affectional bonds persist between parent and adult offspring – if only because death of a parent so often occasions grief and disorganization far beyond what the emancipated adult sons and daughters would have anticipated. As we have argued, the achievement of self-reliance in no way implies the disappearance or even attenuation of affectional bonds.

Parents are not the only figures to which a child may become attached in a relationship akin to that between child and parent. Even in infancy one may become attached to one or perhaps a very few adults other than parents

(Ainsworth, 1967; Schaffer & Emerson, 1964). Nevertheless, remarkably little research has been done on the conditions affecting the development of such attachments or their significance in the child's life. Specifically, there has been no research relevant to Bowlby's hypothesis that there is a hierarchy of attachment figures – the principal attachment figure and one or a few other subsidiary attachment figures. And despite current keen interest in the effects of various kinds of day care on a child's development, research has scarcely begun that could help identify the conditions under which day-care personnel become attachment figures and how they may supplement a child's original attachments to parents or possibly change their nature.

In the school years it seems likely that affectional bonds akin to attachments can be formed to figures who somehow provide a secure base for the child's endeavors even though their caregiving role differs in many particulars from that of the child's parents or other early caregivers. Such further attachment figures might be found among teachers, leaders of youth groups or athletic teams, and older siblings – plus, in adult life, mentors. But certainly not all such persons become attachment figures to all in their charge. Systematic research into such possible attachments is totally lacking, as is any evidence as to how well secure attachments to such figures might compensate for anxious attachments to parents.

As Bowlby (1977) suggested, the psychotherapist or analyst may well serve as an attachment figure to patients – and indeed should. That patients do cast the therapist into such a role is clearly indicated by the phenomena of transference, through which the patient manifests indications that his or her expectations of the therapist are shaped by representational models of parent figures. Bowlby suggested that when a patient has built up trust in the therapist as someone who truly cares about him or her, the patient is enabled to use the therapist as a secure base from which to reexamine representational models – both those based on semantic memory and a possibly conflicting set based on episodic memory – to reappraise them in the light of present-day reality and to reconstruct a set of models less riddled by conflict.

## Affectional bonds of parent to child

It has already been suggested that parental bonds to children differ from attachments of children to parent figures in that the parent, under usual circumstances, relies on the child neither for caregiving nor as a focus of his or her feelings of security. Nevertheless, it is obvious that strong affectional bonds are usually formed between parents and their children.

It has also been suggested that the bond of mother to child has a genetic underpinning. Nevertheless, research is needed to elucidate how experiential factors affect bond formation – not merely the immediately postnatal contact experiences emphasized by Klaus and Kennell (1976) but also experiences long preceding the birth of the child, as well as those that follow it. There is good reason to believe that the quality of a mother's care for her child may be strongly influenced by her own childhood experiences of being mothered (e.g., Wolkind, Hall, & Pawlby, 1977), but many important details remain to be explored in further research, including identification of circumstances that enable a parent, herself badly mothered, to care well for her own children. Also requiring investigation are the dimensions in terms of which qualitative differences in maternal bonds to the baby may be understood.

Earlier, it was suggested that the bond of father to child might have the same kind of genetic foundation as the maternal bond, with the caregiving behavioral system and the function of protection of the child fundamental to both. However, it is at least a possibility that the predisposition of human males to form bonds to their offspring evolved in a somewhat different way than did the basis of the mother–child bond. Relevant data are sparse and inferences difficult to draw about the early evolutionary history of the human species. Nevertheless, the basis of the father–child bond is a tantalizing issue, even though cultural and individual circumstances obviously also play a major part in influencing paternal behavior.

So complementary are the attachments of child to parents and the bonds of parents to child, as well as the behavioral systems relevant to each, that one can scarcely consider one without the other. This implies that the issues raised above about possible attachments of a person to parent like figures – teachers, older siblings, leaders, mentors, therapists, and the like – need to include the caregiving/ protective implications of these various roles. Obviously, the specific behaviors have almost no overlap with maternal caregiving behavior directed toward an infant or young child, so the focus must be on the affective aspects of caring for another, with the specific behaviors (and limitations of behavior) presumably determined by the circumstances of the relationship. For example, the relationship of priest or pastor implies a kind of parent–child bond at least to some parishioners, as indeed the title "father" suggests.

## Sexual bonds

Heterosexual pair bonding is not characteristic of all species. The reproductive behavioral system may achieve its functional outcome without an enduring bond between the partners ensuing. In species in which heterosexual pair bonding does occur, the caregiving system appears to be involved, ensuring that the male shares somehow in giving care to the young, either directly, indirectly by caring for his mate, or both. In most human societies, moreover, marriage customs, whether monogamous or polygynous, tend to foster enduring bonds between heterosexual partners, thus backing up biological predispositions to ensure that young are produced and cared for.

The clinical and research material reported by Bowlby (1973, 1980) clearly implies an attachment component in the affectional bonds between partners in marriage and other long-term relationships. Separation from the partner evokes distress, especially when involuntary and unexpected, whereas permanent loss sets mourning processes in train. Furthermore, it appears that the partners reciprocate in seeking security from and providing it to each other. From what is known about healthy and enduring relationships, in some respects and on some occasions one partner is the caregiver and is relied on by the other to be accessible and responsive, whereas in other respects and on other occasions the roles are reversed.

Thus there seem to be three major behavioral systems involved in forming and maintaining heterosexual pair bonding: (1) the reproductive or mating system, which seems likely to be initially the most important in bond formation, regardless of whether the biological function of reproduction is fulfilled; (2) the caregiving behavioral system, which is involved in two ways – giving care to the partner and sharing with the partner caregiving to the young that may result from the union; and (3) the attachment system, which implies that each partner seeks security – comfort and reassurance – through maintaining contact with the other. Such a view of the heterosexual bond does not seem to be invalidated by the many deviations from the modal pattern that obviously occur. Casual relations, resting only on the sexual component, tend to be short-lived. In some marriages one partner may play mainly the role of caregiver and serve chiefly as attachment figure for the other, and on this basis the bond may endure even if sexual interest has waned. Joint commitment to caring for children may cement a bond when other components have weakened. If the attachment component is anxious and ambivalent, this does not imply that the bond is fragile. Representational models of self and partner derived from a long period of intimate interaction, and influenced also by models of parents and self carried over from childhood, tend to resist revision.

It seems likely that bonds between same-sex adult peers may also have sexual, caregiving, and attachment components, despite the impossibility of the sexual component fulfilling its reproductive function. As in the case of many heterosexual bonds, it seems likely that it is the reciprocal caregiving and attachment components that are responsible when the bond is long-lived.

## Affectional bonds with age peers

Despite much research into children's interaction with other children, little evidence of attachments among them has emerged, except for two relevant studies. A. Freud and Dann (1951) reported that a group of young children, having lost their parents in Nazi extermination camps, found security in one another. Harlow and Harlow (1965) reported that infant rhesus macaques, reared together without a mother figure, clung to one another, apparently finding their only source of security in this contact. Such findings suggest the young child's predisposition to become attached is so strong that in the absence of appropriate parental figures, the child will direct attachment behavior toward familiar figures, no matter how functionally inappropriate they may be. These studies throw no light on the nature of affectional bonds that are ordinarily formed among children.

Harlow and Suomi (e.g., Harlow & Harlow, 1962; Suomi & Harlow, 1972), working with rhesus macaques, have drawn attention to the significance of interactions with age peers as a condition for later normal social development. Findings such as these have led others to turn attention to the entire social network as more important in determining the course of development than attachments or other affectional bonds (e.g., Weinraub, Brooks, & Lewis, 1977). Yet, as Weiss (1975) suggested, the effects of loss of a figure to whom one is bonded differ from the effects of loss of a social network. There are many types of relationships that involve neither attachment nor any other kind of enduring affectional bond (cf. Hinde, 1976). Nevertheless, it is reasonable to expect some relationships to be more significant than others and to differ in the biological functions that they fulfill.

Interactions with playmates, as Harlow and Suomi have implied, may have the important function of providing an opportunity for a child to learn how to get along with others. In a social species such as the human species it may be inferred that underlying social interaction is a sociable or affiliative behavioral system with an essential function, since survival rests in large part on cooperative endeavors. Nevertheless, much as a child may enjoy playmates and be at loose ends when none is available, it seems likely that playmates are interchangeable to a large extent and that the relationship with a playmate would not ordinarily involve an enduring bond. Similarly, an adult may frequently seek the company of specific others who share his or her interests but is unlikely to mourn the loss of a tennis partner or bridge companion; the adult's expectable response would be to try to find a replacement.

In adolescence, and perhaps also earlier, a child may seek security in belonging to a group and may be very upset if cut off from the group, even though the individuals who constitute the group are more or less interchangeable. Similar group affiliations occur in adult life also. If such affiliation can be termed an affectional bond, its nature obviously differs from bonds between individuals. Nevertheless, its significance is not to be minimized, if only because in social species behavior toward familiar conspecifics differs markedly from behavior toward unfamiliar conspecifics.

Yet there is reason to believe that affectional bonds may be formed with specific others who are more or less the same age – bonds between twins, for example. It seems likely that bonds – whether fond and secure or hostile and anxious – may be formed with brothers and sisters. Indeed, separation studies (e.g., Heinicke & Westheimer, 1966) have shown that when siblings, separated from home and parents, are placed in the same unfamiliar environment with unfamiliar caregivers, for each sibling the presence of the other seems to alleviate distress to some extent. Weiss (1982) suggested that strong affectional bonds may be formed between "buddies" in the armed services, presumably with the same kind of reciprocal involvement of caregiving and attachment systems that may be identified in sexual pair bonds but without any necessary inference that the sexual system is also implicated. Such bonds between partners engaged in dangerous enterprises can be viewed as having survival function.

So far, there has been little relevant research into the possibility of bonds (presumably with attachment components) being implicated in friendships in either childhood or adulthood. Since it may be assumed that relationships involving affectional bonds endure substantially longer than most other relationships and have a more significant effect on development throughout the life span, it would seem highly desirable for more research to be directed toward identifying and exploring their nature. Some, but not all, of these will be found to have an attachment component. Nevertheless, in such explorations it is expected that attachment theory and the research that has stemmed from it would provide a useful framework for understanding.

## Notes

1  Even though eight subgroups were also identified – with which we cannot be concerned here – it is inconceivable that one small sample of infants could include all important variants of pattern. It is amazing that the three main patterns (A, B, and C) have proved as stable and useful as they have in the course of extensive research. Nevertheless, researchers have identified some further patterns that do not fit readily into the A, B, and C classifications, perhaps especially in work with "at risk" or maltreated infants. As might be expected, these further patterns seem indicative of variations in anxious attachment (e.g., Main & Weston, 1981). In the light of further research, the classificatory system is in need of refinement and expansion. Meanwhile, it serves most research purposes remarkably well.

2  I am indebted to Robert Weiss for suggesting the relevance to this issue of the emotional significance of different attachment figures and for generally inducing me to round out the picture of childhood loss by including discussion of loss through parental divorce, even though I am not at present prepared to review the relevant literature adequately.

## References

Adam, K. S. (1973) Childhood parental loss, sucidal ideation and suicidal behaviour. In E. J. Anthony & C. Koupernik (Eds.). *The child in his family: The impact of disease and death*. New York: Wiley.

Ainsworth, M. D. S. (1962) The effects of maternal deprivation: A review of findings and controversy in the context of research strategy. In *Deprivation of maternal care: A reassessment of its effects (Public Health papers, No. 14)*. Geneva: World Health Organization.

Ainsworth, M. D. S. (1967) *Infancy in Uganda: Infant care and the growth of love*. Baltimore: Johns Hopkins University Press.

Ainsworth, M. D. S. (1972) Attachment and dependency: A comparison. In J. L. Gewirtz (Ed.), *Attachment and dependency*. Washington, DC: Winston.

Ainsworth, M. D. S. (1979) Attachment as related to mother–infant interaction. In *Advances in the study of behavior (Vol. 9)*. New York: Academic Press.

Ainsworth, M. D. S. (1982) Attachment: Retrospect and prospect. In C. M. Parkes & J. Stevenson-Hinde (Eds.). *The place of attachment in human behavior*. New York: Basic Books.

Ainsworth, M. D. S., & Bell. S. M. (1970) Attachment, exploration, and separation: Illustrated by the behavior of one-year-olds in a strange situation. *Child Development, 41*, 49–67.

Ainsworth, M. D. S., Bell, S. M., & Stayton, D. J. (1971) Individual differences in strange-situation behaviour of one-year-olds. In H. R. Schaffer (Ed.). *The origins of human social relations*. New York: Academic Press.

Ainsworth, M. D. S., Blehar, M. C., Waters, E., & Wall, S. (1978) *Patterns of attachment: A psychological study of the strange situation*. Hillsdale, NJ: Erlbaum.

Ainsworth, M. D. S., & Bowlby, J. (1953) *Research strategy in the study of mother–child separation*. Paris: Courrier de la Centre International de l'Enfance.

Ainsworth, M. D. S., & Wittig, B. A. (1969) Attachment and exploratory behavior of one-year-olds in a strange situation. In B. M. Foss (Ed.). *Determinants of infant behaviour* (Vol. 4). London: Methuen.

Arend, R., Gove, F. L., & Sroufe, L. A. (1979) Continuity of individual adaptation from infancy to kindergarten: A predictive study of ego resiliency and curiosity in preschoolers. *Child Development, 50*, 950–959.

Baumrind, D. (1967) Child care practices anteceding three patterns of preschool behavior. *Genetic Psychology Monographs, 75*, 43–88.

Bell, S. M. (1970) The development of the concept of the object as related to infant–mother attachment. *Child Development, 41*, 291–311.

Bischof, N. (1975) A systems approach towards the functional connections of attachment and fear. *Child Development, 46*, 801–817.

Bower, T. G. R. (1974) *Development in infancy*. San Francisco: Freeman.

Bowlby, J. (1944) Forty-four juvenile thieves: Their characters and home life. *International Journal of Psycho-Analysis, 25*, 19–52; 107–127.

Bowlby, J. (1952) *Maternal care and mental health* (2nd edn.). Monograph Series No. 2. Geneva: World Health Organization.

Bowlby, J. (1969) *Attachment and loss (Vol. 1): Attachment*. New York: Basic Books.

Bowlby, J. (1973) *Attachment and loss (Vol. 2): Separation: Anxiety and anger*. New York: Basic Books.

Bowlby, J. (1977) The making and breaking of affectional bonds. *British Journal of Psychiatry 130*, 201–210; 421–431.

Bowlby, J. (1980) *Attachment and loss (Vol. 3): Loss: Sadness and depression*. New York: Basic Books.

Bretherton, I. (1980) Young children in stressful situations: The supporting role of attachment figures and unfamiliar caregivers. In G. V. Coelho & P. I. Ahmed (Eds.). *Uprooting and development*. New York: Plenum.

Bretherton, I., & Ainsworth, M. D. S. (1974) Responses of one-year-olds to a stranger in a strange situation. In M. Lewis & L. A. Rosenblum. *The origins of fear*. New York: Wiley.

Brown, G. W., & Harris, T. (1978) *The social origins of depression: A study of psychiatric disorder in women*. London: Tavistock.

Connell, D. B. (1976) *Individual differences in attachment: An investigation into stability, implications, and relationships to structure of early language development*. Unpublished doctoral dissertation, Syracuse University.

Egeland, B., & Sroufe, A. (1981) Developmental sequelae of maltreatment of infancy. *New Directions for Child Development, 11*, 77–92.

Erdelyi, M. H. (1974) A new look at the new look: Perceptual defense and vigilance. *Psychological Review, 81*, 1–25.

Feldman, S. S., & Ingham, M. E. (1975) Attachment behavior: A validation study in two age groups. *Child Development, 46*, 319–330.

Fox, N. (1977) Attachment of kibbutz infants to mother and metapelet. *Child Development, 48*, 1228–1239.

Fraiberg, S. (1969) Libidinal object constancy and mental representation. *Psychoanalytic Study of the Child, 24*, 9–47.

Fraiberg. S. *(Ed.). (1980) Clinical studies in infant mental health: The first year of life*. New York: Basic Books.

Freud, A., & Dann, S. (1951) An experiment in group upbringing. *Psychoanalytic Study of the Child, 6*, 127–168.

Freud, S. (1938) *An outline of psychoanalysis*. London: Hogarth.

Furman, E. (1974) *A child's parent dies: Studies in childhood bereavement*. New York: Wiley.

Goldfarb, W. (1943) Effects of early institutional care on adolescent personality. *Journal of Experimental Education, 12*, 106–129.

Gratch, G. (1977) Review of Piagetian infancy research: Object concept development. In W. F. Overton & J. H. Gallagher (Eds.). *Knowledge and development* (Vol. 1). New York: Plenum.

Harlow, H. F. (1958) The nature of love. *American Psychologist, 13*, 673–685.

Harlow, H. F. (1961) The development of affectional patterns in infant monkeys. In B. M. Foss (Ed.). *Determinants of infant behavior*. New York: Wiley.

Harlow, H. F., & Harlow, M. K. (1962) Social deprivation in monkeys. *Scientific American, 207* (5), 136–146.

Harlow, H. F. & Harlow, M. K. (1965) The affectional systems. In A. M. Schrier, H. F. Harlow, & F. Stollnitz (Eds.). *Behavior of non-human primates* (Vol. 2). New York: Academic Press.

Heinicke, C., & Westheimer, I. (1966) *Brief separations*. New York: International Universities Press.

Hetherington, E. M., Cox, M., & Cox, R. (1981) Effects of divorce on parents and children. In M. Lamb (Ed.). *Nontraditional families*. Hillsdale, NJ: Erlbaum.

Hinde, R. A. (1976) On describing relationships. *Journal of Child Psychology and Psychiatry, 17,* 1–19.

Klaus, M. H., & Kennell, J. H. (1976) *Maternal–infant bonding*. St. Louis: Mosby.

Korchen, S. J., & Ruff, G. E. (1964) Personality characteristics of the Mercury astronauts. In G. H. Grosser, H. Wechsler, & M. Greenblatt (Eds.). *The threat of impending disaster: Contributions to the psychology of stress*. Cambridge, Mass: MIT Press.

Kotelchuck, M. (1976) The infant's relationship to the father: Experimental evidence. In M. E. Lamb (Ed.). *The role of the father in child development*. New York: Wiley.

Kuhn, T. S. (1962) *The structure of scientific revolutions*. Chicago: University of Chicago Press.

Lamb, M. E. (1976) Interactions between eight-month-old children and their fathers and mothers. In M. E. Lamb (Ed.). *The role of the father in child development*. New York: Wiley.

Lamb, M. E. (1977) Father–infant and mother–infant interaction in the first year of life. *Child Development, 48,* 167–181.

Lamb, M. E. (1978) Qualitative aspects of mother- and father–infant attachments. *Infant Behavior and Development, 1,* 276–275.

Lieberman, A. F. (1977) Preschoolers' competence with a peer: Influence of attachment and social experience. *Child Development, 48,* 1277–1287.

Londerville, S., & Main, M. (1981) Security of attachment, compliance, and maternal training methods in the second year of life. *Developmental Psychology, 17,* 289–299.

Maccoby, E. E., & Feldman, S. S. (1972) Mother-attachment and stranger-reactions in the third year of life. *Monographs of the Society for Research in Child Development, 37* (1, Serial No. 146), pp.1-86.

Mahler, M. S., Pine, F., & Bergman, A. (1975) *The psychological birth of the human infant*. New York: Basic Books.

Main, M. (1977) Analysis of a peculiar form of reunion behavior seen in some daycare children: Its history and sequelae in children who are home-reared. In R. Webb (Ed.). *Social development in daycare*. Baltimore: Johns Hopkins University Press.

Main. M. (1983) Exploration, play, and cognitive functioning related to infant–mother attachment. *Infant Behavior and Development, 6,* 167–174.

Main, M., & Weston, D. R. (1981) Security of attachment to mother and father: Related to conflict behavior and the readiness to form new relationships. *Child Development, 52,* 932–940.

Marvin, R. S. (1977) An ethological-cognitive model for the attenuation of mother–child attachment behavior. In T. M. Alloway, L. Krames, & P. Pliner (Eds.). *Advances in the study of communication and affect (Vol. 3): The development of social attachments*. New York: Plenum.

Marvin. R. S., & Greenberg, M. T. (1982) Preschoolers' changing conceptions of their mothers: A social-cognitive study of mother–child attachment. In D. Forbes & M. T. Greenberg (Eds.). *New directions in child development: The development of planful behavior in children*. San Francisco: Jossey-Bass.

Matas, L., Arend, R. A., & Sroufe, L. A. (1978) Continuity of adaptation in the second year: The relationship between quality of attachment and later competence. *Child Development, 49,* 547–556.

Parke, R. D. (1979) Perspectives on father–infant interaction. In J. D. Osofsky (Ed.). *Handbook of infant development*. New York: Wiley.

Parkes, C. M. (1972) *Bereavement: Studies of grief in adult life*. London: Tavistock.

Peck, R. F., & Havighurst, R. J. (1960) *The psychology of character development*. New York: Wiley.

Piaget, J. (1926) *The language and thought of the child*. New York: Harcourt, Brace.

Piaget, J. (1954) *The construction of reality in the child*. New York: Basic Books.

Richards, M. P. M. (1974) First steps in becoming social. In M. P. M. Richards (Ed.). *The integration of a child into a social world*. London: Cambridge University Press.

Robertson, J., & Robertson. J. (1971) Young children in brief separation: A fresh look. *Psychoanalytic Study of the Child, 26,* 264–315.

Rosenblatt, J. S., Siegel, H. I., & Mayer, A. D. (1979) Progress in the study of maternal behavior in the rat: Hormonal, non-hormonal, sensory, and developmental aspects. In D. S. Lehrman, R. A. Hinde, & E. Shaw (Eds.). *Advances in the study of behavior* (Vol. 10). New York: Academic Press.

Schaffer, H. R. (1971) *The growth of sociability*. London: Penguin.

Schaffer, H. R., & Emerson, P. E. (1964) The development of social attachments in infancy. *Monographs of the Society for Research in Child Development, 29* (3, Serial No. 94), pp.1-77.

Seligman, M. E. P. (1975) *Helplessness: On depression, development, and death*. San Francisco: Freeman.

Spitz, R. A. (1965) *The first year of life*. New York: International Universities Press.

Sroufe, L. A. (1979) The coherence of individual development: Early care, attachment, and subsequent developmental issues. *American Psychologist, 34*, 834–841.

Sroufe, L. A., & Waters, E. (1977a) Attachment as an organizational construct. *Child Development*, 1977, *48*, 1184–1199. (a)

Sroufe, L. A., & Waters, E. (1977b) Heartrate as a convergent measure in clinical and developmental research. *Merrill-Palmer Quarterly, 23*, 3–28.

Sroufe, L. A., Waters, E., & Matas, L. (1974) Contextual determinants of infant affective response. In M. Lewis & L. A. Rosenblum (Eds.). *The origins of fear*. New York: Wiley.

Suomi. S., & Harlow, H. F. (1972) Social rehabilitation of isolated-reared monkeys. *Developmental Psychology, 6*, 487–496.

Tulving, E. (1972) Episodic and semantic memory. In E. Tulving & W. Donaldson (Eds.). *Organization of memory*. New York: Academic Press.

Vaughn. B., Egeland, B., Sroufe, L. A., & Waters, E. (1979) Individual differences in infant–mother attachment at twelve and eighteen months: Stability and change in families under stress. *Child Development, 50*, 971–975.

Waddington, C. H. (1957) *The strategy of the genes*. London: Allen & Unwin.

Wallerstein, J. S., & Kelly, J. B. (1980) *Surviving the breakup: How children and parents cope with divorce*. New York: Basic Books.

Waters, E. (1978) The reliability and stability of individual differences in infant–mother attachment. *Child Development, 49*, 483–494.

Waters, E. Wippman, J., & Sroufe, L. A. (1979) Attachment, positive affect, and competence in the peer group: Two studies in construct validation. *Child Development, 50*, 821–829.

Weinraub, M., Brooks, J., & Lewis, M. (1977) The social network: A reconsideration of the concept of attachment. *Human Development, 30*, 31–47.

Weiss, R. S. (1975) *Marital separation*. New York: Basic Books.

Weiss, R. S. (1982) Attachment in adult life. In C. M. Parkes & J. Stevenson-Hinde (Eds.). *The place of attachment in human behavior*. New York: Basic Books.

Wolkind, S., Hall, F., & Pawlby, S. (1977) Individual differences in mothering behaviour: A combined epidemiological and observational approach. In P. J. Graham (Ed.). *Epidemiological approaches in child psychiatry*. New York: Academic Press.

Yarrow, L. J. (1967) The development of focused relationships during infancy. In J. Hellmuth (Ed.). *Exceptional infant* (Vol. 1). Seattle: Special Child Publications.

# Reference Note

1. Marvin, R. S., Mossier, D. C., & VanDevender, T. L. *An experimental study of brief separations between mothers and their 4-year-old children*. Unpublished manuscript.

# 4

# Love as Attachment

## *The Integration of Three Behavioral Systems*

### Phillip R. Shaver, Cindy Hazan, and Donna Bradshaw

Research on romantic love has been primarily descriptive and atheoretical. Rubin (1973), for example, developed questionnaires to assess degrees of liking and loving but said relatively little about why these states exist. Walster and Walster (1978), following a popular tradition, distinguished passionate from companionate love but said little about the origins or functions of either. Berscheid and Walster (1974), noting that previous investigators had proceeded without much theorizing, attempted to apply Schachter's (1964) two-factor theory of emotion to passionate love. Unfortunately, since Schachter's theory dealt mainly with mislabeled states of arousal, love perforce became a mislabeled arousal state, robbed of independent existence and purpose. Sternberg and Grajek (1984) tested various psychometric theories of love, taking their lead from psychometric models of intelligence. Since this approach relies on existing measures of love (and of liking, in Sternberg and Grajek's case), the resulting conception of love is like the operational definition of intelligence: love is whatever measures of love measure.

Our own approach (Hazan & Shaver, 1987; Shaver, Hazan, & Bradshaw, 1984) has been to situate love within an evolutionary framework, to ask about its dynamics and possible functions, to consider how it relates to loss and grieving, and to explore how its infantile and childhood forms might be related to its adolescent and adult forms, on the assumption that as Konner (1982) put it, "the evolution of the brain would have to be considered unparsimonious if it were not able to draw upon the same basic capacities of emotion and action in the various settings where strong attachment is called for" (p. 298). Fortunately, a rich theoretical framework, *attachment theory* (Ainsworth, Blehar, Waters, & Wall, 1978; Bowlby, 1969, 1973, 1979, 1980; Bretherton, 1985; Sroufe & Waters, 1977), has already been developed to explain various facets of infant care-giver attachment. To the extent that adolescent and adult romantic love are also attachment processes, many of the concepts and principles of attachment theory should apply to them.

Unfortunately, a major preconception held by some social scientists makes it difficult to consider romantic love an attachment process having emotional dynamics and biological functions akin to those of infant care-giver attachment. According to this preconception, romantic love is a fairly recent invention of Western civilization (for example, Averill, 1985; de Rougement, 1940), in particular, a creation of the courtly love tradition that emerged in thirteenth-century Europe. When one consults sources from over a thousand years earlier, however, love is easy to find. In two fragments attributed to Sappho, a well-known sixth-century BC poet, for example, we encounter

*Source:* Philip R. Shaver, Cindy Hazan, Donna Bradshaw, "Love as Attachment: The Integration of Three Behavioral Systems," pp. 68–99 from *The psychology of Love*, eds. Robert J. Sternberg, Michael L. Barnes (New Haven, CT: Yale University Press, 1988). Reproduced with permission from Authors.

both the pain of unrequited love, thought by some current writers to be a thirteenth-century invention, and the recognition that a lover's reaction to unresponsiveness is like that of a small child:

> It's no use
> Mother dear, I
> can't finish my
> weaving
>         You may
> blame Aphrodite
> soft as she is
> she has almost
> killed me with
> love for that boy      (Sappho, Fragment 12,
>                         1958 translation)
> Afraid of losing you
> I ran fluttering
> like a little girl      (Sappho, Fragment 54,
> after her mother            1958 translation)

The same kinds of examples can be found in the great literatures of early historic times, from China and the Middle East to Greece and Rome (Mellen, 1981). The relative contributions of biology and culture to romantic love are obviously difficult to determine, as are the relative contributions of these factors to any complex social phenomenon. What we claim is the right to hypothesize, in the absence of strong evidence to the contrary, that romantic love has always and everywhere existed as a biological potential whether or not it has been accepted as a basis for marriage and procreation. The same could be said about anger or any other strong emotion over which societies have attempted to exercise control.

This chapter is structured as follows. We begin with a fairly detailed summary of attachment theory, which will be important in our attempt to extend the theory to adult romantic love. We then list some of the observable and theoretical similarities between infant care-giver attachment and adult romantic love. Next, we describe three kinds or styles of attachment identified by Ainsworth and her coworkers (1978) in laboratory studies of mother–infant interaction and report highlights of two empirical studies exploring the possibility that the same three styles characterize adult romantic love. We then assess the limitations of our work to date and suggest how attachment theory might be mined and extended to overcome these limitations. In particular, we discuss the possibility that adult love is an integration of three behavioral systems (discussed by Bowlby): attachment, care giving, and sexuality. These three systems, as Sternberg (1986) and others (for example, Shaver, Hazan, & Bradshaw, 1984) have suggested, operate differently over the course of a relationship, causing the quality of love to change accordingly. Finally, we consider grief, the emotional response to loss of an important attachment figure. One advantage of the attachment-theoretical approach to love is that it helps explain why loss is so painful and why grief involves such strong and irrational-seeming reactions.

## Attachment Theory Summarized

Bowlby's purpose, in his three-volume exploration of attachment, separation, and loss (the processes by which affectional bonds are forged and broken), was to describe and explain, within a functionalist, evolutionary framework, how infants become emotionally attached to their primary care givers and emotionally distressed when separated from them. Extending attachment theory to adult love and loss is an enterprise that Bowlby himself has endorsed. In a 1977 paper (reprinted in Bowlby, 1979), he contended that "attachment behavior [characterizes] human beings from the cradle to the grave." In another paper he pointed out the links between attachment processes and familiar emotions, including love:

Affectional [attachment] bonds and subjective states of strong emotion tend to go together, as every novelist and play-wright knows. Thus, many of the most intense of all human emotions arise during the formation, the maintenance, the disruption and the renewal of affectional bonds – which, for that reason, are sometimes called emotional bonds. In terms of subjective experience, the formation of a bond is described as falling in love, maintaining a bond as loving someone, and losing a partner as grieving over someone. Similarly, the threat of loss arouses anxiety and actual loss causes sorrow; whilst both situations are likely to arouse anger. Finally, the unchallenged maintenance of a bond is experienced as a source of security, and the renewal of a bond as a source of joy. (Bowlby, 1979, p. 69)

Bowlby's attachment theory grew out of observations of the behavior of infants and young children who were separated from their primary care giver (usually mother) for various lengths of time. Bowlby noticed what primate researchers had also observed in the laboratory and the field: when a human or primate infant is separated from its mother, the infant goes through a predictable series of emotional reactions. The first is *protest*, which involves crying, active searching, and resistance to others' soothing efforts. The second is *despair*, which is a state of passivity and obvious sadness. And the third, discussed only with reference to humans, is *detachment*, an active, seemingly defensive disregard for and avoidance of the mother if she returns.

Because of the remarkable similarities between human infants and other primate infants, Bowlby was led to consider the evolutionary significance of infant care-giver attachment and its maintenance in the face of occasional separations. He hypothesized that the major biological function of this affectional bonding system in humans' "environment of evolutionary adaptedness" was to protect infants from predation and other threats to survival. He adopted from ethology and artificial intelligence theory a control systems approach, according to which attachment is a behavioral system, a set of behaviors (crying, smiling, clinging, locomoting, looking, and so on) that function together to achieve a set-goal, in this case a certain degree of proximity to the primary care giver. The set-goal changes systematically in response to illness, pain, darkness, unfamiliar surroundings, and so on – all conditions associated with potential harm.

The attachment system is just one among a number of behavioral systems (for example, care giving, mating, affiliation, and exploration), each with its own set of distinct behaviors and functions. According to Bowlby, however, the attachment system is central and of critical importance for the smooth functioning of the other systems. He and other observers of both human and primate behavior have noticed that when an infant is healthy, alert, unafraid, and in the presence of its mother, it seems interested in exploring and mastering the environment and in establishing affiliative contact with other family and community members. Researchers call this "using the mother as a secure base." When mother is unavailable, the infant becomes preoccupied with regaining her presence, and exploration and socializing fall off dramatically. Thus, exploratory behavior (the exploration system) can be preempted by activation of the attachment system.

Systematic observation reveals that the typical infant checks back periodically, visually and/or physically, to make sure that mother is available and responsive. If she moves or directs her attention elsewhere, the child attempts to regain that attention by vocalizing or returning to her side. When the attachment system is activated strongly, most children cry and seek physical contact with their primary care giver. When the system is quiescent, they play happily, smile easily, share toys and discoveries (such as rocks and pieces of lint) with their care giver, and display warm interest in other people. In this sense, attachment is the basis of happiness, security, and self-confidence.

Bowlby claimed that infants and children construct mental models of themselves and their major social-interaction partners, and that these models regulate a person's social behaviors and feelings throughout life. His entire theory can be summarized in three propositions:

The first [proposition] is that when an individual is confident that an attachment figure will be available to him whenever he desires it, that person will be much less prone to either intense or chronic fear than will an individual who for any reason has no such confidence. The second proposition concerns the sensitive period during which such confidence develops. It postulates that confidence in the availability of attachment figures, or a lack of it, is built up slowly during the years of immaturity – infancy, childhood, and adolescence – and that whatever expectations are developed during those years tend to persist relatively unchanged throughout the rest of life. The third proposition concerns the role of actual experience. It postulates that the varied expectations of the accessibility and responsiveness of attachment figures that individuals develop during the years of immaturity are tolerably accurate reflections of the experiences those individuals have actually had. (Bowlby, 1973, p. 235)

According to Bowlby, mental models of self and relationship partners, and the behavior patterns influenced by them, are central components of personality. Personal continuity, in fact, is primarily due to the persistence of mental models, which are themselves sustained by a fairly stable family setting. The two aspects of mental models – representations of self and representations of relationships – are closely interrelated, as Bowlby explains in the following passage:

> Confidence that an attachment figure is, apart from being accessible, likely to be responsive can be seen to turn on at least two variables: (a) whether or not the attachment figure is judged to be the sort of person who in general responds to calls for support and protection; [and] (b) whether or not the self is judged to be the sort of person towards whom anyone, and the attachment figure in particular, is likely to respond in a helpful way. Logically these variables are independent. In practice they are apt to be confounded. As a result, the model of the attachment figure and the model of the self are likely to develop so as to be complementary and mutually confirming. (1973, p. 238)

Bowlby's belief that these mental models play an important part in determining the fate of a person's feelings and relationships across the life span is still the focus of heated controversy, but it is supported by a growing number of longitudinal studies of social behavior from infancy through the early elementary school years (Dontas, Maratos, Fafoutis, & Karangelis, 1985; Erickson, Sroufe, & Egeland, 1985; Main, Kaplan, & Cassidy, 1985; Sroufe, 1983; Waters, Wippman, & Sroufe, 1979). We take these studies as encouragement for exploring longer-range continuity between childhood attachment and adult romantic love.

## Similarities Between Infant Care-Giver Attachment and Adult Romantic Love

Given the foregoing theoretical background, we are ready to suggest more explicitly that all important love relationships – especially the first ones with parents and later ones with lovers and spouses – are attachments in Bowlby's sense. We begin by examining similarities between infant and adult attachments. Table 4.1 lists the key features of mother–infant attachment and adult romantic love. For every documented feature of attachment there is a parallel feature of love, and for most documented features of love there is either a documented or a plausible infant parallel. (References for the documentation are listed in a note beneath the table.) The two sets of features are so remarkably similar that before rejecting the hypothesis that attachment and love are variants of a single underlying process, one should feel compelled to offer another explanation of the parallels.

In addition to sharing many features, the two kinds of attachment exhibit similar *dynamics*. When the attachment figure (or attachment object, AO) is available and responsive, the infant (or adult lover) feels secure enough to wander off and explore the environment and to interact win others, occasionally checking back with AO. If AO suddenly become unavailable, attachment behaviors such as signaling or moving closer are initiated and maintained, until feelings of security are restored (see Figure 4.1). The loop in the upper right-hand corner of the figure represents the process experienced most often by secure infants and secure lovers. To loop in the bottom left portion of the figure represents the negative, painful side of love relationships, experienced occasionally by every lover but, a explained below, especially characteristic of insecure infants and insecure lovers.

## Three Kinds or Styles of Attachment

The formation during early childhood of a smoothly functioning (that is secure) attachment relationship with a primary care giver, although the norm in American society, is by no means guaranteed. In a test of Bowlby's ideas, Mary Ainsworth found that a mother's sensitivity and responsiveness to her infant's signals and needs during the first year of life are crucial prerequisites for a secure early attachment relationship. Mothers who are slow or inconsistent in responding to their infant's cries or who regularly intrude on or interfere with their infant's desired activities (sometimes to force "affection" on the infant at a particular moment) produce infant who cry more than usual, explore less than usual (even in mother's presence), mingle attachment behaviors with overt expressions of anger, and seem generally anxious. If instead, or in addition, mother frequently rebuffs or rejects the infant's attempts to establish physical contact, the infant may learn to avoid her. On the basis of their observations, Ainsworth and her colleagues delineated three types of Attachment, often called *secure* (characterizing 66 percent of the infants tested), *anxious/ambivalent* (19 percent), and *avoidant* (21 percent). The anxious/ambivalent type

**Table 4.1**　Comparison of the features of attachment and adult romantic love

| Attachment | Romantic Love |
| --- | --- |
| Formation and quality of the attachment bond depends on the attachment object's (AO's) sensitivity and responsiveness. | The love feelings are related to an intense desire for the love object's (LO's) (real or imagined) interest and reciprocation. |
| AO provides a secure base and infant feels competent and safe to explore. | LO's real or imagined reciprocation causes person to feel confident, secure, safe, etc. |
| When AO is present, infant is happier, has a higher threshold for distress, is less afraid of strangers, etc. | When LO is viewed as reciprocating, the lover is happier, more positive about life in general, more outgoing, and kinder to others. |
| When AO is not available, not sensitive, etc., infant is anxious, preoccupied, unable to explore freely. | When LO acts uninterested or rejecting, person is anxious, preoccupied, unable to concentrate, etc. |
| Attachment behaviors include: proximity- and contact-seeking – holding, touching, caressing, kissing, rocking, smiling, crying, following, clinging, etc. | Romantic love is manifest in: wanting to spend time with LO; holding, touching, caressing, kissing, and making love with LO; smiling and laughing; crying; clinging; fearing separation, etc. |
| When afraid, distressed, sick, threatened, etc., infants seek physical contact with AO. | When afraid, distressed, sick, threatened, etc., lovers would like to be held and comforted by LO. |
| Distress at separation or loss: crying, calling for AO, trying to find AO, becoming sad and listless if reunion seems impossible. | Distress at separation or loss: crying, calling for LO, trying to find LO, becoming sad and listless if reunion seems impossible. |
| Upon reunion with AO, infants smile, greet AO with positive vocalization or cry, bounce and jiggle, approach, reach to be picked up, etc. | Upon reunion with LO, or when LO reciprocates after reciprocation was in doubt, the lover feels ecstatic, hugs LO, etc. |
| Infant shares toys, discoveries, etc. with AO. | Lovers like to share experiences, give gifts, etc., and imagine how LO would react to interesting sights, etc. |
| Infant and AO frequently engage in prolonged eye contact; infant seems fascinated with AO's physical features and enjoys touching nose, ears, hair, etc. | Lovers frequently engage in prolonged eye contact and seem fascinated with each other's physical features and like to explore noses, ears, hair, etc. |
| Infant feels fused with AO and, with development, becomes ambivalent about the balance of fusion and autonomy. | Lover sometimes feels fused with LO, and the balance of fusion and autonomy is frequently a matter of concern. |
| Although the infant can be attached to more than one person at a time, there is usually one key relationship (a "hierarchy of attachments"). | Although many adults feel they can and do "love" more than one person, intense love tends to occur with only one partner at a time. |
| Separations, maternal nonresponsiveness, etc., up to a point, increase the intensity of the infant's attachment behaviors (proximity-seeking, clinging, etc.). | Adversity (social disapproval, separations, etc.), up to a point, increases the intensity of the lovers' feelings and commitment to each other. |
| Infant coos, "sings," talks baby talk, etc.; mother talks a combination of baby talk and "motherese." Much nonverbal communication. | Lovers coo, sing, talk baby talk, use soft maternal tones, etc., and much of their communication is nonverbal. |
| The responsive mother senses the infant's needs, "reads the infant's mind, etc. Powerful empathy. | The lover feels almost magically understood and sympathized with, Powerful empathy. |
| Infant experiences AO as powerful, beneficent, all-knowing, etc. In the early stages of development the "good AO" is mentally separate from the "bad AO." | Lover at first ignores or denies LO's negative qualities and perceives LO as powerful, special, all-good, "a miracle," etc. |
| When relationship is not going well, and infant is anxious, it becomes hypervigilant to cues of AO's approval or disapproval. | Before a love relationship becomes secure, the lover is hypersensitive to cues of LO's reciprocation or non-reciprocation, and feelings (ecstasy to despair) are highly dependent on these cues. |

**Table 4.1** (*Continued*)

| Attachment | Romantic Love |
|---|---|
| The infant appears to get tremendous pleasure from AO's approval, applause, attention, etc. | At least early in a relationship, the lover's greatest happiness comes from LO's approval, attention, etc. |

*Sources:* Facts about attachment are derived from Ainsworth et al., 1978; Bell & Ainsworth, 1972; Bowlby, 1969, 1973, 1980; Campos et al., 1975; Cohen & Campos, 1974; Haith, Bergman, & Moore, 1977; Heinicke & Westheimer, 1966; Kaye, 1982; Mahler, Pine, & Bergman, 1975; Morgan & Ricciuti, 1969; Robeson, 1967; Schaffer & Emerson, 1964; Stayton & Ainsworth, 1973; Stern, 1977; Tracy, Lamb, & Ainsworth, 1976; Waters et al., 1979. Facts about adult romantic love are from our own data, plus Driscoll, Davis, & Lipetz, 1972; McCready, 1981 ; Pope et al., 1980; Reedy, Birren, & Schaie, 1981 ; Reik, 1941; Rubin, 1973; Tennov, 1979; Vaillant, 1977; Walster & Walster, 1978; Weiss, 1979.

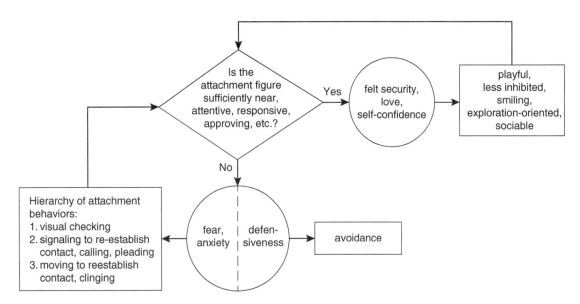

**Figure 4.1**   The dynamics of infant–mother attachment and adult romantic love. The diamond represents a test (as in Miller, Galanter, & Pribram's, 1960, test-operate-test-exit model of behavior); circles represent emotions and squares represent behaviors. The term *sufficiently* in the test question implies that the degree of proximity (and emotional closeness, in the case of adult lovers) is influenced by relationship history and current psychological state (including such things as pain, illness, fatigue, stress, and novelty).

frequently exhibits the behaviors that Bowlby called protest, whereas the avoidant type seems detached. The following quotations (from Ainsworth et al., 1978) provide brief accounts of the three types:

*Secure.* Even when [mother] is out of sight, [the secure infant] nevertheless usually [seems to believe] she is accessible to him and would be responsive should he seek her out or signal to her. It is our hypothesis that expectations of her accessibility and responsiveness have been built up through [the infant's] experience of her generally sensitive responsiveness to his signals and communications. Such experience has been repeatedly confirmed by interactions with her in many different contexts – including feeding, face-to-face [interactions], close bodily contact, and by her response to his crying – throughout the first year. By the end of the first year it is probably only when attachment behavior has already been activated to some extent by conditions such as fatigue, hunger, or illness, or by some unaccustomed and somewhat alarming circumstance, that he protests her departure and/or continuing absence. (p. 312)

*Anxious/Ambivalent.* There is every reason to believe that [anxious/ambivalent] infants are anxious in their attachment to mother. Both at home and in the [unfamiliar laboratory] situation, they cry more than [secure] babies. They manifest more separation anxiety. They do not seem to have confident expectations of the mother's accessibility and responsiveness. Consequently they are unable to use the mother as a secure base from which to explore an unfamiliar situation – at least not as well as [secure] infants. . . . Because they are chronically anxious in relation to mother, they tend to respond to [her] departures in the separation episodes with immediate and intense distress; their attachment behavior has a low threshold for high-intensity activation. (pp. 314–315)

*Avoidant.* [In interpreting the avoidant babies' behavior], we began by noting the similarity between avoidance of the mother in the [laboratory] reunion episodes and the "detachment" behavior that has been observed to result from "major" separation experiences. ... We suggested that both mother avoidance in the [laboratory] situation and detachment during and after longer separations served a defensive function. Our next clue was to note that the mothers of [avoidant] infants were more rejecting than either [secure] or [anxious] mothers. ... One major way in which they rejected their infants was to rebuff infant desire for close bodily contact. [They were also more frequently angry or irritated than the mothers of secure and anxious/ambivalent infants, and less expressive of positive emotions. They were characterized by observers as more rigid and compulsive.] (pp. 316–317)

Notice that all three kinds of infants are "attached," although in different ways, so it makes little sense to talk about varying degrees or intensities of attachment. Instead, Ainsworth and her followers speak of the quality of attachment. This is one of the major ways in which their approach differs from a focus on unidimensional constructs such as attitude, affection, or dependency. A major goal of our recent work has been to apply Ainsworth et al.'s three-category system to the study of adult romantic love. Another goal has been to pursue Bowlby's idea that continuity in relationship style is a matter of mental models of self and relationships. A third goal has been to explore the possibility that the specific characteristics of parent–child relationships identified by Ainsworth et al. as the probable causes of differences in infant attachment styles are also among the determinants of grownups' romantic attachment styles. Details of the studies can be found in Hazan and Shaver (1987); here we summarize the major results.

## Two Studies of Love as Attachment

Our first study was based on a questionnaire that appeared in the *Rocky Mountain News*, Denver's largest circulation newspaper, in the summer of 1985. More than twelve hundred people responded, and we analyzed questionnaires from about half of them (N = 620). The survey included a "Love Quiz" comprising fourteen a priori subscales (for example, trust, jealousy, desire for reciprocation, emotional extremes), based on previous adult love measures and extrapolations from the literature on infant care-giver attachment. Subjects described their "most important" love relationship. We also included questions concerning relationships with parents (attachment history), and mental models of self and relationships. Respondents were grouped according to a single-item measure of attachment type designed by translating Ainsworth et al.'s descriptions of their infant forms into terms appropriate to adult love.

Possible limitations of the first study, especially respondents' self-selection, made it desirable to conduct a conceptual replication. We therefore tested a "captive" university student group (N = 108) and included all measures from the first study plus some new ones. Because of space limitations imposed by newspaper editors, the *Rocky Mountain News* study neglected the self side of mental models, so in the university student study we emphasized that. We also added a single classification item for the care-giving style of each parent, based on Ainsworth et al.'s descriptions of the three major kinds of mothers.

The proportions of each of the three attachment types were highly stable across studies. Table 4.2 shows how the alternatives were worded and provides the percentage of people endorsing each description. In both samples, just over half classified themselves as secure, whereas the other half split fairly evenly between the avoidant and anxious/ambivalent categories. These figures are not terribly different from the proportions reported in Ainsworth et al.'s (1978) study of infant–mother attachment. Interestingly, there were no significant sex differences, which is another parallel between our results and those from infant studies.

People with different self-designated attachment styles also differed in the way they characterized their most important love relationship. (See Table 4.3, which displays means from the *Rocky Mountain News* study.) Secure lovers described love as especially happy, friendly, and trusting, and emphasized being able to accept and support their partner despite the partner's faults. Moreover, their relationships tended to endure longer (10.02 years, on the average, compared with 4.86 years for the anxious/ambivalent and 5.97 years for the avoidant lovers), even though all three groups were the same age, on the average (36 years). Avoidant lovers were characterized by fear of intimacy, emotional highs and lows, and jealousy. They never produced the highest mean on a positive (desirable) feature of love. The anxious/ambivalent lovers experienced love as involving obsession, desire for reciprocation and union, emotional highs and lows, and extreme sexual attraction and jealousy (a pattern of emotions similar to what Tennov, 1979, called "limerence"). These effects of attachment style on love experiences were very similar in the university student study, although not all the subscales yielded significant mean differences with the smaller sample. Once again, there were no important sex differences (see Hazan & Shaver, 1987, for details).

**Table 4.2**  Adult attachment types and their frequencies

**Question:**
Which of the following best describes your feelings?

| *Answers and Percentages:* | Newspaper Sample | University Sample |
|---|---|---|
| **Secure:** | 56% | 56% |
| I find it relatively easy to get close to others and am comfortable depending on them and having them depend on me. I don't often worry about being abandoned or about someone getting too close to me. | | |
| **Avoidant:** | 25% | 23% |
| I am somewhat uncomfortable being close to others; I find it difficult to trust them completely, difficult to allow myself to depend on them. I am nervous when anyone gets too close, and often, love partners want me to be more intimate than I feel comfortable being. | | |
| **Anxious/Ambivalent:** | 19% | 20% |
| I find that others are reluctant to get as close as I would like. I often worry that my partner doesn't really love me or won't want to stay with me. I want to merge completely with another person, and this desire sometimes scares people away. | | |

**Table 4.3**  Attachment style and the experience of love

| | Attachment Type | | |
|---|---|---|---|
| | *Avoidant* | *Anxious/Ambivalent* | *Secure* |
| Happiness | 3.19 | 3.31 | **3.51** |
| Friendship | 3.18 | 3.19 | **3.50** |
| Trust | 3.11 | 3.13 | **3.43** |
| Fear of closeness | **2.30** | 2.15 | **1.88** |
| Acceptance | **2.86** | 3.03 | 3.01 |
| Emotional extremes | **2.75** | **3.05** | **2.36** |
| Jealousy | **2.57** | **2.88** | **2.17** |
| Obsessive preoccupation | 3.01 | **3.29** | 3.01 |
| Sexual attraction | 3.27 | **3.43** | 3.27 |
| Desire for union | 2.81 | **3.25** | 2.69 |
| Desire for reciprocation | 3.24 | **3.55** | 3.22 |
| Love at first sight | 2.91 | **3.17** | 2.97 |

*Note:* Statistically significant differences between means within a row are indicated by bold-face type. Where one mean differs from the other two, which do not significantly differ from each other, that one appears in boldface type. Where one mean differs significantly from one other, those two appear in boldface type. Where all three differ significantly from each other, all three are boldfaced.

We attempted to assess a generalized version of what Bowlby called working models of relationships using the items shown in Table 4.4. Each was either checked or not checked as describing how a respondent generally "view[s] the course of romantic love over time," and how he or she views self and others. Secure lovers more often said that romantic feelings wax and wane but at times reach the intensity experienced at the start of the relationship, and that in some relationships romantic love never fades. Avoidant lovers said that the kind of head-over-heels romantic love depicted in novels and movies doesn't exist in real life, that romantic love rarely lasts, and that it is rare to find a person one can *really* fall in love with. Anxious/ambivalent respondents claimed it is easy to fall in love and said they frequently feel themselves beginning to do so, although (like the avoidant lovers) they rarely find what they would call "real" love. Once again, the results were similar across our two studies and held for both sexes, although there were fewer significant differences for the smaller university sample.

Table 4.4 also includes the self-model items used only in the university student study. Secure respondents described themselves as easy to get to know and as liked by most people, and endorsed the claim that other people are generally well intentioned and good-hearted. Anxious/ambivalent lovers reported having more self-doubts, being misunderstood and under-appreciated, and finding others less willing and able than they are to commit

**Table 4.4**    Attachment style and mental models

| | Avoidant | Anxious/ Ambivalent | Secure |
|---|---|---|---|
| 1. The kind of head-over-heels romantic love depicted in novels and movies doesn't exist in real life. | .25 | .28 | .13 |
| 2. Intense romantic love is common at the beginning of a relationship, but it rarely lasts forever. | **.41** | .34 | .28 |
| 3. Romantic feelings wax and wane over the course of a relationship, but at times they can be as intense as they were at the start. | **.60** | .75 | .79 |
| 4. In some relationships, romantic love really lasts; it doesn't fade with time. | .41 | .46 | **.59** |
| 5. It's easy to fall in love. I feel myself beginning to fall in love often. | .04 | **.20** | .09 |
| 6. It's rare to find someone you can really fall in love with. | .66 | .56 | **.43** |
| 7. I am easier to get to know than most people. | .32 | .32 | **.60** |
| 8. I have more self-doubts than most people. | .48 | .64 | **.18** |
| 9. People almost always like me. | .36 | .41 | **.68** |
| 10. People often misunderstand me or fail to appreciate me. | .36 | .50 | **.18** |
| 11. Few people are as willing and able as I am to commit themselves to a long-term relationship. | .24 | **.59** | .23 |
| 12. People are generally well intentioned and good-hearted. | .44 | .32 | **.72** |

*Note:* Results for the first six items are from the newspaper sample and were replicated in the university sample; results for the last six items are from the university sample only. The system of boldfacing is explained in the note beneath Table 4.3.

themselves to a relationship. The avoidant group generally fell between the extremes set by their secure and anxious/ambivalent counter-parts, and in most cases were closer to the anxious than to the secure lovers.

Attachment history was assessed by asking respondents to describe how each parent had generally behaved toward them during childhood and how the parents had gotten along with each other. Respondents indicated their answers by checking or not checking adjectives such as *caring, critical, intrusive,* and *responsive.* Stepwise multiple regression procedures were used to determine which adjectives discriminated between attachment types considered in pairs (secure versus avoidant, and so on).

In the newspaper sample, mothers of avoidant respondents were characterized as more demanding, more disrespectful, and more critical, when compared with mothers of secure respondents. Fathers of avoidant respondents were characterized as more forceful and uncaring. The relationship between mother and father was described as not affectionate. These results fit well with Ainsworth et al.'s (1978) observations, indicating that mothers of avoidant infants are relatively cold and rejecting. When anxious/ambivalent respondents were compared with secure respondents, their mothers were portrayed as more intrusive and unfair, the fathers were described as more unfair and threatening, and the parental relationship was characterized as unhappy. The term *intrusive* was the main one used by Ainsworth et al. in their description of mothers of anxious/ambivalent infants. "Unfair" may be a child's way of characterizing that kind of parent's inconsistent and unreliable care giving. Finally, when anxious/ambivalent lovers were compared with avoidant lovers, mothers of the former were described as more responsive and funny, and their fathers were portrayed as relatively unfair but affectionate. Nothing about the parental relationship predicted differences between these two groups. This last set of results parallels Ainsworth et al.'s characterization of the mothers of avoidant infants as more uniformly negative than the mothers of anxious/ambivalent infants. In general, the results fit remarkably well with attachment theory and suggest that both mothers and fathers are important in determining their children's long-term attachment styles and that both have the same kinds of effects.

In the university student study, perceptions of relationships with parents also predicted attachment type. The specific adjectives were not identical across studies, but their meanings with respect to attachment theory were similar. The statistical results were stronger for the university students, who averaged eighteen years of age, than for the newspaper readers (who averaged thirty-six years of age), suggesting that the younger the sample, the easier it is to predict their adult attachment styles from descriptions of relationships with parents. In line with this interpretation, when the newspaper readers were divided into younger and older age groups, the connections between love styles and relationships with parents were stronger for the younger group. As distance from parents increases and adult love experiences accumulate, the effect of childhood relationships on adult mental models and behavior patterns decreases. (For more complex analyses of the parent data, see Hazan & Shaver, 1987.)

## Limitations of Our Initial Studies

The results of our first two studies provide encouraging support for an attachment-theory perspective on adult romantic love. Their major short-comings have to do with the preliminary measures of attachment constructs. First, because both questionnaires had to be brief, we were able to inquire about only a single romantic relationship. To increase the chances of detecting features of love experiences that are due to subjects' attachment styles, it might be better to ask about more than one relationship (as, for example, Hindy & Schwarz, 1984, have done). It might also be useful to assess both partners in the relationship, employing a multimethod approach (see Kobak & Sceery, 1988). Roger Kobak, in conjunction with us, is currently beginning such a study, assessing adult attachments via observational coding, intensive interviews, and self-report questionnaires.

Second, our measures were limited in terms of number of items and number of answer alternatives provided for each item. The love subscales contained only a few items each, and the questions about mental models and attachment history received either yes or no answers. In future studies it should be possible to develop highly reliable assessment scales for each of the domains and dimensions we have identified.

Finally, there are reasons to suspect that no amount of psychometric improvement will solve all the problems associated with self-report assessment of attachment-related variables. First of all, people may be unable to articulate exactly how they feel in love relationships. Second, they are unlikely to have anything like perfect recall of past love experiences or of the nature of their relationships with parents, especially during preschool years. Third, they are likely to be defensive and self-serving when recalling and describing some of the events we wish to inquire about. (See George, Kaplan, & Main, 1984, and Kobak & Sceery, 1988, for more probing and complexly scored interview procedures that may solve some of these problems.)

Another important issue has to do with continuity and change in attachment style. For theoretical reasons, we have been interested in exploring continuity between childhood and adulthood, and we consider it important that there is good evidence for some continuity between ages one and six. Nevertheless, it would be overly pessimistic from the perspective of insecurely attached people to conclude that simple continuity between early childhood and adulthood is the rule rather than the exception. The correlations we obtained between parent variables and current attachment type were statistically significant but not terribly strong, especially for older respondents.

There is evidence that thinking about and working through unpleasant childhood experiences helps people change their mental models of relationships (Main et al., 1985). This kind of insight can break the chain of cross-generational continuity, allowing once-insecure parents to respond appropriately to their young children, who then go on to become secure adults. The process by which an insecure person becomes increasingly secure, probably by participating in relationships that disconfirm negative features of experience-based mental models and/or gaining insight into the workings of one's mental models, offers an extremely important topic for future research. Obviously, the results will be especially interesting to research-guided psychotherapists.

Because some critics have called our approach Freudian, we should mention the important differences between familiar Freudian conceptions of infant-to-adult continuity, on the one hand, and the conception offered by attachment theory, on the other. Unlike the Freudian conception, according to which the supposed irrationalities of adult love indicate regression to infancy or fixation at some earlier stage of psychosexual development, attachment theory asserts that social development involves a continuing need for secure attachments and the continual construction, revision, integration, and abstraction of mental models. This latter idea, which is similar to the notion of scripts and schemas in cognitive and social psychology (for example, Fiske & Taylor, 1984), is compatible with the possibility of change based on new information and experiences, although change may become more difficult with repeated, uncorrected use of habitual models or scripts.

Freud argued his case beautifully, if not persuasively, by likening the unconscious mind to the city of Rome, which has been ravaged, revised, and rebuilt many times over the centuries. In the case of the unconscious, according to Freud, it is as if all the previous cities still exist in their original form and on the same site. Bowlby's conception is more in line with actual archaeology. The foundations and present shapes of mental models of self and social life still bear similarities and connections to their predecessors – some of the important historical landmarks, bridges, and crooked streets are still there. But few of the ancient structures exist unaltered or in mental isolation, so simple regression and fixation are unlikely. There is continuity in attachment behavior, but there can also be significant change.

# Three Behavioral Systems: Attachment, Care Giving, and Sexuality

Aside from measurement problems, our attachment-theoretical approach to romantic love must overcome some sizable conceptual obstacles. In our preliminary studies, we chose largely to overlook the fact that child–parent relationships differ in important ways from adult romantic relationships. One of the most striking differences is that romantic love is usually a two-way street between people with approximately equal power and status; both partners are sometimes anxious and security seeking and at other times able providers of security and care. A second important difference is that romantic love almost always involves sexual attraction (Berscheid, 1988), whereas only the most speculative psychoanalysts have claimed that infants' attachments to parents are sexual in nature.

Bowlby (1969) and Ainsworth (for example, 1982, 1985) have already provided the conceptual tools with which to attack this problem. In the same way that exploration and foraging are behavioral systems that differ from attachment, Bowlby and Ainsworth have argued that care giving and mating (or sexual reproduction) are behavioral systems distinct from attachment.

The care-giving system is the one activated in a parent when his or her child displays attachment behaviors. In its optimal form it includes sensitivity and responsiveness, behaviors aimed at soothing the child (holding, patting, rocking), and attempts at problem solution. Like attachment behaviors on the part of infants, care-giving responses on the part of parents can easily be observed among nonhuman primates (and other mammals). In the case of parents and infants, the care-giving and attachment systems are naturally complementary. When the infant's attachment system is active, it elicits care-giving behavior from the parent; when the parent's care-giving system is active, it produces behaviors that ease the child's distress. In the same way that attachment reactions can be distorted by faulty care giving, the care-giving system can be distorted by nonoptimal social-learning experiences. In fact, the various forms of deficient parenting observed by Ainsworth et al. (1978) – including rejection, intrusiveness, and inconsistency – can be viewed as distortions in the parents' care-giving systems that are due to faulty socialization experiences.

The sexual system requires less comment. Animals, including humans, have been constructed by evolution to place a high priority on sexual reproduction. Sexual desires are among the strongest motivators of human behavior, and sexual gratification is one of the greatest human pleasures. The cycle of desire and arousal followed by sexual behavior and orgasm can easily be viewed as an innate system with an important biological function. Perhaps less obvious but nevertheless well documented is the vulnerability of the sexual system to deviations and distortions caused by nonoptimal socialization and sexual experiences. (Consider, for example, the "perversions" that captured Freud's attention and the sexual "dysfunctions" studied by Masters and Johnson, among others.)

Of the three biologically based behavioral systems – attachment, care giving, and sexuality – attachment would seem to be the preeminent system, developmentally speaking. It arises first and adapts itself to whatever care-giving environment happens to be encountered. It seems reasonable to suppose that care giving is learned, at least in its rudimentary forms, by modeling the behavior of primary attachment figures or, less commonly, by responding to an attachment figure's need for care. If so, people should grow up exhibiting the same kinds of care-giving deficiencies evident in their own care givers' behavior, or at least with deficiencies related to those care givers' needs and behaviors, a sad conclusion for which there is growing evidence (for example, Hazan & Shaver, 1987; Main et al., 1985; Ricks, 1985).

Because the attachment system is the first social-behavioral system to develop, it plays an important role in the creation of cognitive models of social life. During the first months and years of life everyone learns what to expect from others, especially attachment figures, and reaches some important conclusions about the self, perhaps both as a care giver and as a love object. Later, when the care-giving system and the sexual system become more fully developed, mental models of the social world constructed during infancy and early childhood are likely to be invoked. Thus, the functioning of all social-behavioral systems is, to a certain degree, influenced by what happens when attachment is first attempted.

Given the division of love into three somewhat independent behavioral systems – attachment, care giving, and sexuality – how might we expect love to develop over time? Clearly, the three systems need not follow the same time course, a fact that allows us to account for the many conceptual schemes developed over the years to explain differences in types of love and changes over time in the form of love. Table 4.5 summarizes some of these schemes.

The first one, a tripartite division proposed by Wilson (1981), is very similar to Bowlby's, which is not surprising given their mutual reliance on evolutionary biology. The second scheme is based on a factor analysis of Rubin's (1973) well-known love scale by Steck, Levitan, McLane, and Kelley (1982). The scale, especially as elaborated by

**Table 4.5** Previous conceptions of love componentscompared with attachment theory's attachment, care-giving, and sexuality components

| Authors | Attachment | Care giving | Sexuality |
|---|---|---|---|
| Wilson (1981) | attachment | parental protection | sex |
| Rubin (1973); Steck et al. (1982) | trust | caring | need |
| Berscheid & Walster (1974); Walster & Walster (1978) | companionate love | | passionate love |
| Sternberg (1986) | intimacy and commitment | | passion |
| Tennov (1979) | limerence | | limerence |
| | love | | |

Steck et al., contains three components very similar to Bowlby's, although to the best of our knowledge the similarities have not been noted before. The remaining three schemes are representative of much of the social psychological literature. Tennov (1979) distinguished between "limerence," on the one hand, a neologism for what Berscheid and Walster (1974, Walster & Walster, 1978) called passionate love, and "love," on the other hand, which the latter authors called companionate love. It is common to claim, as Walster and Walster did, that passionate love precedes and somehow becomes transformed into companionate love, but the reasons for the transformation are usually left vague.

Sternberg's (1986) scheme is a bit different. It includes three rather than two components: passion, intimacy, and commitment, each of which follows its own time course. Passion rises quickly and then typically drops off; commitment gradually rises and then levels off, in a step-function fashion; intimacy grows slowly and steadily over a long period of time. The unique feature of this scheme is the inclusion of commitment, which Sternberg seems to view more as a decision than as an emotional process. Whether all aspects of commitment can be so viewed (for example, the gradual commitment of time and resources to a relationship; the gradual constraints a couple experiences as family and friends begin to view them as a unit) is still a matter of debate (for example, Stanley, 1986).

The advantage of the attachment approach is that the three systems it highlights – attachment, care giving, and sexuality – all make biological sense and have the status of behavioral systems. Whether commitment makes similar sense remains to be seen. Sternberg's (1986) time-course analysis of love, according to which different components of love (passion, commitment, and intimacy) increase (and in some cases decline) at different rates, also applies to the three behavioral systems. Sexual attraction can increase very quickly and pull people into a relationship. Attachment and care giving, both perhaps aspects of what Sternberg calls intimacy, develop more slowly. In a secure relationship, attachment and care giving probably develop in tandem, each person providing responsive kindness and support which the other person comfortably relies upon.

In the various kinds of insecure relationships, the attachment and care-giving components take distorted forms (Bowlby, 1979), three of which are compulsive self-reliance (common among avoidant types), compulsive care giving (another, less common strategy of vulnerability avoidance), and premature attachment (common among anxious/ambivalent lovers, who, as our results indicate, are eager for union and commitment). The exact nature of such relationships and the reasons for their early demise (as revealed by our newspaper sample, in which secure people's relationships lasted twice as long, on the average, as those of insecure people) are high-priority topics for future research. We suspect that the distinction between attachment and care giving will prove important, since a lover can be attached to someone (be dependent for emotional security on that person) without also being an adequate care giver.

It is important to understand, while considering the time course of love, that by calling romantic love an attachment process we do not mean to imply that the early phases of romance are equivalent to *being attached*. Our idea, which needs further development, is that romantic love is a biological process designed by evolution to facilitate attachment between adult sexual partners who, at the time love evolved, were likely to become parents of an infant who would need their reliable care. Romantic love and infant care-giver attachment thus both contribute to reproduction and survival. As Bowlby said in a passage quoted earlier, "The formation of [an attachment] bond is described as falling in love, maintaining a bond as loving someone." The early phases of romance are, when all goes well, the processes of bond formation (and, before the invention of birth control, of sexual reproduction); the long-term result – again, if all goes well – is attachment among members of a nuclear family.

Why does romantic love seem to wane after a period of months or years? The usual reason offered is that sexual attraction just naturally declines, especially among males for whom it supposedly makes evolutionary sense to seek new sexual partners (Wilson, 1981). Another reason may have to do with the dynamics of attachment. If one's lover repeatedly proves to be available and responsive, the fear component of the attachment system (refer back to Figure 4.1) becomes quiescent, and a feeling of security reigns. In childhood, the process of establishing such taken-for-granted security occupies about three years. According to Bowlby (1969), "By most children attachment behavior is exhibited strongly and regularly until almost the end of the third year. Then a change occurs. . . . In many children the change seems to take place almost abruptly, suggesting that at this age some maturational threshold is passed" (pp. 204–205). Surprisingly, and perhaps only coincidentally, the time period most often mentioned in connection with the duration of romantic love is also three years (for example, Tennov, 1979).

When romantic passion wanes, problems in care giving are likely to arise. We suspect that this, rather than the decline of passion per se (which most marital relationships survive), largely accounts for the fact, mentioned earlier, that the relationships of avoidant and anxious/ambivalent respondents to our newspaper survey lasted little more than a few years, on the average. When two lovers are no longer preoccupied by sexual attraction, they can more easily see each other's care-giving deficiencies and will perhaps weigh those more heavily in deciding whether the relationship is rewarding and equitable (Hatfield, Traupmann, Sprecher, Utne, & Hay, 1985).

## Broken Attachments: Grieving for Lost Love

An advantage of the attachment-theoretical approach to adult love is that it helps explain the powerful emotional reactions that accompany broken relationships, whether they come about through separation, divorce, or death. It is hard to see how love-as-an-attitude theorists or love-as-labeled-arousal theorists could say very much about this, whereas attachment theory was designed from the start to deal with separation and loss as well as with love. When loss of a spouse occurs, for example, especially if it occurs abruptly, the typical reaction is similar to separation distress in infancy, including uncontrollable restlessness, difficulty in concentrating, disturbed sleep, anxiety, tension, and anger. These are deep and uncontrollable reactions, which Bowlby argues are biologically designed to regain the lost attachment figure. They therefore seem irrational in situations where contact with the lost figure is temporarily or permanently impossible. Consider the following examples, one involving a three-year-old child whose mother left him in a residential nursery, the other involving a young wife whose husband was killed in a car accident.

> Patrick tried to keep his promise and was not seen crying. [His mother had told him to be a good boy and not to cry; otherwise she would not visit him.] Instead he would nod his head whenever anyone looked at him and assured himself and anybody who cared to listen that his mother would come for him, she would put on his overcoat and would take him home with her again. Whenever a listener seemed to believe him he was satisfied; when anybody contradicted him, he would burst into violent tears. . .
>
> Later an ever-growing list of clothes that his mother was supposed to put on him was added: She will put on my overcoat and my leggings, she will zip up the zipper, she will put on my pixie hat.
>
> When the repetitions of this formula became monotonous and endless, somebody asked him whether he could not stop saying it all over again. Again Patrick tried to be the good boy that his mother wanted him to be. He stopped repeating the formula aloud, but his moving lips showed that he was saying it over and over to himself.
>
> At the same time he substituted for the spoken words gestures that showed the position of his pixie hat, the putting on of an imaginary coat, the zipping of the zipper, etc. . . . While the other children were mostly busy with their toys, playing games, making music, etc., Patrick, totally uninterested, would stand somewhere in a corner, moving his hands and lips with an absolutely tragic expression on his face. (Freud & Burlingham, 1943, p. 89)

Obviously, the attachment system does not relax in response to simple environmental demands that it do so. The same holds for adult attachment. The following passages are taken from an interview with a woman who was notified that her husband had been injured in an accident. When she arrived at the hospital emergency room, they directed her to the morgue, which, if rationality had prevailed, would have indicated that her husband was dead and that calling him was futile.

> We went in and told them what we were looking for and that we wanted to identify him. But he was already identified. They had his name down, just like it was on the cards in his wallet. The man finally came up and took us down. You know, you have to go down, walk down the steps. And I knew he was dead. . .
>
> I walked in and felt his skin. It was just as warm as mine. He was lying there just like he's in bed some nights, with his eyes half opened. And I closed them, and I rubbed his face, and I called him for twenty minutes. And the man told me, "Lady, your husband didn't even go to the accident room. Your husband came right here, because he was dead when he left the scene."
>
> I didn't believe it. I stayed for twenty minutes. I rubbed him, I rubbed his face, I patted him, I rubbed his head. I called him, but he didn't answer. And I knew if I called him he'd answer because he's used to my voice. But he didn't answer me. They said he was dead, but his skin was just as warm as mine. . . . I thought, well, maybe if I stay here and call him, maybe he'll answer me, because he didn't look like he was dead. (Parkes & Weiss, 1983, pp. 83–84)

Weeks later, the young widow was still having what she recognized to be a mysteriously difficult time accepting her husband's death: "It's been like that ever since he died. I listen for the key in that bottom door. . . . I went over and saw him and identified him and still I said, 'Well, he'll be home.' I know he's there, buried, but right now I don't believe it. I have it in my mind that he'll come home. It's a mystery how a grown-up would say that. But I really have it in my mind that he'll come home around 5:00" (Parkes & Weiss, 1983, p. 85). As anyone knows who has been through such an experience, yearning for the lost person can continue for months or years and can be mingled with anger at the person for leaving – even though that, too, is recognized as "irrational." We would say that the attachment system is more primitive than rationality, which is why both intense romantic love and intense grieving for a lost love seem uncontrollable and hence a bit "crazy." The system as a whole, however, does not seem *crazy* at all, given its important biological functions in both infancy and adulthood. It only looks crazy when its goals are unattainable.

The same thing might be said with respect to irrational-seeming religious experiences (Brehm, 1988). Widows and widowers, as well as children like little Patrick, can think so intently of their absent primary attachment figure that he or she seems actually to be present. In fact, it is normal for adults to hallucinate the presence of their dead spouse, to plead with him or her for help (in making important life decisions, for example), and to try to live in ways that would please the person. The attachment figure need not be physically present for such an "interaction" to take place, which makes it more understandable that people have imaginary but very convincing and affecting interactions with rock singers, dead philosophers, and religious figures of all kinds. Attachment, separation distress, and grieving are primarily psychological processes; they require psychological, not physical, interaction partners, Since adult attachment often involves three interwoven behavioral systems – attachment, care giving, and sexuality – it is natural that relations, say, between mystics and their image of Jesus can involve soothing his wounds, drying his tears, and expressing intense feelings that border on sexual passion.

## Conclusion

What lessons can be drawn from our comparison of love and attachment? One implication is that love is a complex dynamic system involving cognitions, emotions, and behaviors. It is not a unidimensional phenomenon, not an attitude, not a simple state of labeled physiological arousal. Consider how impoverished the psychology of infant care-giver bonding would be if the concept of attachment were replaced by the idea that infants have a positive attitude toward their mothers or get physiologically aroused in the presence of their mothers and interpret this as love. These conceptions seem almost facetious until one realizes that they are taken directly from the social psychology of romantic love. If anything, adult love should be more, not less, complicated than infant caregiver attachment, involving as it does a much more differentiated understanding of self, others, and both real and ideal relationships; a much longer history of relationship experiences; more mature feelings of empathy; and adult sexuality.

Another implication, although one that needs further conceptual and empirical analysis, is that love, like early attachment, has biological bases and functions. According to Bowlby (1969), infants emerge from the womb ready for attachment because, in evolutionary history, physical proximity to a care giver greatly increased infants' chances of survival. Subsequent theorists have added that more than immediate biological survival is at stake. The relationship between infant and care giver is the infant's ticket to emotional self-regulation, education about the environment, and training in social skills. Does romantic love have similarly consequential functions? One obvious possibility is that love encourages sexual reproduction; but, as sociobiologists have pointed out, sexual attraction in itself, and hence reproduction, would not require attachment. Thus, the function of attachment between adult lovers may be primarily to increase the likelihood of parental health, stability, and investment in offspring. More speculative is the possibility that the happiness, openness, and care giving associated with adult love fosters good parenting behavior.

A third implication is that romantic love, although perhaps based on a single, general biological system or an interrelated set of systems, takes on somewhat different forms depending on a person's attachment history. Tennov's (1979) well-known distinction between "limerence," a passionate, painful sort of romantic love, and "love," a calmer state of friendship and support, may be similar to our distinction between anxious/ambivalent and secure love. The same distinction may help explain individual differences in religious experiences discussed by Brehm (1988). Perhaps some of the most florid religious experiences, like some of the great human love affairs, depend on the existence of people who are desperately seeking a form of security never attainable in previous relationships.

There are many research-worthy mysteries in the domain of romantic love. We will close by mentioning three. First, what is the role of perceptual and cognitive model building during the early phases of attachment and love? The fact that infants stare with intense interest at their mother for much of the first few months of life, gradually achieving an integrated picture of her that allows for quick recognition (and perhaps contributes to feelings of pleasure and reassurance in her absence), has seemed natural enough to researchers. After all, the infant's nervous system is physically immature and has had no previous experience with visual perception. But what about the seemingly parallel phase of adult love: gazing intently at the partner, being fascinated with his or her physical features, mannerisms, personal history, and so on? What about the dreaming, daydreaming, and cognitive preoccupation with the new love object? Could it be that here, too, the mind seeks a particularly complete representation of the lover, perhaps because, once enshrined at the center of the subject's social network, this person is destined to play a highly significant role in the subject's emotional life?

Second, what role, if any, is played by successive love relationships in childhood? Presumably there is never a direct mental leap from infant attachment to adult love, but instead a long series of infatuations and crushes about which psychologists seem to know almost nothing (for an exception, see Easton, Hatfield & Synodinos, 1984). While writing this chapter, the three of us found that we could easily recall such infatuations, running back at least to kindergarten, and the memories included vivid imagery and still-significant feelings. These memorable relationships, however fragmentary and short-lived they may have been, seem to have left an indelible mark on us. In his book about love, sociologist Jack Douglas (1988; personal communication) argues, mostly on the basis of personal experience, that childhood crush partners form a psychological bridge between parents and subsequent adult romantic partners, and that the kind of people a particular individual finds attractive and lovable can be traced back to parents only through a history of infatuations. This would seem to create problems for our analysis of adult love in terms of three behavioral systems – attachment, care giving, and sexuality. Do all three of these exist in rudimentary forms in childhood crushes? If not, which is primary? Why do memories of crushes seem to involve all the components of romantic love: pleasure, yearning, desire to touch and be near, attempts to be generous and kind, and so on?

Finally, the attachment literature is alive with controversy concerning the role of temperament and care-giver continuity in the determination of temporal stability of attachment styles (Campos, Barrett, Lamb, Goldsmith, & Stenberg, 1983; Lamb, Thompson, Bardner, Charnov, & Estes, 1984; Waters, 1983). These controversies are relevant to our attempt to find connections between early attachment experiences and adult love. If infant temperament is, say, even half as important as parental responsiveness in determining whether the attachment bond will be anxious, secure, or avoidant, and if temperament persists throughout life, part of the continuity in attachment style from infancy to adulthood may be temperamental. And if the stability of attachment behavior between infancy and the early school years is due largely not just to intrapsychic continuity in the child but to stability in the parent–child relationship which is supplied mainly by the parents, then the degree of continuity between infancy and adulthood may vary widely depending on the continuity or discontinuity of a person's actual relationships over time.

Clearly, there is still a great deal to be learned about romantic love. It seems likely that attachment theory will be helpful in mapping the terrain.

# References

Ainsworth, M. D. S. (1982). Attachment: Retrospect and prospect. In C. M. Parkes & J. Stevenson-Hinde (Eds.). *The place of attachment in human behavior* (pp. 3–30). New York: Basic Books.

Ainsworth, M. D. S. (1985). Attachments across the life span. *Bulletin of the New York Academy of Medicine, 61,* 792–811.

Ainsworth, M. D. S., Blehar, M. C., Waters, E., & Wall, S. (1978). *Patterns of attachment: A psychological study of the strange situation.* Hillsdale, NJ: Erlbaum.

Averill, J. R. (1985). The social construction of emotion: With special reference to love. In K. J. Gergen & K. E. Davis (Eds.). *The social construction of the person* (pp. 89–109). New York: Springer-Verlag.

Bell, S. M., & Ainsworth, M. D. S. (1972). Infant crying and maternal responsiveness. *Child Development, 43,* 1171–1190.

Berscheid, E., & Walster, E. (1974). A little bit about love. In T. L. Huston (Ed.). *Foundations of interpersonal attraction* (pp. 355–381). New York: Academic Press.

Berscheid, E. (1988). Some comments on love's anatomy: Or, whatever happened to oldfashioned lust? In R. J. Sternberg, & M. L. Barnes (Eds.). *The psychology of love* (pp. 359–374). New Haven, CT: Yale University Press.

Bowlby, J. (1969). *Attachment and loss: Vol. 1. Attachment.* New York: Basic Books.

Bowlby, J. (1973). *Attachment and loss: Vol. 2. Separation: Anxiety and anger.* New York: Basic Books.

Bowlby, J. (1979). *The making and breaking of affectional bonds.* London: Tavistock.

Bowlby, J. (1980). *Attachment and loss: Vol. 3. Loss.* New York: Basic Books.

Brehm, S. S. (1988). Passionate love. In R. J. Sternberg & M. L. Barnes (Eds.).*The psychology of love* (pp. 232–263). New Haven, CT and London: Yale University Press.

Bretherton, I. (1985). Attachment theory: Retrospect and prospect. *Monographs of the Society for Research in Child Development, 50* (1–2), 3–35.

Campos, J. J., Barrett, K. C., Lamb, M. E., Goldsmith, H. H., & Stenberg, C. (1983). Socioemotional development. In M. M. Haith & J. J. Campos (Eds.). *Handbook of child psychology: Vol. 2. Infancy and psychobiology* (pp. 783–915). New York: Wiley.

Campos, J. J., Emde, R. N., Gaensbauer, T. J., & Henderson, C. (1975). Cardiac and behavioral interrelationships in the reactions of infants to strangers. *Developmental Psychology, 11,* 589–601.

Cohen, L., & Campos, J. (1974). Father, mother, and stranger as elicitors of attachment behaviors in infancy. *Developmental Psychology, 10,* 146–154.

De Rougement, D. (1940). *Love in the Western world.* New York: Harcourt.

Dontas, C., Maratos, O., Fafoutis, M., & Karangelis, A. (1985). Early social development in institutionally reared Greek infants: Attachment and peer interaction. *Monographs of the Society for Research in Child Development, 50* (1–2), 136–146.

Douglas, J. D., & Atwell, F. C. (1988). *Love, intimacy, and sex.* Beverly Hills, CA: Sage.

Driscoll, R., Davis, K. E., & Lipetz, M. E. (1972). Parental influence and romantic love: The Romeo and Juliet effect. *Journal of Personality and Social Psychology, 24,* 1–10.

Erickson, M. F., Sroufe, L. A., & Egeland, B. (1985). The relationship between quality of attachment and behavior problems in preschool in a high-risk sample. *Monographs of the Society for Research in Child Development, 50* (1–2), 147–166.

Fiske, S. T., & Taylor, S. E. (1984). *Social cognition.* Reading, MA: Addison-Wesley.

Freud, A., & Burlingham, D. (1943). *War and children.* New York: International Universities Press.

George, C., Kaplan, N., & Main, M. (1984). *Attachment interview for adults.* Unpublished manuscript, University of California at Berkeley.

Haith, M. M., Bergman, T., & Moore, M. J. (1977). Eye contact and face scanning in early infancy. *Science, 198,* 853–855.

Hatfield, E., Traupmann, J., Sprecher, S., Utne, M., & Hay, J. (1985). Equity and intimate relations: Recent research. In W. Ickes (Ed.). *Compatible and incompatible relationships* (pp. 91–117). New York: Springer-Verlag.

Hazan, C., & Shaver, P. (1987). Romantic love conceptualized as an attachment process. *Journal of Personality and Social Psychology, 52,* 511–524.

Heinicke, C., & Westheimer, I. (1966). *Brief separations.* New York: International Universities Press.

Hindy, C. G., & Schwarz, J. C. (1984). *Individual differences in the tendency toward anxious romantic attachments.* Paper presented at the Second International Conference on Personal Relationships, Madison, WI.

Kaye, K. (1982). *The mental and social life of babies: How parents create persons.* Chicago: University of Chicago Press.

Kobak, R. R., & Sceery, A. (1988). Attachment in late adolescence: Working models, affect regulation, and representations of self and others. *Child Development, 59,* 135–146.

Konner, M. (1982). *The tangled wing: Biological constraints on the human spirit.* New York: Holt, Rinehart, & Winston.

Lamb, M. E., Thompson, R. A., Bardner, W. P., Charnov, E. L., & Estes, D. (1984). Security of infantile attachment as assessed in the "strange situation": Its study and biological interpretation. *Behavioral and Brain Sciences, 7,* 157–181.

Mahler, M. S., Pine, F., & Bergman, A. (1975). *The psychological birth of the human infant.* New York: Basic Books.

Main, M., Kaplan, N., & Cassidy, J. (1985). Security in infancy, childhood, and adulthood: A move to the level of representation. *Monographs of the Society for Research in Child Development, 50* (1–2), 66–104.

McCready, L. E. (1981). *Experiences of being in love: An interview study describing peak times in reciprocal love relationships.* Unpublished doctoral dissertation, New York University.

Mellen, S. L. W. (1981). *The evolution of love.* San Francisco: W. H. Freeman.

Miller, G. A., Galanter, E., & Pribram, K. H. (1960). *Plans and the structure of behavior.* New York: Holt.

Morgan, S., & Ricciuti, H. (1969). Infants' responses to strangers during the first year. In B. Foss (Ed.). *Determinants of infant behavior* (Vol. 4, pp. 253–272). London: Methuen.

Parkes, C. M., & Weiss, R. S. (1983). *Recovery from bereavement.* New York: Basic Books.

Pope, K. S., & Associates. (1980). *On love and loving: Psychological perspectives on the nature and experience of romantic love.* San Francisco: Jossey-Bass.

Reedy, M. N., Birren, J. E., & Schaie, K. W. (1981). Age and sex differences in satisfying love relationships across the adult life span. *Human Development, 24,* 52–66.

Reik, T. (1941). *Of love and lust.* New York: Farrar, Straus, & Cudahy.

Ricks, M. H. (1985). The social transmission of parental behavior: Attachment across generations. *Monographs of the Society for Research in Child Development, 50* (1–2), 211–227.

Robeson, K. S. (1967). The role of eye contact in maternal–infant attachment. *Journal of Child Psychology and Psychiatry, 8,* 13–25.

Rubin, Z. (1973). *Liking and loving: An invitation to social psychology.* New York: Holt, Rinehart, & Winston.

Sappho. (6th C. BC/1958). *Sappho: A new translation* (M. Barnard, Trans.). Chicago: University of Chicago Press.

Schachter, S. (1964). The interaction of cognitive and physiological determinants of emotional state. In L. Berkowitz (Ed.). *Advances in experimental social psychology* (Vol. 1). New York: Academic Press.

Schaffer, H. R., & Emerson, P. (1964). The development of social attachments in infancy. *Monographs of the Society for Research in Child Development, 29* (3, serial no. 94).

Shaver, P., Hazan, C., & Bradshaw, D. (1984). *Infant-caretaker attachment and adult romantic love: Similarities and differences, continuities and discontinuities.* Paper presented at the Second International Conference on Personal Relationships, Madison, WI.

Sroufe, L. A. (1983). Infant–caregiver attachment and patterns of adaptation in preschool: The roots of maladaptation and competence. In M. Perlmutter (Ed.). *Minnesota Symposium on Child Psychology* (Vol. 16, pp. 41–83). Hillsdale, NJ: Erlbaum.

Sroufe, L. A., & Waters, E. (1977). Attachment as an organizational construct. *Child Development, 48,* 1184–1199.

Stanley, S. M. (1986). *Commitment and the maintenance and enhancement of relationships.* Unpublished doctoral dissertation, University of Denver.

Stayton, D., & Ainsworth, M. D. S. (1973). Development of separation behavior in the first year of life: Protest, following, and greeting. *Developmental Psychology, 9,* 213–225.

Steck, L., Levitan, D., McLane, D., & Kelley, H. H. (1982). Care, need, and conceptions of love. *Journal of Personality and Social Psychology, 43,* 481–491.

Stern, D. (1977). *The first relationship: Infant and mother.* Cambridge, MA: Harvard University Press.

Sternberg, R. J. (1986). A triangular theory of love. *Psychological Review, 93,* 119–135.

Sternberg, R. J., & Grajek, S. (1984). The nature of love. *Journal of Personality and Social Psychology, 47,* 312–329.

Tennov, D. (1979). *Love and limerence: The experience of being in love.* New York: Stein & Day.

Tracy, R. L., Lamb, M. E., & Ainsworth, M. D. S. (1976). Infant approach behavior as related to attachment. *Child Development, 47,* 571–578.

Vaillant, G. E. (1977). *Adaptation to life: How the best and the brightest came of age.* Boston: Little, Brown.

Walster, E., & Walster, G. W. (1978). *A new look at love.* Reading, MA: Addison-Wesley.

Waters, E. (1983). The stability of individual differences in infant attachment: Comments on the Thompson, Lamb, and Estes contribution. *Child Development, 54,* 516–520.

Waters, E., Wippman, J., & Sroufe, L. A. (1979). Attachment, positive affect, and competence in the peer group: Two studies in construct validation. *Child Development,* 50, 821–829.

Weiss, R. S. (1979). The emotional impact of marital separation. In G. Levinger & O. C. Moles (Eds.). *Divorce and separation: Context, causes, and consequences.* New York: Basic Books.

Wilson, G. (1981). *The Coolidge effect: An evolutionary account of human sexuality.* New York: Morrow.

# 5

# Relationships, Self, and Individual Adaptation

## L. Alan Sroufe

*The process out of which the self arises is a social process which implies interaction of individuals. . . . Selves can only exist in definite relationships to other selves. No hard-and-fast line can be drawn between our own selves and the selves of others, since our own selves exist and enter as such into our experience only in so far as the selves of others exist and enter as such into our experience also.*

—George Herbert Mead (1934)

The basic thesis underlying this book is that most problems in the early years, while often manifest poignantly in child behavior, are best conceptualized as relationship problems. This position immediately suggests a number of interrelated issues. In general, what justification is there for attributing such a powerful influence to social relationships? Second, if it is the relationship that is disordered, why is the disorder so strongly manifest in infant and child behavior? And how do what begin as disorders in relationships become disorders in individuals, even when they are no longer in the context of that relationship? All of these questions may be approached by considering what is perhaps a more fundamental developmental question, namely, what is the role of social relations in the emergence and formation of the self or individual person?

In this chapter we will present a beginning conceptualization of the self, describe the developmental process by which the self emerges from early relationships, and explore the implications of variations in the self for individual patterns of adaptation. In brief, it will be argued that self should be conceived as an inner organization of attitudes, feelings, expectations, and meanings, which arises from an organized caregiving matrix. That is, the dyadic infant–caregiver organization precedes and gives rise to the organization that is self. The self-organization, in turn, has significance for ongoing adaptation and experience, including later social behavior. Distortions in self-organization are influenced by distortions in prior dyadic organization, and subsequent problems in individual behavioral organization (adaptation) are most clearly manifest in distorted social relationships. The self is a social creation, and it is defined, maintained, and transformed with reference to others. For these reasons social relations are viewed as having such fundamental importance in both normal and pathological development. The answer to the question of how a relationship disorder comes also to be an individual disorder is the same as the explanation of how individual personality is formed within relationships. Each personality, whether healthy or disordered, is a product of the history of vital relationships.

*Source:* L. Alan Sroufe, "Relationships, Self, and Individual Adaptation," pp. 70–94 from *Relationship Disturbances in Early Childhood*, eds. Arnold J. Sameroff, Robert N. Emde (New York: Basic Books, 1989). Copyright © 1992. Reprinted by permission of Basic Books, an imprint of Hachette Book Group, Inc.

*Attachment Theory and Research: A Reader*, First Edition. Edited by Tommie Forslund and Robbie Duschinsky.
© 2021 John Wiley & Sons Ltd. Published 2021 by John Wiley & Sons Ltd.

## An Organizational Perspective

As outlined by Arnold Sameroff (1989), behavior, development, and personality may be viewed within a systems or organizational perspective. Behavior is examined not simply in terms of what the person does or how frequently but in light of how any given behavior is organized with other behaviors and with respect to context. Similarly, development is viewed not simply as the addition of new capacities but in terms of the changing organization of capacities according to the principle of hierarchical integration. Existing capacities and levels of organization are subordinated and integrated into new, more complex levels of organization. Finally, personality no longer is viewed as a collection of static traits or dispositions. It is not a thing or a collection of things that persons possess in certain degrees; rather, it is the organization of attitudes, feelings, expectations, and behaviors of the person across contexts (Block & Block, 1980; Breger, 1974; Loevinger, 1976; Sroufe, 1979a).

The following everyday example may be used to illustrate some of the implications of an organizational viewpoint: A twelve-month-old infant sits playing with a variety of toys on the floor of a laboratory playroom. Her mother sits a short distance away. As the child examines various objects in front of her, a large puzzle piece (a brightly colored carrot) captures her attention. She grasps the carrot with widened eyes. Then, in a smooth motion, she turns and extends it toward the mother, smiling broadly and vocalizing. Mother returns her smile and comments about the carrot.

The significance of this sequence is not in the simple showing of the toy, which would be as commonly manifest toward strangers as toward mothers at this age (Rheingold & Eckerman, 1973), but in the total organization of the behavior. In the first place, one notes the *integration* of the toy show with the other behaviors. (Showing of a toy accompanied by both smiling and vocalizing is rarely directed toward strangers by twelve-month-olds.) Second, one notes the *sequential organization* of the behavior. The child recognizes the object and then directly (as if the sequence has become automated or unitized) shares her delight with the mother. The *meaning* of this organized pattern of behavior ("affective sharing") is fundamentally different from the meaning of toy shows to a stranger ("affiliative gestures"), which are not organized with respect to exploration and mastery of the object world in the same way. In hundreds of cases, one would rarely see an infant in the course of intensive exploration turn and affectively share a discovery with a stranger.

The behavior pattern also reveals the *hierarchically organized* nature of development. One sees the incorporation of earlier visual and object manipulation skills, prelinguistic communication skills, and early attachment behavior (looking, vocalizing, maintaining proximity) into intentional social behavior, all mediated by affect.

One may also look at this example in terms of a changing organization in the dyadic social relationship. First one sees a change in the way the dyadic system meets the infant's need for security. In the early weeks of life caregivers physically hold infants as a means of comforting. Later, by four to six months when the infant is on the caregiver's knee *en face,* the "holding" is with eyes and voice (Brazelton, Koslowski, & Main, 1974). Then, by twelve months, as in our example, looks, shows, vocalization, and the sharing of affect are sufficient for the maintenance of psychological contact. In toddlers, such contact may be maintained even when visual contact is blocked (Carr, Dabbs, & Can, 1975). Second, qualitative change is noted at each point in terms of the increasingly active role played by the infant. By twelve months it is no longer always caregiver picking up and holding the infant; the infant maintains contact as well. We will return to this point later.

The emerging self and individual differences in personality are also best captured in organizational terms. There are indeed individual differences in the quality of affective sharing among infants and in the tendencies to seek and be reassured by physical contact. But even more important are the timing, flexibility, and organization of such behaviors with respect to context. Similarly, in older children one might assess general level of activity or exuberance or capacity for planning and restraint; yet far more informative would be assessments of the child's organization of such capacities with regard to context. The "ego resilient" child is the child who may be spontaneous and exuberant on the playground when circumstances permit and controlled and planful during classroom instruction when circumstances require (Block & Block, 1980).

When personality is viewed in organizational terms, the formative importance of early social relations with primary caregivers becomes apparent. Others, of course, evoke and respond to behaviors of the infant. But beyond this, relationships provide the framework and context within which behaviors are organized. When one asks, organized with respect to what? in the case of the infant's behavior the answer clearly is, *the caregiver.* Finally, as will be a major thesis of this chapter, the relationship is itself an organization (Sroufe and Fleeson, 1986), from which the self emerges.

# The Emergence of the Self

## The dyadic system

Accounting for the emergence of the self presents a basic developmental problem. Self as an inner organization of attitudes, expectations, and feelings cannot be conceived of in the newborn, whose cortex shows little dendritic elaboration and little interconnection with midbrain emotional structures (Minkowski, 1967; Schade, Meeter, & van Goeningen, 1962); yet to posit the self simply as emergent at some later period (something arising from nothing) is a nondevelopmental solution. Louis Sander (1975) has pointed the way to a developmental approach to this problem by postulating that organization exists from the outset, but that the organization resides in the infant–caregiver *dyadic system*. The developmental account, then, traces the origins of the inner organization (self) from the dyadic organization – from dyadic behavioral regulation to self-regulation. From an organizational matrix constructed around the infant, to organized patterns of behavior that make room for increasing participation of the infant, to a "dim recognition" of "his own role in determining action", the "stage is set" for self-regulatory core" (p. 141).

The view that the self is a social product has, of course, been widely held. It is a cornerstone of the theoretical positions of George Herbert Mead (1934) and James Mark Baldwin (1897). Baldwin wrote that the self "is a pole or terminus at one end of an opposition in the sense of personality generally, and that the other pole or terminus is . . . the other person" (p. 15), and further that the child is "at every stage . . . really in part someone else" (p. 30). Soren Kierkegaard (1938) poetically summarized the idea of self as a social product:

> The loving mother teaches her child to walk alone. She is far enough from him so that she cannot actually support him, but she holds out her arms to him. She imitates his movements, and if he totters, she swiftly bends as if to seize him, so that the child might believe that he is not walking alone. . . . And yet, she does more. Her face beckons like a reward, an encouragement. Thus, the child walks alone with his eyes fixed on his mother's face, not on the difficulties in his way. He supports himself by the arms that do not hold him and constantly strives towards the refuge in his mother's embrace, little suspecting that in the very same moment that he is emphasizing his need of her, he is proving that he can without her, because he is walking alone. (p. 85)

The idea of the social origins of self also has been prominent in the work of infant theorists such as Heinz Kohut (1977), Donald Winnicott (1965), Margaret Mahler (Mahler, Pine, & Bergman, 1975), and Mary Ainsworth (1973). Winnicott's famous statement, "There is no such thing as an infant," was meant to capture the basic embeddedness of the infant in the caregiving context. Mahler described a "symbiotic phase," a period of infant–caregiver interconnection that paves the way to individuation. Finally, Ainsworth and Bell (1974) make the same point as Sander when they argue that an infant *can be competent only to the extent that there is a caregiving environment that is alert and responsive to the newborn's reflexive signals*. By responding to the young infant's fluctuating states and primitive signals, the caregiver imbues them with meaning and makes them part of an organized behavioral system. If one wishes to describe an organized relationship between organism and surroundings in the newborn period it can be done only in the context of a responsive caregiving environment. Thus, self, as organization, can be conceived of only within the caregiving relationship system in the early months of life.

## The developmental process

Sander (1975) and others have outlined a series of phases in the evolution of the dyadic organization toward the inner organization of self. These phases are not tasks to be completed; rather, they represent ascending and ongoing issues (see Table 5.1). When this developmental process approach is embraced the self is viewed as *emerging* rather than as *emergent* at any given age (see Sroufe, 1977, pp. 144–145, for a discussion of this distinction).

*Phase 1: Basic regulation* In the first two to three months of life the caregiving system establishes "phase synchrony between mother and infant in regard to the periodicities of relative activity and quiescence" (Sroufe, 1977, p. 137). Infant state and caregiver intervention become coordinated. As Sander concludes here: "One of the features most idiosyncratic during the first three months is the extent to which the infant is helped or compromised

**Table 5.1**　Stages of the emerging self

| Age | Stage |
| --- | --- |
| 0–6 months | The preintentional self |
| 6–12 months | The intentional self |
| 12–24 months | The separate (aware) self |
| 24–60 months | The self-monitoring self |
| Adolescence | The self-reflective self |

in beginning to determine aspects of his own regulation. . . . [For the caregiver] trial and error learning gives way to ideas of what 'works' and to the feeling of confidence that she knows her baby's needs and can specifically meet them" (p. 137). Such physiological regulation may be viewed as the prototype for later psychological regulation, which is characterized by coordinated sequences of behavioral interactions. Such coordination, which is a hallmark of Phase 2, marks the primitive beginnings of inner organization of experience.

*Phase 2: Reciprocal Exchange* Chained interaction sequences become a dominant feature in the second three months of life. Basic state regulation is achieved, the infant is awake and alert more, smiling and cooing are common, and the infant actively participates in social interaction. Several investigators (including Brazelton, Koslowski, & Main, 1974; Stem, 1974) have described the coordinated, give-and-take, dancelike quality of caregiver–infant interactions during this period. However, in the strict sense, "coordination" or "reciprocity" here is in part illusory. The appearance of give and take, with each responding to the other, is largely created by the caregiver's responsiveness to the infant. Careful study has shown that there is a dramatic asynchrony in the conditional probabilities of responsiveness; the caregiver makes adjustments to fit the infant's action, but the infant at this age has little capacity to adjust his or her behavior to fit changes in caregiver behavior (Hayes, 1984). To be sure, sequences exist in which the infant does A, mother does B, infant does C, and mother does D. Within such an established sequence the infant does respond to the mother's behavior. C occurs commonly only following B. But the infant cannot readily follow a new lead of the caregiver, whereas the caregiver commonly follows new leads of the infant (for example, A, B, E, F).

Thus, the caregiver crafts an organized system of coordinated behavioral sequences around the infant. Although the infant cannot achieve such organization independently or by design, during this phase he or she can *participate* in such a highly organized system. The organization is not yet "represented" or internalized schematically (the infant cannot fill in the missing parts). The infant does have action schemes, of course, and therefore is able to follow through on an interactive sequence once started, as long as the caregiver keeps it on track.

Although this higher level of organization remains in the hands of the caregiver, it is of great importance to the infant for two reasons. First, the countless repetitions of such highly organized sequences lay the groundwork for a more initiatory role in the next phase. Second, these sequences commonly culminate in exchanges of obvious pleasure and delight (Sander, 1975; Stern, 1974); in one scheme this phase is referred to as the period of positive affect" (Sroufe, 1977). As Sander puts it, "The affect of joy or delight becomes established as the criterion for precision in the matching of interpersonal reciprocations" (p. 145). Such shared affect represents a reservoir of positive feelings that will be coordinated with the infant's representation (scheme) of the caregiver as it consolidates in the second half year.

*Phase 3: Initiative* In the third three months we see the beginnings of "goal-directed schemes" and "a first *active* bifurcation in the direction of the child's initiative: toward her and away from her" (Sander, 1975, p. 138). Fully freed from the twenty-four-hour state regulation issues and with budding intentionality, the infant can direct activities, both those designed to elicit caregiver responses and those that explicitly elicit caregiver prohibitions. The infant now initiates the games orchestrated by the caregiver in the earlier period and in other ways plays a more active and creative role in maintaining and continuing coordinated exchanges. Now the infant can follow and embellish the caregiver's lead, as, for example, when in response to the caregiver's smile the infant smiles and reaches to the caregiver's face (Greenspan, 1981).

Clearly there is movement toward genuine reciprocity in this phase, and behavior is directed through inner imagery and goals. One sees the emergence of organized greeting sequences (bouncing, smiling vocalization with arms raised) in this phase (Vaughn, 1978), which reflect the rise of intentionality and goal-directed behavior. One sees also a dramatic rise in aversive responses to strangers and in specific affects such as anger (Stenberg, Campos, & Emde, 1983), surprise, and fear (Hyatt, Emde, & Campos, 1979; Vaughn & Sroufe, 1979). These developments point to a coordination of affect and cognition (the emergence of affectively toned schemes), marking the beginnings of an inner organization of experience (Sroufe, 1979b).

The changes in the caregiver–infant dyadic system are so dramatic during this phase that it can well be argued that for the first time the term *relationship* may appropriately replace the concept of organized interaction. This is nicely illustrated by classic research on the effects of hospitalization (Schaffer & Callender, 1959). Two distinct patterns emerged, depending on age. For infants older than seven months, a classic picture of protest to the period of hospitalization was seen: "Protest during the initial hospitalization, negativism to the staff, intervals of subdued behavior and withdrawal, and a period of readjustment after return home, during which [there was] a great deal of insecurity centering around mother's presence" (p. 537) (see also Heinicke & Westheimer, 1966). Infants younger than seven months showed none of these reactions. The reactions of the older group indicate clearly that it is the break in the relationship with the mother that formed the core of the disturbance (p. 537). By seven months the infant has begun internalizing the organized caregiving context. When the infant begins to initiate behavior intentionally based on the known organization, substitute patterns of care will not do. Earlier, hospital staff may stand in stead for the mother, providing stimulation for the infant, general experiences with chained interactions, and shared affect. The transfer back to the mother's care likewise is readily accomplished. But by seven months or so the particular system is being internalized. The organized caregiving matrix begins to become part of a core of emerging inner organization. A particular relationship and a self are emerging.

*Phase 4: Focalization* The increasingly active role for the infant and increased mobility lead to visible changes in the organization of his behavior around the caregiver in the final months of the first year. The caregiver takes on the role of the "home base" (Mahler, Pine, & Bergman, 1975) or "secure base" (Ainsworth, 1973), and the infant centers his expanding exploratory activities around this base. The infant ranges away from the caregiver, drawn by curiosity concerning novel aspects of the environment. But should the baby become fatigued or threatened or otherwise encounter something beyond his capacities (and if the appropriate internal affective signals arise) a retreat to the caregiver or a directed signal brings assistance, reassurance, comfort, and a return to organized exploration. At other times in the course of exploration positive affect arises and routinely is shared with the caregiver. Affect, cognition, and social behavior are smoothly coordinated and organized with respect to the caregiver. Sander uses the term *focalization* to capture how the caregiver has moved to the center of an expanding world. Goal-directed behavior with respect to the caregiver becomes prominent. The infant selects from a repertoire of capacities a signal or behavior suited to the response she intends the caregiver to make (arms raised to signal a desire to be picked up; showing an object for comment). Moreover, should one initiation fail, an alternative is selected as the infant *persists* toward her goal. Both goals and expectations become more specific. Clearly, all of this reflects a new level of organized complexity and must portend advances in inner organization as well.

John Bowlby (1973) describes the emergence of "working models" during this period. A central feature of any child's working model of the world is "his notion of who his attachment figures are, where they may be found, and how they may be expected to respond" (p. 203). By the end of the first year the infant will have developed clear expectations concerning the "availability" of the caregiver. *Availability* in Bowlby's usage includes both the child's expectation that the caregiver will be accessible (present) to satisfy needs and that the caregiver will be responsive. Such models are rooted in the history of interactions over the course of the first year and are viewed by Bowlby as "tolerably accurate reflections" of the infant's actual experience. From the coordinated exchanges orchestrated by the caregiver early in the first year and the caregiver's responsiveness to the infant's intentional signals of need and desire in the second half year the infant learns that the caregiver likely is available and that when the caregiver is available organized behavior may be maintained or reachieved if lost. Such working models will be revealed in the quality and organization of attachment behavior with respect to the caregiver. An infant that expects a caregiver to be responsive will explore confidently in his or her presence, will signal needs intentionally, and will respond quickly to the caregiver's interventions (expecting them to be effective).

Thus, a new level of organization has emerged by the end of the first year, and the flexibly organized, goal-directed quality of the infant's behavior suggests considerable inner organization as well. *The infant responds to new situations in light of his or her past history and purposefully selects behaviors with respect to goals.*

Is this, then, our emergent self? Although a number of compelling arguments could be made in support of a positive response, a process orientation would suggest tracing further the emerging inner organization. The working model of the infant at this time may be better described as a model of the relationship than of the self (Bowlby, 1973; Main, Kaplan, & Cassidy, 1985; Sroufe & Fleeson, 1986). That is, major expectations the infant has concerning her own actions have to do with likely responses of the caregiver (and, to a varying degree, of others).

If she gestures she will receive a response; if she seeks contact she will get it; if she signals a need it will be addressed. Her actions are part of these expectations but the expectations are centered on the caregiver's responsiveness. Moreover, under stress the infant has great difficulty maintaining organized behavior without the caregiver's assistance. It is only later that the child will firmly recognize (be aware of) her own potency as an independent center of action and will be able to deal with stress and frustration more on her own.

To be sure, however, the self is nascent here. Numerous theoreticians have suggested that it is from the attachment relationship that the particular organization of the individual emerges (Ainsworth, 1973; Bowlby, 1973; Erikson, 1963; Greenspan, 1981; Mahler, Pine, and Bergman, 1975; Sroufe dr Waters, 1977). From the sense of trust comes the sense of trustworthiness (Erikson, 1963); or in Bowlby's (1973) words:

> In the working model of the world that anyone builds, a key feature is his notion of who his attachment figures are . . . and how they may be expected to respond. Similarly, in the working model of the self that anyone builds a key feature is how acceptable or unacceptable he himself is in the eyes of his attachment figures. . . . The model of the attachment figure and the model of the self are likely to develop so as to be complementary and mutually nonconfirming. Thus an unwanted child is likely not only to feel unwanted by his parents but to believe that he is essentially unwantable. (pp. 203–204)

*Phase 5: Self-assertion* With the flowering of intentionality and with increased mobility (at about fourteen to twenty months) the toddler more actively pursues his own goals and plans, at times even when these are *explicitly* counter to the wishes of the caregiver. "Guidance of behavior on the basis of the pleasure of realizing *inner aims* can take precedence at times over the more familiar pleasurable reinforcement of finding a coordination with the parental caretaker" (Sander, 1975, p. 141). The child now initiates separations both physically and psychologically. He explores away from the caregiver (Mahler's "practicing"), inevitably engaging objects more on his own. And he operates on the basis of his more autonomous plans. Still, of course, such moves away are balanced by continued bids for reciprocation with the caregiver, and maintaining this balance is forecast by the quality of the earlier relationship. Securely attached infants are as toddlers able to function more autonomously, while still drawing upon the caregiver when challenges exceed their capacities (Matas, Arend, & Sroufe, 1978; Londerville & Main, 1981; Sroufe & Rosenberg, 1980). This is a critical transition toward the emergence of self-awareness and inner organization, which includes a concept of self as action. Through independent action and through the pursuit of inner plans (even which at times conflict with maintaining previous patterns of coordinated behavior) comes the beginning of the sense of being an independent actor.

It should be noted that these changes mark a redefinition of the attachment relationship, not its termination. Autonomy and attachment are not opposites. The attachment relationship provides the springboard for autonomy, and the development of autonomy brings about a transformation in the child–parent attachment. Nonetheless, attachments endure even as autonomy increases.

*Phases 6 and 7: Recognition and Continuity* With the rise of symbolic capacity at eighteen to thirty-six months the toddler can move to a new level of awareness. Behaving autonomously fosters a dim recognition of self as actor, but recognizing that the caregiver is aware of her plan and is, for example, in opposition to it (a recognition greatly assisted by language) brings the "realization that another can be aware of what one is aware of within oneself, i.e., a shared awareness." Sander assumes that this marks the beginning of awareness of a self-organizing core within – "actually a core that from the outset has been operative in the service of regulation at the more biological level but is now in a position to be accorded a new priority in the guidance of behavior" (Sander, 1975, p. 142).

This new level of awareness enables the infant to move toward what Sander has described as *self-constancy*. Drawing upon Jean Piaget's (1952) concepts of object constancy and operations, Sander describes a process wherein the child "perturbs" the dyadic harmony and reachieves it through her purposeful actions and the caregiver's continued cooperativeness. Deliberately acting contrary to her understood perception of the caregiver's intention and yet being reassured that the relationship can be reinstated and remains intact ("reversibility"), the child gains a sense of constancy of the relationship *and* of the self-organizing core.

> The intentional disruption of previously reinforcing and facilitating exchanges with the caretaker disrupts the toddler's newly consolidating self and body representational framework. Reexperiencing his own coherence, again at his own initiative or by out reach from the caretaker, provides a situation from which self constancy as an inner structure can be established. . . . Self as active initiator or as active organizer is thus "conserved." (p. 143)

Parallel to this development is the emergence of mirror self-recognition (Amsterdam, 1972; Lewis & Brooks, 1978; Mans, Cicchetti, & Sroufe, 1978) and "I do it" and "do it myself" assertions early in this phase (Breger, 1974), and the emotions of shame, pride, and guilt as the phase proceeds (Sroufe, 1979b). The beginnings of perspective taking and the roots of empathic response are also seen (Radke-Yarrow, Zahn-Waxler, & Chapman, 1983; Hoffman, 1979; Flavell, 1977) as the child moves toward what Bowlby (1969) calls a "goal-corrected partnership." The child can recognize the caregiver's intentions as separate from his own and can coordinate his behavior in terms of these goals of the other. There is coordination as before, but now it is the coordination of two autonomous and interdependent beings, each recognizing the other. With each new level of self-organization, there is a changed relationship organization, and with reorganizations of the relationship, the self emerges and is transformed.

## Self as Inner Organization

From our developmental/organizational viewpoint, then, the emerging of the inner organization that we will call *self* is properly viewed in relationship and process terms. Exactly when one chooses to posit that a self has emerged is partly semantic. Some might argue that there is rudimentary representation and some regularity in experience, and therefore "self," even in the first half year (Stern, 1985). Others may require intentionality and plans, self-recognition, self-monitoring, or self-reflection, all of which occur at later developmental periods (see Table 5.1).

In the first six months there is limited memory capacity and limited evidence to suggest that experiences are carried forward. In this sense, the concept of self as an ongoing, organized core seems challenging to justify. On the other hand, in the usual case, there is sufficient regularity in the dyadic organization to ensure basic patterns of repeated experience – sequences of motor behavior, tension regulation, and affect. And *these* regularities commonly *are* carried forward to the next phase, when the infant plays a more active role in the regulatory process. Regularities in the interaction become regularities in the relationship and in the self.

By the end of the first year the infant's behavior is based much more on her appraisal of both external and internal parameters. Her immediate and past experiences, as well as her ongoing affective state (mood) provide the context for behavior (Sroufe, Waters, & Matas 1974). Behavior is goal directed, and goals reflect a characteristic inner organization. She recognizes the role of the other in maintaining constancy in affective experience and behavioral organization and acts to utilize that other. Some would argue that this, then, signifies the emergence of the self. Others would point to the lack of awareness of self (including absence of indications of self-recognition) and the rather total dependence of organized behavior on availability of another to suggest that even this degree of inner organization does not qualify as self. Again, however, although the infant may not be *aware* of the continuity of experience, continuity is there. And, in time, from the infant's active efforts in maintaining inner regulation (though centered on another) will come the sense of inner organization that is clearly self.

From this process view of self, it becomes clear that the core of self, the basic inner organization, has to do with regularities in experience cycles of environmental (or state) variation, behavioral disruption, efforts to reinstate organization, and experienced affect. At first such regulation is clearly dyadic regulation; it is highly dependent on the responsiveness of the caregiver. When the caregiver is available and sensitively responsive, periods of disequilibrium are short-lived and reorganization and positive affect routinely follow environmental challenge or negative state change. These repeated experiences of regulation and positive affect (or the converse in the case of nonresponsive care) represent the rudimentary core of what will become the self. [Thus], for this reason, Robert Emde [1983] has put forward the concept of the affective self.

In time the infant comes to play a more active role in this regulatory process and to recognize the other as part of the regulation. Such increased control, which is paralleled by increases in the intensity of regularly occurring positive affective experiences (Sroufe & Waters, 1976), allows the infant to move toward ownership and sharing of the inner experience. The infant comes to recognize the self as competent to elicit the regulatory assistance from the other and, in time, to perturb and reachieve the inner regulation on his or her own.

> The importance of a stable basic regulation has to do with a context in which the child can begin dimly to recognize his own role in determining action. . . . The emergence of autonomy as here proposed is based on the further differentiation of awareness – especially that of inner perception which sets the stage for the "disjoin" of the self-regulatory core. (Sander, 1975, p. 141)

What is carried forward, then, into childhood is an abstracted history of experiences of behavioral and state regulation and their affective product within the relationship, a recognition of others as part of regulation, a recognition of oneself as effective or ineffective in eliciting care, and, finally, a recognition of the self as the author of experience. At their core, the complementary working models of self and other have to do not so much with particular actions or thoughts as with expectations concerning the maintenance of basic regulation and positive affect even in the face of environmental challenge. The core of self lies in patterns of behavioral and affective regulation, which grant continuity to experience despite development and changes in context. As Kohut (1977) has put it:

> It may well be . . . that the sense of the continuity of the self, the sense of our being the same person throughout life – despite the changes in our body and mind, our personality make-up . . . does not emanate solely from the abiding content of the constituents of the nuclear self and from the activities that are established . . . but also from the abiding specific relationship in which the constituents of the self stand to each other. (pp. 179–180)

## Empirical Implications of the Organizational/Relationship Perspective

There are two major empirical implications of this organizational/relationship perspective on self: first, emerging patterns of self-organization, as they are seen in the context of primary infant–caregiver relationships, should be related to earlier patterns of dyadic organization crafted by the caregiver; second, these emerging patterns of self-organization should forecast in specific ways later patterns *of* social adaptation (the child's organization of expectations, attitudes, feelings, and behavior) even outside of the family. That is, the way the child organizes, interprets, and creates experience and the way the child forges new relationships are products of the relationship history. From dyadic organization built through caregiver responsiveness to infant states and signals, to more reciprocal relationship organization in which the infant is an active participant, to a self-organizing child, the inner core of self develops.

### Responsive care and the emergence of self

The nascent self may be glimpsed within the dyadic organization of the attachment relationship. The particular quality of affect regulation within this relationship is presumed to reflect the experience-based expectation, (and dyadic regulatory procedures) developed through the course of interaction. By the end of the first year interactive experiences have become abstracted into particular models of caregiver availability and responsiveness and complementary models of self (which have little definition outside of this context). Feeling states give rise to behavioral tendencies that are expressed in accord with expectations of likely responses by the caregiver and their consequences. If the infant is threatened and expects that an alarm signal to the caregiver will achieve comforting, the signal will be made, *The organization of these feeling states, actions, and expectations is the emerging self.* Its particular form should be the result of the particular history of dyadic interaction. Where various particular actions (mediated by affect) routinely have particular consequences for ongoing regulation, a particular pattern of inner organization (self) emerges. Should these actions lead to consequences that promote smooth regulation of affect and ongoing commerce with the environment, a well-defined, functional self core (and a secure attachment relationship) results.

The proposition that smoothly organized attachment behavior (smooth affect regulation) emerges from a history of responsive care has been amply documented empirically. Ainsworth (for instance, Ainsworth, 1973; Ainsworth, Blehar, Waters, & Wall, 1978) was the first to show that ratings of the caregiver's responsivity at various points in the first year predicted later quality of attachment behavior in both home and laboratory. Infants of mothers who had characteristically responded to their signals promptly and effectively (which entails availability and sensitivity) cried less at home, explored more actively, and showed fewer undesirable behaviors than infants with a history of insensitive care. In a novel laboratory situation, these infants were assessed as securely attached. They used the caregiver as a base for exploration, exploring comfortably in her presence. They actively initiated interaction or contact following brief separations from the caregiver and were readily comforted when distressed (returning again to active exploration). Thus, an infant who has experienced responsive care becomes, by the end of the first year, an active, effective participant in a well-regulated dyadic system. By virtue of this participation and the attendant experiences of effectance, a positive core of self emerges.

Infants with a history of insensitive care were unduly wary in the novel setting and impoverished in their exploration; upon reunion either they were unable to be settled or they avoided contact with the caregiver even when markedly distressed. (In addition to low sensitivity ratings, mothers of these avoidant infants had been previously assessed as characteristically rebuffing their infants whenever the *infant* initiated contact; Main & Stadtman 1981.) Both groups of anxiously attached infants were unable to return to active exploration following reunion with the mother. Active participation in such systems also influences the emerging selves of these infants.

Ainsworth's core finding – namely, the relationship between quality of attachment in her laboratory assessment and sensitivity of care based on extensive home observation earlier in the first year (usually at six months) – has been replicated by several different teams of researchers (Bates, Maslin, & Frankel, 1985; Grossman, Grossman, Spangler, Suess, & Unzer, 1985; Egeland & Farber, 1984). In each of these studies independent coders assessed caregivers' responsiveness and infants' later attachment, and neither set of coders had knowledge of the other's data.

These data provide critical support for the proposition that the nature of the earlier dyadic organization, which depends on the caregiver's responsiveness to the infant's states and signals, provides the groundwork for the later dyadic organization, which, because it is a joint product of two intentional partners, reflects the emerging core of self. In being part of an organized system the infant comes to participate actively in such a system, paving the way for the emergence of an autonomous inner organization (Sroufe & Fleeson, 1986).

## The emerging self as organizer of later experience

The emerging self is the inner organization of attitudes, expectations, and feelings, which derives from the history of affective and behavioral regulation within the caregiving system. As such, it has implications for the ongoing structuring of experience, by taking the child toward or away from certain encounters with the environment, by influencing the style of engaging environmental challenges and opportunities, and by guiding interpretations of experience. Such subsequent encounters with the environment, of course, feed back on the self as the inner organization is consolidated and undergoes continued modification. There is some tendency for continuity in the inner organizing core because (1) there is an active structuring of later experience by the self, (2) early prototypes of inner organization are not readily accessible to conscious awareness, and (3) there is a tendency to form new relationships that are congruent with earlier models. Because of these organizational principles, according to Bowlby (1973), inner models of self, other, and relationships show some resistance to modification even by the end of infancy, become rather firmly established by the end of early childhood, and become quite difficult to modify after adolescence. This is a sophisticated version of the sensitive period hypothesis.

Although Bowlby's entire conceptualization has not been tested, there is now available substantial data concerning the organizing significance of early working models of self and other into the elementary school years. In studies that draw upon Ainsworth's method for assessing quality of attachment in late infancy (twelve to eighteen months), several groups of children have been following for various periods of time through early childhood. The following discussion is based on comparisons of two groups: (1) those Ainsworth calls secure in their attachment and (2) those who show avoidant attachment. (It should be noted that all conclusions are based on studies in which all coders and informants were blind to attachment history.)

Infants in the first group show confident exploration of novel environments in the caregiver's presence; they routinely share positive affective experiences; they show active, positive greetings upon reunions with the caregiver when they are not distressed; and they are active in seeking and maintaining contact upon reunion if they are distressed. Moreover, such contact readily leads to comforting and a return to active exploration. Both the shared interaction and the ease of comforting reveal expectations about the availability of the caregiver and the likelihood of maintaining organized, affectively positive behavior in his or her presence. A working model of themselves as potent, worthy, and capable and of others as available is assumed to be carried forward from such a relationship.

In avoidant attachment relationships there is an absence of active greetings by the infant upon reunion and a failure to seek comforting when distressed. As stress is increased in Ainsworth's procedure by having a second brief separation, avoidance is more marked, with a consequent failure of resumption of active exploration. As described above, such a pattern derives from a history of insensitive care and, specifically, rebuff when the infant signals need. The resulting working model portrays significant others as unavailable in times of emotional arousal and self as unworthy.

*Self as Potent* The idea that from a model of caregiver as available will emerge a complementary model of self as potent has been supported in several studies based on two samples. At both two years and three-and-a-half years, children who had been assessed in infancy as securely attached have been found to be more enthusiastic, affectively positive, and confident in solving problems (Arend, 1984; Matas, Arend, & Sroufe, 1978; Sroufe & Rosenberg, 1980) than children with histories of avoidant attachment. At five years the securely attached children have been shown to exhibit more curiosity on the Banta curiosity box (Arend, Gove, & Sroufe, 1979).

In other studies children with histories of secure attachment were found to have greater ego strength at age three and a half (to be "self-directed" and "forceful in pursuing goals"; Waters, Wippman, & Sroufe, 1979) and to be more "ego resilient" at four to five years (Arend, Gove, & Sroufe, 1979; Sroufe, 1983). In the Alan Sroufe study composites were made of the Q-sorts of three teachers, and these were compared to a criterion Q-sort of the ideal ego-resilient child (confident and flexible in managing impulses, feelings, and desires). For all sixteen children with histories of secure attachment, the correlations between actual description and criterion were all positive and averaged 50; for eleven children with avoidant histories, nine of the correlations were negative and averaged –.13.

In this same study children who had been securely attached were judged by teachers (blind to attachment history) to be dramatically more independent and resourceful, based on Q-sorts, rankings, and ratings. Teachers' judgments were confirmed by observational data; for example, in circle time those with secure histories less often sat by teachers or on their laps; nor did they seek attention through negative behaviors. They did, however, actively greet teachers and use them skillfully as resources; in turn, teachers rated them higher on "seeks attention in positive ways" (Sroufe, Fox, & Pancake, 1983).

Thus, young children with histories of secure attachment are seen to be independent, resourceful, curious, and confident in their approach to the environment. As we will elaborate later, these children, while assertive, are not aggressive, thus confirming the idea that these two characteristics lie on separate developmental pathways (Stechler & Halton, 1987).

*Self as Worthy* In our large-scale study of an urban poverty sample (Egeland & Sroufe, 1981) we have had two opportunities to assess self-esteem. The first was based on a rating made in a "barrier box" situation where the child faced the frustration of an insoluble problem in the caregiver's absence. The rating centered on the child's confidence, ability to maintain flexible organization, and capacity to keep "expecting well." The second opportunity was in the preschool setting mentioned above. In this case the composited Q-sorts of each child were compared to a criterion high-self-esteem Q-sort (Waters, Noyes, Vaughn, & Ricks, 1985). In both cases children with a history of secure attachment were significantly higher on self-esteem. (A simple rank-ordering by the teachers on self-esteem was in accord with this finding.) In addition, based on observer Q-sort descriptions in second and third grades, children with histories of secure attachment were determined to be higher on social competence and lower on anxiety than those with histories of anxious attachment (Sroufe, unpublished data).

Children with histories of avoidant attachment carry forward feelings of low self-worth, isolation, and angry rejection, which they sometimes turn inward. Teachers' ratings in the preschool placed them low on emotional health/self-esteem and confidence. In addition, a depression mega-item was extracted from the composited Q-sort data. The mean for the avoidant group was significantly higher than the mean for the secure group, with five of the ten avoidant subjects being clearly depressed compared to only one of sixteen secure children. Even specific items, such as "appears to feel unworthy; thinks of self as bad," were seen as characteristic for those with avoidant histories and uncharacteristic for those having secure relationships in infancy. Teachers' judgments were corroborated by several sets of ratings, including facial affect (Garber, Cohen, Bacon, Egeland, & Sroufe, 1985).

Self-esteem is an elusive concept, and these findings can perhaps be made more concrete with an example from the Minnesota Preschool Project (Sroufe, 1983). One day in the nursery school several children were dancing to recorded music, a lively and inviting scene. Other children arrived. One child (RA) approached another and asked to dance. The child said no and RA withdrew to a corner and sulked. Another child (RT) entered, approached a potential partner, and also was turned down. This child, however, skipped on to another child, and the second time was successful in soliciting a partner. RT, who had a history of secure attachment, showed no evidence of being "rejected," and her persistent stance led her ultimately to receive further confirmation of her expectation that others are responsive and that she is worthy. RA, on the other hand, *experienced* intense rejection and cut himself off from further opportunities to disconfirm his model of himself as unworthy. He had a history of avoidant attachment. Countless related examples could be provided.

## The self and later relationships

Beyond implications for self-reliance, personal power, inner security, and feelings of self-worth, the relationship perspective makes very specific claims concerning the organization of the self and later personal relationships. Such claims have been pursued in a number of studies.

*Others as Available and Valuable* The tendency of children with secure histories to draw effectively upon their preschool teachers as resources, their active greetings, and their sharing of discoveries already have been mentioned. A child with such a history who is ill or injured will confidently turn to teachers for support. In contrast, it is particularly at such times that those with an avoidant history fail to seek contact. A boy is disappointed and folds his arms and sulks. A girl bumps her head under a table and crawls off to be by herself. A child is upset on the last day of school; she sits frozen and expressionless on a couch. Such reactions are typical of preschoolers with histories of avoidant attachment.

At the same time, preschoolers with histories of secure attachment are more engaged and more affectively positive with peers. They more frequently initiate interactions with positive affect and more frequently respond to bids by others with positive affect (Sroufe, Schork, Motti, Lawroski, & LaFreniere, 1984). They expect interacting with others to be positive, and they convey to others this positive expectation. They are higher ranked socially, they have more friends (Sroufe, 1983; LaFreniere & Sroufe, 1985), and they have deeper relationships (Pancake, 1985). Recently, our observations in second and third grade have confirmed earlier findings (Sroufe, 1983; Waters, Wippman, & Sroufe, 1979) of a link between secure attachment history and later competence with peers.

In addition, Jeanne Block and Jack Block (1980) assembled a mega-item for empathy from their Q-sort – items such as "shows a recognition of others' feelings (empathic)"; "shows concern for moral issues (reciprocity, fairness)"; "is considerate of other children (does not try to take advantage of other children)." By summing the item placements for these items (treating the placement in categories 1–9, from uncharacteristic to characteristic, as a score) total empathy scores were derived from our preschool Q-sorts (Sroufe, 1983). Children with histories of secure attachment had significantly higher empathy scores than those with histories of avoidance. The empathy items were on average characteristic for the secure group, uncharacteristic for the avoidant group. From a history of empathic responsiveness, securely attached children have internalized the capacity for empathy and the disposition to be empathic. What was a characteristic of their early relationship has become part of the core self.

Other striking findings concern the fantasy play of children with histories of avoidance. Despite IQs equivalent to those of children with secure histories, the play of these children lacks complexity and elaboration (Rosenberg, 1984). What is more noteworthy is the almost complete absence of fantasy play concerning people. Such fantasies dominate the play of almost all preschool children and were well represented in the play of those with secure histories in our sample. These data reveal sharp contrasts in the working models of the two groups – one world is richly peopled, the other is not. In addition, when injury or illness entered the fantasy play of the secure children ("He broke his leg, take him to the hospital!") there routinely was a positive resolution ("They fixed it"). Such was not the case for children with histories of avoidant attachment.

*Relations with Peers and Teachers* One noteworthy finding concerns the frequent hostility, unprovoked aggression, and generally negative peer interactions of children with avoidant histories (LaFreniere & Sroufe, 1985; Sroufe, 1983). Sometimes this pattern alternates with emotional distance, and sometimes the latter stance is dominant. We had the opportunity to watch nineteen pairs of children in repeated play sessions as part of our Minnesota Preschool Project (Pancake, 1985), and two sets of findings were noteworthy. First, pairs in which one or both partners had a history of avoidance were rated significantly higher on hostility and lower on commitment than pairs without such a child. (This prediction derived from the notion that if one partner is disposed to be distant or hostile, such a characteristic will pervade the relationship; it takes two to be intimately and positively engaged.) Second, five of the nineteen total pairs were identified as being involved in exploitative relationships, where one child verbally or physically subjugates the partner in an ongoing way (Troy & Sroufe, 1987). In all five cases the "exploiter" had a history of avoidance; the partner had also been anxiously attached (either avoidant or Ainsworth's resistant pattern). Children with secure histories were not observed to be exploitative or victimized. Either role was open to children with histories of avoidance, presumably because of the confluence of hostility and low self-esteem in these children.

The first four comments from the summaries of a clinical judge or four pairs of avoidant-avoidant or avoidant-resistant partners are presented in Table 5.2. These were the only four such pairs observed, and, like all other coders, the judge was blind to histories and all other data. The negative quality of these relationships is apparent.

**Table 5.2**   Observations of pairs of preschool children with anxious (A) or resistant (C) attachment backgrounds

| Dyad 1 (A/A, girls) |
|---|

- This relationship is a vulnerable one – not dependable.
- Poor on "give and take."
- There is some degree of attraction for each other but they are not able to work out their differences well (they bark and snap at each other and usually give up)
- They don't know how to compromise, thus they never really build a mutually satisfying relationship.

| Dyad 2 (A/A, boys) |
|---|

- A very unhealthy relationship, characterized by intense conflict and tension.
- They become locked in steady conflict; neither is capable of altering the interaction into a positive one – they are both highly invested in supporting the negative dynamics.
- They develop an organized pattern of interaction, with TE sometimes approaching SO in a sweet-sounding, coy affective tone, trying to "warm up" to SO, then, as SO responds and begins to cooperate, TE will change his tone to nasty and malicious taunts. This dynamic is repetitive and becomes predictable.
- Both have developed maladaptive coping strategies which are very different; TE is better able to change his affective tone at will and uses it to manipulate SO; SO uses accusations and threats as a way of defending himself and provoking TE; SO is more direct and perhaps more vulnerable.

| Dyad 3 (A/C, girls) |
|---|

- Very unhealthy! This pair is intensely involved in a system of mutual provocation that neither can stop; they are highly invested in supporting the negative dynamics.
- The relationship is supported by the predictability of behavior from both – JL maintains her cold, rejecting manner, while TN persists in setting herself up as the victim of JL's rejections.
- JL leads the play (without initiating interaction with TN), TN tends to crawl around her, following her like a puppy, begging for her attention, taunting and teasing her, yet doing it in a sweet and innocent voice.
- As TN moves closer in, JL moves away, and in one instance JL whispers (3 times), "Go over there and play!" TN doesn't move away, rather she tries to redirect her attention (she won't be left alone).

| Dyad 4 (A/C, boys) |
|---|

- This relationship looks immature and impulsive.
- Not a healthy "give and take" relationship.
- Not good cooperation or balanced exchanges.
- Often play side by side but don't connect, sometimes communicate for brief periods via indirect attention seeking (silly sound effects, "in-role" invitations) – they seem to rely on this as a form of communication or cooperation by doing it at the same time, sometimes rhythmically.
- They do interact, but the interaction is not mutually supportive – they get into negatives more often than positives, fall into nonsense talk, taunting, mimicking (both contribute to negative cooperation).

*Source*: Fury, 1984.

One behavioral example from dyad 3 can illustrate the exquisite "negative empathy" of some of these children. When her partner, NT, complained to LJ of a stomachache, LJ smiled and poked her in the stomach. NT cried out in pain and said, "That hurts," whereupon LJ smiled and poked her again.

Recently we have examined further qualitative aspects of relationships between teachers and children of varying attachment histories (Motti, 1986; Sroufe & Fleeson, 1988). We assumed that teachers would develop characteristic styles of relating to different children and that such styles would be related to the child's relationship history. Teachers have histories, too, but they represent constants, as it were. Thus, variations in the attitudes, expectations, and behavior of a given teacher toward groups of children should reflect the *children's* inner working models of relationships and self as these are brought forward.

The first finding was that teachers do behave in different but characteristic ways toward different children. In fact, intercoder agreement on our rating scales was as high when coders looked at sets of totally different interactions for a given teacher and child as when they made ratings on the same set of interactions (generally agreement was in the .70s).

Moreover, there were clear and notable differences in teachers' behavior depending on the children's attachment history. Teachers expected children with secure histories to comply with requests, to follow classroom rules and standards, and to engage in age-appropriate behavior. They treated them in a matter-of-fact manner. In contrast, children with histories of avoidance were shown more discipline and control, lower expectations for compliance, less warmth, and, at times, even anger. Children with histories of anxious resistant attachment were also controlled more. Yet they were also shown more nurturance and tolerance; that is, teachers, perceiving their emotional immaturity, made more allowances for them, accepting minor infractions of classroom rules and indulging their dependency needs. These ratings were based on independent examination of teachers' behavior by persons with no knowledge of attachment history or other information on the child.

## Conclusion

Clinicians have frequently argued that difficulties in interpersonal relationships derive from low self-esteem, which in turn derives from a lack of nurturance or empathie care (Erikson, 1963; Greenspan, 1981, Kohut, 1977, Sullivan, 1953). The inner organization of attitudes, expectations, feelings, and meanings is a product of relationship history with ongoing implications for the organization of socio-emotional behavior. This hypothesis is not new. The organizational/relationship framework, however, has offered a context in which empirical data concerning this proposition could be gathered. Prospective, longitudinal data, based on groupings of early relationships (inspired by Bowlby's model and Ainsworth's organizational scheme), confirm the link between relationship history and the emerging constellation of inner organization that is self. Moreover, there is continuity within the relationship history itself: the nature of the dyadic interaction orchestrated by the caregiver forecasts the nature of the later attachment relationship, which, by virtue of the infant's active participation, is the framework for the emerging core of self.

Avoidant attachment relationships in late infancy reflect a history of insensitive care and rejection, especially in the context of clearly expressed need or desire on the part of the infant. When caregivers are chronically unavailable emotionally, avoidant attachment is virtually guaranteed (Egeland & Sroufe, 1981). At the same time, such a pattern of attachment reveals an internalized working model the infant has developed of the caregiver as unavailable and unresponsive to emotional need. Thus, the infant fails to seek contact as stress is elevated. Reciprocally, this leads to a model of the self as isolated, unable to achieve emotional closeness, uncared about, and unworthy. Care can be sought only in times of low stress (as when avoidant children sit with thumb in mouth on teachers' laps during storytime). The social world is viewed as alien and unprovoked with anger and hostility. Oftentimes the children behave in ways that elicit further confirmation of their models. They exhibit negative affect and unprovoked aggression, leading other children to reject them. They disrupt classroom routine, exploit the vulnerable, and engage in devious or antisocial behavior (lying, stealing, cheating; Sroufe, 1983), leading even teachers to dislike many of them. Teachers' anger is directed almost exclusively toward these children, and much of the input they receive from teachers is in the form of control. Behaving in terms of the world they have known they create relationships and influence their current environment to confirm their models of self and others (Sroufe & Fleeson, 1986).

One final case example from the Minnesota Preschool Project powerfully illustrates the process of self emerging from relationship history and the ongoing organizational significance of early self-representation. RV experienced chronic rejection and hostility from her mother, which was repeatedly documented. At both twelve months and eighteen months their relationship was classified as avoidant. The interaction with her mother at age two was very angry, and her mother called her a "nasty bitch." By preschool RV vacillated between long bouts of explosive anger and periods of desperate isolation. Nonetheless, one female teacher developed a special fondness for this physically attractive and bright child and stayed emotionally available to her, despite her anger. Late in the term RV reported a dream to this favorite teacher, in which the teacher had, in a fit of rage, thrown her against a wall. The child obviously was shaken by the dream. The teacher, with arm around her, said, "Oh, RV, I would never do that." Astonishingly, RV asked her, "Why?" "Because I like you very much, RV." RV then responded, "Why do you like me?" making it clear that this was a perplexing state of affairs, requiring explanation, not a matter of course.

This interchange allows us a clear look into this child's inner organization – her model of self and other. It also allows us to see the organizing significance of the self. For each child certain material may be more or less readily worked into the existing organization of feelings, attitudes, and expectations. For RV and others like her who have experienced chronic emotional unavailability from their caregivers, it is very difficult to make sense out of another's obvious caring.

There are several reasons that models of self and others are difficult to change (and that there is basic coherence to self-structure over time). First individuals often tend to select partners and form relationships that promote continued enactment of existing working models, although this process generally remains out of awareness (Sroufe & Fleeson, 1986). Second, individuals (certainly including children) tend to elicit input confirming their preexisting models, be that rebuff or positive feedback. But, in addition, as illustrated by RV, countervailing information often is not recognized as such when it does occur. In these ways early self-structures, created in the context of infant–caregiver relationships, in time become self-stabilizing and resistant to change.

It is not the case, however, that change is impossible. Change may be possible at many points during childhood. For example, as Main and Goldwyn (1984) point out, the advent of formal operations in adolescents makes it possible "to step outside a given relationship system and see it operating" (p. 16). Thus, working models of self and others could be modified, most likely in the context of other significant relationships. Understanding the origins of self in relationships, the organizing nature of self, and processes of social exchange that stabilize this organization will be important for understanding the process of growth and change as well as psychopathology.

Return now to the basic questions that initiated this chapter. First, the literature on outcomes of individual differences in infant–caregiver attachment is quite compelling with regard to the importance of early relationships for individual development. Even discontinuity between early attachment and later functioning in childhood has been found to be associated primarily with changes in the child–parent relationship (Erickson, Sroufe, & Egeland, 1985). Second, from this conceptualization it is clear that relationship disorders would be manifest in infant behavior because the infant is so inextricably embedded within the relationship system. Indeed, the infant can be competent only to the extent that there is a well-organized, reciprocating relationship. Finally, the internalization of a relationship disorder poses no mystery. The nature of the dyadic organization – well functioning or disordered – will be embodied in the self-organization.

# References

Ainsworth, M. D. S (1973). The development of infant–mother attachment. In B. Caldwell & H. Ricciuti (Eds.). *Review of child development research* (Vol. 3). Chicago: University of Chicago Press.

Ainsworth, M. D. S., & Bell, S. (1974). Mother–infant interaction and the development of competence. In K. Connelly & J. Bruner (Eds.). *The growth of competence.* New York: Academic Press.

Ainsworth, M. D. S, Bell, S., & Stayton, D. J. (1974). Infant–mother attachment and social development "socialization" as a product of reciprocal responsiveness to signals. In M. P. M. Richard (Ed.). *The integration of a child into a social world* (pp. 99–135). Cambridge: Cambridge University Press.

Ainsworth, M. D. S., Blehar, M. C., Waters, E., & Wall, S. (1978). *Patterns of attachment: A psychological study of the strange situation.* Hillsdale, NJ: Lawrence Erlbaum Associates.

Amsterdam, B. (1972). Mirror self-image reactions before age two. *Developmental Psychobiology, 5,* 297–305.

Arend, R. (1984). *Preschoolers' competence in a barrier situation: Patterns of adaptation and their precursors in infancy.* Unpublished doctoral dissertation, University of Minnesota

Arend, R. A., Gove, F. L., & Sroufe, L. A. (1979). Continuity of individual adaptation from infancy to kindergarten: A predictive study of ego-resiliency and curiosity in preschoolers. *Child Development, 50,* 950–959.

Baldwin, J. M. (1897). *Social and ethical interpretations in mental development.* New York: Macmillan.

Bates, J., Maslin, C., & Frankel, K. (1985). Attachment security, mother–child interaction, and temperament as predictors of behavior problem ratings at aye three years. In I. Bretherton & E. Waters (Eds.). Growing points of attachment theory and research. *Monographs of the Society for Research in Child Development, 50* (1–2, Serial No. 209).

Block, J. H., & Block, J. (1980). The role of ego-control and ego-resiliency in the organization of behavior. In W. A. Collins (Ed.). *Development of cognition, affect, and social relations.* Hillsdale, NJ: Lawrence Erlbaum.

Block, J. H, Block, J., & Morrison, A. (1981). Parental agreement-disagreement on child rearing orientations and gender-related personality correlates in children. *Child Development, 52,* 965–974.

Bowlby, J. (1969). *Attachment and loss: Vol. 1. Attachment.* New York: Basic Books.

Bowlby, J. (1973). *Attachment and loss: Vol 2. Separation, anxiety and anger.* New York. Basic Books.

Brazelton, T. B., Koslowski, B., & Main, M. (1974). The origins of reciprocity: The early mother–infant interaction. In M. Lewis & L. A. Rosenblum (Eds.). *The effects of the infant on its caregiver.* New York: Wiley.

Breger, L. (1974). *From instinct to identity*. Englewood Cliffs, NJ: Prentice Hall

Carr, S., Dabbs, J., & Carr, T. (1975). Mother–infant attachment: the importance of the mother's visual field. *Child Development, 46*, 331–338.

Egeland, B., & Farber, E. (1984). Infant–mother attachment: Factors related to its development and changes over time. *Child Development, 55*, 753–771.

Egeland, B., & Sroufe, L. A. (1981). Developmental sequelae of maltreatment in infancy In R. Rizley & D. Cicchetti (Eds.). *Developmental perspectives in child maltreatmen R. Rizley & D. t*. San Francisco: Jossey-Bass.

Emde, R. N. (1983). The prerepresentational self and its affective core. *Psychoanalytic Study of the Child, 38*, 165–192.

Erickson, M. F., Sroufe, L. A., & Egeland, B. (1985). The relationship of quality of attachment and behavior problems in preschool in a high risk sample. In I. Bretherton & E. Waters (Eds.). Growing points of attachment theory and research. *Monographs of the Society for Research in Child Development, 50* (1–2, Serial No. 209), 147–186.

Erikson, E. (1963). *Childhood and society* (rev. edn.). New York: Norton.

Flavell, J. H. (1977). *Cognitive development*. Englewood Cliffs, NJ: Prentice Hall.

Fury, G. (1984). *Qualitative differences in relationships formed by preschool children with different attachment histories. Unpublished dissertation*, University of Minnesota.

Garber, J., Cohen, E., Bacon, P., Egeland, E., & Sroufe, L. A. (1985, April). *Depression in preschoolers: Reliability and validity of a behavioral observation measure*. Paper presented at the meeting of the Society for Research in Child Development, Toronto.

Gottman, J. M. (1990). How marriages change. In G. R. Patterson (Ed.). *Depression and aggression in family interaction* (pp. 75–101). Hillsdale, NJ: Erlbaum.

Greenspan, S. I. (1981). *Psychopathology and adaptation in infancy and early childhood*. New York: International Universities Press.

Grossman, K., Grossman, K. E., Spangler, G., Suess, G., & Unzer, L. (1985). Maternal sensitivity and newborn's orientation responses as related to quality of attachment in Northern Germany. In I. Bretherton & E. Waters (Eds.). Growing points of attachment theory and research (pp. 229–257). *Monographs of the Society for Research in Child Development, 50 (1–2, Serial No. 209)*.

Hayes, A. (1984). Interaction, engagement, and the origins of communication: Some constructive concerns. In L. Feagans, C. Garvey, & R. Golinkoff (Eds.). *The origins and growth of communications*. Norwood, NJ: Ablex.

Heinicke C., & Westheimer, I. (1966). *Brief separations*. New York: International Universities Press.

Hoffman, M (1979). Development of moral thought, feeling, and behavior. *American Psychologist, 34*, 958–966.

Hyatt, S., Emde, R., & Campos, J. (1979). Facial patterning and infant emotional expression: Happiness, surprise and fear. *Child Development, 50*, 1020–1035.

Kierkegaard, S. (1938). *Purity of heart is to will one thing*. New York: Harper & Row.

Kohut, H. (1977). *The restoration of the self*. New York: International Universities Press.

LaFreniere, P, & Sroufe, L. A. (1985). Profiles of peer competence in the preschool: Interrelations between measures, influence of social ecology, and relation to attachment history. *Developmental Psychology, 21*, 58–68.

Lewis, M., & Brooks, J. (1978). Self-knowledge and emotional development. In M. Lewis & L. Rosenblum (Eds.). *The development of affect*. New York: Plenum.

Londerville, S., & Main, M. (1981). Security of attachment, compliance and maternal training methods in the second year of life. *Developmental Psychology, 17*, 289–299.

Mahler, M. S., Pine, F., & Bergman, A. (1975). *The psychological birth of the human infant: Symbiosis and individuation*. New York: Basic Books.

Main, M., & Cassidy, J. (1988). Categories of response to reunion with the parent at age 6: Predictable from infant attachment classifications and stable over a 1-month period. *Developmental Psychology, 24*, 415–426.

Main, M., & Goldwyn, R. (1984). Predicting rejection of her infant from mother's representation of her own experience: Implications for the abused-abusing intergenerational cycle. *Child Abuse and Neglect, 8*, 203–217.

Main, M., Kaplan, N., & Cassidy, J. (1985). Security in infancy, childhood and adulthood: A move to the level of representation: In I. Bretherton & E. Waters (Eds.). Growing points of attachment the*ory and research. Monographs of the Society for Research in Child Development, 50* (1–2, Serial No. 209).

Main M. & Stadtman, J. (1981). Infant response to rejection of physical contact by the mother: Aggression, avoidance and conflict. *Journal of the American Academy of Child Psychiatry, 20*, 292–307.

Main M. & Weston, D. (1981). The quality of the toddler's relationship to mother and to father: Related to conflict behavior and readiness to establish new relationships. *Child Development, 52*, 932–940.

Mans, L., Cicchetti, D., & Sroufc, L. A. (1978). Mirror reactions of Down's syndrome infants and toddlers Cognitive underpinnings of self-recognition. *Child Development, 46*, 547–556.

Matas, L., Arend, R., & Sroufe, L. A. (1978). Continuity of adaptation in the second year. The relationship between quality of attachment and later competent functioning. *Child Development, 99*, 547–555.

Mead, G. H. (1934). *Mind, self and society*. Chicago: University of Chicago Press.

Minkowski, A. (1967). *Regional development of the brain in early life*. Oxford: Blackwell.

Motti, E. (1986). *Patterns of behaviors of preschool teachers with children of varying developmental histories*. Unpublished doctoral dissertation. University of Minnesota, Minneapolis.

Pancake, V. R. (1985, April). *Continuity between mother–infant attachment and ongoing dyadic peer relationships in preschool*. Paper presented at the biennial meeting of the Society for Research in Child Development, Toronto.

Piaget J. (1952). *The origins of intelligence in children* (2nd edn.). New York: International Universities Press.

Radke-Yarrow, M., Zahn-Waxler, C., & Chapman, M. (1983). Children's prosocial dispositions and behavior. In P. Mussen (Ed.). *Charmichael's manual of child psychology* (Vol. 4) (4th edn.). New York: Wiley.

Rheingold, H., & Eckerman, C. (1973). Fear of the stranger: A critical examination. In H. Reese (Ed.). *Advances in child development and behavior* (Vol. 8). New York: Academic Press.

Rosenberg, D. (1984). *The quality and content of preschool fantasy play. Correlates in concurrent social/personality function and early mother–child attachment relationships. Unpublished doctoral dissertation*, University of Minnesota.

Sameroff, A. J. (1989). Models of developmental regulations: The environtype. In D. Cicchetti (Ed.). *Development and psychopathology* (pp. 41–68). Hillsdale, NJ: Erlbaum.

Sander, L. (1975). Infant and caretaking environment: Investigation and conceptualization of adaptive behavior in a system of increasing complexity. In E. J. Anthony (Ed.). *Explorations in child psychiatry* (pp. 129–166). New York: Plenum.

Schade, J, Meeter, K., & van Goettingen, W. (1962), Maturational aspects of the dendrites of the human cortex. *Acta Morphologische Scandinavica, 5*, 37–48

Schaffer, H., & Callender, M. (1959). Psychologic effects of hospitalization in infancy. *Pediatrics 21*, 528–539

Sroufe, L. A. (1977). *Knowing and enjoying your baby*. New York: Spectrum.

Sroufe, L. A. (1979a). The coherence of individual development. *American Psychologist, 14* 834–841.

Sroufe, L. A. (1979b). Socioemotional development. In J. Osofsky (Ed.). *Handbook of infant development* (pp. 462–516). New York: Wiley.

Sroufe, L. A. (1983). Infant–caregiver attachment and adaptation in the preschool: The roots of competence and maladaptation. In M. Perlmutter (Ed.). *Development of cognition, affect, and social relation* (pp. 41–81). Hillsdale, NJ: Lawrence Erlbaum Associates.

Sroufe, L. A. (1985). Attachment classification from the perspective of infant–caregiver relationships and infant temperament. *Child Development, 56*, 1–14.

Sroufe, L. A., & Fleeson, J. (1986). Attachment and the construction of relationships. In W. Hartup & Z. Rubin (Eds.). *Relationships and development*. Hillsdale, NJ: Lawrence Erlbaum Associates.

Sroufe, L. A., & Fleeson, J. (1988). Relationships within families: Mutual influences. In R. A. Hinde & J. Stevenson-Hinde (Eds.). *The coherence of family relationships* (pp. 27–47) Oxford: Oxford University Press.

Sroufe, L. A., & Fleeson, J. (1988). The coherence of family relationships. In R. A. H. J. Stevenson-Hinde (Ed.). *Relationships within families: Mutual influences* (pp. 27–47). Oxford: Oxford University Press.

Sroufe, L. A., Fox, N., & Pancake, V. (1983). Attachment and dependency in developmental perspective. *Child Development, 54*, 1615–1627.

Sroufe, L. A., Jacobvitz, J., Mangelsdorf, S., DeAngelo, E., & Ward, M. J. (1985). Generational boundary dissolution between mothers and their preschool children: A relationships systems approach. *Child Development, 56*, 17–29.

Sroufe, L. A., & Rosenberg, D. (1980, March). *Coherence of individual adaptation in lower SES infants and toddlers*. Paper presented at the International Conference on Infant Studies, Providence, RI.

Sroufe, L. A., & Rutter, M. (1984). The domain of developmental psychopathology. *Child Development, 55*, 17–29.

Sroufe, L A, Schork, E., Motti, F., Lawroski, N., & LaFreniere, P. (1984). The role of affect in social competence. In C. Izard, J. Kagan, & R. Zajonc (Eds.). *Emotions, cognition and behavior*. New York: Cambridge University Press.

Sroufe, L. A., & Ward, M. J. (1980). Seductive behavior of mothers and toddlers: Occurrence, correlates, and family origins. *Child Development, 51*, 1222–1229.

Sroufe, L. A., & Waters, E. (1976). The ontogenesis of smiling and laughter: A perspective on the organization of development in infancy. *Psychological Review, 85*, 173–189.

Sroufe, L. A., & Waters, E. (1977). Attachment as an organizational construct. *Child Development, 48*, 1184–1199.

Sroufe, L. A., Waters, E., & Matas, L. (1974). Contextual determinants of infant affective responses. In M. Lewis & L. Rosenblum (Eds.). *The origins of fear*. New York: Wiley.

Stechler, G., & Halton, A. (1987). The emergence of assertion and aggression during infancy: A psychoanalytic systems approach. *Journal of the American Psychoanalytic Association, 35*, 821–838.

Stenberg, C., Campos, J., & Emde, R. (1983). The facial expression of anger in seven-month-old infants. *Child Development, 54*, 178–184.

Stern, D. (1974). The goal structure of mother–infant play. *Journal of the American Academy of Child Psychology, 13*, 402–421.

Stern, D. N. (1985). *The interpersonal world of the infant: A view from psychoanalysis and developmental psychology*. New York: Basic Books.

Troy, M., & Sroufe. L. A. (1987). Victimization among preschoolers: The role of attachment relationship history. *Journal of the American Academy of Child and Adolescent Psychiatry, 26,* 166–171.

Uddenberg, N. (1974). Reproductive adaptation in mother and daughter [Supplement]. *Acta Pschiatrica Scandinavica, 254.*

Vaughn, B. *(1978). An ethological study of greeting behaviors in infants from six to nine months of age. Unpublished doctoral dissertation,* University of Minnesota.

Vaughn, B., & Sroufe, L. A. (1979). The temporal relationship between infant heart rate acceleration and crying in an aversive situation. *Child Development 50,* 565–567.

Waters, E. (1978). The stability of individual differences in infant-mother attachments. *Child Development 49,* 483–494.

Waters, E., & Deane, K. E. (1985). Defining and assessing individual differences in attachment relationships. Q-methodologv and the organization of behavior in infancy and early childhood. In I. Bretherton & E. Waters (Eds.). Growing points of attachment theory and research. *Monographs of the Society for Research in Child Development 50* (1–2, Serial No. 209).

Waters, E., Noyes, E., Vaughn, B., & Ricks, M. (1985). Q-sort definitions of social competence and self-esteem: Discriminant validity of related constructs in theory and data. *Developmental Psychology, 21,* 508–522.

Waters, E., Vaughn, B., & Egeland, B. (1980). Individual differences in infant–mother attachment relationship at age one: Antecedents in neonatal behavior in an urban economically disadvantaged sample. *Child Development 51,* 203–216.

Waters, B, Vaughn, B., Egeland, B., & Sroufe, L. A. (1979). Individual differences in infant–mother attachment at 12 and 18 months: Stability and change in families under stress. *Child Development, 50,* 971–975.

Waters, E., Wippman, J., & Sroufe, L. A. (1979). Attachment, positive affect, and competence in the peer group: Two studies in construct validation. *Child Development, 50,* 821–829.

Winnicott, D. (1965). *The maturational processes and the facilitating environment.* New York: International Universities Press.

# 6

# Disorganized/Disoriented Infant Behavior in the Strange Situation, Lapses in the Monitoring of Reasoning and Discourse during the Parent's Adult Attachment Interview, and Dissociative States

## M. Main and E. Hesse

This is a speculative working paper in attachment, focusing upon some first and second-generation effects of traumatic experiences. The paper takes its origins in certain consequences of the theory of attachment as developed by John Bowlby (Bowlby, 1969/1982) – specifically, the consequences of being severely frightened by attachment figures (Main, 1981; Main & Weston, 1982), and/or of interacting with attachment figures who have themselves been traumatized and frightened (Main & Hesse, 1990). For an attached infant, both of these situations are likely to produce conflict, disorganization, and disorientation, and both are inherently without immediate solution.

The paper opens with a brief review of the theory of attachment as developed by John Bowlby and Mary Ainsworth (Bowlby, 1969/82; 1973, 1980; Ainsworth, 1969, 1974, 1990). We emphasize the role of fear in the activation of attachment behavior, and describe the parent–infant separation-and-reunion procedure conducted in an unfamiliar laboratory setting which is known as the Ainsworth Strange Situation (Ainsworth, Blehar, Waters & Wall, 1978). Most infants in low-risk samples have traditionally been expected to show one of three relatively well-organized patterns of behavioral and attention response to the parent in this situation – secure, insecure-avoidant, or insecure-ambivalent – responses which differ depending on whether the parent has been accepting, rejecting, or unpredictably responsive. We suggest that the differing behavioral responses observed in relation to rejecting and unpredictably responsive attachment figures may follow upon alterations in the focus of attention.

In the second section of this paper we describe the discovery of a new, "disorganized/disoriented" ("D") category of infant Strange Situation response (Main & Solomon, 1986, 1990). Infants are placed in this category if they display any of an array of disorganized/disoriented responses to this procedure, including substantially misdirected movements, contradictory movements, prolonged freezing, stereotypies and anomalous gestures and postures. In high-risk samples, infant "D" attachment status has been linked to child maltreatment, which is inherently frightening (Lyons-Ruth, Zoll, Connell & Odom, 1987: Carlson, Cicchetti, Barnett & Braunwald, 1989). In low-risk samples, however, infant "D" attachment status has been linked to parental discussions of loss experiences during the Adult Attachment Interview (George, Kaplan and Main, 1985), and specifically to lapses in the monitoring of reasoning or discourse shown by the parents of "D" infant during these discussions (Main & Hesse, 1990; Ainsworth & Eichberg, 1991). We have suggested that these lapses may occur because the parents are still overwhelmed by these incompletely remembered loss experiences, and that in interactions with the infant they may sometimes appear frightened. Because the attachment figure is the infant's only solution to experiences of fear, whether the parent is frightening or frightened, the infant faces a paradox. We have suggested that the

*Source:* Main, M., & Hesse, E. D, "Disorganized/disoriented infant behavior in the Strange Situation, lapses in the monitoring of reasoning and discourse during the parent's Adult Attachment Interview, and dissociative states," pp. 86-140 from *Attachment and Psychoanalysis*, eds. M. Ammaniti & D. Stern (Gius: Rome, 1992). Reproduced with permission from Dr. Massimo Ammaniti.

disorganized/disoriented behavior exhibited is indicative of the resultant collapse of behavioral, and quite likely attentional, strategies.

In the third section of this paper we elaborate upon a hypothesis developed by Giovanni Liotti which suggests that infant disorganized/disoriented attachment status may be linked to an increased vulnerability to dissociative disorders. He has suggested that vulnerability to these disorders could be increased via self-hypnosis induced by repeated exposure to the paradoxical situation outlined above. His hypothesis has been supported to date by the finding of more frequent maternal loss experiences around the time of birth for patients suffering from dissociative as compared to other disorders, and by a case study involving dissociative disorder (Liotti, Intreccialagli, & Cecere, 1991; Liotti, 1992, 1995). At the phenotypic level, we provide support for Liotti's hypothesis with descriptions of some trance-like states and seemingly dissociated actions observed in disorganized/disoriented infants. Further, a reconsideration of the lapses observed in their parents' discussion of traumatic experiences indicates that they are compatible with narratives that might be expected if the parent has suffered a loss of discourse context due to the intrusion of dissociated ideas, or holds two incompatible ideas regarding a loss or abuse experience in parallel.

In the final section, we briefly review some recent conceptualizations of cognitive processes – specifically, the concepts of working memory and parallel distributed processing. The link between dissociation and trauma is well established, but to date the concept of "trauma" has been essentially *quantitative*. The theory presented here may permit an increased understanding of the *qualitative structure* of trauma insofar as it involves inherently paradoxical interactions with a frightening/frightened attachment figure. Interactions of this kind may lead to: (a) a trance-like looping of attention, and relatedly (b) lapses in working memory. In addition, (c) such interactions may be beyond the infant's capacity for serial processing, and thus encourage the onset of parallel, divided and relatively independent/dissociated mental processes which are poorly remembered.

## Attachment Theory and Infant Response to Separations from the Parent in a Strange Environment

It is now widely accepted that an "attachment behavioral system" has evolved in individuals in ground-living primate species (Bowlby 1969/1982). This system is presumed to facilitate the protection of the younger and/or weaker members of the troop through leading them to continually monitor both the location and accessibility of one or a few group members capable of serving as protective, parental ("attachment") figures. Once a "primary attachment figure" has been selected (usually but not inevitably the infant's biological mother), the primate infant closely monitors her whereabouts, preserving proximity even under non-stressful conditions. If threatening conditions arise, the system becomes highly activated, and the infant is led to seek close proximity and contact with this individual. It should be noted that infants may have more than one attachment figure, and with the primary figure unavailable, one or a few other figures may be sought.

Although Bowlby originally proposed that the biological function of the attachment behavioral system was primarily protection from predation, the full import of the system is probably best understood by considering (1) that it serves *multiple* survival functions, and relatedly, (2) that *maintenance of proximity to a protective older conspecific is in fact the sine qua non of primate infant survival* (Main, 1979). In addition to protection from predation, proximity provides, for example, protection from unfavorable temperature changes, from natural disasters, and from the attacks of conspecifics. Moreover, it is only through the attachment figure that the young primate maintains access to nourishment, and is assured of keeping up with movements of the group.

Human infants and young children are presumed to be highly influenced by the development and operation of the attachment behavioral system. The reader should note the following further points:

1. The attachment behavioral system is conceived of as *continually active,* whether or not attachment behavior is displayed at any particular point in time.
2. This means that, whether or not attachment behavior is manifest at a given time, the attached individual is at some level *attending to (monitoring) the physical location of the attachment figure(s)*. This continual monitoring (attention) cannot always be conscious. It is now widely recognized, however, that we have the capacity for

attending to and processing input which does not reach the usual levels of awareness (see Kihlstrom, 1987 and Baddeley, 1990).

3.   The attached individual must also be alert to the *physical and psychological accessibility* of the attachment figure, the latter including – once cognitive abilities permit – the figure's *likely response to actions which might be taken*. Repeated experiences interacting with a given attachment figure may, for example, indicate that that figure is usually rejecting of attachment behavior, or is unpredictable and difficult to access except in emergencies: in this case the infant may need not only to mark the figure's location, but be aware of special strategies for gaining or maintaining access.

4.   Internal and external conditions are also continually monitored for both *natural* and *learned clues to danger* (Bowlby, 1973). As noted above, any externally threatening situation leads the system to high levels of activation, and to seeking close proximity and contact. In addition, the ill or injured infant may need to maintain close proximity or contact in situations in which a healthy infant can explore, and both are expected to be somewhat more alert to possible danger in unfamiliar environments.

5.   With respect to the relation between attachment and danger, Bowlby noted that the function served by the attachment figure in primate species differs from those served by the mother in many other mammalian species, in a specific and critical way. For many mammals, (1) the mother provides nourishment and opportunities for learning, while separately (2) a den, burrow or other special location provides the haven of safety in times of alarm. In this case, maintenance of proximity to mother is of import, but frightening circumstances will lead the young to seek a special location rather than the mother herself. For the primate infant, in contrast, the attachment figure *is* the single location which the infant must seek in times of alarm (Bowlby, 1958).

6.   The attachment behavioral system in primates is therefore particularly responsive to "natural clues to danger" (Bowlby, 1973), is intimately related to fear, and is activated by frightening conditions of any kind.

The now well-known Ainsworth Strange Situation was designed to illustrate the functioning of the attachment behavioral system in one-year-old human infants by exposing them to combined indications of mild increases in danger – namely, (a) an unfamiliar environment in which (b) the mother briefly leaves. This laboratory procedure was first utilized at the conclusion of Ainsworth's intensive study of a sample of middle-class Baltimore infant–mother dyads observed in the home throughout the first year of life (Ainsworth et at., 1978). Within this 20-minute procedure, the parent twice leaves the infant (once in the company of a stranger, and once alone) and twice returns. Separation episodes are curtailed if the infant becomes more than mildly distressed, and attractive toys are available to the infant throughout the situation.

On the basis of her laboratory observations, Ainsworth developed a three-category (A, B, C) classification system for describing the patterning of the infant's response to the parent with whom it was being observed. Ainsworth and her colleagues reported strong links between the way the infant responded to separation and reunion in this situation and mother–infant interaction in the home situation (Ainsworth et al., 1978).

*Pattern B: Secure.* Ainsworth expected the majority of infants to use mother as a "secure base" for exploration and play when present; to show increasing signs of missing the mother during her absences (crying, calling or searching); to greet her actively on reunion, usually demanding proximity and/or contact; and then, once mother's continuing presence was assured, to return to play. Two-thirds (13/23) of the infants in her original Baltimore study did in fact exhibit this ("secure") response pattern. An examination of home observations showed that the mothers of these infants had been "sensitive to the signals and communications" of their infants. Greater sensitivity to infant signals in the mothers of B (vs. A and C) infants has continued to be noted in succeeding studies, and follow-up studies have repeatedly shown more favorable outcomes for children classified as secure with mother in infancy (see Bretherton, 1985 for a review).

Main (1990) suggested that, since their mothers have been responsive to their signals and communications in other circumstances, the problem presented to secure infants by the Strange Situation is primarily one involving caregiver location. For this reason, both the attention and the behavior of the secure infant can be organized as a relatively simple reflection of environmental changes. Exploration of the new and attractive environment is possible so long as mother is present; diminishes in favor of attachment behavior in her absence; and emerges again once the infant has re-established proximity and/or contact with the mother upon reunion.

*Pattern A: Insecure-avoidant.* A minority of infants showed little or no distress during separation from the mother, actively exploring the toys and the room. When mother returned, they actively avoided and ignored her by turning away, looking away and refusing contact with her before returning to exploration of the environment. The mothers of these infants were found actively rejecting of attachment behavior in the home situation, pushing the infants away in response to bids for access. Succeeding studies also linked the parent's aversion to physical contact with the infant to infant avoidance of the parent under stress (Main & Stadtman, 1981).

Because their caregivers have been rejecting of attachment behavior within the home situation, Group A infants may be faring a more complex problem in the Strange Situation than the simple tracking of shifts in caregiver location (Main, 1990). As in the case of Group C infants (discussed below) their Strange Situation behavior may be influenced not only by changes in caregiver location, but also by the particular difficulties they may have experienced in gaining or maintaining access to their caregivers in other environments. Elsewhere, we have suggested that these physically rejected infants are able to refrain from exhibiting distress and other forms of attachment behavior in the Strange Situation by *minimizing responsiveness to fear-eliciting conditions*.[1] This in turn may be accomplished through an "organized shift of attention" away from the mother and/or her absence (and towards the inanimate environment). Such behavior has the advantage of permitting continued organization, and possibly also of permitting the maintenance of whatever proximity is possible (Main, 1981; Main & Weston, 1982).

*Pattern C: Insecure-ambivalent.* Finally, a few infants were highly distressed by the procedure, some well before the first separation – for example, upon entering the strange environment or in response to the entrance of the stranger. These infants responded to separation from the mother with great distress, yet seemed unable to obtain comfort from her return, continuing to display distress and failing to return to exploration. Several showed anger, alternating or combining with proximity seeking. An examination of the home records showed that the mothers of these infants were not notably rejecting, but rather were insensitive to signals and unpredictable in their responsiveness.

Elsewhere, we have suggested that the infants of parents who are unpredictable, and therefore potentially undependable in an emergency, may need to maximize the display of attachment behavior in circumstances indicating even minimal clues to danger. Note also that, in contrast to Group B infants (whose attentional focus varies with circumstances) and Group A infants (who utilize an organized shift in attention *away from* the attachment figure and her whereabouts), Group C infants appear almost completely *preoccupied with* the attachment figure and her whereabouts throughout the situation.

★

It appears then that, despite relatively reduced maternal sensitivity, Group A and C infants are able to maintain reasonable levels of organization in the face of mildly fear-eliciting conditions, in part by focusing attention either away from or toward (1) the attachment figure and (2) any cues to danger implicit in the situation.[2] This organization will, however, be vulnerable to certain kinds of changes in the situation. For Group A infants, for example, increasing the alarming aspects of the situation should at some point over-ride the ability to utilize a shift in attention – forcing the infant to finally approach the rejecting attachment figure, albeit possibly in a somewhat disorganized manner.[3] Since both Group B and Group C infants approach the attachment figure in response to stressful conditions, they may be somewhat less vulnerable to moderate increases in alarm stemming from the environment external to the dyad.

Note, however, that *all three* patterns of organization should be expected to break down into disorganization if something about the *attachment figure herself* (rather than changes in her location, or placement in an unfamiliar situation) becomes frightening. This is a situation likely to be too alarming and confusing for behavioral organization to be maintained through an "organized shift in attention" (pattern A). At the same time, since the attachment figure is in this case the source of the alarm, organization cannot be maintained through approach behavior (patterns B/C). Infants who repeatedly find something about the mother herself alarming should then fail to exhibit a consistent patterning of behavior and attention across the course of the Strange Situation, and consequently be difficult to categorize *("unclassifiable")* within the A, B, C system.

Finally, as noted above, the attachment behavioral system is presumed to have evolved to maintain and promote proximity and contact with protective individuals in times of danger. Phylogenetically, cues to danger are expected to stem either from the environment, or from internal signals (as when the individual is ill or injured, see Bowlby, 1969/1982). However, if a system has evolved to lead to safety by promoting proximity to an attachment figure in times of distress, it cannot by definition function normally when that figure is the source of the alarm. Alarming parental behavior may not only lead to failures in consistency of patterning (unclassifiability), then, but may also create a breakdown in the functioning of the system: actively *disorganized* and/or *disoriented* behavior should be expected in consequence.

## From "Unclassifiable" to "Disorganized/disoriented" Infant Attachment Status: The Recognition of a New Infant Attachment Category and its Probable Relation to Frightening and/or Frightened Parental Behavior

Above, we argued that, if something about the attachment figure is frightening – whether because the figure is directly threatening, or is herself frightened by some source unidentifiable to the infant – the infant will not be able either to approach the attachment figure, or to successfully minimize responsiveness. In this case, the consistency and organization of Strange Situation behavioral patterning may be lost, and disorganized, disoriented behavior may appear when the infant is exposed to a stressful situation in the company of the parent.

### From "unclassifiable" to "disorganized/disoriented" infant attachment status

Main & Solomon (1990) have provided a brief history of the development of a new, "Disorganized/disoriented" (hereafter, D) category of infant Strange Situation behavior. This category was developed following the increasingly wide-spread recognition that a number of infants in both low-risk (Main & Weston, 1981) and high-risk/ maltreatment samples (Crittenden, 1985; Egeland & Sroufe, 1981; Radke-Yarrow, Cummings, Kuczinski & Chapman, 1985; Spieker & Booth, 1988) were "unclassifiable" within the A, B, C classification system. Some infants, for example, cried and called for the mother during her absence, attempting to open the door (behavior fitting to the B or C attachment categories), then fell silent and sharply avoided and ignored her immediately upon reunion (behavior fitting to the A category). Other infants showed strong proximity seeking immediately upon reunion, and then, having established contact with the mother, turned sharply away and stood motionless in room center (to fit to group B classification instructions, termination of contact should have been followed by a return to exploration and play). In high-risk/maltreatment samples, a peculiar and unclassifiable mix of avoidant and resistant behaviors were frequently observed, leading to the use of an "A-C" attachment category identified somewhat differently across investigations (see especially Crittenden, 1985).

With the aim of better understanding "unclassifiable" attachment status in both low-risk and maltreated infants 12 to 18 months of age, Main & Solomon (1986) first undertook a review of unclassified Strange Situation videotapes available within the Berkeley sample. What the "unclassifiable" infants shared in common was the display of a diverse array of "inexplicable", odd, disorganized, or overtly conflicted behavior patterns in the parent's presence. One "unclassifiable" infant, for example, cried loudly while attempting to gain her mother's lap, then suddenly fell silent and "froze", standing unmoving for several seconds. Other "unclassifiable" infants were observed approaching the parent with head averted; rocking on hands and knees following an abortive approach; moving away from the parent to the wall when apparently frightened by the stranger; screaming for the parent by the door upon separation, then moving silently away upon reunion; raising hand to mouth in an apprehensive gesture immediately upon reunion; and rising to greet the parent on reunion, then falling prone to the floor. Many of these behaviors appeared to be of a type ethologists term "conflict behaviors", that is, behaviors that result from the simultaneous activation of incompatible behavioral systems (see, e.g., Hinde, 1970). Some seemed to involve apprehension, either directly (fearful facial expressions, oblique approaches, vigilant postures) or indirectly (freezing of all movement at parent's entrance). Often, behaviors suggestive of apprehension succeeded and replaced the start, followed rapidly by the inhibition, of approach or signalling behavior.

The most striking theme running through the list of behaviors observed in unclassified infants was that of *disorganization* or, an observed contradiction in movement pattern, corresponding to an inferred contradiction in intention or plan. The term *disorientation* was also used to describe behavior which, while not overtly disorganized, nonetheless indicated a lack of orientation to the present environment (such as immobilized behavior accompanied by a dazed expression).[4] A system for the identification of the new, *"Disorganized and/or disoriented"* infant attachment category was developed (Main & Solomon, 1986). While by definition no exhaustive list of disorganized behaviors could be drawn up, seven thematic headings were identified.[5] The system was refined through repeated study of 200 infant Strange Situation videotapes classified as "D" – half drawn from low-risk and half from high-risk and/or maltreatment samples – and good inter-judge reliability was obtained by investigators working in other laboratories (see Main & Solomon, 1990, for review).

*Linking infant D attachment status to frightening parental behavior.* Above, we argued that disorganized/disoriented behavior would be expected in infants whose parents were frightening. We have in fact informally noted subtly frightening behavior in some parents of D infants filmed during the Strange Situation. These include movements or postures which seem to be part of a pursuit-hunt sequence; threat postures; sudden threat gestures; unpredictable invasions of the infant's personal space, as, parents' hands suddenly silently sliding (from behind) across the infant's throat; and sudden "looming" into the infant's face (Main & Hesse, 1990). A more direct way of supporting the expected link between *frightening* parental behavior and infant "D" attachment status would of course be through studies of infants seen in the Strange Situation with maltreating parents. Two such investigations have been completed, in each of which care was taken to compare the Strange Situation behavior of these infants to that of well-matched controls. About 80% of the infants in maltreating families were judged Disorganized/disoriented in the Strange Situation, as compared to between 20 and 40% of the controls (Carlson, Cicchetti, Barnett & Braunwald, 1989; Lyons-Ruth, Zoll, Connell & Odom, 1987).

*Linking infant D attachment status to the parent's own traumatized/frightened state of mind: Unresolved/disorganizing mental processes surrounding trauma in the parents of D infants in low-risk samples.* Infant "D" attachment status has been assigned to infants in two low-risk, middle-class samples (the Bay Area sample studied by Main and Hesse, 1990, and a similar Charlottesville sample studied by Ainsworth and Eichberg, 1991), the proportions being similar to those observed in the control populations cited above. In these studies, the parent with whom the infant has been observed in the Strange Situation has also been seen in the Adult Attachment Interview (George, Kaplan & Main, 1985), a structured, hour-long interview in which the subject is asked to describe and evaluate a number of attachment-related experiences, including loss of attachment figures through death and any threatening experiences, such as abuse. In both studies, infant D attachment status has been found strongly linked to apparent lapses in metacognitive monitoring associated with the parent's discussion of potentially traumatic experiences (Main & Hesse, 1990; Ainsworth & Eichberg, 1991). In these middle-class samples, lapses in monitoring have chiefly been associated with discussions of loss of important persons through death. Lapses in monitoring during the Adult Attachment Interview have also been linked to infant D attachment status in two poverty samples, however (see ff. 9), where the potentially traumatic experience being discussed is frequently sexual or physical abuse.

Scoring systems have been developed for scoring indices of Unresolved/disorganizing/disorienting (hereafter, U/D) mental processes surrounding the discussion of potentially traumatic experiences in these verbatim speech transcripts. Where lapses are striking enough, the individual is classified as Unresolved/disorganized/disoriented with respect to the experience being described. As in the case of disorganized/disoriented behavior in infants, no exhaustive list of statements indicative of these processes can be completed, but thematic headings can be identified. Specifically, the adult is assigned to Unresolved attachment status if speech surrounding a potentially traumatic event shows one or more of the following characteristics[6]:

a. Lapses in the monitoring of reasoning during discussion of the experience. These include indications of incompatible beliefs, often including indications that the lost person is considered *simultaneously dead and alive* (in a physical, rather than a religious/metaphysical sense). Indications of a belief in having been causal in the death where no material cause was present are also considered as lapses in the monitoring of reasoning, as are efforts to manipulate the mind so as to ignore or alter the fact of the loss. Similar principles are extended to identifying still unresolved/disorganized processes in the discussion of abusive experiences (Main & Goldwyn, 1991).

b. Lapses in the monitoring of discourse during discussion of the experience. These are identified through alterations in the form ("register") of discourse during the discussion of a potentially traumatic experience, suggesting that the individual has suddenly entered into a special state of mind. These alterations include several kinds of disoriented changes in the speaker's manner of response, such as might be shown in sudden attention to extreme details surrounding a death; a sudden change to a eulogistic style of speech; or suddenly raising discussion of a traumatic experience in a completely unrelated context.

c. Reports of extreme (disorganized/disoriented) behavioral reactions. These include reports of displacement of grief reactions, such as extreme reactions to the death of public figures following absence of reaction to the death of a parent, and reports of suicide attempts.[7]

As noted above, the potentially traumatic experience discussed most often by parents in the middle-class Berkeley and Charlottesville samples was loss. Loss in itself was not found related to infant D attachment status in these samples, however, *unless the narrative surrounding the death indicated the continuing presence of unresolved/disorganizing mental processes.* In the Bay Area study, 11 out of 12 mothers (91%) identified as Unresolved/disorganized on the basis of their discussions of loss had had infants who had been judged Disorganized/disoriented five years previously. In contrast, only 3 out of 19 mothers (16%) who had experienced loss, but showed no indications of unresolved/disorganizing mental processes in discussing the loss, had Disorganized infants.[8] In the Charlottesville study, all eight mothers identified as Unresolved/disorganized on the basis of their discussions of loss had infants judged Disorganized with them during the Strange Situation a few months previously (Ainsworth & Eichberg, 1991). As would be expected given the findings of the Bay Area study, the experience of loss in itself was not significantly related to infant D attachment status in the Charlottesville sample.[9]

Main proposed that a frightening attachment figure presents an infant with a paradox which cannot be resolved at the behavioral level – namely, to simultaneously flee from the attachment figure as a source of danger, and to approach the attachment figure as a haven of safety (Main, 1981). Precisely because this paradox is not resolvable in behavioral terms, it should lead to the visible collapse of behavioral strategies observed in disorganized/disoriented behavior (Main & Hesse, 1990). For this reason, infants seen in the Strange Situation with maltreating parents were expected to be Disorganized/disoriented.

On the basis of the Bay Area and Charlottesville studies indicating second-generation effects of loss experiences upon infant D attachment status, we hypothesized that *frightened* as well as frightening parental behavior could place an infant in an irresolvable situation (Main & Hesse, 1990). This frightened behavior was expected to occur at times when the still-traumatized parent responded to (possibly only weakly accessible) memories or ideas surrounding the loss experience. From the infant's point of view, this was expected to be particularly overwhelming because what was frightening the parent would be unidentifiable as to source. The infant's alarm could be further exacerbated by indications that the parent, while indicating the presence of danger, might simultaneously indicate a desire to flee from the vicinity, or even from the infant itself (Main & Hesse, 1990).[10]

We have in fact informally observed frightened behavior in the parents of D infants. These include backing away from a pursuing infant while stammering an entreaty not to approach, and frightened movements and facial expressions as the infant (on lap) reaches towards the parent's face. When the parent appears frightened of an infant's approach, the infant is placed in a paradoxical position in which attempts to approach the attachment figure as a haven of safety leads the figure to still further reduce the infant's safety through increased signs of fear and overt tendencies to flight. Like a frightening attachment figure, then, a mysteriously frightened attachment figure could certainly leave the infant without a behavioral strategy, and lead to the production of disorganized/disoriented behaviors.

## Linking disorganized/disoriented attachment status to increased vulnerability to dissociative disorders: Liotti's hypothesis

As noted earlier, Giovanni Liotti has recently proposed that individuals who were Disorganized/disoriented as infants may be more vulnerable than others to developing dissociative disorders (Liotti et al., 1991; Liotti, 1992; Liotti, 1995). The essential feature of the dissociative disorders as identified in DSMIII-R is "a disturbance or alteration in the normally integrative functions of identity, memory, or consciousness." Minor dissociations are recognized as part of a normal process experienced by many individuals, but the phenomena of dissociation include trance states and ideas of possession, experiences of depersonalization and derealization, fugues, and multiple personality disorder. Dissociation has been documented following a wide variety of traumatic experiences, and a strong link has been established between the development of dissociative symptoms and trauma (Spiegel, 1990; Putnam, 1985).

The phenomena of dissociation are closely linked to the phenomena of hypnosis, and Bliss has summarized evidence suggesting that self-hypnosis in childhood forms the basis for some of the more severe dissociative disorders (1986; see also Breur & Freud, 1895/1986). Hypnotic phenomena are mobilized spontaneously as defenses during assault (Spiegel, 1989), and higher hypnotic susceptibility has been linked to childhood abuse experiences (Nash & Lynn, 1985).

Liotti's hypothesis is based upon the link between dissociative disorders and hypnotic (trance-like) states, and upon the fact that *paradoxical behavioral injunctions* in fact constitute one technique for inducing hypnotic states.

These paradoxical injunctions are seen in "confusion techniques"[11] of hypnotic induction, in which the hypnotist may, for example, very rapidly urge the subject to engage in contradictory movements which cannot be carried out at the same time. Liotti links these paradoxical confusion techniques to the experience of the infant exposed to the paradox of interacting with a frightening and/or frightened attachment figure. If trance-like states are sometimes induced in "D" infants exposed to these interactional patterns, and if early self-hypnotic experiences are in fact linked to later dissociation, then an ability to dissociate may indeed develop:

> Recent theories of hypnotic induction suggest that a trance state is obtained whenever one is unable to assimilate an inescapable interpersonal situation to the cognitive schemata one has been able to construct (Erickson, 1964; Erickson, Rossi and Rossi, 1976). If this is true, then the child interacting with a frightened and frightening attachment figure is likely to experience trance-like states of consciousness during the attachment relationship. This relationship is inescapable, since the child cannot avoid the activation of the attachment system nor the interaction with the frightened and frightening caregiver (Main, 1981; Main & Hesse, 1990). Therefore, the child engaged in a disorganized attachment relationship is likely to be unwittingly subject to a sort of hypnotic induction. . .Blank spells and other dissociative experiences, particularly likely to occur in those suffering from the dissociative disorders, have been equated to trance states due to spontaneous self-hypnosis (Bliss, 1986).

In a first attempt to test this hypothesis, Liotti and his colleagues asked psychiatric patients suffering from dissociative disorders[12] whether their mothers had experienced a major loss during the two years before and two years after their own birth. This question was used because of the link already established between the parent's experience of Unresolved/disorganized responses to loss and infant D attachment status, and because a major maternal loss occurring during or near the patient's infancy could have left the patient particularly vulnerable. The hypothesis was supported. A strong majority of patients suffering from dissociative disorder, but only a small minority of other psychiatric patients, reported that their mothers had indeed experienced such a loss around the time of their birth (Liotti et al., 1991).

Liotti has recently described his clinical work with a 44-year-old patient, "Lisa", who presented with a history of failed psychotherapies and complex disturbances (Liotti, 1995). Her difficulties included frequent thoughts of committing suicide, flickering attention, perceptual distortions and bizarre trance-like states (blank spells, during which she seemed to lose the ability to think and feel). These were accompanied by a peculiar obsessive-compulsive disturbance, triggered at anytime that glassware was broken at home. At such times, she became obsessed with the idea that extremely tiny fragments of glass could escape her attention, be inhaled or ingested by her daughter, and cause her death. As Liotti describes it, the surface of a table, glinting under a ray of light, could have her motionless, tense and trembling for as much as an hour, staring at the glittering surface, in a desperate effort to become certain that no fragment of glass was present.

This obsessive-compulsive pattern had its onset about one year after the birth of her daughter, who was hospitalized for pneumonia at that time. Observing her difficult breathing created a panic state in Lisa. Later, she began thinking of fragments of glass as a possible source of danger to her daughter, and the blank spells, paralysis and obsessive-compulsive behavior began. Her husband, who had recently completed a psychoanalytic treatment, linked Lisa's fear of broken glass to her death instinct, and suggested that a desire to kill her daughter was being transformed into these peculiar fears.

During one of her "blank spells", and in keeping with the initial therapeutic contract in which therapist and client had agreed upon a primary collaborative goal of understanding and overcome her blank spells, her therapist asked her (1) whether her mother had suffered from serious losses just before her birth, or close to it and (2) whether she often looked "frightened and frightening". Lisa replied with the report of "a terrible story". When Lisa was about 18 months old, her newborn sister died. The one-month-old had been taken to the beach, where the mother had a fit of dizziness and the infant fell from her mother's arms, lying for a while with her face in the sand. On the following day she developed a high fever and died within a week. Lisa's mother frequently relived the event in Lisa's presence, looking guilty and frightened, and speaking in a highly incoherent, fragmentary and disorganized fashion. Lisa described having experienced an "uncanny feeling" of impending disaster as she listened to her mother's rehearsal of these events.

In response to a request from Lisa, her therapist then described the connections he had made between frightened/frightening parental behavior, disorganized/disoriented attachment, and trance-like states (Lisa's blank spells). He suggested that Lisa may have entered trance-like states in response to her mother's frightened recounting of these events, and that the uncanny atmosphere she experienced upon listening to these recountings could be a hint that she was then in an altered state of consciousness. Her fears for her daughter might then be connected to an effort to protect a baby from shining little things (sand/glass) that, if inhaled, could harm the baby (note that glass is in fact manufactured from sand).

Lisa did not experience blank spells during therapy for several months following this discussion. In further therapy sessions, new memories intruded, new ways of construing her perceptions and interactions were discussed, and new kinds of interaction were practiced. After two years, the blank spells had faded away, as did Lisa's obsessive-compulsive pattern of behavior.

Liotti suggests that in connecting her mother's narrative regarding a young infant who seemed to have died from a fall into sand, and implied dangers to her own infant from broken glass, Lisa was using a form of semiconscious visual-emotional imaging coming from her childhood memory rather than a formal reasoning. This memory image was likely to correspond to what she had visualized, in an altered state of consciousness, while listening to her mother's tragic narrative. Drawing upon Hilgard's theory of divided consciousness, Liotti suggests that Lisa "was not relating the memories of her mother's dramatic narratives (which were evoked by her daughter's illness) to the frightening, intrusive image of her daughter's dying because of the ingestion of something extremely tiny, hard and shining." He suggests that she failed to attend to the relation between her memories and the intrusive images of her own daughter's death partly because she was in an altered state of consciousness when she constructed the memory images. Research on state dependent learning in fact "suggests that it may be difficult to confront a memory image constructed in a trance with related mental images (either perceptions, fantasies or other memories) constructed in a different state of consciousness (Eagle, 1987, p. 177; Overton, 1977).[13]

### Disorganized/disoriented behavior in infants and unresolved/disorganized mental states in adults: new interpretations following Liotti's hypothesis

Liotti's hypothesis links infant "D" attachment status to increased vulnerability to dissociative disorders via spontaneous hypnotic states. In this section of the paper, we first describe some trance-like behaviors and seemingly "dissociated" actions observed in "D" infants. We next reconsider the parents of D infants, who we have described as Unresolved/disorganized with respect to previous trauma. Given the relation already long established between dissociative disorders and traumatic experiences, it will not be surprising if "lapses in monitoring of reasoning or discourse" now seem to suggest either the co-existence of, or interference from, dissociated ideas surrounding the potentially traumatic experience which is under discussion. Finally, if this is the case, then the parents of "D" infants may be in partially dissociative states at other times as well. Informal videotaped observations suggest that this is so.

*Trance-like behaviors and dissociated actions in infants judged Disorganized/disoriented.* Liotti links the effects of early interactional experiences to increased vulnerability to dissociative disorders. It is not, however, necessary to presume that dissociative/hypnotic states are induced at very early ages for the hypothesis to be affirmed. Thus, it could be that the young infant is immune to entering such states, and begins to respond in this way to paradoxically frightening parental behavior only later. We do know, however, that post-hypnotic amnesia is induced more readily in children than in adults (Hilgard, 1964), and a review of the literature on hypnosis concludes that children are more readily hypnotizable than adults (Chapman, Elkins & Carter, 1982).

We have at present no way of ascertaining whether a 12–18 month old infant can enter into a hypnotic/dissociative state comparable to those experienced by somewhat older children and adults. Insofar as hypnosis and dissociation involve amnesias and alterations in identity, direct evidence will be difficult to interpret for children of these ages even if supplied. At the *phenotypic/descriptive* level, however, a review of our directions for identifying "disorganized/disoriented" behaviors does reveal a surprising resemblance, in some instances, to indications of the presence of hypnotic/dissociative states:

1. Main and Solomon selected the term *disorientation* "to describe behavior which, while not overtly disorganized, nonetheless indicated a lack of orientation to the present environment (such as immobilized behavior accompanied by a dazed expression)" (1990, p. 133). Disorientation in itself is suggestive of a disorder or alteration of consciousness, and two of the seven thematic headings suggested for identifying "D" behavior include numerous behavior examples suggestive of such alterations – "Freezing, stilling, and slowed movements and expression", and "Direct indices of disorganization and disorientation".

"Freezing, stilling and slowed movements and expressions" makes primary reference to immobilized postures accompanied by dazed or trancelike expressions. "Freezing of movement" is defined as a cessation of movement in a posture requiring resistance to gravity. This can be quite dramatic, and an infant may, for example, "freeze" with arms held out waist-high, as though in arrested motion. "Stilling" is defined as cessation of movement in a relatively restful posture. Freezing lasting 20 seconds or more in the parent's presence, and "accompanied by a dazed or trance-like facial expression" leads to assignment to infant D attachment status even if it occurs only once during the Strange Situation (Main & Solomon, 1990, p. 138). Judges are also instructed to consider infant D attachment status on observing "Disorganized wandering, especially when accompanied by disoriented expression" (observed in one infant whose mother was later found to have experienced a clearly unresolved/disorganizing early loss), and "Disoriented facial expression: sudden 'blind' look to eyes where infant had previously used eyes normally" (observed in one infant whose father was later suspected of abuse).

Trancelike and dazed expressions are also frequently mentioned in conjunction with major transitions of behavior and state.[14] For example, judges are to consider immediate D category placement when the infant – in the context of an apparently good mood – assumes a dazed facial expression and undertakes a slow, subtly aggressive movement towards the parent's face (observed in several infants whose parents had suffered major loss). The judge is also to consider assignment to D attachment status when "Immediately following strong proximity seeking and a bright, full greeting with raised arms, the infant moves to the wall or into the center of the room and stills or freezes with a dazed expression" (observed in a maltreated infant, p. 136).

*2. Disorganized* behavior has been broadly defined as an observed contradiction in movement pattern suggesting an inferred contradiction in intention and plan (see Main & Solomon, 1990). In ethological terms, these "disorganized" behaviors are frequently conflict behaviors. Dissociative status need not be implied when, for example, the infant shows signs of fear in smiling to the parent, or makes awkward, repeated stop-start approach movements towards her. These movements and expressions simply imply conflict between approach and flight, and the infant may simply be attached to an abusive parent. Thus, not all disorganized-appearing behavior listed by Main and Solomon need imply more than momentary experiences of conflict, and expressions of conflict between approach and avoidance behavior towards the parent need not imply the intrusion of a dissociated secondary plan or system. Many of the disorganized behaviors observed in the infants of maltreating and traumatized parents may mark uncertainty and indecisiveness rather than dissociated states of mind.

The phenomena of hypnosis (and dissociation) include, however, complex and purposeful actions undertaken outside of the awareness of the actor. In Hilgard's "neodissociation" theory, it is not considered unreasonable to attribute these actions to the operation of dissociated "systems", operating either alongside or outside of the principal system usually associated with consciousness, each producing relatively coherent patterns of behavior with sufficient complexity to represent some degree of internal organization (Hilgard, 1977/86; see also Bowlby, 1980). We may term these *dissociated actions,* and some disorganized behavior does appear in this form.

As a particularly striking example of dissociated action observed in the Strange Situation, we may consider a description of one 12-month old infant who interrupted her strong approach to father on reunion as follows:

> Creeping rapidly forward toward father, she suddenly stopped and turned her head to the side and – while gazing blanking at the wall – slapped a toy and then her empty hand on the floor in a clearly angry gesture, still with head averted and gaze blank. This interruption lasted only three to four seconds. She then continued her strong approach and reached to be picked up (Main & Solomon, 1990, p. 142).

This infant's face remained impassive or expressed good mood also a minute later when, held by father, she three times brought her arm down in a gesture that involved apparently accidental striking of father's face with a toy. The child was identified as D solely on the basis of the above patterning and without any knowledge of the father's history. The father had in fact recently attempted suicide, and was subject to homicidal fantasies. Aside from these brief gestures, the infant appeared secure (p. 142).

Other "disorganized" behaviors which seem indicative of some dissociation (dissociated actions) include sudden distress or angry behavior appearing without warning in the middle of a long period of contented play (p. 137). These may cease as abruptly as they began. In addition, infants have been observed raising arms to the *stranger* (with whom they have already spent several minutes) with a bright greeting ("hi!") as the parent enters the room. They have also been observed following a parent to the door crying, then smiling at the door as though in greeting as it closes. The disorientation implied in these behavior patterns is marked enough to imply a lapsed awareness of the surround. Finally, peculiar fleeting asymmetries of facial expression immediately upon hearing or seeing the parent have been observed intruding upon the infant's greeting to the parent. The immediate response to reunion observed in one seriously maltreated 12 month old infant was as follows:

> The baby hears mother's voice and turns and looks to the door. Her look is initially blank, brows somewhat raised. Looks up at mother, averts gaze for a moment, facial expression then *divides in two* (left vs. right half of face), uplifting left mouth-comer only, in these microseconds her eyes widen and as she looks at mother, the asymmetry makes her appear puzzled, disgusted, or fearful. Her face then breaks into an extremely wide smile (Main & Solomon, 1990, p. 143).

This infant was coded "D" largely on the basis of the intrusion of this peculiar expression. This infant otherwise appeared secure.

The behaviors described may be regarded as candidates for description as *dissociated* to greater and lesser degrees, depending in part upon complexity, duration, and the infant's apparent awareness of the immediate context. The response to reunion displayed by the infant of the father suffering from suicidal and homicidal impulse seems, however, particularly strongly to suggest the momentary intrusion of a secondary intention, plan or system.

3. Although disorganized/disoriented infant behavior may frequently index indecision or confusion without an accompanying alteration in consciousness, it does denote a "collapse of behavioral strategy" (Main & Hesse, 1990). Consequently, we should not be surprised if an accompanying collapse of mental strategy – i.e., a dissociative/trancelike state – is present somewhat more frequently than has been (conservatively) suggested above. We are led to the following further conclusions regarding these diverse behaviors and their origins:

a.  In many instances, these displays may simply signal momentary experiences of conflict which cannot be resolved at the behavioral level. The particular form taken by the observed "cascade" of disorganized/disoriented behavior may then be heavily dependent upon the initial conditions pertaining when the conflict intruded. Infants experiencing this conflict when (i) creeping across the room, (ii) sitting on the parent's lap, (iii) examining a toy, (iv) crying, et alia, will then produce differing displays. Presuming parent–infant interactional patterns remain the same, the same infant observed with the same parent in a second Strange Situation some months later may then display very different (but still disorganized/disoriented) behaviors.
b.  In some cases the disorganized/disoriented display may be frequently rehearsed by the infant in conjunction with particular, repeated experiences with the parent. In this case the display may be predictable and be the product of a dyadic behavioral organization. For example, in several Strange Situations, we have observed immobilization accompanied by trancelike expressions taking place *simultaneously* in parent and infant. Some stilling immediately upon obtaining the parent's lap, and some falls to floor in a peculiar huddled-depressed posture may also have also been rehearsed and repeated in particular interactional contexts.
c.  Dissociation in response to highly stressful experiences is regarded as adaptive in many contexts (Bliss, 1986), the most dramatic of these being the extreme abuse in early childhood which forms the usual background for the development of multiple personality disorder (Kluft, 1985; Putnam, 1985). In this case separate, independent, and coherently organized personality states may develop, each featuring a particular repertoire of memories, feelings and action tendencies. Except in very rare cases, these personality states experience at least a one-way amnesia for one another, and turns are taken in the control of the individual's behavior.

Most of the brief displays of disorganized/disoriented behavior observed in infants in low-risk samples, even if and when indicative of alterations in consciousness, probably have little relation to multiple personality disorder. As noted earlier, however, in maltreatment and other high-risk samples some few infants display such marked avoidance and resistance in the same reunion episodes that the term "A-C" (avoidant/resistant) initially used by many individuals working with such samples, seems warranted (see Main & Solomon, 1990 for review). In some cases the infant may simultaneously scream *for* the parent and stretch as far out of the parent's arms as possible with eyes cast to the side, or dramatically switch from displays of distress and anger to impassive, affectless avoidance and back again.[15]

A consideration of the potential relations between disorganization and dissociation suggested by Liotti may shed new light upon the peculiarities of the "A-C" pattern. Crittenden (Crittenden & Ainsworth, 1989) has suggested that as opposed to D attachment status, A-C may reflect an organized pattern. Although at the *behavioral* level in *infancy*, these rapidly sequential or simultaneous displays of two dramatically opposing insecure response patterns appear highly disorganized,[16] both A and C responses in themselves are organized (Ainsworth et al., 1978). If we are able to conceive of individuals able to function under the alternating control of two of more different, relatively well-organized personality states then at the *mental* as opposed to the behavioral level, infant A-C Strange Situation behavior may represent or forecast the emergence of a kind of multiply-controlled self-organization.

*Lapses in the monitoring of reasoning or discourse during discussions of potentially traumatic experiences: Indicative of lapses into partially dissociative states?* We have identified several infant "D" behavior patterns which are phenotypically compatible with those which would be expected in individuals entering into dissociative states. Since dissociation is traditionally related to trauma, it is now possible to speculate that some of the "D" behaviors observed in maltreatment samples (Carlson et al., 1989; Lyons-Ruth et al., 1987) indicate the infant's lapse into dissociative states as a result of physical abuse. The remaining problem, then, is that of identifying a "cause" for the appearance of phenotypically dissociative phenomena (e.g., the appearance of trance-like states) in infants whose parents are not directly frightening or abusive.

As the reader is aware, a link has been established in low-risk samples between infant "D" attachment status with respect to a particular parent and "lapses in the monitoring of reasoning or discourse" (hereafter, "lapses" or "lapses in monitoring") during that parent's discussion of potentially traumatic events. We have understood these lapses to be indicative of traumatized states of mind and earlier, we suggested that a *traumatized* (frightened) parent may place the infant in an irresolvable paradox similar to the one created by a *traumatizing* (frightening) parent. Further, we noted that observing a frightened/traumatized parent may also be frightening because, responding to memories or external events only idiosyncratically related to memories, the source of the parent's fright is not discernible and/or comprehensible (Main & Hesse, 1990).

Here, we reconsider the nature of the fright exhibited by the still-traumatized parent. We suggest that the lapses of monitoring of reasoning or discourse which identify the parents of "D" infants may often be indicative of the partial intrusion of frightening, normally dissociated memories; that the parents of "D" infants may be in partially dissociative states at other times as well; and that observing a parent in a frightened/dissociative state is in all likelihood inherently frightening.

As is obvious, we have no formal proof that the parents of "D" infants are suffering from dissociative experiences during the Adult Attachment Interview. External assessments bearing on this problem are not yet available (although they are in progress in a study being conducted with Marinus van IJzendoorn). We are, nevertheless, persuaded of the likelihood that dissociative processes may underlie the anomalies observed during interviews with the parents of "D" infants for three reasons:

1. *Dissociation is associated with traumatic/frightening experiences. Similarly, the anomalous patterns of speaking and reasoning discovered in interviews with the parents of "D" infants appeared specifically during their discussions of potentially traumatic/frightening events.* Infant D attachment status has been found associated with lapses in the adult's responses to the two (out of 15) questions in the Adult Attachment Interview dealing specifically with (a) "any threatening experiences" involving parents, and (b) loss of significant figures through death. Since abuse is more frequently a frightening/traumatic experience than is loss, dissociative phenomena would be expected to occur more frequently in conjunction with the discussion of abuse experiences. If, then, the lapses we have identified are indicative of dissociative processes, these lapses should also be more frequently identified during the discussion of abuse. The data do in fact indicate far more frequent lapses in monitoring surrounding these discussions.

2. *Dissociation is identified through "alterations" in consciousness and behavior: Correspondingly, our directions for identifying Unresolved/disorganized responses to trauma have referred to "alterations"/lapses in the monitoring of reasoning or discourse (Main & Goldwyn, 1991).* Transcripts of the hour-long Adult Attachment Interview can be judged Unresolved/disorganized on the basis of one or two sentences – sentences which are conceivably not either remembered or monitored by many subjects. These predictors of infant Disorganized attachment status often appear as a brief anomalies in a transcript in which the speaker otherwise uses well-formed sentences and shows no other evidence of implausible reasoning. For this reason, the anomalous speech appearing in discussions of potentially traumatic events by the parents of D infants could best be described as indicative of a lapse in the monitoring of reasoning as opposed to indicating "irrational" thinking or difficulties with the maintenance of normal discourse as a whole.

3. *Our directions for identifying "lapses in monitoring of reasoning or discourse" appear compatible with directions which might also be used to identify (a) efforts to dissociate memories from awareness (b) current interference from partially*

*dissociated memories, and (c) evidence of co-existing but incompatible and dissociated memories (Main & Goldwyn, 1991). Here, we consider each of these in turn.*

a.   *Lapses suggestive of efforts to dissociate memories from awareness.* One type of lapse in the monitoring of reasoning consists in "psychologically confused statements" in which the subject describes manipulations of his or her mind in the service of "forgetting" bad experiences or bad aspects of attachment figures. Thus, one subject, describing an abusive attachment figure, said that it was "almost better when he died, because then at last I could forget the bad parts of him, and remember just the good". Others described efforts to put bad memories in special places in their minds, or making their minds "just go away".

b.   *Lapses suggestive of current interference from partially dissociated memories.* Lapses in the monitoring of discourse are described as indicating that the speaker has entered "a special state of mind in which she is no longer appropriately conscious of the interview situation." In these and similar cases, we note that "the speaker seems to have lost awareness of the discourse context. . .This lack of immediacy suggests an encapsulation or segregation of the event from normal consciousness" (Main & Goldwyn, 1991). Examples include lapses into a eulogistic style of speech during discussions of a loss ("She was young, she was lovely, she was dearly beloved by all who knew her and who witnessed her as she was torn from us by that most dreaded of diseases, cancer"); sudden, inappropriate attention to detail; sudden inappropriate intrusions into the interview of information regarding a loss or other traumatic experience ("And so, in answer to your question, I didn't have much difficulty with my first year of kindergarten at six. My uncle died when I was seventeen."); and changes into speech forms appropriate to much younger speakers during discussions of early traumatic experiences ("If I didn't tell my mom about my piano lesson, then she'd be really mad, *'cause I'd hided it from,* you know, I hid it from her, and um. . .that's when the punishment came, you know. . .").

     Lapses in the monitoring of discourse are also identified when speakers lose track of the discourse context in a manner suggesting that visual/sensory images/memories are intruding. Asked whether her mother had been abusive, one subject replied, "I know my mother used to hit me. I don't know if you would call it abuse. *I guess another adjective would be pain."* The following is another subtle example:

     –   And what kind of hitting was it, was it spanking, or was it more severe than that?
     –   Uh, maybe, I guess, when I was lying around the house, uh, I don't know, mostly spanking, um, *some sticks,* I guess. *Let me see, what kind of sticks?...um,* mmm. . .yeah, I guess it was mostly spanking as far as I can remember. . .*um, umbrellas.* Let's see, uh, I don't remember. . .uh, one time she hit me with this really big stick, I uh broke a vase. . .cause I was playing with her vase and I broke it. . .*really big stick.*

     Visual/sensory memories are characteristic in hypnotic states, and also occur in association with the "flashbacks" long linked with post-traumatic and other dissociative disorders (as see Hilgard, 1986, and Horowitz, 1976).

c.   *Lapses suggesting the simultaneous existence of incompatible systems of memory and consciousness.* Lapses in the monitoring of reasoning during the discussion of a loss experience include indications of belief that the lost person is simultaneously dead and alive (in the physical, rather than the religious/metaphysical sense). For example, one speaker said of a father who died some years previously, "It's probably better that he is dead, because he can get on with being dead and I can get back to my business". Aspects of this sentence indicating the existence of ideas regarding the father's status as simultaneously dead and not-dead include: (1) use of the present tense; (2) the implication that being dead is something which a dead person can actively "get on" with or "do", i.e., that being dead is an activity; (3) the implication that the deceased and the speaker are leading parallel lives in the present, each "getting on" with something.

Note that Bowlby (1980) discussed such cases extensively, pointing out that a bereaved person is faced with two worlds of plans and memories – the current one, in which the attachment figure is absent, and a second one in which feeling and behavior was organized with respect to the lost person. His analysis of one particular case, that of a young girl (Geraldine) who had lost her mother several years ago, is particularly striking. Struck by Hilgard's (1977) theorizing with respect to the possibilities of more than one executive/control systems operating in divided consciousness, Bowlby suggests that, during Geraldine's fugue states, executive control was given to a system in which she believed her mother to be alive and consequently set out to find her.

If the parents of "D" infants in low-risk samples suffer interference from dissociated or partially dissociated ideas or memories during the course of the Adult Attachment Interview, are they in similar states at other times as well? As mentioned earlier, startling vocal changes have been observed in the mothers of D infants (especially, during greetings). These occasionally take the form of sudden switches to a male register and intonation pattern. In addition, parents of "D" infants have been observed during the Strange Situation in immobilized postures accompanied by trance-like facial expressions (eyes half-open or staring blankly). These trance-like states may last for close to a full minute. Although rare, these and other informal observations (see Main & Hesse, 1990) suggest that some parents of D infants do enter into dissociative states in the infant's presence. Interestingly, during the Strange Situation, these kinds of parental behaviors have been followed almost immediately with D behaviors on the part of the infant.

What effect might the parent's entrance into a partially dissociative state in response to a frightening memory have upon an observing infant? In many cases, dissociative states may not be observable by infants or by adults: for example, in one of the most extreme of the dissociative disorders, multiple personality disorder, the behavior of the individual may appear entirely normal for long periods of time even though frightening memories and alternative personality states are fully dissociated.[17] It may be that only a minority of adults identified as Unresolved/disorganized/disoriented during the Adult Attachment Interview – as many as 15 to 35% of individuals in normal samples by our present estimate – suffer from any clinical form of dissociative disorder, including post-traumatic stress disorder. Nonetheless, the frightened and/or frightening behavior which we believe they exhibit may be at times the product of memories/ideas which are partially dissociated, and this may directly affect the infant and developing child. This may be because the parent's behavior is inherently frightening at times, as in the case of immobilized trancelike states in which the parent appears to be simultaneously "there and not-there". In these and other cases, the parent may additionally be frightening because they appear frightened, while the location of what is frightening remains either completely indiscernible (e.g., located in the parent's memories) or inexplicable (e.g., idiosyncratically associated with the parent's own traumatic experiences).

We suggest that in either case, the ambiguity, confusion and fear surrounding such observations and interactions could lead to the development in the offspring of *frightening ideation untraceable as to source*. These fears would be untraceable specifically because their origin would lie not in any directly traumatic experience, but rather in interactions with an attachment figure suffering from partially dissociated and frightening memories associated with their own history of trauma.

An adult who was raised by a *highly dissociative but nonabusive,* and perhaps even normally sensitive and responsive parent might well be unaware of this perplexing aspect of their experiential history. In addition, they would not be likely to manifest symptoms typically associated with traumatic experiences (symptoms now familiar to most clinicians). Such a person – with a history of unnamable experiences – might be particularly vulnerable to symptomatologies involving panic disorders (above), overwhelming anxiety experiences, and/or concepts of the self as bad or dangerous[18]. As a simple example, a parent who lost a young sibling through poisoning, and occasionally became frightened/dissociated in associated circumstances, could well engender a phobia related to poisoning in the offspring without ever discussing this loss or its concomitants. In similar ways, eerie fantasies involving peculiar or even "supernatural" connections among events, and feelings of inexplicably impending doom could be unrecognized second-generation effects of the parent's partially dissociated traumatic experiences.

Follow-up studies of "D" infants at six years of age do in fact suggest such outcomes. For example, Kaplan (1987) presented six-year-olds in the Bay Area study with six photographs of mild to moderately severe parent–child separations, asking in conjunction with each presentation what the child might feel and what a child might do. As six-year-olds, children who at 12 months of age had been judged Disorganized/disoriented with the mother in the Strange Situation were typically described (by judges blind to all other assessments) as "Fearful/disorganized/disoriented", seeming inexplicably afraid and unable to imagine anything the pictured child could do. Asked what the child would feel or do during the pictured separation, some imagined that the attachment figure or the child would be seriously hurt or killed:

*(Feels?)* She's afraid. *(Why is she afraid?).* Her dad might die and then she'll be by herself. *(Why is she afraid of that?).* Because her mom died and if her mom died, she thinks that her dad might die.

*(Do?)* Probably gonna lock himself up. *(Lock himself up?).* Yeah, probably in his closet. *(Then what will he do?).* Probably kill himself.

Kaplan, 1987, p. 110

Anticipating our immediate theme – the acquisition of mysterious fears through observation of a parent in a dissociative state – Kaplan also noted that some D children "make subtle remarks during the interview, implying that certain actions occur without an agent, that is things are done to them without knowing who the actor is. Such statements have an eerie quality, and suggest invisible actors who are unknown." This outcome appears to us consistent with a history of interacting with a parent mysteriously (frightened by events which are neither observed or known (see also Cassidy, 1986, 1988; Solomon & George, 1991[19]; Wartner, 1987).

## Conclusion

We began this paper with a description of the close tie between fear and attachment, emphasizing the way in which the attachment figure normally provides an infant with the solution to situations which are frightening. We suggested that the "organized" (A and C) patterns of insecure attachment represent solutions to frightening situations for infants whose parent is *unresponsive but not frightening,* and that these behavioral solutions are based on alterations in attention. We proposed that an infant who is, in contrast, directly *frightened by* the parent is locked in a paradox in which impulses to both approach and flee from the parent are operative. Placed in this position, the "D" infant suffers a collapse of both behavioral and attentional strategies.

Liotti (1992) has suggested that "D" infants may be lapsing into hypnotic/dissociative states. We supported his proposal with a description of trancelike states and dissociated actions considered indicative of D attachment status. An analysis of the lapses observed in the narratives of the parents of "D" infants during discussions of traumatic events also appeared to fit to a dissociative model.

This concluding analysis begins with an overview of some current conceptualizations of mental processing. It has recently been established that complex mental activities can take place outside of consciousness, in the form of parallel, distributed, and relatively unlimited processing "nets" which are (a) locally guided and (b) capable of influencing not only mental processes but also actions. The solutions/assessments of some nets may readily contradict others.

Conscious processes are currently identified with "working memory", an intermediary between short and long-term memory held responsible for reasoning and language processing. In direct opposition to parallel distributed processes, its operations are undertaken in coordination with a single overriding "processing goal", and overseen by control processes termed executive and monitoring functions. Working memory is limited by its singular and exclusively serial structure.

We apply these new conceptualizations of mental processes first to the lapses in narratives observed in the parents of "D" infants, and next to the behavior of the infants themselves. We suggest that frightening, paradoxical situations involving attachment figures are unsolvable at the serial level; cannot be avoided through a shift in attention; and will almost inevitably overwhelm the infant's already limited capacities for serial processing. Trancelike and dazed behaviors may then indicate lapses in serial processing. Repeated exposures to traumatic/ abusive paradoxical situations may lead to the development of independent, dissociated "nets" of mental activity – each potentially organized with respect to one of the competing and incompatible goals which cannot have simultaneous access to awareness.

## Parallel Distributed Processing and Working Memory

Parallel distributed processing, or "connectionism" (hereafter, PDP) constitutes a recent reconceptualization of information processing theory (Rumelhart & McClelland, 1986). Earlier versions had left no room for a "cognitive" unconscious: unattended perceptions and memories were presumed unable to influence higher processing, which was understood to consist in serial operations performed upon symbols. As noted earlier, however, Hilgard (1977/1986) had drawn attention to evidence for the existence of complex, deliberate and attention-consuming processes operating outside of awareness. Kihlstrom (1987) summarized additional evidence for the existence of a "cognitive unconscious" based upon studies of subliminal perceptions, automatic processes and implicit memories (see also Eagle, 1987). At about the same time, it was shown that an "exclusive or" proposition (which permits a response if only one, but not both, of two conditions are present) could not be solved by serial means, or by only two "layers" of parallel processors (Minsky & Papert, 1988), but could be "solved" by processes running in parallel and including a hidden layer. This meant that a "computer" model of mind as devoted exclusively to serial symbolic processing was inadequate to account for the existence of complex mental activities outside of our awareness, and did not permit minds to solve problems which in fact are readily solved.

The "computer" metaphor of mind has therefore been supplemented with what is currently called a "brain" metaphor of mind, in which each "node" may be in principle connected to all others. Memories are not presumed to be located in any particular node, but rather in the patterning of relations between nodes, which, operating in parallel on relatively simple problems, are termed "neural nets". Presented with a problem (e.g., the identification of a sound), these nets are presumed (a) to reach a solution through local changes in excitation and inhibition ("computations") and (b) to be capable of generalization.

In contrast to parallel processes, which can handle virtually unlimited data, working memory/consciousness is presumed to be a limited, serial processor. Closely identified with reasoning and language, its central task is that of activating information in long-term memory in order to operate upon it in short term memory in coordination with a current "processing goal". Anderson (1983) has proposed that, in keeping with its limited and serial nature, working memory can contain only one currently active goal at a time.[20] Incompatible goals are, again, not a difficulty for parallel processes.[21]

## Working memory, PDP, and lapses in narrative surrounding trauma

One characteristic of individuals suffering from dissociative disorders is a failure to mark trauma-related memories exclusively as memories rather than immediate perceptions. In an intriguing analysis of this problem, Siegel (1992) has proposed that the unique nature of trauma-specific memories may prevent the reflective, rehearsal modifications which permit their inclusion in an individual's life-narrative. Drawing upon a recent model of memory which simultaneously stores both perceptual and reflective components (Johnson, 1991) he suggests that if a traumatic event is too overwhelming for reflective processing to occur, its encoding may have a predominance of perceptual processing only. In this case, when re-activated, the "High Perception, Low Retrieval" memory configuration is likely to be difficult to identify as originating solely from internal sources.

In light of the above, some "lapses in the monitoring of discourse" observed in narratives surrounding traumatic events can now be understood as (a) lapses in working memory stemming from (b) intrusions from long-term memories which are partially processed as perceptions. In other words, lapses in the monitoring of discourse occurring in the parents of D infants may be attributable to loss of the maintenance of context – a central task of working memory which is especially critical to language production. In some cases, this loss of context may occur because the speaker's limited "working memory" capacity is overwhelmed by being forced to "attend" to frightening memories which are still partially processed perceptually. This is almost certainly the case when visual/sensory memories distort sentence formation. In other instances the speaker may lose the immediate context through a shift to a mental state not presently appropriate, but appropriate to the time of the episode being described (e.g., eulogistic speech).

Lapses in the monitoring of reasoning in the parents of D infants often reveal ideas which cannot be true in the same episode of space and time (e.g., dead/not dead) and violate the "exclusive or" requirement in that sense. At the least, such statements suggest intrusions from segregated processes whose products are not appropriately monitored for compatibility by the "reasoning" function in working memory, possibly again because its limited capabilities are momentarily overwhelmed by frightening material However, lapses in reasoning such as dead/not dead additionally suggest that *two* parallel, incompatible nets of associations may surround these incompatible premises, and that both are momentarily accessed. This would imply the development of dissociated <u>structures</u>, over and above a lapse in serial processing.

## Working memory, parallel processing and infant response to frightening, paradoxical situations involving attachment figures

In a paper remarkable for its elegance, Spiegel (1990) has pointed out that the "PDP" model of mental processing is inherently "contentious and dissociated", and that its emphasis upon local computations operating outside of an overseeing awareness makes special sense in application to the dissociative disorders. Here, we further utilize the PDP model to assist us in taking a developmental approach to these disorders, exploring the consequences of exposing an infant to the "paradox" of the threatening attachment figure discussed earlier.

The paradox presented to a young infant severely frightened by an attachment figure, and with no alternative attachment figures available, is inherently unsolvable. As noted earlier, it does not permit an escape through a shift of attention (one classic solution to animal conflict situations), nor is a behavioral solution available. Unlike the classic "double bind" situation, which involves externally originating conflicting signals, the attached infant is <u>biologically</u> rather than externally driven to perceive/respond to this <u>single</u> element of the environment in completely opposing ways. Moreover its flight and approach tendencies, both vital to survival, are mutually exacerbating. A situation of this kind must lead not only to a collapse of behavioral strategies, but also, we propose, to a "looping" of attention, since it is simultaneously too frightening to permit an attentional escape and too frightening to permit an attentional focus. This should lead to a loss of awareness of the surround, and inevitably a lapse in serial processing.

How does this apply to the two major kinds of phenotypically dissociative behaviors which we have observed in 12 month olds? It is possible that the <u>trancelike states</u> observed in others may represent no more than this kind of lapse in serial processing. In contrast, the <u>dissociated actions</u> observed in some infants may represent a more advanced byproduct of incompatible perceptions, experiences and impulses in which independent "nets" have developed and momentarily control behavior.

## Traumatic abuse involving attachment figures: "D/A-C" attachment status and the development of severe dissociative disorders

While our discussion to this point has been largely devoted to infant D attachment status in relation to interactions with a mildly dissociative, but nonabusive parent, here we consider the infant who is directly maltreated by the parent. Although traumatic experiences involving parental figures (e.g., experiences of battering and sexual abuse) have traditionally been linked to dissociative disorders, to our knowledge no link to dissociative-like behaviors in <u>infancy</u> has been previously recognized. Definitions of trauma have to this point in time been largely quantitative, i.e., as a psychologically distressing event outside the range of normal human experience, usually involving intense fear, terror and helplessness (DSMIII-R). We suggested however at the onset of this presentation that the attachment paradox described above adds a structural or qualitative dimension to our understanding of direct trauma involving an attachment figure. The most extreme of the dissociative disorders may then result not merely from overwhelmingly frightening experiences, but also because these experiences present the infant with an unsolvable paradox. The "structural" component of the paradox involves, of course, incompatible impulses to action, as well as a related, inevitable "looping" of attention.[22]

If, as we believe, maltreated infants frequently have parents who themselves suffer from dissociative disorders, then these infants are likely to be exposed to the paradox we have described in both its mild and its extreme forms. Chronic assaults upon the infant's body would, of course, constitute an extreme form of exposure. Under such conditions the experience of alarm must be far greater, and the propensity to (contradictory) actions will be at an extreme. The infant may, therefore, be vulnerable to the gradual development of independent nets representing incompatible aspects of its experience – nets which contribute not only to confusion of ideation, but also eventually to the control of behavior.

Let us now consider the case of the "D/A-C" infants briefly described above. We propose that these infants may not only be more vulnerable than other D infants to the development of dissociative disorders in general, but may, in addition, be at greater risk of developing the more extreme forms of these disorders. As noted earlier, Crittenden (1985/1988) described an "A-C" pattern of Strange Situation behavior in three to four year-old maltreated children, a pattern associated in her sample with the most severe forms of maltreatment. Our own observations of 12-to-18 month old <u>infants</u> from maltreatment and high-risk samples show that only a few of these infants combine (fractionated) "A" and "C" displays simultaneously or in rapid succession. The behavior of these infants is sufficiently striking, however, that we have urged investigators recoding their videotapes to consider "D/A-C" as a potentially meaningful sub-category (Man & Solomon, 1990).

"D/A-C" infants exhibit the extremes of the two possible behavioral and intentional "solutions" to the paradox created by severe maltreatment: distressed signalling or approach, occasionally accompanied by angry behavior (C) and withdrawal (A). These responses constitute, of course, not only a combination of the two incompatible manipulations of attention available to insecure infants, but also the contradictory <u>actions</u> which the infant exposed to an abusive attachment figure is impelled to take. In light of the above, we suggest that chronic exposure to extreme paradoxical conflict resulting from abuse by attachment figures may be the mechanism linking abuse to the development of differing executive controls on action, each associated with a differing attentional/behavioral structure. Insofar as these structures begin to appear in alternation (rather than in the disorganized-simultaneous forms observed in infancy), we may see them as providing a solution to the attachment paradox. One consciousness cannot solve this paradox, but a divided consciousness can.[23]

The outcome towards which we are heading is the possibility that the rare infant "D/A-C" attachment status (as well as dissociated actions manifest by some D infants[24], and infant "Cannot Classify" status described in Main & Solomon, 1990, but not explored here) may suggest a specific vulnerability to the later development of multiple personality disorder. The essential feature of this disorder is the existence within the person of two or more distinct personalities or personality states, each with its own relatively enduring pattern of perceiving, relating to, and thinking about the environment and the self. At least two of these personalities or personality states recurrently take full control of the person's behavior. The degree of impairment varies from mild to severe, but many high-functioning professionals have been diagnosed with this disorder.

Given the relatively well-organized behavior of many individuals suffering from this disorder, and the extremely disorganized nature of the infant behavior patterns we have been describing, we may well ask whether any phenotypic similarity exists between "D/A-C" (or "D/B") infant behavior patterns and the organized, although alternating personality states appearing in conjunction with the disorder. Interestingly, Putnam (1988, 1989) has suggested that multiple personality disorder may be based upon a normative substrate – specifically, the highly discrete behavioral states observed in newborns (Wolff, 1987) – and that the transitions between these states exhibit properties that are similar to those observed across "switches" of alters in multiple personality disorder.

A review of Putnam's descriptions of behaviors observed during the "switching" process shows a remarkable similarity to those behaviors listed by Main and Solomon (1990) as signs of infant disorganization and disorientation. Thus, the behaviors observed include unresponsive, trance-like states with blank, unseeing eyes; transient facial twitching or grimacing; upward rolls of the eyes; and sudden inexplicable shifts in affect. Any and all of these behaviors would be coded as disorganized/disoriented if observed in infants.

It may be that this apparent similarity in behavior is due to the fact that in each case the origins lie in a temporary lapse in serial processing. For the infant, this lapse is occasioned by its restricted abilities to comprehend and process incompatible, confusing or paradoxical experiences. For the adult, the dissociated nets underlying multiple personality disorder may create similar limitations wherein incompatible memories, often partially confused with incompatible perceptions, cannot be simultaneously processed.

# Summary

1.  For ground-living primate infants, the attachment figure normally provides the solution to all situations involving fear. When the attachment figure has been highly responsive to the infant in times of alarm, the infant is expected to seek the figure in times of alarm, but explore the environment when the figure is present. This behavioral pattern, identified by Ainsworth, is termed "secure" (B), and has been identified in the infant's response to parental leave-taking and return within the Strange Situation.

2.  When the attachment figure is either rejecting, or unpredictably responsive, infants respond to Ainsworth's Strange Situation with one of two "conditional" behavioral strategies, the one involving an organized shift of attention away from the attachment figure and fear-eliciting situations (A), the other involving a preoccupied focus (C).

3.  During the last decade, many investigators working observed that some infants cannot be classified as either A, B, or C in relation to the primary attachment figure. An analysis of unclassified infants conducted by Main and Solomon showed that they exhibit disorganized and/or disoriented (D) behaviors in the parent's presence during the Strange Situation. Main and Hesse interpreted these behaviors as indicating a collapse of behavioral and attentional strategy which would be expected if something about the attachment figure herself is frightening.

4.  Directly maltreating parents have been shown to have D infants. We proposed that parents still frightened by traumatic experiences might also behave in frightening ways in the infant's presence. This hypothesis was based in part on the observation that infant "D" attachment status was linked to lapses in the monitoring of reasoning or discourse during the parent's discussion of traumatic events.

5.  Liotti (1992) noted that frightened/frightening parental behavior was analogous to the "paradoxical behavioral injunction" occasionally used to induce hypnotic/trance states. He proposed that "D" infants might be in trancelike states at times, and that repeated entrance into such states could lead to increased risk with respect to the later development of dissociative disorders.

6.  We provided support for Liotti's hypothesis through a review of some infant behavior patterns previously identified as "disorganized and/or disoriented." Many dazed, disoriented and directly trancelike behaviors had been noted: in addition, some infants had exhibited dissociated actions.

7.  We re-examined the lapses in the monitoring of reasoning or discourse linked to infant "D" attachment status in normal (non-maltreating) samples. These lapses proved compatible with a dissociative model.

8.  This re-examination suggested that some non-abusive, and even otherwise well-treating parents of D infants could suffer from partially dissociative experiences. We suggested that dissociative states observed in a parent could be inherently frightening to witness, and produce mildly dissociative states in the offspring through this mechanism.

9.  Several investigators working with D six-year-olds in normal samples (Kaplan; Cassidy; Wartner; and Solomon & George) reported the development of fearful or aggressive fantasies, as well as, in some cases, the concept of a bad self. Main and Hesse suggested that these sequelae are compatible with interactions with a mysteriously frightened parent. We note further that the offspring of frightened/dissociative parents may develop incomprehensible phobias related to the parent's trauma, or may fear that the self is the cause of the parent's state of fright. Moreover, a frightened parent may provoke mildly aggressive responses in even a young infant, and these may become aggressive fantasies.

10. A number of these sequelae to interactions with a frightened/dissociated parent are compatible with phenomena of concern to Melanie Klein. Note, however, that most of these sequelae, no matter how disturbing to the individual, are concerned with ideation rather than action and do not suggest the development of separate, competing executive controls.

11. Recent theories of cognitive processing suggest that only a portion of mental processing is conscious and "serial", while the greater part – still capable of fairly advanced cognitions – takes place in distributed "nets" of "parallel" activities and is unconscious. Conscious-serial processing is identified with working memory, a mediator between long and short-term memory closely identified with language and reasoning processes. Working memory operates with singular processing goals, and presumably under executive guidance. Parallel processing nets, in contrast, may operate with contradictory goals and are locally guided.

12. We suggest that a number of the lapses in the monitoring of discourse observed in the parents of D infants may signal lapses in working memory. Some lapses in the monitoring of reasoning may additionally signal the development of parallel "nets" associated with incompatible ideas and memories, such as "dead/not dead".

13. A similar analysis is applied to the infant whose attachment figure behaves in a frightening manner. We suggest that this paradox (a) inevitably involves a "looping" of attention and (b) cannot be solved in "serial" fashion.

14. The trancelike states observed in some D infants may then be simply indicative of a lapse out of serial processing, while the "dissociated actions" which sometimes succeed trancelike states may indicate, further, the development and presence of parallel processes and memories which are somewhat dissociated.

15. We examine the special case of the infant whose parent is maltreating, inflicting bodily harm. In this circumstance, the infant may not only be momentarily unable to continue serial processing, but may also be vulnerable to developing parallel and relatively independent/dissociated neural nets which are, for example, associated respectively with flight towards, and flight away from the parent.

16. In some cases, these nets may be conceived of as "solving" the paradox which an abusive parent presents to consciousness. This "solution" results from the creation of a divided consciousness, each division representing one of the action tendencies which are simultaneously engendered when the infant is abused by an attachment figure.

17. Some (rare) "D/A-C" infants exhibit the extremes of the two "insecure" attentional and behavioral strategies, showing "A" and C" behaviors simultaneously. Working with a maltreatment sample of parents and infants, Crittenden observed this pattern of Strange Situation behavior in children three to four years of age, and found it associated with the most severe maltreatment. Because both "A" and "C" encompass full strategies rather than single actions, and because the strategies exhibited are highly incompatible, we suggest that "D/A-C" infants may be more vulnerable than others to developing the more severe of the dissociative disorders.

# Notes

1 Physiological measures and behavior observed in other situations have indicated that, despite their failure to exhibit distress or other forms of attachment behavior in this situation, Group A infants experience stress at least comparable to, and possibly greater than, that experienced by secure infants (Sroufe & Waters, 1977; Main, 1981).

2 As implied above, the patterning of the infant's behavior to a given parent in the Strange Situation is presumed to largely reflect the history of the infant's interactions with that parent. This implies in turn that, providing the parent is living in stable life circumstances, infant Strange Situation responses should be stable, which they are. At the same time, a given infant's Strange Situation response in the company of one parent is frequently different from the same infant's response to the Strange Situation in the company of the other parent, so that an infant whose Strange Situation behavior is insecure-avoidant with mother may well be secure with father or vice versa. However, Strange Situation behavior observed with a particular parent has been observed to change when the parent's life circumstances change markedly, this shift being presumed mediated by changes in parent-infant interaction patterns (see Bretherton, 1985 for a review of these studies).

3 In a study of the stability of infant responses to the Strange Situation over a two-week period, Ainsworth reported increased levels of distress during the second procedure (many infants seemed to recognize the situation). Subjected to the procedure for the second time, Group A infants failed to maintain sufficient avoidance to maintain the Group A classification, and were recoded as B for their proximity-seeking. However, coders reported considerable difficulties in classifying infant responses to the second procedure, suggesting that these infants may well have become disorganized when levels of stress required approach to a historically rejecting mother (see Ainsworth et al, 1978 and Main & Solomon, 1990).

4 Some disorganized/disoriented behaviors are to be expected in neurologically impaired children (as for example, autistic children and children suffering from Down's syndrome). When, however, the coding system is applied to neurologically normal samples, an experiential or interactional base is suggested. This is supported in part through evidence supplied below, i.e., the association of infant D attachment status with parental maltreatment, and with parental unresolved trauma. In addition, infant D/unclassifiable attachment status has been found independent across caregivers in two low-risk samples (see Main & Solomon, 1990, for review). Finally, in a sample of children seen with both parents at one and again at six years of age, infant D attachment status predicted specific dysfluent patterns of parent-child discourse, and controlling/role-inverting parent-child interactions--but only for discourse and interactions with that parent with whom the child had been judged Disorganized five years earlier (Main, Kaplan & Cassidy, 1985; Main & Cassidy, 1988).

5 The following seven thematic headings were used to represent the kinds of disorganized/disoriented behaviors most frequently observed (several examples of behavior of each type were offered): (1) Sequential display of contradictory behavior patterns, (2) Simultaneous display of contradictory behavior patterns, (3) Undirected, misdirected, incomplete and interrupted movements and expressions, (4) Stereotypies, asymmetrical movements, mistimed movements and anomalous postures, (5) Freezing, stilling and slowed movements and expressions, (6) Direct indices of apprehension regarding the parent, and (7) Direct indices of disorganization and disorientation.

6 Note that in the following system, certain indications of affective states which might clinically be considered indicative of incomplete resolution are not considered Unresolved. These include: Reports of lingering grief, crying during the discussion of the experience, expressions of continuing regret for experiences missed with the lost person, or (in the case of abuse) expressions of continuing hatred for the perpetrators.

7 If the speaker convincingly indicates that her mental organization is now entirely different than at the time of this reaction, such reports are not included as indicative of unresolved/disorganized status.

8 Main, DeMoss and Hesse developed a 9-point scale for scoring the degree to which a speaker indicated the presence of disorganized/disorienting (Unresolved) mental processes during the discussion of loss (Main & Goldwyn, 1991). In the Bay Area sample studied by Main & Hesse, fifteen mothers had experienced early loss of an attachment figure. Nine had infants assigned to D attachment status, and six had non-D infants The mean score for Unresolved mental processes for the mothers of the nondisorganized infants was 3.9, while the mean for the mothers of the Disorganized infants was 7.2. Thus, the mother's experience of early loss of an older family member did not in itself lead to infant D attachment status, unless the mother appeared to experience disorganized/disoriented (Unresolved) mental processes in consequence.

9 Two studies of high-stress, black and Hispanic poverty samples have now compared mother's Adult Attachment interview responses to infant Strange Situation attachment status. In one, interviews and Strange Situations were conducted concurrently (Carlson, 1990); in the other, interviews were conducted prenatally, and compared to the infant's response to the Strange Situation approximately 15 months later (Ward & Carlson, 1991). In both studies, the mother's Unresolved attachment status was again predictive of infant D attachment status. The potentially traumatic experience being discussed was, however, frequently sexual or physical abuse.

10 In contrast to frightening parental behaviors, which almost by definition arise from pathological conditions, frightened parental behaviors can have either normal or pathological origins. Frightened parental behaviors resulting from

immediately perceptible dangers (e.g., a parent's response to the infant approaching an apparently dangerous object) should normally differ from those produced by the parent's past traumatic experiences in that (1) ordinarily, the alarm will stem from a source external to the dyad (2) which is both discernible and comprehensible.

11  Plotkin and Schwarz (1985) describe confusion as one of the three chief methods of hypnotic induction, the others being absorption and relaxation. Green (1989) suggests that confusion induction, which consists of many discontinuities, leaves the subject stranded in the moment. This means a radical foreshortening of the temporal dimension, leaving the patient open to increased vulnerability to suggestion as to the "content" of the next moment.

12  Patients suffering from multiple personality disorder were not included in the sample of dissociative disorder patients, because this disorder seems related to later and much more severe traumas from the caregivers (see Ross, 1989 cited in Liotti, 1995).

13  This appears similar to Breur's view (as recounted by Freud) that "what happens in hypnoid hysteria is that an idea becomes pathogenic because it has been received during a special psychical state and has from the first remained outside the ego" (Breur & Freud, 1895/1986).

14  In practice, context is always considered before assignment is made to D attachment status. Although being dazed and motionless in the parent's arms is usually considered disoriented, we have frequently observed it as an otherwise well-organized infant makes the "state" transition from hard crying during separation. Brief bouts of dazed 'stilling' directly upon being picked up after hard crying are then not considered strong markers of disorientation. These assumptions of trancelike and dazed expressions during state changes in infancy are nonetheless interesting, particularly in the light of similar "switches" observed in adults suffering from dissociative disorders (see Putnam, 1989).

15  These patterns occur, again, only very rarely in infancy. A review of about 300 low-risk, Bay Area Strange Situation videotapes revealed at most 3 informal instances, and none using the formal criteria proposed by Speiker and Booth, 1985). In addition, the reader should remember that the term was initially used in many laboratories to reference all infants who were unclassifiable.

16  Because of the behavioral disorganization inevitable to both simultaneous and rapidly sequential display of anger/distress (resistance) and affectless avoidance, "A-C" infant Strange Situation behavior is currently captured by the coding instructions for "D", but regarded as a potentially important subgroup to be set aside for further and potentially separate analysis (Main & Solomon, 1990).

17  The behavior of adults suffering from this disorder may, of course, be somewhat abnormal when *changes* of personality state are in progress (Putnam, 1989), and some personality states may be directly frightened and/or frightening.

18  In work in progress, we suggest that the offspring of a dissociative-frightened parent may occasionally develop the idea they are themselves the source of the parent's alarm. Studies by Cassidy (1986, 1988) and Wartner (1987) show ideas of a "bad" self associated with infant or six-year "D" or "Controlling/D" attachment status.

19  In an important study of six-year-olds and their mothers, Solomon and George (1991) used the sixth-year Controlling/disorganized classification (Main & Cassidy, 1988) to identify children who may have been Disorganized/disoriented with the mother earlier. When children in this D-equivalent category were compared with children in the remaining (A, B, C-equivalent) sixth-year categories in a doll-play session featuring a child-parent separation, Controlling/D children were distinguished from others by the "nightmare" quality of their stories. As opposed to avoidant and ambivalent children, whose separation stories were innocuous, and secure children, who created a crisis followed by the resolution of a happy ending, Controlling/D children told separation stories involving violent fantasies in which increasingly uncontrollable events deteriorated into destruction, chaos, and sometimes the death of the child as well as the parents.

20  With respect to the response of working memory to conflict situations, Dennett (1991) also reviews a model (SOAR) in which conflict situations provide the basis of new mental activities at higher levels.

21  In this one-page overview, we have given the impression of greater unity regarding the entity under consideration than is warranted. There may be several (Squire, 1987) rather than one "working memory", and working memory may (Baddeley, 1992) or may not (Dennett, 1991) be controlled by a central executive.

22  It is interesting that Breuer and Freud (1893-1895) originally attributed the splitting of consciousness in the defense hysterias to incompatible ideation, and described the moment of splitting as "traumatic". The incompatible idea is later "excluded" and forms "an incompatible psychical group".

23  As noted earlier, the "exclusive or" (XOR) problem is presented to infants exposed to the attachment paradox in an insoluble form. While this is not a problem which can be solved by a serially processing machine (Minsky & Papert, 1988), it can of course be solved by adults who can hold more than one item of information in working memory. During extremely traumatic events involving attachment figures, however, even adults may be unable to move beyond the simultaneous toward/away paradox. Processing demands may, in other words, be so immediate in this situation that awareness is not possible. This would mean, in keeping with Siegel's (1992) recent proposal regarding trauma, that reflective processing of the event may vanish, while only perceptual processing remains available.

24  Although it seems likely that children who will later develop multiple personality disorders would exhibit neither A, B or C attachment patterns if seen in the Strange Situation with the abusing parent, the possibilities may be complex than those discussed to this point. Ross (1989) has stated that, among individuals suffering from chronic trauma, those somehow unable to develop multiple personality states in response may be the least functional and the least amenable to later treatment. Given the courage, intelligence, and capacity for relatedness often observed in individuals suffering from this disorder, it is possible that the capacity for developing multiple personality states (including, frequently, a "protector") may be present only in individuals who have had some early experiences of at least partial security. These (D/B) experiences could have occurred with an individual who later became sexually abusive, or (B) with an individual who was not involved in abusive experiences at all.

# References

Ainsworth, M. (1969). Object relations, dependency and attachment. *Child Development, 40*, 969–1025.

Ainsworth, M. D. S. (1990). Epilogue: Some considerations of attachment theory and assessment relevant to the years beyond infancy. In M. T. Greenberg, D. Cicchetti, & M. Cummings (Eds.). *Attachment in the preschool years: Theory, research and intervention* (pp. 463–488). Chicago: University of Chicago Press.

Ainsworth, M. D. S., Bell, S. M., & Stayton, D. J. (1974). Infant–mother attachment and social development: 'Socialisation' as a product of reciprocal responsiveness to signals. In M. J. M. Richards (Ed.). *The integration of a child into a social world* (pp. 9–135). Cambridge: Cambridge University Press.

Ainsworth, M., Blehar, M., Waters, E. & Wall, S. ([1978] 2015). *Patterns of attachment: A psychological study of the strange situation*. Hillsdale: Lawrence Erlbaum.

Ainsworth, M. D. S. & Eichberg, C. G. (1991). Effects on infant-mother attachment of mother's experience related to loss of an attachment figure. In: C.M. Parkes, J. Stevenson-Hinde, & P. Marris (Eds.). *Attachment across the life cycle* (pp. 160–183). New York: Routledge.

Anderson, J. R. (1983). A spreading activation theory of memory. *Journal of Verbal Learning and Verbal Behavior, 22* (3), 261–295.

Baddeley, A. D. (1990). The development of the concept of working memory: implications and contributions of neuropsychology. In Vallar, G. & Shallice, T. (Eds.). *Neuropsychological impairments of short-term memory (pp. 54–73.)* Cambridge: Cambridge University Press.

Bliss, E. L. (1986). *Multiple personality, allied disorders, and hysteria*. New York: Oxford University Press.

Bowlby, J. (1969/1982). *Attachment*. London: Penguin.

Bowlby, J. (1973). *Separation*. London: Pimlico.

Bowlby, J. (1980). *Loss*. New York: Basic Books.

Bretherton, I. (1985). Attachment theory: Retrospect and prospect. *Monographs of the Society for Research in Child Development, 50*, 3–35.

Breuer, J., & Freud, S. (1955). On the psychical mechanism of hysterical phenomena: Preliminary communication from studies on hysteria. In *The standard edition of the complete psychological works of Sigmund Freud, Volume II (1893–1895): Studies on Hysteria* (pp. 1–17). London: Vintage.

Carlson, E. A. (1990). *Individual differences in quality of attachment organization of high risk adolescent mothers Unpublished Doctoral dissertation*, Columbia University.

Carlson, V., Cicchetti, D., Barnett, D., & Braunwald, K. (1989). Finding order in disorganization: Lessons from research on maltreated infants' attachments to their caregivers. In D. Cicchetti & V. Carlson (Eds.). *Child maltreatment: Theory and research on the causes and consequences of child abuse and neglect* (pp. 494–528). Cambridge: Cambridge University Press.

Cassidy, J. A. (1986). *Attachment and the self at age six*. Unpublished doctoral dissertation. University of Virginia.

Cassidy, J. (1988). Child–mother attachment and the self in six-year-olds. *Child Development, 59* (1), 121–34.

Chapman, R. K., Elkins, G. R., & Carter, B. D. (1982). Childhood hypnotic susceptibility: a review. *The Journal of the American Society of Psychosomatic Dentistry and Medicine, 29* (2), 54–63.

Crittenden, P. M. (1985). Maltreated infants: Vulnerability and resilience. *Journal of Child Psychology and Psychiatry, 26* (1), 85–96.

Crittenden, P. M., & Ainsworth, M. D. (1989). Child maltreatment and attachment theory. In D. Cicchetti & V. Carlson (Eds.). *Child maltreatment: Theory and research on the causes and consequences of child abuse and neglect (pp. 432–462)*. New York, NY: Cambridge University Press.

Crittenden, P. M., & Ainsworth, M. D. S. (1989). Child maltreatment and attachment theory. In D. Cicchetti (Ed.). *Handbook of child maltreatment theory and research: A lifespan developmental perspective* (pp. 432–463). Cambridge: Cambridge University Press.

Dennett, D. C. (1991), *Consciousness explained*. Boston: Little, Brown and Company.

Eagle, M.N. (1987). The psychoanalytic and the cognitive unconscious. In R. Stern (Ed.). *Theories of the unconscious and theories of the self* (pp. 155–189). New York: Analytic Press.

Egeland, B., & Sroufe, L.A. (1981). Attachment and early maltreatment. *Child Development, 52* (1): 44–52.

Erickson, M. (1964). A hypnotic technique for resistant patients: The patient, the technique and its rationale and field experiments. *American Journal of Clinical Hypnosis, 7,* 8–32.

Erickson, M. H., Rossi, E. L., & Rossi, S. I. (1976). *Hypnotic realities: The induction of clinical hypnosis and forms of indirect suggestion.* New York: John Wiley.

Green, J. L. (1989). The confusion induction: A phenomenological explication. *Australian Journal of Clinical & Experimental Hypnosis. 17* (1), 45–60.

Hilgard, E. R. (1964). Individual differences in hypnotizability. In J. E. Gordon (Ed.). *Handbook of clinical and experimental hypnosis* (pp. 391–433). New York: Macmillan.

Hilgard, E. R. ([1977] 1986). *Divided consciousness: Multiple controls in human thought and action.* New York: Wiley.

Horowitz, M. J. (1976). *Stress response syndromes.* New York: Aronson.

Johnson, M. K. (1992). MEM: Mechanisms of recollection. *Journal of Cognitive Neuroscience, 4,* 268–280.

Kaplan, N. (1987). *Individual differences in 6-years olds' thoughts about separation: Predicted from attachment to mother at age 1 Unpublished doctoral dissertation.* Department of Psychology, University of California, Berkeley, CA.

Kihlstrom, J. F. (1987). The cognitive unconscious. *Science, 237* (4821), 1445–1452.

Kluft R. P. (1985) The natural history of multiple personality disorder. In R. P. Kluft (Ed.). *Childhood antecedents of multiple personality* (pp. 197–238). Washington, DC: American Psychiatric Press.

Liotti, G. (1992). Disorganized/disoriented attachment in the etiology of the dissociative disorders. *Dissociation, 5*(4), 196–204.

Liotti, G. (1995). Disorganized/disoriented attachment in the psychotherapy of the dissociative disorders. In S. Goldberg, R. Muir, & J. Kerr (Eds.). *Attachment theory: social, developmental, and clinical perspectives* (pp. 343–363). Hillsdale, NJ: Analytic Press.

Liotti, G., Intreccialagli, B., & Cecere, F. (1991). Esperienza di lutto nella madre e predisposizione ai disturbi dissociativi della prole: Uno studio caso-controllo. *Rivista di Psichiatria, 26,* 283–291.

Lyons-Ruth, K., Connell, D., Zoll, D., & Stahl, J. (1987). Infants at social risk: relations among infant maltreatment, maternal behavior, and infant attachment behavior. *Developmental Psychology, 23* (2), 223–232.

Main, M. (1979) The "ultimate" causation of some infant attachment phenomena: Further answers, further phenomena, further questions. *Behavioral and Brain Sciences, 2,* 640–643.

Main, M. (1981). Avoidance in the service of proximity: A working paper. In K. Immelmann, B. Barlow, L. Petrovich & M. Main (Eds.). (1981) *Behavioral development: The Bielefeld interdisciplinary project* (pp. 694–699). Cambridge: Cambridge University Press.

Main, M. (1990). Cross-cultural studies of attachment organization: Recent studies, changing methodologies, and the concept of conditional strategies. *Human Development, 33,* 48–61.

Main, M., & Cassidy, J. (1988). Categories of response to reunion with the parent at age 6: Predictable from infant attachment classifications and stable over a 1-month period. *Developmental Psychology, 24* (3), 415–426.

Main, M., & Goldwyn, R. (1991). *Adult attachment scoring and classification systems.* Unpublished manuscript.

Main, M. & Hesse, E. (1990). Parents' Unresolved Traumatic Experiences are related to Infant Disorganized Attachment Status: Is frightened/frightening parental behavior the linking mechanism? In M. Greenberg, D. Cicchetti & M. Cummings (Eds.). *Attachment in the preschool years* (pp. 161–182). Chicago: University of Chicago Press.

Main, M. & Solomon, J. (1986) Discovery of a new, insecure-disorganized/disoriented attachment pattern. In Yogman, M. & Brazelton, T. B. (Eds.). *Affective development in infancy* (pp. 95–124). Norwood, NJ: Ablex.

Main, M. & Solomon, J. (1990) Procedures for identifying infants as disorganized/disoriented during the Ainsworth Strange Situation. In M. T. Greenberg, D. Cicchetti & E. M. Cummings (Eds.). *Attachment in the preschool years* (pp. 121–160), Chicago: University of Chicago Press.

Main, M., & Stadtman, J. (1981). Infant response to rejection of physical contact by the mother. *Journal of the American Academy of Child Psychiatry, 20* (2), 292–307.

Main, M., & Weston, D. R. (1982). The quality of the toddler's relationship to mother and to father: Related to conflict behavior and the readiness to establish new relationships. *Child Development, 52* (3), 932–940.

Main, M., Kaplan, N. & Cassidy, J. (1985). Security in infancy, childhood, and adulthood: A move to the level of representation. *Monographs of the Society for Research in Child Development, 50,* 66–104.

Minsky, M. & Papert, S. (1988) *Perceptions.* Cambridge, MA: MIT Press.

Nash, M. R., & Lynn, S. J. (1986). Child abuse and hypnotic ability. *Imagination, Cognition and Personality, 5* (3), 211–218.

Overton, D. A. (1977). Drug state dependent learning. In M. E. Jarvik (Ed.). *Psychopharmacology in the practice of medicine* (pp. 73–79). New York: Appleton—Century-Crofts.

Plotkin, W. B., & Schwartz, W. R. (1985). A conceptualization of hypnosis: II. Hypnotic induction procedures and manifestations of the hypnotic state. *Advances in Descriptive Psychology, 4,* 75–101.

Putnam, F. W. (1985). Dissociation as a response to extreme trauma. In R. P. Kluft (Ed.). *Childhood antecedents of multiple personality* (pp. 65–97). Washington DC: American Psychiatric Press.

Putnam, F. W. (1989). Pierre Janet and modern views of dissociation. *Journal of Traumatic Stress, 2* (4), 413–429.

Radke-Yarrow, M., Cummings, E. M., Kuczynski, L., and Chapman, M. (1985). Patterns of attachment in two- and three-year–olds in normal families and families with parental depression. *Child Development, 56,* 884–893.

Ross, C. A. (1989). *Multiple personality disorder: Diagnosis, clinical features, and treatment.* New York: Wiley.

Rumelhart, D. E. & McClelland, J. L. (1986). *On learning the past tenses of English verbs.* Cambridge, MA: MIT Press.

Solomon, J., George, C., & De Jong, A. (1995). Children classified as controlling at age six: Evidence of disorganized representational strategies and aggression at home and at school. *Development and Psychopathology, 7* (3), 447–463.

Spiegel, D. (1990). Trauma, dissociation, and hypnosis. In R. P. Kluft (Ed.). *Incest-related syndromes of adult psychopathology* (pp. 247–261). Washington: American Psychiatric Press.

Spiegel, D. (1990) Hypnosis, dissociation and trauma: Hidden and overt observers. In J. L. Singer (Ed.). *Repression and dissociation: Implications for personality theory, psychopathology and health* (pp. 121–142). Chicago: University of Chicago Press.

Siegel, D. J. (1995). Memory, trauma and psychotherapy: A cognitive science view. *Journal of Psychotherapy Practice and Research, 4* (2), 93–122.

Spieker, S., & Booth, C. (1988). Maternal antecedents of attachment quality. In J. Belsky & T. Nezworski (Eds.). *Clinical implications of attachment* (pp. 95–135). Hillsdale, NJ: Erlbaum.

Squire L. R. (1987) *Memory and brain.* Oxford: Oxford University Press.

Sroufe, L. A., & Waters, E. (1977). Attachment as an organizational construct. *Child Development, 48* (4), 1184–1199.

Ward, M. J., & Carlson, E. A. (1995). Associations among adult attachment representations, maternal sensitivity, and infant–mother attachment in a sample of adolescent mothers. *Child Development, 66* (1), 69–79.

Wartner, U. G., Grossmann, K., Fremmer-Bombik, E., & Suess, G. (1994). Attachment patterns at age six in south Germany: Predictability from infancy and implications for preschool behavior. *Child Development, 65* (4), 1014–1027.

# 7

# The Prototype Hypothesis and the Origins of Attachment Working Models: Adult Relationships with Parents and Romantic Partners

Gretchen Owens, Judith A. Crowell, Helen Pan, Dominique Treboux, Elizabeth O'Connor, and Everett Waters

Freud (1940) viewed the infant–mother relationship as a prototype that influenced the formation and course of later love relationships. Attachment theory shares with psychoanalytic theory the assumption that attachment experience in infancy is a major influence on later love relationships (Bowlby, 1973; Waters, Johnson, & Kondo-Ikemura, 1995). Bowlby (1973, 1980, 1988) preserved Freud's insight regarding the importance of early experiences and took some of the mystery out of the link between early experience and later affect, cognitions, and behavior by proposing that internal "working models" of self and other are constructed out of interactions with the primary attachment figure. He also described these representations as dynamic, in the sense that they are always "under construction" and can change, not only in the course of psychotherapy, but also in light of experiences within later attachment relationships.

Across the life span, individuals may develop attachment-like relationships with several different partners, including mothers, fathers, siblings, and other relatives, nonfamilial caregivers, peers, and – during adolescence and adulthood – romantic partners and spouses. While these relationships differ in a variety of ways, any of them can serve as a context for important attachment experiences (i.e., receiving care, using another as a base for exploration, or using another as a safe haven when aroused or threatened). Attachment researchers have considered parents (or other primary caregivers) as the most influential in terms of the construction of internal working models of attachment and models of the self, but the fact that most people participate in relationships with multiple partners presents current attachment theory with an array of difficult questions. Does early experience leave us with a generalized attachment representation that contributes to the development and course of all later love relationships? Are there also (or instead) representations associated with specific relationships? How are representations of early (child–parent) and later (adult–adult) relationships related? Are there patterns of concordance consistent with the notion that early representations significantly influence the nature of later representations? How do adults' representations of early experience and of current relationships influence the development and quality of romantic relationships? The answers to these questions will shape our understanding of how relationship experience is represented and how past experience influences subsequent relationships.

Empirical research on these questions depends on the design of relevant assessment tools. Although the Strange Situation paradigm (Ainsworth, Blehar, Waters, & Wall, 1978) has long been employed for assessing toddlers' attachments, the first tool to emerge for use with adults was the Adult Attachment Interview (AAI; George, Kaplan, & Main, 1984; Main, Kaplan, & Cassidy, 1985). Rather than focusing on the relationship with a particular

*Source:* Republished with permission of John Wiley & Sons, Inc., from Gretchen Owens et al., "The Prototype Hypothesis and the Origins of Attachment Working Models: Adult Relationships with Parents and Romantic Partners," pp. 216–223 from *Monographs of the Society for Research in Child Development* 60:2-3 (April 1995); permission conveyed through Copyright Clearance Center, Inc.

person, the AAI addresses the individual's overall "state of mind" with regard to attachment (i.e., his or her general way of thinking about attachment relationships). The AAI has opened up a wide range of possibilities for research on adults' and adolescents' attachment-related working models (see van IJzendoorn & Bakermans-Kranenburg, 1996) and relations between current working models of attachment and other variables (Crowell & Treboux, 1995).

In order to examine how closely adults' models of their current love relationships correspond to the generalized attachment models believed to be accessed by the AAI, we developed a parallel instrument, the Current Relationship Interview (CRI), and employed both measures in the first stage of a longitudinal study of engaged couples. In this report, we present data on concordance between AAI and CRI classifications and the relation of a given individual's AAI classification to behavior in a love relationship as described by the partner.

The present data address three principal issues. First, how similar are representations of attachment to parents and representations of attachment to an adult partner in a love relationship (AAI–CRI concordance)? Is the correspondence between AAI and CRI classifications within the individual great enough to suggest that representations of child–parent and current adult love relationships are integrated within a single overall model of attachment? Positive results would lend support to Freud's prototype hypothesis, whereas finding substantial differences in the two representations would suggest that separate models are maintained for different relationships or different types of relationships.

Second, we were interested in testing the degree of similarity between the two partners' descriptions of their current romantic relationship (CRI–CRI concordance) as well as between their descriptions of their respective child-parent relationships (AAI–AAI concordance). Finally, these data address the important issue of learning across relationships (Waters, Kondo-Ikemura, Posada, & Richters, 1990). If, as Sroufe and Fleeson (1986) argue, the child internalizes the roles of both the attached and the caregiving partners and carries this relational history into subsequent relationships, we can predict that someone who has experienced sensitive and responsive care during childhood (i.e., has been securely attached) will be able to provide similar care to an adult partner in future relationships. By evaluating the correspondence between an individual's AAI security classification and his or her partner's description of their current relationship, we test the hypothesis that past experiences in attachment relationships help forecast both a person's behavior and the security of his or her partner in future love relationships. Our data permit evaluation of this hypothesis at the level of overall classifications (concordance between subject's AAI and partner's CRI) and at the level of individual dimensions relevant to attachment security (e.g., love and rejection).

## Method

### Subjects

Subjects were 45 engaged couples, part of a larger sample who volunteered to participate in the Stony Brook Relationship Project, a longitudinal study of relationship formation in young adults. Their ages ranged from 20 to 26 for the women ($M = 23.40$, SD = 1.59) and from 20 to 31 for the men ($M = 25.02$, SD = 2.31). The sample was 92% white, 2% black, and 5% Hispanic. Most were from middle-class, intact homes (72% had parents who were still married, while the parents of 27% of the participants were divorced or separated and of 1% widowed). At the time of the interview, the couples had been dating for a mean of 4.3 years (SD = 2.15), with a range of 1–11 years, including an engagement period that averaged 14 months (range = 1 month–3 years).

### Measures

*Adult attachment interview*
The AAI (George et al., 1984) is a semistructured interview designed to elicit a subject's recollections about relationships with parents and other significant attachment figures during childhood. The interviewer asks about childhood experiences with parents, significant separations and losses during childhood, and the current status of the child–parent relationship.

The scoring system was developed by Mary Main and Ruth Goldwyn in conjunction with the development of the interview. Scoring of the interview is based on (*a*) descriptions of childhood experiences in parent–child relationships, (*b*) the language used to describe past experiences, and (*c*) the ability to give an integrated, believable account of experiences and their meaning (Main & Goldwyn, 1991). The interview is scored from a transcript using scale points that, in the coder's opinion, characterize the degree to which each parent was loving, rejecting, neglecting, involving, and pressuring. A second set of scales is used to assess the subject's state of mind and discourse style: overall coherence of transcript and of thought, idealization, insistence on lack of recall, active anger, derogation, fear of loss, metacognitive monitoring, and passivity of speech. The scale scores are used to assign the adult to one of three major attachment classifications: secure, insecure/dismissing, and insecure/preoccupied. These parallel the secure, avoidant, and resistant/ambivalent classifications of the Ainsworth Strange Situation scoring system (Ainsworth et al., 1978).

Individuals are classified as secure if they can readily and spontaneously describe a wide range of childhood experiences, understand and attach plausible explanations to (good or bad) experiences with their parents, value attachment relationships, and view attachment-related experiences as influential in their development. They are classified as insecure if their reports and explanations lack "coherence," that is, if their responses seem inconsistent or implausible. From this we infer a deficiency in the underlying "working model" that ordinarily links memories of past experience with the meaning and interpretations of past experience. As in the Strange Situation, there are two major subgroups within the insecure group. Individuals classified as insecure/dismissing tend to deny or devalue the effect of early attachment relationships, have difficulty recalling specific events, often idealize experiences, and usually describe an early history of rejection. Those classified as insecure/preoccupied tend to display confusion about their past experiences and are unable to gain insight into early events, and their current relationships with parents tend to be marked by active anger or by passivity and attempts to please parents.

Individuals may be classified as unresolved in addition to one of the three major classifications. These adults have experienced attachment-related traumas such as a loss or abuse. Their discussions of the traumatic experience are characterized by lapses in monitoring of reasoning (e.g., indications of disbelief that the event occurred), lapses in monitoring of discourse (e.g., eulogistic speech in discussing a death), or extreme behavioral responses (e.g., displaced reactions). The scoring system gives the unresolved classification precedence over the major classification in categorizing the individual, and the relationship is considered insecure.

Several recent studies (e.g., Bakermans-Kranenburg & van IJzendoorn, 1993; Crowell et al., 1996) have established the discriminant validity of the security classifications based on ratings of AAI transcripts, demonstrating the validity of the AAI vis-à-vis social desirability, cognitive complexity, narrative style, IQ, or general social adjustment. Researchers have shown that AAI security classifications are stable over a period of 18 months (Benoit & Parker, 1994; Waters et al., 1994). Classifications are also associated with reports of marital conflict (Cohn, Silver, Cowan, Cowan, & Pearson, 1992; O'Connor, Pan, Waters, & Posada, 1995; O'Connor et al., 1993).

*Current relationship interview*

The CRI was devised by Crowell (1990) in order to investigate how adults mentally represent their attachment to a dating or marriage partner, as reflected in how they speak about their relationships. The intent was to design an interview that paralleled the structure and content of the AAI as closely as possible but targeting the current love relationship of the subject. The interview covers the person's dating history, the nature of the present relationship and characteristics of the partner, and routine behaviors within the relationship, especially those related to seeking and providing support. To get an overview of how subjects view their relationship, questions are also included about the effects of the relationship on them, what they have learned from being in the relationship, and their hopes and fears for the future of the relationship.

The scoring system (Owens & Crowell, 1993) also parallels the format of the AAI. The 23 dimensions fall into five general categories, each scored on a nine-point rating scale. Three of the scales assess the person's observations of and experience in adult–adult relationships: how warm the parents' marriage was, the degree of conflict in the parents' marriage, and the intensity of the subject's previous dating relationships. Three scales assess how the person depicts his or her partner along the dimensions of being loving, rejecting of attachment, and open in communication. Six scales describe the rater's impression of the subject: how open he or she is in communicating with the partner, how skilled he or she is at taking another person's perspective, how satisfied he or she is with the partner, how dependent he or she is on the partner or on others, to what extent he or she seems to value intimacy, and how much he or she values autonomy. Four scales measure the subject's and the partner's abilities to assume a caregiving role and a nurturance-seeking (attachment) role. Finally, the subject's discourse style is rated on the same seven dimensions used in the AAI: anger, derogation of partner and of attachment in general, idealization of the partner (or the relationship), passive speech, fear of losing the partner, and overall coherence of the transcript.

These scale scores are used to assign the subject to one of three attachment classifications that parallel the AAI classification system: secure, insecure/dismissing, and insecure/preoccupied. The secure classification is given to subjects who coherently and believably describe the relationship with a partner; in most cases the partner provides security and comfort and is someone in whose availability subjects are confident. Insecure subjects are less coherent in discussing their relationships, less likely to express a valuing of intimacy and/or autonomy, and less able to function as a secure base for the partner. The dismissing classification is assigned when subjects avoid attachment concerns either by denying or minimizing the limitations of a rather unloving partner or by focusing on other facets of life instead of the relationship. Preoccupied subjects appear confused or angry about the relationship or the partner's behavior and may be anxious about the partner's ability to fulfill their needs for support and closeness.

To provide an analogue to the AAI Unresolved Loss and Unresolved Trauma scales, one final scale, Effects of Loss on Present Relationship, was added. On the CRI, the Loss scale is limited to losses of peers (either romantic partners or close friends), but not just through death: distance or dissension may also lead to unresolved feelings that interfere with the present relationship. High scores on this scale lead to a major classification of unresolved; a secondary classification of secure, dismissing, or preoccupied is also assigned.

### Self-report measures

The Dyadic Adjustment Scale (DAS; Spanier, 1976) includes a list of 14 common sources of conflict within relationships (e.g., finances, household tasks, religion); three additional topics pertinent to the engagement period and an open-ended space for "other" were added. For each item, the subject was asked to indicate how often he or she and the partner have disagreed or quarreled about that topic during the previous 6 months. The DAS also includes a scale for reporting satisfaction with the relationship, rated from "extremely unhappy" to "perfectly happy."

### Procedure

Each couple came to the Department of Psychology twice within the 3 months before their wedding date. A battery of tests and questionnaires, two interviews (AAI and CRI), and a videotaped interaction were completed by the end of the two 2-hour sessions. Each subject was individually interviewed with the CRI in the first session and with the AAI in the second session.

The CRIs were scored blind from typed transcripts, without knowledge of the subject's identity or any other information about the subject. Half the transcripts were scored independently by a second coder; disagreements in major classification were resolved in conference with a third coder (JAC). The scorers gave the same classification as secure, dismissing, or preoccupied 85% of the time and agreed on whether the person was secure or insecure 87% of the time ($\kappa = .79$ and $.75$, respectively, $p < .0001$ for both).

Each AAI transcript was scored by one of three researchers who had received AAI training with Mary Main; 25% were also scored by a second rater. Disagreements were resolved in conference. Overall, these scorers achieved 77% agreement for secure/dismissing/preoccupied classifications and 80% agreement for security/insecurity ($\kappa = .56$ and $.60$ respectively, $p < .001$ for both).

## Results

Like the Strange Situation, the AAI and the CRI can be scored in terms of (*a*) a secure–insecure dichotomy, (*b*) one secure and either two or three discrete insecure groups, or (*c*) numerous secure and insecure subgroups. The level of analysis chosen for a particular study depends on theoretical and practical considerations. In our primary analyses, we focus on the secure–insecure dichotomy since this approach affords the greatest statistical power as we address concordance questions. Nonetheless, breakdowns for specific insecure groups (i.e., dismissing, preoccupied, and unresolved) are included wherever they are of descriptive or hypothesis-generating value. Cohen's kappa and Fisher's exact probability test were used to evaluate the significance of the secure/insecure cross-tabulated data, while chi-square was employed for three- and four-group analyses.

## Difference between the percentage of subjects scored as secure on the AAI and on the CRI

For descriptive purposes, we first compared rates of secure attachment attained on the AAI and the CRI. Fifty-six percent of the subjects in the present sample were classified as secure on the AAI; this is comparable to the rates for middle-class nonclinical samples (55%–60%) summarized in van IJzendoorn and Bakermans-Kranenburg's (1996) meta-analysis. Among the insecure subjects, 77% were dismissing; in the van IJzendoorn and Bakermans-Kranenburg samples, insecure subjects were more evenly split between dismissing and preoccupied. A number of factors could contribute to this difference: sampling error, the fact that ours is a community rather than a university sample, or regional differences in child rearing and family behavior.

Attachment theory does not afford a specific prediction about relative rates of security to be expected from AAI and CRI interviews. With the opportunity to construct and revise over many years a working model of the child–parent relationship, one might expect higher rates of security on the AAI than on the CRI. On the other hand, romantic partners (unlike parents) are chosen freely; both courtship and the process of leaving unsatisfying relationships might have been expected to inflate the rate of secure attachment in our CRI data. In actuality, the rates of secure attachment scored from the two interviews were similar: 50 of 90 subjects (56%) for the AAI and 42 of 90 (47%) for the CRI. The difference between these rates was not significant ($p = .42$).

Because the CRI is a new measure, it is also important to consider issues of discriminant validity that have already been addressed for the AAI. In the present case, the most important of these concern the relations of CRI classifications to measures of marital discord and satisfaction. Clearly, on the basis of content alone there should be some association between the CRI and such marital variables; the issue is whether the classifications carry additional unique information. To evaluate this, we calculated point-biserial correlations between CRI secure/insecure assignments and scores from two sections of the DAS: the global satisfaction rating and the total score on the conflict items. Security on the CRI was significantly associated with marital variables ($r = .36$ for satisfaction and $r = -.45$ for conflict, $p < .001$ for both). As expected, the correlations are significant, but they are not nearly so large as to raise concerns that the CRI is little more than a measure of marital satisfaction.

## Similarities between individuals' perspectives on their relationships with parents (AAI) and a romantic partner (CRI)

If attachment working models formed in childhood serve as important prototypes for subsequent conceptualizations of romantic relationships, one would expect significant associations between individuals' AAI and CRI status. Our results support this prediction; overall, 64% of the subjects received the same AAI and CRI ratings as secure or insecure (expected = 49%; $\kappa = .29$, $p < .002$). Of the 50 subjects classified as secure on the AAI, 30 were also secure on the CRI; of the 40 classified as insecure on the AAI, 28 were also insecure on the CRI.[1] Table 7.1 presents the cross-tabulation of subjects' AAI classifications with their own CRI classifications. For descriptive purposes, the complete four-group classifications are presented. As noted earlier, the CRI scoring system includes a set of rating scales that parallel the scales used to score the AAI. To examine similarities between child–parent and romantic partner relationships further, we computed Pearson correlations between corresponding AAI and CRI scales. The results of these analyses are presented in Table 7.2.

Overall, only three of these 11 correlations were significant for the full sample. However, when data from males and females were analyzed separately, a clear sex difference emerged in the pattern of results. In the male subsample, all correlations were positive, and seven of the 11 values reached the conventional level of significance (mean $r$ for significant correlations = .37); in the female subsample, only three of 11 correlations were significant. The pattern of results reveals significant effects from both mother and father for males. For females, on the other hand, past experiences with neither mother nor father correlated with partner scales, while the state-of-mind variables evidenced a stronger paternal influence. Because attachment theory does not specifically predict such differences, these results need to be replicated and extended before engaging in extensive speculation concerning their implications.

The issue of possible sex differences is an important one in attachment research. As Posada, Liu, and Waters (1994) point out, the absence of mean differences between the sexes in Strange Situation data does not preclude sex differences in how infant attachment data relate to other variables. Posada et al. illustrate this point by showing strong sex differences in the correlations of attachment security with socialization outcomes in preschool-aged

**Table 7.1**  Concordance of current relationship interview (CRI) and adult attachment interview (AAI) classifications

| AAI Classifications | CRI Classifications | | | |
|---|---|---|---|---|
| | Secure | Dismissing | Preoccupied | Unresolved |
| Secure | 30 | 14 | 6 | 0 |
| | (33) | (16) | (7) | (0) |
| Dismissing | 6 | 16 | 2 | 0 |
| | (7) | (18) | (2) | (0) |
| Preoccupied | 0 | 1 | 2 | 0 |
| | (0) | (1) | (2) | (0) |
| Unresolved | 6[a] | 3[b] | 2[c] | 2[d] |
| | (7) | (3) | (2) | (2) |

*Note*: Secondary classifications for subjects classified unresolved on the AAI were as follows:

[a] four secure, two dismissing;

[b] one secure, two preoccupied;

[c] one preoccupied, one dismissing/preoccupied; and

[d] one dismissing, one dismissing/preoccupied. Percentages are given in parentheses.

**Table 7.2**  Pearson correlations between analogous adult attachment interview (AAI) and current relationship interview (CRI) scales

| AAI/CRI Scale | Past Experience Scales | | |
|---|---|---|---|
| | Full Sample | Males | Females |
| Mother loving/Partner loving | .15 | .35** | −.03 |
| Mother rejecting/Partner rejecting | .13 | .36** | −.05 |
| Father loving/Partner loving | .09 | .20 | .01 |
| Father rejecting/Partner rejecting | .15 | .36** | −.01 |
| | Current State of Mind/Discourse Style | | |
| Anger at mother/Anger at partner | .14 | .28* | .08 |
| Idealization of mother/Idealization of partner | .14 | .16 | .09 |
| Derogation of mother/Derogation of partner | .05 | .25* | -.15 |
| Anger at father/Anger at partner | .45*** | .45*** | .47*** |
| Idealization of father/Idealization of partner. | .19* | .11 | .26* |
| Derogation of father/Derogation of partner | .11 | .01 | .22 |
| Coherence on AAI/Coherence on CRI | .43*** | .54*** | .33* |

Note: Because positive correlations are expected between comparable AAI and CRI scales, all significance levels are for one-tailed tests.

* $p < .05$.

** $p < .01$.

*** $p < .001$.

children. Sex-related patterns would seem even more likely in adult attachment data. In light of the present results, correlations involving AAI or CRI scales should be computed separately for males and females, and the sexes should be combined only if the results are comparable in both groups.

## Correspondence between AAI security classifications of the two partners in the romantic relationship

In some formulations of the prototype hypothesis, it is proposed that individuals seek out partners with whom they can have relationships similar to those they had with their parents. In the present data, this would be reflected in a tendency for secure individuals to seek secure partners – or perhaps to avoid anxious ones – and for anxious people to enter into relationships with others who are similarly anxious (i.e., preoccupied or dismissing about attachment). This interpretation was not supported by the AAI concordance data; analysis of the correspondence between partners' security on the AAI revealed a 56% concordance rate (25 of 45 pairs; $\kappa = .10$, N.S.; Fisher's exact probability $= .35$). Using a three-group typology, 53% (24 pairs) received the same classification as secure, dismissing, or preoccupied; this dropped to 47% (21 pairs) for the four-group system (which includes a separate unresolved classification).

In their meta-analysis, van IJzendoorn and Bakermans-Kranenburg (1996) found similar levels of concordance when they pooled data from five studies investigating correspondence between spouses' AAI classifications. In their sample, 51% received the same three-group classification as the spouse, comparable to the 53% who matched the partner in ours. Although none of the studies listed by van IJzendoorn and Bakermans-Kranenburg reported significant correspondence, the added statistical power of pooled samples led to significant results in the meta-analysis. The issue, however, is not whether the association is greater than zero but whether it is great enough to suggest that attachment-related prototypes are important in establishing and maintaining romantic relationships. The present results, as well as those of van IJzendoorn and Bakermans-Kranenburg, suggest that prototype effects on partner selection are either weak or operate only in some relationships.

## Correspondence between CRI security of male and female partners

CRI security was concordant (i.e., both partners were classified as secure or as insecure) in 35 of the 45 couples (78%; $\kappa = .56$, $p < .0001$). This strikingly high concordance rate is consistent with two interpretations: one, that people seek out (or stay with) romantic partners whose working models of adult love relationships are similar to their own and, the other, that, over the course of time, the two partners' working models of their shared relationship converge. The validity of these interpretations is an empirical issue; either or both processes could prove to be significant in mate selection. Longitudinal data from dating, rather than engaged, couples could help us evaluate the first hypothesis: if attachment styles act as one of the many filters involved in mate selection (so that people are more likely to find and/or stay with those who share their perspective on romantic relationships), then mismatched couples would be expected to break up with greater frequency than those whose approaches to attachment coincide. Data on the stability of CRI classifications (i.e., tendency toward change leading to similar classifications) during the same interval could address the second hypothesis, that of convergence over time.

## Correspondence between one partner's AAI and the other's CRI

As Bretherton (1990) and Sroufe and Fleeson (1986) have noted, both Ainsworth and Bowlby recognized the importance of bidirectional influences in relationship formation, an issue that is developed further in Oppenheim and Waters's (1995) discussion of the "co-construction processes" through which working models are formed. An important aspect of the co-construction concept is that the ability to formulate a coherent model (perhaps especially early in relationships) is greatly influenced by the coherence of the partner's behavior and discourse. In the present data, such processes would be reflected in relations between one partner's CRI classification and the other partner's AAI classification. We predicted that a person would be more able to form a coherent model of the current relationship (as reflected in a secure CRI) if the partner presented the coherent behavior and discourse associated with a secure AAI classification.

To avoid dependencies in the data, and because the previous analyses alerted us to the possibility of differential patterns in males and females, we examined subject CRI–partner AAI concordance (secure–insecure dichotomy only) separately in male and female subjects. For females, CRI security ratings matched their partners' AAI security in 69% of the cases (31 of 45; $\kappa = .37$, $p = .006$). For males, CRI security matched the partner's AAI security in 64% of the couples (29 of 45; $\kappa = .30$, $p = .02$). These results suggest that, for both sexes, working models of current relationships are constructed in light of the partner's behavior and discourse to a significant degree; they are not merely representations of early experience. Identifying the specific behaviors and discourse processes associated with secure and insecure AAI status deserves high priority in future research.

A person's own AAI status, of course, may also contribute to the process of evolving a working model of a current relationship. Although the present sample is too small to support a formal analysis of such effects, directions for future research become evident when the data are presented separately for AAI-classified secure and insecure subjects, as in Table 7.3. Among *secure* (AAI) subjects with a secure (AAI) partner, 12 of 15 females (80%)

**Table 7.3** Concordance between subjects' security classifications on the current relationship interview (CRI) and the partner's security on the adult attachment interview (AAI) as a function of subject's AAI security

| | Partner's AAI Status | | | |
| | Females | | Males | |
| Status | Secure | Insecure | Secure | Insecure |
|---|---|---|---|---|
| Subjects with secure AAI classification: | | | | |
| Secure on CRI | 12 | 3 | 11 | 4 |
| Insecure on CRI | 3 | 6 | 4 | 7 |
| Subjects with insecure AAI classification: | | | | |
| Secure on CRI | 6 | 3 | 2 | 1 |
| Insecure on CRI | 5 | 7 | 7 | 9 |

and 11 of 15 males (73%) were classified as secure on the CRI. In contrast, among *insecure* (AAI) subjects with a secure (AAI) partner, only six of 11 females (54%) and two of nine males (22%) were classified as secure on the CRI. This suggests that secure (AAI) subjects are better able to benefit from whatever behavioral and discourse-related assets a secure (AAI) partner brings to a relationship (or that insecure subjects are less able to do so).

This complexity is made all the more interesting by indications that there may be sex differences in the relation between AAI and CRI classifications. Among insecure (AAI) subjects with a secure partner, six of 11 females (55%) but only two of nine males (22%) obtained secure CRI classifications. This could represent a greater vulnerability to the partner's characteristics on the part of females. Alternatively, it could reflect a tendency for males to construct working models later in the relationship or to do so over a longer period of time, in which case their models might be better characterized as "under construction" than as insecure. Larger samples and assessment at different points in relationships are necessary to resolve these issues.

## Discussion

Freud's (1940) prototype hypothesis remains a central, if untested, tenet of attachment theory. There are four major challenges to research on the prototype hypothesis. The first is a problem of definition. As Waters and Deane (1982) point out, there are "stronger" and "weaker" versions of the prototype hypothesis. The ability to decide among alternative formulations on the basis of theory alone would be impressive evidence of the power of attachment theory. For the present, however, we cannot deduce much about the nature of attachment representations or their likely effects from theory alone; we are still dependent on an interplay between theory, description, and experimentation.

Measurement and validity issues present a second type of problem. It must be remembered that neither the AAI nor the CRI directly measures the content of a working model. Instead, they provide narratives that are judged to be more or less coherent, and the relation between level of coherence and any underlying working model is inferred, not measured. Research is hampered also by the fact that the AAI and the CRI are expensive to administer and score. Unfortunately, the prospects for more economical measurement are unclear. Self-report measures developed by Hazan and Shaver (1987) and by some others seem to have attachment-related correlates but show little correspondence with AAI classifications (Crowell, Treboux & Waters 1999). The relation between AAI classifications and projective measures is also inconsistent at best (Sroufe, personal communication). It is difficult to measure something until you know what it is; accordingly, it may be better to turn to cognitive psychology rather than psychometrics for solutions. In the meantime, it is important to keep in mind the distance between attachment measures and the constructs with which they are theoretically linked; Meehl (1973) has argued persuasively that work under such conditions is nevertheless philosophically defensible – as well as having been standard procedure throughout the history of science.

A third difficulty arises from the fact that most formulations of the prototype hypothesis presume some degree of continuity or coherence in individual development across 20 or more years. There are few empirical data to confirm such assumptions (Waters, Merrick, Albersheim, & Treboux, 1995), and we have to employ alternative designs that incorporate replication and convergence of diverse strategies. It will be particularly useful to have longitudinal data that can help establish whether the AAI reflects working models that were already present in childhood, as opposed to current models of childhood experiences (as argued by Main). Even then, issues that cannot be resolved by cross-sectional or short-term longitudinal designs will remain to be considered.

A final difficulty in conducting research on the prototype hypothesis has been the problem of age- and construct-appropriate assessment. Clearly, the Strange Situation serves as a reliable anchor for early behavioral assessment, but, until the development of the AAI, there was no way to assess internal working models of attachment. The CRI is particularly important in adding to what can be done in this regard because it permits us to determine whether a single attachment working model characterizes adulthood or whether there exist multiple models that are associated with different relationships. The data presented in this report provide useful information on several aspects of the prototype issue and point to important directions for research on several others, as elaborated in the following sections.

## One model or many?

Several of the analyses that we have presented converge on the conclusion that individuals have multiple, yet related, working models of close relationships, not just a single model developed in the child–parent relationship or completely independent models related to the particulars of specific relationships. First is the fact that, although AAI and CRI concordance for secure/insecure classifications is statistically significant, it is far from perfect (64%); correlations between the individuals' current state of mind toward the two relationships are also moderate at best. (The task of understanding discordant classifications – whether the explanation lies in past experience, previous relationships, or the current relationship – deserves high priority in attachment research. It would be of special interest to know whether unusual or traumatic experiences play a significant role.)

As further evidence that the models being accessed by the AAI and CRI are not identical, AAI and CRI classifications showed different results when we examined the concordance between the two partners as secure or insecure: between-partner concordance for secure/insecure status was only 56% (N.S.) on the AAI yet 78% ($p < .0001$) on the CRI. The much higher value obtained with the CRI suggests that models of current relationships are co-constructed along the lines described by Oppenheim and Waters (1995). Interestingly, infant attachment data show the same pattern: low concordance between infant Strange Situation classifications with mother and with father separately (Fox, Kimmerly, & Schafer, 1991) yet clear consistency between maternal AAI and infant Strange Situation classifications, which assess both dyad members' models of their shared relationship (Main et al., 1985).

These results do not support the notion that formulations of the prototype hypothesis should include predictions of assortative mating based on individuals' generalized state of mind regarding attachment. It is possible, of course, that a person with a particular AAI working model might prefer partners with certain *behavioral* characteristics. However, this would not necessarily entail similarity in attachment working models; the partner's behavior could be just as attractive if it reflected cultural or temperamental characteristics and were unrelated to the partner's attachment working models.

## Behavioral correlates of attachment working models

A second prototype-related issue addressed in this report is whether AAI classifications have behavioral correlates that affect relationship formation. The Bowlby–Ainsworth perspective places considerable emphasis on the child's behavioral manifestations of attachment, particularly the secure-base phenomenon, as well as on the associations between parents' caregiving behaviors and their children's attachment behaviors. Additionally, numerous AAI studies have documented the link between adults' internal attachment representations and their parenting of their children. Thus, insofar as attachment working models influence ordinary behavior in relationships, they are important not only to the individuals who construct them but also to their partners in close relationships.

Perhaps the most intriguing finding from the present research was that the set of expectations, attitudes, and behaviors that individuals presumably learned in the context of early attachment relationships influenced not just their own but also their *partner's* security in the later romantic relationship. We tested the hypothesis that a person would find it difficult to formulate a coherent model of a romantic relationship (i.e., be classified as secure on the CRI) if the partner brought to the relationship an insecure working model (as determined using the AAI). This prediction was based on the expectation that a person with an insecure AAI classification would act in an incoherent and/or inconsistent fashion in the relationship and would be a poor partner in the process of co-constructing an understanding of the relationship. Our results supported this prediction; for both males and females, participants with secure (AAI) partners were more likely (and those with insecure partners less likely) to form secure (CRI) models of the relationship. Consequently, people who had a secure overall perspective on attachment (AAI), but who were paired for whatever reason with an insecure partner, were often able to help the partner attain a secure CRI classification but were themselves twice as likely to be scored insecure rather than secure in the partner relationship.

Thus, it appears that what is internalized during early interactions with the parents is not simply a prototype for the type of partner one will seek out for later relationships, as asserted by Freud, but instead a set of behaviors that allow the individual to recreate aspects of earlier relationships with subsequent partners (as suggested by Sroufe & Fleeson, 1986). In future research, we need to take a closer look at interactions between couples in order to detail the distinguishing behaviors exhibited by individuals from each of the AAI classification groups and to identify the relational patterns that emerge from the two partners' separate approaches to attachment.

Research on the behavioral correlates of the AAI presents an interesting opportunity to examine another of the central tenets of attachment theory, namely, the notion that infant–adult attachments and adult–adult love relationships are the same kind of relationship. For Bowlby and Ainsworth, this implies that both draw on the species-specific attachment control system to regulate secure-base behavior.[2] From this, it follows that some of the same (or analogous) types of interactions and caregiver/partner behavior would be prepotent or even necessary to initiate and maintain such relationships. We might hypothesize, therefore, that experience using the partner as a secure base (see Waters & Deane, 1985) and experience receiving secure-base support from the partner (see Kondo-Ikemura & Waters, 1995) would be stronger correlates of relationship formation or representation than behaviors such as negative affect per se or the generic communication skills commonly assessed in marital therapy research (e.g., Weiss & Heyman, 1990). Sharing developmental antecedents would be an important indication that infant–adult and adult–adult attachments are similar in kind.

## Concluding Comments

Our results are consistent with the notion that early experience influences later relationships. However, we found little support for the "strong" form of the prototype hypothesis, that is, the idea that a working model formed in a child's interactions with his or her primary caregiver subsequently serves as the framework for understanding all later love relationships. Representations of early attachment experience had only a modest effect on conceptualizations of current relationships. However constrained or biased by early experiences, an adult's mental model of his or her romantic relationship is clearly open to ongoing experiences within that relationship. In fact, our CRI concordance results suggest that romantic partners co-construct their conceptualizations of their shared relationship (see also Oppenheim & Waters, 1995).

Representations of the child–parent relationship seem most likely to influence the development and course of adult relationships through effects on behavior. Insecure adults can form secure working models (especially if the partner is secure), but they may behave in ways that engender conflict and also make it difficult for a partner to understand or predict relationship transactions. This conclusion raises a number of important questions. What mechanisms link representations of early attachment experience to behavior in romantic relationships? How does one partner's behavior influence the other's understanding of a romantic relationship? How do representations of an ongoing relationship influence behavior? Research on these questions would benefit from collaboration with cognitive psychologists interested in belief systems and conceptual change and with social psychologists interested in stereotyping, prejudice, persuasion, and attitude change. The relations of attachment working models to interpersonal attraction and relationship formation are also areas in which attachment theorists could profitably collaborate with experts in traditional areas of social psychology (e.g., Shaver & Hazan, 1994; Simpson & Harris, 1994).

# Notes

1 In order to determine whether concordance is a function of how the AAI and CRI classifications are grouped, we also examined AAI-CRI concordance using three groups (secure, dismissing, preoccupied) and four groups (secure, dismissing, preoccupied, unresolved). For the three-group analysis, unresolved subjects were assigned to their secondary (secure, dismissing, or preoccupied) classification. Concordance was significant in both analyses; using three groups concordance was 61% (expected = 41% $\kappa$ = .34, $p$ < .0001), and using four groups it was 56% (expected = 37%; $\kappa$ = .30, $p$ < .0001). For all three analyses, concordance was also significant when males and females were analyzed separately.

2 Although one can construct multiple attachment working models, the nervous system provides only a single attachment control system.

# References

Ainsworth, M. D. S., Blehar, M. C., Waters, E., & Wall, S. (1978). *Patterns of attachment: A psychological study of the Strange Situation.* Hillsdale, NJ: Erlbaum.

Bakermans-Kranenburg, M. J., & van IJzendoorn, M. H. (1993). A psychometric study of the Adult Attachment Interview: Reliability and discriminant validity. *Developmental Psychology, 29* (5), 870879.

Benoit, D., & Parker, K. C. H. (1994). Stability and transmission of attachment across three generations. *Child Development, 65* (5), 1444–1456.

Bowlby, J. (1973). *Attachment and loss: Vol. 2. Separation: anxiety and anger.* New York: Basic Books.

Bowlby, J. (1980). *Attachment and loss: Vol. 3. Loss, sadness, and depression.* New York: Basic Books.

Bowlby, J. ([1969] 1982). *Attachment and loss: Vol. 1. Attachment* (2d edn.). New York: Basic Books.

Bowlby, J. (1988). *A secure Base: parent–child attachment and healthy human development.* New York: Basic Books.

Bretherton, I. (1990). Communication patterns, internal working models, and the intergenerational transmission of attachment relationships. *Infant Mental Health Journal, 11* (3), 237–252.

Cohn, D. A., Silver, D. H., Cowan, C. P., Cowan, P. A., & Pearson, J. (1992). Working models of childhood attachment and couple relationships. *Journal of Family Issues, 13* (4), 432–449.

Crowell, J. A. (1990). *Current Relationship Interview.* Unpublished manuscript, State University of New York at Stony Brook.

Crowell, J. A., & Treboux, D. (1995). A review of adult attachment measures: Implications for theory and research. *Social development, 4* (3), 294–327.

Crowell, J. A., Waters, E., Treboux, D., O'Connor, E., Colon-Downs, C., Feider, O., . . . & Posada, G. (1996). Discriminant validity of the adult attachment interview. *Child Development, 67* (5), 2584–2599.

Crowell, J. A., Treboux, D., & Waters, E. (1999). The Adult Attachment Interview and the Relationship Questionnaire: Relations to reports of mothers and partners. *Personal Relationships, 6* (1), 1–18.

Fox, N. A., Kimmerly, N. L., & Schafer, W. D. (1991). Attachment to mother/attachment to father: A meta-analysis. *Child Development, 62* (1), 210–225

Freud, S. (1940). An outline of psychoanalysis. In J. Strachey (Ed. and Trans.), *The standard edition of the complete psychological works of Sigmund Freud (Vol. 23).* London: Hogarth.

George, C., Kaplan, N., & Main, M. (1984). *Attachment interview for adults.* Unpublished manuscript, University of California.

Hazan, C., & Shaver, P. (1987). Romantic love conceptualized as an attachment process. *Journal of Personality and Social Psychology, 52* (3), 511–524.

Kondo-Ikemura, K., & Waters, E. (1995). Maternal behavior and infant security in old world monkeys: conceptual issues and a methodological bridge between human and nonhuman primate research. *Monographs of the Society for Research in Child Development, 60* (2/3), 97–110.

Main, M., Kaplan, N., & Cassidy, J. (1985). Security in infancy, childhood, and adulthood: A move to the level of representation. In I. Bretherton & E. Waters (Eds.). *Growing points of attachment theory and research.* Monographs of the Society for Research in Child Development, *50* (1–2, Serial No. 209)

Meehl, P. (1973). *Psychodiagnosis: Selected papers.* Minneapolis: University of Minnesota Press.

O'Connor, E., Pan, H., Posada, G., Crowell, J., Waters, E., & Teti, D. (1993, March). The Adult Attachment Interview and women's reports of marital discord and spouses' conflict behavior. *Paper presented at the meeting of the Society for Research in Child Development,* New Orleans.

O'Connor, E., Pan, H., Waters, E., & Posada, G. (1995). Attachment classification, romantic jealousy, and aggression in couples. *Paper presented at the meeting of the Society for Research in Child Development,* Indianapolis.

Oppenheim, D., & Waters, H. S. (1995). Narrative processes and attachment representations: Issues of development and assessment. *Monographs of the Society for Research in Child Development, 60* (2/3), 197–215.

Owens, G., & Crowell, J. (1993). *Current Relationship Interview scoring system.* Unpublished manuscript, State University of New York at Stony Brook.

Posada, G., Liu, X. D., & Waters, E., (1994) *Specific domains of marital discord and attachment security: Girls and boys.* Unpublished manuscript.

Shaver, P. R., & Hazan, C. (1994). *Attachment.* In A. L. Weber & J. H. Harvey (Eds.). *Perspectives on close relationships (pp. 110–130).* Allyn & Bacon.

Simpson, J., & Harris, B. (1994). Interpersonal attraction. In A. Weber & J. Harvey (Eds.). *Perspectives on close relationships.* Boston: Allyn & Bacon.

Spanier, G. (1976). Measuring dyadic adjustment: New scales for assessing the quality of marriage and similar dyads. *Journal of Marriage and the Family, 38* (1), 15–28.

Sroufe, L. A., & Fleeson, J. (1986). Attachment and the construction of relationships. In W. Hartup & Z. Rubin (Eds.). *Relationships and development* (pp. 51–71). Hillsdale, NJ: Erlbaum.

Waters, E. (1978). The reliability and stability of individual differences in infant–mother attachment. *Child Development, 49* (2), 483–494.

Waters, E. (1987). *Attachment Behavior Q-Set (Revision 3.0).* Unpublished instrument, State University of New York at Stony Brook, Department of Psychology.

Waters, E., Crowell, J., Treboux, D., O'Connor, E., Posada, G. & Golby, B. (1993, March). Discriminant validity of the Adult Attachment Interview. *Poster session presented at the 60th Meeting of the Society for Research in Child Development,* New Orleans, LA.

Waters, E., & Deane, K. E. (1982). Infant–mother attachment: Theories, models, recent data, and some tasks for comparative developmental analysis. In L. Hoffman, R. Gandelman, & H. Schiffman (Eds.). *Parenting: Its causes and consequences.* Hillsdale, NJ: Erlbaum.

Waters, E., & Deane, K. E. (1985). Defining and assessing individual differences in attachment relationships: Q-methodology and the organization of behavior in infancy and early childhood. In I. Bretherton & E. Waters (Eds.). *Growing points of attachment theory and research. Monographs of the Society for Research in Child Development, 50* (1–2, Serial No. 209).

Waters, E., Garber, J., Gornal, M., & Vaughn, B. (1983). Q-sort correlates of visual regard among preschool peers: Validation of a behavioral index of social competence. *Developmental Psychology, 19* (4), 550–560.

Waters, E., Hay, D. F., & Richters, J. (1985). Infant–parent attachment and the origins of prosocial and antisocial behavior. In D. Olweus, J. Block, & M. Radke-Yarrow (Eds.). *The origins of prosocial and antisocial behavior.* New York: Academic.

Waters, E., Johnson, S., & Kondo-Ikemura, K. (1995). *Do preschool children love their peers?* Manuscript submitted for publication.

Waters, E., Kondo-Ikemura, K., Posada, G., & Richters, J. E. (1990). Learning to love: Mechanisms and milestones. In M. R. Gunnar & L. A. Sroufe (Eds.). *Self processes and development (Minnesota Symposia on Child Psychology, Vol. 23).* Hillsdale, NJ: Erlbaum.

Waters, E., Merrick, S. K., Albersheim, L. J., & Treboux, D. (1995, March). Attachment security from infancy to early adulthood: A 20-year longitudinal study. In J. A. Crowell & E. Waters (Chairs), *Is the parent–child relationship a prototype of later love relationships? Studies of attachment and working models of attachment. Symposium presented at the meeting of the Society for Research in Child Development,* Indianapolis.

Waters, E., Noyes, D. M., Vaughn, B. E., & Ricks, M. (1985). Q-sort definition of social competence and self-esteem: Discriminant validity of related constructs in theory and data. *Developmental Psychology, 21* (3), 508–552.

Waters, E., Posada, G., & Vaughn, B. E. (1994). *The Attachment Q-Set: Hyper-text advisor.* Unpublished computer software, State University of New York at Stony Brook, Department of Psychology.

Weiss, R. L., & Heyman, R. (1990). Observation of marital interaction. In F. Fincham & T. Bradbury (Eds.). *The psychology of marriage.* New York: Plenum.

Van IJzendoorn, M., & Bakermans-Kranenburg, M. (1996). Attachment Representations in Mothers, Fathers, Adolescents, and Clinical Groups: A Meta-Analytic Search for Normative Data. *Journal of Consulting and Clinical Psychology, 64* (1), 8–21.

# 8

# Dynamics of Romantic Love
## *Comments, Questions, and Future Directions*

### Phillip R. Shaver

I begin with a brief case study, which is followed by a discussion of the points it raises and illustrates. I am especially interested in what we mean when we say that romantic love, or pair bonding, is based on three separate behavioral systems, so I devote several sections to implications of that claim. I then turn to the issue of individual differences in attachment, caregiving, and sex and consider ways of thinking about the fact that individual differences in the functioning of the three systems are interrelated and that priming one system has systematic effects on the others. Finally, toward the end of the chapter I consider how the attachment, or behavioral systems, approach to romantic love and couple relationships is similar to and differs from other theoretical approaches.

## A Reference Case: The Feynmans' Attachment Relationship

Because this book, like most high-level scientific discourse, is quite abstract, even though it deals with some of life's most intense, engaging, and in some cases exceedingly painful and destructive experiences – sexual passion, emotional bonding, affectionate caregiving, rejection and loss, couple violence, and sexual coercion – I begin with a specific and fairly normal example of what we are theorizing about.

### The case

In the early 1940s, while working on the first atomic bomb, the Nobel Prize-winning physicist Richard Feynman wrote almost daily to his young wife, Arline Feynman. Like Richard's behavior throughout his long and eventful life, the letters (edited by Richard's daughter, Michelle Feynman, 2005) are marked by quirky brilliance, a sparkling, devilish sense of humor, intense affection, and sexual attraction. The letters as a whole are remarkable for a variety of reasons, but the most amazing letter, to my mind, is one Richard wrote at age 28, a year and a half after Arline died of tuberculosis:

> I adore you, sweetheart. I want to tell you I love you . . . I always will love you. I find it hard to understand . . . what it means to love you after you are dead – but I still want to comfort you and take care of you – and I want you to love me and take care of me. I want to have problems to discuss with you; I want to do little projects with you. . . . What should we do?

*Source:* Philip R. Shaver, "The Dynamics of Romantic Love: Comments, Questions and Future Directions," pp. 423-456 from *The Dynamics of Romantic Love: Attachment, Caregiving, and Sex*, eds. Mario Mikulincer, Gail S. Goodman (New York, NY: Guilford Press). Reproduced with permission from Guilford Press.

*Attachment Theory and Research: A Reader*, First Edition. Edited by Tommie Forslund and Robbie Duschinsky.

When you were sick you worried because you could not give me something that you wanted to and thought I needed. You needn't have worried. Just as I told you then there was no real need because I loved you in so many ways so much. And now it is clearly even more true – you can give me nothing now yet I love you so that you stand in my way of loving anyone else – but I want [you] to stand there. You, dead, are so much better than anyone else alive.

I don't understand it, for I have met many girls and very nice ones and I don't want to remain alone – but in two or three meetings they all seem ashes. You only are left to me. You are real. My darling wife, I do adore you. I love my wife. My wife is dead.–

P.S. Please excuse my not mailing this – but I don't know your new address. (pp. 68–69)

If anyone doubted that Bowlby's (1969/1982, 1973, 1980) theory of attachment and loss applies to adult romantic love, this letter should help change the person's mind. Richard had Arline's substance and qualities so deeply etched in his mind – in his attachment hierarchy and internal working models, to use Bowlby's terms – her vivid presence was impossible to dislodge even though Richard, who was not religious, believed he would never see her again. Arline's status as what Bowlby called Richard's "primary attachment figure" caused other attractive women, at least for a period of years, to be excluded from that role, perhaps against Richard's "better judgment." Moreover, despite his obvious brilliance in other domains, he couldn't fathom his continuing commitment to and longing for Arline. Notice that Richard was, in attachment theory terms, *attached* or emotionally bonded to Arline; he wished intensely to be near her. But he also wanted to take care of her and be taken care of by her, and he clearly grieved for her. (His daughter Michelle said in her notes on the correspondence that "This letter is well worn – much more so than others – and it appears as though he reread it often.")

## Keeping personal experience and everyday observations in mind

Whatever readers of this volume conclude about love and attachment, I hope they keep the example of Richard and Arline in mind, along with whatever experiences of intense romantic love (pair bonding, in the language of evolutionary psychology) still blaze or smolder in their own memories. Certainly I think about my own experiences when theorizing about love. My wife, Gail Goodman's, brief description of the early years of our courtship refers to some of the memories I consult frequently, memories of a time when I failed to return to a tenured job at New York University after spending a sabbatical year at the University of Denver, where I first met Gail. Despite receiving the academic equivalent of death threats from NYU's psychology department and attorneys, I wanted to stay in Denver with Gail, and I did. I also awkwardly ended relationships with other women whom I cared about in New York so I could pursue what has proven to be a very rewarding 25-year relationship with Gail.

In my opinion, there is no theory of personality, emotions, social relationships, or psychological development that holds much more than a flickering candle to actual experience. Someday there may be, but not today. Thus it behooves us as relationship researchers to keep attachment theory, alternative theories of love such as interdependence theory; the intimacy theory developed by Harry Reis (2006); Art and Elaine Aron's (2006) self-expansion theory; and Ellen Berscheid's (2006) wise conceptual analysis; and our own actual experiences of love in mind. I was delighted to see, when reading Berscheid's lovely essay that she had been moved by Nobel Prize-winner Herbert Simon's casual question, "What about tenderness?" I assume the question grew out of his keen observations of his own and other people's close relationships, not from formal work in artificial intelligence, his insightful but fairly narrow conception of emotions as interrupters of cognition, and his analyses of "satisficing" in organizational economics.

I was also pleased that the Arons (2006) raised the issue of the Jungian "shadow," the aspect of a person or culture that is suppressed or hidden from view and complements or contradicts what is consciously emphasized. The Arons refer to the "archetype of the Divine Child," which is similar to attachment researchers' image of the perfectly secure infant who grows up to be a perfectly loving and happy adult. All of us realize, I hope, that no one is perfectly secure or perfectly "divine" and that to insist on a model of perfect security, rather than a model that acknowledges human complexity, depth, and intrapsychic conflicts and tensions, is bound to be misleading and perhaps even dangerous, because the shadow component of a mind or a culture tends to assert itself in destructive ways. By keeping our own relationships and other real relationships in mind, perhaps we will remember the complexity that even our fairly simple studies reveal: Everyone has had both more and less successful relationships and has enjoyed being loved, as well as having suffered from inevitable attachment injuries. All of us are subject to conflicting motives and impulses, the balance of which changes as a function of social context (presence or absence of partner support), external threats (wars, economic depressions, a partner's serious illness), and internal conditions (self-doubts, "compassion fatigue," and painful negative memories, dreams, or daydreams). It takes effort for anyone to balance and regulate all of the conflicting pushes, pulls, and priorities.

In the attachment field we are so accustomed to glorifying secure attachment that we rarely stop to wonder why there aren't more saints in the world, especially given that Ainsworth and her followers (e.g., Ainsworth, Blehar, Waters, & Wall, 1978; Weinfield, Sroufe, Egeland, & Carlson, 1999) labeled more than half of the middle-class children they studied "securely attached" and that researchers using the Adult Attachment Interview (AAI; e.g., Hesse, 1999; Main, 1995) have declared that more than half of middle-class American adults have a "secure state of mind with respect to attachment." Psychologists have done a great deal of research and administered megatons of psychotherapy over the past hundred or so years; yet human cruelty, damaged children, unfaithful spouses, and wars and violence have not noticeably diminished, let alone disappeared completely. Thus it is worthwhile to keep one eye on everyday experiences and the daily world news, especially experiences and stories that contradict our theories, so that we do not become deluded by theoretical oversimplifications, misleading abstractions, or wishful idealizations.

## Romantic love engages multiple behavioral systems

The fact that Richard Feynman's love for Arline Feynman involved both attachment and caregiving (I'll get to sex in a minute) was evident when he said, "I still want to comfort you and take care of you – and I want you to love me and take care of me." That was not mere rhetoric. He actually *had* taken care of Arline while she was ill, very tenderly, and even though she was living mainly in a tuberculosis sanitarium at the time, she did a great deal, in letters and in the considerable time they spent together, to take care of Richard's emotional, sexual, and other needs. In a letter to Arline written months before she died, Richard said: "Without you I would be empty and weak like I was before I knew you" (Feynman, 2005, p. 48). They both shared their everyday experiences, frustrations, and new discoveries, including discoveries about their own feelings – in ways that fit well with Reis's (2006) insightful discussion of intimacy.

One thing to notice about Richard's wish to care for Arline, as expressed in the letter I quoted, is that this aspect or form of love (i.e., caregiving) is not only what Berscheid (2006) calls an affect, or a feeling. It is also not, as I believe she would agree, an attitude. In my opinion, the psychology of emotions and its extension into the field of close relationships made a mistake when it conceptualized emotions, including forms of love, primarily as "affects, feelings, or attitudes – that is, as subjective states that might be located in an abstract mental space defined by the dimensions of valence and arousal. (For an excellent contemporary example of this approach, with which I disagree despite admiring the author's scope, see Barrett, 2006a, 2006b.)

We can see some of the difficulties inherent in the "affect" or "feeling" conceptualization of love in the following passages (here combined for brevity) from Berscheid (2006):

> The title of this volume (and the title of the conference that preceded it) confused me, undoubtedly because the term "romantic love" itself is confusing. It is often used loosely to refer to any kind of positive *affect* that occurs within a relationship between a man and a woman, especially a relationship that either is progressing toward or has culminated in marriage. . . . However, the term "romantic love" also is used to refer to a particular *kind* of positive affect – or syndrome of emotions, feelings, attitudes, and behaviors – as opposed to other kinds of positive affect that are often observed in a relationship between a man and a woman, which is how I am using the term. (p. 409)

Except for the single word "behaviors" that sneaked in at the end of the inserted, dashed phrase, the passage is all about feelings or affects. (The fact that the term "romantic love" confounds a kind of relationship, a couple relationship that includes sex or at least sexual interests, with a kind of "affect" related to one of several different behavioral systems, only one of which is sexual, is important, and I will return to it later.)

An advantage of conceptualizing romantic love in terms of innate, motivated, dynamic, and generally functional behavioral systems is that focusing our attention on such systems forces us to think about *motives*, *actions*, and *action tendencies* rather than just feelings. Aron and Aron (2006) make a related observation:

> We hypothesized . . . that passionate love is best conceptualized as a goal-oriented motivational state in which the individual is experiencing an intense desire to merge with the partner. That is, we conceive of passionate love as the experience that corresponds to the intense desire to expand the self by including another person in the self. Thus passionate love is not a distinct emotion in its own right (such as sadness or happiness) but rather can evoke a variety of emotions according to whether and how the desire is fulfilled or frustrated, (p. 364)

None of us, I assume, would deny that feelings are important (see Shaver, Morgan, & Wu, 1996, for an example of my own efforts to characterize feelings of love), but I think it is crucial that we tie them theoretically to motives and goals – or, in the language of attachment theory, to innate behavioral systems. The attachment system causes a lonely or distressed person to seek physical and psychological proximity to a comforting protector or supporter; that is, it *moves* the person, both figuratively and literally, in the direction of a real or imagined attachment figure. If the person's goal of seeking proximity is frustrated or rebuffed, he or she is likely to protest, cry, become aggressive, and so on. (Bowlby's books, such as the second and third volume of his Attachment and *Loss* trilogy, published in 1973 and 1980, had subtitles including the words anxiety, anger, sadness, and depression.) The caregiving system influences a person to feel troubled by another person's vulnerability, distress, or need, and it *moves* a compassionate, caring person toward a needy other in ways that can be observed in behavior and detected in the motor cortex of the brain during "compassion meditation" (e.g., Lutz, Greischar, Rowlings, Ricard, & Davidson, 2004). The sexual system does more than cause feelings or affects; it moves a person to engage in sexual activities. Both the desires involved and experienced when behavioral system is activated and the emotions evoked by successfully attaining or failing to attain the behavioral systems' set goals (as Bowlby called them) are affective (felt), but the feelings are not the only parts of that process that have psychological significance.

One of the most important advances in emotion theory in the past few decades, and one to which I tried to make at least a small contribution (e.g., Reis & Shaver, 1988; Schwartz & Shaver, 1987; Shaver et al., 1996; Shaver' Schwartz, Kirson, & O'Connor, 1987), was to place *goals and action tendencies* rather than feelings or affects at the center of the emotion process (e.g., Frijda, 1986; Oatley & Jenkins, 1996). Nancy Collins, AnaMarie Guichard, Máire Ford, and Brooke Feeney (2006), does a marvelous job of showing that caring involves a motivated set of actions and action tendencies, not a mere feeling (although I'm not denying that caring feelings are extremely important; they help us realize, make sense of, and remember our motives and motivational inclinations). If caregiving tendencies did not express themselves in behavior, the caregiving system postulated by Bowlby would never have evolved.

Richard and Arline Feynman did not write a great deal about sex, at least not in the letters published by Richard's daughter (from a subsequent marriage), but the two lovers had been devoted and amorous high school sweethearts who went on to spend many weekends together while Richard was in college and graduate school. Even after they married and her health was declining, Arline wrote to Richard: "I'm so excited and happy and bursting with joy – I think, eat, and sleep 'you' – our life, our love, our marriage. . . . I love you sweetheart – body and soul – I long to be near you again . . . you're a wonderful husband and lover. Come to me soon – I need you and want you" (Feynman, 2005, p. 24). In another letter, after feeling that she might be pregnant, she wrote, "I could rave about you endlessly dear, everything about you seems so extra-special and nice to me – your legs are strong and muscular . . . then there is the baby talk you use sometimes when you love me . . . I adore you" (p. 27). During the final year of her life despite being weak and frequently in pain, Arline wrote, "It's good to know that even if medicine fails, there is always your smile and your hand – it's effective dearest" (p. 34).

As Gail Goodman (2006) explains, I have definitely begun to think of myself as a dirty old man but I can imagine only one activity that Arline might have been referring to when praising Richard's healing hand. Like the attachment and caregiving systems the sexual system motivates actions, not just feelings.

## Still, What About the *Feeling* of "Love"? What Does it Mean to Say "I Love You"?

A big challenge, once we place romantic love and pair bonding in a behavioral systems framework, is to figure out how best to integrate the separate systems and to do so in a way that acknowledges the feeling aspect and the everyday language of love. Certainly, Richard and Arline's letters revealed and expressed strong feelings, and the lovers often used the term "love" for their feelings, although, viewed in terms of behavioral systems theory, they sometimes seemed to be talking about wanting to see each other and be physically close, wanting to be taken care of, wanting to take care of the other, and wanting to "make love" to each other. In accord with my wish not to get lost in abstractions, I wouldn't want to endorse a cybernetic model of behavioral systems that left out experiences, feelings, words, and values. (As a colleague recently asked in an e-mail message, "If we're talking about mechanical behavioral systems rather than human emotions, couldn't two robots be 'in love' and 'pair bonded'?" [Louise Sundararajan, personal communication, 2005]).

Bowlby, the originator of the behavioral system perspective, clearly believed that the operation of the attachment system is closely associated with what we, in ordinary language, call "love":

> Many of the most intense of all human emotions arise during the formation, the maintenance, the disruption and the renewal of affectional bonds – which for that reason are sometimes called emotional bonds. In terms of subjective experience, the formation of a bond is described as falling in love, maintaining a bond as loving someone, and losing a partner as grieving over someone. Similarly, the threat of loss arouses anxiety and actual loss causes sorrow, whilst both situations are likely to arouse anger. Finally, the unchallenged maintenance of a bond is experienced as a source of security, and the renewal as a source of joy. (1979, p. 69)

All of these emotions are evident in the letters exchanged by Richard and Arline Feynman, and one can easily see in their correspondence the kinds of challenges and misunderstandings – usually amounting to unintended breaches of trust or violations of expectations about giving and receiving care – that sometimes cause negative attachment-related emotions to erupt (as demonstrated by other couples in the studies described by Jeff Simpson, Lorne Campbell, and Yanna Weisberg [2006]). The Feynman's interactions, extending over many years, also corresponded well with Collins et al.'s (2006) laboratory experiments on the dynamic interrelation of one partner's attachment needs and the other partner's caregiving efforts.

As explained subsequently, the term "love" is broad enough in every-day language to be associated with an attachment, or "affectional," bond to a caring other, the "care" associated with the caregiving behavioral system, and the sexual attraction and satisfaction associated with the sexual system. That is, the ordinary-language term "love" is used for all of the feelings associated with all three of the behavioral systems that Hazan and I (Hazan & Shaver, 1987) thought were involved in romantic pair-bond or couple relationships, especially the positive feelings, but also many of the negative ones. The idea that "love hurts" has been expressed in countless love songs over the centuries (see Aron & Aron, 2006, for countless examples of the diverse emotions associated with love).

This means, as Ekman (1992) explained when deciding that love is not a basic emotion, that the term "love" is used for just about any notable emotion generated in "romantic love" relationships. Ekman called these relationships "plots," meaning that they involve more than one person, usually in particular kinds of roles relevant to a particular emotion term. According to Ekman, many different discrete emotions arise in such scenarios (jealousy is another example of a "plot" – one that by definition involves three social roles), so there cannot be only a single emotion term that accurately applies to them, and – of great interest to Ekman when he was deciding which emotions are and which are not "basic" – there is no single, easily identifiable facial expression associated with a love plot or a jealousy plot.

As scientists, when we contemplate the workings of the attachment, caregiving, and sexual systems, we move beyond thinking about consciously available feelings in one person's subjective consciousness to a set of partly unconscious motivational processes that cause people to approach, touch, and interact with each other in order to receive protection and comfort, to offer protection or provide support, or to engage in sexual activities. When all three of the behavioral systems are organized around a particular person we have what I mean by "romantic love" (which, when it occurs in only one member of a dyad, can be one-sided and may qualify for the term "infatuation"). When both the attachment, caregiving, and sexual systems of both members of a dyad are organized around each other we have what I would call a "romantic relationship". What matters in these cases is not any particular emotion but the ways in which several behavioral system and kinds of emotion (including but not limited to the ones mentioned in the passage I quoted from Bowlby) are organized around successive interactions, and eventually a relationship, with a particular person. I think Berscheid and I come close to agreeing about this, although I admit that the language and the various constructs involved are devilishly difficult to pin down precisely.

## What about exploration and affiliation?

Several authors (see Mikulincer & Goodman, 2006) mention explicitly or imply that Hazan and I (Hazan & Shaver, 1987; Shaver, Hazan, & Bradshaw, 1988) were too restrictive in characterizing romantic love in terms of only three of the behavioral systems discussed by Bowlby (1969/1982). In particular, we left out the exploration and affiliation systems. This is an important point because the natural link between Bowlby's theory and self-expansion theory as outlined by Aron and Aron (2006) is the exploration system. Bowlby used the term "exploration" to refer to the human infant's very evident curiosity, playfulness, and intense interest in developing personal efficacy and competence (e.g., standing up, walking, making interesting events happen over and over again). Bowlby and Ainsworth placed enormous emphasis on the role of secure attachment in promoting exploration, learning, and personal growth. They might well have called these processes "self-expansion."

Exploration is also important to Collins et al. (2006) because caregiving in an adult relationship often amounts to supporting a partner emotionally and in other ways while he or she attempts to solve personally important problems, achieve desirable goals at work, and so on. Exploration and self-expansion are also obviously important to Reis's (2006) discussion of intimacy. What makes intimacy so exciting and rewarding when it goes well is that a person is helped by a partner to see more deeply and unambivalently into him- or herself and to have previously confusing, hidden, or disapproved aspects of the self understood and, in many cases, genuinely sympathized with or approved of. When this goes on in both directions in a relationship, the two partners come to feel "larger," freer, less conflicted and distorted, and more complete. The result is "self-expanding," without a doubt, and not only because one "includes the other in the self," in the Arons' terms, but also because more of the self has become visible, understood, and accepted by the other and the self.

I have less to say about affiliation per se, but Berscheid (2006) is surely correct that friendship, or companionship, between loving partners is a significant part of love. Simply doing things together, being playful together, and having fun of all kinds together (e.g., leisure activities, home improvement projects, vacationing) are important, as Richard Feynman indicated when he said, "I want to do little projects with you. . . . What should we do?" Also important is the sense of security and identity couple members enjoy based on a shared history.

Thinking about these additional behavioral systems helps me realize that "love," or "romantic love" (meaning the set of forces that draw members of a couple together and cause them to care about each other), is a broad, overarching term used for all of the forces, including sexual attraction and involvement, that cause members of a couple to care for and about each other as specific individuals. "I love him" is a way of saying, "I have a lot of my behavioral systems wrapped firmly around him, and the image of him, in ways that make it very difficult for me to think about trading him in for anyone else." I still think this makes attachment a very central part of the process of this kind of love, along with caring and sex, but it might be appropriate to include exploration and affiliation as well. They both contribute to the emotional force of love, to the selection of one partner rather than another, and to the likelihood that what begins as self-expansion and infatuation will evolve into a lasting attachment.

## Appraisal and bestowal

Another, related way to think about "romantic love" is to notice that anyone with whom I establish a "pair bond" in a mutual, multi-behavioral-system way has a very special *value* to me. *Feeling* that value, and *feeling myself* assigning it to one particular person, especially if it places her ahead of all others in my personal pantheon, or attachment hierarchy, is an important part of what I mean by "loving" that person. And if the sexual behavioral system is involved (in line with the emphasis Berscheid places on that system when using the term "romantic"), then the love is likely to qualify as "romantic."

In Singer's (1984) comprehensive historical study of the philosophy of love, he concluded that the term "love" refers to two related but distinct ways of valuing a person: *appraisal* and *bestowal*. Interestingly, without articulating a theory of the underlying processes, he noticed that when one person "loves" another in the romantic sense, the lover "appraises" the beloved individual as being more valuable (at least to the lover) than other people and as more valuable than most other people believe the lover to be. This kind of appraisal is relatively easy to explain in terms of what the lover "does for me," and in that respect it is somewhat like becoming attached to someone because he or she provides a safe haven and secure base. Harlow (1959), in his famous studies of rhesus monkey infants' attachments to a cloth surrogate mother, called this process "love." According to Singer, the other kind of human valuation, which he calls "bestowal," goes beyond and is more mysterious than appraisal. He claims that bestowal involves both creative imagination and generosity and is therefore a form of "giving":

> Only in relation to our bestowal does another person enjoy the kind of value that love creates. . . . The bestowing of value shows itself . . . in caring about the needs and interests of the beloved, by wishing to benefit or protect her, by delighting in her achievements, by encouraging her independence while also accepting and sustaining her dependency by respecting her individuality, by giving her pleasure, by taking pleasures with her, by feeling glad when she is present and sad when she is not, by sharing ideas and emotions with her, by sympathizing with her weakness and depending upon her strength, by

developing common pursuits, by allowing her to become second nature to him – "her smiles, her frowns her ups, her downs" [to quote a once-popular song] – by wanting children who may perpetuate their love. (pp. 6–7)

Although Singer never says so (he is definitely not an attachment theorist), I think the bestowal process is mainly a product of the caregiving system. Consider how much it helps parents to view their children as special, as cute or beautiful, as potential geniuses, as exceptionally funny, and so on. Often, this allows parents to see and foster the genuine potential in their children that other people do not care enough to notice. For many adults, perhaps including parents themselves, it is as funny to notice this biased parental bestowal of value on a particular child as it to see a romantic Jack go gaga over Jill. But for a child, the parent's special care and bestowal of high value is a godsend. It is what allows the potential to become manifest in reality.

For some reason, the bestowal process has been underemphasized in psychology. This may have something to do with the long immersion of American psychology (and Anglo-American culture generally) in utilitarianism, market economics, and rewards and punishments. It is fairly easy for us to ask and answer the question "What's in it for me (or Jack)?" in terms of rewards and punishments. It is more difficult to say why one person would bestow special value on another through a generous act of imagination. But if my hunch is correct, caregiving, sensitive responsiveness, and bestowal are more important to a lasting romantic "pair bond" relationship than attachment and sex are, even though attachment and sex often contribute to it or follow from it (see Diamond [2006], for intriguing examples of two-way influence).

Although as scientists we may be inclined to view bestowal skeptically or cynically, looking back at Richard Feynman's letter to his dead wife, I think you'll see the bestowal process in full swing, and at least for me it is difficult to smirk about it in that case. Richard really did bestow Arline with precious, and for a while totally irreplaceable, qualities, which made it easy for him to take care of her and difficult for him to "turn her in for a new model" when she died. Why? Although I obviously cannot say for sure, I find it useful to conceptualize Richard as having activated his caregiving system with respect to Arline, even though that may not have been his original reason for being attracted to her. Singer (1984), like Berscheid (1988), realized that the initial attraction in a romantic relationship is often sexual, but he thought romantic love was more than sexual attraction or infatuation:

If a woman is *simply* a means to sexual satisfaction, a man may be said to want her, but not to love her. For his sexual desire to become a part of love, it must function as a way of responding to the character and special properties of this particular woman. Desire wants what it wants for the sake of some private gratification, whereas love demands an interest in that vague complexity we call another person. No wonder lovers sound like metaphysicians, and scientists are more comfortable in the study of desire. For love is an attitude with no clear objective. Through it one human being affirms the significance of another, much as a painter highlights a figure by defining it in a sharpened outline. But the beloved is not a painted figure. She is not static: she is fluid, changing, indefinable – *alive*. The lover is attending to a *person*. And who can say what that is? (p. 8)

I agree with, and even marvel at, most of what Singer says in that passage, except when he says "love is an attitude with no clear objective." When viewed from the perspective of the caregiving system, noticing, appreciating, and bestowing admirable qualities on a particular other person is part of what allows one of us human adults to see more deeply into another (see Diamond [2006], and Reis [2006] for examples), to understand and share each other's goals and perspectives (Aron & Aron, 2006), to take care of one another (Collins et al., 2006), to commit to a relationship partner, to engage in a long-term, mutually supportive relationship with the partner, and often, to wish to have and take care of children with him or her (see Brumbaugh & Fraley 2006). In the same way that the motivational goals of the attachment system is the self's protection, security, expansion, and development, the goal of the caregiving system is the person's protection, security, expansion, and development (Mikulincer, 2006). Contrary to cynical psychologies, I believe that it feels as good to achieve the latter kinds of goals as it does to achieve the former kinds, which is one reason for being hopeful and optimistic about the human species despite its many weaknesses, self-destructive tendencies, and failings.

There may be a sense in which both kinds of rewards, those from the attachment side and those from the caregiving side, become part of an amplifying cycle, for reasons discussed by Aron and Aron (2006) and Reis (2006). As already mentioned, the Arons contend that one of the exciting aspects of a romantic relationship is the rapid self-expansion such a relationship provides to both partners. They can expand their knowledge, identities, emotional repertoires, skills, and capacities by experiencing, understanding, valuing, and incorporating their partner's qualities and perspectives into themselves. This sounds somewhat "selfish" and egotistical at first, partly because of the term self-expansion, but if you consider the example of a parent feeling excited, edified, and rewarded by intimate loving interactions with his (in my case) child, you will notice that the parent's self-expansion comes partly from seeing the world anew through the child's eyes, noticing the profound impact a parent has on a child's feelings and development, appreciating the child's rapidly expanding skills, and empathizing with the child's distress. In other words, it can be "self-expanding" to take care of another person's needs sensitively and responsively.

Reis (2006) explains well, in what is for me a remarkable "expansion" of the theory of intimacy he and I sketched in 1988 (Reis & Shaver, 1988), how two people's sensitivity and responsiveness to each other can enlarge and illuminate *both* people's worlds. When two people see and "feel" deeply into each other, and consequently experience, understand, see and express more of themselves, they *both* "expand" – and not in a *folie á deux* manner. As each person grows, becomes more secure, risks "exploring" more of self, partner, and world (to call again on Bowlby's notion of an exploration behavioral system), and reflects positive feelings back onto the partner, both people's attachment and caregiving systems are gratified renewed, and reinforced. Although this kind of intimacy definitely happens in sexual relationships and can be facilitated by mutually rewarding sexual experiences, the mutual self-expansion that occurs often includes much more than sex.

The double-barreled valuing process – appraisal plus bestowal – is interesting in part because we have all noticed, I'm sure, that when a person falls in love, his or her friends are often perplexed by the extreme value placed on the beloved. Jack's friends find it a little silly, stupid, or crazy, perhaps even embarrassing, that Jack perceives Jill to be so uniquely and incredibly wonderful. To them, although she may be quite all right, she is certainly "nothing special." Murray, Holmes, and Griffin (1996) call this peculiar form of valuation a "positive illusion," but I prefer Singer's term "bestowal" because it avoids the cynicism inherent in the term "illusion." Besides, as Reis (2006) explains, recent research shows that a "positive illusion" has measurably good effects on a partner by virtue of being associated with the bestower's very real sensitive and responsive care. It may be misleading to conceptualize the bestower's perceptions of the "bestowee's" potential as illusory if the bestowee goes on to realize the potential in ways that everyone can see. We might be more accurate to call the bestowal "beneficial discernment" rather than illusion.

## Putting the Three Behavioral Systems Together

The evidence reviewed in *The dynamics of romantic love* (Mikulincer & Goodman, 2006) indicates that the three behavioral systems emphasized by Hazan and me (Hazan & Shaver, 1987) in our theorizing about romantic love – attachment, caregiving, and sex – are systematically interrelated, and in more ways than by simply receiving the blanket designation "love" in everyday discourse. Why is this the case?

As a starting point, notice that secure people (understood here as those who score relatively low on both the attachment insecurity dimensions of anxiety and avoidance; see Mikulincer, 2006) find it relatively easy to get psychologically close to others and, when threatened or stressed, to call on memories of supportive experiences with attachment figures. They are also sensitive and responsive caregivers who allow their relationship partners to cope with challenges autonomously if the partners are inclined to do so but offer well timed and appropriately structured comfort and assistance if that is what is needed (e.g., Collins et al., 2006). In other words, attachment security is related to sensitive and responsive caregiving.

Similarly, people with a secure attachment orientation view sex as a mutually enjoyable way to foster intimacy and affection in the context of a stable relationship (see Cooper et al. [2006], and Gillath & Schachner [2006]). Secure people are not usually sexually anxious, out to prove themselves sexually, or inclined to cynically manipulate or use their sexual partners. We do not know much yet about the interplay between the caregiving and sexual systems, but Gillath's (2006) preliminary experimental studies in which participants were subliminally primed with photographs of naked members of the opposite sex, indicate that priming the sexual system moves people, on average, toward greater self-disclosure and more constructive handling of conflicts – tendencies usually associated with attachment security and supportive caregiving. I can imagine that priming people with a sense of caring might also alter the nature of the sexual inclinations, at least slightly – for example, by causing them to be more partner- than self-oriented.

How can we best conceptualize the relations among the behavioral systems? Bowlby and Ainsworth began their theorizing by portraying attachment security as a "secure base for exploration," which suggested that the attachment system was primary, came first in development, and formed either a solid or a shaky foundation for the other behavioral systems. Following Bowlby and Ainsworth's lead, my coauthors and I have, over the years, tended to treat the attachment-system aspect of romantic love as primary. One reason for doing this is that attachment behavior and attachment styles, or orientations, show up early in infant development, whereas caregiving (e.g., as first indicated, for example, by empathy in 3-year-olds; Kestenbaum, Farber, & Sroufe, 1989) appears next, and sex – at least genital sexuality – appears later. With this developmental progression in mind, we looked initially for predictive links between measures of adult attachment style and measures of caregiving (e.g., Kunce & Shaver, 1994; also Collins et al., 2006; and Mikulincer, Shaver, & Slav, 2006) and sex (e.g., Cooper, Shaver, & Collins, 1998; Davis, Shaver, & Vernon, 2004; Schachner & Shaver, 2004; Tracy, Shaver, Albino, & Cooper, 2003; and Levy, Kelly, & Jack, 2006; Cooper et al., 2006; Davis, 2006; and Gillath & Schachner, 2006).

More recently, however, we have learned that we can experimentally prime any one of the behavioral systems and see causal effects on the others. In other words, at least in adults, the behavioral systems are intertwined, such that activation of one has effects on the others and that individual differences in one tend to be correlated with individual differences in the others. There are, as already mentioned, two ways to think about this. First, we can view the attachment system as appearing first in development because its function, assuring protection (i.e., survival), is biologically crucial. Once a child has a functioning attachment system and has begun to adapt it to the local caregiving environment (i.e., once a fairly stable attachment style has developed), the child's caregiving system comes on line to deal with sibling and peer relationships and to be molded by moral socialization and enculturation. Given that children with different attachment styles act in and experience social relationships somewhat differently, the operating parameters of the caregiving system may be shaped in certain predictable directions. Also important are imitation and modeling of primary caregivers, which create similarities in caregiving between parents and children and between a child's attachment system (shaped by the parents) and his or her caregiving system (modeled on those of the parents).

We know empirically that caregivers' behavior initially causes similarities between caregivers' and children's attachment styles (e.g., de Wolff & van IJzendoorn, 1997; van IJzendoorn, 1995). Parental attachment and caregiving anxieties encourage offspring attachment anxiety, and parental attachment and caregiving avoidance encourage offspring attachment avoidance (perhaps partly for genetic reasons, as discussed later, but probably not primarily for those reasons). The anxious or avoidant child is likely to become an anxious or avoidant caregiver by two routes besides genetic similarity – by reacting systematically to the parent's caregiving regime and by copying the caregiver's behavior through a modeling process.

Once the attachment and caregiving systems have developed in tandem and accommodated to each other, they are available to influence presexual peer relationships and then adolescent and adult sexual relationships. Hence, when we study sexual motives and behavior in college and adult samples, the operating parameters of the sexual system are predictable to some extent from the operating parameters of the attachment and caregiving systems. But also, given that priming the sexual system with pictures of naked members of the opposite sex has effect on the attachment and caregiving systems (see Gillath & Schachner, 2006), it seems likely that once pregenital romantic and fully sexual romantic relationships begin, sexual experiences feed back on the operating parameters of the attachment and caregiving systems. (This remains to be studied).

A second way to think about the empirically documented interrelations among the attachment, caregiving, and sexual systems is to view all of them as being affected by pervasive individual differences in temperament or personality. I have conducted several studies to see whether global attachment styles, or attachment-style dimensions, are completely redundant with one or more of the "Big Five" personality traits: openness to experience, conscientiousness, extroversion, agreeableness, and neuroticism (McCrae & Costa, 1996). They definitely are not. In two of our studies (Noftle & Shaver, 2006; Shaver & Brennan, 1992), we compared attachment-style scales with measures of the "Big Five" traits to see which sets of variables best predicted relationship quality and outcomes. Using different measures of attachment style and different measures of the "Big Five" traits, we found Attachment measures consistently outperformed personality trait measures, using both contemporaneous and longitudinal research designs.

Moreover, in several of our laboratory experiments on both conscious and unconscious mental processes related to attachment style (e.g., Mikulincer, Gillath, & Shaver, 2002; Mikulincer, Shaver, & Slav, 2006), we controlled for neuroticism, general anxiety, self-esteem, or inter-personal trust and still obtained predicted effects of attachment anxiety and avoidance. Simpson, Davis, and other authors of chapters in *The dynamics of romantic love* (Mikulincer and Goodman, 2006) have included similar statistical controls in their studies and obtained similar results: Attachment effects are never fully, and usually not even partially, explained by alternative personality constructs. In a recent study using functional magnetic resonance imaging, we (Gillath, Bunge, Shaver, Wendelken, & Mikulincer, 2005) found different patterns of brain activation associated with neuroticism and attachment anxiety.

Still, the correlation between neuroticism and attachment anxiety is often substantial (around .40 or .45), and the correlation between avoidant attachment and agreeableness or extraversion is often statistically significant, although not large. Graziano and Tobin (2002) have shown that agreeableness is positively related to compassion and altruism in some of the same ways that avoidant attachment is negatively related to those same prosocial states, but it seems unlikely, given the relatively modest correlation between avoidance and agreeableness, that the attachment effects are redundant with the agreeableness effects. Moreover, there is nothing in the conceptualization of the "Big Five" traits that would have led to the huge research program generated over the past 20 years by adult attachment theory. Thus attachment theory and its associated measures are scientifically fruitful, whether or not we think of attachment styles as personality traits.

Whatever kinds of qualities they measure, attachment-style measures might be influenced by genes. In the case of the "Big Five" personality traits, about half of the individual-difference variance is attributable to genetic factors (Bouchard & Loehlin, 2001). To date, only a handful of behavior genetic studies of infant attachment patterns have been published. Four of these studies (Bokhorst et al., 2003; Bakersman-Kranenberg, van IJzendoorn, Bokhorst, & Schuenge J, 2004; O'Connor & Croft, 2001; Ricciuti, 1992) turned up little evidence of heritability but garnered some evidence for effects of shared environment on attachment patterns (as would be expected twins' common caregiving environment mattered). In some cases, however, the sample sizes were small or the attachment-style measure differed substantially from the "gold standard" Strange Situation test (Ainsworth et al., 1978), so the absence of evidence for genetic influences may still not be compelling. In one study (Finkel & Matheny, 2000), the heritability of attachment security, based on a nonstandard measure of security, was estimated to be 25%, and there was no substantial effect of shared environment. But the attachment measure used in that study was more similar than usual to measures of infant temperament, perhaps thereby skewing the results in the direction of genetic determination.

At the adult level, Brussoni, Jang, Livesley, and MacBeth (2000) estimated that 43%, 25%, and 37%, respectively, of the variability in fearful, preoccupied, and secure attachment (assessed with Griffin and Bartholomew's 1994, self-report measures) was attributable to genes, but the four attachment measures were intercorrelated, so the results might all reflect a single genetic influence. Variability in dismissing attachment, however, was not at all attributable to genes in that study. Crawford et al. (2005) used proxy versions of the Experience in Close Relationships (ECR) attachment anxiety and avoidance scales (Brennan, Clark, & Shaver, 1998) and found that roughly 40% of the variance in anxious attachment was attributable to genetic factors but that none of the variance in avoidant attachment was due to genes. Interestingly, in that study about 33% of the variance in avoidance was attributable to shared environment.

These preliminary studies are interesting and thought provoking even if they are not yet totally clear in their implications. It seems possible that similarities and differences in what is tapped by the Strange Situation, the AAI, and self-report measures such as the ECR attachment scales can eventually be illuminated by determining the extent to which they have similar or different genetic determinants. Because the ECR self-report attachment scales share variance with "Big Five" neuroticism and are similar in assessment method, they may be more affected than AAI classifications (Hesse, 1999) by genes.

My goal in touching on the matter of genetic influences is not to prejudge or resolve it, because no one can resolve it at present, but to encourage readers to remain open to whatever the evidence eventually dictates. The large and very systematic network of research findings obtained to date by adult attachment researchers will continue to be quite meaningful and significant, both scientifically and clinically, no matter how behavior genetic studies turn out. Nevertheless, it behooves us to include measures of personality and temperament variables in our studies, to take genes into account by pursuing twin studies or doing actual genetic assessments, and to keep in mind that some of the effects we attribute to attachment history may be due in part to genes or to interactions between genes and attachment history. Eventually, and perhaps not too far in the future, we will be able to examine actual genetic profiles associated with different patterns of scores on attachment, caregiving, and sexual motivation measures. Gillath is beginning to explore the possibilities in my lab at the moment.

To summarize this section, there are systematic links between the attachment, caregiving, and sexual systems and between individual differences in the parameters of the three systems (all of which might be characterized in terms of "hyperactivation" and "deactivation," as Mikulincer [2006] does). We don't know yet whether these links are due to inherent properties of the behavioral systems (e.g., to shared brain mechanisms or to the way they unfold and overlap in development), to the roles played by parental attachment figures in shaping the three systems' parameters, to common influences of central personality traits, or to genes. This uncertainty leaves the field wide open for a variety of future studies.

## Further Questions

### What is adult attachment?

Hazan, Campa, and Gur-Yalsh (2006) ask how we can recognize and confidently assess adult attachment. Investigators of infant attachment generally bypass this question by assuming that a child's primary caregiver, often the child's mother, is likely to be *a* primary if not *the* primary attachment figure. In studies of college students and their romantic partners, we often assume, or at least hope, that most relationships that have lasted beyond a certain point (say, several months) are either genuine attachments or at worst what Bowlby, discussing young infants, called "attachments in the taking." This practice is sometimes questioned, even though the results of studies based on it have generally yielded clear and theory-compatible results.

In their discussion of the problems inherent in delineating adult attachment, Hazan et al. refer to four defining classes of behavior discussed by Bowlby (1969/1982): *proximity maintenance, safe haven, separation distress,* and *secure base.* They say "these features of attachment and the dynamic functioning of the attachment system are most readily observable in the behavior of 12-month-olds in relation to their primary caregivers (typically mothers)" (p. 49). In the case of adults, they say we are surest that adult romantic pair bonds qualify as attachments when we see one partner grieve following the death or loss of the other.

Although I agree with these statements, and in fact chose the example of Richard Feynman's letter to his dead wife partly because it was written while he was grieving, I think one can also see Richard and Arline's attachment to each other in their other letters and behavior (as recounted and reflected in their correspondence well before Arline died). They repeatedly chose to stay together even when there were forces pulling them apart, such as separations entailed by his work or her illness and his parent's concern that it was unwise to marry someone who was becoming increasingly ill. The two lovers traversed great distances to be together, and when that was impossible, they communicated frequently by other means.

Also, although not shown in the letters I quoted, it was evident in others that Arline's and Richard's feelings were buoyed up or brought down depending on the condition and receptiveness of their partner. The two lovers were part of a dynamic dyadic system, and I doubt that a day went by when they were unaware of each other's existence and of the importance to each of the other's well-being. Moreover when they were separated, they longed to get back together and looked forward to seeing and touching each other again.

Thus, although I understand what worries Hazan et al. about having to rely on any particular imperfect indicator of adult attachment, such as behaviors in a single real or artificial situation, self-reports, or physiological reactions in an experimental setting, I believe we can do a decent job of detecting attachment if we combine several such indicators. In the studies in which I have been involved, we have measured attachment by asking to whom a person would turn if he or she needed one or more of the comforts provided by attachment figures (using the WHOTO scale designed by Hazan and Zeifman, 1994, and subsequently adapted by other researchers, including Bartholomew and Fraley), by seeing whose names become more readily available cognitively following subliminal threats (e.g., Mikulincer et al., 2002), by seeing whose names, when encountered subliminally or activated in association with conscious memories of that person's loving kindness, increase a person's activation of other behavioral systems, such as caregiving (e.g., Gillath, Shaver, & Mikulincer, 2005; Mikulincer, Shaver, Gillath, & Nitzberg, 2005).

Because letters seem to be a revealing way to assess adult attachment in the case of Richard and Arline Feynman, we might also use methods and materials such as love letters, e-mail correspondence, experience sampling, daily diaries, and so on to supplement behavioral observations and more general self-reports or self-descriptions. That these methods have great value has already been demonstrated in diary studies by Collins and Feeney (2004), Pietromonaco and Feldman Barrett (1997), Tidwell, Reis, and Shaver (1996), and by some of the other authors of *The dynamics of romantic love* (Mikulincer & Goodman, 2006; e.g., Mikulincer et al., 2006; Simpson et al., 2006).

A valuable supplementary approach might be to study existing correspondence between relationship partners. An example that has fascinated Mikulincer and me is the published correspondence between Gauguin, Van Gogh, and their friends and relatives (see Druick & Zegers, 2001, a book designed for a joint exhibit of the two artists' work). Although I assume these artists were not romantic or sexual partners in a literal sense (see Diamond, 2006, for a pioneering study of the complexity of same-sex attraction and attachment), their relationship had many of the qualities of such a relationship. Gauguin, who left not only his wife and children but also Van Gogh when he moved to Tahiti, was clearly avoidant; and Van Gogh, who fell apart psychologically and famously cut off his ear when Gauguin left their collaborative relationship, was clearly anxious and preoccupied. Van Gogh did everything he possibly could to lure Gauguin into a collaborative relationship and to keep him from jettisoning it, and all the while Gauguin was writing to friends complaining about Van Gogh's annoying leech-like neediness and dependency.

Despite hoping, with Hazan et al., that we can do a better job of operationally identifying adult attachment, it would be a mistake, at least in some research contexts, to draw too sharp a line between attachment and nonattachment relationships. Besides the still undeveloped example of Gauguin and Van Gogh (and related studies of attachment and affiliation by Furman, 1999, and Mikulincer & Selinger, 2001), we might consider studies by Rom and Mikulincer (2003), who built on pioneering work by Smith, Murphy, and Coats (1999) to show that people can be "attached" to groups in which they work and that individual differences in attachment style, measured similarly to the way we measure them in the context of romantic relationships, predict how people feel and behave in the groups to which they are "attached." Moreover, group cohesion, which is related to the degree to which people feel integrated into and sensitively and responsively treated by a particular group, interacts with attachment style to predict work performance (even in the military, which might seem like an odd place to look for "love," although it is surely a context in which threats and fears and the wish for protection are rampant). In a similar vein Kirkpatrick (2004) conducted several studies of "attachment to God" and summarized other researchers' studies of attachment and religion. Many of the individual differences in attachment style documented in the domain of romantic relationships reappear in relation to God and other religious figures, such as the Virgin Mary and the Buddha.

This should not be surprising, because we know that part of what underlies individual differences in attachment style is what Bowlby called "internal working models," cognitive–affective structures that come into play when a person feels threatened or is moved to perceive another person group, or imaginary personage as a possible protector, safe haven, or secure base. Just as the mental structures or working models that originally applied to one's mother can be extended to actual and potential romantic partners (e.g., Zayas & Shoda, 2005), the models (expectations, assumptions, and lists of virtues or scary attributes) that apply to parents and romantic partners can be extended or transferred (Andersen & Chen, 2002) to group leaders, the Buddha, religious mentors, and so on. One of the simplest and most common Buddhist prayers is "I take *refuge* in the Buddha, the Dharma [the Buddha's teachings], and the Sangha [the community of fellow Buddhist practitioners]." This is a way of saying, "The living religious tradition to which I am attached, which includes vivid images of both legendary and currently living exemplary loving and protective individuals, serves me as a safe haven and secure base."

Hazan and colleagues (2006) say that "what distinguishes our attachment figures from everyone else is that, in a very literal sense, they reside inside of us" (a notion that fits well with Aron and Aron's [2006] ideas about "inclusion of the other in the self"):

> Their effects on us do not require their physical presence. We carry around mental images of them that we invoke when we need comforting. We go about our daily business more confidently because we know they are cheering us on and ready to help if needed. Our emotional reactions are tempered by anticipating their embrace or reassuring words. Our physiological homeostasis is sustained beyond immediate interactions because our physiological systems have been conditioned to them. (Hazan et al., 2006, p. 65)

I agree completely. But notice that these statements could apply to any person, symbolic figure, religious entity, group, or even culture to which a person becomes attached.

Mikulincer and I (Mikulincer & Shaver, 2004) have demonstrated in a preliminary way that when people are threatened or worn down by failure, they can call on symbolic residues of past good attachment relationships both to ease their current distress and to bolster their sense of themselves as strong, worthy, self-sustaining people who share some of their attachment figures' admirable qualities. I assume this can be done with Jesus and the Buddha almost as well as it can be done with Mom or "Putzie" (Richard Feynman's "baby talk" term of endearment for his wife Arline). Moreover, Mikulincer, Florian, and Hirschberger (2003) showed that attachment relationships can serve some of the "terror management" functions previously attributed only to self-esteem enhancement and adherence to a cultural worldview. My colleagues and I (Hart, Shaver, & Goldenberg, 2005) recently followed up this work and found that threatening one of the three main security-maintaining strategies (attachment, self-esteem, or worldview) evoked defensive responses in the others, suggesting a common underlying security-maintenance system. Both religions and political ideologies seem well designed to bolster this tripartite security system.

This is a huge and important topic, well beyond the scope of this chapter, but I hope by merely mentioning it to convey why I wouldn't want the effort to pin down a specific definition of attachment to keep us from exploring how some of our insights regarding attachment might extend into other social and psychological domains. In the same way that Bowlby (1969/1982) created attachment theory from very diverse ideas and research findings in psychoanalysis, ethology, cybernetics, cognitive and developmental psychology, and community psychiatry, we or our intellectual offspring can bring together new ideas, issues, and findings to create an intellectual framework and body of knowledge that reaches beyond today's attachment theory.

Perhaps this is an appropriate place to make a different but related point. There is a natural tension among psychological researchers when one theory or approach to research threatens to invade the territory staked out by another or when one subfield's interpretation and use of a seminal theoretical text, such as Bowlby's (1969/1982) first volume in the *Attachment and Loss* trilogy, differs from another subfield's interpretation or use of it. Relationship theorists who are not "attached" to attachment theory are quick to demand that "attachment" be defined more restrictively so that attachment researchers do not invade the territory of closeness researchers, interdependence researchers, group researchers, and so on. Moreover, attachment researchers who use observational or interview assessments of attachment style (e.g., the AAI; Hesse, 1999) are sometimes resistant to findings obtained with self-report questionnaires and social-cognition research paradigms (see, for example, the exchange between Shaver & Mikulincer, 2002a, 2002b, and Waters, Crowell, Elliott, Corcoran, & Treboux, 2002). Similarly, most of us self-report attachment researchers tend to ignore the AAI literature (although Bartholomew, Furman, and Simpson are important exceptions).

In my opinion, a healthy response to this kind of territory marking is to leave the boundaries loose for the time being, not because they should necessarily remain loose forever but because we are making interesting discoveries on all sides of all the fences I have just obliquely referred to and because we might not have made these discoveries if we had subdivided the intellectual territory prematurely and built more solid fences around the subterritories. The attitude I am recommending requires tolerance of ambiguity and openness to uncertainty and exploration, which we know are facilitated by security and impeded by insecurity and defensiveness. Fortunately, these intellectual tensions occur within a shared professional arena in which, to a great extent, we can attain greater courage and security simply by granting it to each other.

My own preference for openness, broad scope, and perhaps even open-minded, temporary fuzziness affects my reading of Brumbaugh and Fraley (2006). They do a heroic job of reviewing gargantuan literatures on biological, cultural, and individual-difference determinants of mating and marriage patterns. In their biological analyses they find modest support for three hypotheses regarding the extension of infant–parent attachment capacities into the realm of adolescent and adult romantic love and mating: the paternal-care hypothesis, the developmental-immaturity or neoteny hypothesis, and the concealed-ovulation hypothesis. None of these hypotheses explains a great deal of the cross-species variance in mating systems, however, and I suspect the reason is twofold: (1) The nature of attachments in adulthood need not be completely explicable in terms of adaptive modules of the brain designed by evolution specifically for adult functions. It seems possible that modules or systems "designed" originally for infant–caregiver attachment simply continue to exist and are used as well in the adult pair-bonding context; and (2) whatever the biological processes involved in adult attachment turn out to be, they interact to such an extent with other emotional and cognitive processes that they are not likely to have a simple, tightly delimited, modular function of the kind imagined by evolutionary psychologists. (For a provocative critical review of the search for such modules in contemporary evolutionary psychology, see Buller 2005.)

An instructive example of another system with the same kind of complexity is human language. Centuries of speculation have gone into trying to determine "*the* function" of human language, but I doubt that it has just one function. Once human language came into existence for whatever primary function or functions it originally served, it became the vehicle for myriad mental and communicative processes that almost certainly do not correspond to a single biological function. Moreover, human language seems to be a case in which there really are no clear phylogenetic antecedents, at least not ones that look anything like human language. There are not such antecedents even among our closest primate cousins (who, you may have noticed, have not said or published much lately).

Another example of an important human activity that involves attachment circuitry but probably not circuitry specifically evolved for its own purpose is religion (Kirkpatrick, 2004). Many scientists have tried to imagine what evolutionary function or functions religion might have had, but Kirkpatrick (2004) argues persuasively that religion is a multidimensional, multicomponent phenomenon that takes advantage of several different evolved behavioral systems without, most likely, being due at all to the evolution of a specific "religion module" in the brain. (For a somewhat different but generally compatible and very interesting analysis, see Rue, 2005).

If many of the processes and functions associated with attachment can be observed in leader–follower, student–teacher, and devotee–God relationships, it doesn't make sense to restrict our consideration of them solely to their child–parent or reproductive relationship contexts. If my intuitions about this matter are correct, we should keep trying to discover how each of the behavioral systems works and what role it plays, separately and in collaboration with other psychological processes, in various social phenomena. It seems possible, for example, that the caregiving system comes into play most directly when a person serves as a parent, less directly but still powerfully when a person cares for a romantic partner, less directly but still notably when the person exhibits compassion and provides altruistic assistance to suffering members of an extended family or tribal or ethnic group and even less directly when the person shows compassion and kindness to needy strangers (Gillath Shaver, & Mikulincer, 2005; Mikulincer et al 2005). The question of whether the caregiving behavioral system evolved specifically for its use in adult romantic or pair-bond relationships or was shaped in additional ways because of genetic payoffs for caregiving in relationships with village members and strangers should remain open.

My unrestricted, wait-and-see attitude extends to the case of recent efforts to determine whether people have a single attachment style in their relationships with parents, siblings, close friends, and various romantic partners (in cases in which there is more than one partner across time). Much of this research is still unpublished, but my impression from hearing about it at conferences and reviewing manuscripts submitted to journals is that the different attachment styles, as measured, are usually substantially correlated despite not being identical across all relationships. Undoubtedly, a person's relationship motives, worries, and behaviors are not the same across all relationships. Many studies show that both partners' attachment styles (and, I assume, caregiving and sexual styles as well, if those were measured) have effects on the relationship and on both partners' measurable feelings about it. For this to be the case (i.e., for there to be joint causality), the partners must affect each other's perceptions, satisfactions, and dissatisfactions. Given that some of these affected states involve trust and distrust, security and insecurity, commitment and infidelity, and many other such issues, the partners' responses to attachment measures should also be affected. This cross-relationship variability must not be so great, however, that it makes "global attachment style" a misleading or meaningless concept, because in many studies (reviewed by Mikulincer & Shaver, 2003, and Shaver & Mikulincer, 2005) we have found that people's scores on global attachment measures predict complex reactions to laboratory and real-world situations. Thus, although it is not unimportant to measure relationship-specific attachment styles, it would be a mistake to ignore a person's general attachment or caregiving or sexual tendencies while pursuing only differences between relationships.

## Relations between attachment theory and other theories and perspectives

Several chapters in *The dynamics of romantic love* (Mikulincer & Goodman, 2006) demonstrate that adopting an attachment theoretical approach to adolescent and adult couple relationships provides a useful perspective on, or a striking alternative to, other theoretical approaches. For example, Bartholomew and Allison (2006) question the reigning feminist perspective on partner violence and abuse and show that both partners' attachment histories and styles contribute to two important dyadic behavior patterns in abusive relationships: pursuing–distancing and pursuing–pursuing. The first pattern tends to occur, the authors say, "in couples with incompatible attachment needs (i.e., closeness vs. distance) . . . [and is generally observed] when individuals with preoccupied tendencies [are] partnered with more avoidant (fearful or dismissing) individuals" (p. 116). In this kind of interaction, either partner is capable of becoming violent, regardless of gender. The pursuing–pursuing pattern tends to occur in couples in which both partners are anxious or preoccupied. Such joint causality has been observed as well in much nonattachment research, in which mutual violence and abuse is predicted by both partners being high on measures of neuroticism or negative affectivity (e.g., Moffitt, Robins, & Caspi, 2001; Robins, Caspi, & Moffitt, 2000, 2002).

Interestingly, Bartholomew and Allison also say that interpersonal problems in abusive relationships are partly a matter of poor caregiving: "When both partners showed preoccupied tendencies, they tended to compete for support and attention from each other. Moreover, neither partner was able to recognize or meet his or her partner's needs, leading to mutual frustration and, at times, aggression" (p. 116). The authors go on to say that future research is likely to reveal that both partners in violent and abusive relationships suffer from "deficits in the ability to effectively ask for care, . . . perceive and appropriately respond to a partner's need for care, and . . . accept and benefit from partner care. . . . In relationships in which a partner's attachment needs are chronically frustrated, caregiving may indirectly fulfill attachment needs and may even serve to inhibit the activation of the attachment system" (p. 118). This is similar to using sexual behavior to serve attachment needs, as described by Davis (2006) and Gillath and Schachner (2006).

Levy, Kelly, and Jack (2006) compare attachment theory with Buss's (1999; Buss, Larsen, & Westen, 1996) evolutionary theory of mating, two alternative ways to explain gender differences in sexual and emotional jealousy. As Levy et al. explain, "Buss et al. . . . found that men tend to view sexual infidelity as more distressful than women do, and women tend to view emotional infidelity as more distressful. They also found that men displayed greater physiological distress than did women while imagining a mate's sexual infidelity" (p. 130). These kinds of data have been viewed by Buss and his colleagues as evidence that men are worried about paternity certainty whereas women, who are pretty certain their children are their own, are worried lest their male partners commit their resources to other women and those women's offspring. Instead, Levy et al. thought the sex differences in kinds of jealousy might be explained by the fact that men are more likely than women to have a dismissingly avoidant attachment style (e.g., Shaver et al., 1996), and because this style has been associated with sexual promiscuity, lack of interest in psychological intimacy (e.g., Davis et al., 2004; Schachner & Shaver, 2002, 2004), and projection of one's own negative traits onto others (Mikulincer & Horesh, 1999) – possibly including attributing sexual infidelity to them – dismissing men might be more sexually than emotionally jealous. If so, this could explain the gender difference in types of jealousy without relying on Buss's theory.

Levy et al. found, in a large-sample study, that dismissing women were roughly 4 times as likely as secure women to say that sexual jealousy was more distressing than emotional jealousy and that dismissing men were nearly 50 times as likely as secure men to say that sexual jealousy was more troubling. Secure individuals of both genders were more likely to find emotional infidelity more distressing than sexual infidelity. Thus, although there were still notable gender differences in kinds of jealous reactions to partner infidelity, there were also important attachment-style differences moderating the gender differences. As the authors point out, the attachment perspective on jealousy suggests social and clinical interventions to reduce male sexual jealousy, which can sometimes escalate to violence or even murder, which the nonattachment version of evolutionary psychology does not.

Some of the studies described by Gillath and Schachner (2006) show that, indeed, augmenting people's sense of security can incline them more toward a stable, long-term relationship, which shows that altering the attachment system can have effects on the sexual system. These results supplement previous studies by our research group (e.g., Gillath, Shaver, Mikulincer, Nitzberg, et al., 2005; Mikulincer et al., 2005) showing that augmenting a person's sense of attachment security causes the person to become more compassionate and altruistic. They also fit with results reported by Mikulincer et al. (2006), which indicate that attachment security fosters gratitude and forgiveness, two prosocial orientations that should contribute to stability and quality of a long-term couple relationship. Combined with Davis's (2006) very comprehensive analysis of the process of sexual coercion, these various clues from attachment research suggest possible methods of intervention to reduce relationship dysfunction and sexual violence.

### Are attachment and sexual attraction incompatible?

Based on two kinds of evidence, Berscheid (2006) provocatively suggests that attachment and sexual attraction might be incompatible. First, sexual attraction and enthusiasm tend to wane over the course of long marriages, even though the partners remain quite attached to each other (Regan & Berscheid, 1999). Second, Wolf (1995) showed, in a fascinating study of an unusual marriage system once practiced in certain areas of Taiwan, that couples who were betrothed and brought up together as young children tended not to have good or long-lasting sexual and marital relationships in adulthood. (The couples were formed by parents when the partners-to-be, especially the girls, were quite young).

I won't dispute the first kind of evidence, because it would require a lengthy analysis and because it does not, in any case, imply that it is the attachment per se that causes or contributes to the decline in sexual excitement. The second kind of evidence deserves attention, however, especially because most readers of this chapter will not have read Wolf's work, as I had not before Berscheid brought it to my attention.

There turn out to be many complexities involved in the special cases of child betrothal discussed by Wolf (1995). First, the child brides-to-be were voluntarily given away by their own parents and placed in adoptive homes, where they were often treated very badly. Here are typical comments from two such brides quoted by Wolf: (1) "When I think of my childhood, I wonder why my fate was so bad. My foster mother beat me too often and too hard. I was always trembling with fear" (p. 61). (2) "They adopt someone else's daughter to do their work. I used to get so angry with my parents because they gave me away. . . . If they hadn't given me away, I probably would have had a very happy life. . . . I felt, 'No one pays attention to me, because I am an adopted daughter' " (p. 63).

Needless to say, there could be many reasons why such women's marriages were not as successful or satisfying, on average, as those of other women raised more normally, without this having anything to do with being attached to their husband-to-be. The live-in future brides often felt heartlessly rejected by their own parents and cruelly mistreated by their future husband's family, including the future husband himself. Wolf (1995) also mentions that couples of this kind tended to get married 2 years earlier, on average, than comparison couples, which in itself might have made their relationships less likely to succeed.

Most important and surprising to me, however, was Wolf's repeated and insistent claim that he was definitely *not* claiming that *adult* attachment interferes with *adult* sexual attraction or marital satisfaction. On p. 16, for example, he says, "That husband and wife commonly form enduring attachments is entirely irrelevant." The reason is that his main idea was that child husbands- and brides-to-be become familiar with each other before they have sexual motives, which then makes it difficult to view their adoptive sibling as a sex partner later on. He would not have advanced a similar hypothesis about a teenage girl adopted into a family with a teenage boy, nor did he believe in any way, shape, or form that adult spouses who were attached could not be sexually attracted to each other. Thus, although it is very important for us to look empirically at how the three behavioral systems under discussion in this book interact with and affect each other, there is no reason at present to predict that sex and attachment or sex and caregiving or caregiving and attachment cannot coexist and function in a mutually coordinated fashion.

# References

Ainsworth, M. D. S., Blehar, M. C., Waters, E., & Wall, S. (1978). *Patterns of attachment: A psychological study of the Strange Situation*. Hillsdale, NJ: Erlbaum.

Andersen, S. M., & Chen, S. (2002). The relational self: An interpersonal social-cognitive theory. *Psychological Review, 109,* 619–645.

Aron, A., & Aron, E. N. (2006). Romantic Relationships from the Perspectives of the Self-Expansion Model and Attachment Theory: Partially Overlapping Circles. In M. Mikulincer & G. S. Goodman (Eds.). *The dynamics of romantic love: Attachment, caregiving, and sex* (pp. 359–382). New York, NY: Guilford Press.

Bakermans-Kranenburg, M. J., van IJzendoorn, M. H., Bokhorst, C. L., & Schuengel, C. (2004). The importance of shared environment in infant–father attachment: A behavioral genetic study of the attachment Q-sort. *Journal of Family Psychology, 18,* 545–549.

Bartholomew, K., & Allison, C. J. (2006). An attachment perspective on abusive dynamics in intimate relationships. In M. Mikulincer & G. S. Goodman (Eds.). *The dynamics of romantic love: Attachment, caregiving, and sex* (pp. 102–127). New York, NY: Guilford Press.

Barrett, L. F. (2006a). Are emotions natural kinds? *Perspectives in Psychological Science, 1,* 28–58.

Barrett, L. F. (2006b). Solving the emotion paradox: Categorization and the experience of emotion. *Personality and Social Psychology Review, 10,* 20–46.

Berscheid, E. (1988). Some comments on love's anatomy: Or, whatever happened to old-fashioned lust? In R. J. Sternberg & M. L. Barnes (Eds.). *The psychology of love* (pp. 359–374). New Haven, CT: Yale University Press.

Berscheid, E. (2006). Seasons of the heart. In M. Mikulincer & G. S. Goodman (Eds.). *The dynamics of romantic love: Attachment, caregiving, and sex* (pp. 404–422). New York, NY: Guilford Press.

Bokhorst, C. L., Bakermans-Kranenburg, M. J., Fearon, P., van IJzendoorn, M. H., Fonagy, P., Schuengel, C., et al. (2003). The importance of shared environment in mother–infant attachment security: A behavioral genetic study. *Child Development, 74*, 1769–1782.

Bouchard, T. J., & Loehlin, J. C. (2001). Genes, evolution, and personality. *Behavior Genetics, 31*, 243–273.

Bowlby, J. (1973). *Attachment and loss: Vol. 2. Separation: Anxiety and anger.* New York: Basic Books.

Bowlby, J. (1979). *The making and breaking of affectional bonds.* London: Tavistock.

Bowlby, J. (1980). *Attachment and loss: Vol. 3. Loss: Sadness and depression.* New York: Basic Books.

Bowlby, J. (1982). *Attachment and loss: Vol. 1. Attachment* (2nd edn.). New York: Basic Books. (Original work published 1969)

Brennan, K. A., Clark, C. L., & Shaver, P. R. (1998). Self-report measurement of adult romantic attachment: An integrative overview. In J. A. Simpson & W. S. Rholes (Eds.). *Attachment theory and close relationships* (pp. 46–76). New York: Guilford Press.

Brumbaugh, C. C., & Fraley, R. C. (2006). The evolution of attachment in romantic relationships. In M. Mikulincer & G. S. Goodman (Eds.). *The dynamics of romantic love: Attachment, caregiving, and sex* (pp. 71–101). New York, NY: Guilford Press.

Brussoni, M. J., Jang, K. L., Livesley, W. J., & MacBeth, T. M. (2000). Genetic and environmental influences on adult attachment styles. *Personal Relationships, 7*, 283–289.

Buller, D. J. (2005). *Adapting minds: Evolutionary psychology and the persistent quest for human nature.* Cambridge, MA: MIT Press.

Buss, D. M. (1999). *Evolutionary psychology: The new science of the mind.* Boston: Allyn & Bacon.

Buss, D. M., Larsen, R. J., & Westen, D. (1996). Sex differences in jealousy: Not gone, not forgotten, and not explained by alternative hypotheses. *Psychological Science, 7*, 373–375.

Collins, N. L., Guichard, A. C., Ford, M. B., & Feeney, B. C. (2006). Responding to need in intimate relationships: Normative processes and individual differences. In M. Mikulincer & G. S. Goodman (Eds.). *The dynamics of romantic love: Attachment, caregiving, and sex* (pp. 149–189). New York, NY: Guilford Press.

Cooper, M. L., Pioli, M., Levitt, A., Talley, A. E., Micheas, L., & Collins, N. L. (2006). Attachment styles, sex motives, and sexual behavior. In M. Mikulincer & G. S. Goodman (Eds.). *The dynamics of romantic love: Attachment, caregiving, and sex* (pp. 243–274). New York, NY: Guilford Press.

Cooper, M. L., Shaver, P. R., & Collins, N. L. (1998). Attachment styles, emotion regulation, and adjustment in adolescence. *Journal of Personality and Social Psychology, 74*, 1380–1397.

Crawford, T. N., John Livesley, W., Jang, K. L., Shaver, P. R., Cohen, P., & Ganiban, J. (2007). Insecure attachment and personality disorder: A twin study of adults. *European Journal of Personality: Published for the European Association of Personality Psychology, 21* (2), 191–208.

Davis, D. (2006). Attachment-Related Pathways to Sexual Coercion. In M. Mikulincer & G. S. Goodman (Eds.). *The dynamics of romantic love: Attachment, caregiving, and sex* (pp. 293–336). New York, NY: Guilford Press.

Davis, D., Shaver, P. R., & Vernon, M. L. (2004). Attachment style and subjective motivations for sex. *Personality and Social Psychology Bulletin, 30*, 1076–1090.

De Wolff, M., & van IJzendoorn, M. H. (1997). Sensitivity and attachment: A meta-analysis on parental antecedents of infant attachment. *Child Development, 68*, 571–591.

Diamond, L. M. (2006). How Do I Love Thee?: Implications of Attachment Theory for Understanding Same-Sex Love and Desire. In M. Mikulincer & G. S. Goodman (Eds.). *The dynamics of romantic love: Attachment, caregiving, and sex* (pp. 275–292). New York, NY: Guilford Press.

Druick D. W., & Zegers, P. K. (2001). *Van Gogh and Gauguin: The studio of the south.* Chicago: Art Institute of Chicago.

Ekman, P. (1992). An argument for basic emotions. *Cognition and Emotion, 6*, 169–200.

Feeney, B. C., & Collins, N. L. (2004). Interpersonal safe haven and secure base caregiving processes in adulthood. In W. S. Rholes, & J. A. Simpson (Eds.). *Adult attachment: Theory, research, and clinical implications* (pp. 300–338). New York, NY: Guilford Press.

Feynman, M. (Ed.). (2005). *Perfectly reasonable deviations from the beaten track: The letters of Richard P. Feynman.* New York: Basic Books.

Finkel, D., & Matheny, A. P. (2000). Genetic and environmental influences on a measure of infant attachment security. *Twin Research, 3*, 242–250.

Frijda, N. H. (1986). *The emotions.* Cambridge, UK: Cambridge University Press.

Furman, W. (1999). Friends and lovers: The role of peer relationships in adolescent romantic relationships. In W. A. Collins & B. Laursen (Eds.). *Minnesota symposia on child psychology: Vol. 30. Relationships as developmental contexts* (pp. 133–154). Mahwah, NJ: Erlbaum.

Gillath, O., Bunge, S. A., Shaver, P. R., Wendelken, C., & Mikulinca; M. (2005). Attachment-style differences and ability to suppress negative thoughts: Exploring the neural correlates. *Neuroimage, 28*, 835–847.

Gillath, O., & Schachner, D. A. (2006). How Do Sexuality and Attachment Interrelate?: Goals, Motives, and Strategies. In M. Mikulincer & G. S. Goodman (Eds.). *The dynamics of romantic love: Attachment, caregiving, and sex* (pp. 337–358). New York, NY: Guilford Press.

Gillath, O., Shaver, P. R., Mikulincer, M. (2005). An attachment-theoretical approach to compassion and altruism. In P. Gilbert (Ed.). *Compassion: Conceptualizations, research, and use in psychotherapy* (pp. 121–147). London: Brunner-Routledge.

Gillath, O., Shaver, P. R., Mikulincer, M., Nitzberg, R. E., Erez, A., & van IJzendoorn, M. H. (2005). Attachment, caregiving, and volunteering: Placing volunteerism in an attachment-theoretical framework. *Personal Relationships, 12,* 425–446.

Goodman, G. S. (2006). Attachment to Attachment Theory: A Personal Perspective on an Attachment Researcher. In M. Mikulincer & G. S. Goodman (Eds.). *The dynamics of romantic love: Attachment, caregiving, and sex* (pp. 3–22). New York, NY: Guilford Press.

Graziano, W. G., & Tobin, R. M. (2002). Agreeableness: Dimension of personality or social desirability artifact? *Journal of Personality, 70,* 695–727.

Griffin, D. W., & Bartholomew, K. (1994). The metaphysics of measurement: The case of adult attachment. In K. Bartholomew & D. Perlman (Eds.). *Advances in personal relationships: Vol. 5. Attachment processes in adulthood* (pp. 17–52). London: Kingsley.

Harlow, H. F. (1959). Love in infant monkeys. *Scientific American, 200,* 68–86.

Hart, J. J., Shaver, P. R., & Goldenberg, J. L. (2005). Attachment, self-esteem, worldviews, and terror management: Evidence for a tripartite security system. *Journal of Personality and Social Psychology, 88,* 999–1013.

Hazan, C., Campa, M., & Gur-Yaish, N. (2006). What is adult attachment? In M. Mikulincer & G. S. Goodman (Eds.). *The dynamics of romantic love: Attachment, caregiving, and sex* (pp. 47–70). New York, NY: Guilford Press.

Hazan, C., & Shaver, P. R. (1987). Romantic love conceptualized as an attachment process. *Journal of Personality and Social Psychology, 52,* 511–524.

Hazan, C., & Zeifman, D. (1994). Sex and the psychological tether. In K. Bartholomew & D. Perlman (Eds.). *Advances in personal relationships: Vol. 5. Attachment processes in adulthood* (pp. 151–177) London: Kingsley.

Hesse, E. (1999). The Adult Attachment Interview: Historical and current perspectives. In J. Cassidy & P. R. Shaver (Eds.). *Handbook of attachment: Theory, research, and clinical applications* (pp. 395–433. New York: Guilford Press.

Kestenbaum, R., Farber, E. A., & Sroufe, L. A. (1989, Summer). Individual differences in empathy among preschoolers: Relation to attachment history. *New Directions for Child Development, 44,* 51–64.

Kirkpatrick, L. A. (2004). *Attachment, evolution, and the psychology of religion.* New York: Guilford Press.

Kunce, L. J., & Shaver, P. R. (1994). An attachment-theoretical approach to *caregiving* in romantic relationships. In K. Bartholomew & D. Perlman (Eds.). *Advances in personal relationships: Vol. 5. Attachment processes in adulthood* (pp. 205–237). London: Kingsley.

Levy, K. N., Kelly, K. M., & Jack, E. L. (2006). Sex differences in jealousy: A matter of evolution or attachment history?. In M. Mikulincer & G. S. Goodman (Eds.). *The dynamics of romantic love: Attachment, caregiving, and sex* (pp. 128–148). New York, NY: Guilford Press.

Lutz, A., Greischar, L. L., Rowlings, N. B., Ricard, M., & Davidson, R. J. (2004). Long-term meditators self-induce high amplitude gamma synchrony during mental practice. *Proceedings of the National Academy of Sciences, 101,* 16369–16373.

Main, M. (1995). Attachment: Overview, with implications for clinical work. In S. Goldberg, R. Muir, & J. Kerr (Eds.). *Attachment theory: Social, developmental, and clinical perspectives* (pp. 407–474). Hillsdale, NJ: Analytic Press.

McCrae, R. R., & Costa, P. T., Jr. (1996). Toward a new generation of personality theories: Theoretical contexts for the five-factor model. In J. S. Wiggins (Ed.). *The five-factor model of personality: Theoretical perspectives* (pp. 51–87). New York: Guilford Press.

Mikulincer, M. (2006). Attachment, caregiving, and sex within romantic relationships: A behavioural systems perspective. In M. Mikulincer & G. S. Goodman (Eds.). *The dynamics of romantic love: Attachment, caregiving, and sex* (pp. 23–44). New York, NY: Guilford Press.

Mikulincer, M., Florian, V., & Hirschberger, G. (2003). The existential function of close relationships: Introducing death into the science of love. *Personality and Social Psychology Review, 7,* 20–40.

Mikulincer, M., Gillath, O., & Shaver, P. R. (2002). Activation of the attachment system in adulthood: Threat-related primes increase the accessibility of mental representations of attachment figures. *Journal of Personality and Social Psychology, 83,* 881–895.

Mikulincer, M., & Horesh, N. (1999). Adult attachment style and the perception of others: The role of projective mechanisms. *Journal of Personality arid Social Psychology, 76,* 1022–1034.

Mikulincer, M., & Selinger, M. (2001). The interplay between attachment and affiliation systems in adolescents' same-sex friendships: The role of attachment style. *Journal of Social and Personal Relationships, 18,* 81–106.

Mikulincer, M., & Shaver, P. R. (2003). The attachment behavioral system in adulthood: Activation, psychodynamics, and interpersonal processes. In M. P. Zanna (Ed.). *Advances in experimental social psychology* (Vol. 35, pp. 53–152). New York: Academic Press.

Mikulincer, M., & Shaver, P. R. (2004). Security-based self-representations in adulthood: Contents and processes. In W. S. Rholes & J. A. Simpson (Eds.). *Adult attachment: Theory, research, and clinical implications* (pp. 159–195). New York: Guilford Press.

Mikulincer, M., Shaver, P. R., Gillath, O., & Nitzberg, R. E. (2005). Attachment, caregiving, and altruism: Boosting attachment security increases compassion and helping. *Journal of Personality and Social Psychology, 89*, 817–839.

Mikulincer, M., Shaver, P. R., & Slav, K. (2006). Attachment, mental representations of others, and gratitude and forgiveness in romantic relationships. In M. Mikulincer & G. S. Goodman (Eds.). *The dynamics of romantic love: Attachment, caregiving, and sex* (pp. 190–215). New York, NY: Guilford Press.

Moffitt, T. E., Robins, R. W., & Caspi, A. (2001). A couples analysis of partner abuse with implications for abuse-prevention policy. *Criminology and Public Policy, 1*, 5–36.

Murray, S. L., Holmes, J. G., & Griffin, D. W. (1996). The benefits of positive illusions: Idealization and the construction of satisfaction in close relationships. *Journal of Personality and Social Psychology, 70*, 79–98.

Noftle, E. E., & Shaver, P. R. (2006). Attachment dimensions and the big five personality traits: Associations and comparative ability to predict relationship quality. *Journal of research in personality, 40* (2), 179–208.

Oatley, K., & Jenkins, J. M (1996). *Understanding emotions.* Cambridge, MA: Blackwell.

O'Connor, T. G., & Croft, C. M. (2001). A twin study of attachment in preschool children. *Child Development, 72*, 1501–1511.

Pietromonaco, P. R., 8c Feldman Barrett, L. (1997). Working models of attachment and daily social interactions. *Journal of Personality and Social Psychology, 73*, 1409–1423.

Regan, P. C., & Berscheid, E. (1999). *Lust: What we know about human sexual desire.* Thousand Oaks, CA: Sage.

Reis, H. T. (2006). Implications of attachment theory for research on intimacy. In M. Mikulincer & G. S. Goodman (Eds.). *The dynamics of romantic love: Attachment, caregiving, and sex* (pp. 383–403). New York, NY: Guilford Press.

Reis, H. T., & Shaver, P. R. (1988). Intimacy as an interpersonal process. In S. Duck (Ed.). *Handbook of research in personal relationships* (pp. 367–389). London: Wiley.

Ricciuti, A. E. (1992). Child–mother attachment: A twin study. *Dissertation Abstracts International, 54*, 3364. (UMI No. 9324873).

Robins, R. W., Caspi, A., & Moffitt, T. E. (2000). Two personalities, one relationship: Both partners' personality traits shape the quality of their relationship. *Journal of Personality and Social Psychology, 79*, 251–259.

Robins, R. W., Caspi, A., & Moffitt, T. E. (2002). It's not just who you're with, it's who you are: Personality and relationship experiences across multiple relationships. *Journal of Personality, 70*, 925–964.

Rom, E., & Mikulincer, M. (2003). Attachment theory and group processes: The association between attachment style and group-related representations, goals, memories, and functioning. *Journal of Personality and Psychology, 84*, 1220–1235.

Rue, L. (2005). *Religion is not about God: How spiritual traditions nurture our biological nature and what to expect when they fail.* New Brunswick, NJ: Rutgers University Press.

Schachner, D. A., & Shaver, P. R. (2002). Attachment style and human mate poaching. *New Review of Social Psychology, 1*, 122–129.

Schachner, D. A., & Shaver, P. R. (2004). Attachment dimensions and motives for sex. *Personal Relationships, 11*, 179–195.

Schwartz, J., & Shaver, P. R. (1987). Emotions and emotion knowledge in interpersonal relations. In W. Jones & D. Perlman (Eds.). *Advances in personal relationships* (Vol. 1, pp. 197–241). Greenwich, CT: JAI Press.

Shaver, P. R., & Brennan, K. A. (1992). Attachment styles and the "big five" personality traits: Their connections with each other and with romantic relationship outcomes. *Personality and Social Psychology Bulletin, 18*, 536–545.

Shaver, P. R., Hazan, C., & Bradshaw, D. (1988). Love as attachment: The integration of three behavioral systems. In R. J. Sternberg & M. Barnes (Eds.). *The psychology of love* (pp. 68–99). New Haven, CT: Yale University Press.

Shaver, P. R., & Mikulincer, M. (2002a). Attachment-related psychodynamics. *Attachment and Human Development, 4*, 133–161.

Shaver, P. R., & Mikulincer, M. (2002b). Dialogue on adult attachment: Diversity and integration. *Attachment and Human Development, 4*, 243–257.

Shaver, P. R., & Mikulincer, M. (2005). Attachment theory and research: Resurrection of the psychodynamic approach to personality. *Journal of Research in Personality 39*, 22–45.

Shaver, P. R., Morgan, H. J., & Wu, S. (1996). Is love a "basic" emotion? *Personal Relationships, 3*, 81–96.

Shaver, P. R., Schwartz, J., Kirson, D., & O'Connor, C. (1987). Emotion knowledge: Further exploration of a prototype approach. *Journal of Personality and Social Psychology, 52*, 1061–1086.

Simpson, J. A., Campbell, L., & Weisberg, Y. J. (2006). Daily Perceptions of Conflict and Support in Romantic Relationships: The Ups and Downs of Anxiously Attached Individuals. In M. Mikulincer & G. S. Goodman (Eds.). *The dynamics of romantic love: attachment, caregiving, and sex* (pp. 216–242). New York, NY: Guilford Press.

Singer, I. (1984). *The nature of love: Vol. 1. Plato to Luther* (2nd edn.). Chicago: University of Chicago Press.

Smith, E. R., Murphy, J., & Coats, S. (1999). Attachment to groups: Theory and measurement. *Journal of Personality and Social Psychology, 77*, 94–110.

Tidwell, M. C. O., Reis, H. T., & Shaver, P. R. (1996). Attachment, attractiveness, and social interaction: A diary study. *Journal of Personality and Social Psychology, 71*, 729–745.

Tracy, J. L., Shaver, P. R., Albino, A. W., & Cooper, M. L. (2003). Attachment styles and adolescent sexuality. In P. Florsheim (Ed.). *Adolescent romance and sexual behavior: Theory, research, and practical implications* (pp. 137–159). Mahwah, NJ: Erlbaum.

Van IJzendoorn, M. H. (1995). Adult attachment representations, parental responsiveness, and infant attachment: A meta-analysis on the predictive validity of the Adult Attachment Interview. *Psychological Bulletin, 117,* 387–403.

Waters, E., Crowell, J., Elliott, M., Corcoran, D., & Treboux, D. (2002). Bowlby's secure base theory and the social/personality psychology of attachment styles: Work(s) in progress. *Attachment and Human Development, 4,* 230–242.

Weinfield, N. S., Sroufe, L. A., Egeland, B., Sc Carlson, E. A. (1999). The nature of individual differences in infant–caregiver attachment. In J. Cassidy & P. R. Shaver (Eds.). *Handbook of attachment: Theory, research, and clinical applications* (pp. 68–88). New York: Guilford Press.

Wolf, A. P. (1995). *Sexual attraction and childhood association: A Chinese brief for Edward Westermarck.* Stanford, CA: Stanford University Press.

Zayas, V., & Shoda, Y. (2005). Do automatic reactions elicited by thoughts of romantic partner, mother, and self relate to adult romantic attachment? *Personality and Social Psychology Bulletin, 31,* 1011–1025.

# 9

# Integrating Temperament and Attachment
## *The Differential Susceptibility Paradigm*

### Marinus H. van IJzendoorn and Marian J. Bakermans-Kranenburg

For years on end, attachment and temperament seemed natural enemies in a deadly war over dominance and territory. At one side of the border, followers of temperament theory basically reduced attachment to temperamental inhibition in the Strange Situation (Kagan, 1995). At the other side, adherents of attachment theory declared temperament obsolete because of its outmoded emphasis on inherited or constitutional individual differences (Sroufe, 1985). Recent research in the fields of both attachment and temperament, however, has shown convincingly that caregiving environments fostering the formation of secure attachment not only shape neurophysiological substrates of temperamental inhibition but also help to regulate infant emotional reactivity (Hane & Fox, 2006). Inspired by the seminal work of Meaney (2010) and his group on the crucial role of caregiving in determining stress reactivity in rodents, the domains of temperament and attachment have come closer to each other in the converging identification of the significance of the caregiving environment. At the same time the idea that the effect of parenting on the child also depends on the child's temperament has almost become a truism.

In recent years temperament and attachment have thus become intertwined more intimately. Although much work still focuses on parenting effects, with the assumption that they apply equally to all children, recent studies have tested the moderating effect of the child's temperament, following Belsky's (1997a) ideas about temperamental differential susceptibility. For example, Klein Velderman, Bakermans-Kranenburg, Juffer, and van IJzendoorn (2006) found that experimentally induced changes in maternal sensitivity exerted greater impact on the attachment security of highly reactive infants than it did on other infants. The very temperamental characteristics of individuals that make them disproportionately vulnerable to adversity may also make them disproportionately likely to benefit from contextual support, which is the core hypothesis of the differential susceptibility paradigm (Ellis, Boyce, Belsky, Bakermans-Kranenburg, & van IJzendoorn, 2011).

In this chapter we describe the various interpretations of the complicated relation between attachment and temperament, and we show how their borders have become permeable. In fact, the differential susceptibility paradigm integrates temperament and attachment in a constructive, complementary, and productive way. Although some decades ago it seemed "never the twain shall meet," a reconciliation is now emerging, and bridges are being built between two major theoretical strands in developmental science. In this chapter we highlight some milestones in this rapprochement, with an emphasis on recent, exciting developments based on the differential susceptibility paradigm as the integrative template of temperament and attachment theory and research.

*Source:* Marinus H. van IJzendoorn, Marian J. Bakermans-Kranenburg, "Integrating Temperament and Attachment: The Differential Susceptibility Paradigm," pp. 403-424 from *Handbook of Temperament*, eds. Marcel Zentner, Rebecca L. Shiner (New York, NY: Guilford Press, 2012). Reproduced with permission from Guilford Press.

# The Nature and Nurture of Attachment and Temperament

## Attachment

*Attachment* has been briefly defined as children's "strong disposition to seek proximity to and contact with a specific figure and to do so in certain situations, notably when they are frightened, tired or ill" (Bowlby, 1969, p. 371). Inspired by Darwinian evolutionary theory and Harlow's (1958) experimental work with rhesus monkeys, Bowlby (1969) was the first to propose that human genetic selection had favored attachment behaviors, since they increased infant–parent proximity, which in turn enhanced the chances for infant survival. Although Bowlby did not use the concept of "inclusive fitness" to hint at the transmission of parental genes into the next generations, he can certainly be considered the first evolutionary psychologist after Darwin (see Simpson & Belsky, 2008, for a more sophisticated treatment of the evolutionary background of attachment). Attachment is considered to be an inborn capacity of every exemplar of the human species. Individual differences in the quality of attachment emerge in the first years of life, and central to attachment theory is the idea that parenting, more specifically, parental sensitive responsiveness to the infant's distress signals, determines whether children develop a secure or an insecure attachment relationship with their primary caregiver (Ainsworth, 1967; Ainsworth, Blehar, Waters, & Wall, 1978).

Individual differences in infant attachment security are typically observed in the Strange Situation, a mildly stressful procedure with two separations from the caregiver in an unfamiliar room, with and without a "stranger" present (Ainsworth et al., 1978). The procedure is supposed to activate the infant's attachment system, and the pattern of behavior observed during the procedure, in particular, upon reunion with the caregiver, is indicative of the quality of the infant–caregiver attachment relationship. When distressed, secure children direct attachment behaviors to their caregivers and take comfort in the reassurance offered by them. Experience has taught securely attached children that they can rely on their caregivers to be there and alleviate their stress. Infants with insecure attachments have not experienced sensitive caregiving and are anxious about the availability of their caregivers. They either avoid showing attachment behavior upon reunion with the caregiver in the Strange Situation procedure because of fear of triggering a negative parental response, or they display anger toward their caregivers, showing ambivalence in the reunion episodes: In the latter case, children seek contact, then resist contact angrily when it is achieved, as if to punish the caregiver for his or her unwanted absence (Sroufe, Egeland, Carlson, & Collins, 2005).

## Temperament

The number of definitions and measures of attachment is limited, and, in fact, the dependence of attachment theory on one or a few "gold standard" assessments has been deplored as too restrictive (Kagan, 1995, 2009). In contrast, the origins of temperament theory are manifold, as are the definitions, interpretations, dimensions, and measures of temperament. Of course, Thomas and Chess (1977), who started their seminal New York Longitudinal Study in 1956, were the singular crucial source of inspiration for many temperament researchers in the 1970s and 1980s of the previous century. Thomas and Chess searched for child characteristics that would influence the course of child development relatively independent of, or in addition to, parenting and other environmental pressures, as they had noted that parenting had only limited success in shaping the development of many children in their clinical practice, as well as in their longitudinal study. They differentiated various temperamental dimensions, including, among others, activity level, rhythmicity, adaptability, sensory threshold, intensity of reaction, mood, and distractibility. Their typology of child temperaments presented the "difficult," the "slow-to-warm," and the "easy" child. In their "goodness-of-fit" concept they pointed at the critical role of the environment in adapting to temperamental features of the individual child, thus preparing the field for a transactional perspective on development emphasizing the combined and evolving interplay of children's constitutional characteristics and the caregiving environment (Sameroff, 1975).

After decades of temperament research, the field has become replete with diverging models and measures, but all temperament researchers seem to agree that temperamental characteristics should appear early in development, show moderate stability, and have distinctive neurobiological indices (Rothbart & Bates, 2006; Zentner &

Bates, 2008). Heritability of temperament is widely considered to be present, albeit in varying degrees depending on the specific temperamental dimension. A large number of temperament dimensions are recognized by temperament researchers (Caspi & Shiner, 2006), but two important dimensions emerging from various temperament models are "behavioral inhibition" (see Kagan, 2012) and "irritability" or "difficultness" (see Bates, Freeland, & Lounsbury, 1979; Deater-Deckard & Wang, 2012). *Inhibition* points at behavior in response to novelty, unfamiliar people, and strange situations, and it is related to harm avoidance and shyness. *Irritability* is aggressive or irritated behavior in response to painful and/or frustrating input, and it is related to difficultness, distress to limitations, and anger proneness. Inhibition is thought to be a rather stable, inherited characteristic influencing the individual's interaction with the environment (without denying a reversed influence), whereas irritability is considered to be the outcome of constitutional and parenting influences, thus leaving considerable room for environmental input (Bates et al., 1979). It seems compatible with the old idea of goodness of fit (Thomas & Chess, 1977). It should be noted that various other temperamental traits have been identified (see Mervielde & De Pauw, 2012), but inhibition and irritability (both lower-order aspects of a broader negative emotionality trait) have received the most attention in research on differential susceptibility.

Similar to evolutionary explanations of attachment, evolutionary pressures have been speculated to be at the root of temperament. Whereas attachment theory assumes that evolution created in all newborns an inborn bias to become attached, temperament theory seems to prefer an evolutionary explanation of temperamental diversity. As Zentner and Bates (2008) argued, temperamental diversity probably evolved as a result of "fluctuating selection." Survival in a variety of ecological niches would require the presence of diversity of temperamental traits suited to each of those niches. Thus, there appears to be no "ideal" temperament independent of context or circumstances. Of course, this view on temperamental diversity does not preclude the idea that temperament traits are related to biological systems that were essential for survival, existing across all humans (e.g., the fight-or-flight system). Individuals, however, may differ in the strengths of these systems, probably due in part to the different contexts they experience (for further elaboration of these ideas see MacDonald, 2012).

One of the earliest pieces of evidence that the benefits of temperament traits depend on context comes from DeVries's (1984, 1987) study of temperament among Masai pastoralists in Kenya. DeVries arrived in Kenya at the height of a 10-year drought, when children and infants were the first in a population to starve. During this particular famine, infant mortality rose to 50%. Of 15 newborn infants observed in the initial study population, he could locate only six by the end of his study; all others had died. Only one of the six infants with difficult, "fussy" temperaments had died, whereas five of the seven with "easy" temperaments had done so. In this case temperamental difficultness appeared to be of vital importance, presumably to attract the mother's attention and elicit her reaction to the infant's hunger signals. The infant's temperament may be an important factor for the child's survival, but, as mentioned before, there appears to be no ideal temperament independent of context. In some circumstances, "easy" children may elicit their parent's sensitive responsiveness, whereas in others a baby's frequent crying may enhance the chance of a parent's adequate response (van IJzendoorn & Bakermans-Kranenburg, 2004).

## Is attachment temperament?

According to Kagan (1995), children's behavior in the Strange Situation is largely determined by temperament. He challenges attachment researchers to disentangle attachment from temperamental features, such as inhibition, and assumes that not much would remain after taking temperament into account. His reasoning is simple and at first sight convincing. The majority of children are not inhibited and do not show excessive distress in strange environments or when confronted with strangers, and if distressed they are soothed rather easily. Kagan describes these children as follows: "These children, who are likely to be classified as securely attached, are temperamentally uninhibited infants who inherited a physiology that mutes a fearful reaction in unfamiliar places" (p. 105). A minority of children with temperamental inhibition responds in a fearful manner to unfamiliar settings, and they start to cry when confronted with a stranger. These children, who can only be comforted by their parent after much effort, are classified as insecurely attached and considered to be at risk for behavior problems in later childhood. Thus, according to this point of view, the patterns of attachment behaviors in the Strange Situation are isomorphic with, or at least largely determined by, temperamental inhibition.

Is insecure attachment essentially temperamental inhibition and, in fact, can attachment not be differentiated from temperament? A first observation would be that secure and insecure children display both high and low levels of distress in the Strange Situation depending on their subclassification, and children acting aloof in the Strange Situation (categorized as avoidantly attached), might show highly irritable behavior at home (see Ainsworth et al., 1978; van den Boom, 1994). We would like to offer two additional strands of argument that run counter to the temperamental redefinition of attachment. The first strand is meta-analytic, and the second strand concerns behavioral and molecular genetics. First, if attachment were simply temperament, and if temperament were based on "inherited physiology," then infants' attachments to their two parents should be largely similar. However, in a meta-analysis of 14 pertinent studies on more than 900 families, we found a modest correlation of $r = .17$ between infant–mother and infant–father attachment, indicating less than 3% overlap in variance (van IJzendoorn & DeWolff, 1997). More important, some overlap between infant–mother and infant–father attachment security might be expected because mothers and fathers tend to interact in similar ways with their children. In terms of attachment representations, we found significant similarity between husbands and wives within the same family in a set of five studies (van IJzendoorn & Bakermans-Kranenburg, 1996). Birds of a feather indeed seem to flock together. Therefore, not only infant temperament but also assortative mating or more direct influences of the partner may cause similarity in attachment and in parenting style of a father and a mother within the same family, resulting in a modest association between infant–mother and infant–father attachment security (van IJzendoorn & DeWolff, 1997).

Second, behavioral and molecular genetics illustrate the divergent roots of individual differences in attachment and temperament. In a twin study we found that about half of the variance in attachment security as observed in the Strange Situation was explained by shared environment, and the other half by unique environmental factors and measurement error (Bokhorst et al., 2003). The role of genetic factors was negligible. In the same study on the same sample, genetic factors explained almost 80% of the variance in temperamental reactivity (and nonshared environmental factors and measurement error more than 20%). Differences in temperamental reactivity were not associated with attachment concordance within twins. Similar results were shown for infant–father attachment and temperamental dependency (Bakermans-Kranenburg, van IJzendoorn, Bokhorst, & Schuengel, 2004), both assessed with the Attachment Q-Sort that also contains temperamental items (Vaughn & Waters, 1990). Attachment security was largely explained by shared environmental (59%) and nonshared environmental (41%) factors, whereas genetic factors explained 66% of the variance in temperamental dependency, with nonshared environmental factors, including measurement error, explaining the remaining 34% of the variance. These results have been found in several other studies (O'Connor & Croft, 2001; Ricciuti, 1992; Roisman & Fraley, 2008).

Molecular genetic analyses also fail to support the temperamental redefinition of attachment. In a genomewide association (GWAS) and pathway analysis on attachment security and temperamental fearfulness in a Dutch sample of about 700 infants, we did not find the same genetic roots for the two phenotypes (Székely et al., 2011). The children of the Generation R Study (Jaddoe et al., 2007) were observed in the Strange Situation at 14 months of age, and at 36 months of age with the Laboratory Temperament Assessment Battery – Preschool Version (Lab-TAB; Goldsmith, Reilly, Lemery, Longley, & Prescott, 1999). Fearful temperament was measured with the Stranger Approach Episode, which indicates social fear when a novel, slightly threatening stranger approaches – quite similar to the first stranger episode of the Strange Situation. As expected, no significant GWAS results for attachment security were found; that is, no pathway was associated with increased chances of secure attachment. For temperamental fearfulness, a significant asparagine and aspartate biosynthesis pathway was found. Aspartate has been proposed to be a glutamate-like neurotransmitter in the central nervous system, as both glutamate and aspartate use the same reuptake mechanisms and have similar postsynaptic effects. It should be noted that in this large sample, attachment security and temperamental fearfulness were again not associated (Székely et al., 2011). Moreover, using a more powerful candidate genes approach in two birth cohort studies including more than 1,000 infants in total, we failed to show associations of attachment security with the genetic "usual suspects" related to the dopamine, serotonin, and oxytocin systems (*DRD4, DRD2, COMT, 5-HTT, OXTR*), with the exception of a co-dominant risk model for *COMT* Val158Met, as children with the Val/Met combination seemed most disorganized. However, this unexpected single finding is difficult to interpret and badly in need of replication (Luijk et al., 2011).

We conclude that attachment cannot be reduced to temperament, most importantly because they are phenotypically different, and show different genetic roots. Whereas there is some evidence for a genetic basis of temperamental differences (see Saudino & Wang, 2012), individual differences in attachment security cannot be ascribed to genetic determinants.

# Three Traditional Views on Temperament and Attachment:
## Orthogonal, Oblique, and Reciprocal

Besides the reductionist view articulated in the previous section (attachment can be reduced to temperament) three other views on the relation between attachment and temperament can be differentiated. The first view considers attachment and temperament as two orthogonal constructs, and the "never the twain shall meet." From an early stage, however, this view was contested by Crockenberg (1981), who sought to study attachment from an interactive perspective, investigating both the simple and interactive effects of early irritability and parental sensitivity on attachment security. This opened ways to consider the relation between attachment and temperament as partially overlapping (oblique) or as reciprocally influencing each other through moderation (reciprocal).

### Temperament and attachment as orthogonal constructs

Reacting to the claim that attachment would merely or essentially be a reflection of temperamental differences, Sroufe (1985) vehemently argued that attachment and temperament constitute *orthogonal* categories, situated at different levels of analysis. In his view, attachment is a relationship construct, characterized by a dyadic origin and nature, whereas temperament is an individual category, characterized by an organismic origin and nature. To try to reduce attachment to temperament (or the other way around) would be a logical category mistake. Sroufe stressed that within a relationship perspective, temperamental differences may influence various aspects of behavior in strange environments and toward a stranger and attachment figures. It does not, however, affect the (dyadic) organization of attachment behavior that is the essence of an attachment classification. The relationship history would override constitutional temperamental differences, and the contribution of temperamental features to Strange Situation behavior or attachment more generally would be negligible (Sroufe, 1985).

The idea that the environment plays a major part in explaining individual differences in quality of the infant–parent attachment relationship is indeed central to attachment theory. Inspired by Ainsworth's seminal work on attachment and childrearing in her Uganda and Baltimore samples (Ainsworth, 1967; Ainsworth et al., 1978), attachment researchers have considered parental sensitivity to be the single most important determinant of infant attachment security, particularly for the three organized attachment strategies: secure, insecure–avoidant, and insecure–ambivalent attachment (Cassidy & Shaver, 2008). Observational and experimental studies of attachment have generally confirmed this core hypothesis, although the combined effect size across numerous correlational studies for the association between parental sensitivity and attachment security is relatively modest. In De Wolff and van IJzendoorn's (1997) meta-analysis, the combined effect amounted to a correlation of $r = .24$. In addition, a large number of experimental studies with attachment-based interventions have documented the causal nature of the relation between parental sensitivity and infant attachment, showing that interventions that more effectively enhanced parental sensitivity also more effectively changed the quality of the attachment relationship (see Bakermans-Kranenburg, van IJzendoorn, & Juffer, 2003, for a meta-analysis on the experimental evidence). Thus, parenting has been proven partly to determine differences in attachment security between children, as elevated levels of parental sensitivity enhance the chance for the child to become secure, whereas lower levels of parental sensitivity lead to a higher risk for insecure attachment. However, these findings certainly leave room for other influences, including those of a more constitutional nature.

### Temperament and attachment related in an oblique way

The oblique point of view acknowledges the environmental influences on attachment security and at the same time stresses the possibility of other determinants, such as temperament, to impact on the child's development of attachment. Several studies have demonstrated that parents' sensitivity to their infants' attachment signals is strongly determined by parents' own secure or insecure mental representation of childhood attachment experiences (Hesse, 2008; Main, Kaplan, & Cassidy, 1985). But parental sensitivity accounts for only one-third of the association between parental attachment representation and infant attachment, leaving a *transmission gap* of unexplained variance in infant attachment security (van IJzendoorn, 1995a, 1995b). Most importantly, although attachment is a relationship construct, at least in the first few years of life, the meta-analyses of correlational and experimental studies on attachment and sensitivity show that attachment is only partly reflected in the interactive history of the parent–infant dyad.

This leaves room for the idea that temperament and attachment are related in an *oblique* way (Belsky & Rovine, 1987; Kochanska, 1998; Marshall & Fox, 2005; Thompson & Lamb, 1984; Vaughn & Bost, 1999). For example, temperamentally inhibited infants may develop an insecure–resistant attachment to their insensitive caregiver, whereas more robust, uninhibited infants may become insecure–avoidant in their attachment to an insensitive parent (Vaughn, Bost, & van IJzendoorn, 2008). Belsky (personal communication, February 10, 2011) even suggests that some temperamentally sturdy and adaptable infants may become securely attached to an insensitive caregiver, explaining the incomplete determination of attachment security by parenting. The sturdiness of temperamentally adaptive children may also explain the remarkable resilience of some orphans growing up in the institutional environment of structural neglect but, against all odds, nevertheless developing secure attachments (van IJzendoorn et al., 2011). Thus, temperament influences the type of insecurity that children develop, and in some cases might even make children less receptive for environmental input.

## Reciprocal: moderating models

Attachment might be a moderator of the influence of earlier temperament on later emotional reactivity to strange environments or persons. Calkins and Fox (1992), for example, found an interaction effect between infants' reactivity to frustration at 5 months and attachment classification at 14 months, predicting inhibition at 24 months. Because inhibition was measured at a later point in time (24 months) than attachment classification (14 months), one may argue that the interaction effect shows the influence of attachment security on inhibition, or is at least not incompatible with this reversed interpretation (van IJzendoorn & Bakermans-Kranenburg, 2004). In the same vein, Nachmias, Gunnar, Mangelsdorf, Parritz, and Buss (1996) examined the moderating role of attachment security in buffering the effects of temperamental inhibition on stress reactivity as assessed by cortisol levels. They assessed cortisol levels before and after a stressful session confronting the child with novel, arousing stimuli, as well as after the Strange Situation. They found no association between behavioral inhibition and security of attachment; they did find that children with higher behavioral inhibition had higher poststress cortisol levels if they were also insecure, but not when they were securely attached to their mother. In a study on behavioral inhibition and heart rate after stressful episodes, Stevenson-Hinde and Marshall (1999) found that low inhibition was associated with high heart rate periods, but only in secure children. Security of attachment can thus be viewed as a buffer against stress or as a moderator of the initial physiological disposition (van IJzendoorn & Bakermans-Kranenburg, 2004).

In the early 1990s Belsky, Fish, and Isabella (1991) showed that infants' change in temperament from 3 to 9 months was predictable from the quality of the rearing environment, and that resultant change in temperament was predictive of attachment security, consistent with the view that attachment reflects, in part, the regulation of temperament. Research examining associations between parenting and temperament has suggested that the caregiving environment supporting the formation of attachment relationships (i.e., parental sensitivity) may also serve to influence and regulate infant reactivity (see Sheese, Voelker, Rothbart, & Posner, 2007, for an example). A paramount example of this line of research is a study by Hane and Fox (2006), who broke through the barrier between attachment and temperament theory by focusing on important indices of fearful temperament (electroencephalographic [EEG] asymmetries in the frontal cortex and fearful reactivity to stimuli in the Lab-TAB assessment) in relation to maternal sensitivity to infants at 9 months of age. The mothers' behavior during a home visit was video-recorded and subsequently rated for degree of sensitivity using the classic Ainsworth sensitivity rating scales central to most of the work on antecedents of attachment (Ainsworth et al., 1978). Relative to infants who experienced highly sensitive maternal care, infants who experienced low sensitive care displayed more temperamental fearfulness and more right frontal asymmetry, an important marker of an infant's disposition toward withdrawal behaviors. Temperament assessed at 4 month of age did not predict these outcomes (Hane & Fox, 2006). This correlational study cannot determine the causal direction of the associations between sensitive parenting and temperamental fearfulness, but the finding that earlier temperament did not predict later fearfulness, whereas maternal sensitivity did, is certainly convergent with a transactional model (Sameroff, 1983) that places sensitive, responsive care in the center of early temperament, as well as attachment, development. Most important, in support of Meaney's (2010) theory of early development based on his extensive studies of rodents,

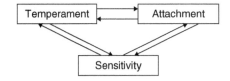

**Figure 9.1**    Various causal pathways between temperament, attachment, and parental sensitivity.

early maternal sensitive care seemed able to change even basic parameters of brain functioning, in the case of Hane and Fox's (2006) study of human infants' patterns of right versus left frontal EEG asymmetry.

In summary, the relations between parenting, attachment, and temperament seem much more complicated and multidirectional than originally conceptualized by Kagan (1995) and Sroufe (1985). A few decades after their debate about the direction of the influences between temperament and attachment, the general consensus seems to be that both temperament and attachment are influencing each other in a transactional way, and both are more or less open to environmental input such as parenting (see Figure 9.1). Despite different origins and a somewhat agonistic tradition, temperament and attachment theory now seem ready for further exploration of mutual fertilization. The differential susceptibility paradigm offers such a new perspective.

## Reconciliation and Integration: Diathesis–Stress and Differential Susceptibility

### Diathesis–stress

Not only has research shown that the caregiving environment may influence and regulate infant reactivity, as we noted earlier, but there is also growing evidence that not all children are equally affected by their caregiving environment. Research on temperament × parenting interactions, or broader temperament × environment interactions, is based on the premise that negative effects of the environment (e.g., inadequate parenting or low-quality day care) are observed in some children but are virtually absent in others. Some children appear to be especially reactive to adversity, whereas other children – lacking such vulnerabilities – do not succumb to a specific adversity and are considered resilient (e.g., Cicchetti, 1993; Masten & Obradović, 2006; also see Lengua & Wachs, 2012), often as a result of personal protective factors such as easygoing temperament, low stress reactivity, or a specific genetic makeup. Implicit in this diathesis–stress framework is the view that children who are vulnerable or resilient due to their personal characteristics thrive similarly in non-adverse and supportive environments. One of the consequences of this focus on developmental psychopathology is that many studies do not measure the full range of either environments or outcomes, but are restricted to just adversity and its absence (e.g., maltreatment vs. no maltreatment) or just dysfunction and its absence (e.g., externalizing behavior problems). However, the temperamental characteristics of individuals that make them disproportionately vulnerable to adversity may also make them benefit more from contextual support. This idea is central to the model of differential susceptibility.

### Differential susceptibility: For better and for worse

According to the differential susceptibility model, individuals characterized by heightened susceptibility are more sensitive to *both* negative and positive environments (i.e., to both risk-promoting and development-enhancing environmental conditions), for better *and* for worse. Several introductions and reviews have been devoted to defining differential susceptibility in contrast to diathesis–stress and cumulative risk (e.g., Bakermans-Kranenburg & van IJzendoorn, 2007; Belsky, 1997a, 1997b, 2005; Belsky, Bakermans-Kranenburg, & van IJzendoorn, 2007; Boyce & Ellis, 2005; Ellis et al., 2011). Temperamental reactivity was one of the differential susceptibility factors taken into account in the first wave of studies pioneered by Belsky, Hsieh, and Crnic (1998), and most of the remainder of this chapter is devoted to a discussion of this temperamental marker of differential susceptibility, though other markers of negative emotionality (including inhibition, irritability, and fearfulness) also appear in this review.

Genetic differential susceptibility was introduced by the Leiden group, with special emphasis on dopamine system-related genes such as *DRD4* (Bakermans-Kranenburg & van IJzendoorn, 2006), whereas physiological factors (i.e., biological reactivity defined by children's autonomic, adrenocortical, or immune reactivity to psychosocial stressors) were introduced by Boyce and his team (1995). Boyce and Ellis (2005) coined the expressive epithets *orchid* and *dandelion* to describe two types of children. More physiologically reactive children displaying heightened sensitivity to both positive and negative environmental influences were given the shorthand designation of *orchid* children, signifying their special susceptibility to both highly stressful and highly nurturing environments. Children low in reactivity, on the other hand, were designated as *dandelion* children, reflecting their relative ability to function adequately in species-typical circumstances of all varieties. Such typologies, though persuasive, should not inadvertently give rise to a misunderstanding; susceptibility is generally considered to be continuously distributed and not as a category that is absent or present (Ellis et al., 2011).

## Defining steps in the test for differential susceptibility

Not all temperament × parenting interactions provide evidence for differential susceptibility. Differential susceptibility needs to be distinguished from other interaction effects, including that of *dual risk*, which arises when the most vulnerable individuals are disproportionately affected in an adverse manner by a negative environment but do not also benefit disproportionately from positive environmental conditions.

The formal test of differential susceptibility consists of five steps (see Figure 9.2; Belsky et al., 2007). Step 1 concerns the application of conventional statistical criteria for evaluating genuine moderation (Dearing & Hamilton, 2006), with some emphasis on excluding interactions with regression lines that do not cross (sometimes referred to as *removable* interactions). The next steps distinguish differential susceptibility from temperament–environment correlations that may reflect rearing experiences evoked by specific child characteristics and from dual-risk models. It is important to ascertain that there is no association between the moderator (i.e., the susceptibility factor) and the environment (Step 2). Belsky and colleagues (1998), examining the effects of infant negative emotionality and parenting on 3-year-old boys' externalizing problems and inhibition, explicitly tested the independence of negative emotionality and parenting as a step in their investigation of differential susceptibility. Had these factors been correlated, the evidence would not have shown that the predictive power of parenting was greater for highly negative infants; it would instead have indicated that either highly negative infants elicit negative parenting or that negative parenting fosters infant negativity. If the susceptibility factor and the outcome are related (Step 3), dual risk – or dual gain, when positive factors are involved – is suggested. For example, early negativity would itself lead to externalizing behavior, but even more so when combined with negative parenting.

1. Is the interaction between the moderator (e.g., temperament) and the environment statistically significant? Do the regression lines cross?
2. Are the moderator and the environment independent?
3. Is the moderator related to the outcome? If the association between the moderator and the outcome is significant, there is no support for differential susceptibility
4. What does the regression plot look like? The prototypical graphical display of the differential susceptibility model is shown if Figure 9.3a. Figure 9.3b shows a main effect of the supposed moderator, independent of the environment. Figures 9.3c and 9.3d represent dual risk or dual gain; the effect of the environment is unidirectional. At one of the extremes of the environmental range there is no difference between the two groups that are distinguished on the basis of the moderator. Figure 9.3e shows contrastive effects; both groups are equally susceptible to environmental influences, though in divergent directions.
5. Is the effect specific to this moderator?

**Figure 9.2** Steps in testing for differential susceptibility. *Source:* Adapted from Belsky, Bakermans-Kranenburg, and van IJzendoorn (2007).

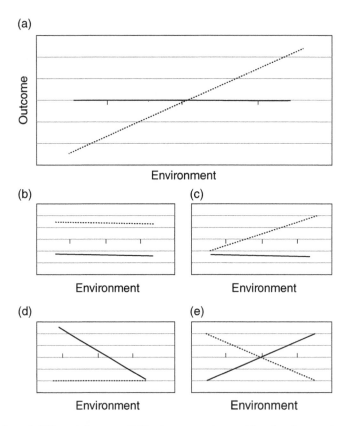

**Figure 9.3**    Graphical display of differential susceptibility in comparison with other interaction effects. *Source:* Bakermans-Kranenburg and van IJzendoorn (2007). *The Association for Psychological Science.* © SAGE Publications.

Differential susceptibility is demonstrated (Step 4) when the moderation reflects a crossover interaction that covers both the positive and the negative aspects of the environment; see Figure 9.3a. The slope for the susceptible subgroup should be significantly different from zero and at the same time significantly steeper than the slope for the nonsusceptible subgroup. The two groups may also show different outcomes independent of the environment. Figure 9.3b displays the results of this scenario; it shows a main effect of the supposed moderator, which in this case is in fact not a moderator. Figure 9.3c and 9.3d represent dual risk or dual gain; the effect of the environment is unidirectional. At one end of the environmental range there is no difference between the two groups (groups distinguished on the basis of the moderator). Figure 9.3e shows contrastive effects; both groups are susceptible to environmental influences, though in divergent directions. As a consequence both slopes are significantly different from zero but in opposite directions, as in the case of positive and negative effects of harsh discipline on, respectively, African American and European American children (Deater-Deckard, Bates, Dodge, & Pettit, 1996). Although clearly different, this is not what is meant in the differential susceptibility model. The specificity of the effect (Step 5 in Figure 9.2) is shown if the model is not replicated when other susceptibility factors are used as moderators (e.g., Bakermans-Kranenburg, van IJzendoorn, Caspers, & Philibert, 2011; Caspi & Moffitt, 2006).

## The Moderating Role of Temperament

When temperament moderates the association between some environmental factor and developmental outcome, it may do so in several ways, as outlined earlier. In the following sections we highlight and illustrate the distinct patterns of interaction. First we review studies with temperamental reactivity or irritability as a *vulnerability* factor, adding to the negative effects of an unsupportive environment. Second, we shift the focus to the bright side of life, where temperament as a *susceptibility* factor enhances the openness to positive influences of a specific subgroup of individuals. Third, we present studies substantiating the bidirectional *for-better-and-for-worse* predictions of the differential susceptibility hypothesis in a single sample. Last, at the end of the chapter, we present the first meta-analytic evidence for differential susceptibility. It should be noted that the discussion of the moderating role of temperament covers a much broader set of concepts and environments than that included in the attachment paradigm.

## Temperament as vulnerability factor

Difficult temperament has more than once been found to increase the vulnerability to negative environmental influences. Here we briefly present some key findings as a background for our treatment of the differential susceptibility model (see Lengua & Wachs, 2012, for an extensive discussion of temperament as a vulnerability factor). For example, in Morrell and Murray's (2003) study, only the highly distressed and irritable 4-month-old boys who experienced coercive and rejecting mothering at this age continued to show evidence, 5 months later, of emotional and behavioral dysregulation. These results reflect a double risk model (Figure 9.3c), where the negative effect of the environment (i.e. coercive, rejecting parenting) is strongest or only apparent in the group of children with a difficult temperament. Other studies have reported similar effects. Belsky and colleagues (1998) observed that infants who scored high in negative emotionality at 12 months of age, and who experienced the least supportive mothering and fathering across their second and third years of life, scored highest on externalizing problems at 36 months of age. Deater-Deckard and Dodge (1997) reported that children rated highest on externalizing behavior problems by teachers across the primary school years were those who experienced the most harsh discipline prior to kindergarten entry and were characterized by mothers at age 5 as being negatively reactive infants. Similarly, in a study on the effects of day care, instability of child care arrangements, as indicated by the number of different care arrangements in the course of a single day or week, was found to be associated with internalizing behavior problems among children with a difficult temperament. In the group of less difficult children, the association between multiple care arrangements and internalizing problems was absent (De Schipper, Tavecchio, van IJzendoorn, & van Zeijl, 2004). These studies illustrate how difficult temperament, in combination with low parental or caregiver support, leads to elevated levels of child problem behaviors.

The generalizability of this dual-risk model of parenting and temperament to non-Western immigrant families with young children was recently supported in a longitudinal study in The Netherlands. We investigated the influence of parenting practices in the prediction of child physical aggression in 94 second-generation Turkish immigrant families with 2-year-old toddlers, and the moderating role of child temperament (Yaman, Mesman, van IJzendoorn, & Bakermans-Kranenburg, 2010). Observational data were obtained for mothers' parenting quality and authoritarian discipline, and maternal reports for child temperament and physical aggression. All measures were repeated 1 year later. Child temperament at age 2 years was a significant predictor of child aggression 1 year later; moreover, toddlers with difficult temperaments were more adversely affected by a lack of positive parenting than were other children.

As in the Yaman and colleagues (2010) study, sometimes a main effect for difficult temperament in the prediction of behavior problems also emerges (which may partly be explained by overlapping items in the measures of the constructs), pointing to the double-risk nature of the pattern of results: Effects are worst for those children who share both temperamental and environmental disadvantages. Essential for a dual-risk model is that children with difficult temperaments are more adversely affected by negative environmental factors (including the lack of positive support), but they do not benefit more from positive environments than do children with more easy temperaments.

## Temperament as susceptibility factor: The bright side

We already noted the preference to focus on adversity and dysfunction in empirical studies. Fortunately, in recent years, a considerable number of studies have included environmental factors or developmental outcomes that reflect what we consider the bright side of life: warm, supportive parenting, attachment security, and prosocial behavior. Where *vulnerability* refers to a unidirectional negative effect of the environment for a subgroup of children (e.g., temperamentally difficult children), *susceptibility* may be used to describe the openness to positive influences of a specific subgroup of individuals.

One of the correlational studies addressing the bright side is that of Denham and colleagues (2000). They reported that the beneficial effects of proactive parenting (i.e., supportive presence, clear limit setting) at age 7 and/or age 9 were most pronounced in the case of children with high levels of disobedient, aggressive, or angry behavior at an earlier time of measurement, even after controlling for problem behavior at the initial measurement occasion. Belsky (1997a, 1997b, 2005) observed that children high in negative emotion, particularly in the early years, appeared to benefit disproportionately from supportive rearing environments. Crockenberg (1981) showed that social support predicted infant attachment security, but only in the case of highly irritable infants. Kochanska (1995) showed the larger effect of gentle parental discipline, deemphasizing power on compliance, in more fearful children compared to less fearful children.

Experimental studies are even more suggestive than the longitudinal correlational evidence. In such experiments, the environment is changed for the better, and susceptible children may profit most from this change. At the same time, this might explain why most interventions are only moderately effective; the average intervention effect may hide a large effect for a subgroup of susceptible children because their larger outcomes are averaged together with the smaller effects for the less-susceptible children. One of the first studies pointing to temperamentally difficult children as being highly susceptible to intervention efforts was van den Boom (1994), who demonstrated the extraordinary effectiveness of an attachment-based intervention on irritable infants and their low-socioeconomic-status (SES) mothers. The intervention helped to elevate the level of maternal sensitivity, which in turn enhanced the children's attachment security. LaFreniere and Capuano (1997) reported intervention effects on anxiously withdrawn children. Mothers in the treatment group started to behave less intrusively, while their children showed an increase in cooperation and enthusiasm during a problem-solving task with the mother, and elevated teacher-rated social competence. Drawing on data from the Infant Health and Development Program, in which premature, low birthweight infants from economically disadvantaged homes were randomly assigned to experimental and control treatment conditions, Blair (2002) examined differential outcomes for infants who varied in negative emotionality. He found that infants who were highly negatively emotional and assigned to the early intervention treatment group scored substantially lower on externalizing problems and higher on cognitive functioning at 3 years of age than did similarly tempered control infants, with no such treatment effect detectable in the case of other infants with less negative emotionality.

Klein Velderman and colleagues (2006) found that experimentally induced changes in maternal sensitivity exerted greater impact on the attachment security of highly negatively reactive infants than it did on other infants. Their Video-Feedback Intervention to Promote Positive Parenting (VIPP; Juffer, Bakermans-Kranenburg, & van IJzendoorn, 2008) effectively enhanced maternal sensitivity. In the group of highly reactive infants, change in pre- to posttest maternal sensitivity and attachment security were significantly correlated, $r = .57$. In the less reactive group, the correlation was $r = .08$. Thus, the experimentally induced change in maternal sensitivity appeared to have a stronger impact on attachment security in the highly reactive infant group; that is, for highly reactive infants, attachment security was significantly associated with their mothers' gains in sensitivity between pre- and posttest. This was not true for less reactive infants; their attachment security was not related to improvements in sensitivity of their mothers. Highly reactive children were more susceptible to experimentally induced environmental change than were less reactive infants. In a similar vein, Cassidy, Woodhouse, Sherman, Stupica, and Lejuez (2011) found that only temperamentally irritable infants profited from a home visit intervention aimed at enhancing attachment security.

It should be noted that in each of the afore-mentioned experiments, random assignment to intervention and control conditions was done according to the experimental manipulation of the environment, not according to temperamental factors in the child. Importantly, the model of differential susceptibility has not yet been tested experimentally in a *randomized controlled trial,* with intervention and control groups stratified according to (temperamental) susceptibility factors.

### Temperament as a factor in bidirectional differential susceptibility

So far we have reviewed studies highlighting the heightened susceptibility of temperamentally difficult children to either positive or negative rearing influences (Figures 9.3c and 9.3d). Even more compelling are data on a single sample substantiating the for-better-*and*-for-worse predictions of the differential susceptibility hypothesis.

Feldman, Greenbaum, and Yirmiya (1999) found that 9-month-olds scoring high on negativity who experienced low levels of synchrony in mother–infant interaction manifested more noncompliance during cleanup at age 2 than other children did. When such infants experienced mutually synchronous mother–infant interaction, however, they displayed greater self-control than did children manifesting much less negativity as infants. Kochanska, Aksan, and Joy (2007) observed that highly fearful 15-month-olds experiencing high levels of power-assertive paternal discipline were most likely to cheat in a game at 38 months, yet when cared for in a supportive manner, such negatively emotional, fearful toddlers manifested the most rule-compatible conduct.

In a study of temperament and maternal discipline in relation to externalizing problems in early childhood, van Zeijl and colleagues (2006, 2007) found that children with difficult temperaments were more susceptible to both negative and positive discipline than were children of relatively easy temperament. Bohlin, Hagekull, and Andersson (2005) found that inhibition moderated the effect of attachment security on social competence at 8 years. For pre-school-age children who showed low levels of behavioral inhibition, attachment security did not make much of a difference for their social competence some years later. In contrast, inhibited children who were insecurely attached showed the lowest levels of social competence, and securely attached inhibited children showed the highest levels of social competence at 8 years. Gilissen, Bakermans-Kranenburg, van IJzendoorn, and van der Veer (2008) showed that temperamentally fearful children were more susceptible to both secure and insecure attachment relationships in their physiological reactivity when looking at fear-inducing film clips. Temperamentally fearful children with less secure relationships showed the highest skin conductance reactivity to the film clip, whereas comparable children with more secure relationships showed the lowest skin conductance activity.

The studies on bidirectional differential susceptibility reviewed thus far all addressed parental care as context or environmental dimension. Evidence for differential susceptibility, for-better-and-for-worse, however, has not been limited to the effects of parental care but includes nonparental care as well. Children in the National Institute of Child Health and Human Development (NICHD) study of early child care who had been temperamentally difficult infants showed the worst outcomes when they experienced inadequate parenting and the best outcomes when they experienced excellent parenting (Bradley & Corwyn, 2008; Stright, Kelley, & Gallagher, 2008). For children who attended child care, the professional caregiver's sensitivity interacted with child temperament in the prediction of children's social competence and behavior problems as assessed with the Child Behavior Checklist (CBCL). Children who had been temperamentally difficult as infants scored low on social competence and high on teacher-reported externalizing behavior problems at 54 months when their caregivers were insensitive, but they scored high on social competence and low on behavior problems when their caregivers were sensitive. For those children who were not difficult in infancy, caregiver sensitivity was not related to social competence and behavior problems at 54 months (Pluess & Belsky, 2009). A much smaller study in The Netherlands showed that fearful children with more stressed professional caregivers (as indicated by an increase in cortisol during the day) showed the lowest levels of well-being in day care, but those with unstressed care-givers (whose cortisol levels decreased over the day) scored higher on caregiver-reported well-being in the child care setting than their less fearful peers (Groeneveld, Vermeer, van IJzendoorn, & Linting, 2012). Thus, fearful infants appear to be more affected by the quality of day care they experience – both negatively and positively – than less fearful children.

Extending the issue of nonparental care beyond kindergarten age, Essex, Armstrong, Burk, Goldsmith, and Boyce (2011) examined the effect of grade 1 teacher–child relationships on mental health symptoms at grade 7. Distinguishing between teacher–child closeness and teacher–child conflict as two only partly overlapping dimensions of the relationship at grade 1, they found that behaviorally inhibited children developed the most severe mental health symptoms by grade 7 under conditions of high grade 1 teacher conflict, but the lowest levels of symptoms under conditions of low teacher conflict. The inhibited children were thus more susceptible to teacher conflict than children with lower levels of inhibition. At the same time, highly *disinhibited* children were more susceptible to teacher–child closeness; they developed the most severe mental health symptoms when they experienced low levels of teacher closeness, and fewest symptoms under conditions of high teacher closeness. The study may point to temperamental inhibition and disinhibition as markers of differential susceptibility dependent on the environmental dimension that is examined. In an environment with conflict, inhibition seems to increase differential susceptibility, whereas in an environment with close contact, disinhibition might operate as a differential susceptibility marker.

## Adult differential susceptibility

Not only children but also *parents* may be differentially susceptible to stressors and supportive experiences. Both positive and negative environmental factors may have more impact on parents who for temperamental or genetic reasons are more susceptible to such influences – with traceable effects on their parenting behavior. We found that parents with a specific genetic makeup (carrying a *DRD4* 7-repeat allele, as well as a *COMT* Val allele) showed increased susceptibility to daily stresses (van IJzendoorn, Bakermans-Kranenburg, & Mesman, 2008). Parents with these gene combinations were less sensitive to their children's needs when they had to deal with many daily hassles, but they showed higher levels of sensitive parenting compared with other parents in the case of few daily hassles. In replicating this study with parents of twins, Fortuna et al. (2011) found that when parents of twins with various birth risks (low gestational age, low birthweight, long stay in neonatal intensive care) were least sensitive to their twins about 3 years later when they were carriers of the *DRD4* 7-repeat allele. Without these child birth risks, parents with the 7-repeat alleles were the most sensitive to their children.

Two other studies involving adults, but not in their parental role, should be mentioned briefly. First, in a study on adults adopted as children, we found that *DRD4* moderated the association of parental problems during the participants' childhood (e.g., parental depression, marital discord) with unresolved loss or trauma (that is associated with post-traumatic stress and dissociative symptoms). Participants with the *DRD4* 7-repeat allele who experienced parental problems had the highest scores for unresolved loss or trauma, whereas participants with the *DRD4* 7-repeat allele who did *not* experience parental problems showed the lowest post-traumatic stress symptoms. Among participants without the *DRD4* 7-repeat allele, the parental problems during childhood did not make much of a difference. Second, in a study on political preferences, more than 2,000 young adults listed up to 10 best friends, and answered one question about political preference: whether they considered themselves to be more conservative, middle-of-the road, or liberal (Settle, Dawes, Christakis, & Fowler, 2010). The authors argued that having more friends would mean more exposure to divergent ideas and worldviews, and thus a more liberal perspective. Without referring to differential susceptibility the authors nevertheless found clear support for the differential susceptibility model: only in carriers of the 7-repeat alleles was having more friends related to more liberal views, and fewer friends, to more conservative attitudes.

The application of the differential susceptibility hypothesis to adults in general and parents in particular is virtually uncharted territory: To our knowledge there is no other published study with temperamental or genetic factors as moderators of environmental effects on parenting. In the Klein Velderman and colleagues' (2006) intervention study, mothers of highly reactive infants profited more from the intervention. They might have been more readily reinforced by their infants' positive behavioral changes in the dyadic context, but an alternative interpretation would be that it was the temperamentally reactive mothers who profited most from intervention efforts. Given that emotional reactivity has been found to be substantially genetically determined (Bokhorst et al., 2003; Goldsmith, Lemery, Buss, & Campos, 1999), the mothers of highly reactive children may have been as temperamentally reactive as their children. Similar to the children's case, differential susceptibility of parents should be tested in an experimental design, with random assignment of parents to the experimental and control conditions based on their supposed (temperamental or genetic) susceptibility.

We therefore advance the exciting hypothesis that adult personality may also be considered a marker of differential susceptibility, and in terms of the Big Five, adults with high levels of Openness to Experience may indeed be highly sensitive personalities (E. Aron, Aron, & Davies, 2005; also see Aron, 2012) across a variety of domains, from parenting to political ideologies, for-better-*and*-for-worse.

It would, of course, be most compelling to test the model of bidirectional differential susceptibility in an experimental design, in order to examine whether the same individuals who profit most from a positive change in the environment would also suffer the most from an experimentally induced deterioration of their environment. A limitation inherent to experiments with human beings is that this is unethical and thus impossible. In limited probabilistic learning tasks (e.g., Klein et al., 2007) or stress paradigms, the use of positive or negative feedback in case of "errors" can experimentally induce changes in the microenvironment of the same subjects, which can then be examined in terms of their impact on immediate outcomes. But this is different than testing the differential susceptibility hypothesis, which involves sustained and at least somewhat enduring change in response to environmental exposures (Ellis et al., 2011). It would simply not be justifiable experimentally to induce negative changes in the caregiving environment. In his seminal work with inhibited rhesus monkeys, Suomi (1997) illustrated the vast potential of studies on nonhuman primates for gaining insight into human development. Perhaps experimental animal models might be used to mimic the basic temperament × environment interactions illustrating the moderating role of temperament in human development for-better-*and*-for-worse.

## Meta-analytic evidence for differential susceptibility: Dopamine-related genes as susceptibility factors

The idea that dopamine-related genetic polymorphisms may play a role in differential susceptibility to the rearing environment is not far-fetched. Low dopaminergic efficiency is associated with decreased attentional and reward mechanisms (Robbins & Everitt, 1999), which may be advantageous or disadvantageous depending on specific environmental characteristics (Suomi, 1997). The role of dopamine in feedback-based learning was tested in a neuroimaging study (Klein et al., 2007). Subjects were grouped according to their *DRD2* genotype. Carriers of the A1-allele had significantly more difficulties learning from negative feedback. Moreover, their posterior medial frontal cortex, involved in feedback monitoring, responded less to negative feedback than did that of their comparison subjects. However, they did not perform worse than comparisons when provided with positive feedback. The study might explain why experimental interventions emphasizing prompt positive feedback trigger the high potentials of children who otherwise show most behavior problems (Bakermans-Kranenburg, van IJzendoorn, Mesman, et al., 2008; Bakermans-Kranenburg, van IJzendoorn, Pijlman, et al., 2008) or display the lowest level of prereading abilities (Kegel, Bus, & van IJzendoorn, 2011).

We conducted a meta-analysis on the role of dopamine-related genes in making children more or less susceptible to rearing influences, for-better-and-for-worse (see Bakermans-Kranenburg & van IJzendoorn, 2011, for details on the studies included in the meta-analysis). Because the number of gene × environment (G × E) interaction studies including dopamine-related gene polymorphisms has steeply increased in recent years, sufficient empirical studies were available to conduct a meta-analysis to explore the effects of G × E interactions on development and to compare the combined effect sizes for both negative and positive effects. The studies included in the meta-analysis examined the moderating role of three dopamine-related genes, *DRD2, DAT,* and *DRD4,* in children up to age 10 years, although most studies did not look explicitly for both the dark and the bright side of differential susceptibility.

We identified 15 pertinent effect sizes on 1,232 subjects, providing data for two meta-analyses of the moderating role of dopamine-related genes on the impact of rearing environment on development (for details, see Bakermans-Kranenburg & van IJzendoorn, 2011). Nine effect sizes concerned vulnerability, that is, susceptibility to *negative* environmental factors. These studies examined the effect of dopamine-related "risk alleles" (*DRD2*-A1, *DAT* 10-repeat, *DRD4* 7-repeat) on the association between adverse rearing environment and behavioral disturbance, such as externalizing behavior, sensation seeking, and attention-deficit/hyperactivity disorder (ADHD). Six effect sizes – enabling a focus on the "bright side" – pertained to moderation of the relation between supportive contexts (e.g., warm, responsive parenting) and positive behavioral outcomes (e.g., effortful control or prosocial behavior), or the absence or reduction of negative behaviors (e.g., decrease in externalizing behavior after intervention). The meta-analyses thus took into account both sides of the differential susceptibility hypothesis but could not directly examine whether the same children who do worse than comparisons in adverse environments also do better in supportive environments – this has simply not yet been tested in empirical studies.

The combined effect size for behavioral disturbance in the presence of adverse rearing influences amounted to $r = .37$ for carriers of the "risk alleles," and $r = .10$ for the comparisons without the risk alleles. The difference was significant *(p = .02)*, supporting the idea that carriers of the risk alleles were more vulnerable to environmental adversity. Turning to the bright side, that is, the association between parental support and better adaptation, we found a combined effect size of $r = .31$ for carriers of the putative risk alleles, whereas the combined effect size for children without the risk alleles was $r = -.03$. Again, the difference was significant *(p < .01)*. Children with alleles that put them at risk for behavioral disturbances in adverse contexts benefited significantly more from parental support than did their counterparts.

The combined effect size for children carrying the risk alleles pertaining to vulnerability was not larger than the combined effect size derived from the positive outcomes. In other words, children with the putative risk alleles were equally susceptible to negative and supportive influences. In fact, the difference between the combined effect sizes of the genetically "at-risk" children and their genetically "low-risk" counterparts were .29 (Fisher's Z) for the vulnerability studies and .35 (Fisher's Z) for studies focusing on the bright side (Bakermans-Kranenburg & van IJzendoorn, 2011). The difference between the combined effect sizes in the second set of studies was thus comparable to and even somewhat larger than the difference in the first set of studies, suggesting that the promotive susceptibility effect is certainly not weaker than the vulnerability effect. In other words, these meta-analytic results provide support for the hypothesis that genetically "vulnerable" individuals are actually more susceptible to the environment, for-better-*and*-for-worse.

## Directions for Future Research

Three critical issues should be high on the agenda for future research. First, the diversity of temperamental characteristics found to play a role in differential susceptibility models points to the question of whether different temperamental features may be identified as susceptibility factors dependent on the specific environmental influence and the specific developmental outcome. Irritable or difficult and inhibited or fearful temperaments have appeared on the stage as susceptibility factors with varying success. The fact that some studies use inhibition or fearfulness, whereas others use irritability or reactivity to distinguish more susceptible individuals from less susceptible individuals, has mostly been passed over in order to stress the converging support for the differential susceptibility model. Future studies should explicitly aim at distinguishing among temperament dimensions such as inhibition, irritability (Zentner & Bates, 2008), and sensory sensitivity (Aron et al., 2005; see also Aron, 2012), and test to what extent these dimensions function as susceptibility factors depending on the specific environmental influences and developmental outcomes. Other (adult) personality traits also deserve more attention as potential markers of differential susceptibility, and Openness to Experience might be a good candidate because it has been found to be associated with dopamine system-related genes.

Temperament has only been one of the differential susceptibility factors taken into account in the first wave of studies pioneered by Belsky and colleagues (1998). Physiological factors (i.e., biological reactivity) were introduced by Boyce and colleagues (1995), whereas genetic differential susceptibility was introduced by the Leiden group (Bakermans-Kranenburg & van IJzendoorn, 2006). The second critical issue concerns the associations between these susceptibility candidates. Their interrelations should be explored because it seems theoretically evident that genetic, endophenotypical, physiological, and phenotypical susceptibility factors would be associated to a larger or smaller degree. For example, it would be critical to know whether dopamine system-related genes are involved in specific temperamental features, and whether the accumulating evidence on the susceptibility role of these genes in fact translates to one of the temperamental dimensions, or whether they operate in an additive (or even interactive) way. There is evidence linking susceptibility factors, but we do not know whether the moderating effect of one susceptibility factor overlaps with the moderating effect of another such factor. Carriers of the *DRD4* 7-repeat alleles might be more temperamentally reactive, but whether these two markers of differential susceptibility have similar roles in similar domains of functioning and in similar contexts remains to be seen. On another score, it has been demonstrated that the carriers of the short variant of the serotonin transporter gene (*5-HTTLPR*) are prone to negative emotionality, and both variants have been found to be markers of differential susceptibility in some studies (see Belsky & Pluess, 2009, for a review). Including various susceptibility factors in the same study (e.g., Essex et al., 2011) creates the opportunity to test interrelations and to examine the varying predictive power of the moderators.

Careful measurement of the environment, the outcome, and the temperamental moderator is a prerequisite for valid tests of the differential susceptibility paradigm. The importance of this third critical issue cannot be overestimated. Kagan (2007, 2009) eloquently argued that temperament should be measured in observational settings, as the concept of temperament refers to a behavioral style, and not to parental or self-perceptions (but see Crockenberg & Leerkes, 2006, who make a case for temperament questionnaires controlling for response biases). Similarly, parenting and other environmental influences should be assessed with greater precision and validity than has been done in several large-scale temperament × parenting or G × E studies, with sometimes disappointing results. As an illustration, two meta-analyses (Munafo, Durrant, Lewis, & Flint, 2009; Risch et al., 2009) failed to find support for the much cited interaction between negative life events and the serotonin transporter gene (*5-HTTLPR*) in depression (Caspi et al., 2003). However, Uher and McGuffin (2010) showed that the method of assessment of environmental adversity was an important determinant of the outcome of the study. Detailed interview-based approaches were associated with significant G × E findings, whereas all nonreplications used self-report questionnaires.

The differential susceptibility paradigm has created myriad opportunities for temperament and attachment researchers to join forces and exploit the best of both theoretical perspectives to gain more insight into human development. It is time to recognize that the battle between two highly influential schools of thought is over, and that "everybody has won, and all must have prizes," to quote Lewis Carroll's *Alice in Wonderland*.

## Further Reading

Bakermans-Kranenburg, M. J., & van IJzendoorn, M. H. (2007). Genetic vulnerability or differential susceptibility in child development: The case of attachment. *Journal of Child Psychology and Psychiatry, 48* (12), 1160–1173.

Ellis, B. J., Boyce, W. T., Belsky, J., Bakermans-Kranenburg, M. J., & van IJzendoorn, M. H. (2011). Differential susceptibility to the environment: A neurodevelopmental theory. *Development and Psychopathology, 23*, 7–28.

Vaughn, B. E., Bost, K. K., & van IJzendoorn, M. H. (2008). Attachment and temperament: Additive and interactive influences on behavior, affect, and cognition during infancy and childhood. In J. Cassidy & P. R. Shaver (Eds.). *Handbook of attachment: Theory, research, and clinical applications* (2nd edn., pp. 192–216). New York: Guilford Press.

## References

Ainsworth, M. D. (1967). *Infancy in Uganda: Infant care and the growth of love*. Baltimore: Johns Hopkins University Press.

Ainsworth, M. D., Blehar, M. C., Waters, E., & Wall, S. (1978). *Patterns of attachment: A psychological study of the Strange Situation*. Hillsdale, NJ: Erlbaum.

Aron, E. N. (2012). Temperament in psychotherapy: Reflections on clinical practice with the trait of sensitivity. In M. Zentner & R.L. Shiner (Eds.). *Handbook of temperament* (pp. 645–672), New York: The Guilford Press.

Aron, E., Aron, A., & Davies, K. M. (2005). Adult shyness: The interaction of temperamental sensitivity and an adverse childhood environment. *Personality and Social Psychology Bulletin, 31*, 181–197.

Bakermans-Kranenburg, M. J., & van IJzendoorn, M. H. (2006). Gene–environment interaction of the dopamine D4 receptor (DRD4) and observed maternal insensitivity predicting externalizing behavior in preschoolers. *Developmental Psychobiology, 48*, 406–409.

Bakermans-Kranenburg, M. J., & van IJzendoorn, M. H. (2007). Genetic vulnerability or differential susceptibility in child development: The case of attachment. *Journal of Child Psychology and Psychiatry, 48* (12), 1160–1173.

Bakermans-Kranenburg, M. J., & van IJzendoorn, M. H. (2011). Differential susceptibility to rearing environment depending on dopamine-related genes: New evidence and a meta-analysis. *Development and Psychopathology, 23*, 39–52.

Bakermans-Kranenburg, M. J., van IJzendoorn, M. H., Bokhorst, C. L., & Schuengel, C. (2004). The importance of shared environment in infant–father attachment: A behavioral genetic study of the Attachment Q-Sort. *Journal of Family Psychology, 18*, 545–549.

Bakermans-Kranenburg, M. J., van IJzendoorn, M. H., Caspers, K., & Philibert, R. (2011). DRD4 genotype moderates the impact of parental problems on unresolved loss or trauma. *Attachment and Human Development, 13* (3), 253–269.

Bakermans-Kranenburg, M. J., van IJzendoorn, M. H., & Juffer, F. (2003). Less is more: Meta-analyses of sensitivity and attachment interventions in early childhood. *Psychological Bulletin, 129*, 195–215.

Bakermans-Kranenburg, M. J., van IJzendoorn, M. H., Mesman, J., Alink, L. R., & Juffer, F. (2008). Effects of an attachment-based intervention on daily cortisol moderated by dopamine receptor D4: R randomized control trial on 1- to 3-year-olds screened for externalizing behavior. *Developmental and Psychopathology, 20*, 805–820.

Bakermans-Kranenburg, M. J., van IJzendoorn, M. H., Pijlman, F. T. A., Mesman, J., & Juffer, F. (2008). Experimental evidence for differential susceptibility: Dopamine D4 receptor polymorphism (DRD4 VNTR) moderates intervention effects on toddlers' externalizing behavior in a randomized trial. *Developmental Psychology, 44*, 293–300.

Bates, J. E., Freeland, C. A. B., & Lounsbury, M. L. (1979). Measurement of infant difficultness. *Child Development, 50*, 794–803.

Belsky, J. (1997a). Variation in susceptibility to rearing influences: An evolutionary argument. *Psychological Inquiry, 8*, 182–186.

Belsky, J. (1997b). Theory testing, effect-size evaluation, and differential susceptibility to rearing influence: The case of mothering and attachment. *Child Development, 68*, 598–600.

Belsky, J. (2005). Differential susceptibility to rearing influence: An evolutionary hypothesis and some evidence. In B. J. Ellis & D. F. Bjorklund (Eds.). *Origins of the social mind: Evolutionary psychology and child development* (pp. 139–163). New York: Guilford Press.

Belsky, J., Bakermans-Kranenburg, M. J., & van IJzendoorn, M. H. (2007). For better and for worse: Differential susceptibility to environmental influences. *Current Directions in Psychological Science, 16* (6), 300–304

Belsky, J., Fish, M., & Isabella, R. (1991). Continuity and discontinuity in infant negative and positive emotionality: Family antecedents and attachment consequences. *Developmental Psychology, 27*, 421–431.

Belsky, J., Hsieh, K., & Crnic, K. (1998). Mothering, fathering, and infant negativity as antecedents of boys' externalizing problems and inhibition at age 3: Differential susceptibility to rearing influence? *Development and Psychopathology, 10*, 301–319.

Belsky, J., & Pluess, M. (2009). Beyond diathesis–stress. *Psychological Bulletin, 135*, 885–908.

Belsky, J., & Rovine, M. (1987). Temperament and attachment security in the Strange Situation: An empirical rapprochement. *Child Development, 58*, 787–795.

Blair, C. (2002). Early intervention for low birth weight preterm infants: The role of negative emotionality in the specification of effects. *Development and Psychopathology, 14*, 311–332.

Bohlin, G., Hagekull, B., & Andersson, A. (2005). Behavioral inhibition as a precursor of peer social competence in early school age: The interplay with attachment and non-parental care. *Merrill–Palmer Quarterly, 51*, 1–19.

Bokhorst, C. L., Bakermans-Kranenburg, M. J., Fearon, P., van IJzendoorn, M. H., Fonagy, P., & Schuengel, C. (2003). The importance of shared environment in mother–infant attachment security: A behavioral genetic study. *Child Development, 74*, 1769–1782.

Bowlby, J. (1969). *Attachment and loss: Vol. 1. Attachment*. London: Penguin.

Boyce, W. T., Chesney, M., Alkon, A., Tschann, J. M., Adams, S., Chesterman, B., et al. (1995). Psychobiologic reactivity to stress and childhood respiratory illnesses: Results of two prospective studies. *Psychosomatic Medicine, 57* (5), 411–422.

Boyce, W. T., & Ellis, B. J. (2005). Biological sensitivity to context: I. An evolutionary–developmental theory of the origins and functions of stress reactivity. *Development and Psychopathology, 17*, 271–301.

Bradley, R. H., & Corwyn, R. F. (2008). Infant temperament, parenting, and externalizing behavior in first grade: A test of the differential susceptibility hypothesis. *Journal of Child Psychology and Psychiatry and Allied Disciplines, 49*, 124–131.

Calkins, S. D., & Fox, N. A. (1992). The relations among infant temperament, security of attachment, and behavioral inhibition at twenty-four months. *Child Development, 3*, 1456–1472.

Caspi, A., & Moffitt, T. E. (2006). Gene–environment interactions in psychiatry: Joining forces with neuroscience. *Nature Reviews Neuroscience, 7*, 583–590.

Caspi, A., & Shiner, R. L. (2006). Personality development. In W. Damon & R. Lerner (Eds.). *Child development: An advanced course* (pp. 181–214). New York: Wiley.

Caspi, A., Sugden, K., Moffitt, T. E., Taylor, A., Craig, I. W., Harrington, H., et al. (2003). Influence of life stress on depression: Moderation by a polymorphism in the 5 HTT gene. *Science, 301*, 386–389.

Cassidy, J., & Shaver, P. R. (Eds.). (2008). *Handbook of attachment: Theory, research, and clinical applications* (2nd edn.). New York: Guilford Press.

Cassidy, J., Woodhouse, S. S., Sherman, L. J., Stupica, B., & Lejuez, C. W. (2011). Enhancing infant attachment security: An examination of treatment efficacy and differential susceptibility. *Development and Psychopathology, 23*, 131–148.

Cicchetti, D. (1993). Developmental psychopathology – reactions, reflections, projections. *Developmental Review, 13*, 471–502.

Crockenberg, S. B. (1981). Infant irritability, mother responsiveness, and social support influences on the security of infant–mother attachment. *Child Development, 52*, 857–865.

Crockenberg, S. C., & Leerkes, E. M. (2006). Infant and maternal behavior moderate reactivity to novelty to predict anxious behavior at 2.5 years. *Development and Psychopathology, 18*, 17–34.

Dearing, E., & Hamilton, L. C. (2006). Contemporary advances and classic advice for analyzing mediating and moderating variables. *Monographs of the Society for Research in Child Development, 71*, 88–104.

Deater-Deckard, K., Bates, J. E., Dodge, K. A., & Pettit, G. S. (1996). Physical discipline among African American and European American mothers: Links to children's externalizing behaviors. *Developmental Psychology, 32*, 1065–1072.

Deater-Deckard, K., & Dodge, K. A. (1997). Externalizing behavior problems and discipline revisited: Nonlinear effects and variation by culture, context, and gender. *Psychological Inquiry, 8* (3), 161–175.

Deater-Deckard, K., & Wang, Z. (2012). Anger and irritability. In M. Zentner & R. Shiner (Eds.). *Handbook of temperament* (pp. 124–144). New York, NY: Guilford Press.

Denham, S. A., Workman, E., Cole, P. M., Weiss-brod, C., Kendziora, K. T., & Zahn-Waxler, C. (2000). Prediction of externalizing behavior problems from early to middle childhood: The role of parental socialization and emotion expression. *Development and Psychopathology, 12* (1), 23–45.

De Schipper, J. C., Tavecchio, L. W. C., van IJzendoorn, M. H., & van Zeijl, J. (2004). Goodness-of-fit in center day care: Relations of temperament, stability, and quality of care with the child's adjustment. *Early Childhood Research Quarterly, 19*, 257–272.

DeVries, M. W. (1984). Temperament and infant mortality among the Masai of East Africa. *American Journal of Psychiatry, 141*, 1189–1194.

DeVries, M. W. (1987). Cry babies, culture and catastrophe. Infant temperament among the Masai. In N. Scheper-Hughes (Ed.). *Anthropological approaches to the treatment and maltreatment of children* (pp. 165–186). Dordrecht, The Netherlands: Reidel.

De Wolff, M., & van IJzendoorn, M. H. (1997). Sensivity and attachment. A meta-analysis on parental antecedents of infant attachment. *Child Development, 68*, 571–591.

Ellis, B. J., Boyce, W. T., Belsky, J., Bakermans-Kranenburg, M. J., & van IJzendoorn, M. H. (2011). Differential susceptibility to the environment: An evolutionary–neurodevelopmental theory. *Development and Psychopathology, 23* (1), 7–28.

Essex, M. J., Armstrong, J. M., Burk, L. R., Goldsmith, H. H., & Boyce, W. T. (2011). Biological sensitivity to context moderates the effects of the early teacher–child relationship on the development of mental health by adolescence. *Development and Psychopathology, 23,* 149–161.

Feldman, R., Greenbaum, C. W., & Yirmiya, N. (1999). Mother–infant affect synchrony as an antecedent of the emergence of self-control. *Developmental Psychology, 35,* 223–231.

Fortuna, K., van IJzendoorn, M. H., Mankuta, D., Kaitz, M., Avinun, R., Ebstein, R. P., et al. (2011). Differential genetic susceptibility to child risk at birth in predicting observed maternal behavior. *PLoS ONE, 6* (5), e19765.

Gilissen, R., Bakermans-Kranenburg, M. J., van IJzendoorn, H. W., & van der Veer, R. (2008). Parent–child relationship, temperament, and physiological reactions to fear-inducing film clips: Further evidence for differential susceptibility. *Journal of Experimental Child Psychology, 99* (3), 182–195.

Goldsmith, H. H., Lemery, K. S., Buss, K. A., & Campos, J. J. (1999). Genetic analyses of focal aspects of infant temperament. *Developmental Psychology, 35* (4), 972–985.

Goldsmith, H. H., Reilly, J., Lemery, K. S., Longley, S., & Prescott, A. (1999). *The laboratory temperament assessment battery: Preschool version.* Unpublished manuscript.

Groeneveld, M. G., Vermeer, H. J., van IJzendoorn, M. H., & Linting, M. (2012). Stress, cortisol, and well-being of caregivers and children in home-based childcare: A case for differential susceptibility. *Child: Care, Health and Development, 38* (2), 251–260.

Hane, A. A., & Fox, N. A. (2006). Ordinary variations in maternal caregiving influence human infants' stress reactivity. *Psychological Science, 17,* 550–556.

Harlow, H. F. (1958). The nature of love. *American Psychologist, 13,* 673–685.

Hesse, E. (2008). The Adult Attachment Interview: Protocol, method of analysis, and empirical studies. In J. Cassidy & P. R. Shaver (Eds.). *Handbook of attachment* (pp. 552–598). New York: Guilford Press.

Jaddoe, V. W., Bakker, R., van Duijn, C. M., van der Heijden, A. J., Lindemans, J., Mackenbach, J. P., et al. (2007). The Generation R Study Biobank: A resource for epidemiological studies in children and their parents. *European Journal of Epidemiology, 22* (12), 917–923.

Juffer, F., Bakermans-Kranenburg, M. J., & van IJzendoorn, M. H. (Eds.). (2008). *Promoting positive parenting.* New York: Taylor & Francis.

Kagan, J. (1995). On attachment. *Harvard Review of Psychiatry, 3,* 104–106.

Kagan, J. (2007). A trio of concerns. *Perspectives on Psychological Science, 2,* 361–376.

Kagan, J. (2009). Two is better than one. *Perspectives on Psychological Science, 4,* 22–23.

Kagan, J. (2012). The biography of behavioral inhibition. In M. Zentner & R. Shiner (Eds.). *Handbook of temperament* (pp. 69–82). New York, NY: Guilford Press.

Kegel, C. A. T., Bus, A. G., & van IJzendoorn, M. H. (2011). Differential susceptibility in early literacy instruction through computer games: The role of the dopamine D4 receptor gene (DRD4). *Mind, Brain and Education, 5,* 71–79.

Klein, T. A., Neumann, J., Reuter, M., Hennig, J., Von Cramon, D. Y., & Ullsperger, M. (2007). Genetically determined learning from errors. *Science, 318,* 1642–1645.

Klein Velderman, M., Bakermans-Kranenburg, M. J., Juffer, F., & van IJzendoorn, M. H. (2006). Effects of attachment-based interventions on maternal sensitivity and infant attachment: Differential susceptibility of highly reactive infants. *Journal of Family Psychology, 20,* 266–274.

Kochanska, G. (1995). Children's temperament, mothers' discipline, and security of attachment: Multiple pathways to emerging internalization. *Child Development, 66* (3), 597–615.

Kochanska, G. (1998). Mother–child relationship, child fearfulness, and emerging attachment: A short-term longitudinal study. *Developmental Psychology, 34,* 480–490.

Kochanska, G., Aksan, N., & Joy, M. E. (2007). Children's fearfulness as a moderator of parenting in early socialization. *Developmental Psychology, 43,* 222–237.

LaFreniere, P. J., & Capuano, F. (1997). Preventive intervention as means of clarifying direction of effects in socialization: Anxious–withdrawn preschoolers case. *Development and Psychopathology, 9,* 551–564.

Lengua, L. J. & Wachs, T. D. (2012). Temperament and risk: Resilient and vulnerable responses to adversity. In M. Zentner & R.L. Shiner (Eds.). *Handbook of temperament* (pp. 519–540). New York: The Guilford Press.

Luijk, M. P. C. M., Roisman, G. I., Haltigan, J. D., Tiemeier, H., Booth-LaForce, C., van IJzendoorn, M. H., et al. (2011). Dopaminergic, serotonergic, and oxytonergic candidate genes associated with infant attachment security and disorganization?: In search of main effects and G × E interactions. *Journal of Child Psychology and Psychiatry, 52*(12), 1295–1307.

MacDonald, K. B. (2012). Temperament and evolution. In M. Zentner & R. Shiner (Eds.). *Handbook of temperament* (pp. 273–296). New York, NY: Guilford Press.

Main, M., Kaplan, N., & Cassidy, J. (1985). Security in infancy, childhood, and adulthood: A move to the level of representation. *Monographs of the Society for Research in Child Development, 50,* 66–106.

Marshall, P. J., & Fox, N. A. (2005). Relations between behavioral reactivity at 4 months and attachment classification at 14 months in a selected sample. *Infant Behavior and Development, 28*, 492–502.

Masten, A. S., & Obradović, J. (2006). Competence and resilience in development. *Annals of the New York Academy of Sciences, 1094*, 13–27.

Meaney, M. J. (2010). Epigenetics and the biological definition of gene × environment interactions. *Child Development, 81*, 41–79.

Mervielde, I., & De Pauw, S. S. (2012). Models of child temperament. In M. Zentner & R. Shiner (Eds.). *Handbook of temperament* (pp. 21–40). New York, NY: Guilford Press.

Morrell, J., & Murray, L. (2003). Parenting and the development of conduct disorder and hyperactive symptoms in childhood: A prospective longitudinal study from 2 months to 8 years. *Journal of Child Psychology and Psychiatry, 44*, 489–508.

Munafo, M. R., Durrant, C., Lewis, G., & Flint, J. (2009). Gene × environment interactions at the serotonin transporter locus. *Biological Psychiatry, 65*, 211–219.

Nachmias, M., Gunnar, M., Mangelsdorf, S., Parritz, R., & Buss, K. (1996). Behavioral inhibition and stress reactivity: The moderating role of attachment security. *Child Development, 67*, 508–522.

O'Connor, T. G., & Croft, C. M. (2001). A twin study of attachment in preschool children. *Child Development, 72*, 1501–1511.

Pappa, I., Szekely, E., Mileva-Seitz, V. R., Luijk, M. P., Bakermans-Kranenburg, M. J., van IJzendoorn, M. H., & Tiemeier, H. (2015). Beyond the usual suspects: a multidimensional genetic exploration of infant attachment disorganization and security. *Attachment & Human Development, 17* (3), 288–301.

Pluess, M., & Belsky, J. (2009). Differential susceptibility to rearing experience: The case of childcare. *Journal of Child Psychology and Psychiatry Allied Disciplines, 50*, 396–404.

Ricciuti, A. E. (1992). Child–mother attachment: A twin study. *Dissertation Abstracts International, 54*, 3364–3364. (University Microfilms No. 9324873)

Risch, N., Herrell, R., Lehner, T., Liang, K., Eaves, L., Hoh, J., et al. (2009). Interaction between the serotonin transporter gene (5-HTTLPR), stressful life events, and risk of depression. *Journal of the American Medical Association, 301* (23), 2462–2471.

Robbins, T. W., & Everitt, B. J. (1999). Motivation and reward. In M. J. Zigmond, F. E. Bloom, S. C. Landis, J. L. Roberts, & L. R. Squire (Eds.). *Fundamental neuroscience* (pp. 1246–1260). San Diego, CA: Academic Press.

Roisman, G. I., & Fraley, R. C. (2008). A behavior-genetic study of parenting quality, infant attachment security, and their covariation in a nationally representative sample. *Developmental Psychology, 44* (3), 831–839.

Rothbart, M. K., & Bates, J. E. (2006). Temperament. In N. Eisenberg, W. Damon, & R. M. Lerner (Eds.). *Handbook of child psychology: Vol. 3. Social, emotional, and personality development (6th edn., pp. 99–166).* Hoboken, NJ: Wiley.

Sameroff, A. (1975). Transactional models in early social-relations. *Human Development, 18*, 65–79.

Sameroff, A. J. (1983). Developmental systems: Contexts and evolution. In P. Mussen (Ed.). *Handbook of child psychology* (Vol. 1, pp. 237–294). New York: Wiley.

Saudino, K. J., & Wang, M. (2012). Quantitative and molecular genetic studies of temperament. In M. Zentner & R. L. Shiner (Eds.). *Handbook of temperament* (pp. 315–346). New York: The Guilford Press.

Settle, J. E., Dawes, C. T., Christakis, N. A., & Fowler, J. H. (2010). Friendships moderate an association between a dopamine gene variant and political ideology. *Journal of Politics, 72*, 1189–1198.

Sheese, B. E., Voelker, P. M., Rothbart, M. K., & Posner, M. I. (2007). Parenting quality interacts with genetic variation in dopamine receptor D4 to influence temperament in early childhood. *Development and Psychopathology, 19*, 1039–1046.

Simpson, J. A., & Belsky, J. (2008). Attachment theory within a modern evolutionary framework. In P. R. Shaver & J. Cassidy (Eds.). *Handbook of attachment: Theory, research, and clinical applications* (2nd edn., pp. 131–157). New York: Guilford Press.

Sroufe, L. A. (1985). Attachment classification from the perspective of infant–caregiver relationships and infant temperament. *Child Development, 56*, 1–14.

Sroufe, L. A., Egeland, B., Carlson, E., & Collins, W. A. (2005). *The development of the person: The Minnesota study of risk and adaptation from birth to adulthood.* New York: Guilford Press.

Stevenson-Hinde, J., & Marshall, P. J. (1999). Behavioral inhibition, heart period, and respiratory sinus arrhythmia: An attachment perspective. *Child Development, 70*, 805–816.

Stright, A. D., Kelley, K., & Gallagher, K. C. (2008). Infant temperament moderates relations between maternal parenting in early childhood and children's adjustment in first grade. *Child Development, 79*, 186–200.

Suomi, S. (1997). Early determinants of behaviour. *British Medical Bulletin, 53*, 170–184.

Thomas, A., & Chess, S. (1977). *Temperament and development.* New York: Brunner/Mazel.

Thompson, R. A., & Lamb, M. E. (1984). Assessing qualitative dimensions of emotional responsiveness in infants: Separation reactions in the strange situation. *Infant Behavior and Development, 7*, 423–445.

Uher, R., & McGuffin, P. (2008). The moderation by the serotonin transporter gene of environmental adversity in the etiology of mental illness: Review and methodological analysis. *Molecular Psychiatry, 13*, 131–146.

Uher, R., & McGuffin, P. (2010). The moderation by the serotonin transporter gene of environmental adversity in the etiology of depression: 2009 update. *Molecular Psychiatry, 15*, 18–22.

Van den Boom, D. C. (1994). The influence of temperament and mothering on attachment and exploration: An experimental manipulation of sensitive responsiveness among lower-class mothers with irritable infants. *Child Development, 65,* 1457–1477.

Van IJzendoorn, M. H. (1995a). Adult attachment representations, parental responsiveness, and infant attachment: A meta-analysis on the predictive validity of the Adult Attachment Interview. *Psychological Bulletin, 117,* 387–403.

Van IJzendoorn, M. H. (1995b). Of the way we are: On temperament, attachment and the transmission gap: A rejoinder to Fox. *Psychological Bulletin, 117,* 411–415.

Van IJzendoorn, M. H., & Bakermans-Kranenburg, M. J. (1996). Attachment representations in mothers, fathers, adolescents, and clinical groups: A meta-analytic search for normative data. *Journal of Consulting and Clinical Psychology, 64,* 8–21.

Van IJzendoorn, M. H., & Bakermans-Kranenburg, M. J. (2004). Maternal sensitivity and infant temperament in the formation of attachment. In G. Bremner & A. Slater (Eds.). *Theories of infant development* (pp. 233–258). London: Blackwell.

Van IJzendoorn, M. H., Bakermans-Kranenburg, M. J., & Mesman, J. (2008). Dopamine system genes associated with parenting in the context of daily hassles. *Genes, Brain and Behavior, 7,* 403–410.

Van IJzendoorn, M. H., & DeWolff, M. W. E. (1997). In search of the absent father: Meta-analyses of infant–father attachment: A rejoinder to our discussants. *Child Development, 68,* 604–609.

Van IJzendoorn, M. H., Palacios, J., Sonuga-Barke, E. J. S., Gunnar, M. R., Vorria, P., McCall, R. B., et al. (2011). Children in institutional care: Delayed development and resilience. *Monographs of the Society for Research of Child Development, 76* (4), 8–30.

Van Zeijl, J., Mesman, J., Stolk, M. N., Alink, L. R. A., van IJzendoorn, M. H., Bakermans-Kranenburg, M. J., et al. (2007). Differential susceptibility to discipline: The moderating effect of child temperament on the association between maternal discipline and early childhood externalizing problems. *Journal of Family Psychology, 21,* 626–636.

Van Zeijl, J., Mesman, J., van IJzendoorn, M. H., Bakermans-Kranenburg, M. J., Juffer, F., Stolk, M. N., et al. (2006). Attachment-based intervention for enhancing sensitive discipline in mothers of 1- to 3-year-old children at risk for externalizing behavior problems: A randomized controlled trial. *Journal of Consulting and Clinical Psychology, 47,* 801–810.

Vaughn, B. E., & Bost, K. K. (1999). Attachment and temperament: Redundant, independent, or interacting influences on interpersonal adaptation and personality development. In J. Cassidy & P. R. Shaver *(Eds.). Handbook of attachment: Theory, research, and clinical applications (pp. 198–225).* New York: Guilford Press.

Vaughn, B. E., Bost, K. K., & van IJzendoorn, M. H. (2008). Attachment and temperament: Additive and interactive influences on behavior, affect, and cognition during infancy and childhood. In J. Cassidy & P. R. Shaver (Eds.). *Handbook of attachment* (pp. 192–216). New York: Guilford Press.

Vaughn, B. E., & Waters, E. (1990). Attachment behavior at home and in the laboratory: Q-sort observations and Strange Situation classifications of one-year-olds. *Child Development, 61,* 1965–1973.

Yaman, A., Mesman, J., van IJzendoorn, M. H., & Bakermans-Kranenburg, M. J. (2010). Parenting and toddler aggression in second-generation immigrant families: The moderating role of child temperament. *Journal of Family Psychology, 24,* 208–211.

Zentner, M., & Bates, J. E. (2008). Child temperament: An integrative review of concepts, research programs, and measures. *European Journal of Developmental Science, 1/2,* 7–37.

# 10

# Annual Research Review

## *Attachment Disorders in Early Childhood: Clinical Presentation, Causes, Correlates, and Treatment*

### Charles H. Zeanah and Mary Margaret Gleason

## Introduction

Attachment disorders were first formally defined as a disorder in the 3rd edition of the *Diagnostic and Statistical Manual of Mental Disorders* [(DSM-III) American Psychiatric Association, 1980], and the criteria were subsequently revised in DSM-III-R (APA, 1987), DSM-IV (APA, 1994), DSM-5 (APA, 2013), and ICD-10 (WHO, 1992). Still, for almost 20 years after appearing in DSM-III, the disorders attracted little attention from investigators, so until DSM-5, revisions to criteria were made largely in the absence of any relevant research (Zeanah, 1996). In fact, the first study directly addressing the validity of any criteria did not appear until 1998 (Boris, Zeanah, Larrieu, Scheeringa, & Heller, 1998).

There is now broad consensus that in early childhood, attachment disorders result from inadequate caregiving environments and encompass two clinical patterns, an emotionally withdrawn/inhibited phenotype and an indiscriminately social/disinhibited phenotype. For purposes of this review, we will use the DSM-5 designations of reactive attachment disorder (RAD) and disinhibited social engagement disorder (DSED) to describe these clinical entities.

In this review, we begin by describing the clinical phenomenology of RAD and DSED, including the historical changes in how these disorders are conceptualized and the rationale for these changes. Next, we consider recent research about the course and correlates of attachment disorders. Finally, we consider the limited data available about intervention and highlight potential new directions for research to enhance our understanding of these disorders.

## Clinical Presentation: Classification and Measurement

Research on disorders of attachment in young children has been conducted by assessing signs with continuous measures and by categorically diagnosing RAD and DSED in maltreated children and currently or formerly institutionalized children. Core features of RAD in young children include the absence of focused attachment behaviors directed toward a preferred caregiver, failure to seek and respond to comforting when distressed, reduced

*Source:* Republished with permission of John Wiley & Sons, Inc., from Charles H. Zeanah, Mary Margaret Gleason, "Annual Research Review: Attachment disorders in early childhood–clinical presentation, causes, correlates, and treatment," pp. 207-222 from *Journal of Child Psychology and Psychiatry* 56:3 (March 2015); permission conveyed through Copyright Clearance Center, Inc.

social and emotional reciprocity, and disturbances of emotion regulation, including reduced positive affect and unexplained fearfulness or irritability. Core behavioral features of DSED include inappropriate approach to unfamiliar adults and lack of wariness of strangers, and a willingness to wander off with strangers. In DSED, children also demonstrate a lack of appropriate social and physical boundaries, such as interacting with adult strangers in overly close proximity (experienced by the adult as intrusive) and by actively seeking close physical contact. By the preschool years, verbal boundaries may be violated as the child asks overly intrusive and overly familiar questions of unfamiliar adults. These behaviors have been reported in numerous studies and comprise a coherent set of objectively defined signs of disorder (O'Connor & Zeanah, 2003; Zeanah, Smyke, & Dumitrescu, 2002).

Still, there have been some changes in how the disorders have been described and defined over the years. We turn next to a brief review of those changes and the rationale underlying them.

## Historical background

At least as early as the mid-20th century, behaviors characterizing two distinct types of attachment disorders were evident in descriptive studies of severely deprived institutionalized young children (Goldfarb, 1945; Levy, 1947; Provence & Lipton, 1962; Spitz, 1945). Somewhat later, studies of the social behavior of young maltreated children also described similar patterns of unusual social and emotional behaviors (Gaensbauer & Harmon, 1982; Gaensbauer & Sands, 1979; George & Main, 1979).

The most important study informing the criteria for contemporary nosologies, was a study by Barbara Tizard and her colleagues of young children being raised in residential nurseries in London (Tizard, 1977). These nurseries had lower child to caregiver ratios than many previous studies of institutionalized children. Also, the children were raised in mixed aged groups and had adequate books and toys available. Nevertheless, caregivers were explicitly discouraged from forming attachments to the children in their care. As a result, the usual confound of material privation in previous studies of institutionalized children was eliminated, and the variable of most interest to study of attachment, caregiver–child relationships, was isolated for study.

The investigators examined children who were abandoned at birth and raised in institutional settings. Of the 26 children who remained institutionalized for the first 4 years of their lives, eight were described as emotionally withdrawn and social unresponsive, 10 others were indiscriminately social, attention seeking and clingy with everyone, including unfamiliar adults, and the remaining eight of the 26 actually formed selective attachments to caregivers (Tizard & Rees, 1975). The two attachment disordered phenotypes in the Tizard study – emotionally withdrawn and indiscriminately social – were later incorporated into criteria in formal nosologies, all of which defined two basic clinical presentations of disordered attachment in young children.

There was general convergence between the DSM-IV and the ICD-10 criteria for attachment disorders. Common features include cross-contextual aberrant social behavior caused by grossly inadequate care, and the two clinical phenotypes of inhibited and disinhibited behavioral patterns. However, ICD-10 divided the subtypes into two distinct disorders, RAD, similar to the emotionally withdrawn/inhibited type of RAD in DSM-IV and disinhibited attachment disorder (DAD), similar to the indiscriminately social/disinhibited type of RAD in DSM-IV. DSM-5 followed the lead of ICD-10, separating the disorders into RAD and DSED.

## Rationale for DSM-5 criteria changes

*One disorder or two?* An implicit controversy concerned the DSM-IV approach of defining the two phenotypes as subtypes of the same disorder or two distinct disorders (as does ICD-10, for example). Part of the original rationale for defining them as subtypes of a unitary disorder was that the phenotypes intended to describe lack of attachment in children who had experienced adverse caregiving – in inhibited RAD, attachment behaviors were not expressed, and in disinhibited RAD, attachment behaviors were expressed nonselectively. As a result, it seemed reasonable to group these two syndromes together, as part of a broad disorder of attachment.

Other than arising in similar conditions of social neglect, however, the two disorders differ in most other important ways, including phenotypic characteristics, correlates, course and response to intervention (Rutter, Kreppner, & Sonuga-Barke, 2009; Zeanah & Smyke, 2014). The phenotypes of the two disorders are in stark contrast with each other. Their psychiatric comorbidities differ, with depressive signs seen in children with RAD and patterns of impulsivity more commonly associated with DSED. For example, RAD resolves nearly completely with access to an adequate attachment figure, whereas DSED can persist in the context of adequate caregiving and a selective attachment relationship. This evidence suggests that these disorders are best conceptualized as two distinct disorders rather than as two subtypes of a single disorder (American Psychiatric Association, 2013; Rutter et al., 2009; Zeanah & Gleason, 2010).

*Reactive attachment disorder.* In DSM-5, the criteria for RAD focus more specifically on absent or aberrant attachment behaviors across settings rather than on social behaviors more generally described in earlier nosologies (see DSM-IV and ICD-10 for contrasts). The change in criteria was guided by evidence from multiple investigations of currently and formerly institutionalized children (Gleason et al., 2011; Smyke, Dumitrescu, & Zeanah, 2002; Tizard & Rees, 1975; Zeanah, Smyke, Koga, & Carlson, 2005), of children in foster care (Oosterman & Schuengel, 2007; Zeanah et al., 2004), and of children in impoverished groups at risk for aberrant parenting behavior (Boris et al., 2004) demonstrating that lack of attachment behaviors is the core deficit of the disorder, and the absence of attachment behaviors directed toward putative primary caregivers that is pathognomonic. Observing a child interacting only with an unfamiliar adult without evidence of how the child interacts with the caregiver would be insufficient to attribute the observed behaviors to RAD.

'Pathogenic care' in DSM-IV and 'parental abuse, neglect or serious mishandling' in ICD-10 was replaced by 'insufficient care' in DSM-5 in order to emphasize that social neglect seems the key necessary condition for the disorder to occur. To date, there are no case reports of young children exhibiting the RAD phenotype as defined by ICD-10 or DSM-5 without at least a reasonable inference of serious emotional neglect, and no cases of the RAD phenotype from abuse without neglect.

DSM-5 also requires that a child have a cognitive age of at least 9 months to ensure that an attachment disorder is not diagnosed in children who are developmentally incapable of demonstrating a focused attachment.

*Disinhibited social engagement disorder.* Guided by extant literature, the DSED phenotype in DSM-5 focuses more on aberrant social behavior. The rationale for defining the indiscriminate behavior phenotype as DSED in DSM-5 as opposed to disinhibited attachment disorder as in ICD-10, is that the data indicate that the core deficit of the disorder is not nonselective attachment behaviors, but more about unmodulated and indiscriminate social behavior, especially initial approaches to and interaction with unfamiliar adults. The justification for the change is supported by the assessment of indiscriminate behavior in numerous studies of institutionalized (Soares et al., 2014; Tizard & Rees, 1975; Zeanah et al., 2002, 2005), post-institutionalized (Bruce, Tarullo, & Gunnar, 2009; Lawler et al., 2014; Smyke et al., 2012), and deprived children in foster care (Bruce et al., 2009; Oosterman & Schuengel, 2007; Pears, Bruce, Fisher, & Kim, 2010; Zeanah et al., 2004). In these studies, what is disinhibited is children's behavior with unfamiliar adults rather than with their putative attachment figures, for whom they may show focused attachment behaviors and preferential comfort seeking.

This point is not without controversy, however. In the Tizard study, for example, institutionalized children were reported as showing separation protest and comfort-seeking from strangers in the residential nurseries (Tizard & Rees, 1975). If attachment behaviors were indiscriminately focused on strangers and familiar caregivers alike, then that suggests disinhibition of attachment. Importantly, however, this conceptualization was developed from observations of affected children living in institutions who may well have had no opportunity to develop focused attachments (see Zeanah et al., 2005). This confound raises the question of whether the indiscriminate behaviors in these studies actually reflected a nonselectivity of attachment behaviors, since many of the studied children may not have had the opportunity to demonstrate selective attachment behaviors. More recent research with children adopted out of institutions has demonstrated that indiscriminate behavior may persist even after children form attachments to adoptive parents (Chisholm, 1998; O'Connor, Marvin, Rutter, Olrick, & Britner, 2003). If a child is adopted and turns selectively to parents for comfort and protection but continues to approach and engage strangers nonselectively, it is less clear that these approaches represent attachment behaviors. What is unresolved is the meaning of approach to strangers – whether that represents and is motivated by attachment, or whether it is motivated by another goal (or not inhibited by stranger wariness as in typical development).

DSM-5 indicates that DSED includes socially disinhibited behavior that must be distinguished from the impulsivity that accompanies ADHD because several lines of evidence suggest that some signs of ADHD and of DSED overlap. Nevertheless, it is clear that children may have ADHD without socially indiscriminate behavior, or socially indiscriminate behavior without ADHD, but there are often moderately strong correlations between the two symptom profiles (Gleason et al., 2011; Roy, Pickles & Rutter, 2004). Rather than make ADHD an exclusion criteria for DSED, it seems more useful to direct attention to its distinction from ADHD.

Tying the phenotype to grossly inadequate caregiving was retained in DSM-5 for the important reason that children who have Williams syndrome – a chromosome 7 deletion syndrome – have been reported to demonstrate phenotypically similar behavior to those with DSED (Dykens, 2003), even though the children are receiving adequate care. This criterion ensures that children with a known biological abnormality do not qualify for the diagnosis of DSED.

In fact, in keeping with the suggestions of social cognitive and behavioral abnormalities of the disorder (Green, 2003; Minnis, Marwick, Arthur, & McLaughlin, 2006; Rutter et al., 2009; Tarullo & Gunnar, 2005), there is now evidence that DSED is predictive of functional impairment, difficulties with close relationships, and more need for special education services (Gleason et al., 2011; Rutter et al., 2007).

## Measurement issues

Studies using continuous measures (Chisholm, 1998; Gleason et al., 2011; O'Connor & Rutter, 2000; O'Connor et al., 2003; Oosterman & Schuengel, 2007; Rutter et al., 2007; Smyke et al., 2002, 2012; Zeanah et al., 2005), and studies using categorical measures (Boris et al., 2004; Gleason et al., 2011; Zeanah et al., 2004) have demonstrated repeatedly that emotionally withdrawn/inhibited and indiscriminately social/disinhibited patterns of behavior can be reliably identified in maltreated, institutionalized, and formerly institutionalized children. Research on international adoptees has focused primarily on indiscriminate behavior, but studies of children being reared in institutions (Zeanah et al., 2005) and maltreated children in foster care (Boris et al., 2004; Oosterman & Schuengel, 2007; Zeanah et al., 2004) have included signs of RAD, as well. Taken as a whole, these studies support their construct validity, but a number of important questions have arisen regarding how these disorders are measured.

Parent report measures of RAD and DSED as defined by DSM-5 have shown acceptable to strong interrater and test–retest reliability in young children who have experienced adverse caregiving (Boris et al., 1998, 2004; Bruce et al., 2009; Chisholm, 1998; Gleason et al., 2011; O'Connor & Rutter, 2000; Oosterman & Schuengel, 2007; Pears et al., 2010; Rutter et al., 2007; Smyke et al., 2002; Zeanah et al., 2004, 2005). Variables assessed by three different interview measures of indiscriminate behavior showed substantial convergence on indiscriminate behavior (Zeanah et al., 2002). In addition, a factor analysis of the items from a parent interview about signs of RAD and DSED in young children identified the two clinical disorders as distinct in a sample of maltreated children in foster care (Oosterman & Schuengel, 2007). Third, among institutionalized young children who were followed longitudinally, signs of RAD and DSED were internally consistent across 4 years (Gleason et al., 2011).

Even stronger evidence of convergence is provided by comparisons between caregiver reports and behavior coded in observational procedures. In the Bucharest Early Intervention Project (BEIP), for example, Zeanah et al. (2005) rated the degree to which the child had developed an attachment to a caregiver during interaction with the caregiver in the Strange Situation Procedure (SSP) (Ainsworth, Blehar, Waters, & Wall, 1978). As predicted, in children 12–31 months of age, more signs of RAD were inversely correlated with the degree to which a child had developed an attachment.

Regarding DSED, Gleason et al. (2011) demonstrated substantial levels of agreement between an interview measure of indiscriminate behavior and an observational procedure designed to assess a young child's willingness to 'go off' with a stranger. Indiscriminate behavior with an unfamiliar adult also has been demonstrated during the SSP both in young children in foster care (Lyons-Ruth, Bureau, Riley, & Atlas-Corbett, 2009) and in institutionalized children and has converged with caregiver report (Oliveira et al., 2012). In children adopted out of foster care and out of institutions, an observational and parent report measure also converged moderately (Bruce et al., 2009).

A recent short-term longitudinal study used a structured laboratory procedure to observe the behavior of young children who were adopted from 13 different countries at ages 16–36 months and then assessed 1–3 months and 8–11 months following adoption (Lawler et al., 2014). As part of a larger assessment protocol, children's behavior during a 10-min interaction with a female adult stranger was coded. Three groups studied included children adopted from institutions, children adopted from foster care and nonadopted children. In the paradigm, the mother was assigned a paperwork task and discouraged from interacting with the child or commenting on the stranger. The child was provided with a picture book. The stranger entered the playroom, and at scripted intervals, she made increasing social overtures to the child. Factor analysis of the child's behavior at both time points yielded a nonphysical social engagement factor (e.g. more responses to stranger overtures, reduced latency to approach), which did not distinguish the groups, and a physical social engagement factor (e.g. more physical intimacy with stranger and shorter latency to touch), which distinguished both adopted groups from the non-adopted group. The investigators concluded that physical social engagement may reflect the core of DSED. Of course, physical engagement in this context *is* social, and more intrusive than nonphysical engagement, so this finding may reflect more extreme sociability, a greater social boundary violation or greater lack of expected reticence to approach. Of course, this physical and social engagement occurred in a laboratory situation in the *presence* of the child's mother. The context in which the social engagement occurs undoubtedly is related to the meaning of the child's sociable behavior and may affect the degree to which it may be considered excessive or deviant.

Although there are some differences among criteria sets and measures used to assess RAD and DSED, these differences appear to be modest. Furthermore, refinements in definitions will no doubt be developed as more is learned. Nevertheless, the preponderance of evidence to date suggests that the two phenotypes are robust and that similar constructs are being identified across studies of different samples in different locations conducted by different research groups. Therefore, in this review we focus less on the nuances of differences among measures and instead accept that their similarities allow considering findings both from studies that have and have not explicitly set out to define attachment disorders. We include studies that have examined 'indiscriminate behavior' to describe signs of DSED and 'inhibited behavior' to describe signs of RAD, whether these are from interviews with parents or from observed behaviors.

## Beyond early childhood

Although this review focuses primarily on RAD and DSED in early childhood, where they have been best studied, we note that other investigators have conducted studies of school age children and adolescents. Because of important phenotypic differences between the disorders in early childhood and in these alternative approaches, we mention this body of work by noting that it is an exception to the general consensus about measurement noted above.

For example, Kay and Green (2013) assessed looked after adolescents (with histories of neglect, emotional abuse, and sexual abuse) and controls and found significantly more signs of indiscriminate behavior with impairment among the looked after children. In advocating for a broader phenotype, they found in addition to the indiscriminate behavior described in DSM-5, factors reflecting attention seeking behavior and superficial relationships. Although they suggested that the broader phenotype resulted from studying a never institutionalized (but still maltreated) sample, this is not clear. Since the phenotype of RAD and DSED in DSM-5 has been demonstrated in young children living in foster care (with no histories of placement in institutions), the different phenotype could reflect developmental differences that emerge in older children.

Minnis and her group have conducted a series of cross-sectional studies relying on various combinations of parent report, standardized observation and structured psychiatric interviews to identify RAD in school aged children (Millward, Kennedy, Towlson, & Minnis, 2006; Minnis et al., 2007, 2009, 2013). These studies have demonstrated reliable identification of RAD in middle childhood, but the measures they used to identify RAD include a broader phenotype and have an unclear relationship to measures used to assess RAD in early childhood. It remains unclear, therefore, whether the findings of population prevalence of 1.4% in a disadvantaged area (Minnis et al., 2013) or high heritability of inhibited and disinhibited types in a large twin study (Minnis et al., 2007) apply to the phenotypes under review.

Given that the definition of RAD differs in these studies in important ways from the disorders as defined in DSM-5 and ICD-10, it is not clear whether the differences reflect developmental changes in RAD and DSED in middle childhood and adolescence or whether what is being described are different disorders altogether. Longitudinal studies from early to middle childhood and adolescence could address this question.

## Causes and Risk

Along with other trauma and stress related disorders, attachment disorders include specification of etiology in the criteria. Thus, social neglect is noted as a necessary though not sufficient requirement for the diagnosis to be entertained.

## Caregiving environments

Children who have experienced seriously adverse, neglectful caregiving environments have demonstrated clear increased risk for RAD and DSED compared to children who are not exposed to adverse caregiving environments (Boris et al., 2004; Bruce et al., 2009; Chisholm, 1998; Gleason et al., 2011; O'Connor & Rutter, 2000; Oosterman & Schuengel, 2007; Pears et al., 2010; Smyke et al., 2002; Van Den Dries et al., 2012; Zeanah et al., 2004, 2005).

One study, for example, demonstrated that increasing signs of RAD and DSED was associated with increasingly adverse caregiving environments. Two groups of young children living in an institution were compared. Those children living on a special unit that restricted the number of caregivers each child encountered in a day had significantly fewer signs of both types of RAD than young children living on a standard unit in the same institution. Thus, the poorer caregiving condition on the standard unit was associated with more signs of RAD and DSED (Smyke et al., 2002).

A threshold of neglect may be necessary for signs of these disorders to appear, but more detailed evaluations of the caregiving environments are needed to determine which components of caregiving are specifically associated with risk. In this regard, Zeanah et al. (2005) examined naturalistic interactions between institutional caregivers and young children in the BEIP, a randomized controlled trial of foster care as an alternative to institutional care (Zeanah, Keyes, & Settles, 2003; Zeanah, Nelson, Fox, Smyke, Marshall, Parker, & Koga 2003). They found a composite variable of caregiving quality was associated with signs of RAD, even after controlling for other child and environmental characteristics. In the same study, however, there was no relationship between caregiving quality and signs of DSED after placement into a family.

In fact, evidence about the relation between concurrent caregiving quality and signs of DSED in young children is mixed. Dobrova-Krol, Bakermans-Kranenburg, van IJzendoorn, and Juffer (2010) found higher levels of positive caregiving among institution-reared children with indiscriminate behavior, an association in the opposite direction as that seen in home-reared controls. In another cross-sectional study, Chinese girls whose adoptive mothers were more sensitive showed less indiscriminate behavior (Van Den Dries, Juffer, van Ijzendoorn, Bakermans-Kranenburg, & Alink, 2012). In a study of postinstututionalized toddlers, Garvin, Tarullo, Van Ryzin, and Gunnar (2012) found that initiation of joint attention at 18 months was inversely correlated with indiscriminate behavior in postinstitutionalized toddlers at 30 months if adoptive parents had lower levels of emotional availability. At higher levels of parents' emotional availability, however, there was no longer a relationship between joint attention and indiscriminate behavior.

Lyons-Ruth et al. (2009), on the other hand, showed that indiscriminate behavior was present in high-risk, family reared infants only if they had been maltreated or if their mothers had had psychiatric hospitalizations. They also found that mothers' disrupted emotional interactions with the infant mediated the relationship between caregiving adversity and indiscriminate behavior.

In a study of institutionalized toddlers in Portugal, Oliveira et al. (2012) found that experiences prior to institutionalization predicted indiscriminate behavior. Specifically, a composite score of maternal prenatal risk, operationalized as having a physical disease, abusing substances, limited prenatal care and preterm birth, predicted indiscriminate behavior, as did emotional neglect. They also demonstrated that neglect mediated the association between maternal prenatal risk and indiscriminate behavior. The same group demonstrated that having a preferred caregiver predicted indiscriminate behavior over and above prenatal and family characteristics (Soares et al., 2014).

Pears et al. (2010), studying children in foster care, founds signs of DSED were related to the number of placement disruptions rather than severity of maltreatment. This is in keeping with the inclusion in DSM-5 of repeated changes in caregivers as a type of insufficient care.

## Child vulnerability factors

Although severe caregiving deficiencies seem necessary for RAD or DSED to develop, they clearly are not sufficient (Bakermans-Kranenberg, Dobrova-Krol & van IJzendoorn, 2011; Bakermans-Kranenburg, Steele, Zeanah, Muhamedrahimov, Vorria, Dobrova-Krol, Steele, van IJzendoorn, Juffer, Gunnar, 2011; Soares, Belsky, Mesquita, Osorio, & Sampaio, 2013; Zeanah & Smyke, 2014). Although the majority of maltreated children and children raised in institutions have insecure or disorganized attachments to biological parents or institutional caregivers

(Carlson, Cicchetti, Barnett, & Braunwald, 1989; O'Connor et al., 2003; Vorria et al., 2003; Zeanah et al., 2005), most do not develop attachment disorders (Boris et al., 2004; Gleason et al., 2011; Zeanah et al., 2004). This raises the question of vulnerability and perpetuating factors that might render some individuals more susceptible to the effects of deprivation or to more persistent social difficulties subsequently.

Most adoption studies have demonstrated that signs of DSED are related to length of time that the child lived in institutional deprivation (Bruce et al., 2009; O'Connor & Rutter, 2000; O'Connor et al., 2003; Rutter et al., 2007). In the English and Romanian Adoptees Study (ERAS), evidence of a sensitive period with regard to adequate caregiving emerged, as 27 of 29 children who showed persistence of indiscriminate behavior through 15 years were adopted after 6 months of age (Rutter et al., 2010).

Mixed results have been reported with respect to IQ, with the ERAS showing no association between mental age at entry into the UK (majority < 24 months) and indiscriminate behaviors at 6 years old, whereas BEIP reported a moderate association between baseline (mean of 22 months) developmental quotient and indiscriminate behaviors at 54 months (Gleason et al., 2014).

Studying children adopted internationally from foster care and from institutions, Johnson, Bruce, Tarullo, and Gunnar (2011) found that only those with stunted growth were at risk for indiscriminate behavior. On the other hand, in the ERAS, there was no clear association between subnutrition and indiscriminate behavior, although some suggestion that head growth partially mediated the association between institutional care and deprivation specific psychological problems including indiscriminate behaviors (Rutter, O'Connor, and the English and Romanian Adoptees (ERA) Study Team, 2004; Sonuga-Barke et al., 2008; Sonuga-Barke et al., 2008).

Using logistic regression, BEIP investigators reported that early disorganized attachment behaviors to caregivers were the sole independent predictor of signs of DSED at 54 months (Gleason et al., 2014). Since disorganized attachment is the most common attachment classification in institutionalized children (Dobrova-Krol et al., 2010; Vorria et al., 2003; Zeanah et al., 2005), these findings raise questions about what early contributors beyond early caregiving in institutionalized young children might be.

Determining whether genetic factors might moderate the effects of deprivation on attachment disorders is another approach to vulnerability factors. Individual differences in genetic polymorphisms plausibly may increase or decrease the risk of children exposed to substantial deprivation developing attachment disorders. No reports to date have identified genetic risks for RAD, but preliminary studies have explored them for DSED.

As noted, indiscriminate behavior has been described anecdotally as occurring in Williams syndrome, though this has not been systematically studied. Soares et al. (2013) have argued that the phenotypic similarities between social behavioral manifestations of Williams syndrome and signs of DSED suggest that children will be most likely to manifest persistent indiscriminate behavior when they carry specific polymorphisms within the critical region for Williams syndrome (region 7q11.23) and experience deprivation in the first year of life.

In a study exploring genetic vulnerability to indiscriminate behavior in children who experienced deprivation, Bakersman-Kranenberg, Dobrova-Krol et al., 2011 and Bakermans-Kranenburg, Steele, et al. 2011 examined whether the serotonin transporter gene (5HTT) moderated the association between institutional care and both disorganized attachment or indiscriminate behavior among young children raised in Ukranian institutions. They found that the long allele of the genotype protected against development of disorganized attachment but did not protect against development of indiscriminate behavior.

Drury et al. (2012), taking another approach, examined vulnerability within the context of BEIP. They examined the effect of the interaction between group status and functional polymorphisms in the serotonin transporter gene (5HTT) and in brain derived neurotrophic factor (BDNF) on levels of indiscriminate behavior over time. They demonstrated that children with the s/s 5httlpr genotype and the met66 carriers of BDNF ('plasticity genotypes') demonstrated the lowest levels of indiscriminate behavior in the children randomized to foster care but the highest levels in children randomized to care as usual (meaning more prolonged institutional care). Children with either the long allele of the 5httlpr or val/val genotype of BDNF demonstrated no difference in levels of indiscriminate behaviors over time and no group by genotype interaction. Although replication is needed, these findings support a 'differential susceptibility' model of gene x environment interactions in children exposed to deprivation (Belsky, Bakermans-Kranenburg, & van IJzendoorn, 2007). The findings also suggest why only some children exposed to serious adversity might develop indiscriminate behavior.

# Correlates of RAD and DSED

## Selective attachment and attachment disorders

A central construct with which attachment disorders must be compared is the presence of and quality of selective attachment to caregivers. Typically, selective attachments are characterized by infant and young child behavior in the Strange Situation and classified as secure, avoidant, resistant, or disorganized. Before considering how this approach maps onto disorders, however, we note studies that have looked at the more basic question of whether children even have a preferred caregiver. The validity of asking institutional caregivers whether young children show preferences is not established, but these caregivers in our experience generally converge in their opinions about which children prefer which caregivers if at all.

In a study of institutionalized Romanian children, Zeanah et al. (2002) found that children 11–68 months who had a 'favorite' caregiver showed similar rates of indiscriminate behavior as their peers without an identified preferred caregiver. In contrast, Soares et al. (2014), studying young children in Portuguese institutions, found that those with a 'preferred caregiver' were less likely to display indiscriminate behavior, after controlling for prenatal and family risk conditions that preceded the child's institutionalization. In neither study was attachment to caregivers formally assessed.

Studies that have assessed attachment using the Strange Situation in currently institutionalized children (Dobrova-Krol et al., 2010; Vorria et al., 2003; Zeanah et al., 2005) have demonstrated children have high levels of disorganized and unclassifiable attachments in the Strange Situation when assessed with their institutional caregivers. Unclassifiable means that the child exhibited so little attachment behavior that it was not possible to identify a pattern of attachment.

With regard to RAD, the only study that has examined both classifications and disorders of attachment is the BEIP (Zeanah, Keyes, et al. 2003; Zeanah, Nelson, et al. 2003). Children between the ages of 11 and 31 months (cognitive age) who were living in institutions following abandonment were assessed with their favorite caregiver. If no favorite was identified, they were seen with a caregiver who worked with them regularly and knew them well. Signs of RAD were assessed by caregiver report. Of children with elevated scores for RAD, 53% were disorganized, 23% were secure, 22% were unclassifiable, and 5% were avoidant. There was no relationship between organized attachment and signs of RAD.

In addition to SSP classifications, investigators in the BEIP assigned a 5-point continuous rating of the degree to which attachment had formed based on behavior in the SSP. As predicted, there was convergence between ratings of fewer attachment behaviors in the SSP and signs of RAD as reported by caregivers. In addition, all of the young children living in institutions who were 'unclassifiable' in the SSP because they demonstrated no attachment behaviors were rated as having elevated signs of RAD (Zeanah et al., 2005). This is strong evidence that the phenotype of RAD is equivalent to lack of selected attachment.

Research relating signs of DSED to selective attachment has yielded a more complicated picture. Lyons-Ruth et al. (2009) studied an impoverished sample and found more indiscriminate behavior (coded from behavior toward the stranger in the SSP) in association with nonsecure attachment. Even so, they found that some securely attached children also exhibited indiscriminate behavior.

In the BEIP, for toddlers living in institutions, classifications of attachment were unrelated to indiscriminate behavior. In the same study, however, at 42 months, security of attachment was moderately and inversely associated with signs of DSED (Gleason et al., 2011). However, there were still some children with secure attachments who also showed high levels of indiscriminate behavior. When attachment classifications in preschool children were dichotomized into typical (secure, avoidant, or ambivalent) versus atypical (disorganized, controlling, or insecure-other), atypical attachment was moderately associated with signs of DSED.

These findings are similar to reports that focused on children adopted out of Romanian institutions. Markovitch et al. (1997) reported that almost half of 3–5 year old adoptees from Romanian institutions who were securely attached to their mothers also exhibited indiscriminate behavior with the stranger, but none of the securely attached control children did so. Chisholm and colleagues also reported some children rated as securely attached also had high levels of indiscriminate behavior (Chisholm, 1998; Chisholm, Carter, Ames, & Morison, 1995). In the ERAS, although there was an association between insecure-other and indiscriminate behavior, there also were securely attached children who also had high levels of indiscriminate behavior (O'Connor et al., 2003). In a study of girls adopted from China out of institutions and foster care, on the other hand, indiscriminate behavior was elevated compared to nonadopted children, but there was no relationship between indiscriminate behavior and either a secure or a disorganized attachment (Van Den Dries et al., 2012).

To summarize, children with fully formed selective attachments do not appear to exhibit signs of RAD. Children with RAD exhibit few or minimal behaviors suggesting that they have formed selective or organized attachments to anyone. Although children with avoidant attachments may seem to lack comfort seeking, and children with resistant attachments may seem to display emotion regulation problems, neither shows the pervasive lack of preference, affective disturbance and lack of responsiveness that is seen in RAD. Furthermore, one would not base a diagnosis solely on a child's behavior in a brief, contrived laboratory paradigm.

In contrast, children with signs of DSED may or may not have selective attachments. In fact, children with DSED may have no attachments, disorganized attachments, insecure attachments or even secure attachments (Bakermans-Kranenberg, Dobrova-Krol et al., 2011; Bakermans-Kranenburg, Steele, et al. 2011; Zeanah & Gleason, 2010). This is one of the major reasons that DSED is not conceptualized as an attachment disorder, though some have argued that the presence of indiscriminate behavior in securely attached children may indicate a lack of true security. Longitudinal studies of securely attached children with and without indiscriminate behavior and insecurely attached children with and without indiscriminate behavior could contribute to our understanding of the relative significance of these patterns of behavior. In children with more extreme or aberrant forms of attachment, such as disorganized or insecure-other, the prevalence of DSED is increased, but attachment disordered behaviors are largely distinct from behaviors seen in different attachment classifications.

What distinguishes disorders of attachment from classifications or patterns of attachment is that the former are clinical conditions that are evident crosscontextually and describe profound disturbances in the child's behavior with caregiving as well as unfamiliar adults (AACAP, 2014; O'Connor & Zeanah, 2003; Zeanah, Mammen, & Lieberman, 1993; Zeanah, Berlin, & Boris, 2011). Insecure or disorganized attachments may be associated with interpersonal difficulties concurrently or subsequently, but they are relationship specific patterns of behavior, so the child's behavior with one adult may be secure and with another insecure. Signs of attachment disorders may have some fluctuations of intensity, but they are present across interactions with different individuals and in different situations. Essentially patterns of attachment operate as risk factors for maladjustment rather than having maladjustment as intrinsic features.

## Clinical correlates and co-morbidity

*Developmental delays.* Serious caregiving adversity is required for a diagnosis of RAD or DSED, and the same deprivation often concomitantly leads to cognitive delays in affected children (Nelson et al., 2007). The extant literature, however, indicates that developmental delays explain neither the signs of RAD nor DSED. In BEIP, RAD was only modestly associated with DQ/IQ in children at 22, 30, and 42 months, and not associated at 54 months. Generally in studies of DSED, cognitive development has either not been associated or only modestly associated with indiscriminate behaviors in young children (Bruce et al., 2009; Chisholm, 1998; O'Connor, Bredenkamp, & Rutter, 1999).

*Autistic spectrum disorders.* The presence of autistic spectrum disorders (ASD) is considered an exclusionary condition for diagnosing RAD (American Psychiatric Association, 2013; World Health Organization, 1992). This exclusionary criterion is intended to distinguish between aberrant social behavior induced by severe neglect and deprivation from that induced by intrinsic central nervous system abnormalities such as autistic spectrum disorders (WHO, 1992; Zeanah, 1996). Both RAD and ASDs are characterized by limited social reciprocity, although RAD is not associated with atypical language development and children with autism may demonstrate focused attachment behaviors (Gleason et al., 2011; Rutgers, Bakermans-Kranenburg, Ijzendoorn, & Berckelaer-Onnes, 2004). The ICD-10 indicates that children with RAD have the capacity for social reciprocity, may have delayed but not stereotyped language (World Health Organization, 1992).

The clinical differential diagnosis is complicated by the findings that 9.2% of previously institutionalized adopted children can demonstrate 'quasi-autism,' in which they meet the diagnostic criteria for autism on the Autism Diagnostic Inventory (Rutter et al., 2007). Quasi-autism is differentiated by normal head circumference, the equal distribution by gender, and most notably, improvement when the child is placed in families. In fact, at age 11, one-quarter of children with quasi-autism at 6 no longer had signs of autism (Rutter et al., 2007). Curiously, in ERAS, children with quasi-autism also showed high rates of co-occurring indiscriminate behavior (Rutter et al., 2010).

*Internalizing and externalizing symptomatology.* Given the emotional impairments in RAD and the intrusive behaviors in DSED, it is reasonable to consider a possible convergence between signs of RAD and internalizing problems and between signs of DSED and externalizing problems. Several studies have identified modest to moderate correlations between signs of RAD and DSED and internalizing and externalizing behavior problems in the predicted directions (O'Connor et al., 2003; Smyke et al., 2002; Zeanah et al., 2002).

The clinical phenotypes of RAD and depression share reduced or absent positive affect and social withdrawal, but few studies have examined this specific association. In BEIP, children showed moderate-high associations between signs of RAD and depression at multiple time points from 22 months to 54 months, but most children with a depressive disorder did not meet criteria for RAD at 54 months (Gleason et al., 2011).

More studies have examined the association between DSED and externalizing behaviors, but findings on this question, have been mixed. Among institutionalized toddlers, Zeanah et al. (2002) found no relationships between caregiver reports of indiscriminate behavior and global ratings of aggression. Similarly, in the BEIP, there was no association between indiscriminate and aggressive behaviors in children 42 months and below (Gleason et al., 2011; Zeanah et al., 2005).

In older children, however, signs of DSED have been more consistently associated with inattention/overactivity and other externalizing behaviors. For example, in BEIP, signs of DSED were associated with signs of ADHD and modestly associated with signs of disruptive behavior disorders at 54 months (Gleason et al., 2011). This outcome replicates similar findings in Romanian adoptees with mean ages of 54–72 months (Chisholm, 1998; Rutter et al., 2007; Stevens et al., 2008). However, despite these correlations, it seems clear from these findings that ADHD and DSED are distinct clinical entities. For example, in BEIP, only 4 of the 20 children who met criteria for ADHD also met criteria for DSED and only 4 of the 16 children who met criteria for DSED also met criteria for ADHD (Gleason et al., 2011).

## Neurobiology

To understand the neurobiology of attachment disorders, we first consider the context provided by recent findings about the neurobiological effects of deprivation from studies of children raised in institutions (see Nelson, Bos, Gunnar, & Sonuga-Barke, 2011; Nelson, Fox, & Zeanah, 2014; for more detailed reviews). Briefly, both structure and functioning of the brain have shown to be altered in currently and formerly institutionalized children, at least for those who were raised in these settings for significant periods of time and beyond 6 months of age. Consistent structural findings are reductions in both gray and white matter volumes in children who experienced institutional deprivation (Eluvathingal et al., 2006; Mehta et al., 2009; Sheridan, Fox, Zeanah, McLaughlin, & Nelson, 2012), compatible with reduced electrical activity in higher frequencies and increased electrical activities in lower frequencies (Marshall & Fox, 2004; Marshall, Reeb, Fox, Nelson, & Zeanah, 2008; Tarullo, Garvin, & Gunnar, 2011; Vanderwert, Marshall, Nelson, Zeanah, & Fox, 2010). These changes may be lasting, but for children placed with families before 24 months, Vanderwert et al. (2010) demonstrated normalization of brain functioning by age 8 years. In addition, specific disruptions in connectivity between amygdala and prefrontal cortex have been demonstrated in postinstitutionalized children (Govindan, Behen, Helder, Makki, & Chugani, 2010).

Because of demonstrated associations between signs of ADHD and indiscriminate behavior (Roy, Pickles & Rutter, 2004; Gleason et al., 2011), several studies have examined inhibitory control, a construct demonstrated to be dependent upon ventral frontostriatal circuitry (Durston et al., 2002). Using laboratory assessments such as the Stroop, go-nogo, or Bear-Dragon task, independent studies have demonstrated predicted inverse associations between inhibitory control and indiscriminate social behaviors in young children, though the convergence has been modest to moderate (Bruce et al., 2009; Gleason et al., 2011; Pears et al., 2010).

Tarullo et al. (2011) assessed in three groups of children: 18-month-old adopted postinstitutionalized children, nonadopted children, and children adopted internationally from foster care. Postinstitutionalized children had an atypical EEG power distribution, with relative power increased in lower frequency bands compared with nonadopted children. Both internationally adopted groups had lower absolute alpha power than nonadopted children. Atypical EEG power distribution at 18 months predicted indiscriminate behavior and poorer inhibitory control at 36 months. Both postinstitutionalized and foster care children were more likely than nonadopted children to exhibit indiscriminate behavior. They proposed that cortical hypo-activation from early deprivation might explain both reduced EEG power and the association with indiscriminate behavior.

Another approach to exploring the neurobiology of indiscriminate behavior has been functional MRI. Olsavsky et al. (2013) used fMRI to demonstrate that children adopted from institutions showed reduced amygdala discrimination between mothers and strangers compared to children with no history of institutional rearing or adoption. Furthermore, reductions in mother–stranger discriminations were moderately associated with indiscriminate behavior, and those children with more prolonged institutional rearing showed reduced amygdala discrimination and more indiscriminate behavior.

All of these findings must be considered preliminary and in need of replication, but they do point to neurobiological susceptibility to the effects of deprivation on signs of DSED. More studies of neurobiological effects of deprivation should include signs of RAD and DSED as an outcome of interest.

## Course and Outcomes

### Stability of signs of RAD

Research is limited that addresses the natural course of RAD. The most relevant data is from BEIP. In this study, children were assessed for signs of RAD and DSED at baseline (mean of 22 months) and again at 30, 42, and 54 months of age (Gleason et al., 2011). Because the design included a care as usual group, it is possible to examine the stability of signs of these disorders in children who did not receive intervention beyond whatever child protection authorities provided for them.

There was at least moderate stability of the level of signs of RAD between each time point in the study for children randomized to care as usual for all comparisons except between 30 and 54 months. By age 54 months, when the trial ended, about half of these children were still living in institutional settings. For those children who remained continuously in institutions, stability of signs was even greater (Gleason et al., 2011).

More studies have examined the stability of signs of DSED, however. In BEIP, signs of DSED were moderately stable from 30 months to 54 months for children with a history of institutional care (Gleason et al., 2011). Among the continuously institutionalized group, stability was slightly higher. Tizard and colleagues reported significant stability in 'overfriendly' and attention seeking behavior from age 4 to 8 years in formerly institutionalized children, and noted that once established, over-friendly behavior was especially resistant to change (Tizard & Hodges, 1978; Tizard & Rees, 1975). At age 16, indiscriminate behavior with caregivers was reduced but evident with peers. Relations with peers were conflicted and superficial, for example, naming a recent acquaintance as a close friend (Hodges & Tizard, 1989).

For children who are adopted out of institutions, signs of DSED seem to show at least modest stability even years after adoption (Chisholm, 1998). In the ERAS, for example, there was modest stability in signs of indiscriminate behavior from six to eleven years of age (Rutter et al., 2007). Furthermore, Rutter et al. (2010) identified a group of 29 children who show continuously elevated signs of DSED from early childhood through 15 years of age. Lawler et al. (2014) showed diminution in signs of physical (but not non-physical) social engagement with a stranger in young children adopted internationally from institutions and foster care over an 8-month beginning 1–3 months after adoption.

### Functional impairment and RAD and DSED

A number of longitudinal studies of children raised in institutions, many of whom have signs of RAD, have implicitly described functional impairment years later, particularly with regard to problematic interpersonal relationships (Chisholm, 1998; Hodges & Tizard, 1989; Rutter et al., 2007). The most direct evidence on this point at least in early childhood, comes from BEIP, in which signs of RAD were associated with concurrently assessed lack of social competence at 30 and 42 months and with functional impairment at 54 months. Signs of RAD at each age predicted future functional impairment in the children randomized to continued institutional care, especially in the children who remained institutionalized through 54 months of age (Gleason et al., 2011).

Similarly, signs of DSED in the same study were concurrently associated with lack of social-emotional competence at 30 and 42 months and with functional impairment at 54 months. Signs of DSED at 42 months predicted impairment at 54 months, but signs at 22 months and 30 months did not (Gleason et al., 2011). The peer relational abnormalities in adolescents in the Tizard study also reflect functional impairment associated with indiscriminate behavior (Hodges & Tizard, 1989).

Rutter et al. (2007) reported an increase in use of mental health services and more special education in children with histories of institutional rearing who showed indiscriminate behavior. Additionally, children showed impaired peer relationships and higher rates of psychopathology. Lyons-Ruth also showed that toddlers who were indiscriminate with strangers showed more aggressive and hyperactive behavior problems in kindergarten (Lyons-Ruth et al., 2009).

## Effects of Intervention

Studies designed as interventions for RAD and DSED are limited. Primarily, the research that has been conducted is the natural experiment provided by adoption of children from deprived institutions into advantaged families. Since signs of RAD and DSED have been identified in young children being raised in institutions (Smyke et al., 2002; Tizard & Rees, 1975; Zeanah et al., 2005), the 'intervention' in these studies is being adopted into families. Implicit in these studies is the notion that the enhanced caregiving following adoption will ameliorate signs of attachment disorders. Because inadequate care is etiologic, it is reasonable to consider that fostering or adoption will lead to elimination or at least substantial reduction of signs of the disorders.

### Intervention for RAD

A striking finding in studies of children adopted out of institutions is that there are no reports of children with RAD. In the Tizard study, although indiscriminate behavior persisted in some children after adoption or return to biological parents, the inhibited phenotype that was evident in institutionalized children at age 4 years was no longer present at age 8 or 16 years (Hodges & Tizard, 1989; Tizard & Hodges, 1978; Tizard & Rees, 1975). In the Canadian and English studies of children adopted from Romanian institutions, signs of DSED were readily apparent, but there were no reports of children with RAD, even in the initial assessments (Chisholm et al., 1995; O'Connor et al., 1999). This suggests that signs of RAD diminish or disappear once the child is placed in a more normative caregiving environment.

A more intentional intervention for RAD was undertaken in BEIP. This RCT demonstrated that signs of RAD were evident in young children living in institutions (average age 22 months) (Zeanah et al., 2005) and that they persisted through 54 months of age (endpoint of the trial) in children randomized to care as usual (Smyke et al., 2012). In contrast, for those randomized to foster care, signs of RAD diminished by the first follow-up at 30 months of age to levels comparable to never institutionalized children, and remained so at 42 and 54 months of age (Smyke et al., 2012). In contrast, those in the care as usual group remained significantly higher than signs of RAD in children in foster care at every follow-up point. For the subset of children in the care as usual group who remained institutionalized through 54 months of age, there was no diminution in signs of RAD over time.

Taken together with the adoption findings, the implication is that once children are placed in families and receive adequate care, signs of RAD in affected children diminish substantially and disappear in most cases. Still more research could be useful. For example, we lack longitudinal studies that could address whether signs of RAD diminish weeks or months after placement in foster care.

Less clear is whether additional interventions beyond family placement may be necessary in children who develop RAD in order to promote secure and healthy attachments. Dozier, Stovall, Albus, and Bates (2001) found that maltreated young children placed in foster care could form secure attachments to their caregivers at rates comparable to never maltreated children but only if foster mothers were themselves securely attached. If the mothers were not securely attached, the probability of disorganized attachments increased substantially. Steele et al. (2008) reported similar findings about maltreated children adopted out of foster care. Since research indicates that secure attachment in young children is fostered by caregivers who are emotionally available and sensitively responsive, evidenced based interventions aimed at these targets are reasonable starting points for augmenting adoptions or fostering for children with RAD (see Bernard et al., 2012; Hoffman, Marvin, Copper, & Powell, 2006; Juffer, Bakersman-Kranenburg, & van IJzendoorn, 2007).

## Intervention for DSED

Tizard's longitudinal study demonstrated both the persistence of indiscriminate behavior and its reduction following adoption (Hodges & Tizard, 1989; Tizard & Hodges, 1978; Tizard & Rees, 1975). Subsequent longitudinal adoption studies have yielded similarly mixed results about the effectiveness of enhanced caregiving in studies of young children adopted out of institutions (Chisholm, 1998; Rutter et al., 2010).

Two longitudinal studies of young children adopted from Romanian institutions in the post-Ceausescu era both demonstrated the persistence of signs of DSED in some children even after they had formed attachments to their adoptive parents. The first was a longitudinal study of young children adopted into Canada from Romanian institutions that found significant increases in parent reports of attachment during the first several years following adoption but no comparable decreases in indiscriminate behavior over time (Chisholm, 1998). Similarly, in the ERAS of children adopted into UK families from Romanian institutions, investigators assessed signs of DSED at ages 4, 6, 11, and 15 years (O'Connor & Rutter, 2000; O'Connor et al., 2003; Rutter et al., 2007, 2010). They reported little change in the numbers of children with high levels of indiscriminate behaviors between 4 and 6 years, but some decline by age 11 years (O'Connor & Rutter, 2000; Rutter et al., 2007). Curiously, however, they did not find that quality of care in adoptive homes was related to indiscriminate behavior. This could mean that there is a threshold of caregiving quality after which remediation of DSED is not further enhanced.

In the BEIP, there was a modest, but statistically significant decline in signs of DSED with the foster care intervention, although rates were significantly lower in the never institutionalized group (Smyke et al., 2012). Importantly, within the foster care group, placement before 24 months of age predicted the lowest level of DSED, compatible with a timing of intervention effect.

As with RAD, the caregiving that should be provided for children with DSED, as best we can determine, is the same caregiving that is known to lead to secure attachment formation. That is, sensitive and responsive care, in which the parent identifies and responds to the child's needs. Evidenced based interventions with maltreated children have been shown to enhance attachment and should be attempted with children with DSED (Bernard et al., 2012; Cicchetti, Rogosch, & Toth, 2006).

Although adequate caregiving seems both to prevent and to ameliorate DSED, the persistence of signs of DSED in some children indicates that additional strategies and approaches beyond an enhancement of caregiving are needed. Given that social cognitive abnormalities plausibly underlie the social boundary violations and disinhibition that characterize the disorder, interventions that target these features seem promising areas to explore.

## Conclusions about interventions for RAD and DSED

In summary, virtually all children with RAD seem to respond to enhanced caregiving, whereas only some with DSED respond to enhanced caregiving. The incomplete remediation for those with DSED could reflect individual differences in responsiveness to caregiving (see Drury et al., 2012) or incomplete remediation in those who were most severely affected initially. The degree to which enhanced care and symptom reduction in these children reduces subsequent social and emotional problems is not yet established. In our view, augmented and additional interventions should be explored both for children diagnosed with RAD and especially DSED.

## Future Directions

Reactive attachment disorder and DSED have been subjected to more systematic research in the past 10 years than in the 25 years that followed their original description in DSM-III (APA, 1980). Though there is now an emerging consensus about the basic phenomenology of the disorders, much remains to be determined. Several directions for research seem promising for illuminating remaining questions:

1.  Given that severe social neglect seems necessary for these disorders to occur, a vexing question is what vulnerability factors might give rise to the very different phenotypes in RAD and DSED. There has been speculation about temperamental differences that might predispose to one or another phenotypes, since both behavioral inhibition and high sociability are known temperamental dispositions (Zeanah & Fox, 2004), but this is exceedingly difficult to study since it is hard to assess temperament in children who will subsequently develop attachment disorders. Also, the underlying neurobiological substrates of these dispositions are not known. In fact, vulnerability has only begun to be explored in DSED, and as yet, no studies have addressed vulnerability to RAD. There is a question of a sensitive period in the vulnerability to DSED, as deprivation that occurs before the first 6 months and after 24 months of age seem far less likely to lead to the clinical picture, but the data remain thin on which this preliminary conclusion rests.

2.  Related to the first point, we have little understanding of the mechanisms by which insufficient care or social neglect lead to the phenotypes defined by RAD and DSED. In particular, although some initial findings about the neurobiology of DSED have appeared, no clear story has yet emerged about either disorder. No studies have addressed the neurobiology of RAD. Progress in understanding the circuitry involved in symptomatology could prove quite useful in better developing more effective interventions.

3.  Although social neglect is broadly implicated in etiology, the specifics of the caregiving insufficiencies that give rise to the two disorders – how similar or different they are – is not known. This is a challenging issue to study for many reasons, but better understanding these features would be useful both for treatment and prevention.

4.  RAD appears exceedingly responsive to enhanced caregiving. Less clear is whether children who recover from RAD remain at risk for subsequent interpersonal difficulties. More longitudinal studies of children diagnosed in the early years with RAD would help us determine which factors increase risk for problematic trajectories.

5.  DESD is less responsive to enhanced caregiving, and additional interventions to remediate signs of the disorder seem indicated, at least in children for whom the disorder persists after placement in a stable family setting. Better elucidation of putative social cognitive abnormalities in affected children could be an important contribution to effective interventions.

6.  These disorders have been studied most systematically in younger children. Follow-ups of the sequelae of these disorders in later childhood, adolescence or adulthood are needed, including peer relationships and interpersonal competence. Also, the question of if and how their symptomatology changes in middle childhood and adolescence needs more careful study. Also, reconciling the different views of the phenomenology of attachment disorders in older children should be a priority. These are additional areas in which longitudinal studies could prove especially valuable.

---

### Key Points

- RAD and DSED represent disorders that appear in some children with histories of living in contexts that limit opportunities to form selective attachments, such as being raised in impersonal institutional settings, social neglect, and frequent changes in foster care.
- Much has been learned in the past decade, although little is known about mechanisms by which insufficient caregiving leads to the two phenotypes of RAD and DSED and also about the longterm sequelae of these disorders.
- RAD is very responsive to enhanced caregiving. But DSED is somewhat less responsive for reasons that are unclear.
- Although high-quality caregiving is an important ingredient to help children recover from both of these disorders, additional interventions may be needed and much remains to be learned about what those additional components should be. More studies of intervention are needed to address these questions.

# References

Ainsworth, M. D. S., Blehar, M. S., Waters, E., & Wall, S. (1978). *Patterns of attachment: A psychological study of the strange situation.* Hillsdale, NJ: Erlbaum.

American Psychiatric Association (1980). *Diagnostic and statistical manual of mental disorders, third edition (DSM-III).* Washington, DC: American Psychiatric Association.

American Psychiatric Association (1987). *Diagnostic and statistical manual of mental disorders, third edition-revised (DSM-III-R).* Washington, DC: American Psychiatric Association.

American Psychiatric Association (1994). *Diagnostic and statistical manual of mental disorders, fourth edition (DSM-IV).* Washington, DC: American Psychiatric Association.

American Psychiatric Association (2013). *Diagnostic and statistical manual of mental disorders, fifth edition (DSM-5).* Washington, DC: American Psychiatric Association.

Bakermans-Kranenberg, M., Dobrova-Krol, N., & van IJzendoorn, M. (2011). Impact of institutional care on attachment disorganization and insecurity of Ukrainian preschoolers: Protective effect of the long variant of the serotonin transporter gene (5HTT). *International Journal of Behavioral Development, 36,* 1–8.

Bakermans-Kranenburg, M. J., Steele, H., Zeanah, C. H., Muhamedrahimov, R. J., Vorria, P., Dobrova-Krol, N. A., . . . & Gunnar, M. R. (2011). Attachment and emotional development in institutional care: Characteristics and catch-up. In R. B. McCall, M. H. van IJzendoorn, F. Juffer, V. K. Groza, & C. J. Groark (Eds.). *Children without permanent parental care: Research, practice, and policy. Monographs of the Society for Research in Child Development,* Serial No. 301, 76, 62–91.

Belsky, J., Bakermans-Kranenburg, M. J., & van IJzendoorn, M. H. (2007). For better and for worse: Differential susceptibility to environmental influences. *Current Directions in Psychological Science, 16,* 300–304.

Bernard, K., Dozier, M., Bick, J., Lewis-Morrarty, E., Lindhiem, O., & Carlson, E. (2012). Enhancing attachment organization among maltreated children: Results of a randomized clinical trial. *Child Development, 83,* 623–636.

Boris, N. W., Hinshaw-Fuselier, S. S., Smyke, A. T., Scheeringa, M. S., Heller, S. S., & Zeanah, C. H. (2004). Comparing criteria for attachment disorders: Establishing reliability and validity in high-risk samples. *Journal of the American Academy of Child and Adolescent Psychiatry, 43,* 568–577.

Boris, N. W., & Zeanah, C. H. (2005). Practice parameter for the assessment and treatment of children and adolescents with reactive attachment disorder of infancy and early childhood. *Journal of the American Academy of Child & Adolescent Psychiatry, 44* (11), 1206–1219.

Boris, N. W., Zeanah, C. H., Larrieu, J. A., Scheeringa, M. S., & Heller, S. S. (1998). Attachment disorders in infancy and early childhood: A preliminary investigation of diagnostic criteria. *American Journal of Psychiatry, 155,* 295–297.

Bruce, J., Tarullo, A. R., & Gunnar, M. R. (2009). Disinhibited social behavior among internationally adopted children. *Development and Psychopathology, 21,* 157–171.

Carlson, V., Cicchetti, D., Barnett, D., & Braunwald, K. (1989). Disorganized/disoriented attachment relationships in maltreated infants. *Developmental Psychology, 25,* 525–531.

Chisholm, K. (1998). A three-year follow-up of attachment and indiscriminate friendliness in children adopted from Romanian orphanages. *Child Development, 69,* 1092–1106.

Chisholm, K., Carter, M. C., Ames, E. W., & Morison, S. J. (1995). Attachment security and indiscriminate friendly behavior in children adopted from Romanian orphanages. *Development and Psychopathology, 7,* 283–294.

Cicchetti, D., Rogosch, F. A., & Toth, S. L. (2006). Fostering secure attachments in infants in maltreating families through preventive interventions. *Development and Psychopathology, 18,* 623–645.

Dobrova-Krol, N. A., Bakermans-Kranenburg, M. J., van IJzendoorn, M. H., & Juffer, F. (2010). The importance of quality of care: Effects of perinatal HIV infection and early institutional rearing on preschoolers' attachment and indiscriminate friendliness. *Journal of Child Psychology Psychiatry, 51,* 1368–1376.

Dozier, M., Stovall, K. C., Albus, K. E., & Bates, B. (2001). Attachment for infants in foster care: The role of caregiver state of mind. *Child Development, 72,* 1467–1477.

Drury, S. S., Gleason, M. M., Theall, K. P., Smyke, A. T., Nelson, C. A., Fox, N. A., & Zeanah, C. H. (2012). Genetic sensitivity to the caregiving context: The influence of 5httlpr and BDNF val66met on indiscriminate social behavior. *Physiology and Behavior, 106,* 728–735.

Durston, S., Thomas, K. M., Yang, Y., Ulug, A. M., Zimmerman, R. D., & Casey, B. J. (2002). A neural basis for the development of inhibitory control. *Developmental Science, 5,* F9–F16.

Dykens, E. M. (2003). Anxiety, fears, and phobias in persons with Williams syndrome. *Developmental Neuropsychology, 23,* 291–316.

Eluvathingal, T. J., Chugani, H. T., Behen, M. E., Juhász, C., Muzik, O., Maqbool, M., . . . & Makki, M. (2006). Abnormal brain connectivity in children after early severe socioemotional deprivation: A diffusion tensor imaging study. *Pediatrics, 117,* 2093–2100.

Gaensbauer, T. J., & Harmon, R. J. (1982). Attachment in abused/neglected and premature infants. In R. N. Emde, & R. J. Harmon (Eds.). *The development of attachment and affiliative systems* (pp. 263–288). New York, NY: Plenum Press.

Gaensbauer, T. J., & Sands, M. (1979). Distorted affective communications in abused/neglected infants and their potential impact on caregivers. *Journal of the American Academy of Child and Adolescent Psychiatry, 18*, 236–250.

Garvin, M. C., Tarullo, A. R., Van Ryzin, M., & Gunnar, M. R. (2012). Post-adoption parenting and socioemotional development in post-institutionalized children. *Development and Psychopathology, 24*, 35–48.

George, M., & Main, M. (1979). Social behavior in maltreated children: Approach, avoidance and aggression. *Child Development, 50*, 306–318.

Gleason, M. M., Fox, N. A., Drury, S., Smyke, A. T., Egger, H. L., Nelson, C. A., Gregas, M. G., & Zeanah, C. H. (2011). The validity of evidence-derived criteria for reactive attachment disorder: Indiscriminately social/disinhibited and emotionally withdrawn/inhibited types. *Journal of the American Academy of Child and Adolescent Psychiatry, 50*, 216–231.

Gleason, M. M., Fox, N. A., Drury, S. S., Smyke, A. T., Nelson, C. A., & Zeanah, C. H. (2014). Indiscriminate behaviors in young children with a history of institutional care. *Pediatrics, 133*, 657–665.

Goldfarb, W. (1945). Effects of psychological deprivation in infancy. *American Journal of Psychiatry, 102*, 18–33.

Govindan, R. J., Behen, M. E., Helder, E., Makki, M. I., & Chugani, H. T. (2010). Altered water diffusivity in cortical association tracts in children with early deprivation identified with Tract-based Spatial Statistics (TBSS). *Cerebral Cortex, 20*, 561–569.

Green, J. (2003). Are attachment disorders best seen as social impairment disorders? *Attachment and Human Development, 5*, 259–264.

Hodges, J., & Tizard, B. (1989). Social and family relationships of ex-institutional adolescents. *Journal of Child Psychology and Psychiatry, 30*, 77–97.

Hoffman, K., Marvin, R., Cooper, G., & Powell, B. (2006). Changing toddlers' and preschoolers' attachment classifications: The Circle of Security Intervention. *Journal of Consulting and Clinical Psychology, 74*, 1017–1026.

Johnson, A., Bruce, J., Tarullo, A. R., & Gunnar, M. R. (2011). Growth delay as an index of allostatic load in young children: Predictions to disinhibited social approach and diurnal cortisol activity. *Development and Psychopathology, 23*, 859–871.

Juffer, F., Bakersman-Kranenburg, M., & van IJzendoorn, M. H. (2007). *Promoting positive parenting: An attachment-based intervention*. Mahwah, NJ: Lawrence Erlbaum.

Kay, C., & Green, J. (2013). Reactive attachment disorder: Systematic evidence beyond the institution. *Journal of Abnormal Psychology, 41*, 571–581.

Lawler, J. M., Hostinar, C. E., Mliner, S., & Gunnar, M. R. (2014). Disinhibited social engagement in post-institutionalized children: Differentiating normal from atypical behavior. *Development and Psychopathology, 26*, 451–464.

Levy, R. J. (1947). Effects of institutional care vs. boarding home care on a group of infants. *Journal of Personality, 15*, 233–241.

Lyons-Ruth, K., Bureau, J.-F., Riley, C. D., & Atlas-Corbett, A. F. (2009). Socially indiscriminate attachment behavior in the strange situation: Convergent and discriminant validity in relation to caregiving risk, later behavior problems, and attachment insecurity. *Development and Psychopathology, 21*, 355–367.

Markovitch, S., Goldberg, S., Gold, A., Washington, J., Wasson, C., Krekewich, K., & Handley-Berry, M. (1997). Determinants of behavioural problems in Romanian children adopted in Ontario. *International Journal of Behavioral Development, 20*, 17–31.

Marshall, P. J., Fox, N. A., & the BEIP Core Group. (2004). A comparison of the electroencephalogram between institutionalized and community children in Romania. *Journal of Cognitive Neuroscience, 16*, 1327–1338.

Marshall, P. J., Reeb, B., Fox, N. A., Nelson, C. A., & Zeanah, C. H. (2008). Effects of early intervention on EEG power and coherence in previously institutionalized children in Romania. *Development and Psychopathology, 20*, 861–880.

Mehta, M. A., Golembo, N. I., Nosarti, C., Colvert, E., Mota, A., Williams, S. C., . . . & Sonuga-Barke, E. J. (2009). Amygdala, hippocampal and corpus callosum size following severe early institutional deprivation: The English and Romanian Adoptees study pilot. *Journal of Child Psychology & Psychiatry, 50*, 943–951.

Millward, R., Kennedy, E., Towlson, K., & Minnis, H. (2006). Reactive attachment disorder in looked after children. *Emotional and Behavioural Difficulties, 11*, 273–279.

Minnis, H., Green, J., O'Connor, T. G., Liew, A., Glaser, D., Taylor, E., . . . & Sadiq, F. A. (2009). An exploratory study of the association between reactive attachment disorder and attachment narratives in early school-age children. *Journal of Child Psychology and Psychiatry, 150*, 931–942.

Minnis, H., Marwick, H., Arthur, J., & McLaughlin, A. (2006). Reactive attachment disorder: A theoretical model beyond attachment. *European Child & Adolescent Psychiatry, 15*, 336.

Minnis, H., McMillan, S., Prichett, R., Young, D., Wallace, B., Butcher, J., . . . & Gillberg, C. (2013). Prevalence of reactive attachment disorder in a deprived population. *British Journal of Psychiatry, 202*, 342–346.

Minnis, H., Reekie, J., Young, D., O'Connor, T., Ronald, A., Gray, A., & Plomin, R. (2007). Genetic, environmental and gender influences on attachment disorder behaviours. *British Journal of Psychiatry, 190*, 490–495.

Nelson, C. A., Bos, K., Gunnar, M., & Sonuga-Barke, E. J. S. (2011). The neurobiological toll of human deprivation. In R. B. McCall, M. H. van IJzendoorn, F. Juffer, V. K. Groza, & C. J. Groark (Eds.). *Children without permanent parental care: Research, practice, and policy. Monographs of the Society for Research in Child Development*, Serial No. 301, 76, 127–146.

Nelson, C. A., Fox, N. A., & Zeanah, C. H. (2014). *Romania's abandoned children: Deprivation, brain development and the struggle for recovery*. Cambridge: Harvard University Press.

Nelson, C. A., Zeanah, C. H., Fox, N. A., Marshall, P. J., Smyke, A. T., & Guthrie, D. (2007). Cognitive recovery in socially deprived young children: The Bucharest early intervention project. *Science, 318*, 1937–1940.

O'Connor, T. G., Bredenkamp, D., & Rutter, M. (1999). Attachment disturbances and disorders in children exposed to early severe deprivation. *Infant Mental Health Journal, 20*, 10–29.

O'Connor, T. G., Marvin, R. S., Rutter, M., Olrick, J. T.,& Britner, P. A. (2003). Child–parent attachment following early institutional deprivation. *Development and Psychopathology, 15*, 19–38.

O'Connor, T. G., & Rutter, M. (2000). Attachment disorder behavior following early severe deprivation: Extension and longitudinal follow-up. *Journal of the American Academy of Child and Adolescent Psychiatry, 39*, 703–712.

O'Connor, T. G., & Zeanah, C. H. (2003). Assessment strategies and treatment approaches. *Attachment and Human Development, 5*, 223–244.

Oliveira, P. S., Soares, I., Martins, C., Silva, J. R., Marques, S., Baptista, J., & Lyons-Ruth, K.(2012). Indiscriminate behavior observed in the strange situation among institutionalized toddlers: Relations to caregiver report and early risk. *Infant Mental Health Journal, 33*, 187–196.

Olsavsky, A. K., Telzer, E. H., Shapiro, M., Humphreys, K. L., Flannery, J., Goff, B., & Tottenham, N. (2013). Indiscriminate amygdala response to mothers and strangers after early maternal deprivation. *Biological Psychiatry, 74*, 853–860.

Oosterman, M., & Schuengel, C. (2007). Autonomic reactivity of children to separation and reunion with foster parents. *Journal of the American Academy of Child and Adolescent Psychiatry, 46*, 1196–1203.

Pears, K. C., Bruce, J., Fisher, P. A., & Kim, H. (2010). Indiscriminate friendliness in maltreated foster children. *Child Maltreatment, 15*, 64–75.

Provence, S., & Lipton, R. C. (1962). *Infants in institutions*. New York, NY: International Universities Press.

Roy, P., Rutter, M., & Pickles, A. (2004). Institutional care: associations between overactivity and lack of selectivity in social relationships. *Journal of Child Psychology and Psychiatry, 45*, 866–873.

Rutgers, A. H., Bakermans-Kranenburg, M. J., Ijzendoorn, M. H., & Berckelaer-Onnes, I. A. (2004). Autism and attachment: A meta-analytic review. *Journal of Child Psychology and Psychiatry, 45*, 1123–1134.

Rutter, M., O'Connor, T. G., & the English and Romanian Adoptees (ERA) Study Team. (2004). Are there biological programming effects for psychological development? Findings from a study of Romanian adoptees. *Developmental Psychology, 40*, 81–94.

Rutter, M., Colvert, E., Kreppner, J., Beckett, C., Castle, J., Groothues C., . . . & Sonuga-Barke, E. J. (2007). Early adolescent outcomes for institutionally-deprived and non-deprived adoptees. *I: Disinhibited attachment. Journal of Child Psychology and Psychiatry, 48*, 17–30.

Rutter, M., Kreppner, J., & Sonuga-Barke, E. (2009). Emanuel Miller Lecture: Attachment insecurity, disinhibited attachment, and attachment disorders: Where do research findings leave the concepts? *Journal of Child Psychology and Psychiatry, 50*, 529–543.

Rutter, M., Sonuga-Barke, E. J., Beckett, C., Castle, J., Kreppner, J., Kumsta, R., . . . & Gunnar, M. R. (2010). Deprivation-specific psychological patterns: Effects of institutional deprivation. *Monographs of the Society for Research in Child Development, 75*, 1–252

Sheridan, M. A., Fox, N. A., Zeanah, C. H., McLaughlin, K. A., & Nelson, C. A. (2012). Variation in neural development as a result of exposure to institutionalization early in childhood. *Proceedings of the National Academy of Sciences, 109*, 12927–12932.

Smyke, A. T., Dumitrescu, A., & Zeanah, C. H. (2002). Disturbances of attachment in young children: I. *The continuum of caretaking casualty. Journal of the American Academy of Child and Adolescent Psychiatry, 41*, 972–982.

Smyke, A. T., Zeanah, C. H., Gleason, M. M., Drury, S. S., Fox, N. A., Nelson, C. A., & Guthrie, D. G. (2012). A randomized controlled trial of foster care vs. institutional care for children with signs of reactive attachment disorder. *American Journal of Psychiatry, 169*, 508–514.

Soares, I., Belsky, J., Mesquita, A. R., Osorio, A., & Sampaio, A. (2013). Why do only some institutionalized children become indiscriminately friendly? Insights from the study of Williams Syndrome. *Child Development Perspectives, 7*, 1–6.

Soares, I., Belsky, J., Oliveira, P., Silva, J., Marquesa, S., Baptista, J., & Martins, C. (2014). Does early family risk and current quality of care predict indiscriminate social behavior in institutionalized Portuguese children? *Attachment & Human Development, 16*, 137–148.

Sonuga-Barke, E. J., Beckett, C., Kreppner, J., Castle, J., Colvert, E., Stevens, S., Hawkins, A., & Rutter, M. (2008). Is sub-nutrition necessary for a poor outcome following early institutional deprivation? *Developmental Medicine & Child Neurology, 50*, 664–671.

Spitz, R. R. (1945). Hospitalism: An inquiry into the genesis of psychiatric conditions in early childhood. *Psychoanalytic Study of the Child, 1*, 54–74.

Steele, M., Hodges, J., Kaniuk, J., Steele, H., Hillman, S., & Asquith, K. (2008). Forecasting outcomes in previously maltreated children: The use of the AAI in a longitudinal adoption study. In H. Steele, & M. Steele (Eds.). *Clinical applications of the adult attachment interview* (pp. 427–451), New York, NY: Guilford Press.

Stevens, S. E., Sonuga-Barke, E. J. S., Kreppner, J., Beckett, C., Castle, J., Colvert, E., . . . & Rutter, M. (2008). Inattention/overactivity following early severe institutional deprivation: Presentations and associations in early adolescence. *Journal of Abnormal Child Psychology, 36* (3), 385–398.

Tarullo, A. R., Garvin, M. C., & Gunnar, M. (2011). Atypical EEG power correlates with indiscriminately friendly behavior in internationally adopted children. *Developmental Psychology, 47,* 417–431.

Tarullo, A. R., & Gunnar, M. (2005). Institutional rearing and deficits in social relatedness: Possible mechanisms and processes. *Cognition, Brain and Behavior, 9,* 329–342.

Tizard, B. (1977). *Adoption: A second chance.* London: Open Books.

Tizard, B., & Hodges, J. (1978). The effect of early institutional rearing on the development of eight-year-old children. *Journal of Child Psychology and Psychiatry, 19,* 99–118.

Tizard, B., & Rees, J. (1975). The effect of early institutional rearing on the behaviour problems and affectional relationships of four-year-old children. *Journal of Child Psychology and Psychiatry, 16,* 61–73.

Van Den Dries, L., Juffer, F., van Ijzendoorn, M. H., Bakermans-Kranenburg, M. J., & Alink, L. R. A. (2012). Infants' responsiveness, attachment, and indiscriminate friendliness after international adoption from institutions or foster care in China: Application of Emotional Availability Scales to adoptive families. *Development and Psychopathology, 24,* 49–64.

Vanderwert, R. E., Marshall, P. J., Nelson, C. A., Zeanah, C. H., & Fox, N. A. (2010). Timing of intervention affects brain electrical activity in children exposed to severe psychosocial neglect. *PLoS ONE, 5,* 1–5.

Vorria, P., Papaligoura, Z., Dunn, J., van IJzendoorn, M., Steele, H., Kontopoulou, A., & Sarafidou, E. (2003). Early experiences and attachment relationships of Greek infants raised in residential group care. *Journal of Child Psychology and Psychiatry, 44,* 1–14.

World Health Organization (1992). *The ICD-10 classification of mental and behavioral disorders: Clinical descriptions and diagnostic guidelines.* Geneva: World Health Organization.

Zeanah, C.H. (1996). Beyond insecurity: A reconceptualization of attachment disorders in infancy. *Journal of Consulting and Clinical Psychology, 64,* 42–52.

Zeanah, C. H., Berlin, L. J., & Boris, N. W. (2011). Practitioner review: Clinical applications of attachment theory and research for infants and young children. *Journal of Child Psychology, Psychiatry and Allied Disciplines, 52,* 819–833.

Zeanah, C. H., & Gleason, M. M. (2010). Reactive attachment disorder: A review for DSM-5. Available from: www.nrvcs.org/nrvattachmentresources/documents/APA%20DSM-5%20Reactive%20Attachment%20Disorder%20Review%5B1%5D.pdf [last accessed 15 October 2014].

Zeanah, C. H., Keyes, A., & Settles, L. (2003). Attachment relationship experiences and child psychopathology. *Annals of the New York Academy of Sciences, 1008,* 1–9.

Zeanah, C. H., Mammen, O., & Lieberman, A. (1993). Disorders of attachment. In C. Zeanah (Ed.). *Handbook of infant mental health* (pp. 332–349), New York, NY: Guilford Press.

Zeanah, C. H., Nelson, C. A., Fox, N. A., Smyke, A. T., Marshall, P., Parker, S., & Koga, S. (2003). Designing research to study the effects of institutionalization on brain and behavioral development: The Bucharest early intervention project. *Development and Psychopathology, 15,* 885–907.

Zeanah, C. H., & Fox, N. A. (2004). Temperament and attachment disorders. *Journal of Consulting Clinical Psychology, 33,* 32–41.

Zeanah, C. H., Scheeringa, M. S., Boris, N. W., Heller, S. S., Smyke, A. T., & Trapani, J. (2004). Reactive attachment disorder in maltreated toddlers. *Child Abuse and Neglect: The International Journal, 28,* 877–888.

Zeanah, C. H., & Smyke, A. T. (2015). Attachment disorders and severe deprivation. In M. Rutter, D. Bishop, D. Pine, S. Scott, J. Stevenson, E. Taylor, & A. Thapar (Eds.). *Rutter's child and adolescent psychiatry* (pp. 795–805), London: Blackwell.

Zeanah, C. H., & Smyke, A. T. (2009). Disorders of attachment. In C. H. Zeanah (Ed.). *Handbook of infant mental health* (3rd edn.) (pp. 421–434). New York, NY: Guilford Press.

Zeanah, C. H., Smyke, A. T., & Dumitrescu, A. (2002). Disturbances of attachment in young children: II. Indiscriminate behavior and institutional care. *Journal of the American Academy of Child and Adolescent Psychiatry, 41,* 983–989.

Zeanah, C. H., Smyke, A. T., Koga, S., Carlson, E., & the BEIP Core Group (2005). Attachment in institutionalized and community children in Romania. *Child Development, 76,* 1015–1028.

# 11

# Attachment Disorders Versus More Common Problems in Looked After and Adopted Children
## Comparing Community and Expert Assessments

Matt Woolgar and Emma Baldock

## Introduction

The ICD-10 diagnoses of Reactive and Disinhibited Attachment Disorders of infancy and early childhood (RAD/DAD; F94.1/F94.2) occur when infants and young children have not had the opportunity to form attachments to primary caregivers, usually because of 'grossly inadequate childcare' or 'extremely frequent changes in caregivers' (World Health Organization [WHO], 1992). Disruptions to early caregiving are almost always present for adopted and looked after children, but are not sufficient to indicate a diagnosis of either RAD or DAD. Indeed, although the prevalence of these attachment disorders is not well-established, they are thought to be uncommon (Haugaard & Hazan, 2004; Zeanah & Smyke, 2009), even in populations experiencing significant social and familial risks (Zeanah, Berlin & Boris, 2011). Nevertheless, there has been a wide dissemination of attachment disorder constructs that are unrelated either to the ICD-10 or DSM-IV diagnostic classifications, or indeed to attachment theory and research (Prior & Glaser, 2006) and many carers of adopted and fostered children request attachment based diagnoses and treatments (Barth, Crea, John, Thoburn & Quinton, 2005). The problem of the overdiagnosis of attachment disorders and generic attachment problems is reflected in the practice parameters for the assessment and treatment of maltreated children (Chaffin et al., 2006), which emphasise the importance of avoiding the 'allure of rare disorders' (Haugaard, 2004, p. 127) especially attachment disorders and attachment problems: 'Although more common diagnoses, such as ADHD, conduct disorder, PTSD or adjustment disorder, may be less exciting, they should be considered as first line diagnoses *before contemplating any rare condition, such as RAD or an unspecified attachment disorder*' (Chaffin et al., 2006, p. 82; italics added). The practice parameter also stresses the importance of neurodevelopmental assessments, especially important in the light of accumulating evidence about the impact of early maltreatment and neglect on neurobiological development (e.g., Gunnar & Fisher, 2006; McCrory, De Brito & Viding, 2010).

Identifying common disorders such as ADHD and conduct disorder facilitates access to evidence based treatments. Similarly, identifying neurodevelopmental problems can clarify complex behaviour and maximise educational opportunities. Unspecified attachment problem constructs, on the other hand, can lead to treatments that are not well grounded in evidence or theory and may even be dangerous (Chaffin et al., 2006). Other guidelines recommend attachment disorders should be assessed by suitably skilled and experienced clinicians, able to consider the full range of possible disorders (American Academy of Child and Adolescent Psychiatry [AACAP] (2005).

*Source:* Republished with permission of John Wiley & Sons, Inc., from Matt Woolgar, Emma Baldock, "Attachment disorders versus more common problems in looked after and adopted children: comparing community and expert assessments," pp. 34–40 from *Child and Adolescent Mental Health* 20:1 (February 2015); permission conveyed through Copyright Clearance Center, Inc.

*Attachment Theory and Research: A Reader*, First Edition. Edited by Tommie Forslund and Robbie Duschinsky.
© 2021 John Wiley & Sons Ltd. Published 2021 by John Wiley & Sons Ltd.

Little is currently known about the prevalence of mental health problems in adopted children in the United Kingdom. However, most are adopted from local authority care and will have been a looked after child at some stage (BAAF, 2011). Fortunately, we have good evidence about the mental health of looked after children within the United Kingdom (Ford, Vostanis, Meltzer & Goodman, 2007; Meltzer, Gatward, Corbin, Goodman, & Ford, 2003) which also provides our best current estimate for the prevalence of psychiatric disorder in the UK adopted population. These studies are based upon a large, nationally representative sample of over 1500 looked after children in the United Kingdom. Mental health data were assessed using a well-validated, structured clinical interview conducted with all carers, and children over the age of 11, supplemented by teacher reports of an abbreviated version. The data for looked after children was compared with over 10,000 children living in private households, split into socially disadvantaged and non-disadvantaged groups. These data reveal significantly elevated rates of common disorders such as conduct problems, ADHD, learning problems and neurodevelopmental disorders compared with children in birth families including those in high levels of social and economic adversity. Interestingly, attachment problems in the same sample were low at around 2%, using an operationalisation broadly consistent with ICD-10 definitions for RAD/DAD (Meltzer et al., 2003), although this excluded criteria relating to the onset of problems before the age of five and evidence of pathogenic care.

The current study explored the hypothesis that there is a tendency to overdiagnose attachment disorders and attachment problems in the populations of looked after and adopted children, at the expense of identifying more common disorders for which there are well-evidenced treatment or management options. We present a case note review of 100 consecutive attendees to a National Child and Adolescent Mental Health Service (CAMHS) service for looked after and adopted children. First we present an analysis of the diagnoses and concerns raised in the referral letters. We then present the rates of psychiatric disorders identified within the specialist service, on the basis of ICD-10 diagnoses and a comprehensive multidisciplinary assessment. Finally, we compared these with the rates of psychiatric disorders reported in a large UK sample of looked after children (Ford et al., 2007). Our predictions were as follows. Higher rates of attachment disorders and attachment problems would be identified in the referral letters than in the specialist multidisciplinary assessment. Secondly, the identification of higher rates of generic attachment problems in the referrals, would have impeded the identification of more common diagnoses. Therefore, it was predicted that for cases identified with attachment problems in the referral letters, there would be fewer problems in total identified in the referral compared with the specialist assessment and, further, that this would be specifically evident for common disorders such as conduct problems and ADHD. Finally, in the light of the recommendation that experienced clinicians should assess these complex presentations, it was predicted that the rates of attachment problems would be lowest amongst professionals with the greatest levels of professional training in child psychiatric diagnosis. That is, the rate would be lowest in the referrals from CAMHS psychiatrists compared with those from GPs, social care and paediatricians.

## Method

### Sample

The files of a consecutive series of 100 cases (49 adopted children and 51 looked after children) referred to a specialist, Tier 4 CAMHS Adoption and Fostering Service across a 4 year-period were accessed and reviewed. A Tier 4 outpatient service offers a specialist multidisciplinary service with capacity for national referrals for specific populations of children and adolescents, in this case adopted and fostered children, with severe and/or complex problems who require highly specialist expertise and/or newly developed ways of working not commonly available across the country.

The study design was approved by the Clinical Audit Office for the South London & Maudsley NHS Foundation Trust. The mean age at referral was 8.6 years ($SD = 3.57$, range 2–17). Sixty-one were boys and 66 were white European. Sixteen were black British, black Caribbean or Latin American and 18 were of dual heritage (a total of 34 from black and minority ethnic groups). Although the gender mix is similar to that reported in Ford et al. (2007), the cases in the current paper represent a younger and more ethnically diverse sample. Thirty-one of the cases were referred by CAMHS psychiatrists and 69 from non-CAMHS sources (10 by paediatricians, 25 by GPs and 34 from social services).

## Data coding

The referral letters and assessment summaries were coded for information regarding diagnoses and problem areas using a standardised and anonymised assessment sheet. The clinic's diagnoses were always made according to ICD-10 multi-axial criteria as part of an assessment conducted by a multidisciplinary team, comprised of consultant child and adolescent psychiatrists, clinical psychologists and mental health social workers. The assessment considered data from previous mental health assessments, school and/or daycare, and social care reports. The intake assessment itself consisted of interviews with the child, carers and the professional network, standardised questionnaires and observations of the child's behaviour with their carers and with strangers (clinic staff). Eighty six children over the age of three were assessed with age-appropriate standardised IQ and literacy assessments. While a primary diagnosis was assigned, as many diagnoses were given as needed to complete the clinical presentation and all identified disorders were recorded.

Although there was variability in the length of referral letters, they all had to be sufficiently detailed about the child's presentation to have met the threshold for commissioning a specialist assessment. All referrals requested a mental health assessment, except for five in which the referral question was about either placement planning or potential breakdown. In three of these five, subsidiary questions were raised about mental health issues such as withdrawn mood or aggressive behaviour.

Referral letters were inspected for the presence of specific diagnoses of attachment disorder, depression, anxiety, conduct disorder, hyperkinetic disorder, autism and related disorders, other neurodevelopmental disorders (e.g., epilepsy, motor/coordination problems, tics etc.) and learning disability. Other disorders such as encopresis, sleep disorders, dyspraxia and adjustment disorder were noted but are not presented in Table 11.1 as no comparable data was presented in Ford et al. (2007)

Referral letters were also inspected for problematic behaviour suggestive of symptoms of psychiatric disorders, for example, a description of 'fighting, stealing and impulsivity' was coded as evidence of conduct disorder and ADHD symptoms.

**Table 11.1** Percentage of psychiatric disorders in ONS data; diagnoses and symptoms in referral letters; and clinic diagnoses (N = 100)

|  | ONS figures (N = 1253) | Referral letters (N = 100) Disorders | Referral letters (N = 100) Symptoms | Clinic assessment disorders (N = 100) All (N = 100) | Clinic assessment disorders (N = 100) Fostering (N = 51) | Clinic assessment disorders (N = 100) Adoption (N = 49) | Agreement between referral and clinic disorders (kappa) |
|---|---|---|---|---|---|---|---|
| Male | 57.1 | | | 61.0 | 58.8 | 63.3 | |
| Older (11 or above) | 59.0 | | | 33.0 | 23.5 | 42.9 | |
| White | 91.6 | | | 66.0 | 56.9 | 75.5 | |
| Any disorder | 46.4 | 30.0 | 82.0 | 64.0 | 60.8 | 67.3 | .26** |
| Anxiety | 11.1 | 5.0 | 14.0 | 8.0 | 5.9 | 10.2 | .26** |
| PTSD | 1.9 | 1.0 | 1.0 | 2.0 | 2.0 | 2.0 | −.01 |
| Depression | 3.4 | 1.0 | 4.0 | 3.0 | 3.9 | 2.0 | −.01 |
| Conduct disorders | 38.9 | 4.0 | 51.0 | 53.0 | 45.1 | 61.2 | .07 |
| ODD | 12.2 | 4.0 | 28.0 | 19.0 | 15.7 | 22.4 | .11 |
| Conduct disorder | 26.7 | 0 | 33.0 | 35.0 | 31.4 | 38.8 | – |
| Hyperkinetic disorders | 8.7 | 12.0 | 23.0 | 31.0 | 27.5 | 34.7 | .29*** |
| Autistic spectrum disorders | 2.6 | 4.0 | 11.0 | 6.0 | 3.9 | 8.2 | .58*** |
| Attachment disorders | 2.5[a] | 16.0 | 1.0 | 4.0 | 5.8 | 2.0 | .04 |
| Other neurodevelopmental disorders | 12.8 | 0 | 6.0 | 12.0 | 11.8 | 12.2 | – |
| Learning disability[b] | 10.7 | 3.0 | 5.0 | 10.0 | 13.7 | 6.1 | .27** |

[a] N = 523, in Meltzer et al. (2003).

[b] Learning Disability as mental age 60% of chronological age in ONS, as stated in the referral letters and as IQ <70 in the clinic assessment.

** $p < .01$;

*** $p < .001$.

The presence of attachment disorders in the referral letters was more complicated. Although described 16 times, only five of these specified a recognised attachment disorder diagnosis, all of which were RAD. The remaining 11 instances were of a generic 'attachment disorder'. In contrast, a more general description of 'attachment problems' was used 26 times in the referral letters. In all 31 children were described as having a recognised attachment disorder, an unspecified attachment disorder and/or attachment problems. Following the terminology used by Chaffin et al. (2006), we refer to this broad conceptualisation of attachment difficulties as 'attachment problems'. Notably, only one child, not part of the 31 with attachment problems, was described with a possible attachment disorder symptom of 'indiscriminate in affections.'

## Attachment disorder diagnoses within the clinical assessment

The identification of attachment disorders is not straightforward and indeed Meltzer et al. (2003, p. 139) specifically excluded attachment disorders from the main body of the ONS report concerned that it would be 'seriously misleading to provide readers with a single "bottom line" estimate of the prevalence of attachment disorders' based only upon a structured interview and the clinical rating of supplementary open-ended questions.

New assessment methodologies and guidelines are emerging for the assessment of attachment disorder (AACAP, 2005; McLaughlin, Espie & Minnis, 2010; Gleason et al., 2011) and they share in common the principle of observing interactions between the child with their carers and with strangers. The clinical assessment of attachment disorder presented here is based upon observations of the child with adult strangers (clinic staff) and with their carers, including separations and reunions – situations which would normally activate the attachment system. Information about the child's social behaviours was also collected from school and any other relevant settings outside of the family home to assess pervasiveness. The diagnosis of either RAD or DAD followed ICD-10 guidelines, and so required evidence of the relevant behaviours in the caregiving history before the age of 5 years and clear evidence of pathology within the attachment system that could not be accounted for by more common disorders such as autism spectrum disorders. In total four children in the clinical assessment were identified with RAD and none with DAD.

## Any axis-I disorder

A summary score was also constructed that summed all the occurrences of diagnosed Axis I disorders for both the referral letters and those resulting from the clinic assessment.

## Data analysis

Agreement between the diagnoses mentioned in the referral letters and those made in the clinic was assessed with kappa values. Similarly, kappa values were used to test whether the identification of an attachment problem obscured the identification of common disorders. Thus, agreement between diagnoses in the referral letters and the clinic for both conduct disorder and ADHD were obtained for the subgroups of referrals which did or did not mention attachment problems. This question was further explored by testing whether referrers who identified attachment problems compared with those who did not were seeing more complex cases, indicated by the number of disorders identified either by referrers or in the clinic. Finally, to test whether CAMHS referrers were identifying fewer attachment problems than other referrers, the proportion of attachment problems identified for each were compared.

## Results

Table 11.1 presents the data from Ford et al. (2007), the comparable diagnoses and symptom-level problem behaviours for the referral letters and the clinic assessment diagnoses. For information, the clinic assessment data are also presented according to adopted and looked after cases. The adoption cases were a slightly older and less diverse sample, and because of these sample differences, no formal testing of the differences between the rates of diagnoses was performed.


## Comparison of psychiatric diagnoses in referrals, clinic and ONS data

Even though this sample had been identified as requiring a specialist Tier 4 mental health assessment the rate of psychiatric disorder in the referral letters was a third lower than the ONS figures for looked after children. Whereas, the proportion of cases with any psychiatric disorder from the clinic assessment is just over a third higher than the ONS rates. Mostly the rates of individual disorder identified in the clinic are comparable with the ONS data, except for ADHD and conduct disorder. Very few referrals to the clinic (4%) considered the possibility of conduct disorders. Referrers were three times more likely to have identified hyperkinetic problems than they were to have considered conduct disorder.

Ford et al. (2007) did not present data specifically about encopresis or enuresis. However, at 6% in this sample, this was a more common clinical diagnosis than RAD/DAD. It was not possible to present comparable data for the literacy or numeracy problems in Ford et al. (2007) (34.3%) because the clinic used a more conservative discrepancy analysis for literacy problems rather than absolute levels of functioning. Eighty-six cases had complete psychometric data, and of these 19.7% were identified as having specific literacy disorders in the clinic assessment (the expected base rate would be less than 2.5%).


## Attachment problems and more common disorders

Attachment disorder and attachment problems were far more often cited in the referral letters than were diagnosed in the clinic assessment.

Of the 16 cases with an attachment disorder diagnosis in the referral letter, only one of these met criteria in the clinic assessment (kappa = .04), but this was not one of the five cases referred with a specific RAD diagnosis. In total, 31 cases were referred with attachment problems in the referral letter, of whom only three were diagnosed in the clinic assessment (kappa = .10). The mean age of the 28 children for whom the referral letter and clinic diagnosis were in disagreement for RAD/DAD was 9.04 (SD = 2.96), whereas the mean age of the three children for whom there was agreement was 5.33 (SD = 4.92).

To assess whether attachment problems in the referral letter obscured the diagnosis of more common disorders, rates of conduct disorder and ADHD were examined within the subsample of 31 cases identified with either attachment disorder or attachment problems at referral.

Fifty-eight percent of these 31 cases were diagnosed with a conduct disorder in the clinic assessment compared with only 3.2% in the referral letter (kappa = .04). In contrast, the clinic assessment identified 35% of the 31 cases as having ADHD, compared to 19% in the referral (kappa = .60). To test whether the reduced identification of conduct disorder could be attributed to an over identification of attachment problems, similar analyses were conducted with the remaining 69 cases who were not identified with attachment problems in the referral letter. Contrary with expectations rates of agreement were also extremely low (kappa = .08), suggesting identifying attachment problems were insufficient to explain the low levels of conduct disorders in the referrals.

To test whether identifying attachment problems obscured the number of domains affected, the total number of disorders identified in the referral letters of the 31 cases referred with attachment problems were compared with the total number of disorders identified in the clinic assessment. The mean number of Axis I diagnoses (excluding attachment problems) in the referral letter for the 31 cases was .38 (SD = .66), compared with 1.45 (SD = 1.17) in the clinic (Wilcoxon Z = 3.69, p < .001). However, as above, more problems were identified in the clinic assessment versus the referral letter for the 69 cases with no attachment problems identified in the referral (Wilcoxon Z = 5.24, p < .001).

While this suggests that attachment problems did not obscure more common disorders, the possibility arises that cases referred with attachment problems were in fact more complex. One index of complexity may be the presence of comorbidity. The total number of identified disorders in the referral letter were not significantly higher in the 31 cases identified with attachment problems compared with the 69 cases without (Mann–Whitney

$Z = 1.35$, $p = .17$, .38 [$SD = .66$] and .21 [$SD = .51$] for those identified with and without attachment problems, respectively). When this comparison was re-run for the number of diagnoses identified in the clinic assessment, the slightly higher number of diagnoses in the 31 cases identified by referrers with attachment problems was not significant (Mann–Whitney $Z = 1.80$, $p = .07$, 1.45 [$SD = 1.17$] and 1.01 [$SD = .89$]).

### Proportion of attachment problems according to referral source

It was predicted that CAMHS services would identify the lowest number of attachment problems in their referrals. However, this was not the case. Eleven CAMHS referrals (35.5%), compared with five non-CAMHS referrals (7%) mentioned attachment disorder in the referral letter ($\chi^2 = 12.69$, $df = 1$, $p < .001$). The pattern was similar for attachment problems, with over half the CAMHS referrals (51%) identifying attachment problems compared with less than a quarter (21%) from non-CAMHS referrers ($\chi^2 = 8.94$, $df = 1$, $p < .01$).

The elevated rate of attachment problems found in referrals from CAMHS psychiatrists might be explained by case complexity as indexed by increased comorbidity. This was partly supported as there were more mental health problems identified in the referral letters from CAMHS (Mann–Whitney $Z = 2.45$, $df = 1$, $p < .05$). However, this complexity was not borne out by the clinical assessment, which found similar numbers of problems for either referral source (Mann–Whitney $Z = 1.31$, $df = 1$, $p = .18$). Thus, although there was a similar number of mental health issues in the cases referred from CAMHS and non-CAMHS sources, the former were more likely to identify a range of problems, even if that complexity was at least in part attributed to attachment problems.

## Discussion

Attachment disorders were construed differently to other disorders in the referral letters. Few referrers who identified an attachment disorder used one of the appropriate terms of either RAD or DAD (five of sixteen) and unlike other disorders these were not supported by descriptions at the symptom level. Indeed many referrers described a generic but unelaborated presentation of attachment problems in addition to attachment disorders. In total attachment problems, that is, specific and nonspecific attachment disorders and/or generic attachment problems, were mentioned in 31% of the referrals, yet only one potential attachment-specific symptom was described and this was for a child in the 69% not identified with attachment problems.

There was some support for a tendency to overdiagnose attachment disorder in adopted and fostered children. In the specialist clinic assessment many common disorders were diagnosed more frequently than RAD/DAD including conduct problems, ADHD, anxiety, autism, encopresis/enuresis, neurodevelopmental problems, learning disability and specific learning disability. Indeed conduct problems were diagnosed 13 times more frequently than RAD/DAD. Yet in each case, an attachment disorder (16%) or attachment problem (31%) was more frequently identified by referrers than one of these more common disorders (between 0% and 12%) in referral letters. Yet the low rates of attachment disorder and higher rates of more common disorders identified in the clinic assessment is consistent with both the practice parameters for maltreated children with attachment problems and also the ONS data for looked after children.

While there was support for the main hypothesis that attachment disorders would be overidentified by referrers, the related hypothesis that this would obscure the identification of more common problems was not well supported. There was only weak evidence for a difference in terms of the total number of diagnoses identified in the clinic between the cases referred with attachment problems and those who were not. Similarly, there was a marked under identification of conduct problems in referral letters compared with the ONS data, regardless of attachment problems. Thus, it was not diagnosing attachment problems that obscured the rates of more common disorders but more worryingly, a tendency to under-identify common disorders more generally. Only 4% of referrals identified conduct disorder compared to almost 10 times that amount being identified in the ONS data, and even more in the specialist clinic assessment. Interestingly, the number of symptoms of common disorders in the referral letters was much greater than the number of disorders diagnosed in the referral letters and much more similar to the rates of disorders diagnosed in the clinic. The notable exception being for attachment problems, for which referrers almost never considered symptoms in the referral letters.

Finally, the practice parameters recommend expert assessments by experienced clinicians, but the hypothesis that CAMHS referrers would be less susceptible to overdiagnosing attachment problems was not supported. Indeed CAMHS referrals were the most likely to identify an attachment problem, even in the absence of evidence that they were referring cases with the most comorbidity. This raises a number of issues, including what constitutes an expert assessment. In particular no referrers indicated concerns about neurodevelopmental problems, even though these are relatively common in the ONS data; the practice parameters suggest paying particular attention to this area; there is converging evidence of the impact of early maltreatment upon neurodevelopment (McCrory et al., 2010); these problems were relatively common in the clinic assessment and there is a collection of studies that demonstrate the specific neuropsychological consequences of extreme neglect in post-institutionalised children (Bos, Fox, Zeanah & Nelson, 2009; Pollak et al., 2010). These latter studies may not be directly compatible with the population of adopted and fostered children from noninstitutional backgrounds but, along with the research outlined above, they do emphasise the importance of considering neurodevelopmental factors in adopted and looked after children's assessments. To some extent neurodevelopmental issues may be clarified in the new ICD-11, in which the draft framework currently proposes replacing DAD with disinhibited social engagement disorder, effectively removing the attachment construct from the diagnosis (WHO, 2012).

The data in this study contribute to the growing concern that the current diagnostic system for attachment problems is inadequate to meet the needs of clinicians working with looked after and adopted children (DeJong, 2010; Minnis, Marwick, Arthur & McLaughlin, 2006). There is confusion about the appropriate diagnostic framework, and an absence of agreed standards for assessing attachment disorders. The ONS data used a narrow and broader definition, and the latter increased the rate almost 10-fold (Meltzer et al., 2003).

The emerging assessment guidelines may help but are time and labour intensive, and also particularly suited to young children (AACAP, 2005; McLaughlin et al., 2010). Indeed the presentation of attachment disorder in children older than 5 years is unclear, yet some referrers identified attachment problems in teenagers and the diagnostic disagreements between the referrals and the clinic were more apparent for older children. Observations of separations and reunions are unlikely to be clinically useful for children beyond infancy and early childhood because the attachment system undergoes significant developmental transitions from infancy through childhood and adolescence into adulthood, moving away from observable behaviours to the level of representation (Allen et al., 2003), yet the attachment disorder phenotype currently lacks elaboration of these transitions.

This study has a number of limitations. First, in the light of the conceptual confusion about attachment disorder constructs and their reliable measurement, the assessments reported here from the specialist clinic cannot claim to be gold standard. Although a multi-informant approach with direct observations was used, we can only say the observed discrepancies between the specialist assessment and the referral letters indicate differences in approach to assessment and formulation. The clinic's assessment methodology, and in particular observations of attachment-specific behaviours, appeared to be very different from the assessments conducted by the referrers and meant that fewer children with attachment disorders were identified in the clinic than in some other services. However, the children who *were* diagnosed with attachment disorders in the clinic did have evidence of specific pathology within the attachment system and the low rate of attachment disorders is consistent with the expert estimates of the prevalence of attachment disorders. Moreover, the formulation derived from the clinic assessment justifies all diagnoses with a variety of evidence, so another service can review the evidence and argue against a diagnosis based on new assessment information or by taking issue with the evidence presented. This transparent approach stands in contrast with the practices criticised by Zeanah (1996) whereby presentations arising from diverse social problems are ascribed to an attachment disorder without an explicit consideration of the alternative causes, in a manner which blurs aetiological factors with the presenting problems.

Secondly, the coding of the diagnoses and problem areas in the referrals was based only upon the information referrers chose to include in the letters. Referrers were not asked to systematically complete a checklist of diagnoses or problem behaviours, and as such it is possible that the under-reporting of common disorders, and conduct disorder in particular, may have reflected their choice to foreground other more complex aspects of the child's presentation. Hence, it is possible that referrers had identified common disorders but they did not prioritise them as core parts of the presentation in the referral letters to Tier 4.

Finally, the findings from this small study cannot be generalised to estimate the prevalence or even ratio of common disorders and attachment disorders more generally in the looked after and adopted populations in the United Kingdom, not least because the referral patterns in a small cohort within a specialist service are likely to be biased in unsystematic ways. Moreover, the use of clinical assessments based on ICD-10, supplemented by observations recommended for DSM-IV RAD-I/II, rather than standardised research measures potentially confounds systematic comparison with existing research findings. Indeed, other types of research are needed to clarify not just the criteria, operationalisation and prevalence of RAD/DAD, but also how these diagnoses fit with other commonly occurring disorders. Probably no single research approach will be adequate to address all these issues. For example, large studies such as that carried out in the United Kingdom for looked after children (Meltzer et al., 2003) would help greatly with planning for the needs of adopted children, to identify the rates of common and rare disorders. In contrast, specific DAD/RAD studies require more intensive observational assessments upon smaller samples, but such studies should be thorough in their identification of more common (but 'less exciting') disorders to relate back to larger prevalence studies and help clarify overlapping phenotypes.

These are interesting research questions we hope to see answered to clarify clinical practice, but in the meantime, based on the practice parameter guidelines for children with attachment problems, it is probably unhelpful to think of disorders such as attachment disorder as being first line diagnoses or as routinely trumping more common disorders in looked after or adopted children. The practice parameters recommend identifying common problems and treating them with evidence based approaches. Mental health interventions specifically for attachment disorders in looked after or adopted children remain in the earliest stages of development (Buckner, Lopez, Dunkel & Joiner, 2008) and the best evidence is to promote stable placements with sensitive carers (Rutter, Kreppner & Sonuga-Barke, 2009; Zeanah et al., 2011). In contrast with the recommendations within the practice parameters, many services working with looked after and adopted children continue to have an overriding belief in attachment issues as the primary explanatory factor for their clients' problems (Barth et al., 2005; Prior & Glaser, 2006). This has the potential to lead to conflict between different service models, in part fuelled by the confusion in diagnostic categories and the competing treatment plans that follow from these. The victims of this confusion are likely to be the looked after and adopted children who miss out on access to the evidence based treatments and educational support that could help them (Woolgar & Scott, 2013).

---

### Key Practitioner Message

- Consistent with the practice parameters (Chaffin et al., 2006) assessments of looked after and adopted children should prioritise the identification of common disorders to open up evidence-based care pathways
- Services for looked after and adopted children should offer multidisciplinary assessments by specialist teams, with expertise in the wide range of problems likely to present, including assessment of neurodevelopmental and neuropsychological problems
- Attachment disorders should always be specified as RAD and/or DAD and not as generic attachment problems. Diagnosis requires significantly more than either disruptions to attachment relationships or a history of pathogenic care. Assessment should always include evidence of pathology within the attachment system, for example, using observational assessments with primary caregivers in contexts likely to activate the attachment system
- RAD and/or DAD formulations should describe in detail the evidence for and against these disorders versus more common disorders, considering evidence of attachment-specific symptoms, as well as any broader attachment-related issues not part of the RAD/DAD phenotype

---

### References

Allen, J. P., McElhaney, K. B., Land, D. J., Kuperminc, G. P., Moore, C. W., O'Beirne-Kelly, H., & Kilmer, S.L. (2003). A secure base in adolescence: markers of attachment security in the mother-adolescent relationship. *Child Development, 74,* 292–307.

American Academy of Child and Adolescent Psychiatry (AACAP) (2005). Practice parameter for the assessment and treatment of children and adolescents with reactive attachment disorder of infancy and early childhood. *Journal of the American Academy of Child and Adolescent Psychiatry, 44,* 1206–1219.

BAAF (2011). Summary statistics on children in care and children adopted from care. *British Association Adoption & Fostering.* Available from: http://www.baaf.org.uk/res/stat-england#afc [last accessed December 2013].

Barth, R. P., Crea, T. M., John, K., Thoburn, J., & Quinton, D. (2005). Beyond attachment theory and therapy: Towards sensitive and evidence-based interventions with foster and adoptive families in distress. *Child & Family Social Work, 10,* 257–268.

Bos, K. J., Fox, N., Zeanah, C. H., & Nelson, C. A. (2009). Effects of early psychosocial deprivation on the development of memory and executive function. *Frontiers in Behavioral Neuroscience, 3,* 16.

Buckner, J. D., Lopez, C., Dunkel, S., & Joiner, T. E., Jr (2008). Behavior management training for the treatment of reactive attachment disorder. *Child Maltreatment, 13,* 289–297.

Chaffin, M., Hanson, R., Saunders, B. E., Nichols, T., Barnett, D., Zeanah, C., . . . & Miller-Perrin, C. (2006). Report of the APSAC task force on attachment therapy, reactive attachment disorder, and attachment problems. *Child Maltreatment, 11,* 76–89.

DeJong, M. (2010). Some reflections on the use of psychiatric diagnosis in the looked after or "in care" child population. *Clinical Child Psychology & Psychiatry, 15,* 589–599.

Ford, T., Vostanis, P., Meltzer, H., & Goodman, R. (2007). Psychiatric disorder among British children looked after by local authorities: Comparison with children living in private households. *British Journal of Psychiatry, 190,* 319–325.

Gleason, M. M., Fox, N. A., Drury, S., Smyke, A., Egger, H. L., Nelson, C. A., . . . & Zeanah, C. H. (2011). Validity of evidence-derived criteria for reactive attachment disorder: Indiscriminately social/disinhibited and emotionally withdrawn/inhibited types. *Journal of the American Academy of Child and Adolescent Psychiatry, 50,* 216–231.

Gunnar, M. R., Fisher, P. A., & The Early Experience, Stress, and Prevention Network. (2006). Bringing basic research on early experience and stress neurobiology to bear on preventive interventions for neglected and maltreated children. *Development and Psychopathology, 18,* 651–677.

Haugaard, J. J. (2004). Recognizing and treating uncommon behavioral and emotional disorders in children and adolescents who have been severely maltreated: Introduction. *Child Maltreatment, 9,* 123–130.

Haugaard, J. J., & Hazan, C. (2004). Child maltreatment in children and adolescents who have been severely maltreated: Reactive attachment disorder. *Child Maltreatment, 9,* 154–160.

McCrory, E., De Brito, S., & Viding, E. (2010). Research review: The neurobiology and genetics of maltreatment and adversity. *Journal of Child Psychology & Psychiatry & Allied Disciplines, 15,* 1079–1095.

McLaughlin, A., Espie, C., & Minnis, H. (2010). Development of a brief waiting room observation for behaviours typical of reactive attachment disorder. *Child and Adolescent Mental Health, 15,* 73–79.

Meltzer, H., Gatward, R., Corbin, T., Goodman, R., & Ford, T. (2003). The mental health of young people looked after by local authorities in England. London: The Stationary Office.

Minnis, H., Marwick, H., Arthur, J., & McLaughlin, A. (2006). Reactive attachment disorder – A theoretical model beyond attachment. *European Child & Adolescent Psychiatry, 15,* 336–342.

Pollak, S. D., Nelson, C. A., Schlaak, M. F., Roeber, B. J., Wewerka, S. S., Wiik, K. L., . . . & Gunnar, M. R. (2010). Neurodevelopmental effects of early deprivation in postinstitutionalized children. *Child Development, 81,* 224–236.

Prior, V., & Glaser, D. (2006). Understanding attachment and attachment disorders: Theory, evidence and practice. London: Jessica Kingsley.

Rutter, M., Kreppner, J., & Sonuga-Barke, E. (2009). Emanuel Miller Lecture: Attachment insecurity, disinhibited attachment, and attachment disorders: where do research findings leave the concepts? *Journal of Child Psychology & Psychiatry & Allied Disciplines, 50,* 529–543.

Woolgar, M. J., & Scott, S. (2013). The negative consequences of over-diagnosing attachment disorders in adopted children: the importance of comprehensive formulations. *Clinical Child Psychology & Psychiatry, 19,* 355–366.

World Health Organization (WHO) (1992). The ICD-10 classification of mental and behavioural disorders: Clinical descriptions and diagnostic guidelines. Geneva: World Health Organization.

World Health Organization (WHO). (2012). Disinhibited social engagement disorder. In ICD-11 Beta. Available from: http://apps.who.int/classifications/icd11/browse/f/en#/http%3a%2f%2fid.who.int%2ficd%2fentity%2f467941148 [last accessed December 2013].

Zeanah, C. H. (1996). Beyond insecurity: A reconceptualization of attachment disorders in infancy. *Journal of Consulting and Clinical Psychology, 64,* 42–52.

Zeanah, C. H., Berlin, L. J., & Boris, N. W. (2011). Practitioner review: Clinical applications of attachment theory and research for infants and young children. *Journal of Child Psychology and Psychiatry, 52,* 819–833.

Zeanah, C. H. J., & Smyke, A. T. (2009). Attachment disorders. In C. Zeanah (Ed.). *Handbook of Infant Mental Health* (3rd edn., pp. 421–434). London: Guilford Press.

# 12

# Attachment in the Early Life Course

## *Meta-Analytic Evidence for Its Role in Socioemotional Development*

Ashley M. Groh, R. M. Pasco Fearon, Marinus H. van IJzendoorn,
Marian J. Bakermans-Kranenburg, and Glenn I. Roisman

Attachment theory (Bowlby, 1982; Ainsworth, 1982) has been a generative theoretical framework for investigating the developmental origins and legacy of children's early experiences with parents. Attachment theory proposes that parents' sensitive caregiving, not children's endogenous characteristics, primarily determines individual differences in attachment security (Sroufe, 1985). Specifically, experiences of parental (in)sensitivity are encoded by children into an internal working model encompassing views of the self, others, and the nature of relationships that influences developmental adaptation (Bowlby, 1973; Bretherton & Munholland 2008). Thus, attachment theory claims that early attachment security should be largely independent of children's individual characteristics (e.g., temperament) and predicts more optimal socioemotional outcomes (including higher quality interpersonal relationships and fewer externalizing and internalizing problems).

These claims have received much attention in almost five decades of research on attachment (Berlin et al., 2008; DeKlyen & Greenberg, 2008; Fearon & Belsky, 2016; Vaughn & Bost, 2016). However, findings have not always converged, and together with the sheer size of the literature, range of correlates examined, and diversity of samples investigated, reviewers have found it difficult to draw conclusions about the significance of early attachment for socioemotional (mal)adaptation. Meta-analysis provides a structured, principled way to quantitatively summarize complex literatures, test theories, and generate new hypotheses. Accordingly, we conducted quantitative reviews examining the relation between early attachment and children's peer competence (i.e., social skills, the quality of children's interactions with peers, and social status; Groh et al., 2014), externalizing symptoms (i.e., aggression, oppositional problems, conduct problems, and hostility; Fearon et al., 2010), internalizing symptoms (i.e., depression, anxiety, social withdrawal, and somatic complaints; Groh et al., 2012), and temperament (i.e., negative emotional reactivity and regulation; Groh et al., 2017).

We addressed questions about the developmental significance of early attachment security versus insecurity by quantifying the association between early attachment and adaptation within these developmental domains and comparing meta-analytic associations across developmental domains to examine whether early security has narrow or broad significance (Belsky & Cassidy, 1994). We also examined the dynamic nature of these meta-analytic associations over childhood to determine whether the predictive significance of early attachment endures or diminishes over time (Sroufe et al., 1990), and we tested whether the effects of attachment vary by population (e.g., clinical status, sex, socioeconomic adversity). For each developmental domain, we examined the relative significance of patterns of insecurity, as some insecure classifications may be linked more closely to some outcomes than others. We restricted our focus to studies that began in early childhood, and we used standardized observational assessments of attachment to be reasonably confident that we were examining common studies using

*Source:* Republished with permission of John Wiley & Sons, Inc., from Ashley M. Groh et al., "Attachment in the Early Life Course: Meta-Analytic Evidence for Its Role in Socioemotional Development", pp. 70–76 from *Child Development Perspectives* 11:1 (March 2017); permission conveyed through Copyright Clearance Center, Inc.

similar definitions and measurement frames, uncontaminated by shared method variance or informant bias. Because relatively few studies have examined attachment between children and *fathers*, there were either too few studies to include in the meta-analysis (Fearon et al., 2010) or the few studies limited the conclusions we could draw (Groh et al., 2012, 2014, 2017). In this article, we summarize findings from this work in relation to mother–child attachment, first focusing on findings for secure versus insecure infants and then on those for patterns of insecurity and disorganization. We also discuss their meaning and significance for ongoing research.

## The Developmental Significance of Early Attachment Security

### Sequelae and origins of early attachment security

According to attachment theory, early security may have the strongest implications for children's peer relationships, and important yet weaker implications for psychopathology (Belsky & Cassidy, 1994). By carving the literature on attachment into distinct developmental domains, our meta-analyses estimated more precisely the association between security and (mal)adaptation within these domains and allowed us to evaluate the relative significance of attachment *across* developmental domains. Early security was associated with greater social competence ($d = .39$; Groh et al., 2014), fewer externalizing problems ($d = .31$; Fearon et al., 2010), and to a lesser extent, fewer internalizing problems ($d = .15$; Groh et al., 2012). Moreover, early security was associated most strongly with children's subsequent interactions with peers (i.e., social competence and externalizing difficulties, which often manifest in peer contexts) and weakly with internalizing symptoms (see Figure 12.1).

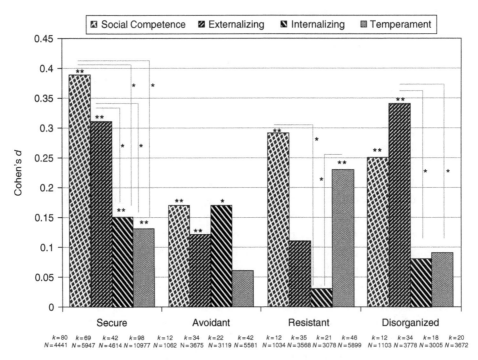

**Figure 12.1** Combined effect sizes for the four attachment categories for social competence with peers, externalizing symptoms, internalizing symptoms, and temperament. *Note:* Secure = secure versus insecure; Avoidant = insecure avoidant versus not avoidant; Resistant = insecure resistant versus not resistant; Disorganized = disorganized versus not disorganized. Effect sizes are presented in the direction of hypotheses. Thus, security was associated meta-analytically with higher levels of social competence and lower levels of externalizing and internalizing symptomatology, whereas insecure subtypes were associated meta-analytically with lower levels of social competence and higher levels of externalizing and internalizing symptomatology. Security and avoidance were associated meta-analytically with lower levels of negative temperament, whereas resistance and disorganization were associated meta-analytically with higher levels of negative temperament. Asterisks over bars indicate significant combined effect sizes. Asterisks along lines indicate significant differences between the combined effect sizes. $N$ = total number of children; $k$ = number of independent studies. *p < .05. **p < .01.

By traditional standards, the effect sizes between early security and children's peer competence and externalizing symptomatology were modest, falling between Cohen's (1988) criteria for small ($d = .20$) and medium ($d = .50$) effects, suggesting that any simplistic notion that security *determines* peer interactions in childhood and aggressive behavior is likely incorrect. However, meta-analytic associations should be considered in the context of other studies examining similar phenomena and using similar methods (McCartney & Rosenthal, 2000). In that respect, the combined effect sizes are not trivial, as they are comparable to the meta-analytic associations between parenting and delinquency ($d = .39$; Hoeve et al., 2009) and parenting and relational aggression ($d = .22$; Kawabata et al., 2011). These meta-analytic associations gain greater significance considering that they are relatively free from measurement bias and occur over lengthy periods. In contrast, the association between insecurity and internalizing problems was weak, a finding we return to later.

Regarding the origins of attachment, security is thought to be rooted in the caregiving environment and thus to have little relation to temperament (Sroufe, 1985). In our meta-analysis, attachment security was associated with lower levels of negative temperament ($d = .13$; Groh et al., 2017). However, this association was significantly weaker than that between security and social competence and externalizing (but not internalizing) problems (see Figure 12.1), providing little evidence that temperament *determines* security status.

## The legacy of attachment security across childhood

Supporting the idea that attachment has enduring significance for developmental (mal)adaptation (Sroufe et al., 1990), we found that associations between security and children's peer competence and internalizing symptoms did not vary according to age of outcome assessment (Groh et al., 2012, 2014), the association between attachment and externalizing problems *increased* with age (Fearon et al., 2010), and the temporal lag between attachment and outcome assessments did not moderate any of the meta-analytic associations. As these meta-analyses comprised children from 1 to 12–14 years and the lag between attachment and outcome assessments ranged from 0 months to 13 years, these findings suggest that, although modest, the significance of early security for children's socioemotional adaptation does not wane from infancy to early adolescence. However, these studies cannot determine whether such stability is due to the early effects of attachment on stable psychobiological structures or continuity in caregiving, a point we return to later.

## Moderators of meta-analytic associations with attachment security

We examined whether the meta-analytic associations between early security and socioemotional adaptation were moderated by factors that have been linked with or indicate psychological problems (e.g., parent or child diagnosed with psychiatric disorder; prenatal exposure to drugs), children's sex, or socioeconomic status. The association between insecurity and externalizing symptomatology was stronger when either the child or the parent had been diagnosed with a psychiatric disorder (see Figure 12.2; Fearon et al., 2010). In addition, children's sex moderated the association between insecurity and externalizing problems, with a stronger association for boys (Fearon et al., 2010), supporting the claim that insecurity might be linked with externalizing problems in boys but not the related assertion that insecurity might be linked to internalizing symptoms in girls (DeKlyen & Greenberg, 2008). Socioeconomic status did not significantly moderate any of the meta-analytic associations (Fearon et al., 2010; Groh et al., 2012, 2014), providing little support for a diathesis–stress model in which the effect of insecurity is strongest in economically deprived populations. These findings suggest that early insecurity places boys and children from clinical populations (i.e., children or parents with psychiatric difficulties) at heightened risk for externalizing problems, but that such factors play little role in amplifying the negative impact of insecurity on peer competence and internalizing problems.

## The Developmental Significance of Early Avoidant, Resistant, and Disorganized Attachments

In the meta-analyses, we examined the shared and distinctive significance of early avoidant, resistant, and disorganized attachments (see Figure 12.1). Consistent with expectations that all patterns of insecurity might undermine social competence (Berlin et al., 2008), early avoidant, resistant, and disorganized attachments were negatively

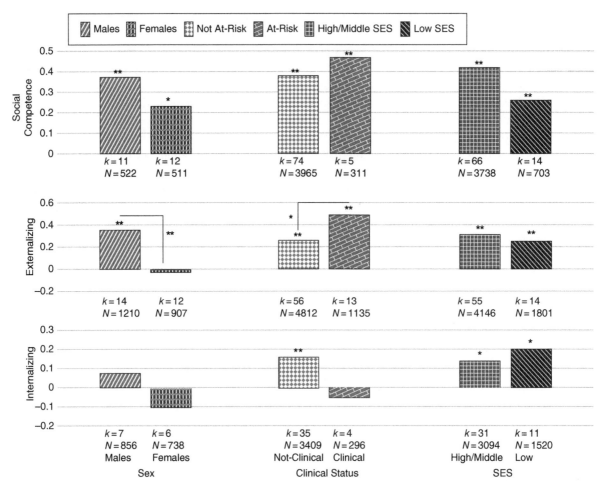

**Figure 12.2**　Combined effect sizes for secure versus insecure infants and children's peer competence, externalizing symptoms, and internalizing symptoms by children's sex, clinical status, and socioeconomic status. *Note:* Top graph displays effect sizes for the association between security (vs. insecurity) and children's peer competence. Middle and bottom graphs display effect sizes for the association between insecurity (vs. security) and children's externalizing and internalizing symptoms, respectively. For each outcome domain, effect sizes for (in)security are displayed by child sex, clinical status (not clinical vs. parent/child clinical), and SES (high/middle vs. low). Positive effect sizes indicate the association was in the direction of hypotheses (e.g., security was associated meta-analytically with higher levels of social competence for girls). Negative effect sizes indicate the association was in the opposite direction of hypotheses (e.g., insecurity was associated meta-analytically with lower levels of internalizing problems for girls). Asterisks over bars indicate significant combined effect sizes. Asterisks along lines indicate significant differences between the combined effect sizes. SES = socioeconomic status; $N$ = total number of children; $k$ = number of independent studies. $^{*}p < .05.$ $^{**}p < .01.$

associated with peer competence and the 85% CI for the point estimates overlapped, suggesting that each pattern of insecurity was associated comparably with less peer competence (Groh et al., 2014). Regarding psychopathology, a somewhat unanticipated pattern emerged: Avoidance was significantly associated with externalizing *and* internalizing problems, whereas resistance was not significantly associated with either symptom domain (Fearon et al., 2010; Groh et al., 2012), providing little support for the claim that avoidant and resistant attachments serve as distinctive diatheses for externalizing versus internalizing problems, respectively (Sroufe, 2003). Moreover, early disorganization placed children at the greatest risk for externalizing problems (relative to other insecure categories), but was not significantly associated with internalizing problems (Fearon et al., 2010; Groh et al., 2012), suggesting that instead of having broad implications for psychopathology (Carlson, 1998), the significance of disorganization was restricted to the externalizing domain. Consistent with conclusions from prior narrative reviews (Vaughn & Bost, 2008; Van IJzendoorn & Bakermans-Kranenburg, 2012), the association between insecurity and negative temperament was primarily due to resistant attachment, as neither avoidance nor disorganization was significantly associated with temperament (Groh et al., 2017).

Findings from our meta-analysis on internalizing symptomatology converged with those from a similar meta-analysis (Madigan et al., 2013), but diverged from other quantitative and narrative reviews (Brumariu & Kerns, 2010; Colonnesi et al., 2011). This might be because of the scope of the reviews. Our meta-analysis and one of the others (Madigan et al., 2013) included only studies that assessed early attachment via observation to help rule out potential inflation of associations due to shared method variance and to evaluate a central tenet of attachment theory that *early* attachments have enduring significance for development (Sroufe et al., 1990). The other reviews (Brumariu & Kerns, 2010; Colonnesi et al., 2011) included studies that used self-reports of attachment and internalizing symptoms, which might have inflated effect sizes artificially, and studies that used attachment measures administered in childhood and adolescence (i.e., 1–18 years). Thus, only one meta-analysis (Madigan et al., 2013) might be considered an independent replication of ours; it corroborated evidence that early avoidant, but not resistant or disorganized, attachment is significantly associated with internalizing symptoms.

## Looking Ahead and Conclusion

Our meta-analyses, comprising the most comprehensive set of quantitative reviews of the literature on the developmental significance of early attachment, provided evidence that early attachment security is only weakly associated with infant temperament, has enduring significance for children's socioemotional (mal)adjustment, and is more strongly involved in social competence and externalizing problems than internalizing problems. Moreover, the findings underscored the across-the-board significance of all insecure attachment patterns for social competence, the broad (yet weak) significance of avoidant attachment for externalizing and internalizing symptomatology, and the relatively heightened significance of disorganized attachment for externalizing outcomes. These results are crucial for indicating not only the importance, but also the limits, of attachment for informing models of psychopathology and adjustment. In addition, even the stronger associations were modest. Our findings also challenge the claim that avoidance is important for externalizing problems, resistance for internalizing problems, and disorganization for general psychological problems (Carlson, 1998; Sroufe, 2003). Next, we suggest how researchers might address these issues.

One potential reason for the modest meta-analytic associations and partial support for the differential significance of insecure subtypes concerns possible limits in assessing infant attachment. Specifically, the factor structure of infant attachment as assessed by the Strange Situation (Ainsworth et al., 1978) may be best reflected by two weakly correlated factors of attachment-related avoidance and resistance (disorganization loaded on the resistance factor, albeit not strongly; Fraley & Spieker, 2003). In contrast to this two-factor solution, the standard coding system (including disorganized attachment and on which we based our meta-analyses) treats insecure patterns of attachment as mutually exclusive, which might have limited the ability of research to detect distinctive implications of patterns of insecurity. That said, findings from our meta-analyses *did* differ for resistant and disorganized attachments in two domains, which might be interpreted as inconsistent with the finding that disorganization and resistance load on a common factor. Thus, we need research on the factor structure of early attachment, especially in high-risk groups where greater variation in disorganization is typical. Similarly, we need more work comparing the predictive significance of the two-factor versus standard coding approaches for children's adaptation in the outcome domains examined here. Moreover, this work is limited by its reliance on a few scales that were not designed with psychometric modeling in mind or to capture all relevant aspects of attachment behavior. Further innovation in measuring attachment phenomena is important.

Nearly all studies on attachment and internalizing symptomatology used parent and teacher reports of symptoms. Given the less public nature of internalizing symptoms, parents and teachers might find it difficult to report on such symptoms. Research on attachment and externalizing problems also relies on such reports, and our meta-analysis revealed that studies that use parent reports ($d = .22$) and teacher reports ($d = .30$) produced smaller effect sizes than those that use direct observations ($d = .58$; Fearon et al., 2010). Finally, despite the appreciation of developmental changes in peer relationships (e.g., increasing importance of intimacy), many studies on attachment and peer competence have not used measures sensitive to such changes; in fact, nearly half used reports of children's general social skills. Research on the implications of attachment would benefit from observational and multi-informant measures, including reports by clinicians and children, that capture variation in outcomes more successfully.

Except in the case of children's externalizing problems, our meta-analyses provided limited evidence that the impact of early (in)security was magnified when children experienced potential risk factors. Researchers might explore whether other factors increase or attenuate associations between attachment and different outcomes. Specifically, given theoretical arguments (Rutter, 1979) and evidence (Belsky & Fearon, 2002) that the negative impact of insecurity increases when children experience many risk factors, researchers should focus on children experiencing more than one risk factor. Researchers might also consider individual factors that make children differentially susceptible to context (Belsky, 1997; Ellis et al., 2011). Indeed, given our finding that insecurity was weakly associated with temperament (Groh et al., 2014), one way to reconcile the attachment and temperament literatures might be to consider whether children's negative temperamental reactivity, conceptualized as a susceptibility factor, heightens the impact of early security on outcomes —for better and for worse (van IJzendoorn & Bakermans-Kranenburg, 2012; Vaughn & Bost, 2016).

Studies on the implications of attachment generally feature small samples that are underpowered to detect the meta-analytic associations reported here (median $N = 44$, 51, and 56 and median power for one-tailed tests = 37, 30, and 15% for studies on peer competence, externalizing, and internalizing outcomes, respectively), increasing the risk of false positives and negatives. Small, underpowered samples are particularly problematic for studies examining the significance of resistant and disorganized attachments for internalizing problems because these attachment patterns are relatively uncommon (Mesman et al., 2016). Given that some of the most surprising meta-analytic findings emerged in this outcome domain, larger, well-powered investigations on attachment and internalizing symptomatology are needed. We call for multisite investigations aimed at replicating a key prediction that insecurity, generally, and resistant and disorganized attachments, specifically, heighten risk for internalizing symptomatology. A successful example of such an effort to replicate a target set of findings across many laboratories exists (Klein et al., 2014) and provides a useful model for testing this prediction. Ideally, such efforts would compare two-factor and traditional approaches to attachment, use trained observers to measure internalizing symptomatology, and examine the role of cumulative psychosocial risk and individual susceptibility factors.

Our meta-analyses provided evidence that, although modest, attachment–outcome associations do not wane over the early life course, providing support for the claim that early attachments have enduring significance for socioemotional development. Given such evidence, we need theory-driven studies that address mediating processes that account for such enduring effects. According to attachment theory, internal working models are among the mechanisms linking early attachment experiences to later outcomes (Bowlby, 1973; Bretherton & Munholland, 2008), and in recent years, advances have been made in our understanding of the nature of such models. Drawing on evidence from cognitive psychology that similarities across repeated experiences are summarized in the form of scripts, attachment scholars have argued that repeated secure base interactions are represented in the form of a secure base script (an understanding that when attachment problems arise, attachment figures consistently provide support in overcoming the problem; Bretherton, 1987; Waters & Waters, 2006). Although access to a secure base script in adulthood is predicted by attachment-relevant experiences in childhood (Steele et al., 2014; Schoenmaker et al., 2015) and associated with attachment-relevant behavior (e.g., sensitivity, Coppola et al., 2006), we need further research on the development of such knowledge in childhood and its role in explicating links between early attachment and socioemotional adjustment.

In addition to internal working models, other mechanisms have been proposed to explain associations between attachment and later outcomes, including social information processing (Dykas & Cassidy, 2011), emotional reactivity and regulation (Cassidy, 1994), and continuity in caregiving (Lamb et al., 1984). Given that attachment relationships serve as a context in which children's stress is regulated, another mechanism by which early experiences might be carried forward is via the effect of attachment on neurobiological systems involved in regulating stress. Indeed, in some studies, attachment has been linked with children's physiological responding within attachment-relevant contexts (see Fearon et al., 2016), highlighting the need for further research into potential neurobiological mechanisms. Furthermore, studies have started to cast light on novel correlates of security at the level of brain structure and function (Coan, 2016) which may provide clues to the mechanisms linking attachment to emotion and behavior.

Despite this wealth of theory, few studies have programmatically tested competing explanations regarding the mechanisms mediating between attachment and children's later (mal)adaptation, making it unclear whether the meta-analytic associations reported here are due to effects of attachment on the psychobiological mediators described earlier or stability in the caregiving environment. Researchers should test these possibilities by adopting many methods so neurobiological (e.g., hypothalamic–pituitary–adrenal axis function, neural activity), cognitive (e.g., internal working models, social attributions), emotional (emotion regulation), and social (e.g., continuity in care) mechanisms are examined simultaneously to tease apart their unique versus joint contribution. In conceptualizing how these multilevel mechanisms might explain attachment–outcome associations, researchers might draw on a cascade model in which associations between early attachment and competencies in subsequently developing domains of socioemotional development arise from the spreading effect of (in)security on functioning across many levels (including cognitive, emotional, and neurobiological) that may or may not depend on the ongoing quality of caregiving. Researchers could test this model through large-scale longitudinal interventions. Such studies may be important for understanding why and how attachment affects development and why, under some circumstances, it does not, information crucial for developing appropriately targeted interventions.

In summary, our meta-analyses of nearly five decades of research on early attachment relationships provide evidence consistent with claims made by attachment theory that attachment security is not determined by infants' temperamental characteristics and have long-term significance for children's socioemotional development. However, researchers need to go beyond current measurement models, place more emphasis on mediating and moderating mechanisms, and conduct joint, multisite efforts to replicate, refine, and extend core findings in attachment research.

# References

Ainsworth, M. D. S. (1982). Attachment: Retrospect and prospect. In C. M. Parkes & J. Stevenson-Hinde (Eds.). *The place of attachment in human behavior* (pp. 3–30). New York, NY: Basic Books.

Ainsworth, M. D. S., Blehar, M. C., Waters, E., & Wall, S. (1978). *Patterns of attachment: A psychological study of the strange situation (Vol. xviii)*. Hillsdale, NJ: Erlbaum.

Belsky, J. (1997). Theory testing, effect-size evaluation, and differential susceptibility to rearing influence: The case of mothering and attachment. *Child Development, 64*, 598–600. doi:10.2307/1132110

Belsky, J., & Cassidy, J. (1994). Attachment theory and evidence. In M. Rutter & D. Hay (Eds.). *Development through life* (pp. 373–402). London: Blackwell.

Belsky, J., & Fearon, R. (2002). Infant–mother attachment security, contextual risk, and early development: A moderational analysis. *Development and Psychopathology, 14*, 293–310. doi:10.1017/S0954579402002067

Berlin, L. J., Cassidy, J., & Appleyard, K. (2008). The influence of early attachments on other relationships. In J. Cassidy & P. R. Shaver (Eds.). *Handbook of attachment: Theory, research, and clinical applications* (2nd edn., pp. 333–347). New York, NY: Guilford.

Bowlby, J. (1973). *Attachment and loss: Vol. 2. Separation: Anxiety and anger*. New York, NY: Basic Books.

Bowlby, J. (1982). *Attachment and loss: Vol. 1. Attachment*. New York, NY: Basic Books. (Original work published 1969).

Bretherton, I. (1987). New perspectives on attachment relations: Security, communication, and working models. In J. Osofsky (Ed.). *Handbook of infant development* (2nd edn., pp. 1061–1100). New York, NY: Wiley.

Bretherton, I., & Munholland, K. A. (2008). Internal working models in attachment relationships: Elaborating a central construct in attachment theory. In J. Cassidy & P. R. Shaver (Eds.). *Handbook of attachment: Theory, research, and clinical applications* (2nd edn., pp. 102–127). New York, NY: Guilford.

Brumariu, L. E., & Kerns, K. K. (2010). Parent–child attachment and internalizing symptoms in childhood and adolescence: A review of empirical findings and future directions. *Development and Psychopathology, 22*, 177–203. doi:10.1017/S0954579409990344

Carlson, E. A. (1998). A prospective longitudinal study of attachment disorganization / disorientation. *Child Development, 69*, 1107–1128. doi:10.2307/1132365

Cassidy, J. (1994). Emotion regulation: Influences of attachment relationships. *Monographs of the Society for Research in Child Development, 59* (Serial No. 2/3), 228–249. doi:10.1111/j.1540-5834.1994.tb01287.x

Coan, J. A. (2016). Towards a neuroscience of attachment. In J. Cassidy & P. R. Shaver (Eds.). *Handbook of attachment: Theory, research, and clinical applications* (3rd edn., pp. 242–269). New York, NY: Guilford.

Cohen, J. (1988). *Statistical power analysis for the behavioral sciences* (2nd edn.). Hillsdale, NJ: Erlbaum.

Colonnesi, C., Draijer, E. M., Stams, G. J. J. M., Van der Bruggem, C. O., Bogels, S. M., & Noom, M. J. (2011). The relation between insecure attachment and child anxiety: A meta-analytic study. *Journal of Child Clinical and Adolescent Psychology, 40*, 630–645. doi:10.1080/15374416.2011.581623

Coppola, G., Vaughn, B. E., Cassibba, R., & Costantini, A. (2006). The attachment script representation procedure in an Italian sample: Associations with Adult Attachment Interview scales and with maternal sensitivity. *Attachment & Human Development, 8*, 209–219. doi:10.1080/14616730600856065

DeKlyen, M., & Greenberg, M. T. (2008). Attachment and psychopathology in childhood. In J. Cassidy & P. R. Shaver (Eds.). *Handbook of attachment: Theory, research and clinical applications* (2nd edn., pp. 637–665). New York, NY: Guilford.

Dykas, M. J., & Cassidy, J. (2011). Attachment and the processing of social information across the life span: Theory and evidence. *Psychological Bulletin, 137*, 19–46. doi:10.1037/a0021367

Ellis, B. J., Boyce, W. T., Belsky, J., Bakermans-Kranenburg, M. J., & Van IJzendoorn, M. H. (2011). Differential susceptibility to the environment: An evolutionary neurodevelopmental theory. *Development and Psychopathology, 23*, 7–28. doi:10.1017/S0954579410000611

Fearon, R. P., Bakermans-Kranenburg, M. J., Van IJzendoorn, M. H., Lapsley, A., & Roisman, G. I. (2010). The significance of insecure attachment and disorganization in the development of children's externalizing behavior: A meta-analytic study. *Child Development, 81*, 435–456. doi:10.1111/j.1467-8624.2009.01405.x

Fearon, R. M. P., & Belsky, J. (2016). Precursors of attachment security. In J. Cassidy & P. R. Shaver (Eds.). *Handbook of attachment: Theory, research, and clinical applications* (3rd edn., pp. 291–313). New York, NY: Guilford.

Fearon, R. P., Groh, A. M., Bakermans-Kranenburg, M. J., Van IJzendoorn, M. H., & Roisman, G. I. (2016). Attachment and development psychopathology. In D. Cicchetti (Ed.). *Developmental psychopathology, volume one, theory and method* (3rd edn., pp. 325–384). New York, NY: Wiley.

Fraley, R. C., & Spieker, S. J. (2003). Are infant attachment patterns continuously or categorically distributed? A taxometric analysis of strange situation behavior. *Developmental Psychology, 39*, 387–404. doi:10.1037/0012-1649.39.3.387

Groh, A. M., Fearon, R. P., Bakermans-Kranenburg, M. J., Van IJzendoorn, M. H., Steele, R. D., & Roisman, G. I. (2014). The significance of attachment security for children's social competence with peers: A meta-analytic study. *Attachment & Human Development, 16*, 103–136. doi:10.1080/14616734.2014.883636

Groh, A. M., Narayan, A. J., Bakermans-Kranenburg, M. J., Roisman, G. I., Vaughn, B. E., Fearon, R. P., & Van IJzendoorn, M. H. (2017). Attachment and temperament in the early life course: A meta-analytic review. *Child Development. 88* (3), 770–795

Groh, A. M., Roisman, G. I., Van IJzendoorn, M. H., Bakermans-Kranenburg, M. J., & Fearon, R. M. P. (2012). The significance of insecure and disorganized attachment for children's internalizing symptoms: A meta-analytic study. *Child Development, 83*, 591–610. doi:10.1111/j.1467-8624.2011.01711.x

Hoeve, M., Semon Dubas, J., Eichelsheim, V. I., Van der Laan, P. H., Smeenk, W., & Gerris, J. R. M. (2009). The relationship between parenting and delinquency: A meta-analysis. *Journal of Abnormal Child Psychology, 37*, 749–775. doi:10.1007/s10802-009-9310-8

Kawabata, Y., Alink, L. R. A., Tseng, W., Van IJzendoorn, M. H., & Crick, N. R. (2011). Maternal and paternal parenting styles associated with relational aggression in children and adolescents: A conceptual analysis and meta-analytic review. *Developmental Review, 31*, 240–278. doi:10.1016/j.dr.2011.08.001

Klein, R. A., Ratliff, K. A., Vianello, M., Adams, R. B., Jr., Bahník, Š., Bernstein, M. J., . . . Nosek, B. A. (2014). Investigating variation in replicability: A "many labs" replication project. *Social Psychology, 45*, 142–152. doi:10.1027/1864-9335/a000178

Lamb, M. E., Thompson, R. A., Gardner, W. P., Charnov, E. L., & Estes, D. (1984). Security of infantile attachment as assessed in the strange situation: Its study and biological interpretation. *Behavioral and Brain Sciences, 7*, 127–171. doi:10.1017/S0140525X00026522

Madigan, S., Atkinson, L., Laurin, K., & Benoit, D. (2013). Attachment and internalizing behavior in early childhood: A meta-analysis. *Developmental Psychology, 49*, 672–689. doi:10.1037/a0028793

McCartney, K., & Rosenthal, R. (2000). Effect size, practical importance, and social policy for children. *Child Development, 71*, 173–180. doi:10.1111/1467-8624.00131

Mesman, J., Van IJzendoorn, M. H., & Sagi-Schwartz, A. (2016). Cross-cultural patterns of attachment: Universal and contextual dimensions. In J. Cassidy & P. R. Shaver (Eds.). *Handbook of attachment: Theory, research, and clinical applications* (3rd edn., pp. 852–877). New York, NY: Guilford.

Rutter, M. (1979). Protective factors in children's responses to stress and disadvantage. In M. W. Kent & J. E. Rolf (Eds.). *Primary prevention in psychopathology: Social competence in children* (pp. 49–74). Hanover, NH: University Press of New England.

Schoenmaker, C., Juffer, F., Van IJzendoorn, M. H., Linting, M., Van der Voort, A., & Bakermans-Kranenburg, M. J. (2015). From maternal sensitivity in infancy to adult attachment representations: A longitudinal adoption study with secure base scripts. *Attachment & Human Development, 17*, 241–256. doi:10.1080/14616734.2015.1037315

Sroufe, L. A. (1985). Attachment classification from the perspective of infant–caregiver relationships and infant temperament. *Child Development, 56*, 1–14. doi:10.2307/1130168

Sroufe, L. A. (2003). Attachment categories as reflections of multiple dimensions: Comment on Fraley and Spieker (2003). *Developmental Psychology, 39*, 413–416. doi:10.1037/0012-1649.39.3.413

Sroufe, L. A., Egeland, B., & Kreutzer, T. (1990). The fate of early experience following developmental change: Longitudinal approaches to individual adaptation in childhood. *Child Development, 61*, 1363–1373. doi:10.1111/j.1467-8624.1990.tb02867.x

Steele, R. D., Waters, T. E. A., Bost, K. K., Vaughn, B. E., Truitt, W., Waters, H. S., . . . Roisman, G. I. (2014). Caregiving antecedents of secure base script knowledge: A comparative analysis of young adult attachment representations. *Developmental Psychology, 50*, 2526–2538. doi:10.1037/a0037992

Van IJzendoorn, M. H., & Bakermans-Kranenburg, M. J. (2012). Integrating temperament and attachment. In M. Zentner & R. L. Shiner (Eds.). *Handbook of temperament* (pp. 403–424). New York, NY: Guilford.

Vaughn, B. E., & Bost, K. K. (2016). Attachment and temperament as intersecting developmental products and interacting developmental contexts throughout infancy and childhood. In J. Cassidy & P. R. Shaver (Eds.). *Handbook of attachment: Theory, research, and clinical applications* (3rd edn., pp. 202–222). New York, NY: Guilford.

Waters, H. S., & Waters, E. (2006). The attachment working model concept: Among other things, we build script-like representations of secure base experiences. *Attachment & Human Development, 8,* 185–197. doi:10.1080/14616730600856016

# Attachment and Biobehavioral Catch-up

## Addressing the Needs of Infants and Toddlers Exposed to Inadequate or Problematic Caregiving

### Mary Dozier and Kristin Bernard

## Introduction

Sensitive parental care during infancy is critical for optimal development. Thus, caregiving that is inadequate (as in neglect) or problematic (as in abuse or frightening behavior) undermines children's development of behavioral and biological regulation. Attachment and Biobehavioral Catch-up (ABC; Dozier et al., 2014) is a 10-session home visiting program that was designed to target the issues that are especially challenging for infants who experience inadequate or problematic parenting. This brief review aims to (a) establish the empirical and theoretical basis for ABC, (b) provide an overview of the ABC model for infants, (c) present research evidence that supports the efficacy of ABC in improving parental sensitivity, and child attachment and other behavioral and biological outcomes, (d) introduce a novel adaptation of ABC for toddlers exposed to early adversity, an underserved population with unique needs, and (e) describe efforts to disseminate ABC with fidelity.

## The Importance of Caregiving in Infancy

Infancy represents an important period for developing brain architecture (Shonkoff et al., 2012), for developing the seeds of self-regulation (Hofer, 1994), and for forming attachments with primary caregivers (Bowlby, 1982; Fearon & Roisman, 2017). The evolutionary history of humans has resulted in a protracted period of immaturity; infants are almost fully dependent on parents or primary caregivers as co-regulators of physiology and behavior (Hofer, 1994). The attachment system evolved as a mechanism that promoted infants' chances of proximity to caregivers under conditions of threat (Bowlby, 1982).

Sensitive, responsive parenting has been posited as key to optimal development in infancy (Ainsworth, 1967; Verhage et al., 2016; Fearon & Roisman, 2017). At least partially on the basis of early experience, the developing brain makes connections between neurons in simple circuits and eventually between brain regions in complex circuits (Belsky & de Haan, 2011; Tottenham, 2012). The developing brain architecture is therefore differentially affected when young children have responsive parents than when they do not. Further, self-regulatory capabilities develop most optimally when the caregiver can serve as a co-regulator for the child; over time and as the result of many experiences of having challenging experiences scaffolded by the sensitive caregiver, the child gradually takes

*Source:* Reprinted from Mary Dozier, Kristin Bernard, "Attachment and Biobehavioral Catch-up: Addressing the Needs of Infants and Toddlers Exposed to Inadequate or Problematic Caregiving," pp. 111–117 from *Current Opinion in Psychology* 15:1 (2017) with permission from Elsevier.

over regulatory functions effectively him or herself (Hofer, 1994; Raver, 1996; Bernier et al., 2015). Secure, organized attachments develop when the caregiver is emotionally available and responsive to the infant's distress (Van Ijzendoorn, 1995; Fearon & Roisman, 2017).

## Effects of Inadequate Caregiving

On the other hand, when caregivers do not provide sensitive, nurturing care, or are insensitive or frightening, it becomes more likely that brain development does not proceed optimally (Tottenham, 2012; Belsky & de Haan, 2011; Teicher & Samson, 2016), more likely that children fail to develop adequate self-regulatory functions (Bernard et al., 2010), and more likely that they develop disorganized rather than organized attachments (Dozier et al., 2001; Cyr et al., 2010). Taken together, these resulting changes in brain structure and function, physiological and behavioral regulation, and attachment exacerbate risk for mental and physical problems across the lifespan (Fearon et al., 2010; Bernard et al., 2015a; Nusslock & Miller, 2016).

For these children who have experienced adversity, responsive care is especially important so as to remediate effects of adversity. Indeed, longitudinal, correlational studies suggest that responsive parenting can buffer children in the face of adversity (e.g., Miller et al., 2011; Asok et al., 2013). Although responsive care is essential for children who have experienced early adversity, many parents are unable to provide this kind of buffering care. Mothers' own histories of childhood maltreatment interfere with their executive functioning and physiological regulation, which in turn leads to insensitive parenting (Gonzalez et al., 2013). Additionally, high levels of current parenting stress have been shown to explain the link between mothers' histories of adversity and insensitive parenting (Pereira et al., 2012). Parents providing foster or adoptive care may also struggle to respond in sensitive ways because children previously exposed to adverse caregiving may fail to signal their needs for nurturance clearly (Dozier et al., 2001; Stovall-McClough & Dozier, 2004). Thus, both biological and non-biological parents face challenges that may interfere with providing vulnerable children with the enhanced parental care that they may need.

## Attachment and Biobehavioral Catch-up

Attachment and Biobehavioral Catch-up (ABC) was designed to target three parenting behaviors that are key to child regulation of behavior and physiology. First, because non-nurturing care is associated with disorganized attachment for vulnerable children (Dozier et al., 2001), ABC intervenes to help parents behave in nurturing ways when their children are distressed. Second, to target children's self-regulatory issues, including difficulty regulating physiology, emotions, and behavior, ABC helps parents follow their children's lead. This has been referred to as 'serve and return interactions' (Shonkoff & Bales, 2011), and as contingent responsiveness (Raver, 1996; Mcquaid et al., 2009). The third target of ABC is reducing frightening behavior, such as yelling, grabbing roughly, and intruding in the child's space, because such behavior undermines children's ability to develop organized attachments (Schuengel et al., 1999), and develop adequate regulatory capabilities (Bernard & Dozier, 2010).

The focus of the ABC intervention is squarely on changing parental behaviors. This focus is apparent in a variety of ways, including the choice of where the intervention is implemented, who is included in sessions, and how it is implemented. First, the intervention is implemented in parents' homes, with office or clinic intervention sessions not recommended. Second, other family members (e.g., boyfriends, grandparents, other children) are invited to join sessions. Parents therefore are practicing new parenting behaviors in the environments in which they live (e.g., grandmother disagreeing with session content, three children vying for attention, etc.).

Third, and key to successful implementation of the intervention is frequent 'in the moment' comments about relevant parent behaviors made by the parent coach. Every time that parents follow their child's lead (or fail to do so), or are nurturing when their child is distressed (or fail to be nurturing), is an opportunity for the parent coach to make a comment. An in the moment comment may contain up to three components; the parent coach may (1) describe the child's behavior and parent's response (e.g., "He cried and you picked him up"), (2) label the intervention target (e.g., "That was a great example of being nurturing when he was distressed"), and/or (3) indicate a potential outcome of the parent's response (e.g., "He will learn trust because he gets a response from you so quickly"). Parent coaches are expected to make comments in at least 50% of the opportunities they have, and at a pace of at least one per minute. Therefore, across a one-hour intervention session, parents should be hearing feedback (most of it positive) about 60 times regarding their following their child's lead and nurturing their child. The frequency of in the moment comments, as well as their quality (*e.g.*, percentage that correctly label the intervention target, average number of components included in comments), has been found to predict the magnitude of change in parent sensitivity (Caron et al., 2018). Parent coaches make in the moment comments throughout each session while also covering content related to one of the three intervention targets: providing nurturance (Sessions 1 and 2), following the child's lead (Sessions 3–5), or avoiding frightening behavior (Session 6). In each session, the parent coach defines the intervention target, presents a research-based rationale for its importance, guides a discussion with the parent regarding the target, presents video examples (both standard videos and video clips from the target dyad), and/or provides feedback during structured parent–child interaction activities. In Sessions 7 and 8, the parent coach further encourages the intervention targets by helping the parent identify 'voices from the past' that interfere with sensitive parenting. Finally, the parent coach consolidates gains and celebrates changes in Sessions 9 and 10. Importantly, throughout all 10 sessions, the parent coach prioritizes in the moment commenting above manual content—interrupting themselves frequently to comment on nurturance and following the lead. These frequent interruptions serve to constantly bring the attention back to the parent's responses toward the child, sending the message to the parent that her interactions with the child are always most important.

Several properties of ABC are consistent with qualities that have distinguished effective interventions in the literature. First, ABC is short-term (i.e., 10 one-hour sessions, delivered once per week), consistent with findings from a meta-analysis of 70 attachment-based interventions showing that programs with shorter durations were *more effective* than those with longer durations (>16 sessions) (Bakermans-Kranenburg et al., 2003). Even for multi-risk families, interventions that had fewer than 16 sessions were most effective for changing sensitive parenting and child attachment. Second, also consistent with meta-analytic findings (Bakermans-Kranenburg et al., 2003), ABC's focus is solely on changing parenting *behaviors*. The meta-analysis found that interventions that focused specifically on changing parents' behaviors were more effective than interventions that focused on changing parents' internal representations (i.e., parents' cognitive models about attachment) or providing social support. Actually, interventions with an exclusively behavioral focus were even more effective than those that tried to change behavior *and* provide social support or change internal representations, suggesting that a very targeted approach is ideal. Third, the ABC intervention is conducted with parents and children together after infants are at least 6 months of age, allowing parents to practice and receive feedback on the target skills; metaanalytic findings (Bakermans-Kranenburg et al., 2003) demonstrated that parenting interventions conducted prenatally were less effective than those conducted after the birth of children, perhaps because a didactic approach (without the opportunity to practice and receive feedback) is not sufficient for changing behavior.

## Efficacy of ABC

By increasing nurturance in response to distress, increasing following the lead, and reducing frightening behavior, ABC is expected to improve children's attachment quality and self-regulation; in turn, these early competencies, along with ongoing enhanced parenting, are expected to support long-term outcomes of improved inhibitory control, peer relations, emotion regulation, and physiological regulation (See Figure 13.1).

In randomized clinical trials, children and parents who receive ABC were compared to children and parents in a control group, who received a comparison intervention. The comparison intervention, referred to as DEF (i.e., Developmental Education for Families), was also 10 sessions, delivered in the home, and involved video feedback. However, the comparison intervention focused specifically on language and motor development, and avoided topics related to parent sensitivity. With some exceptions (Bakermans-Kranenburg et al., 2003; Berlin et al., 2014), ABC has primarily been tested in our lab.

Parents assigned to the ABC intervention showed greater sensitivity and lower levels of intrusiveness at post-intervention than parents assigned to the control intervention (Bick & Dozier, 2013; Bernard et al., 2015b; Yarger et al., 2016). In a study of parents' brain activity, assessed using event-related potentials (ERP), parents who received ABC showed a larger enhancement of ERP responses for emotional faces relative to neutral faces than

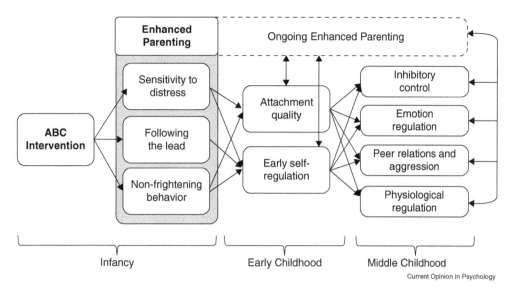

**Figure 13.1** Conceptual model for anticipated effects of ABC on key outcomes in early childhood and middle childhood.

parents who received a control intervention (Bernard et al., 2015b). Whereas ABC parents' brain activity to children's emotional faces was similar to low-risk comparison parents, the attenuated responses to emotional faces seen among parents in the control intervention mirrored brain responses of neglectful parents in a previous study (Rodrigo et al., 2011).

Children who received ABC showed enhanced functioning across key developmental domains. More of the children in the ABC intervention group had secure attachments as assessed in the strange situation, and fewer had disorganized attachments, than children in the control group (Bernard et al., 2012). Children in the ABC group also had more normative patterns of cortisol production at post-intervention than children in the control group (Bernard et al., 2015c), with these effects persisting three years post-intervention (Bernard et al., 2015d). As toddlers, children in the ABC intervention showed lower anger during a frustrating problem-solving task than children in the control group (Lind et al., 2014). Finally, children in the ABC group also showed more optimal inhibitory control and cognitive flexibility several years after the intervention than children in the control group (Lewis-Morrarty et al., 2012; Lind et al., 2017).

## Unique Needs of Toddlers Exposed to Adversity

Toddlerhood represents a developmental period of increasing autonomy, with children typically becoming more independent in regulating emotions and behavior (Calkins & Leerkes, 2011). Children with a history of early adversity, however, often struggle to develop self-regulatory competencies, showing poorer executive functioning (Pears & Fisher, 2005) and higher externalizing behavior (Bernard et al., 2015a) than typically-developing peers. Difficult child behaviors such as aggression, defiance, and hyperactivity may directly interfere with receiving sensitive care, as these behaviors can challenge parents' own emotion regulation abilities. In response, parents may be harsh or threatening, setting limits in coercive ways. Thus, toddlers who experience early adversity are especially in need of intervention if they are to develop good self-regulation.

## ABC for Toddlers

A number of attachment-based parenting programs, such as ABC, has been developed for infants (Bakermans-Kranenburg et al., 2005; Cyr & Alink, 2017), and a number of behavior-management parenting programs has been developed for preschoolers (Fisher & Kim, 2007; Thomas & Zimmer-Gembeck, 2012; Fisher & Skowron, 2017; Gardner & Leijten, 2017). However, parenting interventions for toddlers that address attachment needs for nurturing and responsive relationships *and* behavioral needs for help regulating emerging dysregulation are lacking. A notable exception is the Video-feed-back Intervention to promote Positive Parenting and Sensitive Discipline

(VIPP-SD), which aims to enhance sensitive parenting especially in the context of limitsetting for young children with behavior problems (Van Zeijl et al., 2006).

ABC for Toddlers (ABC-T) also addresses this gap. In addition to helping parents respond in nurturing ways to children's distress and follow children's lead with delight, ABC-T helps parents serve as co-regulators of children's emerging behavioral dysregulation. Parents learn strategies to help toddlers settle in the context of a supportive relationship. ABC-T encourages parents to remain physically and psychologically available and sensitive when children are showing destructive or aggressive behaviors. Strategies include: staying calm and labeling the child's emotion, avoiding power struggles and lecturing, remaining close and providing nurturance, and resuming following the child's lead with delight when the child is calm. Similar to ABC for infants, ABC-T coaches provide frequent in the moment comments to celebrate, reinforce, and scaffold parents' behaviors with regard to each of the targets. In a randomized clinical trial, ABC-T has been found to improve foster children's cognitive flexibility and reduce foster children's attention problems (Lind et al., 2017). In ongoing research, it will be critical to examine whether ABC-T reduces externalizing behaviors, such as aggression and non-compliance, in addition to the related constructs of cognitive self-control.

## Success in Disseminating ABC

Often when interventions with strong efficacy results are implemented in community settings, the effects are substantially smaller than in the lab (Weisz et al., 1995; Durlak & DuPre, 2008; Hulleman & Cordray, 2009). Although ABC has not yet been tested in a randomized clinical trial in the community, pre-intervention and post-intervention sensitivity data aggregated for 108 dyads, seen by 38 coaches across 5 dissemination sites, show a large effect size ($d$ = .83, Roben et al., 2017), which is at least as large as effect sizes seen in efficacy studies. The successful dissemination of ABC is likely the result of first identifying the active ingredient for parent behavior change (i.e., in the moment commenting) and then developing training, supervision, and fidelity monitoring that enhance this active ingredient. The fidelity-monitoring system that quantifies the frequency and quality of in the moment comments is used in weekly supervision. The parent coach and her fidelity supervisor code a randomly selected 5-min segment from one of the coach's sessions each week. In that 5-min clip, each coder identifies every opportunity to comment (i.e., any time that the parent behaved in a way that was consistent or inconsistent with a target, such as being nurturing or not nurturing). For every opportunity, the coder then identifies whether the parent coach commented, and if she did, rates a number of indicators about the quality of the comment (e.g., on-target vs. off-target, number of components included). Summary information for the video, including the frequency of comments, percent of comments that were on-target, and number of missed opportunities to comment, is used in weekly fidelity supervision to enhance the coach's skill in commenting. Although the self-coding has been shown to lead to improved commenting in a case study (Meade et al., 2018), ongoing work about ABC supervision aims to understand what approaches to supervision are most effective in improving and maintaining parent coach fidelity.

## Summary

Infants and toddlers with histories of inadequate or problematic parenting are especially in need of sensitive care to develop self-regulation. By helping parents nurture children in times of distress, follow children's lead, and avoid behaving in frightening ways, ABC enhances secure and organized attachments, cortisol regulation, and behavioral outcomes. Evidence of ABC's efficacy informs models of developmental psychopathology, highlighting the critical role of sensitive parenting for young children's healthy development. Following models of differential susceptibility (Belsky et al., 2007; Bakermans-Kranenburg et al., 2008; Overbeek, 2017), future research should examine what factors in children and parents predict the magnitude of changes seen in outcomes as a result of ABC. Such evidence about moderators of treatment effectiveness can help in targeting interventions to those most likely to benefit, and tailoring interventions to those that may need a different or more intensive approach. These future directions, and others, are critical for ensuring that interventions, such as ABC, are meeting the needs of high risk parents and vulnerable infants.

# References

Ainsworth, M. D. S. (1967). *Infancy in Uganda: Infant care and growth of love.* Baltimore, MD: Johns Hopkins University Press.

Asok, A., Bernard, K., Roth, T. L., Rosen, J. B., & Dozier, M. (2013). Parental responsiveness moderates the association between early-life stress and reduced telomere length. *Developmental Psychopathology, 25,* 577–585 http://dx.doi.org/10.1017/S0954579413000011.

Bakermans-Kranenburg, M. J,. van IJzendoorn, M. H., & Juffer, F. (2003). Less is more: meta-analyses of sensitivity and attachment interventions in early childhood. *Psychological Bulletin, 129,* 195–215 http://www.ncbi.nlm.nih.gov/pubmed/12696839.

Bakermans-Kranenburg, M. J., van IJzendoorn, M. H., & Juffer, F. (2005). Disorganized infant attachment and preventive interventions: a review and meta-analysis. *Infant Mental Health, 26,* 191–216 http://dx.doi.org/10.1002/imhj.20046.

Bakermans-Kranenburg, M. J., van IJzendoorn, M. H., Mesman, J., Alink, L. R. A., & Juffer, F. (2008). Effects of an attachment-based intervention on daily cortisol moderated by dopamine receptor D4: a randomized control trial on 1- to 3-year-olds screened for externalizing behavior. *Developmental Psychopathology, 20,* 805–2820 http://dx.doi.org/10.1017/S0954579408000382.

Belsky, J., & de Haan, M. (2011). Annual research review: parenting and children's brain development: the end of the beginning. *Journal of Child Psychology & Psychiatry, 52,* 409–428 http://dx.doi.org/10.1111/j.1469-7610.2010.02281.x.

Belsky, J., Bakermans-Kranenburg, M. J., & van IJzendoorn, M. H. (2007). For better and for worse: differential susceptibility to environmental influences. *Current Directions in Psychological Science, 16,* 300–304 http://dx.doi.org/10.1111/j.1467-8721.2007.00525.x.

Berlin, L. J., Shanahan, M., & Appleyard Carmody, K. (2014). Promoting supportive parenting in new mothers with substance-use problems: a pilot randomized trial of residential treatment plus an attachment-based parenting program. *Infant Mental Health, 35,* 81–85 http://dx.doi.org/10.1002/imhj.21427.

Bernard, K., Butzin-Dozier, Z., Rittenhouse, J., & Dozier, M. (2010). Cortisol production patterns in young children living with birth parents vs children placed in foster care following involvement of Child Protective Services. *Archives of Pediatric and Adolescent Medicine, 164,* 438–443 http://dx.doi.org/10.1001/archpediatrics.2010.54.

Bernard, K., & Dozier, M. (2010). Examining infants' cortisol responses to laboratory tasks among children varying in attachment disorganization: stress reactivity or return to baseline? *Developmental Psychology, 46,* 1771–1778.

Bernard, K., Dozier, M., Bick, J., & Gordon, M. K. (2015). Intervening to enhance cortisol regulation among children at risk for neglect: results of a randomized clinical trial. *Developmental Psychopathology, 27,* 829–841 http://www.journals.cambridge.org/abstract_S095457941400073X.

Bernard, K., Dozier, M., Bick, J., Lewis-Morrarty, E., Lindhiem, O., & Carlson, E. (2012). Enhancing attachment organization among maltreated children: results of a randomized clinical trial. *Child Development, 83,* 623–636.

Bernard, K., Zwerling, J., & Dozier, M. (2015a). Effects of early adversity on young children's diurnal cortisol rhythms and externalizing behavior. *Developmental Psychobiology, 57,* 935–947.

Bernard, K., Simons, R., & Dozier, M. (2015b). Effects of an attachment-based intervention on child protective services-referred mothers' event-related potentials to children's emotions. *Child Development 2015, 86,* 1673–1684.

Bernard, K., Hostinar, C. E., & Dozier, M. (2015c). Intervention effects on diurnal cortisol rhythms of child protective services-referred infants in early childhood. *JAMA Pediatrics 169* (2), 112–119 http://dx.doi.org/10.1001/jamapediatrics.2014.2369.

Bernier, A., Beauchamp, M. H., Carlson, S. M., & Lalonde, G. (2015). A secure base from which to regulate: attachment security in toddlerhood as a predictor of executive functioning at school entry. *Developmental Psychology, 51,* 1177–1189 http://dx.doi.org/10.1037/dev0000032.

Bick, J., & Dozier, M. (2013). The effectiveness of an attachment-based intervention in promoting foster mothers' sensitivity toward foster infants. *Infant Mental Health, 34,* 95–103 http://dx.doi. org/10.1002/imhj.21373.

Bowlby, J. (1982), *Attachment and loss.* London: Hogarth Press

Calkins, S. D., & Leerkes, E. M. (2011). Early attachment processes and the development of emotional self-regulation. In K. D. Vohs & R. F. Baumeister. (Eds.). *Handbook of self-regulation: Research, theory, and applications,* 2nd edn. (pp. 355–373), New York, NY: Guilford Press.

Caron, E. B., Bernard, K., & Dozier, M. (2018). In vivo feedback predicts parent behavior change in the Attachment and Biobehavioral Catch-up intervention. *Journal of Clinical Child & Adolescent Psychology, 47* (1), 35–S46.

Cyr, C., & Alink, L. R. (2017). Child maltreatment: the central roles of parenting capacities and attachment. *Current Opinion in Psychology, 15,* 81–86.

Cyr, C., Euser, E. M., Bakermans-Kranenburg, M. J. & van IJzendoorn, M. H. (2010). Attachment security and disorganization in maltreating and high-risk families: a series of meta-analyses. *Developmental Psychopathology, 22,* 87–108 http://dx.doi.org/10.1017/S0954579409990289.

Dozier, M., Meade, E. B., & Bernard, K. (2014). Attachment and biobehavioral catch-up: an intervention for parents at risk of maltreating their infants and toddlers. In S. Timmer, & A. Urquiza (Eds.). *Evidence-based approaches for the treatment of child maltreatment* (pp. 43–60). New York, NY: Springer. http://dx.doi.org/10.1007/978-94-007-7404-9_4.

Dozier, M., Stovall, K. C., Albus, K. E., & Bates, B. (2001). Attachment for infants in foster care: the role of caregiver state of mind. *Child Development*, *72*, 1467–1477 http://www.ncbi.nlm.nih.gov/pubmed/11699682.

Durlak, J. A., & DuPre, E. P. (2008). Implementation matters: a review of research on the influence of implementation on program outcomes and the factors affecting implementation. *American Journal of Community Psychology*, *41*, 327–350 http://dx.doi.org/10.1007/s10464-008-9165-0.

Fearon, R. P., Bakermans-Kranenburg, M. J., van IJzendoorn, M. H., Lapsley, A-M., & Roisman, G. I. (2010). The significance of insecure attachment and disorganization in the development of children's externalizing behavior: a meta-analytic study. *Child Development*, *81*, 435–456 http://dx.doi.org/10.1111/j.1467-8624.2009.01405.x.

Fearon, R. P., & Roisman, G. I. (2017). Attachment theory: progress and future directions. *Current Opinion in Psychology*, *15*, 131–136.

Fisher, P.A., & Kim, H. K. (2007). Intervention effects on foster preschoolers' attachment-related behaviors from a randomized trial. *Preventative Science*, *8*, 161–170 http://dx.doi.org/10.1007/s11121-007-0066-5.

Fisher, P. A., & Skowron, E. A. (2017). Social-learning parenting intervention research in the era of translational neuroscience. *Current Opinion in Psychology*, *15*, 168–173.

Gardner, F., & Leijten, P. (2017). Incredible Years parenting interventions: Current effectiveness research and future directions. *Current Opinion in Psychology*, *15*, 99–104.

Gonzalez, A., Jenkins, J. M., Steiner, M., & Fleming, A. S. (2012). Maternal early life experiences and parenting: the mediating role of cortisol and executive function. *Journal of the American Academy of Child & Adolescent Psychiatry*, *51*, 673–682 http://dx.doi.org/10.1016/j.jaac.2012.04.003.

Hofer, M. (1994). Hidden regulators in attachment separation, and loss. *Monographs of the Society for Research in Child Development*, *59*, 192–207.

Hulleman, C. S., & Cordray, D. S. (2009). Moving from the lab to the field: The role of fidelity and achieved relative intervention strength. *Journal of Research on Educational Effectiveness*, *2* (1), 88–110.

Kotch, J. B., Lewis, T., Hussey, J. M., English, D., Thompson, R., Litrownik, A. J., Runyan, D. K., Bangdiwala, S. I., Margolis, B., & Dubowitz, H. (2008). Importance of early neglect for childhood aggression. *Pediatrics*, *121*, 725–731 http://dx.doi.org/10.1542/peds.2006-3622.

Lewis-Morrarty, E., Dozier, M., Bernard, K., Terracciano, S. M., & Moore, S. V. (2012). Cognitive flexibility and theory of mind outcomes among foster children: preschool follow-up results of a randomized clinical trial. *Journal of Adolescent Health*, *51*, 17–22 http://dx.doi.org/10.1016/j.jadohealth.2012.05.005.

Lind, T., Bernard, K., Ross, E., & Dozier, M. (2014). Intervention effects on negative affect of CPS-referred children: results of a randomized clinical trial. *Child Abuse & Neglect 38*, 1459–1467 http://www.pubmedcentral.nih.gov/articlerender.fcgi?artid=4160393&tool=pmcentrez&rendertype=abstract.

Lind, T., Raby, K. L., Caron, E. B., Roben, C. K., & Dozier, M. (2017). Enhancing executive functioning among toddlers in foster care with an attachment-based intervention. *Development and Psychopathology*, *29* (2), 575–586.

Mcquaid, N., Bibok, M., & Carpendale, J. (2009). Relation between maternal contingent responsiveness and infant social expectations. *Infancy*, *14*, 390–401 http://dx.doi.org/10.1080/15250000902839955.

Meade, E., Dozier, M., & Bernard, K. (2014). Using video feedback as a tool in training parent coaches: promising results from a single-subject design. *Attachment & Human Development*, *16*, 356–370 http://www.ncbi.nlm.nih.gov/pubmed/24972104.

Miller, G. E., Lachman, M. E., Chen, E., Gruenewald, T. L., Karlamangla, A. S., & Seeman, T. E. (2011). Pathways to resilience: maternal nurturance as a buffer against the effects of childhood poverty on metabolic syndrome at midlife. *Psychological Science*, *22*, 1591–1599 http://dx. doi.org/10.1177/0956797611419170.

Nusslock, R., & Miller, G. E. (2016). Early-life adversity and physical and emotional health across the lifespan: a neuroimmune network hypothesis. *Biological Psychiatry*, *80*, 23–32 http://dx.doi.org/10.1016/j.biopsych.2015.05.017.

Overbeek, G. (2017). Parenting intervention effects on children's externalizing behavior: the moderating role of genotype and temperament. *Current Opinion in Psychology*, *15*, 143–148.

Pears, K., & Fisher, P. A. (2005). Developmental, cognitive, and neuropsychological functioning in preschool-aged foster children: Associations with prior maltreatment and placement history. *Journal of Developmental & Behavioral Pediatrics*, *26* (2), 112–122.

Pereira, J., Vickers, K., Atkinson, L., Gonzalez, A., Wekerle, C., & Levitan, R. (2012). Parenting stress mediates between maternal maltreatment history and maternal sensitivity in a community sample. *Child Abuse & Neglect*, *36*, 433–437 http://dx.doi.org/10.1016/j.chiabu.2012.01.006.

Raver, C. C. (1996). Relations between social contingency in mother–child interaction and 2-year-olds' social competence. *Developmental Psychology*, *32*, 850–859 http://dx.doi.org/10.1037/0012-1649.32.5.850.

Roben, C. K., Dozier, M., Caron, E. B., & Bernard, K. (2017). Moving an evidence-based parenting program into the community. *Child Development*, *88* (5), 1447–1452.

Rodrigo, M. J., León, I., Quiñones, I., Lage, A., Byrne, S., & Bobes, M. A. (2011). Brain and personality bases of insensitivity to infant cues in neglectful mothers: an event-related potential study. *Developmental Psychopathology*, *23*, 163–176 http://dx.doi.org/10.1017/S0954579410000714.

Schuengel, C., Bakermans-Kranenburg, M. J., & van IJzendoorn, M. H. (1999). Frightening maternal behavior linking unresolved loss and disorganized infant attachment. *Journal of Consulting & Clinical Psychology, 67*, 54–63 http://www.ncbi.nlm.nih.gov/pubmed/10028209.

Shonkoff, J. P., & Bales, S. N. (2011). Science does not speak for itself: translating child development research for the public and its policymakers. *Child Development, 82*, 17–32 http://dx.doi.org/10.1111/j.1467-8624.2010.01538.x.

Shonkoff, J. P., Richter, L., van der Gaag, J., & Bhutta, Z. A. (2012). An integrated scientific framework for child survival and early childhood development. *Pediatrics, 129*, e460–472 http://dx.doi.org/10.1542/peds.2011-0366.

Stovall-McClough, K. C., & Dozier, M: (2004). Forming attachments in foster care: infant attachment behaviors during the first 2 months of placement. *Developmental Psychopathology, 16*, 253–271 http://www.ncbi.nlm.nih.gov/pubmed/15487595.

Tottenham, N. (2012). Human amygdala development in the absence of species-expected caregiving. *Developmental Psychobiology, 54*, 598–611 http://dx.doi.org/10.1002/dev.20531.

Teicher, M. H. & Samson, J. A. (2016). Annual research review: enduring neurobiological effects of childhood abuse and neglect. *Journal of Child Psychology & Psychiatry, 57*, 241–266 http://dx.doi.org/10.1111/jcpp.12507.

Thomas, R., & Zimmer-Gembeck, M. J. (2012). Parent–child interaction therapy: an evidence-based treatment for child maltreatment. *Child Maltreatment, 17*, 253–266 http://dx.doi.org/10.1177/1077559512459555.

Van IJzendoorn, M. H. (1995). Adult attachment representations, parental responsiveness, and infant attachment: a metaanalysis on the predictive validity of the Adult Attachment Interview. *Psychological Bulletin, 117*, 387–403 http://www.ncbi.nlm.nih.gov/pubmed/7777645.

Van Zeijl, J., Mesman, J., van IJzendoorn, M. H., Bakermans-Kranenburg, M.J., Juffer, F., Stolk, M. N., Koot, H. M., & Alink, L. R. A. (2006). Attachment-based intervention for enhancing sensitive discipline in mothers of 1- to 3-year-old children at risk for externalizing behavior problems: a randomized controlled trial. *Journal of Consulting & Clinical Psychology, 74*, 994–1005 http://dx.doi.org/10.1037/0022-006X.74.6.994.

Verhage, M. L., Schuengel, C., Madigan, S., Fearon, R. M. P., Oosterman, M., Cassibba, R., Bakermans-Kranenburg, M. J., & van IJzendoorn, M. H. (2016). Narrowing the transmission gap: a synthesis of three decades of research on intergenerational transmission of attachment. *Psychological Bulletin, 142*, 337–366 http://dx.doi.org/10.1037/bul0000038.

Weisz, J. R., Donenberg, G. R., Han, S. S., & Weiss, B. (1995). Bridging the gap between laboratory and clinic in child and adolescent psychotherapy. *Journal of Consulting & Clinical Psychology, 63*, 688–701 http://www.ncbi.nlm.nih.gov/pubmed/7593861.

Yarger, H. A., Hoye, J. R., & Dozier, M. (2016). Trajectories of change in Attachment and Biobehavioral Catch-up among high-risk mothers: a randomized clinical trial. *Infant Mental Health, 37*, 525–536 http://dx.doi.org/10.1002/imhj.21585.

# 14

# Children's Multiple Attachment Relationships and Representations in Different Family Contexts

## Fabien Bacro, Tommie Forslund, and Pehr Granqvist

There is wide and longstanding consensus that children can – and often do – develop multiple attachment relationships (Bowlby, 1969; Cassidy, 2016; Howes & Spieker, 2016). However, there is still no consensus regarding the nature, structure and relative importance of each attachment relationship in children's development. In fact, these questions have received scarce empirical attention (Bacro & Florin, 2009); particularly considering that attachment research has been grappling with inconsistent links between attachment quality and subsequent development (Forslund & Granqvist, 2017).

Women's participation in the labor force has increased considerably in the modern Western societies, fathers claim their place as direct caregivers, and parental roles have consequently become more egalitarian. Many children are also confronted with parental separation or divorce and come to live with only one parent, in alternating residence, and/or with one or more step-parents. Furthermore, adoptees and children placed in foster care experience prolonged or permanent separations from their parents and face the challenge of developing attachment relationships to new principal attachment figures.

In this chapter, we review theory and research, including research of our own, which addresses how family contexts may influence children's attachment representations. The chapter aims to provide new insights into the multiplicity and organization of children's attachment relationships, building on research that is not yet published in English. We first examine how children's attachment relationships become organized in two-parent heterosexual families, then turn to divorced and separated families, and conclude with attachment representations and behavior problems among children in foster care.

## Attachment Representations

According to Bowlby (1969), human infants are evolutionarily predisposed to develop behavioral control systems. One such system is the attachment system. The primary function of this system in infancy is to maintain physical proximity with caregivers, but as the child develops, the goal is more generally to ensure the availability of the caregiver when distressed or alarmed. Consequently, the privileged relationships that most children develop with their principal caregivers follow from the caregivers acting as "safe havens" by responding with comfort to attachment behaviors. However, attachment figures also serve an important role as "secure bases" from which children

*Source:* Fabien Bacro, Pehr Granqvist, Tommie Forslund, *Children's Multiple Attachment Relationships and Representations in Different Family Context.* © 2021 John Wiley & Sons, Inc.

*Attachment Theory and Research: A Reader*, First Edition. Edited by Tommie Forslund and Robbie Duschinsky.
© 2021 John Wiley & Sons Ltd. Published 2021 by John Wiley & Sons Ltd.

explore the environment (Ainsworth, 1982; Bowlby, 1988). Attachment relationships are lasting ones that involve non-exchangeable persons and involuntary separations are consequently painful (Cassidy, 2016).

Children are thought to develop cognitive-affective representations, or "internal working models" (IWM) of self and others (Bowlby, 1969), as a function of their caregivers' characteristic responses to proximity and comfort-seeking behaviors. The IWMs guide children's interpretations of external events and organization of attachment behaviors; children therefore become active co-creators of their subsequent experiences. Stated differently, the IWMs are progressively integrated into personality (Bretherton, 1998).

There is robust support for attachment theory's core notions with a widespread consensus that caregiving influences attachment quality (van IJzendoorn & De Wolff, 1997), which in turn is predictive of subsequent development (Groh et al., 2017). However, the sensitivity of one particular caregiver only accounts for a moderate proportion of variance in children's attachment quality (Verhage et al., 2016), despite arduous work refining the assessment of pertinent caregiver behaviors (Bernier et al., 2014).

Importantly, various moderators typically are invoked to explain inconsistent findings and unsatisfyingly modest effects sizes, including the role of children's multiple attachment relationships. Thus, knowledge regarding the multiplicity of children's attachment relationships, such as when and how experiences with specific attachment figures may lead children to develop more general expectations about relationships, and their importance for children's development, may inform pertinent research questions (Bacro & Florin, 2009).

## The Multiplicity of Attachment Relationships and Their Organization

Already in 1964, Schaffer and Emerson found that although the majority of infants formed a privileged relationship with their mother, their most familiar caregiver, most also had an attachment to their father, a grandparent, and/or another family member. Bowlby (1969) concluded in the first volume of *Attachment and Loss* that children tend to form multiple attachment relationships that he argued are organized into a hierarchy. However, he believed that it is only from around three years of age that children feel safe with subsidiary attachment figures in the absence of their primary caregivers. Similarly, Ainsworth (1982) observed that children directed their attachment behaviors preferentially toward their primary attachment figure when distressed. Along these lines, some authors argue that children tend to develop a small hierarchy of three to four attachments (Bretherton, 1980; Cassidy, 2016).

Van IJzendoorn, Sagi & Lambermon (1992) have distinguished three theoretical models, further developed by Howes (1999) and Howes and Spieker (2008, 2016), to explain how attachment relationships become organized and influence development; the hierarchical model, the integrative model and the independent model. First, the traditional "hierarchical" model is based on Bowlby's (1969) hypothesis that children organize their attachment relationships hierarchically, with the relation with their most familiar caregiver – usually the mother – at the top of the hierarchy. This *principal attachment* is assumed to have the greatest influence on child development, particularly on relational development. According to Bowlby then, the quality of children's principal attachment relationship should influence all subsidiary attachment relationships and the child–father attachment should tend to be dependent on child–mother attachment.

To account for inconsistent findings, Bretherton (1985) elaborated on Bowlby's model and proposed that children may first construct relationship-specific models that, over time, become integrated into a single model composed of two representations: one of the attachment figures and one of the child him-/herself. Retaining the hierarchical notion, the principal attachment would still exert the greatest influence on development. The hierarchical model is still the most widespread, likely reflecting Bowlby's influence.

The second model that was proposed, the "integrative" model, postulates that attachment relationships are independent of one another but become integrated into a holistic representation with equal weights. Consequently, children's multiple attachment relationships should predict development better as a whole than separately. Following the proposed development of a holistic representation, different relationships should exert common effects on development. In contrast to the hierarchical model, the integrative model emphasizes influences by attachment figures beyond the primary one. Consequently, this model also acknowledges the potential of compensation mechanism. For example, a secure attachment with the father may buffer against negative effects of an insecure attachment with the mother.

Finally, the "independent" model postulates that children's attachment relationships are independent of one another and that they have independent influences on children's development. In contrast to the other models, the independent model predicts that each relationship may influence distinct domains of development if attachment figures adopt different parenting roles. For example, whereas mothers may often adopt the primary role of safe haven (comforting the child when distressed), fathers may adopt the principal role of secure base (providing cognitive stimulation and supporting exploration and autonomy; Bernier et al., 2014; Grossmann ct al., 2002). Indeed, it has been proposed that an attachment to the mother and father may be captured by partially different behaviors and have differential effects on development (Lucassen et al., 2011).

In sum, three central points can differentiate the three models: (i) preference for a principal caregiver, (ii) qualitative correspondence between relationships, and (iii) the influence of different relationships on development (Bacro & Florin, 2009). In the next section, we review research examining these points in two-parent heterosexual families.

## Preference for the mother over the father?

Already in the 1970s, Lamb (1976a, b, c) conducted a series of studies in which children were observed during a procedure similar to the Strange Situation (Ainsworth & Wittig, 1969). Children were first observed with their mother and father together, then separately with each parent, and finally with both parents and a stranger. Lamb distinguished between "attachment behaviors" (e.g., reaching out, touching), and "affiliative behaviors" (e.g., smiling, vocalizing). Interestingly, children were more likely to direct their attachment behaviors to the mother than the father at twelve and eighteen months, but only in the presence of a stranger. Affiliative behaviors at eighteen months were more frequent with the father (1976a), and when observed at home and presumably when not distressed, children showed no preference for their mothers over their fathers (Lamb, 1977a). On the contrary, children engaged in more attachment and affiliative behavior with their fathers when observed at home at two years of age (Lamb, 1977b). According to this set of studies, any hierarchical structure may be limited to a brief developmental period and to particular contexts, such as stressful situations (Lamb, 1997).

To further address the question of whether children "prefer" their mother over their father, Bacro and Florin (2008) explored attachment representations with each parent in 138 French preschool children. Attachment representations were examined with an adaptation of the Attachment Story Completion Task (ASCT), a doll-play method in which children complete story stems about fictional children in attachment-related situations (Bretherton et al., 1990; Miljkovitch et al., 2003). Children completed the stories once for each parent separately, with a coding procedure adapted to allow for separate examination of attachment representations. A factor analysis revealed four factors: representation of parental support, representation of parental availability, appropriateness of emotions expressed in response to the stories and cooperation during the task. Whereas children expressed more appropriate emotions when completing the stories with the mother figure, fathers were described as equally supportive and even more available (Bacro & Florin, 2008). Thus, preschool children may expect that they can rely as much or even more upon their father's presence in times of need.

Research with school-aged children has generally relied on self-perceived attachment security on Kern's Security Scale (Kerns et al., 1996). For instance, Belgian school-age children described themselves as more secure with their mother than their father (Verschueren & Marcoen, 2005), and American school-age boys described their fathers as less available than their mothers (Lieberman et al., 1999). To further this line of research, Bacro (2011) examined perceived attachment security to mothers and fathers in 210 school-aged children using a French adaptation of the Security Scale. Children reported higher attachment security with their mothers, but the difference was small (Cohen's $d = .17$).

## Correspondence between attachment quality to mother and father?

Contrary to Bowlby's (1969) hierarchical model, the first study that assessed the correspondence between child–mother and child–father attachment quality suggested qualitative independence (Main & Weston, 1981). An early meta-analysis of studies using the Strange Situation reported that attachment quality to mother and father was significantly, albeit weakly related (Fox et al., 1991). Similarly, a subsequent meta-analysis found that attachment to mothers accounted for only 3 percent of the variance in child–father attachment quality (van IJzendoorn & De Wolff, 1997). Studies with older children have also suggested that whilst child–father and child–mother attachment tend to be related, they also show notable independence (e.g., Dubeau & Moss, 1998). Our own research discussed above also addressed this question (Bacro & Florin, 2008). The associations between children's perceptions of maternal and paternal supportiveness and availability were weaker than the association for appropriateness of expression of emotions. Psychological availability and supportiveness are, of course, crucial in fostering felt security, and the pattern of associations would suggest a fair degree of independence between representations.

Another question pertains to how qualitative correspondence develops over time. Correspondence could either be stable, increase or decrease, and the three different models would suggest partially different trajectories. The hierarchical model suggests stability, since the principal attachment relationship should influence other relationships. However, because IWMs are "working" models of others they should transform if those other relationships consistently disconfirm the initial expectations. The integrative model would suggest increasing correspondence, since relationship-specific representations should give way to holistic ones. The independent model does not propose a distinct trajectory but suggests that correspondence should fluctuate depending on the association between the attachment figure's sensitivity. The independent model also acknowledges the possibility of decreasing correspondence. Verschueren and Marcoen (2005) found that the association between children's security to mother and father, though correlated, diminished from eight to eleven years as a function of child age. In the same vein, we also found that the correlation between self-reported attachment to mother and father decreased in strength from eight to twelve years (Bacro, 2011).

## The influence of attachment to mother and father on child development

For Bowlby, the principal importance of the mother, or a permanent mother-substitute, was a natural consequence of how he perceived that caregiving responsibilities were arranged in most societies, with mothers usually occupying the principal caregiving role. Fast forward to the present, and research on child–father attachment is considerably less extensive, and the majority of studies on attachment quality and child development are based on child–mother attachment. The theoretical emphasis on mothers has arguably become self-perpetuating; whereas attachment to the mother has been systematically controlled in studies examining the effects of attachment to the father, the reverse is rarely true. Attachment theory has been critiqued for an over-emphasis on mothers and not adequately acknowledging that cooperative parenting by additional adults and older siblings may have been the norm through ancestral history (Hrdy, 2006). Family system theories and ecological models have also suggested that child attachment and development is determined by factors on multiple levels, including whole-family interactions and inter-caregiver alliance (e.g., Gallegos et al., 2010; Belsky, 1984).

Research that has included attachment to the father, and sometimes to a professional child-care provider, also indicated that the entire network of attachment relationships taken together may be a better predictor of development than each relationship separately (Suess et al., 1992; van IJzendoorn et al., 1992). For example, Boldt and colleagues (2014) found that a cumulative index of security to mother and father was the best predictor of children's behavior problems and social competence. Such findings attest to the importance of relationships beyond a principal attachment, but they do not favor the integrative or the independent model over one another.

Some studies have suggested common and integrative effects and that attachment quality to fathers may sometimes exert a comparatively stronger influence (Bacro & Florin, 2009). Complicating interpretations, attachment quality to both parents taken together has often yielded the strongest effects. For instance, Bureau et al. (2017) found that attachment insecurity to fathers was a better predictor of preschoolers conduct problems than attachment to mothers. However, insecurity to both parents predicted the highest levels of problems. Similarly, Kochanska and Kim (2013) found that insecurity with fathers in infancy was the strongest predictor of teacher-rated externalizing behavior problems and self-reported behavior problems in school-age children. That being said, children who had been insecure with both parents had more externalizing problems than children who had been secure with at least one parent.

Other studies have suggested that child–father attachment may have independent effects on cognitive development, consistent with suggestions that fathers may often adopt a primary role in supporting exploration. For example, Easterbrooks and Goldberg (1984) found that attachment security to fathers was a particularly robust predictor of children's performance in a problem-solving task. To examine this question further, Bacro (2012) examined the relations among school-age children's perceptions of attachment security with mother and father, academic self-concept and school performance in language mastery. Considering that fathers have been found to be more demanding than mothers regarding use of language (Tomasello et al., 1990) and academic achievement (McGrath & Repetti, 2000), it was hypothesized that language mastery would be associated with attachment to father but not mother. Perceived attachment security was assessed with Kerns Security Scale and academic self-concept with the Self Perception Profile (Harter, 1982; Pierrehumbert et al., 1987). Children's grade point averages in language mastery and a written word identification test were used to assess language mastery.

Perceived attachment to father was the only predictor of language mastery, even after controlling for sex, age and cognitive performance. Finally, academic self-concept mediated the relation between perceived attachment to father and language mastery (Bacro, 2012).

## Integrated discussion

Taken together, empirical research has provided some challenges to the hierarchical model (Bowlby, 1969). For instance, children may not show a consistent or strong preference for a principal attachment figure beyond infancy (Bacro & Florin, 2009). A tentative conclusion is that relationships with other caregivers, such as fathers, may become increasingly important beyond infancy since parental roles often become increasingly egalitarian with increased age.

Most studies have been conducted with children from middle-class families, in countries with high expectations regarding paternal involvement, and with most children attending day-care. As a result, most children have been raised by multiple adults with whom they may develop attachments. Moreover, attachment behavior may be preferentially directed toward a principal attachment figure specifically during distress (Umemura et al., 2013). Yet, few studies have accounted for children's emotional states, raising the question of whether the attachment system has been meaningfully activated. Furthermore, most studies with school-aged children have evaluated attachment using self-report instruments. These questionnaires assess children's consciously available *perceptions* of their attachment relationships, and these do not necessarily correspond with *attachment representations*. Though children's perceptions of their attachment relationships should be grounded in the same cognitive-affective structures as their attachment representations, the latter should also entail organizational and unconscious processes that, in the case of insecurity, may include defensive mechanisms such as shifting of attention and defensive exclusion to protect the individual from anxiety (Bowlby, 1973). Accessibility of attachment-related information may therefore be influenced (Verschueren & Marcoen, 2005).

Despite these methodological limitations, it is intriguing that some studies have suggested that attachment to fathers may be particularly important in relation to cognitive development and academically related achievements. Fathers' increasing involvement coincides with children's growing development of executive functioning (EF), which is crucial for self-regulation and which has been linked to caregiver sensitivity, autonomy support and child attachment (Bernier et al., 2012). It is therefore interesting that secure base behavior, such as sensitivity in play (Lucassen et al., 2011) and autonomy support (Grossman et al., 2002), have been proposed as particularly important in attachment to fathers. This would suggest that domain-specific effects of attachment to mother and father reflect how caregiving responsibilities are typically arranged across children's maturational periods, developmental domains and the cultural contexts in which children develop and caregiving roles are differentially allocated. Such differences certainly need not imply anything endemic or essential to the biological sex of the parents.

As a whole, research suggests that multiple attachment relationships may play important roles in child development. This raises many questions about the impact of specific life contexts on the development and the organization of children's attachment relations and representations. In the next section, we therefore focus on parental separation and custody arrangements in separated and divorced families.

## The Effects of Parental Separation and Custody Arrangements on Children's Attachment Relationships and Representations

Parental separation and divorce are common in Western societies, and the influence of different custody arrangements on attachment has become a source of debate (Altenhofen et al., 2010; Baudé & Zaouche-Gaudron, 2013; Tornello et al., 2013). Whereas some have argued that children need a stable relationship with a residential parent, and that overnight stays with the other parent can be a source of insecurity, others have argued that frequent switches may be needed for young children whose object permanence is not fully developed to be able to keep both parents in mind (Kelly & Lamb, 2000). Remarkably few studies have examined this question empirically.

Separation and divorce are typically very stressful life events for parents and children (Feeney & Monin, 2016). For parents, the separation from their partner often corresponds to the dissolution of their principal attachment relationship. Consequently, they have to reorganize their IWMs of the spousal relationship and often transform their bond into an affiliative relationship. Most of the time, they must also come to an agreement about how to share parental responsibilities. In some cases, parental separation or divorce may reduce conflict and increase parents' ability to respond to children's attachment needs. However, it is more often a source of stress that may have repercussions on parenting and attentional availability, which in turn may affect children's IWMs (Page & Bretherton, 2001).

Children of separated parents have been found to be less secure and more disorganized with their mothers than children living with both parents (Altenhofen et al., 2010; Solomon & George, 1999; Tornello et al., 2013). The only study to date on fathers reported similar results, with children more likely to be disorganized (Solomon & George, 1999). Moreover, overnight stays with fathers have been associated with decreased security with the residential parent (i.e., the mother). For example, Solomon and George (1999) found that disorganized attachment with mothers was elevated among children who occasionally spent nights with their father. Similarly, Tornello and colleagues (2013) found that children who spent frequent nights with their father (>1 night/week during the first year, > 35 percent of nights during the third year) were less likely to be secure with their mothers. At first glance, these results would suggest that shared custody arrangements that include frequent separations from the residential parent may have a negative impact on attachment security.

The relationship between parental separation and child attachment may also depend on contextual factors, such as inter-parental conflict (Feeney & Monin, 2016). For example, Solomon and George (1999) found that disorganized attachment was elevated if inter-parental communication was poor and inter-parental conflict was high. Furthermore, inter-parental conflict has been associated with decreased maternal emotional availability, in turn predictive of child insecurity (Altenhofen et al., 2010). Nair and Murray (2005) also reported that "educational style" mediated the association between parental separation and child attachment; separated mothers were less democratic, which the authors interpreted as denoting lower sensitivity, cooperativeness and emotional accessibility.

To further the knowledge on the role of the quality of the relationship between separated parents for child attachment, Bacro (2016) examined the relations among custody arrangements, attachment representations and parenting alliance in fifty-four families with three-to-five-year-old children. Thirty children lived with both their parents, twelve in fully alternating residence (joint custody) and twelve with their mother as custodial parent. We examined attachment representations with the Attachment Story Completion Task (Miljkovitch & Pierrehumbert, 2008) and mothers' perceptions of their parenting alliance with fathers with the Parenting Alliance Questionnaire (Rouyer et al., 2015). Attachment quality was related to custody arrangement: children in alternating residence were less secure and more disorganized than children living with both parents. However, insecurity and disorganization was negatively correlated with parenting alliance when children lived in alternating residence. Critically, differences in security and disorganization did not remain after controlling for parenting alliance.

In sum, children from separated and divorced families tend to be less secure and more disorganized. However, rather than a direct effect of custody arrangements per se, empirical research has highlighted the importance of the parental relationship – particularly the parenting alliance. More research is clearly needed, particularly given the high rates of parental separation and divorce. Moreover, the child's age may constitute a moderator, with parental separation perhaps less influential as children develop and the objective of the attachment system moves from physical proximity to psychological closeness (felt security). The respective role of different attachment relationships in children's development also requires more attention. It is notable that no study has examined attachment development among children who have fully alternating residence before establishing attachments to their parents (e.g., from birth) and therefore do not experience a sudden change in caregiver availability following separation or divorce. It is quite possible that children will develop secure attachments to both caregivers in such settings (Main et al., 2011). Finally, we stress the possibility that divorce followed by complete and chronic separation of the child from one of its parents may be akin to a traumatic loss for the child, which could itself produce child disorganization (Solomon & George, 2011). Although chronic separation is occasionally warranted (e.g., from a seriously maltreating parent), it is imperative for most children to be able to maintain contact with both parents after a divorce. With these considerations in mind we turn to attachment representations among children in foster care

## Placement Trajectories, Attachment Representations and Behavior Problems of Children in Foster Care

Foster care placement includes prolonged or permanent separation from *both* parents and repeated or multiple separations from parental figures. Children in foster care constitute a particularly vulnerable population in which some have experienced maltreatment (Cook et al., 2005, Scheeringa & Zeanah, 2001, Spinazzola et al., 2005). Additionally, these children are sometimes taken out of their parents' care in great haste and in a context of fear and conflict, potentially representing a traumatic separation experience in its own right. These children must often cope with unstable placement trajectories and multiple placements in which they have to repeatedly create new attachment relationships (Bacro et al., 2015). Mental disorders are also common, with disruptive disorders most common (Bronsard et al., 2016).

Although the risks associated with unstable placements are well recognized, they are still common and little is known about the processes that may explain the impact of placement experiences on child development (Pasalich et al., 2016). Theoretically, multiple and extended separations from attachment figures should have a negative impact on children's feeling of security and reinforce negative, potentially disorganized models of self and others (Granqvist, 2016; Granqvist et al., 2017; Hazen et al., 2015). Several studies have also found that children in foster care are less secure and more disorganized than children living with their parents (Bernier et al., 2005; Quiroga & Hamilton-Giachritsis, 2016; Stovall & Dozier, 1998). To the best of our knowledge, however, only one study has examined the impact of number of placements on attachment quality to foster mothers. This longitudinal intervention study found that the number of placements was related to externalizing behavior problems and that insecure attachment to the foster mothers mediated this link (Pasalich et al., 2016).

Disorganized attachment, however, was not examined in this study, despite being the type of insecurity most strongly associated with externalizing behavior problems (Fearon et al., 2010). Toussaint and colleagues (2018) therefore examined disorganized attachment in relation to children's placement trajectories and behavior problems, hypothesizing that disorganization would mediate a presumed relation between number of placements and behavior problems. The study included forty children aged four to ten years who were temporarily placed in foster care because of abuse or neglect. Attachment representations were examined with the Attachment Story Completion Task (Miljkovitch & Pierrehumbert, 2008) and social workers rated behavior problems on the Child Behavior Check List (Achenbach & Rescorla, 2000, 2001). First, prevalence of behavior problems was high; a small majority of the children obtained an internalizing problem score and a general psychopathology score in the borderline or clinical range. A substantial minority of the children were also in the borderline and clinical range for externalizing problems. In addition, the number of placements was strongly correlated with attachment disorganization and externalizing behavior problems, which in turn were correlated. Finally, attachment disorganization fully mediated the relation between placements and externalizing problems (Toussaint et al., 2018).

Though the study by Toussaint and colleagues (2018) was cross-sectional, rendering process direction ambiguous, the results are consistent with the longitudinal findings by Pasalich and colleagues (2016). Jointly, these findings suggest that multiple separations from caregivers can cause not only insecurity but also disorganization, which in turn may lead to externalizing behavior problems. The findings also corroborate Bowlby's (1944) research into the long-term effects of early child–caregiver separations, which demonstrated antisocial outcomes. Bowlby (1988) argued for a close link between fear and anger, which he regarded as a natural reaction to threats of separation (i.e., separation anxiety) and actual losses (i.e., mourning). The prospect of an "anger–fear complex" is intriguing given the centrality of fear and alarm in the emergence of disorganized attachment and its association with externalizing problems (Fearon et al., 2010). An anger–fear complex has also been found to mediate the relation between disorganized attachment and symptoms of oppositional defiant disorder (Forslund et al., 2018). Numerous placements, including repeated losses of attachment figures and threats of further losses, may conceivably give rise to high levels of unmodulated fear and anger, disorganized attachment representations and externalizing behavior problems.

The study by Toussaint et al. (2018), along with multiple sources of converging findings, suggest that out-of-home placements can have adverse ramifications, especially in the context of poor stability of placement. For example, abused children placed in out-of-home care have been found to show elevated levels of behavior problems, even in comparison with children who were still living with their maltreating parents (Lawrence et al., 2006). Further, 25 percent of Dutch adolescents placed in residential and foster care reported having been physically abused in their institution or foster family (Euser et al., 2014). These findings suggest that, contrary to the hopes and expectations of welfare professionals, children placed in out-of-home care are not well protected against violence or maltreatment. Thus, politicians and social service professionals must be careful not to assume that out-of-home care is always effective. Attachment-based caregiving interventions, however, have been found to be effective in helping parents increase sensitivity and avoid frightening behavior (Dozier et al., 2014). When possible, evidence-based caregiving interventions should be used as a first step in order to avoid the negative effects associated with breakdowns of children's attachment relationships (e.g., Granqvist et al., 2017).

# Conclusions

The attachment system has likely served children well by increasing chances of survival through the maintenance of proximity to caregivers. The openness of the system to environmental calibration has arguably facilitated its ability to function adaptively in different caregiving contexts. The notion of multiple attachment relationships likewise harmonizes with the flexibility that serves as a trademark for our species. Multiple attachments may not only have buffered against difficulties in principal relationships, including losses of attachment figures to predators and other natural dangers, but may also have served the child's developmental needs better (van IJzendoorn, 2005).

Attachment security and organization, however, depend on sufficient relationship stability and attachment quality is therefore vulnerable to prolonged separations from attachment figures and psychological inaccessibility. Similarly, attachment quality may be vulnerable to low quality co-parenting, as sometimes occurs following divorce and parental separation. Unfortunately, studies examining the development of attachment relationships in these life contexts are inadequate, especially among young children. With few exceptions, research has focused on the mother, who has typically been assumed to be the principal attachment figure. The diversity and complexity of family constellations have not been adequately taken into account. With the high rates of parental separation and the development of assisted reproductive methods, many children live in single-parent, step-parent and alternating residence families through the course of their development (Zadeh et al., 2017). Other children are separated from their parents and live in foster care for a longer or shorter period, with more or less success. Therefore, we call for a concerted body of research to help better understand the factors that allow children to develop and maintain secure attachment relationships and representations across this diversifying family landscape.

# References

Achenbach, T. M., & Rescorla, L. A. (2000). *Manual for the ASEBA preschool forms & profiles*. Burlington, VT: University of Vermont, Research Center for Children, Youth, & Families.

Ainsworth, M. D. S. (1967). *Infancy in Uganda: Infant care and the growth of love*. Baltimore: Johns Hopkins University Press.

Ainsworth, M. D. S. (1982). Attachment: retrospect and prospect. In C. M. Parkes and J. Stevenson-Hinde (Eds.). *The place of attachment in human behavior (pp. 3–30)*. Basic Books.

Ainsworth, M. D. S., Bell, S. M., & Stayton, D. (1971). Individual differences in Strange Situation behavior of one-year-olds. In H. R. Schaffer (Ed.), *The origins of human social relations (pp. 17–57)*. Academic Press.

Ainsworth, M. D. S., & Wittig, B. A. (1969). Attachment and exploratory behavior of one year-olds in a strange situation. In B. M. Foss (Ed.), *Determinants of infant behavior (Vol. 4, pp. 111–136)*. Methuen.

Altenhofen, S., Biringen, Z., & Mergler, R. (2010). Families experiencing divorce: Age at onset of overnight stays, conflict, and emotional availability as predictors of child attachment, *Journal of Divorce & Remarriage, 51*, 141–156.

Bacro, F. (2011). Validation francophone de l'échelle de sécurité des perceptions d'attachement au père et à la mère (Kerns, Klepac, & Cole, 1996). *Revue Européenne de Psychologie Appliquée, 61*, 213–221.

Bacro, F. (2012). Perceived attachment security to father, academic self-concept and school performance in language mastery. *Journal of Child and Family Studies, 21*, 992–1002.

Bacro, F. (2016, September). Attachment representations of 3-to-5-years-old children from separated families. *Paper presented at the 57th meeting of the French Psychological Society*, Nanterre, France.

Bacro, F., & Florin, A. (2008). Spécificité des modèles internes opérants : les représentations d'attachement au père et à la mère chez des enfants de 3 à 5 ans. *Enfance, 60* (2), 108–119.

Bacro, F., & Florin, A. (2009). La relation père-enfant, la nature et l'organisation des relations d'attachement. *Canadian Psychology, 50*, 230–240.

Bacro, F., Rambaud, A., Humbert, C., & Sellenet, C. (2015). Les parcours de placement et la qualité de vie des enfants de 6 à 11 ans accueillis dans des institutions relevant de la protection de l'enfance. *L'Encéphale, 41* (5), 412–419.

Baude, A., & Zaouche Gaudron, C. (2013). L'adaptation socio-affective d'enfants de quatre à 12 ans en résidence alternée: une approche écosystémique. *Neuropsychiatrie de l'enfance et de l'adolescence, 6*, 347–356.

Belsky, J. (1984). The determinants of parenting: A process model. *Child Development, 55*, 83–96.

Bernier, A., Ackerman, J., & Stovall-McClough, C. (2004). Predicting the quality of attachment relationships in foster care dyads from infants' initial behaviors upon placement. *Infant Behavior & Development, 27*, 366–381.

Bernier, A., Carlson, S. M., & Whipple, N. (2010). From external regulation to self-regulation: Early parenting precursors of young children's executive functioning. *Child Development, 81* (1), 326–339.

Bernier, A., Carlson, S. M., Deschênes, M., & Matte-Gagné, C. (2012). Social factors in the development of early executive functioning: A closer look at the caregiving environment. *Developmental science*, 15 (1), 12–24.

Bernier, A., Matte-Gagné, C., Bélanger, M. and Whipple, N. (2014), Taking stock of two decades of attachment transmission gap: Broadening the assessment of maternal behavior. *Child Development*, 85, 1852–1865.

Boldt, L. J., Kochanska, G., Yoon, J. E., & Nordling, J. K. (2014). Children's attachment to both parents from toddler age to middle childhood: Links to adaptive and maladaptive outcomes. *Attachment and Human Development*, 16, 211–229.

Bowlby, J. (1944). Forty-four juvenile thieves: Their characters and home life (I &II). *International Journal of Psychoanalysis*, 25, 154–178 & 107–127.

Bowlby, J. (1969). *Attachment and loss*. Vol.1. Attachment. Hogarth

Bowlby, J. (1988). *A secure base* (new edn.). Routledge Ltd.

Bretherton, I. (1980). Young children in stressful situations: The supporting role of attachment figures and unfamiliar caregivers. In G. V. Coelho & P. I. Ahmed (Eds.). *Uprooting and development (pp. 179–210)*. Plenum Press.

Bretherton, I. (1985). Attachment theory: Retrospect and prospect. In I. Bretherton & E. Waters (Eds.), Growing points of attachment theory and research. *Monographs of the Society for Research in Child Development*, 50 (1–2, serial No. 209), 3–35.

Bretherton, I. (1998). Internal working models and communication in attachment relationships: A commentary of the review by Raphaële Miljkovitch. In A. Braconnier & J. Sipos (Eds.), *Le bébé et les interactions précoces (pp. 79–88)*. PUF.

Bretherton, I., & Munholland, K. A. (2016). Internal working model construct in light of contemporary neuroimaging research. In J. Cassidy & P. H. Shaver (Eds.). *Handbook of attachment: Theory, research, and clinical applications, 3rd edn. (pp. 63–88)*. Guilford Press.

Bretherton, I., Ridgeway, D., & Cassidy, J. (1990). Assessing internal working models of the attachment relationships: An attachment story completion task for 3-year-olds. In M. T. Greenberg, D. Cicchetti, & E. M. Cummings (Eds.). *Attachment in the preschool years. Theory, research, and intervention (pp. 273–308)*. University of Chicago Press.

Bronsard, G., Alessandrini, M., Fond, G., Loundou, A., Auquier, P., Tordjman, S., & Boyer, L. (2016). The prevalence of mental disorders among children and adolescents in the child welfare system: A systematic review and meta-analysis. *Medicine*, 95 (7), 2622.

Bureau, J. F., Martin, J., Yurkowski, K., Schmiedel, S., Quan, J., Moss, E., Deneault, A. A., & Pallanca, D. (2016). Correlates of child–father and child–mother attachment in the preschool years. *Attachment and Human Development*, 19 (2), 130–150.

Cassidy, J. (1988). Child–mother attachment and the self in 6-year-olds. *Child Development*, 59, 121–124.

Cassidy, J. (2016). The nature of the child's ties. In J. Cassidy & P. H. Shaver (Eds.). *Handbook of attachment: Theory, research, and clinical applications, 3rd edn.(pp. 3–24)*. Guilford Press.

Chotart, C., Guimard, P., Acier, D., & Bacro, F. (2017). *Custody arrangements, parenting alliance and attachment representations of 3-to5-years-old children with separated parents (Unpublished manuscript)*.

Cook, A., Spinazzola, J., Lanktree, C., Blaustein, M., & Cloitre, M. (2005). Complex trauma in children and adolescents. *Psychiatric Annals*, 35, 390–398.

Dozier, M., Meade, E. B., & Bernard, K. (2014). Attachment and biobehavioral catch-up: An intervention for parents at risk of maltreating their infants and toddlers. In S. Timmer & A. Urquiza (Eds.). *Evidence-based approaches for the treatment of child maltreatment (pp. 43–59)*. Springer.

Dubeau, D., & Moss, E. (1998). La théorie de l'attachement résiste-t-elle au charme des pères? Approche comparative des caractéristiques maternelles et paternelles durant la période préscolaire. *Enfance*, 50, 82–102.

Easterbrooks, M. A., & Goldberg, W. A. (1984). Toddler development in the family: Impact of father involvement and parenting characteristics. *Child Development*, 55, 740–752.

Euser, S., Alink, L. R. A., Tharner, A., Van IJzendoorn, M. H., Bakermans-Kranenburg, M. J. (2014). Out of home placement to promote safety? The prevalence of physical abuse in residential and foster care. *Children and Youth Services Review*, 37, 64–70.

Fearon, R. P., Bakermans-Kranenburg, M. J., Van IJzendoorn, M. H., Lapsley, A.-M., & Roisman, G. I. (2010). The significance of insecure attachment and disorganization in the development of children's externalizing behavior: A meta-analytic study. *Child Development*, 81 (2), 435–456.

Feeney, B. C., & Monin, J. (2016). Divorce through the lens of attachment theory. In J. Cassidy & P. H. Shaver (Eds.). *Handbook of attachment: Theory, research, and clinical applications, 3rd edn. (pp. 941–965)*. Guilford Press.

Forslund, T., & Granqvist, P. (2017). Effects of attachment quality and organization. In T. Shackelford, & V. Weekes-Shackelford (Eds.). *Encyclopedia of Evolutionary Psychological Science*. Springer.

Forslund, T., Peltola, M. J., & Brocki, K. C. (2018). *Disorganized Attachment Representations, Externalizing Behavior Problems, and Socio-Emotional Competences* (Doctoral dissertation, Uppsala University, Uppsala, Sweden). Retrieved from http://uu.diva-portal.org/smash/record.jsf?pid=diva2%3A1250329&dswid=-1568.

Fox, N. A., Kimmerly, N. L., & Schafer, W. D. (1991). Attachment to mother/attachment to father: A meta-analysis. *Child Development*, 62, 210–225.

Gallegos, M. I., Murphy, S. E., Benner, A. D., Jacobvitz, D. B., & Hazen, N. L. (2017). Marital, parental, and whole-family predictors of toddlers' emotion regulation: The role of parental emotional withdrawal. *Journal of Family Psychology, 31* (3), 294.

Granqvist, P. (2016). Observations of disorganized behaviours yield no magic wand: Response to Shemmings. *Attachment & Human Development, 18 (6)*, 529–533.

Granqvist, P., Sroufe, L. A., Dozier, M., Hesse, E., Steele, M., [. . .], & Duschinsky, R. (2017). Disorganized attachment in infancy: Review of the phenomenon and its implications for clinicians and policy-makers. *Attachment & Human Development.* Advance online publication. Doi: 10.1080/14616734.2017.1354040.

Groh, A. M., Fearon, R. P., Bakermans-Kranenburg, M. J., Van IJzendoorn, M. H., Steele, R. D., & Roisman, G. I. (2014). The significance of attachment security for children's social competence with peers: A meta-analytic study. *Attachment & human development, 16* (2), 103–136.

Groh, A. M., Fearon, R. P., van IJzendoorn, M. H., Bakermans-Kranenburg, M. J., & Roisman, G. I. (2017). Attachment in the early life course: Meta-analytic evidence for its role in socioemotional development. *Child Development Perspectives, 11* (1), 70–76.

Groh, A. M., Roisman, G. I., Van IJzendoorn, M. H., Bakermans-Kranenburg, M. J., & Fearon, R. P. (2012). The significance of insecure and disorganized attachment for children's internalizing symptoms: A meta-analytic study. *Child Development, 83*, 591–610.

Grossmann, K., Grossmann, K. E., Fremmer-Bombik, E., Kindler, H., Scheuerer-Englisch, H., & Zimmermann, P. (2002). The uniqueness of the child–father attachment relationship: Fathers' sensitive and challenging play as a pivotal variable in a 16-year longitudinal study. *Social Development, 11*, 307–331.

Harter, S. (1982). The perceived competence scale. *Child Development, 53*, 87–97.

Hazen, N. L., Allen, S. D., Christopher, C. H., Umemura, T., & Jacobvitz, D. B. (2015). Very extensive nonmaternal care predicts mother–infant attachment disorganization: Convergent evidence from two samples. *Development and Psychopathology, 27*, 649–661.

Howes, C. (1999). Attachment relationships in the context of multiple caregivers. In J. Cassidy & P. H. Shaver (Eds.). *Handbook of attachment: Theory, research, and clinical applications (pp. 671–687).* Guilford Press.

Howes, C. & Spieker, S. J. (2008). Attachment relationships in the context of multiple caregivers. In J. Cassidy & P. H. Shaver (Eds.). *Handbook of attachment: Theory, research, and clinical applications, 2nd edn.(pp. 317–332).* Guilford Press.

Howes, C., & Spieker, S. J. (2016). Attachment relationships in the context of multiple caregivers. In J. Cassidy & P. H. Shaver (Eds.). *Handbook of attachment: Theory, research, and clinical applications, 3rd edn. (pp. 314–329).* New York, NY: Guilford Press.

Hrdy, S. B. (2011). *Mothers and others.* Harvard University Press.

Kelly, J. B. and Lamb, M. E. 2000. Using child development research to make appropriate custody and access decisions. *Family and Conciliation Courts Review, 38* (3): 297–311.

Kerns, K. A., Klepac, L. & Cole, A. (1996). Peer relationships and preadolescents' perceptions of security in the child–mother relationship. *Developmental Psychology, 32*, 457–466.

Kochanska, G., & Kim, S. (2013). Early attachment organization with both parents and future behavior problems: From infancy to middle childhood. *Child Development, 84*, 283–296.

Lamb, M. E. (1976a). Effects of stress and cohort on mother and father infant interaction. *Developmental Psychology, 12*, 435–443.

Lamb, M. E. (1976b). Interaction between two-year-olds and their mothers and fathers. *Psychological Reports, 38*, 347–350.

Lamb, M. E. (1976c). Twelve-month-olds and their parents: Interaction in a laboratory playroom. *Developmental Psychology, 12*, 237–244.

Lamb, M. E. (1977a). Father–infant and mother–infant interaction in the first year of life. *Child Development, 48*, 167–181.

Lamb, M. E. (1977b). The development of mother–infant and father–infant attachments in the second year of life. *Developmental Psychology, 13*, 631–648.

Lamb, M. E. (1997). L'influence du père sur le développement de l'enfant. *Enfance, 49*, 337–350.

Lawrence C. R., Carlson E. A., Egeland B. (2006). The impact of foster care on development. *Development and Psychopathology, 18*, 57–76.

Lieberman, M., Doyle, A. B. & Markiewicz, D. (1999). Developmental patterns in security of attachment to mother and father in late childhood and early adolescence: Associations with peer relations. *Child Development, 70*, 202–213.

Lucassen, N., Tharner, A., Van IJzendoorn, M. H., Bakermans-Kranenburg, M. J., Volling, B. L., Verhulst, F. C., & Tiemeier, H. (2011). The association between paternal sensitivity and infant–father attachment security: A meta-analysis of three decades of research. *Journal of Family Psychology, 25* (6), 986.

Main, M., & Solomon, J. (1988). Discovery of an insecure disorganized-disoriented attachment pattern. In T. B. Brazelton & M. W. Yogman (Eds.). *Affective development in infancy (pp. 95–124).* Ablex.

Main, M., Hesse, E., & Hesse, S. (2011). Attachment theory and research: Overview with suggested applications to child custody. *Family Court Review, 49* (3), 426–463.

Main, M. & Weston, D. (1981). Security of attachment to mother and father: Related to conflict behavior and readiness to establish new relationships. *Child Development, 52*, 932–940.

Matas, L., Arend, R. A., & Sroufe, L. A. (1978). Continuity of adaptation in the second year: The relationship between quality of attachment and later competence. *Child Development, 49*, 547–556.

Miljkovitch, R., Moss, E., Bernier, A., Pascuzzo, K., & Sander, E. (2015). Refining the assessment of internal working models: the Attachment Multiple Model Interview. *Attachment & Human Development, 17*, 492–521.

Miljkovitch, R., & Pierrehumbert, B. (2008). Des stratégies comportementales d'attachement aux stratégies représentationnelles : Construction et validité des cartes de codage pour les histoires à compléter. *Enfance, 60*, 22–30.

Miljkovitch, R., Pierrehumbert, B., Karmaniola, A., & Halfon, O. (2003). Les représentations d'attachement du jeune enfant. *Développement d'un système de codage pour les histoires à compléter. Devenir, 15*, 143–177.

Moss, E., & Saint-Laurent, D. (2001). Attachment at school-age and school performance. *Developmental Psychology, 37*, 107–119.

Murray, A. D., & Yingling, J. L. (2000). Competence in language at 24 months: Relations with attachment security and home stimulation. *The Journal of Genetic Psychology, 161*, 133–140.

Nair, H., & Murray, A. D. (2005). Predictors of attachment security in preschool children from intact and divorced families. *The Journal of Genetic Psychology, 166* (3), 245–263.

Page, T., & Bretherton, I. (2001). Mother– and father–child attachment themes as represented in the story completions of preschoolers in postdivorce families: Linkages with teacher ratings of social competence. *Attachment and Human Development, 3*, 1–29.

Pasalich, D. S., Fleming, C. B., Oxford, M. L., Zheng, Y., & Spieker, S. (2016). Can parenting intervention prevent cascading effects from placement instability to insecure attachment to externalizing problems in maltreated toddlers? *Child Maltreatment, 21* (3), 175–185.

Pierrehumbert, B., Plancherel, B. & Jankech-Carretta, C. (1987). Image de soi et perception de compétences propres chez l'enfant. *Revue de Psychologie Appliquée, 37*, 359–377.

Quiroga, M. G., & Hamilton-Giachritsis, C. (2016). Attachment styles in children living in alternative care: A systematic review of the literature. *Child & Youth Care Forum, 45*, 625–653.

Rouyer, V., Huet-Gueye, M., Baude, A., Mieyaa, Y. (2015). French adaptation of the Parenting Alliance Inventory: Issues in defining and measuring coparenting. *Family Science, 6* (1), 194–200.

Scheeringa, M. S., & Zeanah, C. H. (2001). A relational perspective on PTSD in early childhood. *Journal of Traumatic Stress, 14* (4), 799–815.

Solomon, J., & Biringen, Z. (2001). Another look at the developmental research: Commentary on Kelly and Lamb's "Using child development research to make appropriate custody and access decisions for young children." *Family Court Review, 39* (4), 355–364.

Solomon, J., & George, C. (1999). The development of attachment in separated and divorced families. Effects of overnight visitation, parent and couple variables. *Attachment & Human Development, 1* (1), 2–33.

Spangler, G., & Grossman, K. (1999). Individual and physiological correlates of attachment disorganization in infancy. In J. Solomon & C. George (Eds.) *Attachment disorganization (pp. 95–124)*. Guilford Press.

Spinazzola, J., Ford, J. D., Zucker, M., van der Kolk, B. A., Silva, S., Smith, S. F., & Blaustein, M. (2005). Survey evaluates complex trauma exposure, outcome, and intervention among children and adolescents. *Psychiatric Annals, 35* (5), 433–439.

Stovall, K. C., & Dozier, M. (1998). Infants in foster care: An attachment theory perspective. *Adoption Quarterly, 2* (1), 55–88.

Suess, G. J., Grossmann, K. E. & Sroufe, L. A. (1992). Effects of infant attachment to mother and father on quality of adaptation in prechool: From dyadic to individual organization of the self. *International Journal of Behavioral Development, 15*, 43–65.

Thompson, R. A. (2016). Early attachment and later development: Reframing the questions. In J. Cassidy & P. H. Shaver (Eds.). *Handbook of attachment: Theory, research, and clinical applications, 3rd edn. (pp. 330–348)*. Guilford Press.

Tornello, S. L., Emery, R., Rowen, J., Potter, D., Ocker, B., & Xu, Y. (2013). Overnight custody arrangements, attachment, and adjustment among very young children. *Journal of Marriage and Family, 75*, 871–885.

Toussaint, E., Florin, A., Schneider, B., & Bacro, F. (2018). Les problèmes de comportement, les representations d'attachement et le parcours de placement d'enfants relevant de la protection de l'enfance. *Neuropsychiatrie de L'Enfance et de l'Adolescence, 66* (6), 335–343.

Umemura, T., Jacobvitz, D., Messina, S., & Hazen, N. (2013). Do toddlers prefer the primary caregiver or the parent with whom they feel more secure? The role of toddler emotion. *Infant Behavior and Development, 36* (1), 102–114.

Van IJzendoorn, M. H. (2005). Attachment in social networks: toward an evolutionary social network model. *Human Development, 48* (1–2), 85–88.

Van IJzendoorn, M. H., & De Wolff, M. S. (1997). In search of absent father-Meta-analyses of infant–father attachment: A rejoinder to our discussants. *Child Development, 68*, 604–609.

Van IJzendoorn, M. H., Dijkstra, J. & Bus, A. G. (1995). Attachment, intelligence, and language : A meta-analysis. *Social Development, 4*, 115–128.

Van IJzendoorn, M. H., Sagi, A., & Lambermon, M. W. (1992). The multiple caretaker paradox: Some data from Holland and Israel. *New Directions in Child Development, 57,* 5–24.

Van IJzendoorn, M. H. & Van Vliet-Visser, S. (1988). The relationship between quality of attachment in infancy and IQ in kindergarten. *The Journal of Genetic Psychology, 149,* 23–28.

Verhage, M. L., Schuengel, C., Madigan, S., Fearon, R. M., Oosterman, M., Cassibba, R., ... & van IJzendoorn, M. H. (2016). Narrowing the transmission gap: A synthesis of three decades of research on intergenerational transmission of attachment. *Psychological Bulletin, 142* (4), 337.

Verschueren, K. & Marcoen, A. (1999). Representation of self and socioemotional competence in kindergartners: Differential and combined effects of attachment to mother and to father. *Child Development, 70,* 183–201.

Verschueren, K. & Marcoen, A. (2005). Perceived security of attachment to mother and father: Developmental differences and relations to self-worth and peer relationships at school. In K. Kerns & R. Richardson (Eds.). *Attachment in middle childhood (pp. 212–230).* Guilford Press.

Waters, E., & Deane, K. E. (1985). Defining and assessing individual differences in attachment relationships: Q-methodology and the organization of behavior in infancy and early childhood. In I. Bretherton & E. Waters (Eds.). *Monographs of the Society for Research in Child Development, 50* (1–2, serial No. 209), 41–103.

West, K., Mathews, B., & Kerns, K. A. (2013). Mother–child attachment and cognitive performance in middle childhood: An examination of mediating mechanisms. *Early Childhood Research Quarterly, 28,* 259–270.

Zadeh, S., Jones, C. M., Basi, T., & Golombok, S. (2017). Children's thoughts and feelings about their donor and security of attachment to their solo mothers in middle childhood. *Human Reproduction (Oxford, England), 32* (4), 868–875.

# 15

# New Correlates of Disorganization from a West-African Dataset, and Shared Rhythmic Touch as a Hidden Pathway to Infant Attachment Security

Mary McMahan True

This chapter is a hybrid with two sections, the first consisting of empirical findings and the second a theoretical proposition. Both sections are informed by my observations of infant care practices in rural, agrarian communities in Western Africa (True, 1994; True et al., 2001). The objective of the empirical section is to investigate two nonexclusive hypotheses that may explain the lack of avoidant classifications among the Dogon infants, and a concomitant high level of disorganized classifications. Whereas the *"relational hypothesis"* is based on maternal contact aversion and dysfluent communication, the *"over-stress hypothesis"* is based on potential "false-positive" D-classifications due to the strange situation procedure perhaps being too stressful for Dogon infants. The hypotheses are grounded in Dogon infant care practice, which I characterize by a high degree of shared rhythmic interaction, feeding on demand and continuous infant–caregiver contact, with even brief separations very uncommon. The empirical section also examines whether the Dogon distribution of strange situation classifications is congruent with that of Western samples and other non-Western samples. In terms of theory, I propose the hypothesis that frequent shared rhythmic touch with caregivers may operate as a pathway to secure attachment relationships. The chapter begins with a description of the West African research project, and continues with a review of the literature relevant to the two empirical hypotheses and the theoretical proposition. This includes a discussion of West African care practice and how it contrasts with Western care practices. After presenting the empirical analyses, I discuss the strange situation procedure from a cross-cultural perspective, drawing from what the pioneers in attachment theory had to say. I also call for a renewed focus on unstructured observations and discuss how the West African findings of rhythmic touch may inform interventions.

Portions of this paper were presented at the biennial meeting of the Society for Research in Child Development; Tampa, Florida, April, 2003.

This research was supported by grants from the National Institute of Mental Health, the University of California at Berkeley, and Saint Mary's College of California, contributions from the Malian Ministry of Public Health and the Italian aid organization DGCS. This paper was substantially improved by the thoughtful comments and editing of Tommie Forslund and Robbie Duschinsky. Finally, I am especially grateful to my colleagues in Mali and to the Dogon families who so generously participated in this research.

Correspondence concerning this article should be addressed to Mary McMahan True, Psychology Dept., Saint Mary's College, Moraga, CA 94618. E-mail: mtrue@stmarys-ca.edu.

# Background

This chapter is based on observations I made in Niger and Mali, West Africa, while completing my doctoral work. I went to West Africa motivated to continue research in infant attachment begun by Mary Ainsworth (1967) in Uganda in the 1950s. As a student of Mary Main I was well prepared in the theory and measures of attachment behavior. I also had something not available in Ainsworth's time: The ability to videotape observations.

My first observations – conducted in a small village in Niger – taught me two things. The first was what it is like to care for an infant in a subsistence agrarian context. Initially, I noticed what was missing: electricity, running water, telephones and transportation. Also missing were the things commonly found in infant care in the US: diapers, strollers, high chairs, cribs and bottles. With time, I came to notice what was present – an incredibly rich and involving social context. Like the infants I observed, I was rarely alone. Every event of my daily life was seemingly watched and discussed by my fellow villagers. When I returned to Berkeley I experienced a loneliness I had not anticipated.

The second was more directly related to my academic goals. I learned how to observe infants' attachment patterns outside the Strange Situation Procedure (SSP; Ainsworth et al., 1978). On my daily rounds through the village, I saw that every few weeks, the mothers dressed up, gathered their infant's United Nations health card, and walked to the local health center for a well-baby exam (the Infant Weigh-In). The exam involved weighing of the infants followed by a ten-minute interview. I soon realized that the exam exposed the infants to a series of mild to moderate stressors not unlike those experienced by Western infants in the SSP. These included being in a new place, being with a stranger, and being taken from the mother's arms. On my return, I learned that these similarities had also been noted by Ainsworth (1977): The "situation closest to this (SSP) that occurred with the Ganda infants was visiting the well-baby clinic" (p. 124).

I filmed about a dozen well-baby exams in Niger. On returning to Berkeley, I saw that the large majority of the infants displayed behavioral and communication patterns associated with secure attachment relationships (True, 1994). On average, the infants became mildly distressed when put on the scale and then turned towards their mother and signaled to be taken off the scale. Once back in their mother's arms, the majority was calmed and visually explored the room. However, a minority showed avoidance of the mother while on the scale; either they never turned their torso towards her, or they only gave her a second's glance. Another minority, similarly to resistant infants, were not calmed by their mother's attempts to offer comfort. Lastly, some infants showed contextually odd behaviors, analogous to those of infants in disorganized relationships.

Based on these observations I was asked to join an Italian research team in Mali to observe infant–mother attachment relationships among the Dogon. My colleagues, Fatimata Oumar and Lelia Pisani, had worked together for ten years on projects involving the well-being of Malian mothers and infants. We filmed forty-nine mother–infant pairs in multiple contexts, including the home, well-infant exams and the SSP (True et al., 2001). This allowed us to investigate central propositions regarding development of organized attachment patterns. It also allowed us to investigate two emerging hypotheses related to the development of infant disorganization. The first predicted an association between disorganization and maternal frightening/frightened (Fr/Fr) behaviors (Main & Hesse, 1990), and the second predicted a linkage between disorganization and dysfluent communication (Lyons-Ruth & Jacobvitz, 1999).

Our first report supported both hypotheses (True et al., 2001). Maternal Fr/Fr behaviors predicted infant disorganization in the SSP. Dysfluent communication in the Weigh-In was also higher for disorganized pairs than secure pairs. However, we also found that whereas maternal sensitivity predicted communication in the Infant Weigh, it did not predict attachment security in the SSP. Finally, we compared the Dogon SSP distribution with that of a meta-analysis of Western samples (van IJzendoorn et al., 1999). Descriptively, there was a higher distribution of secure classifications among the Dogon infants–mother dyads (67 percent vs. 55 percent), a lower distribution of avoidant classifications (0 percent vs. 22 percent), a similar distribution of resistant classifications (8 percent vs. 8 percent), and a higher distribution of disorganized classifications (25 percent vs. 15 percent). There was also a significant difference between the distributions, which was due to the lack of avoidant classifications among the Dogon dyads.

The primary research question that motivated the present study was therefore: "Why were there no avoidant classifications among the Dogon?" Before elaborating on the two hypotheses I investigate, I will put them in the context of attachment theory and Dogon infant care practices.

# Theoretical and Empirical Background

## The attachment system and the organized patterns of attachment

Bowlby (1958) articulated the fundamental proposition of attachment theory when he stated that infants' efforts to maintain proximity to or communication with their caregivers (also termed "attachment figures") – especially when distressed – manifest a biologically-based behavioral system. The system is considered to be experience-dependent and, over the first year of life, infants develop an "organization of attention, expectation, affect and behavior" based on their experiences with their caregivers (Reisz et al., 2017). This organization is thought to guide infants' subsequent behavior, especially in times of distress (Sroufe & Waters, 1977).

Ainsworth's (1967) ethnographic research in Uganda provided the first empirical support for Bowlby's theory; the majority of infants showed the expected behavioral organization by increasing proximity to their mothers when distressed. However, she also observed that a minority of infants did not seek proximity, or sought proximity but failed to be comforted by their mothers' attempts to console them. Ainsworth's subsequent Baltimore study extended these findings and demonstrated individual differences in attachment behavioral organization, which in turn were meaningfully related to individual differences in maternal behaviors (Ainsworth, et al., 1978).

As in Uganda, the majority of infants increased proximity to their mother under distress and were calmed by their mother's presence and attempts to comfort them (termed the "secure" pattern of attachment organization). In extensive home observations, the mothers of these infants were sensitive to their infants' signals. In addition, Ainsworth observed two patterns of anxious or "insecure" attachment organization in the SSP. The first of these included infants who organized their attention and behaviors away from their mothers upon her return after a separation (termed insecure-avoidant). Mothers of these infants displayed the highest levels of rejecting behavior in the home observations – including aversion to close contact and comfortable holding of their infants – in spite of the effectiveness of soothing contact in regulating infant distress (Main, 1990). The second pattern of insecure organization included infants who approached their mothers on her return in the SSP, but whose behaviors were organized by anger and who could not be calmed by their mothers to return to play (termed insecure-resistant). In home observations, mothers of these infants were highly inconsistent in their interactions with their infants, being sensitive and responsive at times and, at other times, unresponsive.

## Disorganized/disoriented attachment

A fourth classification was later introduced by Main and Solomon (1986, 1990), based on reviews of 200 unclassifiable SSPs and observations that Bowlby had made of contradictory behavior patterns under high stress (Reisz et al., 2017). The central feature of this classification – termed disorganized/disoriented – is an inability to maintain an organized pattern of behaviors (cf. strategy) in relation to the caregiver during the SSP.

Main and Solomon (1990) described seven themes of disorganized/disoriented behaviors (henceforth termed disorganized or "D" for brevity). The first five themes describe indices of (presumed) approach-avoidance conflict, including; (I) sequential displays of contradictory behavior patterns; (II) simultaneous display of contradictory behavior patterns; (III) undirected, misdirected, incomplete and interrupted movements; (IV) stereotypies, asymmetrical movements, mistimed movements and anomalous postures; and (V) freezing, stilling and slowed movements or expressions. The final two themes reflect (VI) direct indices of apprehension regarding the parent and (VII) direct indices of dissociation/disorientation. Each behavior that corresponds to any of the seven indices is initially given a score for its intensity (1–9), with infants receiving ratings over five on one or more behaviors classified as in disorganized relationships.

Meta-analyses suggest that approximately 15 percent of infant–mother dyads from low-risk samples are classified as D (van IJzendoorn et al., 1999). D-rates are higher in high-risk samples (e.g., substance abuse, unresolved parental trauma, living in violence-prone neighborhoods), with the highest D-rates in maltreatment samples (Cyr et al., 2010). Studies of developmental outcomes report that D is moderately predictive of lowered social competence and externalizing problems such as hostile-aggressive behaviors (Groh et al., 2014; Fearon et al., 2010). Links between D and internalizing problems have also been reported (Carlson, 1998; Lyons-Ruth & Jacobvitz, 2016), although meta-analytical research has provided conflicting findings (Groh et al., 2012).

## Pathways to disorganized attachment

In research conducted in the West, D is the attachment category most predictive of poor developmental outcomes, and a large body of research has focused on its etiology (see Lyons-Ruth & Jacobvitz, 2016). Interestingly, Bowlby's (mostly unpublished) writings regarding the origins of disorganization have proved prescient and congruent with later research findings (Reisz et al., 2017). Bowlby proposed three pathways to disorganized behaviors. The first pathway involves experiencing threat directly from the attachment figure, which he argued would lead to a conflict between two motivational systems. The first being an approach system motivating the infant to go to the parent as a safe haven, and the second being a withdrawal/fear system motivating the infant to move away from the parent as a source of alarm. In short, disorganization is the outward display of an internal conflict of opposing motives. The second pathway involves fear or anxiety that is not coming directly from the attachment figure; however, the infant does not believe in the attachment figure's ability to manage or assuage the distress. He writes: "It is no less natural to feel afraid when lines of communication with base are in jeopardy than when something occurs in front of us that alarms us" (cited in Reitz et al., 2017; p. 119). The third pathway pertains to long-term separations from the attachment figure. I organize the review below around the first two pathways, as they are most relevant to our previous findings and the present study.

### Fr/Fr behavior as a pathway to infant disorganization

Main and Hesse (1990) proposed, consistent with Bowlby's first pathway, that alarming behavior that come directly from the attachment figure (frightening/frightened behavior) is the primary developmental precursor to infant D as it leads to a situation of unassuaged distress. Main and Hesse (1990) discerned six types of behaviors that predict infant disorganization: threatening, frightened, dissociative, timid or differential, role-reversing and disorganized behavior. The hypothesis has been supported empirically, with a moderate meta-analytic association between Fr/Fr and D ($r = .32$; Madigan et al., 2006). This association corresponds well to the one we found in the Dogon sample ($r = .39$; True et al., 2001).

### Dysfluent communication as a pathway to disorganized attachment

A number of attachment theorists have come to adopt a wider view on precursors to infant D. Consistent with Bowlby's second pathway, they propose that infant D can stem from (severe enough) caregiver unresponsiveness to their infant's distress and need for solace (Lyons-Ruth & Jacobvitz, 2016). For instance, Lyons-Ruth (2007) argues that "The more general caregiving mechanism related to D may be the lack of effective caregiver regulation of fearful arousal, rather than explicit fear of the caregiver herself" (p. 609). Absence of effective caregiver regulation – also termed dysfluent or dysregulating communication – can presumably come in many forms, including; withdrawal in response to infants' distress; highly incongruent responses; negative intrusive, role-confused, disoriented responses; or other affective communication errors (Lyons-Ruth & Jacobvitz, 1999, 2016). Meta-analytic associations between dysfluent communication and infant D have also been reported (Lyons-Ruth & Jacobvitz, 2016; Madigan et al., 2006), and the association was found in the Dogon study as well ($r = .35$).

### Disorganization and micro-analysis of communication patterns

It has been argued that investigation of the etiology of D necessitates fine-tuned analyses of caregiver–infant interactions, as opposed to the more global rating scales that are typically used (Madigan et al., 2006). Studies using microanalysis of face-to-face communication have also proved fruitful. For instance, Jaffe and colleagues (2001) measured the temporal rhythms of vocal dialogs between four-month-old infants and their mothers. Pairs with infants later classified as secure demonstrated moderate levels of temporal coordination. In contrast, pairs with infants later classified as D showed idiosyncratic patterns similar to adults where there are angry exchanges, with each partner's communication highly contingent on their partner's communication. Moreover, the infants later classified as D displayed an approach/avoidance conflict, leaning and looking away at the same time as they made approach signals (i.e., distress vocalizations). A follow-up study with four- to six-month-old infants reported congruent findings: in dyads where infants were later classified D there were "many forms of intrapersonal and interpersonal conflict, intermodal discordance or contradiction" (Beebe & Steele, 2013, pp. 597–598). Such early conflict and discordance may affect infants' ability to develop a consistent and organized strategy for dealing with distress, the lack of which is the hallmark of disorganized relationships.

*Bodily versus face-to-face communication*

Infants and caregivers in Western cultures typically communicate in "distal" patterns through face-to-face and verbal interactions, and it therefore makes sense to assess Western infant–caregiver communication in this context. However, this is not the case in many non-Western contexts, where infant care is more "proximal" through close and continual physical proximity (Keller et al., 2009). Fortunately, individual differences in bodily-focused, dyadic communications can also be measured (Shai & Belsky, 2017). Physical actions are not simply behaviors; rather, they operate as signals of intention and emotion to a communicative partner. Shai and Belsky (2017) therefore observed individual differences in dyadic bodily communications – parental embodied mentalization (PEM) – by rating caregivers' ability to read their infants' intent, to respond to it appropriately, and, if needed, to repair previous responses. Consistent with findings suggesting that avoidant infants often experience conflicted physical interactions with their mothers, Shai and Meins (2018) found that higher PEM distinguished secure infants from avoidant infants, though not from disorganized or resistant infants.

## Dogon infant care practices

Dogon infant care practices have three central features, with physical contact a major means of caregiver–infant interaction. The first is prompt responding to distress. Indeed, we found that infant cries and fusses were responded to, on average, in five seconds (Pisani et al., 2005). In comparison, American caregivers have been found to respond, on average, in thirty seconds (Bell & Ainsworth, 1972). The second feature is near-constant bodily contact, with Dogon infants in bodily contact with or within arm's reach of a caregiver 90 percent of the time during their first year (Pisani, 1988). Bodily contact typically includes shared rhythmic touch, which not only occurs when mothers breastfeed or massage their infants, but also when they carry them in soft carriers while working. The third feature is breastfeeding on demand, for nourishment and for calming of distress. Mothers wear a loose blouse (or none at all) to give their infants free access to the breast, and infants soon learn to signal their desire to breastfeed with pulls at the mother's shirt. Breastfeeding bouts are frequent and short and often occur several times per hour. According to Ainsworth, the feeding system and the attachment system are intertwined when "the baby is fed contingent on his own behavior and when the baby is breastfed, so that the food-providing source and the attachment figure are one and the same" (Ainsworth, 1977; p. 128). These conditions clearly apply to the Dogon.

## Two hypotheses linking the lack of avoidant classifications among the Dogon to disorganization

The first hypothesis is that infants whose mothers show discomfort holding them – suggesting maternal aversion to close contact – can get caught in an approach/avoidance conflict when experiencing distress. On the one hand, the infants are encouraged to approach their caregivers, due to the cultural norm that distress should be met promptly with breastfeeding. On the other hand, mothers' who are high in contact aversion may simultaneously communicate to their infants, through their postures, not to approach. The regularity of such conflict may preclude development of an avoidant strategy. Since infant D is assumed to stem from mother–infant relationship dynamics, I call this the *"relational hypothesis."* The second hypothesis is that Dogon infants may experience unintended high levels of stress in the SSP since they are rarely left alone, or left alone with a stranger in a strange place. That is, even if Dogon infants develop an avoidant strategy for dealing with contact aversive mothers, the strategy may be prone to collapse under the stress of the SSP. Because this hypothesis is linked to a possible procedural flaw leading to infant overstress, I call this the "overstress *hypothesis."*

*The relational hypothesis*

In Western samples, infant avoidance is associated with maternal rejection, intrusiveness and aversion to close bodily contact (Ainsworth et al., 1978; Isabella, 1993; Main, 1990). Maternal aversion to contact has been described as movements that prevent ventral-to-ventral contact with the infant (Main & Stadtman, 1981). In fact, Main (1990) hypothesized that infants whose proximity-seeking is rebuffed will become caught in an approach/avoidance conflict. This is because rejection will increase the activation of the infant's attachment system and, hence, the motivation to approach the caregiver. At the same time, the infant will be motivated to move away from the caregiver and the pain of being rebuffed when closeness is most needed. Main (1990) described avoidance – a shift in attention away from an inaccessible caregiver and the feelings it produces – as decreasing the threat of conflict and, consequently, behavioral disorganization. Main (1990) also demonstrated that the threat of disorganization is real for infants of contact-averse mothers in three separate studies. Maternal contact aversion in home observations and play situations, which are presumably less distressing than the SSP, was strongly associated with infant conflict behavior (*rs* = .44, .55, .63).

Approximately 15 percent of the Dogon mothers showed contact aversion in the home (True et al., 2003). However, the Dogon mothers cannot ignore or completely rebuff their infants' signals to breastfeed, as this would be culturally inappropriate. Breastmilk is infants' major source of nourishment and, in a context where 15–20 percent die during their first year, custom dictates that mothers respond to their infants' initiatives to feed. Consequently, Dogon infants may not get consistent experiences of physical rejection on which to build an avoidant attachment strategy. Often enough, their cues are met with the comfort of warm milk and some degree of contact. However, an approach-avoidance dynamic may nonetheless be in play when mothers are contact averse. Though each mother will find a way to handle the conflict, the resolution may result in contradictory and dysfluent communication, the everyday nature of which may dampen infants' ability to develop a coherent strategy and result in D (Beebe & Steele, 2013).

*The overstress hypothesis*

The SSP was designed to elicit mild to moderate distress in infants accustomed to brief separations (Ainsworth et al., 1978). However, when Ainsworth re-administered the SSP after two weeks, to assess its reliability, she discovered that the infants showed higher levels of stress than intended, and that their behavior changed. Mary Main, then a student of Ainsworth, also observed that the infants who were classified as avoidant in the first SSP approached their caregivers in the second SSP, albeit displaying conflict behavior. The implication is that an avoidant strategy will collapse under too much stress. This reasoning fits with Bowlby's writings, in which he stated that "above a certain level, however, efficiency (emotional organization) may be diminished; and, when in an experimental situation total stimulation is very greatly increased, behavior becomes completely disorganized" (cited in Reisz et al., 2017, pp. 96–97).

Overstress in the SSP has also been empirically linked to unexpected high rates of D-classifications (Granqvist et al., 2016). Swedish middle-class infants who had experienced a second SSP less than forty-three days after the first and who experienced the full three-minute separation episode in spite of showing marked distress were disproportionately likely to be classified as disorganized. While there is no direct support for the proposal that the SSP is more stressful for Dogon infants than for Western infants there is indirect support: Dogon infants were more likely to show distress (crying) in the SSP (85 percent) than in the Weigh-In (54 percent; True, 1994). It is important to note that we took great care to avoid overstress in the SSP due to extended separations, with separations curtailed if infants showed marked distress signals for ten seconds (True, 1994; True et al., 2001). Nonetheless, infants are left alone in the SSP, and this is a very rare experience for Dogon infants, whereas the mother is always nearby in the Weigh-In, in keeping with Dogon care practices.

## SSP distributions in non-Western countries

It is unclear whether the lack of avoidant classifications among the Dogon is anomalous or congruent with other non-Western cultures. To date, nine studies in non-Western populations have used the ABCD Strange Situation classification and are published in English (see Mesman et al., 2016; Mooya et al., 2016; Zreik et al, 2017). As stated above, an objective of the current study is to construct an aggregate non-Western distribution to compare with a Western aggregate and with the Dogon sample.

Provision of validating data for the SSP in different cultures is a central issue in the field. Cross-cultural validation of the D classification is of particular concern, as this was the most common insecure classification among the Dogon. Several studies in collectivistic cultures have examined maternal sensitivity to support the validity of a two-way difference between secure and insecure patterns of attachment in the SSP. However, there has been little investigation of, or support for, theory-based differences in caregiver interactions related to the avoidant, resistant and disorganized (insecure) attachment classifications (e.g., Zreik et al., 2017). Moreover, meta-analyses in primarily individualistic cultures have indicated that maternal sensitivity does not predict D-classifications (Mesman et al., 2016; van IJzendoorn et al., 1999).

## Protective behaviors in Dogon infant care practices

A major critique of attachment research is that the primary predictor of secure infant–mother attachment relationships – maternal sensitivity – is culturally biased (Keller et al., 2009, 2018). The argument is that the concept presumes that infants are communicative agents who express desires and needs that are best served by contingent responsiveness. These assumptions may differ from those in collective cultures where infants are not viewed as autonomous beings in need of a sense of personal efficacy. Infant care also appears more culturally rote among the Dogon than among Western caregivers. For example, most Dogon infants were given the breast immediately on distress signals, suggesting that maternal consideration of multiple appropriate responses is not common among Dogon mothers (Pisani et al., 2005). Caregiver proximity is also a given in rural Mali – rather than a decision to be made – since there are constant dangers such as open fires and snakes.

By focusing on contingent responsiveness in moment-to-moment interactions attachment researchers can miss non-contingent caregiving practices which provide the infant an ongoing experience of connection and safety. There is evidence that when distressed infants are carried, the infants show reduced levels of crying, bodily movement and heart rate beyond the effects of just being held (Cascio et al., 2019). This is important theoretically as a caregiver's inability to assuage infant distress is increasingly recognized as a key variable in the development of D (e.g., Beebe & Steele, 2013).

Shared rhythmic interaction between caregiver and infant may, in fact, operate as a hidden factor in the development of secure attachment relationships. Prenatally, the fetus experiences not only the constancy of the mother's heartbeat, but also the rhythmic motion of lanugo hairs while moving in the amniotic fluid (Cascio et al., 2019). Postnatal rhythmic interaction begins in the first weeks of infants' lives and represents an intermodal form of sensory communication (Stern, 1977). For example, an infant's gurgle may be met by a similar rhythm in his mother's tapping on its stomach. A seminal study by Condon and Sandler (1974) found that young infants' hand movements were synchronous with their parents' patterning of speech. Blind children have moreover been shown to change their hand movements in accordance with their caregiver's rhythm, suggesting an inborn ability to detect and express rhythmic interactions (Trevarthen & Aitken, 2001).

In a series of experimental studies with rat dams and their pups, Myran Hofer and colleagues have demonstrated that specific maternal behaviors regulate specific infant physiological processes (for a review, see Hofer, 2006). For example, a dam's tactile stimulation decreased her pups stressed hyperactivity in separation episodes. In unpublished papers, Bowlby actually expressed support for Hofer's research as providing insight into possible mechanisms for the development of secure attachment relationships (R. Duschinsky, 2019, personal communication). Recent findings in social neuroscience research report a "correspondence between gentle, caress-like stroking and the activation of low-threshold unmyelinated peripheral afferent C-touch (CT) fibers" (Cascio et al., 2019, p. 5). This activation is associated with positive affect, and there is indirect evidence that CT fibers mediate oxytocin release during affiliative and nurturing touch.

In multiple studies, Ruth Feldman and her colleagues have demonstrated how synchronous interactions between parents and their young infants operate to regulate physiological processes (see Feldman, 2015, for a review). This includes a positive feedback loop for release of oxytocin for both parent and infant, as well as coordinated heart rates. Synchrony has also been linked to developmental outcomes, including positive affiliative behaviors and emotional regulation skills in childhood. In a small experimental study with mothers of newborns, Anisfeld and colleagues (1990) found that the use of soft infant carriers – which by their nature promote shared rhythmic interaction – might facilitate the development of secure attachment relationships. Mothers who were randomly assigned a soft infant carrier (rather than a plastic infant carrier) were more sensitive when their infants were three months old, and their infants had higher rates of secure attachment at twelve months of age. Importantly, the use of soft infant carrier overlaps with non-Western care practices, where infants are frequently carried on their mothers' backs while they work. This finding, though in need of replication, suggests that non-Western care practices that facilitate shared rhythmic touch may facilitate the development of secure attachment relationships.

The most common form of shared rhythm examined in Western studies of interactive rhythms involve face-to-face communication (Beebe & Steele, 2013; Feldman, 2015). Our observations among the Dogon did capture moments of face-to-face rhythmic interaction. However, this was not the most typical form of shared rhythmic interaction. Much of the shared rhythm took place in close bodily contact: while the infants were on their mothers' backs as they pounded, shifted and ground the millet; during the infant's daily post-bath massage; while breast-feeding; and while co-sleeping. The predominance of rhythmic touch in West African infant care is supported by two recent studies comparing modes of tactile interaction between Western and non-Western mothers. First, West African immigrant mothers were found more likely to initiate motor stimulation with their infants than Italian mothers, and they had longer periods of rhythmic tactile and rhythmic motor interaction with their infants (Carra et al., 2014). Second, West African Nso-mothers were more likely to match their motor stimulation and touches with rhythmic vocalizing and protosongs than German middle-class mothers (Demuth, 2008).

## Aims of the present study

The first objective of the present study was to investigate the relational and overstress hypotheses for the lack of avoidant SSP classifications in the Dogon sample. The relational hypothesis states that maternal contact aversion will explain variance in infant disorganization in the SSP, above and beyond the variance explained by Fr/Fr caregiver behavior. The overstress hypothesis states that maternal contact aversion will be associated with infant avoidance in the Weigh-In but not in the SSP, because the avoidant strategy collapses during the (overly) stressful SSP for Dogon infants. The hypotheses are not mutually exclusive.

The second objective was to construct an aggregate of SSP distributions in non-Western cultures to enable comparisons of (I) the Dogon distribution with distributions for other non-Western countries and (II) non-Western and Western distributions.

The third objective was to illustrate the everyday occurrence of shared touch and rhythmic interaction among Dogon mothers and their infants.

# Methods

## Participants

The participants were forty-two mother–infant dyads from the Dogon ethnic group of Western Mali. The total sample size was forty-nine, but seven dyads had to be excluded due to severe infant malnutrition. Fifteen mother–infant pairs lived in rural/agrarian villages, the rest in a town of approximately 9,000 people. There were no differences between the village and town samples on background variables, except for maternal sensitivity in one home observation (True et al., 2001). The infants (eighteen boys, twenty-four girls) were between ten and eleven and-a-half months old at the beginning of data collection ($M = 10.6$; $SD = .4$). There was a 20 percent infant mortality rate in the first year, most commonly caused by pathogens acting synergistically with undernutrition (Straussman, 1997). All mothers except for the two who were first-time mothers reported a lifetime loss of one or more children.

## Measures

### The strange situation procedure

Infants and mothers were observed in the standard ABCD procedure (Ainsworth et al., 1978; Main & Solomon, 1990). The SSP was filmed in a semi-private outdoor alcove that normally served as a waiting area for the town's Health Center. Donna Weston coded the procedure and Judith Solomon and Mary Main reliability coded 44 percent of the SSPs. Reliability was high for the major classifications (88 percent), the continuous ratings of D (.83), and avoidance (.79). Many infants signaled to breastfeed, particularly in the second reunion, and this was coded as contact maintenance.

### The infant weigh-in

The setting was the town's medical clinic, mirroring a typical West-African infant exam room (see Figure 15.1). A research assistant weighed the infants and then talked with the mothers about the infants' health. The procedure lasted three minutes and consisted of two linked episodes that were repeated once. The first was a thirty-second placement of the infants on the scale next to the stranger, during which the mothers were asked to stay in sight of

**Figure 15.1**    Setting for weigh-in procedure.

but not touch their infants. The mothers then picked up and held their infants for ninety seconds before a second set of the two episodes.

The Weigh-In was coded using five-point rating scales of infant and maternal communication behaviors. The rating scales were designed to be consistent with Grice's (1975) concept of communication violations, which also served as a foundation of the Adult Attachment Interview (George et al., 1985). Infant positive communication was operationalized as direct signaling while on the scale, and maternal positive communication as cooperation with her infant's signals. Infant negative communication – considered violations of coherence and cooperativeness – was operationalized as avoidance (e.g., not looking or turning towards the mother while on the scale), resistance (e.g., kicking on the pick-up), and disorganization (e.g., holding an arm up against gravity for over five seconds). Maternal negative communication – considered violations of coherence and cooperativeness – was operationalized as withdrawal (e.g., moving away while the infant was on the scale), overriding of infant negativity (smiling when the infant was crying), and Fr/Fr behaviors (e.g., stilling for over ten seconds while the infant was on the scale).

The highest rating of negative communication for each pair was used as a summary measure of communication violations. The coding was done by Betty Repacholi. Using data from two Weigh-In procedures filmed six weeks apart, the communication violations scale showed strong inter-rater reliability ($r = .87$), and acceptable test-retest reliability ($r = .71$). Inter-rater reliability was particularly strong for avoidance ($r = .95$).

*Infant distress in the weigh-in and strange situation procedure*
Distress in the Weigh-In was assessed using a five-point scale (1 = no fusses/cries; 3 = intermittent fusses/cries; 5 = full crying without interruption), with infants judged distressed if rated higher than 2 (brief fuss). Inter-rater reliability for distress/no distress was 92 percent ($n = 16$). Distress in the SSP was assessed using the SSP coders' transcripts, with infants coded as distressed if they cried during either of the separation–reunion episodes. Inter-rater reliability was 100 percent ($n = 12$ episodes).

*Maternal aversion to contact*
Maternal aversion to contact was assessed during fifteen-minute (videotaped) observations while the mothers were occupied with caregiving and cooking chores. The observations were coded using Sue Lyon's (1992) adaptation of Townsend and Mains' (Main, 1990) 9-point rating scale "Parental avoidance of tactual contact with the infant" (outlined below). The adaption consisted of the addition of three items designed to capture aversion

while holding or breastfeeding the infant (identified by *), resulting in a scale with ten behavioral indices. Ratings on all indices were averaged into a summary score of contact aversion. Aversion to contact in the breastfeeding situation was often most shown through index b.

a    Keeping body midline angled away from the infant
b    Keeping shoulders back rather than curved toward the infant
c    Keeping the knees up or in some other position so that there is no opportunity for the infant to reach the chest/lap/stomach
d    Moving the head or neck back uncomfortably while holding the infant
e    Moving into or remaining in uncomfortable postures, the relaxation of which would bring the parent into contact with the infant
f    Folding the arms across the stomach as though to prevent the child's body from touching the parent's ventral surface, especially when the child is seated upon the parent's lap
g    Wincing or flinching as the child moves into closer contact
h*    Holding the infant away from the parent's body, though infant may want to approach
i*    While breastfeeding, placing/holding the infant so that his only contact with the mother is with her nipple
j*    Leaning away from the infant especially while holding

### Maternal frightening/frightened behavior

Fr/Fr behaviors were assessed with "Frightening, Frightened, Timid, Dissociated or Disorganized Behavior on the Part of the Parent" (Main & Hesse, 1990). Three different observations were used to examine Fr/Fr behaviors: the two separate home observations, and the first infant Weigh-In, as it had the most complete sample. The highest rating from the three observations was used as a measure of Fr/Fr behavior for each mother. Inter-rater reliabilities were .71 and .84 for the home observations and .74 for the Weigh-In.

### Non-Western SSP distribution

Studies were initially sought in Mesman and colleagues' (2016) cross-cultural review of patterns of attachment. Studies were included if they used the standard ABCD procedure and published in English. There is a growing consensus that caregiving practices in non-Arab Israel is primarily Western and distal (Feldman & Masalha, 2010; Mesman et al, 2016; Zreik, et al., 2017). In comparison to previous summaries of non-Western distributions, I therefore excluded Israeli studies, resulting in seven studies being included from Mesman and colleagues (2016). A literature search (Google Scholar and Psychnet) revealed two additional studies, published after 2015, that were also included. An aggregate SSP distribution of non-Western samples was constructed based on these nine studies.

# Results

## Descriptive statistics

Descriptive statistics for Dogon infant–mother communication and interaction are presented in Table 15.1. The distributions of attachment classifications are presented in Figure 15.2 and Table 15.2. The distribution of SSP-classifications in the non-Western aggregated sample was 61 percent secure; 7 percent avoidant; 14 percent resistant; and 18 percent disorganized. The distribution of SSP-classifications in the North-American low-risk population (van IJzendoorn et al., 1999), which has been used for comparison purposes in a recent study of Zambian infants (Mooya et al., 2017), was 55 percent secure; 23 percent avoidant; 7 percent resistant; and 15 percent disorganized.

## Tests of research hypotheses

### Comparison of SSP distributions

There was a significant difference between the non-Western and North American distributions, $\chi^2$ (3) = 11.45, $p < .01$. The difference was due to lower percentages of avoidant classifications in the non-Western samples: $\chi^2$ (1) = 4.11, $p < .05$.

**Table 15.1**  Descriptive statistics for dysfluent communication, maternal contact aversion and Fr/Fr behavior, and infant attachment behavior ($n = 39$)

|                              | M    | SD   | Range |
| ---------------------------- | ---- | ---- | ----- |
| Dysfluent Communication      | 2.83 | 1.31 | 1–5   |
| Maternal Contact Aversion    | 2.91 | 1.47 | 1–6   |
| Maternal Fr/Fr Behaviors     | 1.53 | .87  | 1–5   |
| Infant SSP Security          | 5.23 | 2.05 | 2–8.5 |
| Infant SSP Disorganization   | 3.04 | 2.13 | 1–8   |
| Infant SSP Avoidance         | 2.36 | 1.19 | 1–4.5 |
| Infant WI Avoidance          | 1.88 | 1.20 | 1–4.5 |

Fr/Fr = Frightening/Frightened. SSP = Strange Situation Procedure. WI = Weigh-In.

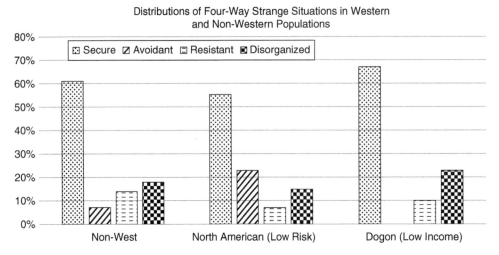

**Figure 15.2**  Four-Way Distributions of SSP-Classifications in the Dogon sample, North American samples, and non-Western samples.

**Table 15.2**  Distribution of non-West SSP classifications and correlating measures

| Country      | n  | Attachment Distribution (%) | | | | Author(s)              | Corr. Measures     |
| ------------ | -- | ---- | --- | ---- | ---- | ---------------------- | ------------------ |
|              |    | Sec. | Av. | Res. | Dis. |                        |                    |
| Mexico       | 66 | 55   | 5   | 15   | 25   | Gojman et al. (2012)   | AAI, M. Sens       |
| Mali         | 39 | 67   | 0   | 8    | 25   | True et al. (2001)     | Fr/Fr, D. Comm.    |
| S. Africa    | 98 | 62   | 4   | 8    | 26   | Tomlinson et al. (2005)| Fr/Fr, Depression  |
| Zambia       | 41 | 46   | 20  | 5    | 29   | Mooya et al. (2016)    |                    |
| Korea        | 87 | 72   | 1   | 18   | 9    | Jin et al. (2012)      | M. Sens            |
| China/Xi'an  | 61 | 58   | 13  | 16   | 13   | Archer et al. (2012)   |                    |
| China/Shg.   | 62 | 68   | 7   | 22   | 3    | Ding et al. (2008)     | M. Sens            |
| Indonesia    | 46 | 52   | 7   | 20   | 22   | Zevalkink et al. 1999) | M. Support         |
| Israel/Arab  | 85 | 67   | 4   | 13   | 16   | Zreik et al. (2014)    | M. Sens            |
| **Mean (%)** |    |      |     |      |      |                        |                    |
| **Non-West★**|    | 61   | 7   | 14   | 18   |                        |                    |
| **N. America★** |  | 55  | 23  | 7    | 15   | (From Mooya et al. (2016) |                 |

★Chi2 Non-West and North American ABCD comparison: 11.45, p < .01
★Chi2 Non-West and North American Secure vs. Insecure comparison: .33, p > .05
*Note:* AAI = Adult Attachment Interview, M. Sens = Maternal Sensitivity, D. Comm. = Dyadic Communication, M Support = Maternal Support in Play.

The ratio of secure to insecure classifications did not differ, $\chi^2 (1) = .33$, $p > .05$. Contrary to expectations, there was also a significant difference between the Dogon sample and the non-Western distribution $\chi^2 (3) = 10.04$, $p < .05$. The difference was due to a lower percentage of avoidant classifications in the Dogon sample (0 percent) than the non-Western distribution (7 percent). This finding is discussed below in terms of the "overstress hypothesis." The ratio of secure to insecure classifications was not different between the Dogon sample and the non-Western distribution, $\chi^2 (1) = .78$, $p > .05$.

### The relational hypothesis

As reported in an earlier publication (True, et al., 2001) infant disorganization was associated with maternal Fr/Fr ($r = .39$, $p < .05$). To examine the relational hypothesis concerning contact aversion, a hierarchical regression analysis was conducted with maternal Fr/Fr behavior and maternal contact aversion entered sequentially as predictors of infant disorganization. The predictors contributed significantly to explained variance in infant disorganization, $F (2, 38) = 8.01$, $p = .001$, and the inclusion of maternal contact aversion doubled the amount of explained variance from 13 percent to 27 percent ($p = .008$), giving support to the relational hypothesis.

### The overstress hypothesis

There was a significant difference in infant distress between the Weigh-In (64 percent) and the SSP (88 percent), $\chi^2 (1) = 5.6$, $p < .05$, representing an increase in distress of 40 percent from the Weigh-In to the SSP. Maternal contact aversion was associated with infant avoidance in the Weigh-In ($r = .32$, $p < .05$), but not the SSP ($r = .07$, $p > .05$). A post hoc analysis also showed that infant avoidance in the Weigh-In was associated with infant D in the SSP ($r = .31$, $p = .05$). These findings give support to the over-stress hypothesis.

## Case by case analyses

Case analyses were conducted of the ten infants classified as disorganized in the SSP. These are intended to provide an additional window into the potentially multiple and overlapping correlates to infant disorganization.

### The relational hypothesis

Mothers of seven D-infants were rated above the sample mean of 2.99 on contact aversion, providing partial support for the relational hypothesis. It should be noted, however, that Main (1990) reported mean contact aversion of 7.2 for the six mothers of avoidant infants in Ainsworth's sample.

### The overstress hypothesis

Three of the D-infants whose mothers displayed contact aversion displayed moderate to high avoidance in the Weigh-In, without any indices of disorganization. However, these infants showed moderate to high avoidance in the first SSP reunion and disorganization in the second reunion. This pattern of findings gives partial support to the hypothesis that avoidant patterns may be prone to collapse in the SSP if stress becomes too high.

### Overlap between dysfluent communication and Fr/Fr behaviors

All but one of the ten mother–infant pairs where the infant had been classified as D in the SSP showed dysfluent communication in the Weigh-In. The most frequent types of maternal dysfluent communication were affective errors such as smiling or turning away when their infants showed distress. Six of the nine mothers who showed dysfluent communication were also rated in the low to moderate range of Fr/Fr behaviors. The single mother who was coded as high in Fr/Fr, due to stilling in her infant's presence, was also coded as high in communication violations in the Weigh-In (as was her infant).

## Discussion

The primary objective of this study was to investigate why there were no avoidant SSP classifications in the Dogon sample. I examined two nonexclusive hypotheses grounded in Dogon infant care practices. First, the *"relational hypothesis"* suggests that the Dogon care practices of breastfeeding on demand and breastfeeding to soothe distress may preclude infants' development of an avoidant organization of attachment behavior. Second, the *"overstress hypothesis"* suggests that the near constant proximity between Dogon infants and their caregivers may result in overstress in the SSP. Both hypotheses were partially supported. The standard predictor of avoidance in Western infants, maternal contact aversion, predicted infant D over and above maternal Fr/Fr behavior, which is the standard predictor of infant D in Western infants.

My thinking consequently broadened to examine why contact aversion may predict D in a non-Western sample such as the Dogon, and whether the Dogon sample is representative of other non-Western cultures. The Dogon infants showed more distress in the SSP than the Weigh-In, as indexed by frequency of crying. Maternal contact aversion was also associated with infant avoidance in the Weigh-In, suggesting that the SSP may be too stressful for Dogon infants and result in "false-positive" D-classifications. There was a lower distribution of avoidant classifications in the non-Western distribution than the Western distribution. However, the Dogon sample also differed from the non-Western distribution by an even lower frequency of avoidant classifications. These findings will be further discussed below.

## The relational hypothesis

The central proposition is that distressed infants of contact-aversive mothers may experience conflicting and disorganizing motivations to both approach and withdraw from their mothers. They are motivated to approach their mother and breastfeed, to reduce their distress, and simultaneously motivated to avoid their physically unwelcoming mother. I see maternal contact aversion as dysfluent physical communication, because such caregivers respond to their infants' cues for physical contact with a conflicted mix of behaviors. On the one hand, they allow their infants access to the breast; on the other hand, they do not provide ventral-to-ventral closeness or a relaxed body. The following excerpt from the second SSP reunion describes the behavior of an infant whose mother was rated very high on contact aversion. The infant displayed high avoidance during both separations in the Weigh-In and the first SSP reunion.

*"He approached his mother to breastfeed. Initially, he climbed up on his mother's lap. As he did so, she did not lean in towards him. After 40 seconds, the infant turned awkwardly away from his mother's torso and moved across her lap and looked up to her. He saw a non-engaged face and he experienced no additional physical contact. He then stood on the ground and pulled the breast away from his mother's body to breastfeed while she clearly leaned away and he pushed against her with his foot on her torso. He never settled."*

This patterning of interactions – though uncommon in the sample– is consistent with Beebe and Steele's (2013) remarks regarding communication between mothers and four-month-old-infants who were later classified as D. The mothers and infants displayed conflict, between and within themselves, often in the form of conflicting actions and affective communication, all of which may work against infants' ability to develop organized strategies for dealing with distress.

## The overstress hypothesis

The central proposition is that infants of contact aversive Dogon mothers may in fact develop an avoidant strategy, but that it collapses in the SSP due to overstress. This possibility, which was acknowledged already by Bowlby (Reisz et al., 2017), was also supported by the present findings; maternal contact aversion was associated with infant avoidance in the (lower stress) Weigh-In, but not in the (higher stress) SSP. The findings of the exploratory case-by-case analyses were consistent with this hypothesis; three D-infants (30 percent) of contact aversive mothers displayed the pattern predicted by the overstress hypothesis. Studies in the US and Sweden have connected overstress in the SSP with increased disorganization (Granqvist et al., 2016; Main, 1990). However, this is to my knowledge the first study suggesting procedurally linked "false positive" D classifications in non-Western contexts.

## Non-Western and Dogon SSP distributions

The non-Western and Western four-way distributions differed, due to lower rates of avoidant classifications in the non-Western distribution. However, the ratio of secure to insecure classifications did not differ. This is consistent with conclusions from previous research on non-Western samples (Mesman et al., 2016; Zreik et al., 2017).

Contrary to my expectations, the Dogon SSP distribution also differed from the aggregated non-Western samples, due to an even lower rate of avoidant classifications. However, the Dogon sample was not an extreme outlier; the presence of even one avoidant classification would have resulted in the distribution being similar to that of the non-Western distribution. Moreover, as discussed above, it is likely that there were three missed avoidant classifications due to the overstress of the SSP for the Dogon sample.

Van IJzendoorn and colleagues (2018) recently argued for the importance of high scientific standards in attachment research, given the replication problem within the social sciences. This is encouraging for researchers in non-Western contexts, including myself, who call for more observational research that test the validity of the different insecure classifications in different cultures (Jin et al., 2012; Posada, 2013; Zreik, et al., 2017). The problem is particularly apparent with regard to the D-classification (see Table 15.2). I could only find nine samples eligible for inclusion in the non-Western distribution. All results from the comparisons including the non-Western distribution should therefore be interpreted with caution. Of course, the scarcity of research using the four-way classification in West African samples is an important finding in of itself, pointing to a need for further research. Moreover, only three of the nine studies that used four-way classifications included data on the validity of D through assessment of pertinent caregiver behavior. In comparison, seven of the nine studies reported a relationship between infant security and measures of maternal sensitivity. Furthermore, no distinction was made between rural, peri-urban, and urban samples in the non-Western aggregate. This is another important limitation, since emigration from urban areas is increasing and traditional care practices are being modified (Carra et al, 2014.).

## Ramifications of overstress in the SSP

The similarity between the non-Western SSP distributions, in combination with similar infant care practices, suggest that infant overstress in the SSP may not be specific to the Dogon sample. Inaccurate "false-positive" D-classifications are of special concern, since D has been highlighted as a risk factor for mental health problems in Western countries (Fearon, et al., 2010; Lyons-Ruth & Jacobvitz, 2016).

Two other concerns about the D-classification need to be raised that are also of relevance to research conducted in the West. First, there is a well-documented tendency among researchers and practitioners to assume a connection between contextual risk factors and D-classifications (Granqvist et al., 2017). There is, indeed, strong evidence for a connection between number of risk factors and frequency of D-classifications (Cyr et al., 2010). However, I find that the usage of risk factors such as poverty as a proxy for validating observations is concerning. One reason is that it may diminish the possibility of discovering cultural caregiving practices that buffer against insecurity in otherwise high-risk contexts. Researchers from Peru, Indonesia, South Africa and Mali have, against expectations, reported high sensitivity among low-income mothers and infant security (Fourment et al, 2018; Tomlinson et al, 2005; True et al., 2001; Zevalkink et al., 1999).

A second concern regarding D-classifications is that infants from high-risk environments may already be in a high state of biological arousal when entering the SSP, due to a continuous state of high biological arousal (Cyr et al., 2010). Such over-arousal may – similarly to illness – make the SSP too stressful and result in overstress. This is an important future question for attachment research. Given these considerations, I believe that SSP-distributions from non-Western samples should not be published without validating data for the SSP in general and for the D classification in particular.

## The pioneers' view of the strange situation

Ainsworth actually designed the SSP as a validation procedure for her extensive observations of infant–mother interaction quality and maternal sensitivity. In Uganda, Ainsworth conducted naturalistic observations over nine months, with bi-weekly two- to three-hour home visits (Ainsworth, 1967). Similarly, in the Baltimore study, she observed mothers and infants over eleven months, with two to three-hour home visits every three weeks (Ainsworth et al., 1978). Her intensive observations of maternal sensitivity, and of infants' development of attachment behavioral organization, led to discoveries that have since defined the field.

The relative importance of the methodologies for assessing caregiver behavior and child attachment has essentially been flipped. The SSP is now considered the gold standard for assessing infant–caregiver attachment relationships, with observational data of caregiver sensitivity used to validate the SSP classifications. In an interview near the end of her career, Ainsworth actually expressed dissatisfaction (three times) about how observational fieldwork on infant–caregiver interactions had receded as a research method in the field (Ainsworth & Marvin, 1995). In a similar vein, Grossmann and his colleagues (1986) wrote:

> Ainsworth's empirical (i.e., observational) work has had an outstanding and justified reception in the scientific work. The Strange Situation has served as a validation procedure, aiming at the very core of the function of attachment. However, the adoption of this procedure as "the" operationalization of the concept of attachment per se implies a grave and dangerous misunderstanding. This misunderstanding is embedded in the unjustified tendency to treat instruments of search and discovery as if they were instrument of proof. (p. 130)

Their views are rooted in experience. The Grossmanns conducted the first replication of Ainsworth's Baltimore study, and found an unexpected SSP distribution with two-thirds classified as in insecure relationships, the majority of which were avoidant (Grossmann et al., 1986). The Grossmanns were concerned that the distribution would be seen as reflecting the supposedly "harsh parenting practices" of Northern Germany. They therefore conducted a thorough two-year analysis of the communication patterns in the SSP, and found that the SSP was not stressful enough for some German infants. Consequently, the infants were less likely to show the proximity-seeking behaviors indicative of a secure attachment relationship.

## A return to unstructured observational methodologies

Ongoing studies, nonetheless, do provide examples of high-quality observational research. For instance, Posada has used both ethnographic and Western approaches to observe maternal sensitivity and infant attachment security in Colombia for over thirty years (Posada et al., 2016). In his most extensive study, he trained local researchers who then conducted eight two-hour home visits (Posada et al., 2004). Four visits provided narrative data of unstructured observations of maternal sensitivity, two of the visits narrative data for the Maternal Behavioral Q-Sort (Pederson & Moran, 1995), and two visits observational data for the Attachment Q-Sort (AQS, Waters, 1995). A new set of local researchers then used the ethnographic home observation data of maternal sensitivity to delineate and describe components of maternal infant care. Many items were congruent with factors in Ainsworth's (1974) maternal sensitivity scale, including promptness of response, interactive smoothness, response effectiveness and quality of physical contact. There was also a strong correlation between the ethnographic components of infant security and the attachment Q-sort of infant security. By providing systematic and thorough use of insider information, the Posada study provides a strong model for attachment research in cultural contexts outside predominantly Western populations.

## Pathways to secure attachment relationships: insights from the Dogon

Unstructured observations allow the researcher to discover otherwise hidden factors of interest. The Dogon study – while designed with attachment-based measures and methods – provided unexpected insights by virtue of the fifty hours of films available. It was apparent in the films, as well as in unplanned spot observations, that infant–mother (caregiver) proximity is a constant, and that proximity often entails mutual touch and shared rhythm – while the infant was on the mother's back while she worked as well as during breastfeeding and co-sleeping. It is important to note that infants did not initiate many of the shared interactions; these interactions were part and parcel of the cultural context of their care.

In all, the Dogon observations suggest that the large majority of infants are "bathed in a sea of rhythmic interaction with a sensitive caregiver" (Perry, 2011, personal notes). An example of this is presented below, from a five-minute morning interaction between an eleven-month-old infant and her mother, who was preparing the family's first meal.

*"After greeting the visitors, the mother (M) stands up and moves the infant (I) to her back, wrapping her in a cloth that supports her. M goes to the bowl in which she pounds millet. M's pounding of the grain is loud and distinctly rhythmic. I is a passive recipient of M's touch and rhythm for about 90 secs. I squirms and leans out of the holding cloth to try to reach M's breast. M begins singing I's*

*name in rhythm to the pounding. I persists in leaning over M's side. After 60 sec from I's first signal to breastfeed, M puts down her pounding tool and takes I off of her back. M sits on a stool about one yard from the cooking fire and continues with other tasks of preparing the meal. Upon sitting, I leans over and into the M to begin breastfeeding, I continues breastfeeding for 30 seconds. I then switches to the other breast for 20 seconds before switching back to the first breast and unlatching."*

The interaction is in stark contrast to the discordant communications described by Beebe and Steele (2013). Though this pair also displayed conflicting goals, they worked it out in a harmonious set of physical interactions that included shared intermodal rhythm, when the mother sang her infant's name in rhythm to her pounding.

## Interventions informed by non-Western infant care practices

It has been argued that it is time to prioritize development and evaluation of attachment-based intervention programs (Granqvist et al., 2017, Van IJzendoorn et al., 2018). There are many reasons to consider non-Western "proximal" infant care practices involving caregiver touch and shared rhythm. First, the practices can begin at birth. Secondly, interactive rhythm and touch affects infants' developing neural pathways, release of affiliative hormones, regulation of stress and, possibly, the expression of genes related to the development of the stress response system (Feldman, 2015; Feldman, Singer & Zagoory, 2010; Hofer, 2006; Schore, 2001; Weaver et al., 2004). It is important to note, as well, that tactile and rhythmic interaction provide infants with a sense of maternal availability whether they are stressed or not.

Traditionally non-Western and proximal infant care practices are inexpensive and available to non-maternal caregivers as well (Keller & Otto, 2009). Kangaroo care, in which parents hold infants skin to skin and chest to chest, is the most well-researched infant care practice based on non-Western infant care (Feldman et al., 2002; Field, 1995). The Kangaroo Method of treating premature infants was developed in Venezuela as a practical and cost-effective alternative to neonatal care units (Field, 1995). Research in both Western and non-Western samples have shown that skin-to-skin contact increases premature infants' weight gain and state maturation, and that it allows infants to leave the hospital sooner. Mothers and fathers of premature infants assigned to kangaroo care have also been found to display higher sensitivity than caregivers assigned to traditional hospital care (Feldman et al., 2002). Premature infants whose mothers provide nurturing touch have also been found more likely to develop secure attachment relationships (Weiss et al., 2000). Given the benefits to interaction quality there is no reason to restrict skin-to-skin care to premature infants.

The use of soft, body-to-body infant carriers while caregivers go about daily life is not only an ancient custom; it is a common feature of non-Western infant care. An experimental study with at-risk mothers of newborns, though in need of replication, suggested that soft carriers can play an important role in enhancing maternal sensitivity and infant attachment security (Anisfeld et al., 1990). Provision of soft infant carriers may well be the most cost-effective attachment-based intervention.

## Conclusions

The present findings suggest four main conclusions. First, there were multiple overlapping correlates of infant disorganization, giving support to both a relational hypothesis and an overstress hypotheses of infant D. These correlates included dysfluent communication, maternal Fr/Fr behaviors and infant overstress in the SSP. Second, the aggregate distribution of nine non-Western samples differed from the Western distribution. The difference was due to lower rates of avoidant classifications in the non-Western samples, including the Dogon sample studied here. This finding – taken together with the possibility of "false-positive" D classifications – indicates how essential validation of the SSP is when used in new cultural contexts. Third, there is a paucity of non-structured observational studies of infant–caregiver interactions in non-Western contexts. Such studies are not only essential for cross-cultural validation of attachment measures and development of theory. Such studies also allow for the discovery of cultural caregiving practices that enhance infants' likelihood of developing secure attachment relationships and can consequently inform intervention practices and education of clinicians and social workers. Fourth, our observations of Dogon mother–infant interactions emphasized rhythmic and shared touch as integral to infant care, factors which may facilitate infant attachment security and which warrant further investigation.

# References

Ainsworth, M. D. S. (1967). *Infancy in Uganda: Infant care and the growth of love.* Johns Hopkins University Press.

Ainsworth, M. D. S. (1977). Infant development and mother–infant interaction among Ganda and American families. In P. H. Leidermann, S. R. Tulkin, & A. Rosenfeld (Eds.). *Culture and infancy: Variations in the human experience (pp. 119–148).* Academic Press.

Ainsworth, M. D. S., Bell, S. M., & Stayton, D. J. (1974). Infant–mother attachment and social development. In M. P. Richards (Ed.), *The introduction of the child into a social world (pp. 99–135).* Cambridge University Press.

Ainsworth, M. D. S., Blehar, M. C., Waters, E., & Wall, S. (1978). *Patterns of attachment: a psychological study of the strange situation.* Erlbaum.

Ainsworth, M. D. S & Marvin, R. (1995). On the shaping of attachment theory and research. *Monographs of the Society for Research in Child Development, caregiving, cultural, and cognitive perspectives on secure-base behavior and working models: New growing points of attachment theory and research, Vol. 60, No. 2/3, pp. 2–21.*

Anisfeld, E., Casper, V., Nozyce, M., & Cunningham, N. (1990). Does infant carrying promote attachment? An experimental study of the effects of increased physical contact on the development of attachment. *Child Development, 61* (5), 1617–1627.

Archer, M., Steele, M., Lan, J., Jin, X., Herreros, F. & Steele, H. (2015). Attachment between infants and mothers in China: Strange Situation procedure findings to data and a new sample. *International Journal of Behavioral Development, 39* (6) 485–491.

Beebe, B., & Steele, M. (2013). How does microanalysis of mother–infant communication inform maternal sensitivity and infant attachment? *Attachment & Human Development, 15* (5–6), 583–602.

Bell, S. M., & Ainsworth, M. D. S. (1972). Infant crying and maternal responsiveness. *Child Development, 43* (4), 1171–1190.

Bowlby, J. (1958). The nature of the child's tie to his mother. *International Journal of Psycho-Analysis, 39,* 350–373.

Carlson, E. A. (1998). A prospective longitudinal study of disorganized/disoriented attachment. *Child Development, 69* (4), 1107–1128.

Carra, C., Lavelli, M., & Keller, H. (2014). Differences in practices of body stimulation during the first 3 months: Ethnotheories and behaviors of Italian mothers and West African immigrant mothers. *Infant Behavior and Development, 37* (1), 5–15.

Cascio, C. J., Moore, D., and McGlone, F. 2019. Social touch and human development. *Developmental Cognitive Neuroscience, 35,* 5–11.

Condon, W. S., & Sander, L. W. (1974). Neonate movement is synchronized with adult speech. *Interactional participation and language acquisition. Science, 183,* 99–101.

Cyr, C., Euser, E. M., Bakermans-Kranenburg, M. J., & Van Ijzendoorn, M. H. (2010). Attachment security and disorganization in maltreating and high-risk families: A series of meta-analyses. *Development and Psychopathology, 22* (1), 87–108.

Demuth, C. (2008). *Talking to infants: How culture is instantiated in early mother–infant interactions. The case of Cameroonian farming Nso and North German middle class families (Unpublished doctoral dissertation).* University of Osnabruck, Germany.

Ding, Y. H., Xu, X., Want, Z., Hi, H., & Want, W. (2012). Study of mother–infant attachment patterns and influence facts in Shanghai. *Early Human Development, 88* (5), 295–300.

Fearon, R. P., Bakermans-Kranenburg, M. J., Van IJzendoorn, M. H., Lapsley, A. M., & Roisman, G. I. (2010). The significance of insecure attachment and disorganization in the development of children's externalizing behavior: a meta-analytic study. *Child Development, 81* (2), 435–456.

Feldman, R. (2015). Sensitive periods in human social development: New insights from research on oxytocin, synchrony, and high-risk parenting. *Development and Psychopathology, 27* (2), 369–395.

Feldman, R., Eidelman, A. I., Sirota, L., & Weller, A. (2002). Comparison of skin-to-skin (kangaroo) and traditional care: parenting outcomes and preterm infant development. *Pediatrics, 110* (1), 16–26.

Feldman, R., & Masalha, S. (2010). Parent–child and triadic antecedents of children's social competence: Cultural specificity, shared process. *Developmental Psychology, 46* (2), 455–467.

Feldman, R., Singer, M., & Zagory, O. (2010). Touch attenuates infants' physiological reactivity to stress. *Developmental science, 13* (2), 271–278.

Field, T. (1995). Massage therapy for infants and children. *Journal of Developmental and Behavioral Pediatrics, 16* (2), 105–111.

Fourment, K., Nóblega, M., Conde, G., del Prado, J. N., & Mesman, J. (2018). Maternal sensitivity in rural Andean and Amazonian Peru. *Attachment & Human Development, published online.* https://doi.org/10.1080/14616734.2018.1454055

George, C., Kaplan, N., & Main, M. (1985). *Adult Attachment Interview protocol (Unpublished manuscript).* Berkeley, CA: University of California.

Gojman, S., Millan, S., Carlson, E., Sanchez, G., Rodarte, A., and Conzalez, P., et al. (2012). Intergenerational relations of attachment: A research synthesis of urban/rural Mexican samples. *Attachment and Human Development, 14* (6), 553–566.

Granqvist, P., Hesse, E., Fransson, M., Main, M., Hagekull, B., & Bohlin, G. (2016). Prior participation in the strange situation and overstress jointly facilitate disorganized behaviours: implications for theory, research and practice. *Attachment & Human Development, 18* (3), 235–249.

Granqvist, P., Sroufe, L. A., Dozier, M., Hesse, E., Steele, M., van Ijzendoorn, M., Solomon, J., Schuengel, C., Fearon, P., Bakermans-Kranenburg, M., Steele, H., Cassidy, J., Carlson, E., Madigan, S., Jacobvitz, D., Foster, S., Behrens, K., Rifkin-Graboi, A., Gribneau, N, . . . & Steele, H. (2017). Disorganized attachment in infancy: a review of the phenomenon and its implications for clinicians and policy-makers. *Attachment & Human Development, 19* (6), 534–558.

Grice, H. P. (1975). Logic and conversation. In P. Cole & J. Moral (Eds.). *Syntax and semantics, 3, pp. 41–58.* Academic Press.

Groh, A. M., Fearon, R. P., Bakermans-Kranenburg, M. J., Van IJzendoorn, M. H., Steele, R. D., & Roisman, G. I. (2014). The significance of attachment security for children's social competence with peers: A meta-analytic study. *Attachment & Human Development, 16* (2), 103–136.

Groh, A. M., Roisman, G. I., van IJzendoorn, M. H., Bakermans-Kranenburg, M. J., & Fearon, R. (2012). The significance of insecure and disorganized attachment for children's internalizing symptoms: A meta-analytic study. *Child Development, 83* (2), 591–610.

Grossmann, K., Grossmann, K., & Schwan, A. (1986). Capturing the wider view of attachment: A re-analysis of Ainsworth's Strange Situation. In C. E. Izard & P. B. Read (Eds.). *Measuring emotions in infants and children (pp. 124–171),* Cambridge University Press.

Hofer, M. A. (2006). Psychobiological roots of early attachment. *Current Directions in Psychological Science, 15* (2), 84–88.

Isabella, R. A. (1993). Origins of attachment: Maternal interactive behavior across the first year. *Child Development, 64,* 605–621.

Jaffe, J., Beebe, B., Feldstein, S., & Jasnow, M. D. (2001). Rhythms of dialogue in infancy. *Monographs of the Society for Research in Child Development,* 1–149.

Jin, M. K., Jacobvitz, D., Hazen, N., & Jung, S. H. (2012). Maternal sensitivity and infant attachment security in Korea: Cross-cultural validation of the Strange Situation. *Attachment & Human Development, 14* (1), 33–44.

Keller, H., Bard, K., Morelli, G., Chaudhary, N., Vicedo, M., Rosabal-Coto, M., Schediecker G., Murray, M., & Gottlieb, A. (2018). The myth of universal sensitive responsiveness: Comment on Mesman et al. (2017). *Child Development, 89* (5), 1921–1928.

Keller, H., Borke, J., Staufenbiel, T., Yovsi, R. D., Abels, M., Papaligoura, Z., Jensen, H., Lohaus, A., Chaudhary, N., Lo, W., & Su, Y. (2009). Distal and proximal parenting as alternative parenting strategies during infants' early months of life: A cross-cultural study. *International Journal of Behavioral Development, 33* (5), 412–420.

Keller, H., & Otto, H. (2009). The cultural socialization of emotion regulation during infancy. *Journal of Cross-Cultural Psychology, 40* (6), 996–1011.

Lyon's (1992). *Quality of maternal holding and infant behavior in the Strange Situation (Unpublished manuscript),* University of California at Berkeley.

Lyons-Ruth, K. (2007). The interface between attachment and intersubjectivity: Perspective from the longitudinal study of disorganized attachment. *Psychoanalytic Inquiry, 26* (4), 595–616.

Lyons-Ruth, K., & Jacobvitz, D. (1999). Attachment disorganization: Unresolved loss, relational violence, and lapses in behavioral and attentional strategies. In J. Cassidy & P. R. Shaver (Eds.). *Handbook of attachment: Theory, research, and clinical applications (pp. 520–554).* The Guilford Press.

Lyons-Ruth, K., & Jacobvitz, D. (2016). Attachment disorganization from infancy to adulthood: Neurobiological correlates, parenting contexts, and pathways to disorder. In J. Cassidy & P. R. Saver (Eds.). *Handbook of attachment: Theory, research, and clinical applications (3rd edn.), 667–695.* The Guilford Press.

Madigan, S., Bakermans-Kranenburg, M. J., Van Ijzendoorn, M. H., Moran, G., Pederson, D. R., & Benoit, D. (2006). Unresolved states of mind, anomalous parental behavior, and disorganized attachment: A review and meta-analysis of a transmission gap. *Attachment & Human Development, 8* (2), 89–111.

Main, M. (1990). Parental aversion to infant-initiated contact is correlated with the parent's own rejection during childhood: The effects of experience on signals of security with respect to attachment. In K. E. Barnard & T. Berry Brazelton (Eds.). *The foundation of experience (pp. 461–495).* International Universities Press.

Main, M., & Hesse, E. (1990). Parents' unresolved traumatic experiences are related to infant disorganized attachment status: is frightened and/or frightening parental behavior the linking mechanism. In M. T. Greenberg, D. Cicchetti, & E. M. Cummings (Eds.). *The John D. and Catherine T. MacArthur Foundation series on mental health and development. Attachment in the preschool years: Theory, research, and intervention (pp. 161–182).* University of Chicago Press.

Main, M., & Solomon, J. (1986). Discovery of an insecure-disorganized/disoriented attachment pattern. In T.B. Brazelton & M.W. Yogman (Eds), *Affective development in infancy, pp. 95–124.* Ablex Publishing Corporation.

Main, M., & Solomon, J. (1990). Procedures for identifying infants as disorganized/disoriented during the Ainsworth Strange Situation. *Attachment in the preschool years: Theory, research, and intervention, 1,* 121–160.

Main, M., & Stadtman, J. (1981). Infant response to rejection of physical contact by the mother. *Journal of the American Academy of Child Psychiatry, 20* (2), 292–307.

Mesman, J., Van Ijzendoorn, M. H., & Sagi-Schwartz, A. (2016). Cross-cultural patterns of attachment, 852–877. In J. Cassidy & P. R. Saver (Eds.). *Handbook of attachment: Theory, research, and clinical applications (3rd edn.), 667–695.* The Guilford Press.

Mooya, H., Sichimba, F., & Bakermans-Kranenburg, M. (2016). Infant–mother and infant–sibling attachment in Zambia. *Attachment & Human Development, 18* (6), 618–635.

Pederson, D. R., & Moran, G. (1995). A categorical description of infant–mother relationships in the home and its relation to Q-sort measures of infant–mother interaction. *Monographs of the Society for Research in Child Development, 60* (2–3), 111–132.

Perry, B. D. (2010). Trauma, love & the brain: Using neuroscience and the power of human connection to help children heal. Napa Infant–Parent Mental Health Interdisciplinary training. Napa, CA.

Pisani, L. (1988). Mere, enfant et entourage dans une communsute africain : Enquete pilote. In P. Coppo (Ed.), *Medecine Traditionnelle : Psychiatrie et Psychologie en Afrique*, 189–206.

Pisani, L., True, M., & Oumar, F. W. (2005). The relationship between infant growth, infant–mother attachment, and maternal sensitivity among Mali's Dogons. *Devenir, 17* (4), 287–302.

Posada, G. (2013). Piecing together the sensitivity construct: Ethology and cross-cultural research. *Attachment & Human Development, 15* (5–6), 637–656.

Posada, G., Carbonell, O. A., Alzate, G., & Plata, S. J. (2004). Through Colombian lenses: ethnographic and conventional analyses of maternal care and their associations with secure base behavior. *Developmental Psychology, 40* (4), 508.

Posada, G., Trumbell, J., Noblega, M., Plata, S., Peña, P., Carbonell, O. A., & Lu, T. (2016). Maternal sensitivity and child secure base use in early childhood: Studies in different cultural contexts. *Child Development, 87* (1), 297–311.

Reisz, S., Duschinsky, R., & Siegel, D. J. (2017). Disorganized attachment and defense: exploring John Bowlby's unpublished reflections. *Attachment & Human Development, 20* (2), 107–134.

Shai, D., & Belsky, J. (2017). Parental embodied mentalizing: How the nonverbal dance between parents and infants predicts children's social functioning. *Attachment & Human Development, 19 (2)*, 191–219.

Shai, D., & Meins, E. (2018). Parental embodied mentalizing and its relation to mind-mindedness, sensitivity, and attachment security. *Infancy, 23* (6), 1–16.

Schore, A. N. (2001). Effects of a secure attachment relationship on right brain development, affect regulation, and infant mental health. *Infant Mental Health Journal: Official Publication of the World Association for Infant Mental Health, 22* (1–2), 7–66.

Sroufe, L. A., & Waters, E. (1977). Attachment as an organizational construct. *Child Development, 48* (4), 1184–1199.

Stern, D. N., 1977. *The first relationship: Infant and mother.* Harvard University Press.

Straussman, B. I. (1997). Polygyny as a risk factor for child mortality among the Dogon. *Current Anthropology, 38* (4), 688–695.

Tomlinson, M., Cooper, P., & Murray, L. (2005). The mother–infant relationship and infant attachment in a South African peri-urban settlement. *Child Development, 76* (5), 1044–1054.

Trevarthen, C., & Aitken, K. J. (2001). Infant intersubjectivity: Research, theory, and clinical applications. *The Journal of Child Psychology and Psychiatry and Allied Disciplines, 42* (1), 3–48.

True, M. M. (1994). *Mother–infant attachment and communication among the Dogon of Mali (Unpublished dissertation).* University of California at Berkeley.

True, M., Lyon, S., Pisani, L., Oumar, F. (2003). *Another pathway to infant disorganization: Insights from an African dataset.* Paper presented at the biennial meeting of the Society for Research in Child Development, Tampa, FL.

True, M., Pisani, L., & Omar, F. (2001). Infant–mother attachment among the Dogon of Mali. *Child Development, 72* (5), 1451–1466.

Van IJzendoorn, M. H., Bakermans, J. J., Steele, M. and Granqvist, P. (2018), Diagnostic use of Crittenden's attachment measures in family court is not beyond a reasonable doubt. *Infant Mental Health Journal, 39* (6), 642–646.

Van IJzendoorn, M. H., Schuengel, C., & Bakermans-Kranenburg, M. J. (1999), Disorganized attachment in early childhood: Meta-analysis of precursors, concomitants, and sequelae. *Developmental Psychopathology, 11* (2), 225–249.

Waters, E. (1995). Appendix A: The attachment Q-set (version 3.0). *Monographs of the society for research in child development*, 234–246.

Weaver, I. C., Cervoni, N., Champagne, F. A., D'Alessio, A. C., Shakti, S., Seckl, J. R. Dymov, S., Szyf, M., & Meaney, M. J. (2004). Epigenic programming by maternal behavior (2004). *Nature Neuroscience, 7* (8), 847–854.

Weiss, S. J., Wilson, P., Hertenstein, M. J. & Campos, R. (2000). The tactile context of mother's caregiving: Implications for attachment of low-birth weight infants. *Infant Behavior and Development, 23* (1), 91–111.

Zevalkink, J., Riksen-Walraven, J. M., & Van Lieshout, C. F. (1999). Attachment in the Indonesian caregiving context. *Social Development, 8* (1), 21–40.

Zreik, G., Oppenheim, D., & Sagi-Schwartz, A. (2017). Infant attachment and maternal sensitivity in the Arab minority in Israel. *Child Development, 88* (4), 1338–1349.

# Index

Please note that page references to Tables will be followed by the letter 't'

*Attachment Theory and Research: A Reader*, First Edition. Edited by Tommie Forslund and Robbie Duschinsky.
© 2021 John Wiley & Sons Ltd. Published 2021 by John Wiley & Sons Ltd.